THE NEW BOOK OF KNOWLEDGE

N

VOLUME 13

THE NEW BOOK OF KNOWLEDGE

Scholastic Library Publishing, Inc.
Danbury, Connecticut

ISBN 0-7172-0540-1 (set)

The publishers wish to thank the following for permission to use copyrighted material:
E. P. Dutton & Co., Inc., for "Habits of the Hippopotamus" from *Gaily the Troubadour* by Arthur
    Guiterman, copyright 1936 by E. P. Dutton & Co., Inc.
Greenwillow Books, a division of William Morrow & Company, Inc., for "Jellyfish Stew" from *The New
    Kid on the Block* by Jack Prelutsky, copyright 1984 by Jack Prelutsky.
Little, Brown and Company for "Eletelephony" from *Tirra Lirra* by Laura E. Richards.
J. B. Lippincott Company for "The Reason for the Pelican" from *The Reason for the Pelican* by John
    Ciardi, copyright © 1955 by the Curtis Publishing Company.
Dover Publications, Inc., for stanza from "Nonsense Verse" by Gelett Burgess.

N, the 14th letter in the English alphabet, was also the 14th letter in the ancient Hebrew and Phoenician alphabets and was the 13th letter in the classical Greek alphabet. The Hebrews and Phoenicians called it *nu*. The Greeks called it *nu*.

Some language scholars believe that the Phoenician word *nun* meant "fish," and that the letter represented a fish. Others believe that it meant "snake." The letter *nun* looked like this: ⌐

The Greeks based their alphabet on that of the Phoenicians. Unlike the Phoenician letters, which were names for objects, the Greek letter names were just names for sounds. *Nu* was simply the name the Greeks gave the letter N.

The early Greeks wrote from right to left, as the Phoenicians and Hebrews had. After 500 B.C., however, most Greek writing ran from left to right, and *nu*, like many other letters, became reversed. Since the time of the Greeks the letter N has changed little. When the Romans learned the Greek alphabet from the Etruscans, they gave the letter a more regular shape but pronounced it as the Greeks had. The Roman form is the one used in English today.

In English the letter N is most frequently pronounced as in the word *not*. In some words, such as *hymn* and *column*, the N is silent.

An important use of the letter N is in the word *an*, meaning "one," or "a particular thing." *An* is almost always used instead of *a* before words that start with vowels. We say "an apple" instead of "a apple" and "an oar" instead of "a oar" because it gives a smoother sound.

In chemistry, N is the symbol for the element nitrogen, Na is the symbol for sodium, and Ni the symbol for nickel. N is also found in some abbreviations. For example, it stands for north on maps, and in many organization names it denotes national, as in N.E.A., or the National Education Association.

Reviewed by Mario Pei
Author, *The Story of Language*

See also ALPHABET.

SOME WAYS TO REPRESENT N:

Nn 𝒩𝓃

The **manuscript** or printed forms of the letter (left) are highly readable. The **cursive** letters (right) are formed from slanted flowing strokes joining one letter to the next.

The **Manual Alphabet** (left) enables a deaf person to communicate by forming letters with the fingers of one hand. **Braille** (right) is a system by which a blind person can use fingertips to "read" raised dots that stand for letters.

The **International Code of Signals** is a special group of flags used to send and receive messages at sea. Each letter is represented by a different flag.

International Morse Code is used to send messages by radio signals. Each letter is expressed as a combination of dots (•) and dashes (——).

NAILS, SCREWS, AND RIVETS

If you were building a birdhouse, how would you hold the parts together? A birdhouse made of wood could be fastened with nails or screws. If you made it out of sheet metal, screws would still be a good option, or you could use rivets. The kind of fastener you use depends on several factors: What materials are being joined? Must the joint be very strong? Is it a permanent joint or does it need to come apart easily? Nails, screws, and rivets are three of the most common kinds of fasteners used in construction, and they come in many different sizes and styles.

▶ **NAILS**

Nails are usually used for joining pieces of wood or for fastening other materials to wood. Nails are hammered into place and are held there mostly by friction.

The oldest style of nail is the **cut nail**, which is cut from sheets of iron or steel. Cut nails are tapered on one face so they are wide at the top, or head, and narrow at the tip. The head is rectangular. All-purpose nails made from round steel wire are called **common nails**. They have round flat heads and measure between 1 and 6 inches (2.5 and 15 centimeters) long. Smaller nails like these are called **wire nails**. Nails 6 inches or longer are usually called **spikes**.

There are many kinds of nails designed for specific uses. A **finishing nail** has a much smaller head than a common nail. When countersunk, or driven below the surface of the wood, it is almost invisible. Small finishing nails, about ½ inch to 1¼ inches (1.3 to 3.2 centimeters) long, are usually called **brads**. **Roofing nails** have large heads and are used to hold tar paper or shingles to a roof. They are coated with zinc to keep them from rusting. **Masonry nails** are especially hard so

they can be driven into concrete. **Double-headed nails** have one head above the other; they are driven in as far as the first head, leaving the upper head exposed so they can be easily pulled out. They are used for scaffolds and other temporary structures. **Staples** are U-shaped nails that are driven in with a hammer or a staple gun. **Upholstery tacks** have decorative round heads and are used to fasten fabric to the frame of a piece of furniture. Small, sharp **carpet tacks** are used to hold carpeting to the floor.

On construction sites, most nailing is done with an electric or pneumatic (air-powered) nailer rather than with a hammer. These handheld machines place each nail with one powerful blow. The nails are packaged in sleeves and feed the nailer like bullets in a machine gun. These machines save time and are easier to use than a regular hammer.

▶ **SCREWS**

A screw is like a nail with a spiral ridge, called a thread, cut around the shaft. When the screw is turned into the wood or other material, the thread provides a stronger grip than a nail. The heads of most screws have either a straight slot or an X-shaped slot (called a Phillips head) into which the screwdriver is placed. But there are many other different style heads made for special

cut nail	common nail	finishing nail	wire nail	roofing nail

LENGTHS OF COMMONLY USED NAILS

The length of a nail is typically given in the penny system, which originated in England during the 1400's. Originally it meant the cost of 100 nails; a fivepenny nail was a nail that cost fivepence (5 pennies) per hundred. In the table below, the letter "d" stands for "penny."

2d = 1 inch		**10d** = 3 inches	
3d = 1¼ inches		**12d** = 3¼ inches	
4d = 1½ inches		**16d** = 3½ inches	
5d = 1¾ inches		**20d** = 4 inches	
6d = 2 inches		**30d** = 4½ inches	
7d = 2¼ inches		**40d** = 5 inches	
8d = 2½ inches		**50d** = 5½ inches	
9d = 2¾ inches		**60d** = 6 inches	

screwdrivers. Because the slotted heads make driving and removing screws easy, parts joined with screws are easier to take apart and put back together again.

Machine screws and **bolts** have flat tips and shafts that are not tapered. They are driven into threaded holes in the material to be joined or into **nuts**, six-sided pieces of metal with a threaded hole in the center. As the machine screw or bolt is turned it moves into the hole, and its threads are held by the threads of the hole. Nuts and bolts are used where strength is required and when it is possible to reach both sides of the objects to be joined together. To make a joint, a hole slightly larger than the bolt is drilled through all the parts to be fastened. The bolt is slipped through the hole and tightened into the nut, which makes the joint secure by pressing the parts tightly together.

Most bolts have hexagonal heads. Machine screws, which are usually smaller than bolts, may have flat or round heads or heads differently shaped for special purposes.

Many specialized fastening systems use a screw or bolt. **Toggles** are helpful for mounting heavy cabinets or mirrors on a wall. Toggles are pushed through a drilled hole, expand inside the wall, and hold securely when the screw is tightened. Bolts and special nuts called **cross dowels** are used to assemble objects like bedposts and rails, where the rail is too long for a bolt to go through. The cross dowel fits in a hole drilled across the rail in a position that the bolt can reach.

Screws with pointed tips are called **self-tapping screws** because they create their own threads as they are driven into wood or other material (to "tap" means to create a thread). **Wood screws** are probably the most familiar kind of self-tapping screw. Their thread tapers to the pointed end and they have flat or

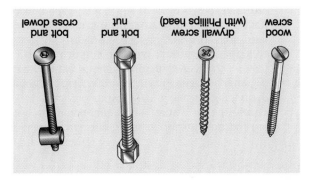

rounded heads. **Drywall** or **sheetrock screws** are used to hold wall materials to the wood framing of a house. They have threads that cut through wood more easily than standard wood screws. They are sharper and less tapered than wood screws so they are less likely to split the wood. **Lag screws** are large wood screws with hexagonal heads (called hex heads) that are turned with a wrench.

▶ RIVETS

Rivets are the most permanent kind of fastener. They look like sawn-off nails and are used to join thin pieces of many kinds of materials, including plastic, metal, fabric, and leather. The brass disks that reinforce the pocket corners on your jeans are rivets.

A rivet is placed through holes in the parts to be joined. Then the end of the rivet is pressed or hammered (called bucking) to form a second head called the point. Large rivets such as those used in buildings are heated first to soften them before bucking. Some small rivets are made hollow to lighten them and make their ends easier to buck.

Blind rivets are used when the point side of the rivet cannot be reached, such as behind a wall. The most common kind of hollow rivet is the **pop-rivet**. It consists of a hollow rivet with a peg, or mandrel, through its center. After the rivet is inserted through a hole, a special tool pulls back on the mandrel and causes the end of the rivet to spread. When the rivet is fully tightened, the mandrel breaks off. Another type of blind rivet uses an explosive charge to form the point.

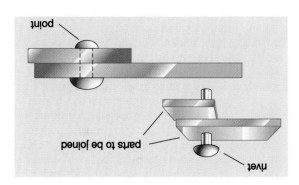

Frank Masterson
President, Industrial Fasteners Institute
Revised by Richard Starr
Author, *Woodworking With Your Kids*

NAMES AND NICKNAMES

Our names are an important part of our identity—a way to distinguish ourselves from everyone else. Each of us comes into the world with a family name, or surname. Our parents then give us another name, a personal one, that is called a given name, and friends and family sometimes call us by a special name, or nickname.

▶FAMILY NAMES

The first family names came about in a number of ways. Often, a man was named after the place in which he lived. Landowners in Europe in the Middle Ages often took their family names from the physical features of their property. Thus, families in England might take the name Lake, Pond, or Pool. Others might be called Brook or Rivers. Other physical features might form the basis of family names such as Cape, Hill, Shaw (an old word for a wood), Dale, Moore, Marsh, Stone, and others. Details of the landscape, such as trees, have provided names like Hawthorne, Ash, and Linden. In other countries, physical features formed the basis of such names as Rio, Rivera, and Montana in Spain; Strom, Berg, and Stein in Germany; Marais and Montaigne in France.

Prepositions often formed a part of many English family names, as in the "by" of Bywaters and the "under" of Underwood. This practice was also used in France—*du* or *de*, meaning "of," often formed part of a family name. The first Du Pont was the man "of the bridge" (*pont* is French for "bridge").

Family names also came from a person's work or craft. A person who looked after sheep, a sheep-herd, might take the name Shepherd. The name Coward is a form of "cow-herd." All over Europe the family name of ironworkers might refer to their craft— Smith in England, Ferraro in Italy, Schmidt in Germany, and Kowal in Poland.

In Anglo-Saxon England, peasants who used rough farm carts, also called "wains," might take the name Carter, Wainer, or Wheeler. At that same time, the Norman French rulers of England called the maker of fine men's cloths a *tailleur*. This became the source of the family name of Taylor. The workers who provided material for the *tailleur* might take the name of Spinner or Weaver.

Place-Names

During the medieval period in Europe, the use of place-names as family names grew. When people moved from one settlement to another, they were often called by the name of their native village or town.

The Scandinavian and German invaders of England sometimes tacked words of their own onto the names of the towns and villages they occupied. Many of these place-names later became family names. The word "thorp," or "thorpe," meaning "farm" or "hamlet," was attached in this way. It often took the form "throp," found in such place-names and family names as Winthrop and Calthrop. The word "wick," meaning "village," was another addition of this kind, and family names such as Pickwick were drawn from place-names with this ending. Often, "wick" was softened into "wich," as in the name Greenwich ("a green place"). Sometimes the "wick" was put first, as in Wickham.

Names ending in "by" come from the short Scandinavian word for "settlement." The name Kirby, for example, is a family name derived from "a settlement with a church." "Ham," originally a shortened form of "homestead," forms the last part of names such as Denham, Haversham, and Gresham. "Ton," an old form of "town," is found in names such as Hilton, Walton, Hampton, and Washington.

The words "ley," "lee," or "lea," meaning "meadow," are found as endings of many English names. The name Priestley may indicate who owned the meadow; Farley suggests a distant meadow. The Germanic and Dutch words for field—*veld*, *velt*, and *Feld*—are found frequently in names such as Roosevelt ("rose field") and Blumenfeld ("flowery field"). The French word for field—*champ*— is found in names like Beauchamp ("beautiful field"), which became Beecham in English.

Use of "Son"

In many places, a common means of forming a family name was to add the word "son" to the father's given name, as in Johnson, Jackson, and many others. Sometimes, as in the name Smithson, a new name was created by adding "son" to the family name instead of to the given name. The "son" ending takes the form of *sen* in Denmark and Norway, *nen* in Finland, *ez* in Spain, and *ski* in Poland.

In Scotland and Ireland, the Gaelic word *mac*, meaning "son," was put in front of the father's name, as in MacDonald. This was sometimes shortened to Mc or even M'. While the Irish used Mac for "son," they used O for "grandson." Thus MacBrian was the son of Brian and O'Brian was Brian's grandson.

The Welsh word for "son"—*ap*—was also put before a name, but the "a" was commonly dropped. Therefore, the children of Howell became Powell; those of Richard became Price or Preece. Sometimes the letter B replaced P, so the descendants of Owen were called Bowen and those of Evan were Bevan.

Another tendency in the British Isles was to shorten the word "son" into the single letter s. Thus the son of Richard became Richards, and the son of John became Johnson or Jones (especially in Wales). The Norman French rulers of England put the word *fils*, for "son," in front of a name. In English, this became Fitz. Many descendants of the Norman French took part in the English conquest of Ireland and settled there. As a result, there are many Fitzgeralds, Fitzherberts, and Fitzpatricks.

Other cultures have also formed names using their words for "son," or "son of." For example, Arabs and Jews often use "son of" in their names. In Arabic, it is *ibn*, as in ibn-Saud. In Hebrew, it is *ben*, as in Ben-Gurion.

Personal Characteristics

Physical features, such as a person's coloring, have often been a source of family names. A man with a red or ruddy complexion might be named Red, Reid, Read, or Read in England; Rousseau or Rouse in France; Rossi in Italy; Roth in Germany; and Flynn in Ireland. A person of fair coloring might be called White in England, Bianco in Italy, Le Blanc in France, and Weiss in Germany.

In addition to coloring, size and strength have also been the source of names, as in Little, Small, Power, and Strong. Conspicuous parts of the body have provided names such as Brain, Head, Legge, and Foot. People who have personality characteristics similar to those of certain animals have been named after them. A cunning man might be called Fox; a valiant one, Lion; a sturdy one, Bull; a gentle one, Lamb; a powerful one, Eagle or Falcon, after these powerful birds of prey.

Trends and Confusions

Societies have differed in the methods they use to form family names. The patronymic method—naming the son after the father, as in Johnson or Johansen—has appealed especially to the Scandinavians, the Semitic people of the Middle East, and the Celtic peoples of Scotland, Wales, and Ireland. The geographic method—using place-names as the basis of family names—has been favored in England and Germany. The professional method—forming a family name from a person's craft, as in Smith and Ferraro—has been used in many societies. Others have used the matronymic method—forming a name based on the mother's name. Presumably, Mollison was Molly's son and Margetson was the child of a Margaret. The matronymic has been used quite frequently in Spain and Latin America. In these societies, the patronymic is often followed by y, meaning "and," and then the mother's name. An example is Antonio Machado y Ruiz, the name of a famous Spanish poet.

The source and form of family names has been complicated by a variety of factors. In earlier times, when little was put in writing, spelling was a matter of personal choice. The pronunciation of words also varied greatly from one place to another, even within a single country. Names were not fixed, but changeable. During the Elizabethan period in England there were more than eighty different ways of spelling "Shakespeare."

A further complication has been caused by the fact that a particular word might have several different meanings. *Barn* in Denmark and "bairn" in Scotland means "child." But there is also the barn that stores a farmer's crops, once called a barton in English. So there are several possible explanations of Barnes or Barton as a family name.

Confusion also arises when a word has changed its meaning. The word "silly" in Shakespearean times meant "simple," not "foolish." People named Seeley were originally called Silly; and their name meant good, innocent persons, not a family of fools. On the other hand, their name might mean they had come from a meadow "ley" by the sea. Another source of confusion is that some names may come from either a profession or a locality. A Potter could be a man who makes pots or one who came from Poitiers in France.

POPULAR GIVEN NAMES

Their Meanings and Origins

It is not certain what a given name first meant. Many names are ancient and their original meanings have been lost or changed. Popularly accepted meanings are given for the names that follow. ("Dim." is the abbreviation for "diminutive"— a shortened form of a name. "Fem." means "feminine," and "var." means "variant" or variations.)

GIRLS' NAMES

NAME	ORIGIN	MEANING
Alice	Greek	Truth
Amanda	Latin	Lovable
Amy	Old French	Beloved
Ann, Anne	Hebrew	Grace, mercy, prayer
Ashley	Old English	Ash wood or meadow
Barbara	Greek	Stranger or foreign
Caroline, Carolyn	Fem. of Charles	
Casey	Gaelic	Brave
Catherine, Katherine	Greek	Pure
Christina, Christine	Greek	The anointed
Claire, Clare	Latin	Clear, bright
Danielle	Fem. of Daniel	
Deborah	Hebrew	Bee
Diana, Diane	Latin	Divine
Dorothy	Greek	Gift of God
Eleanor	Var. of Helen	
Elizabeth, Beth	Hebrew	Consecrated to God
Emily	Latin	To flatter
Erica	Norse	Ever powerful
Faith	Latin	Trusting or faithful
Gale, Gail	Old English	Gay, lively
Gloria	Latin	Glory
Hannah	Hebrew	God has favored me
Helen	Greek	Light or sun
Irene	Greek	Peace
Jane, Jean, Joan	Fem. of John	
Jennifer	Old English	White cheeked or fair
Jessica	Hebrew	God beholds
Judith	Hebrew	The praised
Julia, Julie	Latin	Youthful
Kelly	Gaelic	Warrior
Laura, Lauren	Fem. of Laurence	
Lillian	Greek	Lily
Martha	Aramaic	Lady
Mary	Latin, Hebrew	Star of the sea; bitter
Megan	Old English	Great
Melissa	Greek	Honeybee
Michelle	French fem. of Michael	
Nancy	Dim. of Ann	
Nicole	Fem. of Nicholas	
Pamela	Greek	All sweetness
Patricia	Fem. of Patrick	
Rachel	Hebrew	Ewe
Rebecca	Hebrew	Captive (literally "bound")
Ruth	Hebrew	Compassionate
Samantha	Aramaic	Listener
Sarah	Hebrew	Princess
Shirley	Old English	Bright meadow
Sharon	Hebrew	Level plain
Stacey, Stacy	Greek	One who is reborn
Stephanie	Fem. of Stephen	
Susan, Susannah	Hebrew	Lily
Theresa	Greek	Harvester
Tracey	Gaelic	Battler
Vanessa	Greek	Butterfly
Victoria	Latin	Victory
Virginia	Latin	Virgin, pure

BOYS' NAMES

NAME	ORIGIN	MEANING
Aaron	Hebrew	Enlightened
Adam	Hebrew	Man of red earth
Alan, Allen	Celtic	Comely, fair
Andrew	Greek	Manly
Anthony	Latin	Beyond praise
Benjamin	Hebrew	Son of the right hand
Brandon	Old English	Sword
Brent	Old English	Steep hill
Brian, Bryan	Celtic	The strong
Charles	Germanic	Manly, strong
Christopher	Greek	Christ-bearer
Craig	Gaelic	Crag-dweller
Daniel	Hebrew	God is my judge
David	Hebrew	Beloved of God
Derek	Germanic	Ruler of the people
Douglas	Celtic	From the dark water
Edward	Old English	Happy guardian
Eric, Erik	Old Norse	Ever ruler
Frederick	Germanic	Peaceful ruler
Gerald	Germanic	Mighty with a spear
Gregory	Greek	Vigilant
Harold	Anglo-Saxon	Strong in battle
Henry	Germanic	Ruler of the home
James	Hebrew	The supplanter
Jason	Greek	Healer
Jeffrey	Germanic	Heavenly peace
Jeremy	Var. of Jeremiah	Appointed by God
John, Jonathan	Hebrew	God's gift
Joseph	Hebrew	He shall increase
Joshua	Hebrew	God is my salvation
Justin	Latin	Just
Keith	Celtic	From the battle place
Kenneth	Gaelic	Handsome
Kevin	Var. of Kenneth	
Kyle	Gaelic	Fair and handsome
Laurence, Lawrence	Latin	Crowned with laurel
Lewis, Louis	Germanic	Renowned warrior
Mark	Latin	Warlike
Matthew	Hebrew	Gift from God
Michael	Hebrew	Who is like God
Nathan	Hebrew	Gift
Nicholas	Greek	Victory of the people
Patrick	Latin	Of noble birth
Peter	Greek	Rock
Philip	Greek	Lover of horses
Richard	Germanic	Stern ruler
Robert	Germanic	Bright fame
Ryan	Gaelic	Little king
Samuel	Hebrew	God has heard
Scott	Old English	A Scotsman
Sean, Shawn	Irish var. of John	
Stephen, Steven	Greek	Crown
Thomas	Aramaic	Twin
Timothy	Greek	Honoring God
Tyler	Old English	Worker with tiles
Walter	Germanic	Powerful warrior
William	Germanic	Strong protector
Zachary	Hebrew	God has remembered

▶ **GIVEN NAMES**

In many countries, a first name is formally given to a child at baptism. Hence, the first name is often spoken of as one's "Christian name," which may be a shortened form of "christening name." "Given name" is a more accurate term, however, since it applies to people of any religion or background. When a child receives two given names, the second one is called the "middle name." In some societies children receive several given names. Given names come from a variety of sources.

Greek and Latin Names

Many given names come from ancient Greek and Latin. The name Helene or Helen comes from the Greek word *helios*, which means "sun." The Greek word *margarites*, meaning "pearl," is the source of the name Margaret or Marguerite. *Theas*, the Greek word for God, is the source of Theodore or Theodora; and Timothy is a form of the Greek name Timotheos, meaning "one who honors God." Greek words are also the root of such names as Alice ("truth"), Katherine ("pure"), Irene ("peace"), Phyllis ("green leaf"), Andrew ("manly"), Gregory ("vigilant"), and Philip ("lover of horses").

From the Latin word *caelum*, meaning "sky," comes Celia ("heavenly one"). The Latin name Carolus was the basis of the names Charles, Charlotte, Caroline, and Carol. The name Justin comes from the Latin word *justus*, meaning "just," and Claire comes from the Latin *clarus*, meaning "bright and clear." Latin is also the basis of such names as Gloria ("glory"), Virginia ("pure"), Valerie ("valor"), Lawrence ("crowned with laurel"), Patrick ("of noble birth"), and Victor ("conqueror").

Biblical Names

The Bible is the source of a large number of given names, many handed down for generations. The name Jeremiah, described as a man appointed by the Lord, is a source of Jeremy. Other popular boys' names include Daniel ("God is my judge"), David ("beloved of God"), and Jonathan ("God's gift"). Names from the New Testament include Matthew, Mark, Luke, John, and Peter. Biblical names for girls include Sarah ("princess"), Deborah ("bee"), Judith ("the praised"), and Ruth ("compassionate").

Other Sources

In naming their children, parents sometimes choose names that honor famous persons, such as Alexander, Jefferson, Lincoln, and Lee. There are almost a hundred names for girls taken from the names of flowers. Parents might also choose names from characters in books or use the names of well-known entertainers, artists, musicians, or writers. Some parents have made up names or given unusual spellings to existing names to create names that are unique and distinctive.

▶ **NICKNAMES**

The word "nickname" comes from an old English term, "an ekename," which was often shortened to "nekename." The word "eke" meant "additional," so an ekename, or nickname, is an extra name.

There are various types of nicknames. The most common ones in the United States and England are derived from given names. Michael becomes Mike; Robert becomes Bob; Elizabeth becomes Liz; Patricia becomes Pat; and so on. Some nicknames are based on a physical characteristic. A thin person may be known as Slim. Lefty would indicate left-handedness. People with sour expressions might be given the nickname Smiley.

A person's place of origin gives rise to nicknames as well. Aussie is commonly used to refer to any Australian, while Kiwi refers to someone from New Zealand. Limey for someone from England came about because years ago English sailors were given limes on long voyages to avoid developing scurvy. In the United States, many states have special names for people that developed from some event in the state's history or from a special feature of its geography or economy. For example, Hawkeye refers to a native of Iowa, Hoosier a native of Indiana, and Nutmegger for a native of Connecticut.

Occupations have also contributed their share of nicknames. For example, Dusty was originally a nickname for a person working in a grain mill. During working hours, millers were usually covered with white dust. Its use with the surname Rhodes makes an obvious pun—Dusty Rhodes (Roads).

IVOR BROWN
Author, *A Word in Your Ear*

Reviewed by ALAN BENJAMIN
Author, *A Treasury of Baby Names*

NAMIBIA

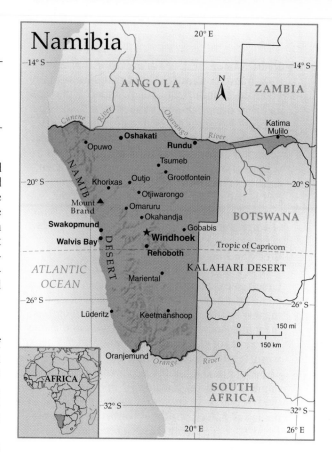

Namibia is a large but thinly populated country in southwestern Africa. It is bordered by Angola on the north, Botswana on the east, the Republic of South Africa on the southeast and south, and the Atlantic Ocean on the west. Formerly known as South-West Africa, Namibia was once a colony of Germany and was later administered by the Republic of South Africa. Namibia gained complete independence in 1990.

▶ PEOPLE

Most Namibians are black Africans of Bantu, Khoikhoi, or San origin. More than half belong to the largest Bantu group, the Ovambo, who live mainly in the north. Whites, people of mixed ancestry, and refugees from war-torn Angola make up a small percentage of the population.

English is the official language, although only about 10 percent of the population speaks it. Most people speak Afrikaans. German and various African languages are also spoken. Most people are Christians.

▶ LAND

Namibia is made up of three physical regions: a high central plateau that occupies most of the territory; the Namib Desert along the coast of the Atlantic Ocean; and the Kalahari Desert in the east. The plateau is the most heavily populated region and the site of the capital and largest city, Windhoek.

Namibia's climate is generally hot and very dry, with limited rainfall. As a result, water is scarce. The only large permanent rivers are those that border the country and flow only a short distance within it. These include the Orange River in the south and the Cunene and Okavango rivers in the north. The country's highest point is Mount Brand, with an elevation of 8,443 feet (2,573 meters).

▶ ECONOMY

Namibia's economy is based primarily on mineral exports, agriculture, and fisheries products. Mining is the major industry, and about half of Namibia's export income comes from diamonds. Fluorite, copper, uranium, gold, lead, tin, lithium, cadmium, and zinc are also mined. In addition, Namibia is believed to have deposits of oil,

A Namibian girl herds goats. Although many Namibians grow crops and raise livestock, agriculture is limited because the country is so hot and dry.

FACTS and figures

REPUBLIC OF NAMIBIA is the official name of the country.

LOCATION: Southwestern Africa.

AREA: 318,694 sq mi (825,418 km²).

POPULATION: 2,000,000 (estimate).

CAPITAL AND LARGEST CITY: Windhoek.

MAJOR LANGUAGES: English (official), African languages, Afrikaans.

MAJOR RELIGIOUS GROUP: Christian.

GOVERNMENT: Republic. **Head of state and government**—president. **Legislature**—National Assembly and National Council.

CHIEF PRODUCTS: Agricultural—millet, sorghum, peanuts, livestock, fish. **Manufactured**—cement, unrefined copper, refined lead. **Mineral**—diamonds, copper, uranium, gold, lead, tin, lithium, cadmium, zinc, salt, vanadium, natural gas.

► **MAJOR CITIES**

Windhoek, Namibia's capital and only major city, has a population of about 234,000. It is the nation's center of commerce, industry, and transportation.

► **HISTORY AND GOVERNMENT**

The San and the Khoikhoi were the region's original inhabitants. They were followed by the Bantu. The Portuguese explored the area in the 1400's. Other Europeans arrived later. In 1892, Germany established its colony of South-West Africa. Between 1892 and 1905 the Germans violently repressed an uprising by the Herero, a Bantu group, and the Nama, a Khoikhoi group. An estimated 60,000 Herero were killed, and thousands more became refugees.

During World War I (1914–18), the colony was taken over by South Africa. It was then administered by South Africa under the League of Nations. South Africa established a policy of apartheid (separation of the races).

After World War II (1939–45), the United Nations wanted Namibia (still known as South-West Africa) to be placed under a U.N. trusteeship. South Africa refused. In 1966 the United Nations, as successor to the League of Nations, voted to assume control of the territory, which it renamed Namibia in 1968. South Africa rejected this, although the International Court of Justice, in 1971, declared its occupation of Namibia illegal. The South-West Africa People's Organization (SWAPO) waged a guerrilla war against the South African administration. Operating from bases in Angola, the group demanded independence under black majority rule.

Independence. South Africa had linked its withdrawal from Namibia to the removal of large numbers of Cuban troops from Angola. Talks on this issue started in 1988, and the Cuban military withdrawal began in 1989.

In 1989, elections were held for a constituent assembly to write a constitution for Namibia. The elections, observed by United Nations officials, gave SWAPO a majority of seats in the assembly. Independence was declared on March 21, 1990. SWAPO leader Sam Nujoma became the country's first president. He was re-elected in 1994 and 1999.

Under the 1990 constitution, Namibia is a republic headed by a president, who governs with the assistance of a Council of Ministers, led by a prime minister. The president and most members of the lower house of the legislature, the National Assembly, are elected for 5-year terms. Members of the advisory upper house, the National Council, serve 6-year terms. The constitution also made the practice of apartheid a crime.

In the late 1990's, unequal distribution of land became a major political issue. Approximately 4,000 white farmers owned more than one-third of the land. In 1999, laws were passed that called for redistribution, but this did not produce much change. The government has since made further efforts to redistribute property, particularly commercial farmland. In 2004, SWAPO candidate Hifikepunye Pohamba was elected president.

PAUL J. KAISER
African Studies Center
University of Pennsylvania

---

coal, and iron ore. Other natural resources include natural gas and hydroelectric power.

Most Namibians herd livestock and grow basic food crops, such as millet and corn, for their own use. Only a very small percentage of the land is suitable for agriculture. White farmers raise most of the commercial livestock. The pelts of Karakul sheep, sold as Persian lamb, are exported.

Service industries make up about 30 percent of Namibia's economy and include tourism, finance, insurance, real estate, business activities, and government services.

NAPOLEON I (1769–1821)

Napoleon Bonaparte, emperor of France from 1804 to 1814, was the greatest general of his day. In 1799, following the French Revolution, he built an empire that stretched across Europe, from Spain in the west to Russia in the east. In addition to his military conquests, Napoleon was a great statesman, dedicated to making France a modern state. He created a system of civil government that gave more power and opportunity to the citizens of France and provided them, for the first time, with a code of laws that protected the rights of the common people.

Napoleon was born to Carlo and Letizia Buonaparte on August 15, 1769, in Ajaccio, Corsica, an island under French rule. In 1778 he obtained a scholarship to a military academy at Brienne, France, and later attended the *École Militaire* (military school) in Paris. In 1785, Napoleon was commissioned a second lieutenant in the artillery, and for the next several years he served at various obscure army posts.

▶ HIS RISE TO FAME

In 1793, Napoleon went to Paris seeking an assignment. This was a critical time in French history. The French Revolution, a bloody civil war that had begun in 1789, had led France into war with Austria, Prussia, Great Britain, Holland, and Spain. Napoleon was sent to the French city of Toulon, an important French naval base on the Mediterranean Sea that had been seized by anti-revolutionary forces and turned over to the British. Placed in charge of the artillery, Napoleon planned a bombardment that helped recapture the base. At the age of 24 he was promoted to brigadier general.

In March 1796, Napoleon was given the command of the French army in Italy, where his spectacular successes led to the acquisition of Lombardy, the city of Nice, and the duchy of Savoy. Then in 1797 he crossed the Alps to advance on Vienna, the capital of Austria. The Austrians called for an armistice (truce) and gave up several territories to France, notably the Belgian provinces. By this time, Napoleon had become famous.

In a daring scheme to extend European power, Napoleon invaded Egypt in 1798. He defeated the Mamelukes, the Egyptian cav-

Napoleon I was only 30 years old when he seized power in France in 1799. Ambition, he said, is "so natural to me...that it is like the blood that flows in my veins."

alry, at the battles of Shubra Khit and Embabeh (or the Battle of the Pyramids). But Napoleon was no mere conqueror. Having overrun Egypt, he sponsored a major program of intellectual and archaeological study of the country and then sought to introduce social reforms. Despite his victories on land, Napoleon was defeated at sea in the Battle of the Nile, where the French fleet was virtually destroyed by Great Britain's most celebrated admiral, Horatio Nelson.

▶ NAPOLEON RULES FRANCE

In 1799, Napoleon returned to Paris. On November 9, with the aid of his followers, he overthrew the unpopular French government in what is now known as the Coup d'État of 18 Brumaire. A consulate of three men was established to govern France. But Napoleon, named First Consul, held all the power.

Napoleon brought stability to France after the hardships of revolution and civil war. The **Concordat**, signed with Pope Pius VII in

On December 2, 1804, with the overwhelming support of the French people, Napoleon crowned himself emperor of France. He then crowned his wife Joséphine empress.

1801, restored good relations between the church and the state. Also a reformer, he helped draw up the **Code Napoleon** (1804) which, to this day, remains the basis of civil law in France and more than 25 other countries. He also reorganized France's financial, local, and judicial administration.

Nevertheless, Napoleon devoted most of his energies to foreign policy and war. In 1800 he won a brilliant victory over the Austrians at Marengo. Austria was forced to sign the Treaty of Lunéville (1801). With Austria defeated, Great Britain also made peace with Napoleon and signed the Treaty of Amiens (1802). The French so admired Napoleon for his accomplishments that in 1802 they named him Consul for Life. Then in 1804, with the support of the people, Napoleon crowned himself emperor.

Eager to ensure his own succession, in 1809 Napoleon divorced his beloved wife, Empress Joséphine, because they could not have children. The following year he made a prestigious marriage with Marie-Louise, a daughter of the Austrian emperor Francis I. In 1811 his son, François Charles Joseph, or Napoleon II, was born and titled King of Rome.

▶ THE NAPOLEONIC WARS

When Napoleon seized power, he began to pursue his dream to conquer all of Europe. The series of wars in which he engaged to achieve this goal are called the Napoleonic Wars. They took place almost continuously from the time he took power until his famous final defeat at the Battle of Waterloo in 1815.

Major Campaigns

On October 21, 1805, British admiral Lord Nelson defeated the French and Spanish fleets at the Battle of Trafalgar, off the coast of Spain. Vanquished at sea, Napoleon then tried to subdue the British by ruining their economy. From 1806 until 1814, he carried out an economic blockade, called the **Continental System**, by forbidding countries under his influence to trade with the British. In retaliation, Great Britain seized all ships trading with France. (One of the causes of the War of 1812 between Great Britain and the United States was that the British seized American trade ships bound for Europe.)

Despite the loss at Trafalgar, Napoleon continued to win his battles on land. Self confident and ruthless, he made swift decisions.

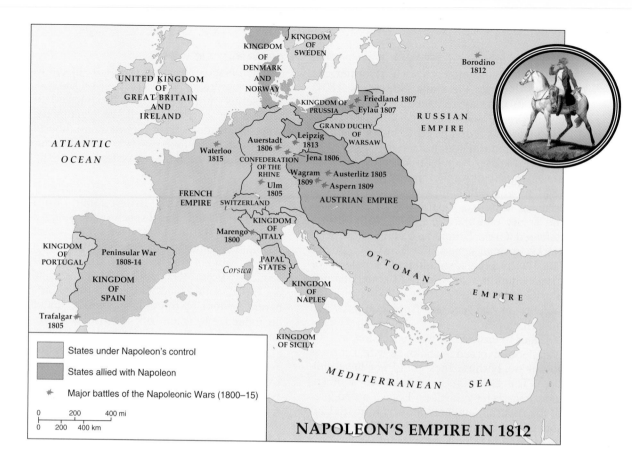

NAPOLEON'S EMPIRE IN 1812

Map labels:

KINGDOM OF SWEDEN

KINGDOM OF DENMARK AND NORWAY

UNITED KINGDOM OF GREAT BRITAIN AND IRELAND

ATLANTIC OCEAN

Borodino 1812

RUSSIAN EMPIRE

KINGDOM OF PRUSSIA

Friedland 1807
Eylau 1807

GRAND DUCHY OF WARSAW

Auerstadt 1806

Leipzig 1813

Waterloo 1815

CONFEDERATION OF THE RHINE

Jena 1806

Wagram 1809

Austerlitz 1805

Aspern 1809

Ulm 1805

FRENCH EMPIRE

SWITZERLAND

AUSTRIAN EMPIRE

KINGDOM OF ITALY

Marengo 1800

KINGDOM OF PORTUGAL

Peninsular War 1808-14

Corsica

PAPAL STATES

KINGDOM OF SPAIN

KINGDOM OF NAPLES

OTTOMAN EMPIRE

Trafalgar 1805

KINGDOM OF SICILY

MEDITERRANEAN SEA

Legend:
- States under Napoleon's control
- States allied with Napoleon
- Major battles of the Napoleonic Wars (1800–15)

0   200   400 mi
0   200   400 km

moved his troops rapidly, and concentrated the strength of his forces where they could be used to the best advantage.

On October 20, 1805, Napoleon's army won a stunning victory over the Austrians at Ulm, in Germany. Six weeks later, on December 2, he crushed the Russians and Austrians at Austerlitz (in the present-day Czech Republic). The Russians retreated, and the Austrians surrendered, giving up territorial possessions in Italy as well as Germany. This paved the way for Napoleon to take control over much of Germany, which in 1806 he reorganized as the Confederation of the Rhine. This brought an end to the Holy Roman Empire, which had governed German lands for more than a thousand years.

In 1806, Napoleon set his sights on conquering Prussia, the strongest of the remaining independent German states. On October 14, he defeated the poorly commanded Prussian armies at Jena and at Auerstadt. On October 24, he seized Berlin, the Prussian capital. Moving eastward, he then marched his army into and occupied the Grand Duchy of Warsaw. The following year, Napoleon conquered Russian armies at the battles of Eylau and Friedland. By the Treaties of Tilsit (1807), he made peace with the Russians and forced Prussia to give up half its territory.

Napoleon now dominated Europe from Spain to the borders of Russia. To guarantee

In 1813, after Napoleon's failed invasion of Russia, the British artist and caricaturist George Cruikshank parodied the disastrous defeat in his cartoon *Russians Teaching Boney to Dance*, a sarcastic reference to Bonaparte.

control, he placed his brothers on the thrones of Naples and Spain (Joseph), Holland (Louis), and Westphalia (Jérôme). Only Great Britain remained undefeated, for although Napoleon ruled the continent, Britain still controlled the seas.

In 1808 a popular uprising against the French broke out in Spain and Portugal. This struggle, called the Peninsular War, dragged on for more than five years, draining France of troops and resources. Meanwhile, the Austrians again rose up against Napoleon. French troops occupied Vienna on May 13, 1809.

▶ NAPOLEON'S DECLINE

In 1812, Napoleon decided to invade Russia because, among other reasons, the Russians refused to cooperate with his blockade of Great Britain. This decision was the worst mistake of his career. On September 7, he defeated but failed to destroy the Russians at Borodino, a battle in which he lost about a quarter of his army. He then advanced on an undefended Moscow. When he entered the city on September 14, it had been set on fire, probably by the Russians, who preferred to burn their city rather than have it taken by the French. Napoleon's capture of Moscow failed to bring victory, and he decided to retreat. But a combination of harsh winter weather, Russian attacks, and the collapse of the French supply system devastated Napoleon's Grand Army.

After the failure of the Russian campaign, Napoleon's dominance of Europe rapidly unraveled. Austria, Prussia, Russia, and Sweden allied themselves against France. Napoleon's newly recruited army of 200,000 inexperienced men was outmaneuvered and badly beaten by the converging allied forces at the Battle of Leipzig, October 16–19, 1813. Meanwhile, Britain's Arthur Wellesley (the great general who would later be given the title Duke of Wellington) had driven the French from Spain and started to invade France from the south. Napoleon gathered a new army and fought a series of desperate battles to hold back the Prussians and Austrians, who were invading from the north. But the allies advanced steadily and captured Paris on March 30, 1814.

Exile to Elba

Napoleon was forced to abdicate (give up) his throne and was exiled to the island of Elba near Corsica. The French royal family, whose former king, Louis XVI, had been executed during the revolution, was restored to power under Louis XVIII. Napoleon's son and heir was taken by his mother to Austria. He never saw his father again.

The Hundred Days

Louis XVIII was not a popular king, and many people longed to see Napoleon return. On March 1, 1815, Napoleon returned to France, beginning a second

THE CONGRESS OF VIENNA (1814–15)

During Napoleon's first period of exile, representatives of the great European powers gathered in the Austrian capital of Vienna to reorganize the governments of the continent and restore the balance of power. The leading figures at the Congress were its host Emperor Francis I of Austria and his foreign minister Prince Klemens von Metternich; Viscount Castlereagh of Great Britain; Czar Alexander I and Count Karl Robert Nesselrode of Russia; King Frederick William III and Prince Karl August von Hardenberg of Prussia; and Charles Maurice de Talleyrand-Périgord of France. The Congress restored many of the monarchies that had been toppled by Napoleon and his relatives. A Kingdom of the Netherlands was created (including what is now Belgium), and a new confederation of German states was formed to replace the old Holy Roman Empire. Switzerland was re-established as an independent nation. Part of Poland (the former Grand Duchy of Warsaw) became a kingdom under the rule of the Russian czar, while other Polish territories went to Prussia and Austria. Prussia also received Saxony, the Rhineland, and Westphalia, while Austria acquired Lombardy and Venetia in northern Italy. Norway, formerly a part of Denmark, was given to Sweden. Most important, the Congress succeeded in establishing relative peace and stability in Europe for the next one hundred years.

In 1815, Napoleon returned from exile and briefly regained power until his defeat at the Battle of Waterloo. To this day, the term "Waterloo" is generally used to indicate a great failure.

reign known as the Hundred Days. Supporters flocked to him, and his advance on Paris became a triumph. King Louis XVIII fled. Other European powers, unwilling to see Napoleon return, began to gather their armies.

On June 18, Napoleon fought his last great battle at Waterloo (in present-day Belgium) against an allied army of British and Dutch troops under the command of the British hero Arthur Wellesley, the future Duke of Wellington. Prussian reinforcements, led by General von Blücher, came to Wellesley's aid, enabling the allies to win the historic battle.

Exile to St. Helena

Thoroughly defeated, Napoleon surrendered to the British, who transported him as a prisoner to the barren island of St. Helena in the South Atlantic. He remained there until his death on May 5, 1821. Although there were rumors that Napoleon was poisoned, most of the evidence suggests otherwise. In 1840 his remains were moved to Paris, where they now rest in a great marble tomb in the Hôtel des Invalides, one of Paris' great landmarks.

JEREMY BLACK
Author, *European Warfare, 1660–1815*
See also FRENCH REVOLUTION; JOSÉPHINE, EMPRESS; WELLINGTON, DUKE OF.

NAPOLEON III (1808–1873)

Louis Napoleon Bonaparte, or Napoleon III, was emperor of France from 1852 until 1870, a reign known as the Second Empire. He was born Charles Louis Napoleon Bonaparte on April 20, 1808. His father, Louis, was Napoleon I's brother.

When Napoleon I's son, Napoleon II, died in 1832, Louis Napoleon asserted his claim to his uncle's imperial heritage. He led two unsuccessful uprisings against the French monarchy and was sentenced to life imprisonment. But in 1846 he managed to escape to England. When the Revolution of 1848 finally toppled French king Louis Philippe, Louis Napoleon promised to restore order and was elected president.

At first Louis Napoleon was a strict ruler who censored the press and imprisoned his opponents, but in an 1852 coup d'état, he declared himself emperor with the people's approval. In the 1860's, when popular support began to decline, he transferred power to the legislature, and the government became known as the Liberal Empire.

During the reign of Napoleon III, there was a marked increase in trade and industry. The emperor's vast public-works programs included a national network of railways and the modernization and beautification of Paris, under the direction of city planner Baron George Eugène Haussmann.

In foreign policy, Napoleon III wanted to restore France to the position of great influence it had enjoyed under his uncle's reign. Victories in the Crimean War (1853–56) and other wars expanded France's colonial empire. However, Napoleon III's pursuit of popularity led him into more risky ventures. In 1870 he was lured by Prussian prime minister Otto von Bismarck into the Franco-Prussian War, for which France was unprepared. The defeat of Napoleon's army at Sedan led to his fall from power in 1871. He joined his wife, the empress Eugénie, in exile in England, where he died on January 9, 1873.

MICHAEL HUGHES
University College of Wales

NARCISSUS. See GREEK MYTHOLOGY (Profiles).

NARCOTICS

Narcotics are powerful drugs that temporarily dull the senses and produce drowsiness and sleep. For centuries, doctors have used narcotics as painkillers, or **analgesics,** but the use of narcotics presents a serious danger. Narcotics are capable of causing drug dependence.

The most common narcotics are the opiates, all of which are highly addictive. Some of the opiates are produced naturally from plants; others are made synthetically in laboratories. An example of a natural opiate is **opium,** a drug known since ancient times. Opium is the dried juice obtained from the unripe seed capsule of a certain type of poppy plant, *Papaver somniferum*. From the days of the Greeks and Romans, opium was one of the most commonly used medicines.

In the early 1800's, scientists derived **morphine,** another natural opiate, from opium. Morphine is a pure chemical substance and has replaced opium as a painkiller in medical use. Scientists also isolated **codeine,** a weaker narcotic than morphine, in pure form from opium. In the late 1800's, chemists tried to develop other drugs that had the same painkilling effects as morphine. Again from opium they derived **heroin,** which today is the most widely abused narcotic.

In the 1900's, chemists developed opiates in the laboratory with chemical structures quite different from those of morphine, heroin, and opium. However, many of these drugs have painkilling effects that are almost exactly like those of the opium narcotics. Several synthetic narcotics, including Demerol and Darvon, are now used widely as medicines to relieve pain. Even though they are less likely to cause drug dependence, the potential exists for using these drugs incorrectly.

The Effects of Narcotics. All narcotics are alike in their effects on the body. They act on nearly all the body systems, but their strongest and most noticeable effects are on the nervous system. Narcotics reduce the activity of the central nervous system, which is made up of the brain and spinal cord. The result is that all behavior is reduced, irritability and anxiety are lessened, and drowsiness and sleep take place. Even low doses of narcotics may cause a person to slip in and out of awareness.

For a person who is sick or in severe pain, the effects that narcotics produce can provide much-needed relief. In fact, the ability of narcotics to relieve pain is their most important medical application.

Unfortunately, the narcotic analgesics can be dangerous if not used properly. Doses only slightly higher than those used to relieve pain can produce a serious slowing down of breathing. The precise effects on a particular individual depend on the type of narcotic, how much is taken, the way it is taken, and how often it is taken.

When the drugs are taken repeatedly, major changes in their effects on the body take place. Over time, taking the same amount does not result in the same effect. Higher doses are needed to have the same effect. This steady loss of effectiveness is known as **tolerance.** Narcotics are especially dangerous because tolerance to them builds quickly. This means that when people are dependent upon narcotics they not only have a desire for the drugs that keeps returning, but they also feel they need more and more of the drug each time.

Legal Measures. Before 1914, anyone could buy preparations of narcotics in the United States without a prescription. In 1914 the United States Congress passed the Harrison Act to control the import, manufacture, and overall distribution of narcotics. In 1930, Congress established the Bureau of Narcotics to regulate the medicinal uses of narcotics and to prevent their illegal distribution. Since then, other laws have been passed to strengthen controls over the manufacture, distribution, and possession of narcotics. The Drug Enforcement Administration, organized within the Justice Department in 1973, enforces U.S. narcotics and substance abuse laws.

Since the early 1900's, nations have recognized that narcotics traffic calls for international cooperation. National governments, the United Nations, and the international criminal police organization known as Interpol work together to combat drug trafficking.

AMELIA ARRIA
Center for Substance Abuse Research (CESAR)
University of Maryland, College Park

See also DRUG ABUSE.

NASA. See SPACE AGENCIES AND CENTERS.

NASHUA. See NEW HAMPSHIRE (Cities).

NASHVILLE

Nashville, the capital of Tennessee, is located on the Cumberland River in the north central part of the state. Known as Music City, U.S.A., Nashville is the largest country music recording center in the world. The city is also nicknamed the Athens of the South for its many institutions of higher learning and its Greek Revival-style buildings.

Nashville covers 533 square miles (1,380 square kilometers) and is the second largest city in Tennessee (although the population of its metropolitan area now surpasses that of Memphis, the state's largest city). About 570,000 people live within the city limits.

Nashville has a thriving economy. Among the city's largest employers are banking, insurance, printing, and publishing companies; the music industry; and tourism. Nashville is a major producer of chemicals, food products, clothing, textiles, airplane parts, and tires. Automobiles are assembled in nearby Smyrna and Spring Hill.

In the 1950's, Nashville began building its music industry. Today it ranks with Los Angeles and New York in the production, publication, and distribution of many styles of music. A downtown convention center, an international airport, and the successful Opryland Hotel complex have also made Nashville a popular business convention center.

The city has many tourist attractions. Opryland USA, a family amusement complex that is home to the legendary Grand Ole Opry, draws millions of visitors each year. Other popular attractions include Music Row (with

the Country Music Hall of Fame); the Hermitage, home of President Andrew Jackson; Belle Meade, a restored pre–Civil War mansion; the Cheekwood Botanical Gardens and Fine Arts Center; and the Parthenon, a replica of the famous temple in Athens, Greece. Also in Nashville is the Tennessee Performing Arts Center. Hockey fans root for the Nashville Predators at Gaylord Entertainment Center. Football fans cheer the Tennessee Titans at Adelphia Coliseum.

Nashville is the home of 16 institutions of higher learning. Vanderbilt University, with its highly regarded medical and law schools, is one of the nation's top universities. Other area schools include Meharry Medical College, Fisk University, Belmont University, and Tennessee State University.

Nashville was founded in 1779 by John Donelson and James Robertson, who came from North Carolina in search of fertile farmland. They established a fort on the west bank of the Cumberland River and named it Nashborough after the Revolutionary War general Francis Nash. The settlement was named Nashville in 1784 and was granted a city charter in 1806. It has served as the capital of Tennessee since 1827. Nashville was also the site of one of the last decisive battles of the Civil War, in December 1864.

In 1963, Nashville and Davidson County combined their governments, providing for a mayor and a 40-member legislative council. This system has since served as a model for other city governments.

Reviewed by WAYNE C. MOORE
Tennessee State Library and
Archives

Nashville, the capital of Tennessee, is situated on the Cumberland River. A center of government and manufacturing, the city is perhaps best known as the home of the country music industry.

NASSER, GAMAL ABDEL (1918–1970)

Gamal Abdel Nasser, president of Egypt from 1956 to 1970, was a leading figure in the Arab world. He was born near Alexandria on January 15, 1918, and as a youth took part in demonstrations against British domination of Egypt. Egypt had been a British protectorate from 1914 until 1922, and British influence remained strong.

Nasser graduated from the Royal Military Academy in 1938 and entered the army, rising to the rank of lieutenant colonel. After Egypt's defeat in the Arab-Israeli war of 1948–49, Nasser and other young officers decided that the government had to be changed. In 1952 they staged a military coup that forced King Farouk from the throne. They made Egypt a republic in 1953, with Nasser as deputy premier. He became premier in 1954 and president in 1956.

In 1956, Nasser took control of the Suez Canal, which had been under mostly British and French ownership, and closed it to Israeli ships. This provoked an invasion by Israel, Britain, and France, but their troops were quickly withdrawn under pressure from the United States and the Soviet Union. Nasser's political victory increased his reputation in the Arab world. Arab unity was one of Nasser's main goals, and in 1958 he merged Egypt with Syria in a federation called the United Arab Republic. But political differences caused its collapse in 1961.

In 1967, Nasser demanded the withdrawal of United Nations peacekeeping forces that had been stationed in the Sinai area since the war of 1956. He also closed the Gulf of Aqaba to Israeli ships. These actions led to war between Israel and Egypt. After Israel's swift victory, Nasser offered to resign but remained in office due to popular support.

During his presidency, numerous jobs were created, and many Egyptian farmers received their own land. Nasser was especially proud of the Aswan High Dam, built to control floods and provide irrigation for a vast area, which began operation in 1968. Nasser died suddenly from a heart attack on September 28, 1970.

Reviewed by DON PERETZ
State University of New York at Binghamton

NAST, THOMAS (1840–1902)

Thomas Nast is considered the first important American cartoonist. Symbols created by him are still popular today, including Uncle Sam, the Democratic donkey, the Republican elephant, and Santa Claus.

Nast was born on September 27, 1840, in Landau, Germany. He attended the National Academy of Design after moving with his family to New York City. As a teenager, Nast worked as an artist for *Frank Leslie's Illustrated Newspaper.* (Before the rise of photojournalism, drawing pictures to accompany newspaper stories was an important job.) From 1858 to 1861, Nast contributed sketches to the *New York Illustrated News* and several other newspapers.

A Nast Santa Claus

In 1862, Nast took a job with *Harper's Weekly* and began to develop modern political cartoons—pictures with captions that sway public opinion. His influential Civil War cartoons, "After the Battle" and "Emancipation," led President Abraham Lincoln to call him "our best recruiting sergeant."

Nast gained national fame for his assaults against political injustice. Between 1869 and 1871, he used a tiger as the symbol for Tammany Hall, a corrupt New York political organization. This series of cartoons attacking Tammany Hall led to the eventual imprisonment of its leader, William "Boss" Tweed. During the presidential campaign of 1874, Nast popularized the elephant and the donkey as symbols of the Republican and Democratic parties.

Nast died on December 7, 1902, while serving as U.S. consul at Guayaquil, Ecuador.

Reviewed by JUDITH D. HINES
Education Manager, The Newseum

NATION, CARRY. See PROHIBITION (Profiles).

NATIONAL ANTHEMS AND PATRIOTIC SONGS

A national anthem is a patriotic song that is sung or played on official occasions, as a special sign of respect for a country. National anthems and patriotic songs serve to unite a people in their common hopes and ideals. Singing these songs may make people feel a deeper sense of loyalty to their country.

Patriotic songs have often been written during times of war or crisis. Sometimes they describe events in the war, such as a particular battle. Sometimes a song is a prayer for the safety of a country or its ruler. Some patriotic songs praise the natural beauty of a country or express the hopes of its people.

The origin of many national anthems is unknown. Often a melody was already popular as a folk song when someone set a patriotic text to it. Only a few melodies were actually written to be national anthems.

Several older national anthems and patriotic songs have the same melodies but different words. Some of them have even been sung as war songs by opposing armies in the same battle. The British anthem, "God Save the Queen" has provided the melody for patriotic songs in Denmark, Germany, Russia, Switzerland, and all English-speaking areas of the world. In the United States the words of "America" are sung to this same melody.

▶ FAMOUS NATIONAL ANTHEMS

Some of the world's best-known national anthems are discussed below. To find the names of national anthems of other countries, consult the fact boxes in the articles on those countries.

United States. The national anthem of the United States was written during the War of 1812. In 1814, Francis Scott Key (1779–1843), a Baltimore lawyer, was sent on a mission to the British fleet anchored off Fort McHenry, near Baltimore. He went to arrange the release of an American physician held captive on one of the British ships. On the night of September 13, 1814, while Key was on board one of the British ships, the British attacked Fort McHenry. All night long Key watched the attack. When he saw the American flag at dawn still flying over the fort, he was so moved that he wrote the words of "The Star-Spangled Banner," for which he used the back of an envelope. Key had a specific tune in mind to go with the words he wrote. This tune, "To Anacreon in Heaven," was a popular English song written by John Stafford Smith (1750–1836).

The day after the battle Key went to a tavern in Baltimore, where a singer introduced the new song. Soon a Baltimore newspaper published the verses under the title "The Defense of Fort McHenry." After that both the verses and the tune appeared in several songbooks, where the song acquired its title, "The Star-Spangled Banner." It was made the official national anthem by act of Congress on March 3, 1931.

The Former Soviet Union. The "Hymn of the Soviet Union" was written during World War II to replace "The International," the original Soviet anthem. "The International" was the anthem of world revolution. It offended the countries allied with the Soviet Union in World War II. The words of the "Hymn of the Soviet Union" were written by Sergey Mikhalkov and I. Registan and set to music by A. V. Aleksandrov. With the breakup of the Soviet Union in 1991, each new country was expected to have its own anthem.

Germany. The tune of "Song of Germany" (*Deutschlandlied*), the national anthem of the Federal Republic of Germany, was written by the great composer Joseph Haydn. It was originally used for the national anthem of Austria and was first performed on February 12, 1797, the birthday of the Austrian emperor.

In 1922 the poem "Song of Germany" was set to Haydn's melody and became the official German anthem. The text was written by H. A. Hoffmann von Fallersleben (1798–1874). In the 1950's it became the official anthem of West Germany. It remained the national anthem after East and West Germany were reunited in 1990.

Netherlands. "William of Nassau" (*Wilhelmus van Nassouwe*), the anthem of the Netherlands, is the oldest of national anthems. It dates from the 16th century, when the Netherlands was trying to achieve its independence from Spain. The leader of the Dutch nobles opposing the king of Spain was William (the Silent) of Nassau, Prince of Orange. The words of the anthem, whose authorship is not definitely known, were set to a folk tune. The oldest surviving edition of the words and tune together dates from 1626.

The Star-Spangled Banner

Words by Francis Scott Key

Music by John Stafford Smith

On the shore dimly seen through the mists of the deep,
Where the foe's haughty host in dread silence reposes,
What is that which the breeze, o'er the towering steep,
As it fitfully blows, half conceals, half discloses?
Now it catches the gleam of the morning's first beam,
In full glory reflected now shines in the stream;
'Tis the star-spangled banner, O, long may it wave
O'er the land of the free and the home of the brave!

O! thus be it ever when freemen shall stand
Between their loved homes and the war's desolation,
Blessed with vict'ry and peace, may the heav'n rescued land
Praise the Pow'r that hath made and preserved us a nation!
Then conquer we must, when our cause it is just,
And this be our motto: "In God is our trust,"
And the star-spangled banner in triumph shall wave
O'er the land of the free and the home of the brave!

O Canada

English Version by R.S. Weir

Music by Calixa Lavallée

O Can-a-da! Our home and na-tive land! True pa-triot love in all thy sons com-mand. With glow-ing hearts we see thee rise, the True North strong and free! From far and wide, O Can-a-da, We stand on guard for thee. God keep our land glo-rious and free! O Can-a-da, we stand on guard for thee. O Can-a-da, we stand on guard for thee!

God Save the Queen

God save our gra-cious Queen, Long live our no-ble Queen, God save the Queen: Send her vic-to-ri-ous, hap-py and glo-ri-ous, Long to reign o-ver us: God save the Queen.

"America," with words by Samuel Francis Smith, is sung to the tune of "God Save the Queen":

My country 'tis of thee,
Sweet land of liberty,
Of thee I sing;
Land where my fathers died,
Land of the pilgrims' pride,
From ev'ry mountainside,
Let freedom ring.

My native country, thee,
Land of the noble free,
Thy name I love;
I love thy rocks and rills,
Thy woods and templed hills,
My heart with rapture fills,
Like that above.

Great Britain. "God Save the Queen" is the national anthem of the United Kingdom of Great Britain and Northern Ireland. Its dignity and solemnity express the devotion of the British to their sovereign. The origin of this anthem is not definitely known. It first appeared in print in 1744. But the earliest known version of the tune appeared in 1619 in a keyboard piece by the English composer John Bull (1563–1628). The first public performance of the anthem took place on September 28, 1745, at the Theatre Royal, Drury Lane, London.

The British national anthem has been called the mother of national anthems because it has been used in so many countries. During the Revolutionary period in America, it was sung to such words as "God save George Washington" and "God save America." The same melody has been used in classical music.

Canada. The Canadian national anthem, "O Canada," was written in honor of an official visit to the city of Quebec in 1880 by the Governor-General of Canada and Princess Louise of England. It became the official national anthem in 1980. The original French text, *O Canada! terre de nos aïeux,* was written by Sir Adolphe Routhier (1839–1920). The music is by Calixa Lavallée (1842–91). The most widely sung English version was written by Robert Stanley Weir (1856–1926). "God Save the Queen" is the royal anthem.

France. The *Marseillaise,* the French national anthem, was the battle song of the French Revolutionary period (1789–1815). The words and music were written by Claude Joseph Rouget de Lisle (1760–1836), a captain in the French Army in Strasbourg. On April 24, 1792, word reached Strasbourg that France had declared war on Austria. At a ban-

La Marseillaise

Words and Music by Claude Joseph Rouget de Lisle

quet the mayor of Strasbourg asked Rouget de Lisle to write a war song. The song was written that night, and the next day it was sung by the mayor. It quickly spread throughout France. In July a battalion of volunteers from Marseilles sang the song as they marched into Paris. Because of this the song was called the ''March of Marseilles,'' and later *La Marseillaise.* It was declared the official national anthem in July, 1795.

Italy. The Italian national anthem, called the ''Hymn of Mameli,'' was the most popular song of the Italian revolution of 1848. The words were written by Goffredo Mameli and the music by Michele Novaro. The hymn always remained a popular patriotic song. However, the *Marcia Reale* (Royal March) was Italy's official anthem through the years of the Italian monarchy. But when the republic was declared in 1946, the popular old hymn became the new republic's anthem.

Japan. The words of *Kimigayo,* the national anthem of Japan, were taken from an ancient poem whose author has long been forgotten. The tune was composed by the court musician Hiromori Hayashi and was first used in 1880 on the birthday of Emperor Meiji. It was played without harmony on traditional Japanese instruments. The German bandmaster of the Japanese Navy, Franz von Eckert, harmonized the tune so that it could be played by the band. In 1893 this version became the official national anthem. The English translation is by Sakuzo Takada.

▶PATRIOTIC SONGS OF THE UNITED STATES

America's first patriotic songs came out of the Revolutionary period. As rebellion mounted, American colonists found an outlet for their emotions in political songs. Verses about timely issues were printed on sheets of paper called broadsides, which were sold in the streets for a penny apiece. Since these verses were set to tunes that were already familiar, the colonists lost no time in singing the new songs.

One of the first patriotic songs written in America was by John Dickinson (1732–1808), a New England lawyer. In 1768 a new import tax, which the colonists regarded as unjust, was imposed in Massachusetts. Dickinson's response to the tax was the "Liberty Song," in which he proclaimed that "not as slaves but as freemen our money we'll give." It was sung to the tune "Heart of Oak," written by the English composer William Boyce.

"Yankee Doodle" was the most famous song of the Revolutionary War. The words were written in 1755 during the French and Indian War. A British army doctor, Richard Schuckburgh (?–1773), wanted to ridicule the shabby-looking colonial soldiers. He improvised some nonsense lines about "Yankee Doodle" and set them to the tune of an English song, "Lucy Locket." No one knows the source of this tune, but it had long been familiar as a nursery song.

"Yankee Doodle" was a favorite of British soldiers whenever they wanted to make fun of the colonists. However, during the Revolution the colonists made it their battle cry of freedom. They sang it at Lexington in 1775 at the beginning of the war and at Yorktown in 1781 when the British surrendered.

"Hail Columbia" appeared in 1798, at a time when war threatened, following clashes between French and American ships on the high seas. It was written by a Philadelphian, Joseph Hopkinson (1770–1842). Hopkinson wrote a stirring poem in praise of his country. He set it to a melody by Philip Phile (1734–93), "The President's March," which had been written in honor of George Washington. For a quarter of a century, "Hail Columbia" was regarded as the national anthem. It was played daily on every American ship when the colors were lowered at sunset.

In 1831, Lowell Mason (1792–1872), one of America's most important music educators, asked the clergyman Samuel Francis Smith (1808–95) to write a new patriotic hymn for America's schoolchildren. Smith's hymn, "America," was set to the tune of "God Save the Queen." It was sung for the first time in Boston, on July 4, 1831, during a children's celebration of American independence. Today it is America's most popular patriotic song.

There is a good deal of mystery surrounding the writing of "Columbia, the Gem of the Ocean." It was first sung at the Chinese Museum in Philadelphia in 1842 by David T. Shaw. The authorship of this song has never been determined.

Civil War Songs

"Dixie" was the most popular song in the South during the American Civil War (1861–65). However, it was written by a Northerner, Dan Emmett (1815–1904), in 1859 for a minstrel show in New York. "Dixie" was probably first heard in the South in 1860 in Charleston, South Carolina. When the war broke out, fighting words were added to the song and it became the battle song of the South. "Dixie" was sung wherever Southern

Yankee Doodle

Words and Music Traditional

Yan-kee Doo-dle went to town,
Rid-ing on a po-ny, Stuck a fea-ther
in his cap, And called it ma-ca-ro-ni.
Yan-kee Doo-dle keep it up,
Yan-kee Doo-dle dan-dy, Mind the mu-sic
and the step, And with the girls be han-dy.

troops gathered or fought. When the South surrendered, President Lincoln asked a band outside the White House to play the song. He confessed that ''Dixie'' had long been one of his favorites.

An interesting thing about Civil War songs is that the favorite song of the South was written by a Northerner and the favorite song of the North, ''The Battle Hymn of the Republic,'' was set to a Southern tune. This tune, with different words, had been popular during the 1850's at the camp meetings of Negro congregations. One of the most popular songs using this tune was ''John Brown's Body,'' which is still sung today.

The words of ''The Battle Hymn'' were written in 1861 by a Northerner, Julia Ward Howe (1819–1910), a poetess and pioneer suffragette. By the end of 1862 it had become the war song of the North.

Two other popular battle hymns of the North were ''The Battle Cry of Freedom'' and ''Marching Through Georgia.'' The first was the work of George F. Root (1820–95) and second was prompted by President Lincoln's call for volunteers in 1863. ''Marching through Georgia'' was written in 1865 by Henry Clay Work (1832–84), a Northern printer. It was inspired by General Sherman's historic march through Georgia to the sea.

From 1895 to the Present

''America the Beautiful'' was written in 1895 by Katherine Lee Bates (1859–1929), a professor of English at Wellesley College. It was inspired by her trip to the top of Pikes Peak, where she was overwhelmed by the natural beauty of the American continent. She wrote these lines as a poem in praise of America and had no intention of using them in a song. But some unknown person combined her poem with the melody of ''Materna,'' which Samuel A. Ward (1814–84) had written in 1882. Words and music seemed made for each other. Today ''America the Beautiful'' is so highly regarded that many people would like to have it for the national anthem.

Among the songs of the armed services, the Navy's ''Anchors Aweigh'' is the oldest still in use. It was composed in about 1900 by Charles Z. Zimmermann to words by A. H. Miles and R. Lovell and was published in 1906. The ''Caisson Song'' was written for the artillery in 1908. Lieutenant Edmund L. Gruber, stationed with the 5th Artillery in the Philippines, was the author and composer. ''The Marines' Hymn'' was first published in 1918. The author was Colonel Henry C. Davis of the Marine Corps. The tune was taken from a comic opera of the 1800's, *Geneviève de Brabant*, by Jacques Offenbach.

''Over There,'' by George M. Cohan (1878–1942), was the most famous song of World War I. Cohan, a successful playwright, actor, and composer, wrote ''Over There'' in 1917, when he heard that America had declared war on Germany. Cohan was later awarded a congressional medal for this song.

''God Bless America,'' by Irving Berlin (1888–1989), was the most popular song of World War II. It was written in 1938 at the request of Kate Smith, the celebrated radio singer, who wanted a patriotic song for her radio show. It was adopted by the American people as one of their favorite patriotic songs. The song brought Berlin a special gold medal.

DAVID EWEN
Author, *Music for the Millions*,
The Home Book of Musical Knowledge

Dixie

Words and Music by Daniel D. Emmett

Refrain

NATIONAL ARCHIVES

The National Archives and Records Administration (NARA), an independent agency of the executive branch of the United States government since 1985, preserves historical records of national importance dating back to 1774. NARA was established by an act of Congress in 1934. Its original headquarters are located in Washington, D.C., between the White House and the Capitol building. Today a second main branch is located in College Park, Maryland.

The Collection. Preserved within NARA are approximately 4 billion pieces of paper; 7 million still photographs; 9 million aerial photographs; 2 million maps and charts; 2 million architectural and engineering plans; 110,000 reels of motion picture film; and 200,000 sound and video recordings. New materials are added continuously.

The most famous documents held by the National Archives are the Declaration of Independence, the Constitution of the United States, and the Bill of Rights, collectively known as the Charters of Freedom. These documents are on permanent display in the Washington, D.C., facility and are visited by more than 1 million people every year. Other important documents housed there include the Louisiana Purchase Treaty of 1803 and the Emancipation Proclamation.

Many of the nation's most treasured documents, such as the U.S. Constitution and the Bill of Rights, are placed in the National Archives for safekeeping.

Additional Facilities. In addition to the two main offices, NARA has 13 regional archives and 15 records centers located throughout the country. Each holds unique historical records of local interest. Other NARA offices include the Office of the Federal Register, which compiles and edits important publications relating to the activities of the federal government, and the National Historical Publications and Records Commission, which provides grants to state and local governments, libraries, and associations for the care of historical records.

The National Archives administers eleven of the nation's 16 presidential libraries, which preserve the papers and other historical materials of Presidents Herbert Hoover, Franklin D. Roosevelt, Harry S. Truman, Dwight D. Eisenhower, John F. Kennedy, Lyndon B. Johnson, Gerald R. Ford, Jimmy Carter, Ronald Reagan, George Bush, and Bill Clinton. NARA also administers Richard Nixon's presidential papers; however, his library is independently operated. Through a variety of public programs, the presidential libraries and corresponding museums provide unique resources for citizens and scholars alike to learn more about each president and the American political system.

Using the National Archives. The materials contained within the National Archives can be viewed by anyone in the world, not only by U.S. citizens. However, a photo identification is required to enter. To handle original materials and documents, one must obtain a research card from the archives and be at least 16 years of age.

Lawyers often use the National Archives to research previous court cases. Scholars study original documents while researching any number of subjects. However, the most common use of the archives is for genealogical research. People can find information about their ancestors by researching old census records, ships' passenger lists, and military service records. Many of these materials are available on microfilm. Research cards are not required to view microfilmed materials. Many interesting NARA documents and photographs that have high research value may also be accessed electronically through the NARA Web site.

Office of Public Affairs
The National Archives and Records Administration

NATIONAL ASSOCIATION FOR THE ADVANCEMENT OF COLORED PEOPLE (NAACP)

The National Association for the Advancement of Colored People (NAACP) is the oldest and the largest civil rights organization in the United States. Its principal goal is to ensure the rights of minority Americans by eliminating "all barriers to political, educational, social, and economic equality." In order to achieve this goal, the NAACP relies on the press, the court system, education, voting, and public petitions against the government and other organizations.

The NAACP has more than 2,200 branches in all 50 states, the District of Columbia, Japan, and Germany. These branches are divided into seven regions and are governed by a board of directors. NAACP headquarters are located in Baltimore, Maryland. Membership exceeds 500,000.

History. On February 12, 1909, on the one hundredth anniversary of

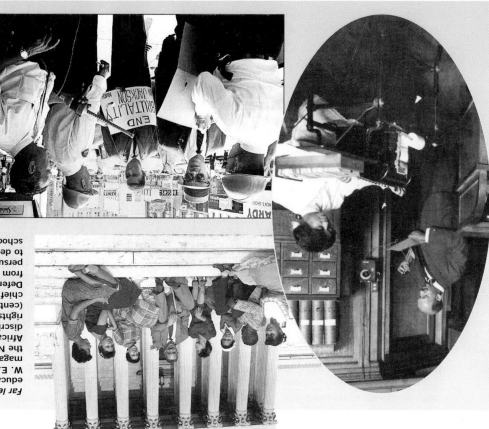

Far left: From 1910 to 1934, the educator and civil rights crusader W. E. B. Du Bois edited *Crisis,* a magazine that became the voice of the NAACP. Du Bois encouraged African Americans to fight discrimination and demand equal rights. *Top:* Thurgood Marshall (center) served as the director and chief counsel of the NAACP Legal Defense and Educational Fund from 1940 to 1961. In 1954 he persuaded the U.S. Supreme Court to declare segregation in public schools unconstitutional. Marshall later petitioned the Court to take action to ensure that black children would be protected from angry white separatists. Pictured here with Marshall in 1958 are six of the nine students known as the Little Rock Nine and their adviser, Daisy Bates, who led the fight to desegregate schools in Arkansas. *Bottom:* In 1963, NAACP executive secretary Roy Wilkins and field secretary Medgar Evers were arrested in Jackson, Mississippi, simply for protesting violence against African Americans.

President Abraham Lincoln's birthday, sixty prominent American citizens—both black and white—called for a national conference in New York City to renew "the struggle for civil and political liberty." A distinguished group of African American leaders and professionals added their voices to the movement. Among them were W. E. B. Du Bois, who had organized the Niagara Movement in 1905 to fight discrimination, and Ida Wells-Barnett, a journalist whose eloquent editorials had focused national attention on the lynchings (murders by mob violence, particularly by hanging) of African Americans.

Participants in the 1909 conference agreed to work toward the abolition of forced segregation (separation of the races); to promote civil rights under the protection of law; and to put an end to racial violence. In 1911, the group was officially incorporated as the National Association for the Advancement of Colored People.

The NAACP's first major campaign was to lobby the U.S. gov-

Clockwise from bottom: Walter F. White served as executive director of the NAACP from 1931 until his death in 1955. Part African American, he experienced intense racism while growing up in the South. His successor, Roy Wilkins, served from 1955 to 1977 and guided the NAACP through the troubled years of the civil rights movement. As chairman from 1995 to 1998, Myrlie Evers-Williams revitalized the NAACP.

ernment to enact anti-lynching laws. In 1919, to educate the public, NAACP leaders risked their lives by conducting first-hand investigations of violent acts against African Americans and then publicizing their findings. By the 1930's, Congress had enacted no laws, but the number of lynchings had declined due to public awareness and pressure.

During the Great Depression of the 1930's, the NAACP turned its focus on racial discrimination. A threat to "march on Washington" prompted President Franklin Roosevelt to create a Fair Employment Practices Committee to prevent discrimination when hiring for federally funded jobs. Then in 1941, when the nation entered World War II, the NAACP tried to end segregation in the U.S. Armed Forces. This goal was achieved in 1948, under President Harry S. Truman, three years after the war had ended.

The next goal of the NAACP was to end segregation in the public schools system. Thurgood Marshall, a lawyer for the NAACP, led the fight to the U.S. Supreme Court, which finally, in *Brown* v. *Board of Education of Topeka* (1954), ruled it unconstitutional for public schools to separate children by race. Although this was an unparalleled victory, many struggles lay ahead.

On December 1, 1955, an NAACP branch secretary in Montgomery, Alabama, named Rosa Parks refused to give up her seat to a white man on a public bus. Overnight she became a model of conduct for millions of Americans seeking nonviolent ways to protest discrimination. Many people consider her action the beginning of the modern civil rights movement.

The NAACP sponsored peaceful marches and sit-ins around the country to raise public awareness about the effects and moral injustices of racial discrimination. It also encouraged African Americans to register to vote. These efforts, among others, resulted in the Civil Rights acts of 1960 and 1964, the Voting Rights Act of 1965, and the Fair Housing Act of 1968.

The NAACP had finally achieved the civil rights protections it had been seeking from the federal government for nearly sixty years. Today the NAACP continues to fight against discrimination and for the civil liberties of all minority American citizens.

Reviewed by JIM MURRAY
Librarian, NAACP Henry Lee Moon Library and Civil Rights Archives

See also CIVIL RIGHTS MOVEMENT; DU BOIS, W. E. B.; SEGREGATION; SPINGARN MEDAL.

NATIONAL CEMETERIES

On July 17, 1862, in the second year of the U.S. Civil War, President Abraham Lincoln signed legislation that authorized the creation of 14 national cemeteries "…for the soldiers who shall die in the service of the country."

These were the first national cemeteries established in the United States. Previously, soldiers had been buried in fields and churchyards, or close to the battlefields, hospitals, and prison camps where they had died.

Today, more than 2.5 million Americans are buried in 136 national cemeteries in the United States and Puerto Rico. They now include the military veterans of every war and conflict in American history, from the Revolutionary War to the very latest times. Two of the cemeteries are administered by the Department of the Army, and 14 are managed by the National Park Service, a branch of the Department of the Interior, because they are important historical sites. The remaining 120 are administered by the National Cemetery Administration (NCA), a division of the U.S. Department of Veterans Affairs.

Department of the Army

The Department of the Army manages two national cemeteries. One of them is the Soldiers Home National Cemetery in Washington, D.C. The other, Arlington National Cemetery, is perhaps the most famous of all the national cemeteries.

Arlington National Cemetery is a 612-acre (248-hectare) cemetery located in Virginia, directly across the Potomac River from Washington, D.C. The grounds once belonged to George Washington Parke Custis, the grandson of First Lady Martha Washington.

Custis' daughter, Mary Ann Randolph Custis, was born at Arlington and continued to live there after her marriage in 1831 to Lieutenant Robert E. Lee, who later became the leading general and hero of the Confederacy during the Civil War. When the war came, federal troops occupied Arlington Heights and turned the Lee mansion into a command headquarters. The Lees never lived at Arlington again.

Arlington National Cemetery was begun on May 13, 1864, when the first military burial took place there. The old Lee mansion was used as an administrative office for the cemetery until 1925, when plans were made to restore it to its original condition. In 1933 it became a national memorial, called the

Arlington House, The Robert E. Lee Memorial, overlooks the grave site of President John F. Kennedy in Arlington National Cemetery.

Custis-Lee Mansion, under the National Park Service. In 1972 it was renamed Arlington House, The Robert E. Lee Memorial.

Today, more than 260,000 people are buried at Arlington National Cemetery. Among the notable people buried there are Generals John J. Pershing and George C. Marshall, Admirals Robert E. Peary and Richard E. Byrd, and Presidents William Howard Taft and John F. Kennedy. An eternal flame flickers above President Kennedy's grave.

The Tomb of the Unknown Soldier honors the unidentified remains of the soldiers who fought in World War I, World War II, the Korean War, and the Vietnam War. This tomb is guarded by sentries day and night. Other memorials include the Tomb of the Unknown Dead of the Civil War, the Confederate Monument, and the mast of the battleship *Maine*, which honors those who died in the explosion that caused the Spanish-American War in 1898.

After the Battle of Gettysburg in 1863, more than 3,700 Union soldiers were buried in Gettysburg National Cemetery. Many of the unidentified soldiers share a common grave *(inset)*.

National Park Service

Because of their importance as historical sites, 14 national cemeteries are managed by the National Park Service, which is a division of the Department of the Interior. Included among those are the Gettysburg National Cemetery in Pennsylvania and Andersonville National Cemetery in Georgia.

Gettysburg National Cemetery adjoins Gettysburg National Military Park. It honors those who died in this famous Civil War battle (July 1–3, 1863). Abraham Lincoln delivered his Gettysburg Address at the dedication ceremonies of this cemetery on November 19, 1863. More than 3,700 Union soldiers are buried there.

Andersonville National Cemetery, contained within Andersonville National Historic Site, is located on the site occupied by Andersonville Prison during the Civil War. The prison was established by the Confederates in 1864 and held 42,000 Union prisoners before the end of the war. More than 12,000 perished within its gates, and many were buried there. For a list of the national cemeteries administered by the National Park Service, see the article NATIONAL PARK SYSTEM in this volume.

National Cemetery Administration

The National Cemetery Administration (NCA), which is administered by the U.S. Department of Veterans Affairs (VA), includes 120 cemeteries in 39 states and Puerto Rico.

The VA is constructing new cemeteries, such as the Tahoma National Cemetery near Seattle, Washington, and has acquired land in other parts of the country for future sites. The VA will also expand some of the existing national cemeteries by acquiring adjoining lands. In addition, the VA has awarded more than 125 grants totaling more than $165 million to 31 states and the Commonwealths of Guam and the Northern Marianas through the State Cemetery Grants program to develop, expand, or improve dozens of state-run veterans' cemeteries.

National cemeteries hold the remains of hundreds of thousands of men and women, who fought and died to preserve the freedom of the United States throughout its history. More than 650 holders of the Medal of Honor are buried in national cemeteries, and each of their graves is marked with a special headstone. For example, Captain Thomas Custer, the first person to receive two Medals

Who can be buried in a U.S. national cemetery?

In the beginning the national cemeteries were meant to be battle monuments to the Union soldiers who died during the Civil War. But by 1881, Civil War veterans were requesting plots in the cemeteries as future burial space for themselves and their families, so the federal government slowly changed its policies. A law passed in 1948 made the following persons eligible for burial in national cemeteries: all persons dying on active duty in the Armed Forces of the United States; veterans who received an honorable discharge from active service; and the husbands or wives and dependent children of persons in both groups. Later many others became eligible, including members of the Reserves, National Guard, and Reserve Officers' Training Corps as well as some members of the National Oceanic and Atmospheric Administration, Public Health Service, and World War II Merchant Marines who die of causes related to their service. Due to overcrowding, Arlington is the only national cemetery where additional burial restrictions apply.

of Honor, is buried at Fort Leavenworth National Cemetery in eastern Kansas. He died, along with his more famous brother, Lieutenant Colonel George Armstrong Custer, at the Battle of the Little Bighorn on June 25, 1876.

The largest of all the national cemeteries is Calverton National Cemetery on Long Island, New York. It covers an area of 1,045 acres (418 hectares). Approximately 7,000 burials are conducted there each year. The cemetery contains a special memorial plaque honoring the memory of Captain Nathan Hale, the Revolutionary War hero, who was hanged as a spy by the commander of the British army.

The smallest national cemetery is the Hampton, Virginia, National Cemetery. Established for the emergency burial of victims

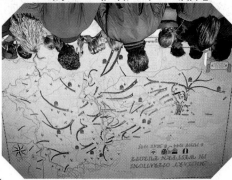

Exhibits, such as this diagram of the invasion of Normandy at a World War II cemetery in France, explain the history of the battles in which American soldiers lost their lives.

of a yellow fever epidemic in 1898, this cemetery contains only 21 headstones.

Another site is the National Memorial Cemetery of the Pacific, located near Honolulu, which was dedicated after World War II ended in 1945. Known as the Punchbowl, the cemetery is contained within the crater of a dormant volcano. It offers a spectacular vista of the Hawaiian capital and is the state's leading tourist attraction. The legendary World War II news correspondent Ernie Pyle, who gained the admiration of American servicemen around the world for his reports on life in combat, is buried there. It is also the grave site of U.S. Air Force Lieutenant Colonel Ellison S. Onizuka, a native of Hawaii, whose life ended tragically in the 1986 Challenger space shuttle disaster.

American Battle Monuments Commission

Not all American soldiers are buried on American soil. In 1923, the American Battle Monuments Commission (ABMC) was created to administer military burial grounds in foreign lands. Today the ABMC administers 24 American cemeteries overseas. Eight of the cemeteries were established after World War I—six in France and one each in England and Belgium. Fourteen more were added after World War II, five in France, two each in Belgium and Italy, and one each in England, the Netherlands, Luxembourg, Tunisia, and the Philippines. Two others include the Mexico City National Cemetery, which contains the dead of the Mexican War (1846-48), and the Corozal American Cemetery in Panama City, Republic of Panama, which was established in the early 1900's when the Panama Canal was under construction. More than 124,000 U.S. war dead are buried in ABMC cemeteries, which are closed to further burials.

KEN MCKINNON
National Cemetery Administration
United States Department of Veterans Affairs

See also Unknown Soldier.

NATIONAL FOREST SYSTEM

How would you like to see some of the oldest living things on Earth? The largest glacier that can be reached by a road? A spring that flows at the rate of 78 million gallons (295 million liters) a day? A rock formation 1 billion years old? The deepest canyon in the United States? A place where you can jump up and down on the ground and shake a person standing 150 feet (46 meters) away? Or a volcano that erupted violently in 1980?

Where can you find each of these wonders? They are not in one place, to be sure. But you can see them,

National forests are public lands set aside for everyone's use and enjoyment. *Left:* The Grand Mesa, Uncompahgre, and Gunnison National Forest in Colorado, with almost 3 million acres (1.2 million hectares), is the third largest national forest in the "Lower 48" states. *Below:* Shoshone National Forest is one of ten national forests in Wyoming.

and many other natural wonders, by visiting some of the national forests of the United States. For the answers to these questions, see Wonders of the National Forests on the opposite page.

The national forests belong to the people of the United States. They are part of the National Forest System, which administers 155 national forests and 20 national grasslands, stretching from Alaska to Puerto Rico. These areas cover more than 191 million acres (77 million hectares), or one-twelfth of the nation's total land area. These lands are protected and managed by the Forest Service, an agency of the United States Department of Agriculture. Other parts of the Forest Service include State and Private Forestry, which oversees programs for state and private landowners; International Forestry, which helps promote global environmental stability; and Forest Research, which pursues scientific knowledge and develops new forest products and technology.

To most people, the word "forest" means trees. It is true that the national forests provide timber, but they are not just timberlands. They also include open grasslands, high alpine tundra, and rivers and streams. People come to the national forests to hike, camp, fish, hunt, and enjoy other recreational activities. The forests also provide watersheds, minerals, habitats for fish and wildlife, forage food for livestock, and products from trees, such as lumber, pulp, and firewood.

▶ HISTORY AND MANAGEMENT

The first forest reserve in the United States was set aside in Wyoming in 1891 by a proclamation of President Benjamin Harrison. There was no plan for operation or protection of the reserves until 1897, when Congress passed an act that gave this responsibility to the General Land Office of the Department of the Interior. The Division of Forestry (later renamed the Bureau of Forestry) within the Department of Agriculture was called on only for aid and advice. But in 1905 the bureau was given control of the forest reserves and renamed the Forest Service. The name "forest reserve" was changed to "national forest." Under Gifford Pinchot, the first chief of the Forest Service, a program for scientific management of the forest was rapidly developed. Pinchot was a

WONDERS OF THE NATIONAL FORESTS

- Among the world's oldest living things—4,000 years old or more—are the bristle-cone pine trees in Inyo National Forest, in California and Nevada.
- The largest glacier that can be reached by a road is in Tongass National Forest, in Alaska.
- Alexander Spring in Florida's Ocala National Forest flows at the rate of 78 million gallons (295 million liters) a day.
- A 1-billion-year-old rock formation can be seen in Ashley National Forest, in Utah.
- The deepest gorge in the United States (7,900 feet or 2,408 meters) is Hells Canyon of the Snake River in Payette National Forest, in Idaho.
- If you jump up and down in Cranberry Glades in West Virginia's Monongahela National Forest, you will shake a person standing 150 feet (46 meters) away. This is because Cranberry Glades is a bog, which has a wet, spongy mat of vegetation for a floor.
- In 1980, Mount St. Helens in Gifford Pinchot National Forest, in Washington, erupted suddenly. The volcano had been inactive since 1857.

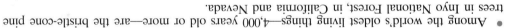

The eruption of Mount St. Helens on May 18, 1980, killed dozens of people and demolished the surrounding landscape, including millions of trees.

forestry expert and one of the nation's great conservationists.

In 1911, Congress passed the Weeks Law, which provided for the purchase of forest lands for watershed protection. Most of the eastern national forests were acquired in this way. The protection of the watersheds under Forest Service management improved the supply of freshwater and helped reduce soil erosion. It also preserved vast areas of recreational land, including most of the wilderness east of the Mississippi River.

White Mountain National Forest in New Hampshire is just one place to view New England's spectacular fall foliage.

About one-third of the timber harvested in the United States comes from national forests. Logs are carted away to be processed into thousands of different products.

▶ FOREST RANGERS

Forest rangers are highly trained professionals. They must earn a college degree and acquire special knowledge of how to manage and protect the forest and grazing lands.

Managing a national forest requires teams of individuals, each with training in a special field, such as business management, computers, engineering, forestry, hydrology (the study of water), recreation management, social science, or wildlife biology.

▶ RESEARCH AND ASSISTANCE

In addition to administering the National Forest System, the Forest Service conducts research through a network of eight Regional Forest and Range Experiment Stations, the Forest Products Laboratory in Madison, Wisconsin, and seventy field sites. The Forest Service also directs programs to encourage better management and protection of forest-lands that are not under federal ownership.

▶ WILDERNESS AND OTHER SPECIAL AREAS

Under the terms of the Wilderness Act of 1964, the Forest Service administers about 35 million acres (14 million hectares) of undeveloped land called wilderness. These areas are preserved for the enjoyment of people and for scientific purposes, such as biodiversity. Trees may not be cut, and structures, roads, and machinery are prohibited. The Forest Service also administers areas within the national forests that Congress has established as national recreation areas and as wild and scenic rivers.

The national grasslands came under Forest Service management in 1953. They are lands that were abandoned during the Dust Bowl of the 1930's, when drought and wind combined to blow soil off areas of the Great Plains.

▶ MULTIPLE USE AND ECOSYSTEM MANAGEMENT

The Forest Service manages the National Forest System, which is dedicated to multiple use. This means the lands are managed to provide the greatest combination of benefits for the greatest number of people, now and in the future.

The Forest Service also uses ecosystem management to care for the national forests and grasslands. Under ecosystem management, Forest Service specialists consider all

Did you know that...

some forests actually need fire? In many forests, especially in the western United States where there is little moisture, dead branches, twigs, needles, and leaves quickly become dry and brittle. When a fire starts, perhaps due to lightning or human carelessness, a dry forest can immediately become engulfed in flames.

To decrease the risk of raging fires, Forest Service rangers actually *start fires*,

called prescribed fires, that they can carefully control. In this way, they can burn away the dry brush that would cause an unplanned fire to spread and burn out of control. After a forest has been treated with a prescribed, or controlled, fire, it is possible that when an unplanned fire does occur, it will not have enough "fuel" to get hot enough to burn most of the larger trees.

parts of a landscape or area—animals, plants, minerals, and the needs of people—so that the lands can be used and enjoyed while being protected for the future. More than sixty endangered species of wildlife, fish, and plants are protected in the national forests. Hunting and fishing are allowed under laws of the individual states.

Many people have businesses that depend on the natural resources found in the national forests. For more than one hundred years, national forests have been an important source of wood. Today, about 5 percent of the nation's annual timber harvest comes from these public lands. Mining is also allowed. Businesses pay the government for permits to harvest the trees and mine the land. Other examples of businesses that depend on national forest resources include ski resorts and livestock ranching.

NATIONAL FORESTS AND GRASSLANDS IN THE UNITED STATES

NATIONAL FORESTS

NATIONAL GRASSLANDS

SPECIAL NATIONAL FOREST AREAS

NAME   ***LOCATION**

NATIONAL RECREATION AREAS (areas that provide places for recreation in a variety of natural settings):

Arapaho	Arapaho (Colorado)
Flaming Gorge	Ashley (Utah, Wyoming)
Hells Canyon	Nez Perce, Payette, Wallowa-Whitman (Idaho, Oregon)
Mount Rogers	Jefferson (Virginia)
Oregon Dunes	Siuslaw (Oregon)
Rattlesnake	Lolo (Montana)
Sawtooth	Boise, Challis, Sawtooth (Idaho)
Spruce Knob–Seneca Rocks	Monongahela (West Virginia)
†Whiskeytown-Shasta-Trinity	Shasta, Trinity (California)

WILD AND SCENIC RIVERS (rivers or parts of rivers preserved in their natural, free-flowing state):

Chattooga	Chattahoochee, Sumter, Nantahala (Georgia, S. Carolina, N. Carolina)
Clearwater, Middle Fork	Bitterroot, Nez Perce, Clearwater (Idaho)
Eleven Point	Mark Twain (Missouri)
Feather, Middle Fork	Plumas (California)
Flathead	Flathead (Montana)
Rapid	Nez Perce, Payette (Idaho)
Rio Grande	Carson (New Mexico)
Rogue	Siskiyou (Oregon)
Skagit	Mt. Baker–Snoqualmie (Washington)
St. Croix–Namekagon	Chequamegon (Wisconsin)
Salmon, Middle Fork	Boise, Challis, Payette, Salmon (Idaho)
Snake	Nez Perce, Payette, Wallowa-Whitman (Idaho, Oregon)

*National forest(s) and state(s)
†Administration shared with National Park Service

required to sustain different forms of life.

Each year national forests become more important. More people depend on forests for the natural resources they provide, and it is becoming increasingly difficult to meet all demands for using and conserving them.

Many people, especially in small towns and communities, depend on the national forests for their jobs. For example, they may cut trees for industries that make products from their lumber and pulp. Or they may graze their cattle in the national

Flaming Gorge National Recreation Area is located within the Ashley National Forest in the states of Utah and Wyoming.

▶ BALANCING USES AND NEEDS AND RESOLVING CONFLICTS

While the rivers, lakes, campgrounds, rangelands, wilderness areas, timber, minerals, and wildlife in the national forests belong to all Americans, it is almost impossible to satisfy the many different desires of all the people in a country as large as the United States. The Forest Service strives to produce the best combination of ways to meet the public's claims for natural resources for both commercial and recreational uses while still maintaining the ecosystem—the balance in nature

forests and grasslands. At the same time, other people are concerned about the possible effects of such activities on the land. The Forest Service tries to find compromises among different demands. One of its most important tools is the public involvement process, which provides citizens with an opportunity to state their beliefs on these issues by writing letters, attending meetings, or forming special interest groups.

CHRIS HOLMES
Acting Director, Public Affairs Office
U.S. Department of Agriculture, Forest Service

See also CONSERVATION; FORESTS AND FORESTRY; NATIONAL PARK SYSTEM; ROOSEVELT, THEODORE.

The National Gallery in London ranks among the world's greatest art museums. Its more than 2,000 paintings represent nearly 700 years of European art.

NATIONAL GALLERY (LONDON)

The National Gallery in London is a public museum financed by the British government. Its collection of more than 2,000 European paintings is smaller than many other national collections. But the museum is famous for the high quality of its works.

The National Gallery was founded in 1824, when the British Parliament voted to buy an important group of paintings from the collection of John Julius Angerstein, a wealthy merchant who had died the year before. The reason for buying the collection was that Parliament did not want the paintings to be taken out of the country. Many of these paintings are among the most famous that the museum owns.

The National Gallery was first opened in Angerstein's town house in London. But as the collection grew, the house soon became very crowded. In 1833, work was begun on a new building in Trafalgar Square. This building was opened in 1838 and is still in use today. It was enlarged with the addition of the Sainsbury Wing in 1991.

The gallery's collection includes examples of the main schools of European painting

from about 1250 to 1920. Especially notable are masterpieces of Italian Renaissance painting by such artists as Leonardo da Vinci, Raphael, Michelangelo, and Titian.

The collection also contains outstanding works by northern European artists, including Hans Holbein the Younger, Peter Paul Rubens, and Rembrandt van Rijn. Among the other famous artists represented in the gallery are Spanish painters Diego Velázquez and Francisco Goya and French painters Nicholas Poussin and Eugène Delacroix.

Although the gallery exhibits a select group of works by British artists, including William Hogarth, John Constable, and J. M. W. Turner, most of the British paintings are now in the Tate Gallery. This museum was founded in 1897 as an annex to the National Gallery. It has been an independent museum since 1955. The Tate also houses modern British and foreign sculpture and modern foreign paintings.

To help the public appreciate the collection, the gallery offers educational services such as guided tours, public lectures, audiovisual shows, and programs for schoolchildren.

Reviewed by A. H. PEPPIN
National Gallery (London)

Left: The original building of the National Gallery of Art, now called the West Building, was opened in 1941. Right: The modern East Building was opened in 1978.

NATIONAL GALLERY OF ART (WASHINGTON, D.C.)

The National Gallery of Art in Washington, D.C., contains one of the world's finest collections of Western European painting, sculpture, and graphic arts, as well as American art from the colonial period to the present time. It has what is often considered to be the most complete survey of Italian painting and sculpture in the Western Hemisphere, including the portrait *Ginevra de' Benci*. This is the only painting outside Europe generally acknowledged to be by Leonardo da Vinci. The National Gallery also has fine groups of paintings by Rembrandt and by the French impressionists and notable examples of American, British, German, Flemish, and Spanish art.

All the works have been given by private citizens or purchased with their donated funds. More than 400 donors have contributed to the gallery's collections, which have grown to more than 40,000 works. Funds from the federal government support the operation and maintenance of the gallery.

▶ THE COLLECTION

The gallery was established in 1937 with funds provided by Andrew W. Mellon. Mellon was a banker and industrialist who served as secretary of the treasury from 1921 to 1932. In 1936 he wrote to President Franklin D. Roosevelt, offering to build a gallery of art that would belong to the people of the United States. To start the gallery, he said that he would donate his own fine collection, which included about 150 paintings and sculptures dating from the 13th century to the 19th century. He also donated funds to erect a building to house these works of art.

The collection given by Mellon included such masterpieces as Raphael's *Alba Madonna,* Jan van Eyck's *Annunciation,* Sandro Botticelli's *Adoration of the Magi,* and nine works by Rembrandt. Also in Mellon's original gift were a portrait of George Washington by Gilbert Stuart (one of three that Stuart painted of Washington from life) and *The Washington Family* by Edward Savage.

Over the years, other major collections have become part of the gallery's holdings. Out-

standing Italian paintings and sculptures from the 13th century to the 18th century were given in the 1940's by Samuel H. Kress and his brother Rush H. Kress. They also added distinguished 18th-century French works of art and fine early German paintings.

The collection of P. A. B. Widener was given to the gallery after his death in 1915 by his son Joseph Widener. It includes works by Rembrandt, Anthony van Dyck, and Jan Vermeer. Other works in the Widener collection include Spanish, English, and French paintings and examples of Italian and French sculpture and decorative arts.

Among more recent donors was Chester Dale. He gave American and French works during his lifetime and on his death in 1962 bequeathed the rest of his extensive collection of French paintings of the 19th and 20th centuries. Dale's collection included *A Girl with a Watering Can* by Pierre Auguste Renoir. Ailsa Mellon Bruce, a daughter of Andrew W. Mellon, bequeathed her collection of French paintings on her death in 1969. She

Right: *A Girl with a Watering Can* (1876), by Pierre Auguste Renoir, is in the Chester Dale Collection at the National Gallery. Below: *The Adoration of the Magi* (1482?), by Sandro Botticelli, from the Mellon Collection.

Inside the East Building. Above: A mobile by Alexander Calder hangs in the inner court. Below: This room, designed for temporary exhibits, displays the sculpture of David Smith.

also provided funds for acquiring several masterworks, among them the portrait of Ginevra de' Benci. The gifts of Paul Mellon, president of the National Gallery of Art and son of Andrew W. Mellon, include paintings by the American artist George Catlin, as well as works by the French artists Paul Cézanne, Paul Gauguin, Édouard Manet, and Edgar Degas. Paul Mellon also lent a group of French impressionist and post-impressionist paintings.

Prints, drawings, and other works given by Lessing J. Rosenwald have formed the nucleus of the gallery's collection of graphic arts. Contemporary American graphics given by the Woodward Foundation have further strengthened the gallery's holdings in this field.

▶ THE BUILDINGS

The gallery's original building is now called the West Building. It was designed by John Russell Pope in the neoclassic style and was opened on March 17, 1941. This building is one of the largest marble structures in the world, with more than 46,000 square meters (500,000 square feet) of floor space. Pope designed it to be large enough to provide for the growth of the collection.

On June 1, 1978, a second building—the East Building—was opened to the public. It was the gift of Paul Mellon, Ailsa Mellon Bruce, and the A. W. Mellon Educational and Charitable Trust. Triangular in design, the East Building has nearly 41,500 square meters (450,000 square feet) of floor space. It was designed by I. M. Pei to provide flexible exhibition areas for the gallery's growing collection of contemporary art and for special exhibitions. Walls and ceilings can be altered to show each exhibit to its best advantage.

The Center for Advanced Study in the Visual Arts is also in the East Building. It includes a library, photographic archives (storage files for preserving photographs), and offices for the staff and visiting scholars.

The two buildings are connected by a large underground concourse, which contains public dining facilities and work areas for gallery staff. A central air-conditioning system adds to the comfort of visitors and staff and helps to preserve the works of art by keeping levels of temperature and humidity constant.

Reviewed by J. CARTER BROWN
Director, National Gallery of Art

In *The Habitant Farm* (1856), Cornelius Krieghoff painted a picture of life on a Quebec farm.

NATIONAL GALLERY OF CANADA

The National Gallery of Canada, in Ottawa, is a public museum, owned by the people of Canada. It houses the world's largest single collection of Canadian art, but works of art from Europe and Asia are also represented.

The early history of the National Gallery is linked with the founding of the Royal Canadian Academy of Arts in 1880. Both were begun with the help of the Marquis of Lorne, the governor-general of Canada, and his wife, Princess Louise, a daughter of Queen Victoria.

In spite of a snowstorm, a large group of people arrived by sleigh to see the gallery's first exhibition. It was made up of 17 works of art donated by artists who were members of the Royal Canadian Academy.

In 1913, an act of Parliament recognized the National Gallery and stated that its purpose was to encourage public interest in art and to promote Canadian art. The National Gallery was declared one of the National Museums of Canada in 1968.

► THE COLLECTIONS

Over the years the collections of the National Gallery have grown steadily. They now include more than 30,000 works of art—paintings, sculpture, prints, drawings, decorative art objects, and photographs. More than one half of them are by Canadians.

In developing the Canadian collection, the curators look for works of art that will help explain the growth and history of art in Canada. The collection includes works by such well-known 19th- and 20th-century artists as Antoine Sébastien Plamondon, Cornelius Krieghoff, Tom Thomson and the Toronto painters known as the Group of Seven, as well as works by Emily Carr, Paul Emile Borduas, and Alex Colville. The best and most imaginative works by Canadian artists of today are also represented.

Works from other countries, especially countries from which Canadians have come, help Canadians trace the traditions of their own art. The curators of the European collection have chosen works that show how art

Above: *Portrait of Soeur Saint-Alphonse* (1841), by Antoine Sébastien Plamondon.

The Jack Pine (1916–17), by Tom Thomson, a painter of Canada's rugged north.

has developed from the Middle Ages to the present. Works by masters such as Bernini, Rembrandt, Jordaens, Turner, and Cézanne are included. Other collections include art from Asian countries, fine-art photographs, and examples of the decorative arts such as silver objects and fine furniture.

Some works of art are purchased by the National Gallery, but many others are donated. Two important donations are the Douglas Duncan collection of Canadian prints and drawings and the Henry Birks collection of Canadian silver. The Heeramaneck collection of South Asian art is another notable gift. It includes stone and wood sculpture and miniature paintings from India.

Parts of the National Gallery's collection are always on exhibit. About 20 special exhibitions are prepared each year. Many of them are sent on tour across Canada. Some are also shown in other countries, including Britain, France, Italy, and the United States.

▶ SPECIAL SERVICES

Because many works of art become fragile as they get older and can be easily damaged, the National Gallery has established a spe-cial laboratory, the Restoration and Conservation Laboratory. The experts in this laboratory, who are called conservators, perform scientific tests on each piece of art to determine the best kind of care and treatment. The conservators also offer advice to other museums and galleries on handling their collections. And they provide private owners with information on caring for their works of art.

The Reference Library of the National Gallery maintains records of all publications on Canadian art. These records are a valuable tool for researchers and art historians. In its Documentation Centre, the library also keeps up-to-date records of the life and work of many Canadian artists.

The Education Department of the National Gallery helps visitors understand and appreciate what they see. Each year thousands of people are given conducted tours. Many others attend lectures and gallery talks. The Education Department also has special films and programs for children.

LORNA JOHNSON
Education Services
National Gallery of Canada

NATIONAL GEOGRAPHIC SOCIETY

The National Geographic Society is one of the largest nonprofit educational and scientific organizations in the world. It gathers and publishes information on science, technology, nature, and world cultures.

Headquartered in Washington, D.C., the National Geographic Society was founded in 1888 by a group of scientists and explorers who wanted to collect and distribute geographical information. Today the Society supports a wide range of projects and activities, including environmental conservation, scientific research and explorations, anthropological and archaeological studies, and educational programs.

The Society has sponsored some of the most important studies and expeditions of modern times. Among these are Robert E. Peary's historic expedition to the North Pole; the primate research of Jane Goodall and Dian Fossey; the many discoveries of early

human fossils by the Leakey family; the underwater explorations of Jacques-Yves Cousteau; and Robert Ballard's discovery of the wreck of the ocean liner *Titanic*.

National Geographic magazine, the Society's official journal, is famous for its authoritative articles and stunning photography. It is published in twenty languages throughout the world. Other publications include *National Geographic Traveler*, which provides information for travelers; *National Geographic Explorer!*, a classroom magazine for children in grades three through six; and *National Geographic Adventure*, which chronicles adventurous people and exciting places. The Society also produces books, maps, and many award-winning videos and CD-ROM's. The Society's cable network, National Geographic Channel, along with its popular television program *National Geographic EXPLORER*, brings the wonders of the world to millions of people every day.

Reviewed by ELLEN SISKIND
National Geographic Society

NATIONAL GUARD

The National Guard is a reserve component of the United States armed forces. It is made up of part-time citizen-soldiers who assist the Army and the Air Force in combat and perform a wide variety of civil services for states and local communities.

Members of the National Guard are volunteers—that is, they enlist of their own free will. Anyone between 17 and 35 years of age who can meet the physical, educational, and legal (such as U.S. citizenship) qualifications may join.

After no less than twelve weeks of basic training, Guard members return to civilian life. They then spend one weekend each month and an additional 15 days each year in training. Their pay is the same as that of active soldiers and aviators of the same rank in the Army and the Air Force.

The federal government and state governments share the cost of the National Guard. The states build armories, which are buildings used as storage places for weapons and as drill centers. The federal government provides pay and equipment.

In the wake of terrorist attacks against the United States in 2001, the National Guard was mobilized to provide extra security at the nation's airports.

The National Guard is a federal force when it is called up, or mobilized, by the president. It is a state force at all other times, with each unit reporting to the governor of the state or territory to which it belongs. The District of Columbia's National Guard unit reports to its commanding general. The Guard is linked to the Army and the Air Force by the National Guard Bureau.

A national emergency such as a war is not the only alarm that causes Guard units to be called up. They may be mobilized to provide relief to victims of earthquakes, floods, or tornadoes; to participate in counterdrug operations; and to conduct search-and-rescue operations.

▶ **HISTORY**

Militia units were first formed in 1636 to defend the colonies from attacks by Native Americans, and the militias later fought the British during the Revolutionary War. When the Marquis de Lafayette (a Revolutionary War hero) visited New York in 1824, the New York Militia renamed itself the Battalion of National Guards in honor of the Garde Nationale de Paris, a force he had commanded in France. By 1896 most state militias were known as National Guard units.

The National Guard helped win the War of 1812, the Mexican War, the U.S. Civil War, and the Spanish-American War. It was state-controlled until 1903, when Congress passed the Dick Act. This act let the federal government take a more active part in training and equipping the militia. It also allowed the president to call Guard units to active duty.

The National Defense Act of 1916 organized the National Guard like the Army, and it would be part of the Army when called into federal service. Later defense acts put the Guard under both the state and federal governments.

The National Guard fought overseas in both world wars. With the founding of the Air National Guard in 1947, the National Guard was divided into two separate divisions, one serving the Army and one serving the Air Force. Since then, the Army National Guard and the Air National Guard have played vital roles in every major U.S. conflict.

Reviewed by LA VERN E. WEBER
Deputy Commanding General
United States Army Forces Command

NATIONAL HONOR SOCIETY

The National Honor Society™ (NHS) and National Junior Honor Society™ (NJHS) are school-based organizations that were first formed in the 1920's to recognize the achievements of outstanding high school and middle school students. It is estimated that more than 1 million students currently participate in these organizations. The NHS and NJHS have more than 20,000 chapters in every state, as well as Puerto Rico, many U.S. territories, and Canada.

Students are selected to become members of the NHS or NJHS through chapters established in their schools. The local selection process is based on the national guidelines. To be eligible, one must have at least a B average (85 percent) or its equivalent.

Students who are named to these organizations must also show leadership at school through their activities and attitudes, be individuals of good character, and be involved in school or community service.

In addition to recognition for one's accomplishments, membership in the NHS and NJHS allows students to participate in Honor Society projects and activities, both locally and nationally.

The National Honor Society was established in 1921 by the National Association of Secondary School Principals (NASSP) under the direction of Dr. Edward Rynearson, a principal from Pittsburgh, Pennsylvania. Though many local and regional honor societies existed at the time, NHS was the first national organization of its kind. In 1929, the NASSP formed the National Junior Honor Society for middle-level students.

Both the NHS and NJHS are sponsored and supervised by the NASSP, which appoints a National Council to oversee operations. The administration of both organizations is handled by the NASSP, headquartered in Reston, Virginia.

DAVID CORDTS
National Association of
Secondary School Principals

NATIONAL INSTITUTES OF HEALTH

The National Institutes of Health (NIH) is the U.S. federal government's main agency for the support of medical research. The NIH is part of the Public Health Service, which is part of the Department of Health and Human Services.

The mission of the NIH is to discover information about living organisms and to apply that knowledge to promote human health and reduce disease. To meet this goal, the NIH conducts medical research on its own campuses in Bethesda, Maryland, and at satellite locations, and it awards grants to scientists at institutions throughout the United States.

The NIH is made up of a number of institutes, centers, and offices. The research conducted at each focuses on specific areas of human health. The institutes of the NIH are listed in the box to the right.

The NIH began as a one-room laboratory of hygiene in 1887. It has grown to become one of the world's foremost medical research centers.

NIH INSTITUTES

National Cancer Institute
National Eye Institute
National Heart, Lung, and Blood Institute
National Human Genome Research Institute
National Institute on Aging
National Institute on Alcohol Abuse and Alcoholism
National Institute of Allergy and Infectious Diseases
National Institute of Arthritis and Musculoskeletal and Skin Diseases
National Institute of Biomedical Imaging and Bioengineering
National Institute of Child Health and Human Development
National Institute on Deafness and Other Communication Disorders
National Institute of Dental and Craniofacial Research
National Institute of Diabetes and Digestive and Kidney Diseases
National Institute on Drug Abuse
National Institute of Environmental Health Sciences
National Institute of General Medical Sciences
National Institute of Mental Health
National Institute of Neurological Disorders and Stroke
National Institute of Nursing Research
National Library of Medicine

Reviewed by VICTORIA A. HARDEN
Director, Office of NIH History
National Institutes of Health

NATIONAL ORGANIZATION FOR WOMEN (NOW)

The National Organization for Women (NOW) is the largest organization of women's rights activists in the United States. It was formed in 1966 to promote equality between men and women and currently has about 500,000 members and 550 chapters.

Since its founding, NOW has fought to end discrimination against women in the workplace, schools, government, legal system, and all other sectors of society. It works to ensure that women have access to the same jobs and professional opportunities as men and that they are paid equal salaries for equal work. The organization also supports reproductive rights, including safe and legal abortion and access to birth control, as well as the right of gays and lesbians to be free from discrimination. In addition, it seeks to achieve a guarantee of equality for women through an amendment to the U.S. Constitution.

NOW fights to end all violence against women and encourages society to recognize the value of women's work in the home.

The organization works closely with other groups on civil rights, welfare rights, economic justice, and other issues. It also works with international women's groups to promote the health and welfare of women around the world.

NOW organizes mass marches, rallies, pickets, and nonviolent civil disobedience. It initiates class-action lawsuits and lobbies for laws that benefit women. It also strives to increase the number of women in politics and other positions of leadership.

Some people and organizations oppose NOW, particularly those who disagree with its position on reproductive rights. NOW has also been criticized by those who believe in preserving traditional roles for women.

NOW has four elected national officers, a national board of directors, and various national-issues committees.

KIM GANDY
President, National Organization for Women

See also WOMEN'S RIGHTS MOVEMENT.

NATIONAL PARK SYSTEM

Can you imagine hiking into a canyon that is 277 miles (446 kilometers) long and 1 mile (1.6 kilometers) deep? Or seeing the world's tallest tree? Or climbing the highest mountain in the "Lower 48" states? Every year, thousands of people do these things in the Grand Canyon, Redwoods, and Sequoia national parks, just three of the hundreds of special places in the U.S. National Park System, administered by the National Park Service.

The National Park System is a collection of the most beautiful, as well as the most historic, places in the country. They have been set aside to be enjoyed but also to be protected for many generations to come. There are more than 365 units of the National Park System that are visited every year by approximately 280 million visitors from all over the world. The system contains more than 80 million acres (36 million hectares) of land. This is slightly less than 4 percent of the total land area of the United States. This remarkable collection of natural places, monuments, historic sites, and other areas is one of America's finest accomplishments.

Establishing and protecting the national parks depends upon vision, care, and hard work. The U.S. National Park System is viewed with pride by Americans and with ad-

miration by people of other countries. In fact, more than 100 other countries have used the United States' park system as a model for establishing their own collections of natural and historic places.

▶ **THE FIRST NATIONAL PARKS**

In 1872, the United States government dedicated the world's first national park, an area to be preserved in its natural condition. It consisted of land surrounding the Yellowstone River in what is now northwestern Wyoming. This area had been explored by John Colter, a former member of the Lewis and Clark expedition (1804–06), and fur trappers, such as Jim Bridger. They told stories of a beautiful land with rivers, waterfalls, hot springs, and geysers.

In 1870, while camping by a river in the Yellowstone area, members of a government-sponsored expedition led by Henry Washburn discussed the idea of establishing a park that would belong to all Americans. This idea grew in popularity and eventually resulted in congressional legislation that established Yellowstone National Park.

Yellowstone was just the start. Other national parks were later established at Yosemite (1890), Sequoia (1890), and Glacier (1910), each created by a specific act of Congress. By 1906 there were eight national parks. In that year, Congress approved the Act for the Preservation of American Antiquities. It authorized the president to set aside lands owned or controlled by the United States that contained historic landmarks, historic or prehistoric structures, and other objects of historical or scientific interest. These sites are called national monuments.

Under the authority of this act, President Theodore Roosevelt set aside Devils Tower, a tall volcanic formation in northeastern Wyoming, as the first national monument. During the early years, national parks and monuments were managed by a variety of agencies of the federal government.

The National Park Service

In 1916 Congress established the National Park Service to manage the various parks and monuments already in existence. Congress called on the new agency to "conserve the scenery and the natural and historic objects and the wild life therein and to provide

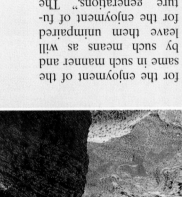

for the enjoyment of the same in such manner and by such means as will leave them unimpaired for the enjoyment of future generations." The National Park Service was placed within the Department of the Interior, an executive department of the U.S. government that has a variety of responsibilities concerning public lands in the United States.

The first director of the National Park Service was Stephen Mather, a businessman and conservationist, who helped create the new agency. Mather served as director from 1917

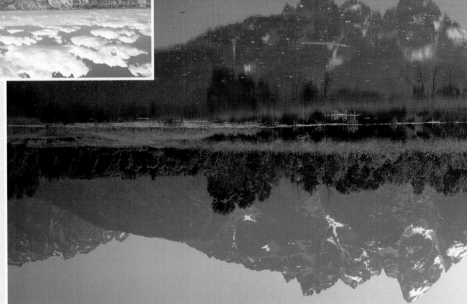

Left: Grand Teton National Park in Wyoming features forests, clear lakes, and the stunning mountains of the Teton Range of the Rocky Mountains. *Below:* The Grand Canyon in Arizona is one of the nation's most visited national parks. Tourists from all over the world come to see its spectacularly colored layers of limestone, sandstone, shale, and other rocks. *Bottom:* A park ranger answers questions at Padre Island National Seashore in Texas.

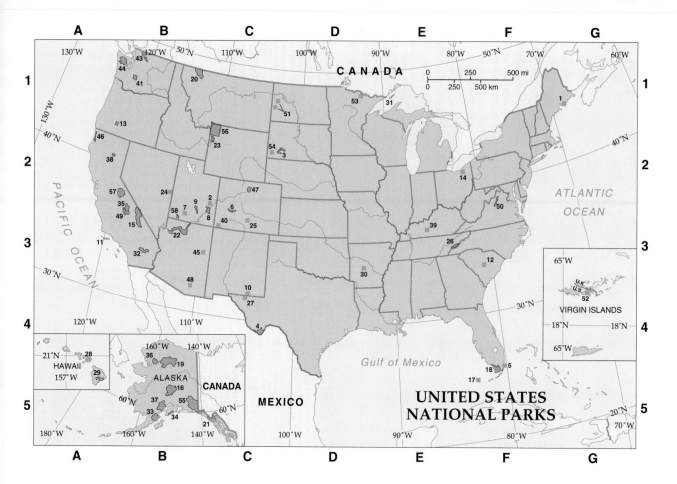

UNITED STATES
NATIONAL PARKS

#	Name (Year Founded)	Location	Outstanding Features
1	Acadia (1919)	Maine (G1)	Rugged coastline and seascape
2	Arches (1971)	Utah (C2)	Desert landscape, rock formations
3	Badlands (1978)	S. Dakota (C2)	Arid climate, fossils, wildlife
4	Big Bend (1944)	Texas (C4)	Mountainous desert along Rio Grande
5	Biscayne (1980)	Florida (F4)	Coral reef, seascape
6	Black Canyon of the Gunnison (1999)	Colorado (C3)	Deep river gorge
7	Bryce Canyon (1928)	Utah (B3)	Colorful rock ranges in desert
8	Canyonlands (1964)	Utah (C3)	Undeveloped desert and canyons
9	Capitol Reef (1971)	Utah (B3)	Colorful rock formations, gorges
10	Carlsbad Caverns (1930)	New Mex. (C4)	Largest known caves in world
11	Channel Islands (1980)	California (A3)	Wild islands in Pacific Ocean
12	Congaree (2003)	S. Carolina (F3)	Old-growth hardwood forest
13	Crater Lake (1902)	Oregon (A2)	Deep, clear lake formed by volcano
14	Cuyahoga Valley (2000)	Ohio (E2)	Historic villages, remains of the Ohio and Erie Canals
15	Death Valley (1994)	California (B3)	Lowest point in Western Hemisphere
16	Denali (1980)	Alaska (B5)	Highest mountain in North America
17	Dry Tortugas (1992)	Florida (F5)	Seascape, historic remnants
18	Everglades (1934)	Florida (F5)	Marshes, rivers, abundant wildlife
19	Gates of Arctic (1980)	Alaska (B4)	Mountainous, remote wilderness
20	Glacier (1910)	Montana (B1)	Mountainous lakes, grizzly bears
21	Glacier Bay (1980)	Alaska (C5)	Coastline glaciers, whales
22	Grand Canyon (1919)	Arizona (B3)	Immense gorge, whitewater rafting
23	Grand Teton (1929)	Wyoming (C2)	Scenic mountains, clear lakes
24	Great Basin (1986)	Nevada (B2)	Mountains and caves
25	Great Sand Dunes (2000)	Colorado (C3)	America's tallest sand dunes
26	Great Smoky Mountains (1930)	Tennessee (E3)	Heavily forested mountains
27	Guadalupe Mountains (1972)	Texas (C4)	Mountainous desert, wildflowers
28	Haleakala (1960)	Hawaii (A4)	Lush vegetation, dormant volcano
29	Hawaii Volcanoes (1961)	Hawaii (A5)	Active volcanic area, vegetation
30	Hot Springs (1921)	Arkansas (D3)	Mineral hot springs, historic resort
31	Isle Royale (1931)	Michigan (E1)	Northern lakes, moose, wolves
32	Joshua Tree (1994)	California (B3)	Joshua trees and desert wildlife
33	Katmai (1980)	Alaska (B5)	Remote wilderness, fishing, bears
34	Kenai Fjords (1980)	Alaska (B5)	Seacoast, marine mammals and birds
35	Kings Canyon (1890)	California (B3)	High mountains, giant trees
36	Kobuk Valley (1980)	Alaska (B4)	Arctic ecosystem, wolves, bears
37	Lake Clark (1980)	Alaska (B5)	Mountainous seacoast, glaciers
38	Lassen Volcanic (1916)	California (A2)	Volcanic mountains, hot springs
39	Mammoth Cave (1941)	Kentucky (E3)	Vast cave system, underground river
40	Mesa Verde (1906)	Colorado (C3)	Remote desert, cliff dwellings
41	Mount Rainier (1899)	Washington (B1)	Single-peak mountain, wildflowers
42	National Park of American Samoa (1988)	American Samoa (off map)	Rain forests, coral reefs
43	North Cascades (1968)	Washington (B1)	Alpine landscape, mountain lakes
44	Olympic (1938)	Washington (B1)	Mountains, coastline, rain forest
45	Petrified Forest (1962)	Arizona (B3)	Painted Desert, petrified trees
46	Redwood (1968)	California (A2)	Coastal redwoods, world's tallest trees
47	Rocky Mountain (1915)	Colorado (C2)	Dozens of peaks over 10,000 feet
48	Saguaro (1994)	Arizona (B3)	Giant cacti in Sonoran Desert
49	Sequoia (1890)	California (B3)	Mt. Whitney, giant sequoia trees
50	Shenandoah (1935)	Virginia (F2)	Mountain forests, Skyline Drive views
51	Theodore Roosevelt (1978)	N. Dakota (C1)	River valley, historic ranch
52	Virgin Islands (1956)	U.S. V.I. (G4)	Beaches, lush vegetation
53	Voyageurs (1975)	Minnesota (D1)	Lakes, canoeing, fishing, wildlife
54	Wind Cave (1903)	S. Dakota (C2)	Limestone caverns, buffalo
55	Wrangell-St. Elias (1980)	Alaska (B5)	Immense wilderness, wildlife
56	Yellowstone (1872)	Wyoming (C2)	Waterfalls, geysers, wildlife
57	Yosemite (1890)	California (A2)	Mountains, valleys, waterfalls
58	Zion (1919)	Utah (B3)	Colorful desert valley

▶ ORGANIZATION

National parks, established by acts of Congress, are usually fairly large land or water areas containing many natural resources. Na-tional monuments are generally smaller than parks and contain at least one significant fea-ture. They can be established by Congress or by a presidential proclamation. National his-toric sites are authorized by Congress or by the secretary of the interior, who is a member of the president's cabinet. Other units are created by congressional legislation. The sys-tem has expanded through individual actions rather than as the result of a comprehensive plan.

As of 1995, the National Park System was made up of 367 units. Park units can be found in every state except Delaware. The National

(text continued on page 50)

providing historic and natural preservation.

In 1935, Congress passed the Historic Sites Act, designating historic preservation as a na-tional policy. This act also created the Advi-sory Board on National Parks, Historic Sites, Buildings, and Monuments and firmly estab-lished a role for the National Park Service in

to 1929. During this period, the agency grew and developed many of its procedures.

Above: Mineral deposits from flowing water form terraces at Mammoth Hot Springs in Wyoming. Yellowstone National Park in Wyoming. Yellowstone is the nation's oldest national park.

Right: Mount McKinley, North America's highest mountain, is the crowning point of Denali National Park and Preserve in Alaska.

REFLECTION POND

A BLOCK OF ICE FROM MCKINLEY'S ANCIENT GLACIERS MELTED TO FORM THIS KETTLE HOLE POND, REFLECTING THE BEAUTY OF ITS MOUNTAIN HERITAGE

NATIONAL PRESERVES

Areas having "national preserve" as a part of their official names are established to protect natural areas with rare or endangered animals and plants. Activities such as hunting and fishing or the extraction of fuels and other minerals may be permitted if they do not harm the natural values.

ANIAKCHAK, ALASKA
BERING LAND BRIDGE, ALASKA
BIG CYPRESS, FLORIDA
BIG THICKET, TEXAS
DENALI, ALASKA
GATES OF THE ARCTIC, ALASKA
GLACIER BAY, ALASKA
GREAT SAND DUNES, COLORADO
KATMAI, ALASKA
LAKE CLARK, ALASKA
LITTLE RIVER CANYON, ALABAMA
MOJAVE, CALIFORNIA
NOATAK, ALASKA
TALL GRASS PRAIRIE, KANSAS
TIMUCUAN ECOLOGICAL AND
        HISTORIC, FLORIDA
WRANGELL-ST. ELIAS, ALASKA
YUKON-CHARLEY RIVERS, ALASKA

Opposite page, top: Haleakala National Park on the island of Maui in Hawaii features the crater of Haleakala, an inactive volcano. *Left:* The heavily forested Great Smoky Mountains National Park lies between Tennessee and North Carolina. *Below:* The Appalachian National Scenic Trail extends 2,143 miles (3,448 kilometers) along the Appalachian Mountains, from Mount Katahdin in Maine to Springer Mountain in Georgia.

WONDER QUESTION

What is the largest U.S. national park?

Wrangell-St. Elias National Park and Preserve in southeastern Alaska encompasses more than 8.3 million acres (3.4 million hectares), which is nearly four times larger than Yellowstone National Park. The park's three mountain ranges contain nine of the nation's 16 tallest mountain peaks, including Mount St. Elias, which at 18,008 feet (5,489 meters) is the second highest mountain in the United States, after Mount McKinley. The park also contains the largest group of glaciers in North America.

Park Service is organized into three levels to manage all the different units. Central headquarters, located in Washington, D.C., is responsible for overall planning and budgeting. Ten regional offices are located throughout the country to provide communication and coordination between headquarters and the individual units. They are located in Anchorage, Atlanta, Boston, Denver, Omaha, Philadelphia, San Francisco, Santa Fe, Seattle, and Washington, D.C. Each unit has its own personnel who manage daily activities.

Most units are headed by a superintendent who oversees a staff of rangers. The rangers manage campgrounds, clean park areas, provide law enforcement, lead nature hikes, and provide many other services to visitors. The National Park System has expanded dramatically since the 1960's. Much of this expansion has resulted from adding new types of park units, such as wild and scenic rivers and urban parks.

▸ **CURRENT CHALLENGES**

The National Park System is faced by many challenges within the park

(text continued on page 56)

NATIONAL MONUMENTS

The title "national monument" has been given to a variety of national treasures, including natural areas, prehistoric ruins, forts, fossil sites, and other historic landmarks.

In 1904, President Theodore Roosevelt (on left) and conservationist John Muir stood together on Glacier Point in Yosemite National Park in California. Muir, who first visited Yosemite in 1868, worked tirelessly to ensure the preservation of its natural wonders.

AGATE FOSSIL BEDS, NEBRASKA

ALIBATES FLINT QUARRIES, TEXAS

ANIAKCHAK, ALASKA

AZTEC RUINS, NEW MEXICO

BANDELIER, NEW MEXICO

BOOKER T. WASHINGTON, VIRGINIA

BUCK ISLAND REEF, VIRGIN ISLANDS

CABRILLO, CALIFORNIA

CANYON DE CHELLY, ARIZONA

CAPE KRUSENSTERN, ALASKA

CAPULIN VOLCANO, NEW MEXICO

CASA GRANDE RUINS, ARIZONA

CASTILLO DE SAN MARCOS, FLORIDA

CASTLE CLINTON, NEW YORK

CEDAR BREAKS, UTAH

CHIRICAHUA, ARIZONA

COLORADO, COLORADO

CRATERS OF THE MOON, IDAHO

DEVILS POSTPILE, CALIFORNIA

DEVILS TOWER, WYOMING

DINOSAUR, COLORADO/UTAH

EFFIGY MOUNDS, IOWA

EL MALPAIS, NEW MEXICO

EL MORRO, NEW MEXICO

FLORISSANT FOSSIL BEDS, COLORADO

FORT FREDERICA, GEORGIA

FORT MATANZAS, FLORIDA

FORT McHENRY, MARYLAND

FORT PULASKI, GEORGIA

FORT STANWIX, NEW YORK

FORT SUMTER, SOUTH CAROLINA

FORT UNION, NEW MEXICO

FOSSIL BUTTE, WYOMING

GEORGE WASHINGTON BIRTHPLACE, VIRGINIA

GEORGE WASHINGTON CARVER, MISSOURI

GILA CLIFF DWELLINGS, NEW MEXICO

GRAND PORTAGE, MINNESOTA

HAGERMAN FOSSIL BEDS, IDAHO

HOHOKAM PIMA, ARIZONA

HOMESTEAD, NEBRASKA

HOVENWEEP, COLORADO/UTAH

JEWEL CAVE, SOUTH DAKOTA

JOHN DAY FOSSIL BEDS, OREGON

LAVA BEDS, CALIFORNIA

LITTLE BIGHORN BATTLEFIELD, MONTANA

MONTEZUMA CASTLE, ARIZONA

MUIR WOODS, CALIFORNIA

Devils Tower in Wyoming was the nation's first national monument, designated by President Theodore Roosevelt in 1906.

Above: Wupatki National Monument in Arizona contains prehistoric dwellings built by the ancestors of today's Pueblo Indians. The circular amphitheater shown here, measuring 50 feet (15 meters) in diameter, probably served as a ceremonial gathering place.

Left: The Statue of Liberty, located on Liberty Island in New York Harbor, is one of the most popular of the national monuments. Every year, about 4 million people come to see it. The national monument includes the American Museum of Immigration, located in the base of the statue, and nearby Ellis Island.

NATURAL BRIDGES, UTAH
NAVAJO, ARIZONA
OCMULGEE, GEORGIA
OREGON CAVES, OREGON
ORGAN PIPE CACTUS, ARIZONA
PETROGLYPH, NEW MEXICO
PINNACLES, CALIFORNIA
PIPE SPRING, ARIZONA
PIPESTONE, MINNESOTA
POVERTY POINT, LOUISIANA
RAINBOW BRIDGE, UTAH
RUSSELL CAVE, ALABAMA
SALINAS PUEBLO MISSIONS, NEW MEXICO
SCOTTS BLUFF, NEBRASKA
STATUE OF LIBERTY, NEW YORK/NEW JERSEY
SUNSET CRATER VOLCANO, ARIZONA
TIMPANOGOS CAVE, UTAH
TONTO, ARIZONA
TUZIGOOT, ARIZONA
WALNUT CANYON, ARIZONA
WHITE SANDS, NEW MEXICO
WUPATKI, ARIZONA
YUCCA HOUSE, COLORADO

NATIONAL MEMORIALS

The title "national memorial" is most often used for sites or structures that commemorate ideas, events, or persons of national importance.

ARKANSAS POST, ARKANSAS

ARLINGTON HOUSE, THE ROBERT E. LEE MEMORIAL, VIRGINIA

CHAMIZAL, TEXAS

CORONADO, ARIZONA

DE SOTO, FLORIDA

FEDERAL HALL, NEW YORK

FORT CAROLINE, FLORIDA

FORT CLATSOP, OREGON

FRANKLIN DELANO ROOSEVELT MEMORIAL, DISTRICT OF COLUMBIA

GENERAL GRANT, NEW YORK

HAMILTON GRANGE, NEW YORK

JEFFERSON NATIONAL EXPANSION MEMORIAL, MISSOURI

JOHNSTOWN FLOOD, PENNSYLVANIA

KOREAN WAR VETERANS, DISTRICT OF COLUMBIA

LINCOLN BOYHOOD, INDIANA

LINCOLN MEMORIAL, DISTRICT OF COLUMBIA

LYNDON BAINES JOHNSON MEMORIAL GROVE ON THE POTOMAC, DISTRICT OF COLUMBIA

MOUNT RUSHMORE, SOUTH DAKOTA

OKLAHOMA CITY NATIONAL MEMORIAL, OKLAHOMA

PERRY'S VICTORY AND INTERNATIONAL PEACE MEMORIAL, OHIO

ROGER WILLIAMS, RHODE ISLAND

THADDEUS KOSCIUSZKO, PENNSYLVANIA

THEODORE ROOSEVELT ISLAND, DISTRICT OF COLUMBIA

THOMAS JEFFERSON (JEFFERSON MEMORIAL), DISTRICT OF COLUMBIA

USS *ARIZONA*, HAWAII

VIETNAM VETERANS, DISTRICT OF COLUMBIA

WASHINGTON MONUMENT, DISTRICT OF COLUMBIA

WRIGHT BROTHERS, NORTH CAROLINA

How do areas qualify to become part of the U.S. National Park System?

Each unit of the National Park System is unique in that it represents some significant aspect of the nation's natural, recreational, or cultural heritage. For a unit to be officially designated, it should have national significance and represent a quality not already featured in the system. The land must also be attainable. The National Park Service reviews proposed areas and then submits recommendations to Congress.

NATIONAL MILITARY PARKS

CHICKAMAUGA AND CHATTANOOGA, GEORGIA/TENNESSEE

FREDERICKSBURG AND SPOTSYLVANIA COUNTY BATTLEFIELDS MEMORIAL, VIRGINIA

GETTYSBURG, PENNSYLVANIA

GUILFORD COURTHOUSE, NORTH CAROLINA

HORSESHOE BEND, ALABAMA

KINGS MOUNTAIN, SOUTH CAROLINA

PEA RIDGE, ARKANSAS

SHILOH, TENNESSEE

VICKSBURG, MISSISSIPPI

Above: Johnstown Flood National Memorial in Pennsylvania recalls the floods that devastated the city in 1889, 1936, and 1977. *Left:* The names of more than 58,000 dead or missing Americans are carved on the walls of the Vietnam Veterans Memorial in Washington, D.C.

The Virginia Memorial is one of hundreds of Civil War monuments erected on the battlefields of Gettysburg, Pennsylvania.

NATIONAL HISTORIC SITES

Areas having "national historic site," as part of their official names preserve places and commemorate persons and events important in the nation's past.

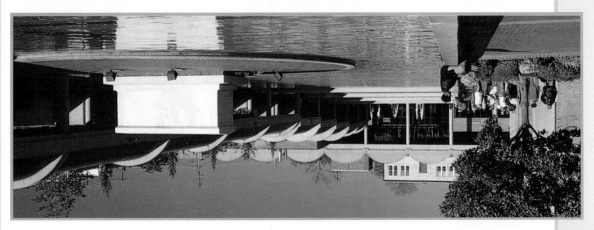

Ford's Theatre, where President Abraham Lincoln was assassinated in 1865, is preserved as a national historic site.

The Martin Luther King, Jr., National Historic Site includes the tomb of the slain civil rights leader.

ABRAHAM LINCOLN BIRTHPLACE, KENTUCKY
ADAMS, MASSACHUSETTS
ALLEGHENY PORTAGE RAILROAD, PENNSYLVANIA
ANDERSONVILLE, GEORGIA
ANDREW JOHNSON, TENNESSEE
BENT'S OLD FORT, COLORADO
BOSTON AFRICAN AMERICAN, MASSACHUSETTS
BROWN v. BOARD OF EDUCATION, KANSAS
CARL SANDBURG HOME, NORTH CAROLINA
CHARLES PINCKNEY, SOUTH CAROLINA
CHRISTIANSTED, VIRGIN ISLANDS
CLARA BARTON, MARYLAND
EDGAR ALLAN POE, PENNSYLVANIA
EDISON, NEW JERSEY
EISENHOWER, PENNSYLVANIA
ELEANOR ROOSEVELT, NEW YORK
EUGENE O'NEILL, CALIFORNIA
FORD'S THEATRE, DISTRICT OF COLUMBIA
FORT BOWIE, ARIZONA
FORT DAVIS, TEXAS
FORT LARAMIE, WYOMING
FORT LARNED, KANSAS
FORT POINT, CALIFORNIA
FORT RALEIGH, NORTH CAROLINA
FORT SCOTT, KANSAS
FORT SMITH, ARKANSAS/OKLAHOMA
FORT UNION TRADING POST, MONTANA/NORTH DAKOTA
FORT VANCOUVER, WASHINGTON
FREDERICK DOUGLASS, DISTRICT OF COLUMBIA
FREDERICK LAW OLMSTED, MASSACHUSETTS
FRIENDSHIP HILL, PENNSYLVANIA
GOLDEN SPIKE, UTAH
GRANT-KOHRS RANCH, MONTANA
HAMPTON, MARYLAND
HARRY S. TRUMAN, MISSOURI
HERBERT HOOVER, IOWA
HOME OF FRANKLIN D. ROOSEVELT, NEW YORK

HOPEWELL FURNACE, PENNSYLVANIA
HUBBELL TRADING POST, ARIZONA
JAMES A. GARFIELD, OHIO
JIMMY CARTER, GEORGIA
JOHN FITZGERALD KENNEDY, MASSACHUSETTS
JOHN MUIR, CALIFORNIA
KNIFE RIVER INDIAN VILLAGES, NORTH DAKOTA
LINCOLN HOME, ILLINOIS
LONGFELLOW, MASSACHUSETTS
MAGGIE L. WALKER, VIRGINIA
MANZANAR, CALIFORNIA
MARTIN LUTHER KING, JR., GEORGIA
MARTIN VAN BUREN, NEW YORK
MARY McLEOD BETHUNE COUNCIL HOUSE, DISTRICT OF COLUMBIA
NICODEMUS, KANSAS
NINETY SIX, SOUTH CAROLINA
PALO ALTO BATTLEFIELD, TEXAS
PENNSYLVANIA AVENUE, DISTRICT OF COLUMBIA
PUUKOHOLA HEIAU, HAWAII
SAGAMORE HILL, NEW YORK
SAINT-GAUDENS, NEW HAMPSHIRE
SAINT PAUL'S CHURCH, NEW YORK
SALEM MARITIME, MASSACHUSETTS
SAND CREEK MASSACRE, COLORADO
SAN JUAN, PUERTO RICO
SAUGUS IRON WORKS, MASSACHUSETTS
SPRINGFIELD ARMORY, MASSACHUSETTS
STEAMTOWN, PENNSYLVANIA
THEODORE ROOSEVELT BIRTHPLACE, NEW YORK
THEODORE ROOSEVELT INAUGURAL, NEW YORK
THOMAS COLE, NEW YORK
THOMAS STONE, MARYLAND
TUSKEGEE INSTITUTE, ALABAMA
ULYSSES S. GRANT, MISSOURI
VANDERBILT MANSION, NEW YORK
WASHITA BATTLEFIELD, OKLAHOMA
WEIR FARM, CONNECTICUT
WHITMAN MISSION, WASHINGTON
WILLIAM HOWARD TAFT, OHIO

NATIONAL HISTORICAL PARKS

National historical parks usually are larger in physical extent and more complex than national historic sites.

APPOMATTOX COURT HOUSE, VIRGINIA

BOSTON, MASSACHUSETTS

CANE RIVER CREOLE, LOUISIANA

CHACO CULTURE, NEW MEXICO

CHESAPEAKE AND OHIO CANAL, MARYLAND/DISTRICT OF COLUMBIA/WEST VIRGINIA

COLONIAL, VIRGINIA

CUMBERLAND GAP, KENTUCKY/VIRGINIA/TENNESSEE

DAYTON AVIATION HERITAGE, OHIO

GEORGE ROGERS CLARK, INDIANA

HARPERS FERRY, WEST VIRGINIA/MARYLAND

HOPEWELL CULTURE, OHIO

INDEPENDENCE, PENNSYLVANIA

JEAN LAFITTE, LOUISIANA

KALAUPAPA, HAWAII

KALOKO-HONOKOHAU, HAWAII

KEWEENAW, MICHIGAN

KLONDIKE GOLD RUSH, ALASKA/WASHINGTON

LOWELL, MASSACHUSETTS

LYNDON B. JOHNSON, TEXAS

MARSH-BILLINGS, VERMONT

MINUTE MAN, MASSACHUSETTS

MORRISTOWN, NEW JERSEY

NATCHEZ, MISSISSIPPI

NEW ORLEANS JAZZ, LOUISIANA

NEZ PERCE, IDAHO

PECOS, NEW MEXICO

PU'UHONUA O HONAUNAU, HAWAII.

SALT RIVER BAY, U.S. VIRGIN ISLANDS

SAN ANTONIO MISSIONS, TEXAS

SAN FRANCISCO MARITIME, CALIFORNIA

SAN JUAN ISLAND, WASHINGTON

SARATOGA, NEW YORK

SITKA, ALASKA

TUMACACORI, ARIZONA

VALLEY FORGE, PENNSYLVANIA

WAR IN THE PACIFIC, GUAM

WOMEN'S RIGHTS, NEW YORK

ZUNI-CIBOLA, NEW MEXICO

The Women's Rights National Historical Park in Seneca Falls, New York, honors the pioneers of the women's rights movement.

OTHER NATIONAL PARKLANDS

CATOCTIN MOUNTAIN PARK, MARYLAND

CONSTITUTION GARDENS, DISTRICT OF COLUMBIA

FORT WASHINGTON PARK, MARYLAND

GREENBELT PARK, MARYLAND

NATIONAL CAPITAL PARKS, DISTRICT OF COLUMBIA/MARYLAND/VIRGINIA

NATIONAL MALL, DISTRICT OF COLUMBIA

PISCATAWAY PARK, MARYLAND

PRINCE WILLIAM FOREST PARK, VIRGINIA

ROCK CREEK PARK, DISTRICT OF COLUMBIA

WHITE HOUSE, DISTRICT OF COLUMBIA

WOLF TRAP FARM PARK FOR THE PERFORMING ARTS, VIRGINIA

NATIONAL BATTLEFIELDS, NATIONAL BATTLEFIELD PARKS, AND NATIONAL BATTLEFIELD SITE

ANTIETAM, MARYLAND

BIG HOLE, MONTANA

BRICES CROSS ROADS, MISSISSIPPI

COWPENS, SOUTH CAROLINA

FORT DONELSON, KENTUCKY/TENNESSEE

FORT NECESSITY, PENNSYLVANIA

KENNESAW MOUNTAIN, GEORGIA

MANASSAS, VIRGINIA

MONACACY, MARYLAND

MOORES CREEK, NORTH CAROLINA

PETERSBURG, VIRGINIA

RICHMOND, VIRGINIA

STONES RIVER, TENNESSEE

TUPELO, MISSISSIPPI

WILSON'S CREEK, MISSOURI

NATIONAL CEMETERIES

The following national cemeteries are associated with historical units of the National Park System and are administered by the National Park Service in conjunction with those units. Some of the cemeteries are legally separate from the associated historical units; others have been incorporated into the units.

ANDERSONVILLE, GEORGIA

ANDREW JOHNSON, TENNESSEE

ANTIETAM, MARYLAND

BATTLEGROUND, DISTRICT OF COLUMBIA

CHALMETTE, LOUISIANA

CUSTER BATTLEFIELD, MONTANA

FORT DONELSON, TENNESSEE

FREDERICKSBURG, VIRGINIA

GETTYSBURG, PENNSYLVANIA

PITTSBURG LANDING (SHILOH), TENNESSEE

POPLAR GROVE (PETERSBURG), VIRGINIA

STONES RIVER, TENNESSEE

VICKSBURG, MISSISSIPPI

YORKTOWN, VIRGINIA

NATIONAL RESERVES

CITY OF ROCKS NATIONAL RESERVE, IDAHO

EBEY'S LANDING NATIONAL HISTORICAL RESERVE, WASHINGTON

Originally the term "national recreation area" was used for units surrounding reservoirs (artificial lakes) created by dams built by other federal agencies. But the idea of recreation areas has grown to include other lands and waters set aside for recreational use by acts of Congress. These include seashores, lakeshores, rivers and riverways, parkways, and scenic trails.

NATIONAL RECREATION AREAS

AMISTAD, TEXAS
BIGHORN CANYON, MONTANA/WYOMING
BOSTON HARBOR ISLANDS, MASSACHUSETTS
CHATTAHOOCHEE RIVER, GEORGIA
CHICKASAW, OKLAHOMA
COULEE DAM, WASHINGTON
CURECANTI, COLORADO
DELAWARE WATER GAP,
NEW JERSEY/PENNSYLVANIA
GATEWAY, NEW JERSEY/NEW YORK
GAULEY RIVER, WEST VIRGINIA
GLEN CANYON, ARIZONA/UTAH
GOLDEN GATE, CALIFORNIA
LAKE CHELAN, WASHINGTON
LAKE MEAD, ARIZONA/NEVADA
LAKE MEREDITH, TEXAS
ROSS LAKE, WASHINGTON
SANTA MONICA MOUNTAINS, CALIFORNIA
WHISKEYTOWN-SHASTA-TRINITY,
CALIFORNIA

NATIONAL SCENIC TRAILS

APPALACHIAN, MAINE/NEW
HAMPSHIRE/VERMONT/MASSACHUSETTS/
CONNECTICUT/NEW YORK/NEW
JERSEY/PENNSYLVANIA/MARYLAND/WEST
VIRGINIA/VIRGINIA/TENNESSEE/NORTH
CAROLINA/GEORGIA
NATCHEZ TRACE,
MISSISSIPPI/ALABAMA/TENNESSEE
POTOMAC HERITAGE, DISTRICT OF
COLUMBIA/MARYLAND/VIRGINIA/WEST
VIRGINIA/PENNSYLVANIA

NATIONAL LAKESHORES

APOSTLE ISLANDS, WISCONSIN
INDIANA DUNES, INDIANA
PICTURED ROCKS, MICHIGAN
SLEEPING BEAR DUNES, MICHIGAN

NATIONAL RIVERS

BIG SOUTH FORK NATIONAL RIVER AND
RECREATION AREA, KENTUCKY/TENNESSEE
BUFFALO NATIONAL RIVER, ARKANSAS
MISSISSIPPI NATIONAL RIVER AND
RECREATION AREA, MINNESOTA
NEW RIVER GORGE NATIONAL RIVER, WEST
VIRGINIA
NIOBRARA NATIONAL SCENIC RIVERWAY,
NEBRASKA/SOUTH DAKOTA
OZARK NATIONAL SCENIC RIVERWAYS,
MISSOURI

Wild ponies roam the dunes on Assateague Island National Seashore between Maryland and Virginia.

NATIONAL SEASHORES

ASSATEAGUE ISLAND,
MARYLAND/VIRGINIA
CANAVERAL, FLORIDA
CAPE COD,
MASSACHUSETTS
CAPE HATTERAS,
NORTH CAROLINA
CAPE LOOKOUT,
NORTH CAROLINA
CUMBERLAND ISLAND,
GEORGIA
FIRE ISLAND, NEW
YORK
GULF ISLANDS,
FLORIDA/MISSISSIPPI
PADRE ISLAND, TEXAS
POINT REYES,
CALIFORNIA

INTERNATIONAL
HISTORIC SITE

SAINT CROIX ISLAND,
MAINE

NATIONAL WILD AND SCENIC RIVERS

ALAGNAK WILD RIVER, ALASKA
BLUESTONE SCENIC RIVER, WEST VIRGINIA
DELAWARE NATIONAL SCENIC RIVER, PENNSYLVANIA/NEW
JERSEY/NEW YORK
GREAT EGG HARBOR SCENIC AND RECREATIONAL RIVER,
NEW JERSEY
MISSOURI NATIONAL RECREATIONAL RIVER, SOUTH
DAKOTA/NEBRASKA
OBED WILD AND SCENIC RIVER, TENNESSEE
RIO GRANDE WILD AND SCENIC RIVER, TEXAS
SAINT CROIX NATIONAL SCENIC RIVERWAY,
WISCONSIN/MINNESOTA
UPPER DELAWARE SCENIC AND RECREATIONAL RIVER,
PENNSYLVANIA/NEW YORK

NATIONAL PARKWAYS

BLUE RIDGE PARKWAY, NORTH CAROLINA/VIRGINIA
GEORGE WASHINGTON MEMORIAL PARKWAY,
VIRGINIA/MARYLAND
JOHN D. ROCKEFELLER, JR., MEMORIAL PARKWAY,
WYOMING
NATCHEZ TRACE PARKWAY,
MISSISSIPPI/ALABAMA/TENNESSEE

AFFILIATED AREAS

The following areas preserve important parts of the nation's heritage. They are called affiliated areas because they receive technical or financial assistance from the National Park Service, but they are not federally owned or directly administered by the National Park Service.

ALEUTIAN WORLD WAR II NATIONAL HISTORIC AREA, ALASKA

AMERICAN MEMORIAL PARK, SAIPAN, NORTHERN MARIANA ISLANDS

BENJAMIN FRANKLIN NATIONAL MEMORIAL, PENNSYLVANIA

BLACKSTONE RIVER VALLEY NATIONAL HERITAGE CORRIDOR, MASSACHUSETTS/RHODE ISLAND

CHICAGO PORTAGE NATIONAL HISTORIC SITE, ILLINOIS

CHIMNEY ROCK NATIONAL HISTORIC SITE, NEBRASKA

DAVID BERGER NATIONAL MEMORIAL, OHIO

DELAWARE AND LEHIGH NAVIGATION CANAL NATIONAL HERITAGE CORRIDOR, PENNSYLVANIA

FATHER MARQUETTE NATIONAL MEMORIAL, MICHIGAN

GLORIA DEI (OLD SWEDES') CHURCH NATIONAL HISTORIC SITE, PENNSYLVANIA

GREEN SPRINGS HISTORIC DISTRICT, VIRGINIA

HISTORIC CAMDEN, SOUTH CAROLINA

ICE AGE NATIONAL SCENIC TRAIL, WISCONSIN

ICE AGE NATIONAL SCIENTIFIC RESERVE, WISCONSIN

ILLINOIS AND MICHIGAN CANAL NATIONAL HERITAGE CORRIDOR, ILLINOIS

INTERNATIONAL PEACE GARDEN, NORTH DAKOTA/MANITOBA, CANADA

JAMESTOWN NATIONAL HISTORIC SITE, VIRGINIA

LEWIS AND CLARK NATIONAL HISTORIC TRAIL, MISSOURI TO OREGON

MCLOUGHLIN HOUSE NATIONAL HISTORIC SITE, OREGON

PINELANDS NATIONAL RESERVE, NEW JERSEY

PORT CHICAGO NAVAL MAGAZINE NATIONAL MEMORIAL, CALIFORNIA

QUINEBAUG AND SHETUCKET RIVER VALLEY NATIONAL HERITAGE CORRIDOR, CONNECTICUT

ROOSEVELT CAMPOBELLO INTERNATIONAL PARK, NEW BRUNSWICK (CANADA)

SEWELL-BELMONT HOUSE, DISTRICT OF COLUMBIA

TOURO SYNAGOGUE NATIONAL HISTORIC SITE, RHODE ISLAND

ture caused by smog from automobiles; and the wearing down of paths, roads, and bridges.

The National Park System also faces threats from outside the parks' boundaries. Air and water pollution from nearby cities and communities can affect natural conditions inside the parks. Rivers in many parks are affected by dams that have been built outside park borders. Park managers, however, have little control over these hazards.

The employees of the National Park Service have attempted to protect the parks by meeting these challenges. Because it is part of the federal government, the agency must depend upon Congress and the president for its budget, management guidelines, and approval of its plans. But because these politicians are elected, American citizens have the final say in how their parks are to be managed and protected.

▶ **NATIONAL PARK SYSTEMS AROUND THE WORLD**

Lord James Bryce, who served as the British ambassador to the United States from 1907 to 1913, once said the National Park System was "the best idea you [Americans] ever had." The first national park outside the United States was established in 1879 in Australia, at a site, now called Royal, in New South Wales. Canadians established Banff, in Alberta, in 1887. Eventually the governments of more than 100 nations created their own national park systems.

National park systems provide crucial protection for some of the world's most precious plants and animals. Australia's Great Barrier Reef Marine Park, for example, contains the world's largest system of corals and associated life-forms, including thousands of fish and sea creatures. Costa Rica's extensive system of parks provides the strongest protection in the world for tropical rain forests and all the plant and animal species that live in them. African national parks, such as Kruger in South Africa and Serengeti in Tanzania, provide the only remaining areas on the continent where people can still see animals like lions and African elephants in their natural environments.

All of these places face serious challenges similar to those in the United States. Many countries rely on tourists and visitors to supply the funds needed to continue protecting

units. The most obvious of these is overcrowding. The number of annual recreational visitors increased from 190 million in 1980 to 270 million by the mid-1990's. Nearly half of the visits occur in the summer months, and many are confined to the most popular units, such as the Great Smoky Mountains. Other problems have resulted due to the large crowds, such as a rise in crime; damage to na-

International Organizations

In the late 1940's, following World War II, various individuals and organizations suggested international discussions on park management to compare national efforts. The International Union for the Conservation of Nature and Natural Resources (IUCN) evolved from a conference held in France in 1948. The IUCN has since become an organization that compiles lists on national parks, publishes data, and helps countries plan their park systems. The IUCN has headquarters in Gland, Switzerland.

The first World Conference on National Parks convened in Seattle in 1962. Ever since, these conferences have been held in different places every ten years. The 1972 conference led to the establishment of the World Heritage Convention. More than 100 nations have signed on to this convention, making it the world's most ratified international conservation agreement. The World Heritage Convention calls for international recognition and cooperation in protecting sites of outstanding cultural value to people throughout the world. The World Heritage Convention now lists more than 100 sites all over the globe. American national parks on the list include Yellowstone, Yosemite, and the Grand Canyon.

WILLIAM R. LOWRY
Washington University

See also BANFF NATIONAL PARK; CONSERVATION; GLACIER NATIONAL PARK; GRAND CANYON NATIONAL PARK; INDEPENDENCE HALL; JAMESTOWN; JASPER NATIONAL PARK; LIBERTY, STATUE OF; WHITE HOUSE; YELLOWSTONE NATIONAL PARK; YOSEMITE NATIONAL PARK; and articles on the states of the United States and the provinces of Canada.

NATO. See NORTH ATLANTIC TREATY ORGANIZATION.

the parks. System managers must therefore be careful to attract enough visitors, but not too many, and monitor tourist activities so that they do not destroy the parks' natural conditions.

Right: Serengeti National Park in Tanzania, Africa, is one of the world's most famous wildlife refuges. *Below:* Banff, Canada's oldest national park, is renowned for its beautiful glacial lakes and Rocky Mountain views.

A chef cooks on a gas range. Many cooks prefer natural gas because the desired level of heat is quickly reached and easily controlled.

NATURAL GAS

When someone says "gas," do you think of the fuel we use to run most cars and trucks? Many people do, but "gas" used in this way is short for "gasoline," a liquid fuel, not a gas.

Natural gas is a "real" gas fuel and an important energy source. It is found deep within the Earth, and it is produced on every continent except Antarctica. It supplies about 24 percent of the energy used in the United States and nearly 25 percent of the world's energy.

Natural gas is made up of hydrocarbons (organic compounds containing only carbon and hydrogen atoms). It consists mostly of the hydrocarbon methane, but other hydrocarbons are usually present as well.

Like coal and petroleum, natural gas is a fossil fuel, so called because it was probably formed millions of years ago from fossils (the remains of dead plants and animals). But natural gas burns cleaner than coal and petroleum, releasing fewer pollutants. This makes it a very efficient source of energy.

▶ USES

Natural gas has a wide variety of applications. One of the most common uses is residential heating. In 2003, more than half the heated homes in the United States used natural gas for heating. Natural gas can also be used for cooling, with natural gas-powered air conditioners. Natural gas appliances, such as hot-water heaters and clothes driers, are increasingly popular. Many home cooks and professional chefs prefer cooking with a natural gas range because it gives the desired amount of heat instantly, and the temperature is easily controlled.

Many industries also use natural gas, not only for space heating and cooling but also for manufacturing, especially when efficiency, cleanliness, and temperature control are important. For example, factories that make glass and pottery use natural gas as a source of heat. Food that is canned or frozen is prepared with heat from natural gas, and dairies use it to pasteurize milk.

Natural gas also has a number of specialized industrial uses. For example, in the plastics industry, moisture can cause cracks and other damage to certain types of plastics during the manufacturing process. Natural gas is used as a drying agent to enable manufacturers to control the amount of moisture in the air. In addition, the hydrogen and carbon that make up natural gas can be rearranged and combined with other elements to make many industrial products, including nylon, fertilizers, and plastics.

Natural gas is also used to generate electricity. In the most basic method, gas is used to heat water in large boilers at electric generating plants. The steam that comes from the boiling water is used to turn a turbine, which creates an electrical current. Also used are highly efficient natural gas turbines, in which the energy released from burning natural gas is used to power the generator.

Natural gas fuel cells are also becoming an important technology for the generation of electricity. A fuel cell is a kind of battery that changes the chemical energy of a fuel directly into electrical energy. Research into fuel cell technology is expected to greatly expand the potential use of natural gas for distributed, or localized, electrical production.

Natural gas has been used to fuel vehicles since the 1930's. Today there are more than 1.5 million natural gas vehicles (NGV's) in use worldwide. Vehicles fueled with natural gas meet strict environmental emissions standards. But high initial costs have so far prevented the mass production of NGV's.

▶ FORMATION OF NATURAL GAS

It is thought that natural gas was formed millions of years ago, when much of the land was covered by oceans. The remains of tiny plants and animals that lived in the water were deposited on the ocean floor. They were covered by layers of mud, washed into the ocean from the land. Bacteria and chemicals worked on the remains of these once-living things. Meanwhile more layers of mud were deposited. During long ages, some of the mud turned into porous rocks (rocks that have tiny holes, or pores) under the heat and pressure of the enormous weight above them. The fossil remains were thereby converted into oil, natural gas, and other hydrocarbons. The gas filled the pores in the rocks, and over the years it seeped through the pores from one part of the rock to another. When it came to a space surrounded by rocks without pores—called impermeable rock—the gas was trapped in one spot.

▶ EXPLORATION AND EXTRACTION

By mapping the Earth according to the locations of porous and impermeable rocks, geologists can identify areas where natural gas is likely to be found. Then further tests are performed—usually by geophysicists—to gain more detailed data. For example, seismic waves sent underground can determine whether layers of rock are dense or porous. Computers may be used to assemble the data into a "map" of the underground location.

Left: Computer images compiled from seismic data help scientists locate natural gas deposits. *Below:* Once a deposit is confirmed, a well is drilled and the gas extracted. This drilling platform is located on the Louisiana coast.

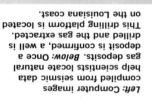

If the data indicates a high probability of a gas deposit, then an exploratory well will be drilled. This is done with special drills, much like the ones used to drill water wells. Sometimes the holes go as deep as 30,000 feet (9,100 meters). But most wells are about 5,000 feet deep (1,500 meters). Offshore gas wells may be much deeper. If significant deposits of natural gas are located, the well will be completed and the gas extracted.

▶ PROCESSING AND TRANSPORT

Once it is extracted, natural gas must be processed to remove water, oil, and other substances. Then it is ready for transport. A network of interstate pipelines carries the gas from its point of origin to local utilities or distribution companies. The gas is compressed to reduce its mass and to push it through the pipe, which typically measures between 24 and 36 inches (60 and 90 centimeters) in diameter.

From the distribution companies, smaller pipes carry the gas to consumers. Prior to distribution, a distinctive odor is added to the gas to make it easier to detect a leak.

This is an important safety precaution: Because natural gas is colorless and odorless, a leak might otherwise go unnoticed and could cause an explosion. Once it reaches its final destination, the gas passes through a meter, which enables the gas company to bill the customer correctly.

In situations where it is impractical to transport natural gas by pipeline, the gas may be cooled and condensed into liquid form, known as liquefied natural gas (LNG). One unit of LNG takes up only about $\frac{1}{600}$ the volume of a unit of natural gas. This makes it possible to store natural gas and transport it over long distances. LNG is typically transported by oceangoing tankers. When LNG is heated, it expands back into a gas and is ready for use.

A network of pipelines transports natural gas from its point of origin to local distribution companies and thence to consumers.

▶ WHERE NATURAL GAS IS PRODUCED

The countries that produce the most natural gas are the United States, Russia, Canada, the United Kingdom, Algeria, Indonesia, Iran, the Netherlands, Norway, and Uzbekistan. These ten countries account for more than 70 percent of world production. U.S. production comes mainly from the Gulf of Mexico and five states: Louisiana, New Mexico, Oklahoma, Texas, and Wyoming. Canada's production comes mainly from Alberta, British Columbia, and offshore from Nova Scotia.

Proved reserves of natural gas are distributed around the globe. (Proved reserves are deposits from which natural gas could be produced economically using current technology.) The nations of the former Soviet Union hold the largest reserves. Together with the Middle East, they hold more than 70 percent of total reserves. Other countries with large proved reserves include the United States, Venezuela, and Indonesia.

The natural gas supply is supplemented by manufacturing synthetic natural gas (SNG) from petroleum hydrocarbons or coal.

In the future, natural gas may be extracted from **hydrates**, special forms of ice. (For more information, see the Wonder Question, Is there a new source of energy in the oceans? in OCEANOGRAPHY in Volume O.)

▶ HISTORY

Although natural gas is millions of years old, it was not until recent times that people learned to extract it and put it to use. In the ancient world, mysterious flames rising from the ground were thought to be a sign from the gods. In fact they were caused by natural gas seeping from underground that had been ignited, for example by lightning. In ancient Greece, a temple was built over one such flame. About 500 B.C. the Chinese used surface deposits of natural gas to boil seawater, separating out the salt and making it drinkable.

The British were the first to manufacture natural gas from coal, using it for lighting by the late 1700's. In North America, Native Americans ignited gases that had seeped into and around Lake Erie. In the early 1800's, a gunsmith named William Hart dug a well at such a site, in nearby Fredonia, New York, to extract natural gas. He piped it through hollow logs to nearby buildings, where it was used to provide lighting. The first U.S. natural gas company was later founded in Fredonia.

But without a good way to transport it, natural gas was little used. When it was found alongside deposits of petroleum, it was usually burned, or flamed off. It was not until the 1950's, when new technologies enabled the construction of reliable pipeline systems, that natural gas became widely used.

BETSY HARVEY KRAFT
Author, *Oil and Natural Gas*
Reviewed by MARK STULTZ
Natural Gas Supply Association

See also FUELS; GASES; PETROLEUM AND PETROLEUM REFINING.

NATURALIZATION

People are usually citizens of the country where they were born (natural-born citizens) or of the country where their parents have citizenship. A person who wants to become a citizen of another country must go through a process called naturalization. Most countries make naturalization easier for the immediate family of natural-born and naturalized citizens and for foreigners who work in the adopted country.

Becoming a U.S. Citizen. In general, people are considered U.S. citizens if they were born in the United States, including, in most cases, Puerto Rico, Guam, and the U.S. Virgin Islands, or if they were born abroad to a U.S. citizen.

Those who want to become naturalized U.S. citizens must meet requirements set by the U.S. government. These include being at least 18 years old (different rules apply to children), and, in most cases, having permanent resident status. (Permanent residents are immigrants who apply for and are granted the right to live permanently in the United States by the U.S. government.) Applicants for citizenship must also pass tests showing that they can read, write, and speak basic English and that they have a basic knowledge of U.S. history and government. There are exceptions to these requirements for older people.

Applicants are also expected to have good moral character. Those who do not—for example, those who have committed certain crimes, including murder—are not eligible to become U.S. citizens.

Another major requirement is the willingness of the applicants to support and defend the United States and its Constitution. Those seeking to become citizens must show this willingness by taking the Oath of Allegiance to the United States. In fact, they do not officially become U.S. citizens until they take this oath.

The Naturalization Process. There is no set time period for obtaining U.S. citizenship through naturalization. The first step is to file an application with U.S. Citizenship and Immigration Services (USCIS), a bureau of the U.S. Department of Homeland Security. The application must include a personal photograph, appropriate documents, and fees. Next comes fingerprinting and then an interview with an immigration officer from USCIS. At the interview, the applicant is asked about his or her background, time in the United States, character, and willingness to take the oath of allegiance. Unless exempt, the applicant is asked to read out loud and write one or two simple sentences in English and either answer verbally or take a written multiple-choice civics test.

As a result of the interview, USCIS may grant, deny or continue the naturalization application. If the case is continued, the applicant must either come back for a second interview or provide additional documents. The most common reasons for having a case continued are when the applicant fails the English or civics test or fails to provide proper documentation. Applicants who are denied citizenship may appeal.

Those who are granted a citizenship attend a naturalization oath ceremony, where they express their loyalty to the United States by reciting the oath of allegiance and receive their certificate of naturalization, which can be used as proof of their citizenship.

Each year, USCIS welcomes more than 450,000 citizens during naturalization ceremonies across the United States. That includes thousands of members of the U.S. armed forces, who may take a faster route to naturalization as a result of their service.

New citizens have most of the rights of natural-born Americans. One exception is the right to become president of the United States, which is restricted to natural-born citizens. But naturalized citizens may vote, serve on juries, and hold many other offices.

Reviewed by CHRISTOPHER S. BENTLEY
Senior Public Affairs Officer
U.S. Citizenship and Immigration Services

See also ALIENS; CITIZENSHIP.

NATURAL NUMBERS. See NUMBERS AND NUMBER SYSTEMS.

NATURAL RESOURCES

Natural resources are those elements of nature that are of use to people. Anything that is part of the world of nature becomes a natural resource when people use it to supply their needs or serve their wants.

The natural resources we think of most often are those that are used directly by people. But each element of nature affects the others. We have learned that if a thing is needed by any part of nature, then people depend on it, too.

▶WHAT ARE OUR RESOURCES?

Air and water are two important natural resources—people need air and water to live. Land is a natural resource if people can use it to grow crops for food. Stone is a natural resource. It was so useful for making tools that the first known period of human culture was called the Stone Age. Stone, along with sand and gravel, continues to be very useful—not for making tools but for construction of buildings and roads and for many other purposes. Wildlife is a resource. Wild animals are used for food, skin, and fur. Forests are natural resources. The wood from trees is used to build houses and to make paper and many other products.

Sometimes several natural features may combine to form a natural resource. A combination of good climate, fertile soils, and good drainage forms valuable cropland. The usefulness of cropland may vary from place to place with the characteristics of these features. A short growing season or low rainfall can make fertile soil less valuable as a resource. Poor soils can limit farming in a region with a good climate.

Usefulness to people is very important in determining whether or not a material is thought of as a natural resource. The example of the nonmetallic mineral known as stone helps us understand this fact. We understand it even more clearly when we think of the periods of human culture known as the Bronze and the Iron ages. Those periods, following the Stone Age, are so called because people learned during those times how to work with certain metallic ores and put them to use in making metal tools and weapons. Iron tools were much more useful than tools made of stone. Then ways of making steel were developed, and steel proved to be ever so much more useful than iron for many purposes.

As it was in past ages, so it is in modern times. Through technical developments, people "discover" natural resources or find new uses for known resources. Bauxite, the ore from which aluminum is made, was not known as a natural resource until a way was

Farmers have been producing rice crops in the Philippines for more than 3,000 years by terracing the hilly land. Rainwater is held in the terraces by clay and stone walls.

found, in the 1880's, to refine it cheaply enough for everyday use. Because people have learned how to use uranium as a source of energy, uranium ore is now classified as a mineral fuel, along with coal, petroleum, and natural gas. But before nuclear fission was discovered, uranium was not a valuable material.

Natural resources also include things that are used only indirectly by people. For example, wetlands (marshes and bogs) are a natural resource because they provide a home for wildlife. They may also hold water that would otherwise flood farmlands. In short, people need the whole vast mix of nature.

The Ecosphere

Natural resources exist where living and nonliving things are linked together. Such a mix is found only in a thin band around the earth, called the **ecosphere** (or **biosphere**). If the earth were an apple, the ecosphere would be like its skin in thickness.

The living things in the ecosphere are plants and animals. They are the living environment. The nonliving things are the **atmosphere** (the air), the **hydrosphere** (water), and the **lithosphere** (soil and rocks). They are the physical environment. These spheres are mixed together in a flow of energy from the sun, called the **energy cycle.**

The sun's energy is our most basic natural resource. Through the energy cycle, energy from the sun provides us with food. Plants convert (change) the energy in sunlight to oxygen and sugar. All living things use the oxygen and sugar. Some living things eat plants and use their sugars. Some of these creatures are eaten in turn by other animals. And as plants and animals die and decay, they are converted by bacteria and fungi into chemicals. The chemicals enter the soil and nourish plants. Thus, energy moves in a great cycle. All of the elements of this cycle—living and nonliving—are needed by people. In a broad sense, these are all natural resources.

Human and Cultural Resources

One major life-form and one major class of things cannot be called natural resources. The life-form is people—ourselves. We are certainly part of nature. But only people have the intelligence to acquire knowledge and invent on a large scale. The term "human resources" is used to refer to this ability. Another term,

"cultural resources," refers to all the things people make—ranging from cars, houses, and factories to great novels and works of art.

Human and cultural resources could not exist without natural resources. People could not build machines, for example, without metals and fuels. But just as natural resources affect human and cultural resources, human and cultural resources affect natural resources.

► HOW PEOPLE AFFECT RESOURCES

People have the ability to change their environment and improve resources. Progress in science and technology is increasing this ability. Dams can be built across streams, and the water can be channeled through canals to turn dry lands into croplands. With reseeding programs and other management techniques, people can turn low-quality forests into forests producing needed goods.

But people can also change their environment so that resources are reduced in value or destroyed. People dump wastes into streams, killing fish or making the water unfit to drink. Factories and cars release smoke into the air, making the air unfit to breathe. These are examples of pollution.

Copper is a valuable resource in the United States. This open-pit mine in Utah is large enough to seat 10 million people around its continuous, circular "benches."

Windmill generators turn the energy of the prevailing wind into electricity on this "wind farm." The transformers in the foreground distribute the power to users.

People also use natural resources carelessly. They farm carelessly, and the soil washes or blows away. They cut down too many trees from forests, and less valuable trees grow in place of those that were cut. They waste the supplies of minerals in the earth.

▶ CONSERVING RESOURCES

How can people reduce their loss of natural resources? One way is to make better use of the world's food supply. Food moves from simple to more complex life-forms in a path called the **food chain.** For example, a steer eats corn, and people then eat the steer. But at each step of the chain, some energy is lost. The steer uses only 10 percent of the energy in the corn. And people use only 10 percent of the energy in the steer. People can get more energy by shortening the food chain—that is, by using the corn as food instead of the steer. Or the steer could feed on grass, which people cannot eat directly. Then the energy of the corn used to feed the steer would not be lost.

We can also increase the usefulness of natural resources by **substitution** and **conversion.** If supplies of oil are low, we may substitute coal, wood, or natural gas. Oil may be burned directly to heat our homes. Or it may be converted to electricity—used to heat a boiler that will produce steam to drive an electric generator. Wise substitution and conversion can extend the life of natural resources.

We can often substitute a **renewable** resource for a **nonrenewable** resource. The mineral resources of the earth are considered nonrenewable. Once they are used, they will be gone forever. For example, there is only a certain amount of coal in the earth, and it took millions of years to form. In terms of the length of human life, coal is a nonrenewable resource. The same is true for other fossil fuels, such as petroleum and natural gas.

In contrast, sunlight is constantly being renewed. No amount of use will make it less available. If we rely on nonrenewable fossil fuels for our heat, sooner or later we will run out. But if we use solar energy, we will never be short. Wind power and water power are other renewable resources that can be used to produce electricity. Forests are also a renewable resource. Wood can be used as fuel or for construction, in place of metal.

Still another way to conserve natural resources is to **recycle** (re-use) them. The metal from aluminum cans can be recycled to make new products. Wastepaper can be used to make new paper products. The fact that some resources may run out does not mean that we should not use them. It means that we should use them wisely.

▶ NATURAL RESOURCES AND THE WORLD

Since the Industrial Revolution of the 1700's and 1800's, two things have placed great demands on the earth's natural resources. First, the world's population has grown dramatically. This has increased the need for food and resources of all kinds. Second, machines have increased the need for nonrenewable resources, such as minerals and fuels. At the same time, machines have made it easier to extract these resources from the earth. The nonrenewable resources are being used up faster than ever before.

These changes have helped to create a gap between rich countries and poor countries. The powerful countries today are often those that control the most resources.

Distribution of Natural Resources

Nations are not equally rich in natural resources. Some regions are rich in cropland, forestland, or minerals. Some have a good supply of several natural resources. Some have very little. Only a few nations are rich in most of the important resources. And some nations own valuable resources but are unable to develop them.

The location of a resource is important. How close are other important resources or industries? A patch of fertile land far away in a mountainous area does not have the same value as similar land located near a large market. Is the resource near a system of transportation? The upper Amazon River basin in South America is rich in forests. But the lumber industry has not been developed very much because of limited means of transportation.

The distribution of resources stimulates trade between countries. No country has within its borders all the resources it needs. For example, the United States needs large amounts of high-quality manganese for making steel. The manganese is imported from

By developing and exporting oil from their vast reserves, Saudi Arabia and other Middle Eastern countries have achieved great wealth and powerful influence in world affairs.

As cities and towns grow, there are more people to feed but less land available for farming. New methods to increase crop yields become increasingly important.

Brazil, South Africa, and other countries. The countries of Western Europe need raw materials for their factories. They buy these materials from countries that have a surplus of them. Finished products are often exchanged for raw materials.

Rich and Poor

Because mineral resources are expensive to develop, only the world's wealthiest nations can afford them. Continuous demand for these resources also gives wealthier countries the power to control markets or buy up resources from poorer nations.

A country's natural resources can determine its global influence. The major petroleum-exporting countries are an example. In the 1970's, growing demand for petroleum caused a shift in world wealth and power. The United States, Japan, and Western Europe—which depend on other countries for some or all of their petroleum—began buying more oil from the Middle East, South America, and Africa. As the exporting countries with the greatest

oil reserves grew richer from oil revenues, they also became more influential in world affairs.

The greater use of natural resources has brought about a great increase in material wealth for many of the world's people. But many nations still depend largely on agriculture. They are poor in resources, and the economic value of their production is low. These countries are at a disadvantage in trade with the industrialized countries. Their people lack formal education, modern medicines, and other products that are enjoyed by the people of the wealthy countries.

▶ THE FUTURE

Economists try to find out how to best use natural resources to satisfy the needs of people. In the past, only the resources that were used directly were considered important. The chief concern was how much value a resource had in the marketplace.

We have learned that the resources people use indirectly are just as important as those that are used directly. Wetlands can be just as important as farmlands. If people are to enjoy a good quality of life, they must learn to use resources without harming the environment.

People have shown a great ability to destroy natural resources. They can undo in a short time what has taken nature millions of years to develop. But nature has shown a great ability to absorb and adjust to a certain amount of pollution. And the natural resources of the earth remain great. Still, the earth is a closed system—that is, it contains a finite amount of air, water, soil, and minerals.

Hope for the future lies in the fact that people are concerned about the environment. This concern is reflected in the work of agencies of the United Nations and of the environmental protection agencies that have been formed in many countries. These groups aim to work with nature, not against it.

People in many countries are also aware of the need to conserve resources and to use renewable resources. To plan for the future, we must practice more conservation. And we must manage natural resources for the benefit of all the peoples of the world.

HARRY B. KIRCHER
Southern Illinois University at Edwardsville

See also CONSERVATION.

NATURE, STUDY OF

People who study nature look at the world around them carefully and patiently to find out how plants and animals live and grow. Collectors unearthing fossils, bird watchers gazing through telescopes, wildlife biologists observing the behavior of wolf packs, and pond investigators peering at one-celled animals through microscopes all are studying different parts of nature.

"The world is watching: one cannot walk through a meadow or forest without a ripple of report spreading out. . . . The thrush darts back, the jay squalls, a beetle scuttles under the grasses, and the signal is passed along."

Gary Snyder
The Practice of the Wild

From the beginning of human time, there have been naturalists—people who study nature. The first naturalists studied the nature around them as they collected plants and berries, caught fish, and hunted wild animals. By gathering plants for food, people learned how to tell which ones were poisonous, which ones if left to grow would get tastier in time, and which ones were simply beautiful. By studying animal tracks, hunters learned that they could find out how long ago an animal had passed by and how fast it was traveling.

As the early naturalists studied, observed, and experimented, they learned to plant seeds and raise their own domesticated animals.

They also learned how to use clay, stone, and metals to make tools and utensils. With their newly made instruments, they hunted, cooked, built houses, and made clothes.

▶ **HOW PEOPLE STUDY NATURE**

There are several ways to explore the natural world. Some naturalists study living things by observing them; others conduct experiments; still others gather specimens to make collections. Whatever method is chosen, the basic equipment is the same: A naturalist needs to have curiosity about animals and plants and about the relationships of living things to each other and to their surroundings.

Observing Nature. One way to study plants or animals is to investigate them in their habitat, the place where they live. Individual species, or kinds, of animals and plants have food, water, climate, and behavior needs that determine where they can survive. Nature is all around us, not just in parks and wild places. Some environments are richer than others, but there are things to study in small backyards or city apartments, too. Even puddles or rotting logs can be intriguing places to study living things.

Naturalists who want to study a specific plant or animal might begin by doing some library research about its life and habitat. The next job is to find it in its natural habitat. Often the best way to learn if a particular plant or animal lives in an area is to ask people who work in parks. Gardeners, farmers, hunters, and people who fish also know a lot about what plants and animals live near them.

Once a likely habitat is found, the naturalist looks for clues to the species' existence. When the animal or plant is tracked down, pictures can be taken and notes can be made about the species' appearance, shelter, and life cycle. If an animal is being studied, some behaviors that can be observed include what it feeds on, how it feeds its young, what it does when it is not searching for food, and how it communicates with other animals. Every visit to its habitat provides new information: when it is most active, when it mates, when it molts. The investigator can check the surroundings to find out what other living things are in the same area and how they interact. Samples of the soil can be taken to examine later under a microscope. The observer can write down the air temperature, weather, and time of year.

Over time habitats may change. If long-term pesticide use or weather changes destroy a species' favorite foods, the species will have to adapt to eating other foods or find a better territory. Other events may cause changes in the life cycle of a plant or animal. A natural scientist has to be a good detective in order to find out what things make a habitat healthy for plant and animal life.

Nature Experiments. Anyone can grow plants indoors and conduct experiments on the different effects of food, water, light, and temperature on plant growth. The algae and mosses that grow on damp rocks and bricks and the lichens that grow on trees are easy to collect and examine.

Pets are also good subjects for observation experiments. Because small animals such as mice, guinea pigs, and gerbils mature quickly, it is possible to study them from the time they are born. Notice what foods they like and dislike. Find out how to take their body temperatures. Note how they act around strange objects and animals. Use a magnifying glass or microscope to study their hairs, feathers, and parasites such as fleas and lice.

Nature Collections. Another way to study nature is by making a collection. Some observers concentrate on one kind of plant, animal, or rock and spend a lifetime collecting samples. They learn how to preserve their treasures and make cases or books to display them. Many collectors also make drawings and paintings of the plants or animals they have preserved. Sometimes these drawings become the collection itself.

At times naturalists have pursued their interests without thinking about the effects on the natural world. They have collected too many specimens, collected rare or protected species, or even destroyed habitats. As you discover the natural world, never harm or disturb the living things that you study and never remove a rare or protected species from its habitat.

Along with looking directly at the natural world, setting up an indoor laboratory, or making up collections, it is useful to visit science and natural history museums, botanical gardens, zoos, pet shops, and libraries. Here you will find displays, people to answer questions, classes for young naturalists, and interesting shops with books on nature and simple nature study equipment. They are all wonderful places to get new ideas.

The Natural World of a Tree

A tree is the largest flowering plant on the earth. It supplies a community of plants and animals with food and shelter. By exploring the life of a tree, a naturalist can find out about life cycles, food chains, and the relationships among living things.

The life cycle of a tree, as well as that of its lodgers, can be determined by observing a tree throughout the year.

Parts of a tree, such as the leaves, flowers, and fruits, can be used to identify the kind of tree.

Observing the behavior of animals found in a tree can reveal which animals make their homes in the tree and which ones only visit to search for food.

A close examination can uncover harmful elements within a tree's community that can destroy the tree's leaves, bark, and roots.

When the area around a tree is inspected, the tree's effects on the surrounding environment, including other plant life, can be discovered.

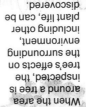

▶ NATURALISTS AND THEIR CONTRIBUTIONS

Naturalists use and share their knowledge of living things and the environment in a variety of ways. Some naturalists identify and classify the plants and animals they find. It was in the 1700's that a Swedish biologist named Carolus Linnaeus attempted to name everything in the natural world. He sent his students all over the world to collect samples. He then developed a method of identifying and naming each species using Latin names. Scientists still use Linnaeus' system.

Others use the information they find through their observations to develop new ways of looking at the world. In 1831 when the ship H.M.S. *Beagle* began its five-year journey around the world, Englishman Charles Darwin was aboard. As he traveled, Darwin observed the great assortment of living things. He worked out theories about how animal and plant species develop and change through time. Years later, Darwin explained his theories of evolution in his famous work, *On the Origin of Species* (1859).

Still other naturalists work to conserve and protect the natural environment and educate the public about the delicate balance of nature. The American writer Henry David Thoreau wrote about his observations of nature in the woods of Massachusetts. His book *Walden* (1854) inspired many other naturalists. Another American, John Muir, was influential in saving wilderness areas. He was responsible for convincing the United States government to create Yosemite National Park, which it did in 1890. He also started the Sierra Club, an organization to help protect wilderness and to teach people about nature.

In the 1960's, American Rachel Carson was a biologist with the U.S. Fish and Wildlife Service. She wrote *Silent Spring*, a book about the overuse of poisonous chemicals. Through her book, she made millions of people aware of environmental pollution. This awareness led many national governments to pass laws that control the use of dangerous chemicals.

▶ PROTECTING THE NATURAL WORLD

Not so long ago much of the world was wild. As human populations grew, people began to cut deeper into the wilderness. Wilderness areas and their resources disappeared as people cleared away forests, dammed rivers, killed wildlife, and mined minerals.

The threat of an ever-dwindling wilderness prompted people to make sure that there would always be places where people could go to enjoy the natural world. Women and men in many countries convinced their governments to establish parks that would be safe havens for plants and animals. This is how Yellowstone National Park, the world's first national park, was created in 1872.

Today there are many nature organizations that continue the education and conservation efforts begun by those concerned naturalists. Many of the organizations have special programs for young people. Most of these groups deal with environmental problems as well as teach about nature. The National Audubon Society, Adopt-a-Stream, and the Izaak Walton League are just three of the many organizations that have programs for young people who are interested in learning about the natural world and who are willing to help make it a healthy place for all living things.

JUDITH KOHL
Coauthor, *The View from the Oak*

See also ANIMALS; BIOLOGY; BIRDS; BOTANY; CARSON, RACHEL; EARTH; ECOLOGY; ENDANGERED SPECIES; ENVIRONMENT; LIFE; LINNAEUS, CAROLUS; MUIR, JOHN; PLANTS; TAXONOMY; ZOOS.

Above: John Muir had a deep love and respect for the natural world, especially what he called "wild places and wild creatures." His devotion to the land guided him as he sought to study, preserve, and protect American lands.

Below: A love of the outdoors that began in childhood fueled Rachel Carson's passionate concern for the environment. Her belief that human activities could tragically upset the balance of nature led her to sound the alarm about the careless use of pesticides.

NAURU

Nauru—the world's smallest independent republic—is a tiny island nation located in the west central Pacific Ocean. It has only one important natural resource—phosphate rock. This mineral is so valuable for making fertilizer that Nauru once had one of the world's highest incomes per person. Today, however, phosphate deposits are almost exhausted; as a result, Nauru faces severe economic hardship. Nauru does not have an official capital.

People. Nauruans are descended from various Pacific island peoples. Almost half the total population is made up of foreign workers who mine the phosphate, but citizenship is restricted to native Nauruans. Nauruan is the official language, but English is widely spoken. Christianity is the primary religion.

Land. Nauru is an oval-shaped coral island. A narrow green coastal strip, where most of the people live, encircles the island. In the interior is a plateau that, as a result of phosphate mining, resembles the barren landscape of the moon. The highest point in Nauru rises to 225 feet (69 meters). Nauru has no rivers. The climate is hot and humid.

FACTS and figures

REPUBLIC OF NAURU is the official name of the country.

LOCATION: West central Pacific Ocean.

AREA: 8 sq mi (21 km²).

POPULATION: 13,000 (estimate).

CAPITAL AND LARGEST CITY: Nauru has no formal capital city. The seat of government is located in the Yaren District.

MAJOR LANGUAGES: Nauruan (official), English.

MAJOR RELIGIOUS GROUP: Christian (Protestant, Roman Catholic).

GOVERNMENT: Republic. Head of state and government—president. Legislature—Parliament.

CHIEF PRODUCTS: Agricultural—coconuts, pandanus, fish. Manufactured—coconut products. Mineral—phosphate.

MONETARY UNIT: Australian dollar (1 dollar = 100 cents).

Economy. Most Nauruans work for the government or in the declining phosphate industry, which is owned by the government. Attempts to create other sources of income have failed. Nauru once assisted other Pacific island countries in need, but it is now dependent on overseas aid. Fish, coconuts, pandanus (fruit-bearing trees), and a few vegetables are the only edible natural resources. Nauruans pay no taxes.

History and Government. British sailors were the first Europeans to visit the island, in 1798. Nauru was colonized by Germany in 1888. After World War I (1914–18), it came under the control of Australia as a mandated territory of the League of Nations. During World War II, Japan occupied the island from 1942 to 1945. Following World War II, Nauru became a trust territory of the United Nations, again administered by Australia. Nauru gained its independence in 1968. It became a member of the United Nations in 1999.

Nauru is a republic. The one-house legislature, the Parliament, is composed of 18 members elected for 3-year terms. The president, elected by Parliament, serves as head of state and government and leads the cabinet, which is responsible to the Parliament.

JOHN MILES
Senior Political Affairs Officer, United Nations
Reviewed by DOUG MUNRO
Victoria University of Wellington

NAVAJO INDIANS. See INDIANS, AMERICAN.

Nauru

PACIFIC OCEAN

166°55' E
0°31' S
166°55' E

MENENG POINT
YAREN DISTRICT
CENTRAL PLATEAU
Buada Lagoon
Anibare Bay
ANNA POINT

N

0 1 mi
0 1 km

ASIA
AUSTRALIA
PACIFIC OCEAN

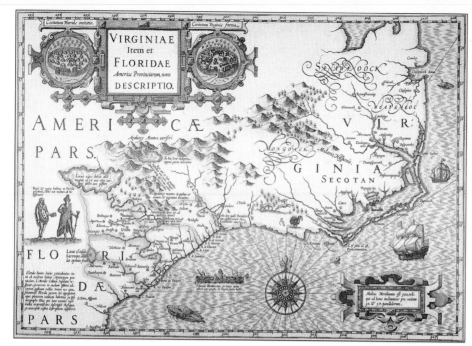

From the earliest days of sailing, nautical charts have been an indispensable navigation tool for ships near land. This chart from the 1600's (*left*) helped early navigators pilot their ships along the southeastern coast of the present-day United States. This contemporary chart of Block Island (*below*) indicates water depths near the shore as well as prominent landmarks that can help a ship establish its location.

NAVIGATION

Many birds and animals seem to have a built-in sense of direction. Migrating birds travel great distances each year. And you may have read stories of cats and dogs that find their way home from far away.

People do not have this sense. If you were put down in the middle of a forest or far out at sea, no inner sense would tell you which way to go to get home. To find your way, you would have to navigate.

Navigation is the science of finding your way. The word "navigation" comes from Latin words meaning "ship" and "move," and originally it referred only to finding your way at sea. But today people also use navigation to accurately find their way when traveling under water, in the air, in space, and on land.

There are four main navigation systems—piloting, celestial navigation, dead reckoning, and electronic navigation. Each is sometimes used alone, but more often a navigator uses a combination of these systems.

▶ PILOTING

If you can see the shore from a ship, you can establish your location. You have only to recognize hills, mountains, or beaches to be fairly certain of where you are. Finding your way by using such landmarks is called piloting.

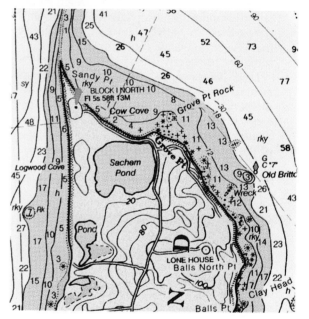

The earliest navigators sailed from one familiar landmark to another along the coast. Land was never out of their sight for very long. As they sailed, they could find the depth of the water by dropping a weighted rope over the side of the ship. In this way they could avoid running aground in shallow coastal waters.

Eventually the Phoenicians, the Vikings, and the Polynesians developed better ways of navigating. They used the sun and the stars to find their way across open seas. But piloting remained a useful system of navigation. And several developments have made piloting easier than it was in the early days of sailing.

Charts, Buoys, and Lighthouses

If you were going to a friend's house for the first time, you might use a map to help you find the house. A chart is a map made especially for navigators. Aeronautical charts are used by airplane pilots. They show landmarks such as towns and bridges and indicate heights of mountains. Nautical charts are used at sea. They show coastal waters, indicating channels and water depths and navigational aids such as buoys and lighthouses.

Buoys are floats that mark channels, dangerous rocks, and the like. The color and design of a buoy tells the navigator how to proceed. For example, navigators often memorize the phrase "red, right returning." This means that to stay in safe waters on returning to port, they should keep red buoys on the right side of the vessel.

Lighthouses also mark dangerous waters. Each lighthouse has its own pattern of flashing lights. Thus navigators can find their ships' location at night by identifying the light pattern and consulting their charts.

Finding Direction

A navigator must know the direction to steer to get to a certain place. The chart may show, for example, that the ship must sail to the northeast. But with no landmarks in sight, which way is northeast? The navigator finds this direction by using a compass.

About 1200, sailors began to use compasses to show them the direction of north. They found that if a small, thin piece of magnetized iron swings freely, it always points in the north-south direction. They called such a piece of iron a magnetic needle.

The first sailor's—or mariner's—compasses were made by inserting a magnetic needle through a piece of straw. The straw was then floated in a bowl of water. Later the needle was attached to a round card marked with the directions north, south, east, and west and points in between (the "points" of the compass). This combination of needle and card is called a magnetic compass.

Today's compass is a magnetic needle mounted on a pivot. The needle is attracted to the magnetic poles—the north magnetic pole or the south magnetic pole. The north magnetic pole is located on Bathurst Island, in northern Canada, not at the geographic, or true, North Pole. Therefore, a compass needle usually points not to true geographical north but close to it. Adjustments are made by using a table that lists the variations between true and magnetic north for any place on the globe.

WONDER QUESTION

What is a ship's log?

Before the invention of the chronometer, navigators could only estimate the distance their ship traveled during a particular length of time. To make this estimate, early English sailors used a device called a **log**. This was a piece of wood that was fixed to a long piece of rope and dropped over the stern of a ship. The rope was let out as the ship sailed away from the floating log. The speed of the ship could be calculated by measuring the amount of rope let out in a given time. The navigator could then calculate about

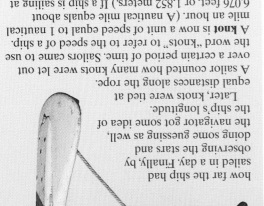

how far the ship had sailed in a day. Finally, by observing the stars and doing some guessing as well, the navigator got some idea of the ship's longitude.

Later, knots were tied at equal distances along the rope. A sailor counted how many knots were let out over a certain period of time. Sailors came to use the word "knots" to refer to the speed of a ship. A **knot** is now a unit of speed equal to 1 nautical mile an hour. (A nautical mile equals about 6,076 feet, or 1,852 meters.) If a ship is sailing at a speed of 15 knots, it is moving at 15 nautical miles an hour. The measurements taken using the log were recorded in a book, later called a logbook. Today a logbook is usually just called a log, and it contains not only the record of the ship's distance traveled but also of any shipboard event worth noting during the voyage.

A magnetic compass cannot be used inside modern steel ships. These ships contain a great deal of metal that affects where a magnetic needle points. In most large modern ships, a different kind of instrument, called a gyrocompass, is used.

The gyrocompass, invented in 1908, is really a gyroscope mounted in a special way. Like all gyroscopes, the gyrocompass has a heavy wheel spinning on an axle. An electric motor drives the wheel. No matter how the ship moves, the axle of the gyrocompass automatically adjusts itself so that it points to true north.

Latitude and Longitude

When a ship is out of the sight of land, its navigator cannot tell one part of the sea from another. Charts are of no help, and even a compass is of little use by itself. To know which way to steer, the navigator must first know exactly where the ship is.

If you wanted to meet a friend downtown, you might say "Meet me at the corner of Elm Street and Main Street." Your friend could look on a map and find out just where to go. At sea or in the air, where there are no roads, navigators use latitude and longitude to locate places.

Latitude and longitude are imaginary lines. Lines of latitude show the distance north or south of the equator. Every place on the equator has a latitude of zero degrees (0°). Every other place has a latitude that is measured by its distance from the equator. For example, Miami, Florida, has a latitude of 26 degrees north. Places south of the equator have a south latitude. For example, Buenos Aires, Argentina, has a latitude of about 35 degrees south.

Longitude indicates how far east or west a place is. But east or west of where? Map makers had to agree on a longitude that would be zero degrees. They decided that zero degrees would be the line of longitude that goes through Greenwich, England. This line is called the prime meridian. Thus New York City's longitude is 74 degrees west (of Greenwich) and Tokyo's longitude is 140 degrees east (of Greenwich).

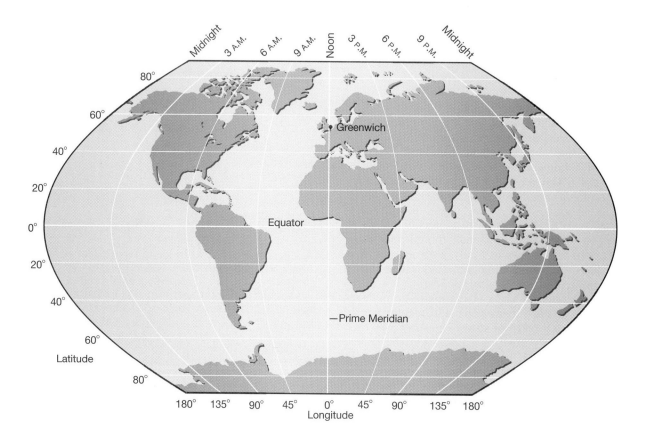

In celestial navigation, a ship's latitude can be determined by measuring the angle between a celestial object and the horizon.

▶ CELESTIAL NAVIGATION

Early navigators guessed their position by following the stars and estimating the strength of the wind. But they could not be sure where they were. Later navigators learned to "take a fix" (find their position) by observing the stars, the sun, the moon, and the planets. This is called celestial navigation.

Finding Latitude by the Stars

To a ship on the equator, certain stars will seem to be directly overhead. But as the ship sails north, those stars seem to slip gradually lower in the sky. Other stars appear to move overhead. Thus a navigator can find the ship's latitude by measuring the distance the stars seem to be above the horizon.

The navigator must know the positions of the stars at different seasons. But some stars hardly change their positions, and they are easy to navigate by. The North Star (Polaris) always seems to be just above the North Pole. It can be seen from anywhere in the Northern Hemisphere. A navigator can keep a steady course east or west by making sure that the North Star stays at the same place above the horizon. In the Southern Hemisphere, a constellation called the Southern Cross is used the same way.

Early navigators used simple instruments to measure their latitude. One instrument, called a **quadrant**, was made of a piece of flat wood or metal shaped like a quarter-circle. A scale was drawn on its rounded edge. The navigator sighted a star through holes in the instrument, and the star's height above the horizon could be read from the scale.

One of the most widely used instruments was the **astrolabe**. This was a heavy metal disk marked with a scale around it and containing a star map. A ring was attached at the top so that the disk could hang from one finger. A bar with sighting holes and pointers at the ends was attached to the center of the disk. The navigator turned the bar until the star was visible through the sighting holes. The figures at the pointers gave the height of the star above the horizon.

It was important to measure the distance between the sun and the horizon to find the latitude during the day-time. Navigators also needed to know exactly when the sun reached its greatest height in the sky. This told them the noon time. But since looking directly at the sun is dangerous, the **backstaff** was invented in 1594. The person using it stood facing away from the sun, and the shadow cast by the sun on the backstaff was used to show its height in the sky.

In 1730, John Hadley, an Englishman, and Thomas Godfrey, an American, each invented an instrument called an **octant**. An octant is shaped like a pie wedge, with a scale encompassing an eighth of a circle (45 degrees) marked on its rounded edge. One end of a swinging arm is attached to the point of the octant. A movable mirror is fixed at that end of the arm. The other end extends to the scale. The octant calculated the height of a star or the sun above the horizon, but it could only measure angles up to 90 degrees.

The octant was gradually changed into the **sextant**, which has the same basic shape but has a scale encompassing a sixth of a circle (60 degrees) and is capable of measuring angles up to 120 degrees. A telescope is mounted on the sextant (unlike on most octants), and a glass, half clear and half mirror, is mounted in front of the telescope. The sextant is still the navigator's main instrument for observing celestial bodies. To "shoot the sun," the navigator looks at the horizon through the telescope and the clear glass, moving the mirror until the reflection of the sun seems to touch the horizon. The scale end of the arm then shows the height of the sun.

Finding and Measuring Longitude

To find longitude the navigator must know the exact time at Greenwich, England, and the exact time aboard ship. If the ship's time is earlier than Greenwich time, its longitude is west of Greenwich. If a ship's time is later than Greenwich time, the ship's longitude is east. It is 15 degrees east or west for each hour's difference in time.

In 1735, John Harrison of England made the first truly accurate clock, or **chronometer**, that could be used at sea. The chronometer told Greenwich time. By observing the sun, a navigator found the time it was aboard the ship. Then, by comparing the ship's time with Greenwich time, the navigator could work out the ship's longitude.

A navigator uses a sextant to "shoot the sun." The height of the sun above the horizon is indicated on the curved scale at the bottom of the sextant.

Chronometers are usually mounted on two brass rings fixed inside a box. No matter how the ship rolls about in a rough sea, the rings keep the chronometer level.

Today all ships have radios and receive time signals from observatories such as the U.S. Naval Observatory in Washington, D.C., and the Royal Greenwich Observatory in Sussex, England. These signals are produced by atomic clocks.

▶ DEAD RECKONING

A navigator can also take a fix by using a method called dead reckoning. In this method the navigator notes the direction and speed of the ship's travel since the last fix was taken. Then the navigator makes corrections for winds and ocean currents that may have forced the ship off course. From this information a new, more accurate fix is calculated. The navigator can then determine the direction to steer the ship to keep it on course.

Dead reckoning is used in navigating aircraft and submarines as well as ships. Finding a position by dead reckoning alone is not as accurate as finding a position by celestial navigation. But it is useful because the navigator can take a fix at any time of day or night, in bad weather, and underwater.

▶ ELECTRONIC NAVIGATION

Today a navigator can find a position with the help of an electronic device such as radar, a radio beacon, loran, or a Doppler system.

A ship or airplane can carry a radar device that provides a "picture" of the port or region the craft enters. Ground or port controllers can also use radar to keep track of all the aircraft or ships in an area. Radio beacons are used a great deal in air navigation. The beacons send out signals that an aircraft can identify to find its way from place to place. A loran (*lo*ng-*ra*nge *n*avigation) system is useful to both air and marine navigators. It provides information on direction and distance.

A Doppler system provides a navigator with information on the speed, height, and sideways motion of an aircraft. In Doppler navigation, radio waves are sent out from the aircraft and reflected back from the land to give the navigator information about the speed of the aircraft. Using radar beams pointed forward, downward, and to the sides of the aircraft, a Doppler system can give accurate information on the movement and direction of the plane. Radio navigation systems are useful in almost every kind of weather.

For more information, see the article RADAR AND SONAR in Volume QR.

Inertial Guidance

Another electronic navigation system is inertial guidance, a modern form of dead reckoning. This system is based on precise information about the speed and direction of a craft. A device called an inertial navigator provides this information. Inertial guidance systems are used in nuclear submarines, military planes, long-range guided missiles, and spacecraft. They are also used in some satellites.

Global Positioning System

A group of 24 satellites, called the Global Positioning System (GPS), continually transmits radio signals to all points on Earth. A device called a GPS receiver compares time delays between signals from at least four of the satellites. Using this data, the device calculates its latitude, longitude, and altitude. GPS has greatly enhanced marine navigation through Electronic Charting Systems that receive signals from the satellites and automatically display the ship's position on digital charts.

The Global Positioning System is used in other forms of navigation. For instance, GPS receivers are now installed in many automobiles to help people find their destination while driving. And hikers can use the GPS to determine their location as well as map popular routes.

◀ NAVIGATION IN SPACE TRAVEL

Navigation in space is much more complicated than navigation on land, at sea, or in the air. An unmanned probe uses land-based navigation systems such as Doppler to measure its speed and radar to determine its distance from Earth. A probe can take photographs of celestial objects to establish both its location and the location of the objects. Once a probe's speed, distance, and position are known, signals sent from Earth can make small corrections in its course so it will safely rendezvous with its target or targets.

Navigation in the space shuttle is even more complex, since the craft not only must maneuver in space but within the Earth's atmosphere as well. Among the electronic navigation aids used by a shuttle are radar; inertial guidance systems; automatic star trackers; and an air data system, which, by sensing air pressure and temperature, helps establish the craft's speed and altitude and

Today's portable GPS receivers can help people find their way through the streets of a city or the hiking trails of the country.

provides information necessary for steering and braking.

Space travel would be next to impossible without computers. They make course corrections much faster and much more precisely than any person can. On manned flights, however, astronauts may still need to take manual star sightings to correct errors by automatic systems.

COLIN A. RONAN
Fellow of the Royal Astronomical Society

Reviewed by LT. CORNELL C. THOMPSON
Branch Chief, Navigation Information Service
U.S. Coast Guard

See also GYROSCOPE; LATITUDE AND LONGITUDE; RADAR AND SONAR.

NAVRATILOVA, MARTINA. See TENNIS (Great Players).

NAVY. See UNITED STATES, ARMED FORCES OF THE.

NAZCA. See INDIANS, AMERICAN (Empires and Other Extended Groups).

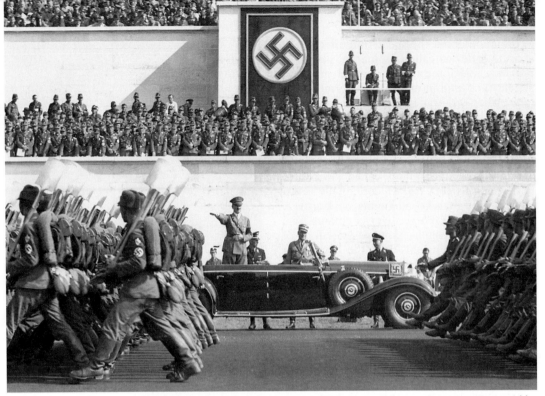

Nazi führer (leader) Adolf Hitler salutes his German soldiers as they goose-step past his reviewing stand during a Nazi Party convention in Nuremberg, 1933.

NAZISM

National Socialism, or Nazism, was a German political movement founded in Munich, Germany, about 1920. Its full title was the National Socialist German Workers' Party (Nazi, for short).

The words "National" and "Socialism" give the key to the direction, or goals, of this movement in its early days. It was led from 1921 to 1945 by Adolf Hitler, a violent German nationalist who played on the bitterness many Germans felt after World War I (1914–18). They had lost the war, and they believed that the harsh demands other nations made on them in the Treaty of Versailles (1919) were unfair. Hitler claimed that the German Army had never been beaten. Instead, Germany had lost because it had been betrayed by the German politicians who came to power at the end of the war in November 1918. Hitler demanded that these "November criminals" be driven from office. He wanted their power handed over to those who would free Germany from the Versailles Treaty and restore it to greatness.

This was one side of National Socialism—its appeal to German nationalism. But the other side, socialism, was equally important, at least in the beginning. Hitler criticized Germany's other nationalist parties for being too traditionalist and "respectable." He attacked the elitist attitude of conservative politicians. He said that they knew nothing about the way the majority of Germans—the working people—lived. Hitler wanted to win their support for German nationalism by linking nationalism to a radical program of social reform.

This was the original two-part program of National Socialism. First, the Nazis told the people that Germans were the greatest people in the world and promised to restore Germany's military power. Second, they promised to carry out radical changes in Germany and to get rid of the leaders who had failed to provide jobs for the people.

The Nazis, like the Fascists (a similar group that organized in Italy), promised much to the workers to win their support. But the Nazis did not believe in equal rights for everyone. They believed that the strong

cept their leadership without question.

Features of National Socialism. The most prominent feature of National Socialism was its racism. Hitler preached that the Germans belonged to a Nordic, or Aryan, master race. He said that Aryans alone had the ability and the right to rule. They were threatened by the inferior races, not only by the black and yellow peoples of Africa and Asia but also by the Slavs of eastern Europe. But the Nazis believed that their greatest enemies were the Jews. They claimed that the Jews were carrying on a worldwide conspiracy to crush the Aryan race. Hitler attacked the Jews for all the evils that had happened to Germany. He said they were to blame for the "stab in the back" that had lost World War I for Germany and for everything that had gone wrong since then. He said that the Jews were the leaders of the Socialist and Communist parties that were working for a revolution that would set the German people against one another. At the same time, he said that the Jews had great financial power and made their profits by cheating the common people. For all these reasons, Hitler believed that the Nazis must clear the Jews out of Germany.

Like the Italian Fascist dictator Benito Mussolini, Hitler glorified war. The Nazis recruited a private army of storm troopers, dressed in brown shirts, with military ranks. Their emblem was the swastika (a cross with the arms bent at right angles) and their salute was the outstretched arm and the greeting "Heil Hitler!" ("Hail Hitler"). The Brownshirts were tough street fighters who broke up rival political meetings and harassed Germans who were against Hitler.

Hitler's Rise to Power. It was in Munich, in November 1923, that Hitler made his first attempt at a National Socialist revolution. He tried to take over the government of Bavaria. But the attempt failed, and he was sent to prison. While there, he wrote the first part of his book *Mein Kampf* ("My Struggle"), which became the bible of the Nazi movement. After his failure, Hitler made up his mind not to risk another attempt at seizing power by force. Instead, he would try to win it legally. But when Hitler got out of prison in December 1924, Germany was no longer so ready for a change. There was less of the widespread unrest that had swept Germany right after the war. The Nazis began to attract a mass following only when the economic crisis of 1929–30 hit Germany and millions were left without jobs. In the general election of September 1930, the Nazis won 107 seats in the Reichstag (parliament). The new government seemed a welcome break with Germany's past, and Hitler became a national figure overnight.

Between 1930 and 1933, the Nazis increased their votes until they became the largest single party in the country. A great part of their success was due to the use of propaganda and publicity on a scale no one had seen before. Giant rallies and military-style parades excited the people. Hitler used these tricks to build up the impression of a mass movement that could not be stopped.

All this campaigning required money. Hitler was able to get money from important business people by making them believe that only the Nazis could save Germany from a Communist revolution. The same argument persuaded the old-style conservative leaders and the army to work with Hitler. They disliked Nazi radicalism and despised Hitler as an upstart. But the Nazis were the only party that could defeat the opposition.

Germany under the Nazis. On January 30, 1933, after much bargaining, Hitler became chancellor of a coalition (combination) government. The other parties that shared in the government thought they could use the Nazis to win their own goals. They discovered that they were mistaken—but it was too late. A fire in the Reichstag building on February 27, 1933, gave Hitler an excuse to declare that the Communists were plotting an armed uprising against the government. Fearing revolution, the people gave Hitler 44 percent of the votes in a new election. At once, Hitler demanded complete power to do anything necessary to secure the safety of the country. He got this power in the Enabling Act of March 21, 1933. He used it to set up a single-party dictatorship.

As dictator, Hitler suppressed all other political parties and the trade unions. He placed Nazis in all key positions, including control of the police. Anyone who protested was thrown into prison. Many Jews were beaten and robbed.

Even this did not go far enough for many Nazis. They wanted still more jobs in the

Consult the Index to find more information in *The New Book of Knowledge* about the following people associated with the Nazis: dictator Adolf Hitler; political leader Hermann Goering; and military leaders Karl Doenitz, Alfred Jodl, and Erwin Rommel.

Adolf Eichmann

Joseph Goebbels

Martin Ludwig Bormann

(1900?-45), born in Halberstadt, Germany, was one of the most powerful Nazi political leaders. He has often been called Hitler's "evil genius." Bormann joined the Nazi Party in 1925. When Hitler came to power in 1933, he gave Bormann a position under Rudolf Hess, head of the Nazi Party cabinet. When Hess flew to Scotland in 1941, Bormann took his position, and in 1943 he became Hitler's private secretary. He was last seen alive on May 1, 1945, one day after Hitler committed suicide. Speculation that Bormann had escaped to South America ended in 1972, when a skeleton found in Berlin was declared to be his. DNA testing confirmed this in 1998.

(Karl) Adolf Eichmann (1906–62), born in Solingen, Germany, was an SS officer and the head of Nazi Germany's Race and Resettlement Office. In this position he was instrumental in the mass murder of European Jews during World War II. He established a convoy system to take Jews to concentration camps, where he had gas chambers installed to kill large numbers of victims all at once. At the end of the war, Eichmann escaped to Argentina. In 1960 he was discovered and kidnapped by Israeli agents and flown to Israel, where he was tried for crimes against humanity. Found guilty, Eichmann was sentenced to death and hanged on May 31, 1962.

(Paul) Joseph Goebbels (1897–1945), born in Rheydt, Germany, was Nazi Germany's minister of propaganda and public instruction. Goebbels joined the Nazi Party in 1924. Hitler gave Goebbels the important propaganda ministry when he came to power in 1933. In this position, Goebbels had total control over the press, radio, theater, film, literature, and art. He used censorship to block or distort the news, and propaganda to espouse Nazi policy, including anti-Semitism. In the latter part of World War II, as German armies were being routed by the Russians and Allied bombers were devastating German cities, Goebbels fought to keep German morale high. But on May 1, 1945, with Germany's defeat just days away, Goebbels poisoned his six children and then shot his wife and himself.

(Walter Richard) Rudolf Hess (1894–1987), born in Alexandria, Egypt, was an original member of the Nazi Party and a close friend of Hitler. His fanatical devotion to Hitler and to the Nazi cause led

army, in government, and in business. Hitler found himself in difficulty. His brown-shirted storm troopers had been useful for frightening his opponents. But now that Hitler was in power, their demands were a nuisance.

The crisis came in the summer of 1934. The aged president of Germany, Paul von Hindenburg, was dying. Hitler knew that if he wanted to become president as well as chancellor, he must have the support of the conservative army leaders. To get that support, he must prove to them that the socialist part of the Nazi revolution was over. On June 30, 1934, he carried out a purge of the party. Some of the best-known party officials—including Ernst Roehm and Gregor Strasser—were shot, and the Nazi Party's Brownshirt army was broken up. Their place was taken by the more reliable blackshirted SS (*Schutzstaffel*—"Protection Squad"), Hitler's official police.

In this way, Hitler broke with the radical side of National Socialism, the idea of a social revolution. The other side, German nationalism, became all the stronger. The whole na-

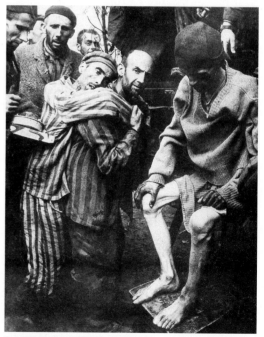

Survivors of the Nazi concentration camps were liberated by Allied troops in 1945. By the end of World War II, Hitler and the Nazis had murdered approximately 6 million Jews and millions of other "undesirables" in the Holocaust.

tion was mobilized to build up Germany's strength as a great power. One by one, Hitler began to ignore the provisions of the Treaty of Versailles. He built up Germany's armed forces into one of the world's great fighting machines. This gave him power to threaten war against anyone who tried to stop his plans to extend Germany's frontiers.

World War II and the Holocaust. As Hitler began taking land from other countries, European nations saw their choice. They must either submit to German domination of Europe, or they must fight. Even after they made up their minds to fight and World War II began in 1939, Hitler swept from victory to victory. In 1941 he attacked the Union of Soviet Socialist Republics (Soviet Union) and set up Nazi control of eastern Europe. The Slavic peoples of Poland and the Soviet Union were robbed of everything they owned and were forced to work like slaves for the benefit of Germany.

At the same time, the Nazi SS, on Hitler's orders, set to work on wiping out the Jewish people by systematic murder. Jews and other prisoners were herded like animals into concentration camps, where they became slave laborers or were exterminated. Many millions of people, including Germans, died in what is now called the Holocaust before Hitler was defeated and the Nazi empire overthrown in 1945.

Since 1945 there have been small Nazi movements in several countries, including Germany. The American Nazi Party was founded in the United States in 1959 by George Lincoln Rockwell, who adopted the swastika symbol and many of Hitler's racist policies. Some extreme groups have even claimed that the crimes against humanity committed by Hitler in World War II did not happen. But most people view the rise and fall of National Socialism as one of the most horrible episodes in human history, never to be repeated.

ALAN BULLOCK
Author, *Hitler, A Study in Tyranny*

See also FASCISM; HITLER, ADOLF; HOLOCAUST; WORLD WAR II.

NEANDERTHALS. See PREHISTORIC PEOPLE.

Hitler to name Hess second in line, after Goering, as his successor. In May 1941, Hess astonished everyone—including Hitler—by flying from Germany to Great Britain to negotiate peace between the two countries. Instead, he was imprisoned in the Tower of London. He remained there until after the war. In October 1945, he was sent back to Germany to stand trial as a war criminal at Nuremberg. Sentenced to life imprisonment, Hess committed suicide in Spandau Prison in 1987.

Reinhard Tristan Eugen Heydrich (1904-42), born in Halle, Germany, was one of the most feared Nazis and a leading advocate of the systematic murder of European Jews. Heydrich joined the Nazi Party and the SS in 1931, became deputy head of the secret police (Gestapo) in 1934, and was named chief of the Reich Central Security Office in 1939. He engineered Kristallnacht, the 1938 pogrom (organized massacre) of the Jews. He convened the 1942 Wannsee Conference, where the "final solution" of the Jewish

Rudolf Hess

problem" (genocide) was planned. And he constructed the death camps, where the Jews and other "undesirables" were murdered in gas chambers. Appointed governor of Bohemia and Moravia, in occupied Czechoslovakia, Heydrich was assassinated on June 4, 1942, by Czech agents. In revenge, the Germans destroyed the Czech village of Lidice and murdered the entire adult male population.

Heinrich Himmler (1900-45), born in Munich, Germany, was the chief administrator of the SS and the secret police (Gestapo), the organizations that carried out terror and genocide in Nazi Germany and Nazi-occupied Europe. His power

Heinrich Himmler

was exceeded only by that of Hitler. Himmler, an anti-Semite, was a member of the Nazi Party from its beginning in the 1920's. During World War II, he led the SS and the Gestapo in their systematic extermination of 6 million Jews and millions of others in concentration camps. In 1943 he became Germany's minister of the interior. After the Allied victory in 1945, Himmler was captured by British troops. He escaped trial at Nuremberg, along with several other Nazi leaders, by poisoning himself.

Albert Speer (1905-81), born in Mannheim, Germany, was an architect who designed the imposing monuments and stadiums that symbolized Hitler's vision for Germany's Third Reich (empire). Later he served as minister of armaments (1942-45). At Nuremberg, Speer was found guilty of using slave labor to increase weapons production. He was sentenced to 20 years at Spandau Prison, where he wrote the autobiographical *Inside the Third Reich* (1970) and *Spandau: The Secret Diaries* (1976).

NEBRASKA

The name Nebraska is derived from the Oto Indian word nebrathka, *meaning "flat water." This is the name the Indians used to describe the shallow Platte River that cuts through the center of the state. Nebraska's nickname, the Cornhusker State, was inspired by corn, the state's most important crop. Most of the corn grown there is used to feed cattle and hogs, Nebraska's most valuable farm products.*

State flag

Nebraska is a midwestern state that lies roughly near the center of the United States. Nearly one-third of the state's residents live in one of two urban centers—Omaha, situated in the east along the Missouri River, and Lincoln, the state capital. Most are descendants of the immigrants who came from Scandinavia and northern Europe in the late 1800's.

Nebraska has long served as an important route between the eastern United States and the West. The broad valley of the Platte River eased transportation across the plains for early fur traders, wagon trains of western pioneers, and the Pony Express mail route. Later the nation's first transcontinental railroad cut across the state, joining east and west.

Those who have traveled along the Platte River valley, a level plain of corn and alfalfa fields, have witnessed only a small part of Nebraska's geographic variety. This image of Nebraska does not take into account the forested bluffs that overlook the Missouri River in the east, the striking canyons and plateaus in the southwest, the wavelike, grass-covered dunes of the Sand Hills in the north, or the buttes and pine-covered cliffs that tower over the Niobrara River in the northwest.

Nebraska is one of the nation's leading agricultural states. Farming has shaped much of Nebraska's history and has remained an important part of the state's economy. Nebraskans have long recognized the value of their fertile soils and abundant groundwater, and they have sought to prevent the decline of these resources as caused by erosion, overuse, and pollution.

As early as 1872, under the leadership of J. Sterling Morton, Arbor Day was founded in Nebraska. Now celebrated nationwide, this special day is set aside for planting trees, not only to protect the soil from erosion but to add beauty to the landscape as well.

▶LAND

Nebraska rises gradually from the Missouri River in the east to the far western section of the state, known as the Panhandle. Much of the state is covered by a windblown material called loess, deposits of fine-grained sand, silt, and clay that are the source of Nebraska's highly fertile soils. Few places on earth have larger loess deposits.

Land Regions

No clear boundary line exists between the state's two landform regions, the Dissected Till Plains and the Great Plains.

The Dissected Till Plains, which are part of a larger region known as the Central Lowland, cover the eastern quarter of the state. During the Ice Age, glaciers covered much of this region. When the glaciers melted thousands of years ago, they left behind large quantities of drift deposits in the form of boulders, gravel, sand, and other earth materials called till. The addition of windblown loess deposits on the Till Plains created a fertile land of low, rolling hills.

The Great Plains, covering the rest of the state, is part of a broad region that stretches all the way from Texas to the Canadian prov-

Nebraska, a midwestern plains state, is known for its agricultural products. Grain elevators store the bounty of its corn and wheat harvests, while cattle graze on its vast rangelands. Children in one of Nebraska's many small towns raise the flag outside their small schoolhouse.

FACTS AND FIGURES

Capital: Lincoln.

Statehood: March 1, 1867; 37th state.

State Motto: *Equality before the law.*

State Song: *"Beautiful Nebraska."*

Nickname: Cornhusker State.

Abbreviations: NE; Nebr.; Neb.

Location: Central United States; bordered on the north by South Dakota, on the east by Iowa and Missouri, on the south by Kansas and Colorado, and on the west by Wyoming.

Area: 77,358 sq mi (200,358 km²); rank, 16th.

Population: 1,711,263 (2000 census): rank, 38th.

Elevation: *Highest*—5,426 ft (1,654 m) in Kimball County; *lowest*—840 ft (256 m) on the Missouri River in Richardson County.

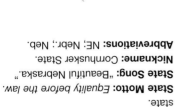

State bird: Western meadowlark

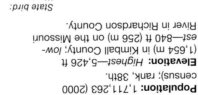

State tree: Cottonwood

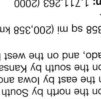

State flower: Goldenrod

ince of Alberta. This region has a fairly level surface. However, in some areas the landscape is interrupted by deep canyons and valleys. Nebraska's highest elevation, 5,426 feet (1,654 meters) above sea level, is located in this region.

The most unique region of Nebraska is the **Sand Hills**, located across the north central part of the state. Covering approximately 19,300 square miles (50,000 square kilometers), it is the largest sand-dune area in the Western Hemisphere. The dunes, formed during the past 8,000 years, are covered by grasses, which keep the sand stabilized. The Sand Hills region is an important ranching and cattle-grazing area.

Grass-covered sand dunes distinguish the landscape of the Sand Hills country, the largest sand-dune area in the Western Hemisphere.

To the west of the Sand Hills lies a region of high plains, made up of badlands, buttes, rugged hills, and canyons, known as the **Pine Ridge**.

To the east and south of the Sand Hills are the **Loess Hills**, where streams have cut steep-sided canyons into the plateaus. The only large level areas of the state are the **Loess Plain** of central Nebraska and the **Platte Valley**, where rich soil has been deposited by the Platte River. These regions are the most productive agricultural areas of the state.

Rivers and Lakes

All of Nebraska lies within the Missouri River drainage basin. The Platte River, formed by the North Platte and South Platte rivers, runs the length of the state. It carries water, especially snowmelt, from the Rocky Mountains eastward to its mouth near Plattsmouth on the Missouri River. In the spring the Platte is a full, wide river, but in late summer, its flow often slows to a trickle. The riverbed is wide and sandy, with many small islands and sandbars.

The most important tributaries of the Platte are the Loup and Elkhorn rivers. The Niobrara River lies near Nebraska's northern border. A portion of it has been designated as part of the National, Wild, and Scenic Rivers system and has gained much attention for its natural beauty and uses for recreation. Other important rivers in Nebraska include the Republican, Big Blue, and Little Blue, all of which flow into the Kansas River, a tributary of the Missouri.

Nebraska has more than 1,000 small lakes in the Sand Hills. Most of these have resulted from abundant groundwater and a high water table. Most larger lakes in the state are reservoirs that have been created by damming rivers for irrigation, flood control, or hydroelectric power. The largest of these is Lake McConaughy, formed by Kingsley Dam on the North Platte River.

Climate

Nebraska has what is known as a continental climate, with cold winters, hot summers, and low amounts of rainfall. January temperatures average 23°F (-5°C), but colder temperatures are common. July temperatures average 76°F (24°C), but most summers have at least a few days with temperatures above 100°F (38°C).

Precipitation in Nebraska is usually low because air masses from the west lose most of their moisture in the form of rain and snow over the Rocky Mountains, leaving dry air to move across the Great Plains. The driest part of the state is the Panhandle, where less than 15 inches (380 millimeters) of rain falls each year. The wettest part of the state is the southeast corner, where as much as 36 inches (915 millimeters) falls annually. Most precipitation occurs during the growing season, between April and September.

Nebraska is known for its extreme weather conditions. Rainfall can be vastly different from year to year, with heavy storms and floods in one year and drought in the next. In the wintertime, major blizzards have been known to close all roads, isolating some farm families for days. In the summertime, heavy thunderstorms, hail, and occasional tornadoes can damage crops, buildings, and trees. Temperatures may change dramatically within a single day.

Plant and Animal Life

The natural vegetation of Nebraska was once mostly prairie grasses. Wooded areas were originally concentrated near rivers and in parts of the Panhandle. Environmentalists, concerned about the lack of trees, have made special efforts to plant forests to prevent soil erosion. The Nebraska National Forest at Halsey in the Sand Hills is one of the largest planted forests in the world.

Wildlife is plentiful in much of Nebraska. Deer are found throughout the state, and

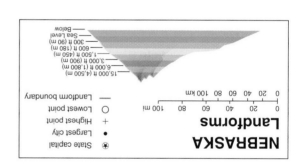

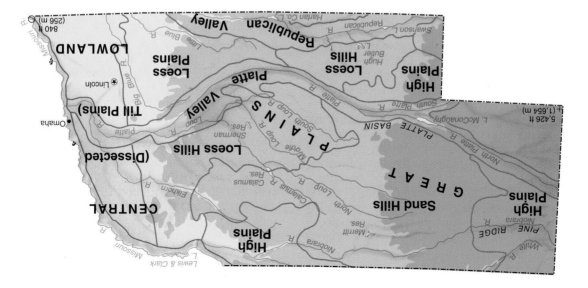

Every spring, enormous flocks of sandhill cranes congregate along the banks and sandbars of Nebraska's Platte River on their migration route to Canada.

pronghorn (American antelope) are common in the Sand Hills. Millions of sandhill cranes pause along the Platte River during their annual migrations north. Other wildlife include freshwater fish, game birds, hawks, eagles, prairie dogs, gophers, squirrels, coyotes, and jackrabbits.

Natural Resources

Nebraska's soil and water are its most valuable natural resources. Together they have made Nebraska one of the leading agricultural states in the nation. Except for the Sand Hills, most of the state's soils are loams—various mixtures of clay, silt, and sand.

Much of central Nebraska lies over the Ogallala aquifer, a huge underground water supply used heavily for irrigation. Rapid expansion of agricultural irrigation has caused concern that the groundwater supplies are being used up faster than they are being replenished. Conservation efforts, such as the use of more efficient irrigation systems, are helping to preserve this priceless resource.

Nebraska has more irrigated farmland than any other state but California. Mechanical irrigation systems draw water from the Ogallala aquifer, a huge underground reservoir.

▶ PEOPLE

Nebraska's first inhabitants were Native Americans of the Oto, Omaha, Missouri, Ponca, and Pawnee tribes. Arapaho, Cheyenne, and Dakota Sioux also hunted bison on Nebraska's plains. Native Americans now make up only 1 percent of the state's population. They live primarily in the cities, in the northern Panhandle, and on three reservations designated for their use.

It was not until the 1850's that white pioneers began to settle the region. Most of these newcomers came from Illinois, Iowa, and Ohio. Between 1870 and 1890 they were joined by about 1 million European immigrants, notably Germans, Irish, Czechs, Swedes, and Danes, whose descendants make up the majority of today's population. African Americans make up 4 percent of the population and Hispanic Americans make up almost 6 percent. Both are concentrated in and around Lincoln and Omaha and in the Platte Valley.

Although Nebraska is considered an agricultural state, about two-thirds of its people live in cities or towns of more than 2,500 residents. Rural population density is greatest in the eastern quarter of the state. The western half of the state is quite sparsely populated. For example, Cherry County, which is larger than the entire state of Connecticut, has fewer than 6,200 residents.

Education

Public schooling in Nebraska dates back to 1875, when it was provided for in the state's first constitution. In those days, when most Nebraskans lived in rural areas, the state contained more than 10,000 school districts, most of which simply had a one-room country schoolhouse. Today most schools are much larger, but there are still a few one-room schools in some rural areas.

The leading institution of higher learning is the University of Nebraska, established in Lincoln in 1869. Branch campuses also are located in Omaha and Kearney. In addition to its acclaimed scholastic reputation, the university's football team, the Nebraska Cornhuskers, is consistently ranked among the best in the nation. On Saturdays during the football season, nearly 70,000 fans don red hats, sweaters, and jackets to cheer their team on at Lincoln's Memorial Stadium.

on the archaeology and history of the state.

Libraries, Museums, and the Arts

More than 260 public libraries serve communities throughout the state. Love Memorial Library at the University of Nebraska at Lincoln is an important research center. The Nebraska State Historical Society houses a large collection of historical books and documents and also contains extensive museum displays

Other state-supported colleges are located in Peru, Chadron, and Wayne. Private universities include Creighton University in Omaha, Doane College in Crete, Dana College in Blair, Midland Lutheran College in Fremont, Concordia College in Seward, Hastings College in Hastings, and Nebraska Wesleyan University and Union College in Lincoln.

Other interesting museums include the University of Nebraska State Museum with its large collection of prehistoric animal fossils, the Museum of the Fur Trade in Chadron, the Stuhr Museum of the Prairie Pioneer in Grand Island, and Omaha's Great Plains Black Museum and Western Heritage Museum. The Joslyn Art Museum in Omaha has one of the largest collections of art of the American West, including works by Karl Bodmer and George Catlin. Sheldon Memorial Art Gallery at the University of Nebraska at Lincoln houses a collection of 20th-century works. The Museum of Nebraska Art in Kearney displays the work of Nebraska artists. The Strategic Air Command Museum in Bellevue has aircraft on display. Also of interest is the Henry Doorly Zoo in Omaha.

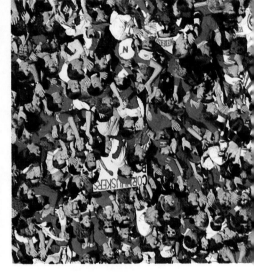

Left: Football fans at the University of Nebraska cheer for the Cornhuskers, one of the nation's most consistently high-ranked teams. *Right:* Ashfall Fossil Beds State Historical Park, near Royal, is a branch of the University of Nebraska State Museum. The Rhino Barn features the preserved remains of mammals that were smothered by ash in a massive volcanic eruption 10 million years ago.

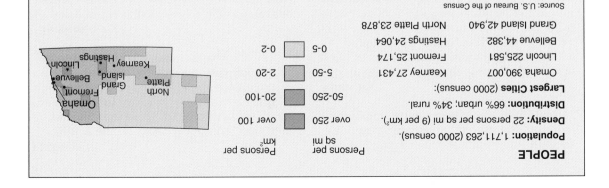

PEOPLE

Population: 1,711,263 (2000 census).

Density: 22 persons per sq mi (9 per km²).

Distribution: 66% urban; 34% rural.

Largest Cities (2000 census):

Omaha 390,007	Kearney 27,431
Lincoln 225,581	Fremont 25,174
Bellevue 44,382	Hastings 24,064
Grand Island 42,940	North Platte 23,878

Persons per sq mi	Persons per km²
over 100	over 250
20–100	50–250
2–20	5–50
0–2	0–5

Source: U.S. Bureau of the Census

▶ECONOMY

Agriculture is Nebraska's most important economic activity. It involves not only farming but many types of businesses related to farming, such as the production of agricultural tools, irrigation equipment, food products, seed, fertilizer, and livestock feed.

Services

Despite the importance of agriculture, the service sector of Nebraska's economy produces more than 70 percent of the gross state product (GSP). Wholesale and retail trade, especially of farm supplies and food products, are as valuable as the state's banking, real estate, and insurance activities. This is significant considering that several large financial and insurance companies are headquartered in Omaha.

Personal services, such as medical care, recreation, tourism, and the repair of goods and machinery contribute significantly to Nebraska's service income. Government activities include the operation of public schools and military bases. Transportation, communica-tion, and utilities include railroad and trucking businesses, telephone companies, newspapers, radio stations, and power companies.

Agriculture

Nebraska is one of the leading agricultural states in the nation. It is regularly among the top producers of cattle, hogs, corn, wheat, grain sorghum, alfalfa, dry beans, and sugar beets. About half of all farmland is used for growing crops. The other half is used as pasture or rangeland.

Livestock contributes about two-thirds of Nebraska's farm income. Cattle are fattened in feedlots throughout the state. Cattle ranching is concentrated in the Sand Hills and in the

Left: Much of the seed corn produced in Nebraska is used to feed herds of livestock. *Above:* In preparation for slaughter, cattle are fattened in feedlots located throughout the state.

PRODUCTS AND INDUSTRIES

Agriculture: Cattle, hogs, corn, hay, soybeans, wheat, sorghum, sugar beets, beans, popcorn.

Manufacturing: Food processing, electrical machinery, farm equipment, scientific instruments, transportation equipment.

Minerals: Petroleum, sand and gravel, limestone, natural gas.

Services: Wholesale and retail trade; finance, insurance, and real estate; business, social, and personal services; transportation, communication, and utilities; government.

*Gross state product is the total value of goods and services produced in a year.

Percentage of Gross State Product* by Industry

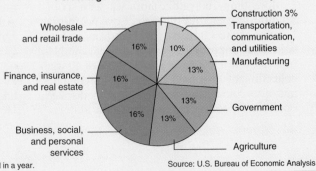

Wholesale and retail trade — 16%
Finance, insurance, and real estate — 16%
Business, social, and personal services — 16%
13%
13%
13%
10%
Construction 3%
Transportation, communication, and utilities
Manufacturing
Government
Agriculture

Source: U.S. Bureau of Economic Analysis

► **CITIES**

Omaha and Lincoln, both located in the eastern part of Nebraska, are the only two large cities in the state. Lincoln, the smaller of the two, is more than five times larger than Bellevue, Nebraska's third most populous city. Most of Nebraska's smaller cities, with populations between 10,000 and 40,000, are located in the Platte River valley.

Lincoln, Nebraska's capital city, was a tiny village surrounded by empty prairie when it was selected as the seat of government in 1867. Named after Abraham Lincoln, the 16th president of the United States, the city today contains more than 225,000 people. Lincoln is also a center for education in the state and is the home of the main campus of the University of Nebraska. Local manufacturing industries make rubber products, electrical equipment, machinery, pharmaceuticals, and transportation equipment.

Omaha, Nebraska's largest city, has a population of about 390,000. Established in 1854 on the west bank of the Missouri River, it served as Nebraska's first territorial capital (1855–77).

Omaha, Nebraska's largest city, is an important transportation and manufacturing center. It is also home to some of the nation's largest insurance corporations.

northern Panhandle, where grass is abundant but rainfall is not sufficient for crop production. Hogs also are raised.

The state's leading crop is corn. Nebraska cornfields cover about 6 million acres (2.4 million hectares) and most are irrigated with water from reservoirs and underground wells. Nebraska has more irrigated land than any other state except California.

Manufacturing

Many of Nebraska's manufacturing activities relate to agriculture. The state traditionally has been a leader in meat packing and food processing as well as in the preparation of livestock feed. Now it is also an important producer of irrigation equipment and other farm machinery. Other manufactured products include electrical equipment, scientific instruments, transportation equipment, fabricated metals, and pharmaceuticals.

Transportation

Transportation has been important to Nebraska's economy since the early 1800's. Wagon trains of people migrating to Oregon and California followed the Platte River on their journey westward and called this section of the Oregon Trail the Great Platte River Road. Ox-drawn wagons were once used to haul goods from the Missouri River to mining communities in Colorado. Construction of the nation's first transcontinental railroad began, westward from Omaha, after the Pacific Railroad Act was passed in 1862. Railroad companies are still important employers in Nebraska. The two largest, Union Pacific and Burlington Northern, have extensive rail networks for transporting agricultural products and manufactured goods. Water transportation is less extensive. The state's only navigable waterway is the Missouri River, which carries heavy barge traffic as far north as Sioux City, Iowa.

Communication

Newspapers have been published in Nebraska since it became a territory in 1854. Today there are about 20 daily newspapers and more than 100 weekly newspapers published. The *Omaha World-Herald* is the largest daily, reaching households in every county. Nebraska has more than 85 radio stations and 14 television stations.

Places of Interest

Czech Festival, in Wilber

Scotts Bluff National Monument, near Gering

Buffalo Bill Ranch State Historical Park, in North Platte

Fort Robinson State Park, near Crawford

Agate Fossil Beds National Monument, in Harrison, is one of the richest sources of prehistoric fossils in the United States. Quarries there contain fossilized bones of animals that lived as long as 19 million years ago. Scenic bluffs at the site overlook the Niobrara River.

Arbor Lodge State Historical Park, in Nebraska City, stands as a memorial to J. Sterling Morton, the founder of Arbor Day. Located on the grounds are Morton's Victorian-style mansion, beautifully landscaped gardens, an orchard, and an arboretum containing hundreds of different varieties of trees and shrubs.

Buffalo Bill Ranch State Historical Park, in North Platte, was the ranch of Buffalo Bill Cody, known for his famous Wild West Show. His house, preserved as a museum, contains exhibits and artifacts. In the summer, rodeos are held.

Chimney Rock National Historic Site, near Bayard, was a well-known landmark and campsite for frontier travelers on the Oregon Trail. Located along the North Platte River, it is a cone-shaped rock formation that towers 500 feet (153 meters) above the prairie.

Fort Niobrara National Wildlife Refuge, north of Valentine, maintains sizable herds of elk, buffalo, antelope, and Texas longhorn cattle. Whitewater canoeing is popular on the wild and scenic Niobrara River.

Homestead National Monument, near Beatrice, preserves the site of one of the first claims in Nebraska under the Homestead Act of 1862. The monument includes a restored pioneer cabin, a museum, and demonstrations of pioneer activities. Daniel Freeman, who made the claim, and his wife are buried at the site.

Nebraska National Forest, established in the Sand Hills region in 1902, is the largest planned forest in the country. It is also a popular recreational area.

Scotts Bluff National Monument, near Gering, is a majestic natural landmark that rises along the North Platte River and the old Oregon Trail. Visitors can still see deep ruts that were carved by the wheels of the wagon trains that passed the famous landmark.

Wilber is known as the Czech Capital of the United States. The town houses a museum and hosts a festival every August, featuring polka dancing and traditional Czech costumes.

State Parks. For more information about state parks and recreation areas, contact the Parks Division, Nebraska Game and Parks Commission, P.O. Box 30370, Lincoln, Nebraska 68503.

Omaha is a leading railroad, manufacturing, and food-processing center and for many years was a leader in meat-packing. Today's manufactures include machinery, electrical equipment, and chemicals. The city also is an important center for insurance corporations.

Since the 1950's, Omaha's suburbs have expanded rapidly. Today they cover two counties and even extend into Iowa, creating a greater metropolitan area containing more than 700,000 people.

▶ HISTORY

The first people to settle in the central Great Plains arrived more than 10,000 years ago. These early hunters followed the movements of such game animals as mammoths and bison. By A.D. 1100, these prehistoric peoples had developed agriculture in eastern and central Nebraska, where they raised corn, beans, squash, and sunflowers, made pottery, and traded with other peoples.

By the late 1700's, Nebraska's Native American population consisted of a variety of different tribes, with nomadic hunters in the western part of the state and village-dwelling farmers in the east. The largest of the farming groups were the Missouri, Omaha, Oto, and Ponca tribes. The Pawnee, Cheyenne, Arapaho, and the Dakota Sioux hunted bison on the plains.

European Exploration

Spanish and French explorers were the first Europeans to reach Nebraska. In 1720 the Spanish sent Pedro de Villasur on an expedition there to remove the French, who had begun to trade with the Indians. The French explorers Pierre and Paul Mallet traveled across Nebraska in 1739 seeking a route to Santa Fe.

The vast Louisiana Territory, which included Nebraska, twice changed hands between Spain and France before France sold it to the United States in 1803. The following year, President Thomas Jefferson sent the experienced frontiersmen Meriwether Lewis and William Clark on an expedition to explore the region and report back on its nature and resources. Lewis and Clark described the entire Nebraska region as a "garden," rich in resources and well-suited for agriculture. Later explorers in Nebraska, namely Zebulon Pike (1806), Stephen Long (1820), and John C. Frémont (1842), disagreed with Lewis and

▶ GOVERNMENT

Nebraska's first constitution was adopted in 1866, one year before the territory became a state. The present constitution, adopted in 1875, was revised considerably in 1920.

Nebraska's government has three branches. The executive branch is headed by a governor who is elected to a 4-year term. Other officials of the executive branch include the secretary of state, attorney general, and treasurer.

Nebraska has the only unicameral, or one-house, state legislature in the nation. Its members, called senators, are elected to 4-year terms on a nonpartisan ballot, which means that a candidate's political affiliation is not listed at the voting booths. The highest court is the state supreme court. The major trial courts are district courts.

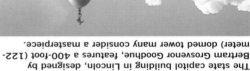

The state capitol building in Lincoln, designed by Bertram Grosvenor Goodhue, features a 400-foot (122-meter) domed tower many consider a masterpiece.

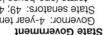

GOVERNMENT

State Government
Governor: 4-year term
State senators: 49; 4-year terms (one-house legislature)
Number of counties: 93

Federal Government
U.S. senators: 2
U.S. representatives: 3
Number of electoral votes: 5

For the name of the current governor, see STATE GOVERNMENTS in Volume S. For the names of current U.S. senators and representatives, see UNITED STATES, CONGRESS OF THE in Volume U-V.

Clark's impressions and pronounced most of it unfit for permanent settlement.

Early in the 1800's, fur trappers, traders, missionaries, and travelers moved across Nebraska. Then in 1840 began the great western migration. For the next 25 years, hundreds of thousands of pioneers in wagon trains followed the Oregon Trail through Nebraska on their way to California and Oregon. The Mormon Trail to Utah and the Denver Trail to Colorado also cut through Nebraska.

Although the U.S. government built several forts for the protection of travelers, and trading posts were established along the Missouri River, no other settlement took place there until the 1850's. In fact, for several decades the federal government prohibited white families from establishing homes in what was then called "Indian country."

Settlement and Statehood

The active settlement of Nebraska began only after the territory was established by the Kansas-Nebraska Act of 1854, which introduced the concept of popular sovereignty to territorial government. For the first time, settlers were allowed to determine for themselves whether or not they would permit slavery in their territory, and most Nebraskans were decidedly against it. (For more information, see the article KANSAS-NEBRASKA ACT in Volume J-K.)

The original territory of Nebraska extended from the present northern boundary of Kansas all the way to the Canadian border. Omaha was made the territorial capital. By the time Nebraska became a state on March 1, 1867, several other territories had been carved out of the Nebraska Territory and the new state was reduced to its current size.

During the 1800's various treaties were negotiated with various Native American groups that transferred Indian lands to the U.S. government, thus opening up the land to white settlement. The Native Americans were given parcels of land called reservations, but much of this land was later reclaimed by the government. Eventually, most of Nebraska's native population was forced to migrate to reservations in Oklahoma.

In 1862, the U.S. Congress passed the Homestead Act. According to this law, anyone who was the head of a household and at least 21 years of age was qualified to receive

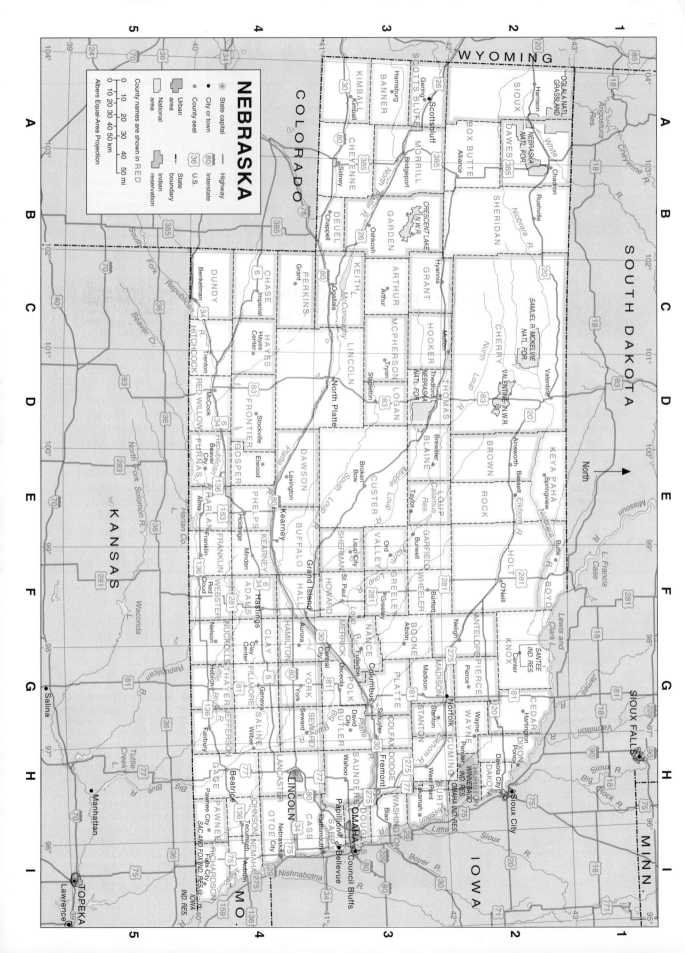

Famous People

Consult the Index to find more information in *The New Book of Knowledge* about the following celebrated people, who were either born in or are otherwise associated with Nebraska: Native American leaders Red Cloud (1822–1909) and Crazy Horse (1849?–77); Black Muslim leader Malcolm X (1925–65); three-time Democratic presidential candidate William Jennings Bryan (1860–1925); President Gerald R. Ford (1913–); Western showman Buffalo Bill Cody (1846–1917); U.S. senator George W. Norris (1861–1944); dancer and actor Fred Astaire (1899–1987); actors Henry Fonda (1905–82) and Marlon Brando (1924–2004); and silent-screen comedian Harold Lloyd (1893–1971).

Johnny Carson (1925–2005), a popular television comedian and entertainer, was born in Corning, Iowa, but grew up in

Norfolk. He began his career in show business in the 1940's as an amateur magician and radio announcer in Omaha. In the 1950's he moved to Los Angeles, California. He hosted the show *Who Do You Trust?* (1957–62), until he replaced Jack Parr as host of NBC's *The Tonight Show* (1962–92). For thirty years, Carson's charm and quick wit made *The Tonight Show* the most popular of all the late-night television shows.

Willa Sibert Cather (1873–1947), one of the most important American novelists of the early 1900's, was born in Back Creek Valley, Virginia, but grew up in Red Cloud (1884–90). Many of her stories, notably *O Pioneers!* (1913) and *My Ántonia* (1918) drew on childhood memories in

Willa Cather

---

a free 160-acre (65-hectare) parcel of land on which to settle. Thousands moved into Nebraska from eastern and other midwestern states and from Europe. Within ten years, the population had increased fivefold. Rapid growth continued, and by 1890 Nebraska had more than 1 million residents.

Farming Challenges

Most people who came to Nebraska in the 1800's planned to farm, although some moved to the cities growing up on the western frontier. Most of the farmers were accustomed to climates with adequate and predictable amounts of rainfall for agriculture and did not imagine that farming in Nebraska would be very different. However, many soon faced enormous difficulties. In 1874 farmers were challenged by great invasions of grasshoppers, which devoured their crops and left many families without resources or food. Then in the 1890's, a severe drought struck with devastating results, and for several years, some farmers harvested nothing at all. Many people gave up and returned East or moved to cities to look for work.

Farmers realized they needed to adopt new farming methods if they expected

In the mid-1800's, pioneers followed the Oregon Trail through Nebraska on their journey west to California and Oregon. Chimney Rock (background, left), which rises near the border of present-day Wyoming, was one of the landmarks by which the migrants measured the distance they had traveled.

to stay in Nebraska. They began experimenting with crops that were more suitable for dry conditions. Wheat and sorghum began to replace corn. Some farmers began irrigating their crops; others turned from crop production to livestock grazing. New techniques for tilling the soil and conserving soil moisture were tried.

During the Great Depression of the 1930's, low prices for farm products crippled the state's economy, but even more disastrous was a severe drought that ruined many farmers. Crops were destroyed by the dry conditions and by dust storms, producing an even greater concern for soil conservation. Programs were started to plant trees in areas called shelterbelts to reduce wind erosion of valuable soils. Numerous irrigation projects and reservoirs were created to protect farmers from dry seasons. Conditions improved during America's World War II years (1941–45) when farmers received record prices for their crops. Industrial growth also brought prosperity.

Modern Times

By the 1960's, business in Nebraska became less directly connected to agriculture than it once had been. Low labor costs, high labor productivity, and easy access to markets outside the state began to expand Nebraska's manufacturing and service industries. Businesses, such as insurance companies and manufacturers of electrical and transportation equipment, machinery, and scientific instruments, diversified the state's economy and allowed more Nebraskans to live in urban areas rather than on farms or in small towns.

Today Nebraska's farms are fewer, larger, more specialized, and more mechanized than they once were. They also are more dependent on groundwater for crop production and are at risk when water tables decline.

Modern farm equipment, such as large tractors, combine harvesters, and mechanical irrigation systems, has greatly reduced the need for manual farm labor. As a result, the number of farms and farmers has decreased steadily in the state since the 1930's. In 1935 there were more than 130,000 farms in Nebraska and their average size was about 350 acres (142 hectares). In contrast, by 1987 there were only about 60,000 farms, although they averaged 750 acres (300 hectares) in size. Economic conditions in the 1980's also contributed to Nebraska's shrinking number of farms.

Because Nebraska's farm products are now shipped all over the world, its farms are increasingly dependent on distant customers and favorable international trade policies. However, Nebraska's increasingly diversified economy makes the state able and willing to respond to ever changing market conditions.

BRADLEY H. BALTENSPERGER
Author, *Nebraska: A Geography*

---

neer themes. Some of Cather's other well-known works include *Death Comes for the Archbishop* (1927) and *One of Ours* (1922), which won the Pulitzer Prize for fiction in 1923. The Willa Cather Historical Center in Red Cloud commemorates her life and work. For more information, see AMERICAN LITERATURE: The Early 1900's in Volume A.

Edward Joseph Flanagan (1886–1948), a Roman Catholic priest, was born in Ballymoe, Ireland, and emigrated to the United States in 1904. After entering the priesthood, he moved to O'Neill, Nebraska, and became a social worker at a Workingmen's Hostel in Omaha, where he helped homeless men and delinquent boys. In 1917 he founded Boys Town in Douglas County. The community, which was run by the hundreds of boys it sheltered, gained widespread support. To this day it continues to provide a home, education, health care, and counseling to boys, and now also girls, in need.

Mari Susette Sandoz (1901–66), a writer and historian, was born to Swiss immigrant parents in Sheridan County.

Buffalo Bill Cody

William Jennings Bryan

Her writings focused on the history and folklore of the Nebraska plains and cattle country of the Old West. Among her best works of nonfiction are *Crazy Horse* (1942), *The Cattlemen* (1958), and *These Were the Sioux* (1961). Her outstanding novels include *Slogum House* (1930) and *Capital City* (1939).

Darryl Francis Zanuck (1902–79), born in Wahoo, was a Hollywood film producer and president (1962–71) of 20th-Century Fox. Zanuck's most celebrated film productions include *The Grapes of Wrath* (1940), *The Longest Day* (1962), and three Academy Award winners for Best Picture, *How Green Was My Valley* (1941), *Gentleman's Agreement* (1947), and *All About Eve* (1950).

NEBULAS

A nebula is a vast cloud of dust and gases. The word "nebula" comes from the Latin word for "mist" or "cloud." The plural form is nebulas or nebulae.

Even though a few bright nebulas can be seen with the naked eye, astronomers use telescopes or other special instruments to study them. Nebulas are classified into three general types—diffuse nebulas, planetary nebulas, and nebulas that are formed by supernovas, or exploding stars.

Diffuse nebulas, the most frequent type, look like ragged clouds. Hot stars within a diffuse nebula make its dust and gases glow, and some glow very brightly. These bright kinds are called **emission nebulas**. The hot gases in emission nebulas glow with colors. In photographs, these nebulas often look red because they are very rich in hydrogen, which gives off red light. The Great Nebula in the constellation Orion is an emission nebula. It can be seen by the naked eye, appearing as a fuzzy patch of light below the three stars in Orion's belt.

Some diffuse nebulas are not as bright as emission nebulas. The dust grains in these nebulas shine only because they are reflecting starlight. An example of this type, which is called a **reflection nebula**, is the nebula in the Pleiades star cluster.

A **dark nebula**, a third type of diffuse nebula, is too far from any stars to emit or to reflect starlight. Because its dust particles block out the light of stars behind it, it appears as a dark patch in the night sky. In the Southern Hemisphere, a very obvious dark nebula is the Coalsack, just next to the Southern Cross. The constellation Orion contains the dark Horsehead Nebula, which can be seen in the photograph below.

New stars often form within diffuse nebulas, usually within regions that are so dense that gravity causes them to collapse upon themselves. As these regions of the nebulas collapse, their central temperatures rise incredibly high, high enough to cause the process of new star formation to begin.

Planetary nebulas are circular in shape. They are not planets but are called planetary only because they look like planets when seen through a low-powered telescope. A planetary nebula is made to shine by a star at its center. The star is quite old, and its hot core is exposed. The nebula forms as the star's outer layers of gas spew outward. Planetary nebulas sometimes look like a ring or a doughnut. The Ring Nebula, in the constellation Lyra, is an example of one that has this appearance.

Supernova is the name given to a star that explodes so forcefully that it is almost completely destroyed. The explosion hurls out threadlike filaments of hot gas, which once made up the atmosphere of the star, and a nebula forms. A supernova was observed in the constellation Taurus in the year 1054. Today the remains of this supernova form the Crab Nebula. Remains of supernovas also occur in formations shaped like loops, while others look like veils.

GERALD S. HAWKINS
Author, *Mindsteps to the Cosmos*
Reviewed by
WILLIAM A. GUTSCH, JR.
Chairman, American Museum-
Hayden Planetarium

See also ASTRONOMY; STARS.

The Horsehead Nebula in the constellation Orion is a dark nebula—too far from any stars to emit or to reflect starlight.

NEEDLECRAFT

The art or craft of creating designs on fabric with needle and thread goes back hundreds of years. Embroidery, quilting, appliqué, and other forms of needlecraft have long been used to transform plain pieces of fabric and simple items of clothing into works of art.

The early civilizations of China, Japan, Egypt, Persia, India, the Mediterranean lands, and Peru produced distinctive styles of decorative stitching. During the Middle Ages, heavy pieces of fabric were appliquéd or embroidered and hung on the walls of European castles and houses. Besides being decorative, they stopped the wind from coming in through cracks between the stones.

In the 1300's in England, beautiful gold thread and silk embroidery designs were made for churches. Called *Opus Anglicanum* ("English work"), the designs were exported all over the then known world. With increasing luxury of dress and furniture in the 1500's, this kind of work for churches began to decline, and the great period of magnificent clothing and beautiful domestic embroidery in Europe began. Trade with China and Japan brought an Eastern influence. The four-poster bed, with curtains for warmth as well as for decoration, became a centerpiece for exquisite stitching. Many bed hangings were stitched in "crewels" (fine wool on linen) in bold designs of trees and flowering branches with springing animals.

Various forms of needlecraft were brought to the American colonies by the early European settlers. Many of the designs and patterns were of English origin. They were used to decorate household items, such as chair coverings and bed quilts. Samplers—which use a variety of stitches to create pictures, verses, letters of the alphabet, and the like—were made by young girls in the colonies.

As machines took over the task of making clothing and other items that had once been made at home, decorative hand-stitching became less a part of everyday life. Today museums around the world have rooms filled with collections of needlecraft from the past. Although needlecraft itself is very old, the basic stitches have not changed a great deal through the years, and many of the old designs are still popular.

▶ EMBROIDERY

Embroidery is decorative stitching on fabric. It is often used to decorate clothing and linens. Different cultures have their own styles of embroidery, but the same basic stitches are used everywhere.

All embroidery was once done by hand. Today sewing machines are frequently equipped with an attachment that makes machine embroidery possible. Yet hand embroidery continues to be a popular craft.

Materials

Embroidery may be worked in one or more kinds of threads, ranging from a single strand of embroidery floss to thick knitting yarns. Popular threads for embroidery are three-strand crewel wools and six-strand cotton embroidery floss. These threads may be combined in one piece of needlework, following the tradition begun in England in the 1700's. Both wool and cotton threads may be separated to give the thickness desired.

Embroidery may be done on any number of fabrics. Silk or cotton may be used as a backing for very fine pieces. Fabrics of heavier texture, such as hopsack or bold-weave linen, may be used for coarser work. Interesting effects are obtained by embroidering patterned fabric, such as gingham or mattress ticking, because the base fabric becomes a pattern for the decorative stitching.

Embroidery needles range in size from 1 (large) to 10 (fine). The size is determined by the thickness of the thread being used.

Needlework can turn plain cloth into luxurious fabric. This decorative jacket, made in England, dates from about 1700.

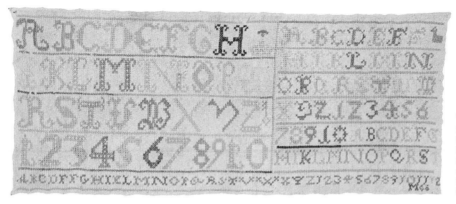

Young girls once practiced embroidery stitches in needlework projects called samplers. Letters of the alphabet and numbers were commonly used for this work.

Technique

Embroidery is best learned by practicing basic stitches on a small piece of fabric that has been marked with a simple pattern. Using embroidery hoops will help keep the stitches smooth and even. The area to be stitched is centered over the smaller of the two hoops. The fabric is pulled tight and then secured by the larger hoop.

After threading the needle, a knot is made at the end of the thread. The first stitch is pulled through, leaving the knot a short distance away on the front of the fabric. To fasten the thread, two small stitches are made on any line of the design near where the work is begun. These stitches will be covered by others as you work, and the waste knot will be cut off the surface. To end off each piece of thread, repeat the process, making two small stitches into any line of the design. Then bring the thread to the surface and cut it off.

Some Basic Embroidery Stitches

There are many popular and useful embroidery stitches. Some are shown on the opposite page. **Backstitch** is useful for outlining. The **split stitch** adapts well to curving shapes because it is firm and smooth. The **straight stitch** is simply a single stitch that can be worked in any direction. When straight stitches are placed closely side by side to fill in an area, the stitch is called **satin stitch**.

More advanced embroidery stitches are **French knots**, which are often used to create the centers of flowers. The basic **chain stitch** is a versatile stitch that can be used for outlining or filling. A series of single chain stitches worked in a circle is called the **lazy daisy stitch**.

Some Popular Styles of Embroidery

Cross-stitch. Cross-stitch, one of the oldest embroidery stitches, still enjoys great popularity. It is the simple crossing of two stitches of equal size. Cross-stitch may be worked on stamped, evenly woven cotton or linen or on gingham check.

Counted Cross-stitch. Counted cross-stitch is a form of embroidery that may have originated in ancient Greece, but historical examples have been found all over the world. The craft has a particularly long tradition in Denmark. This traditional form of cross-stitch is done on evenweave fabric, following a pattern marked on graph paper.

The woven pattern of the cloth used for counted cross-stitch must be visible so that tiny cross-stitches may be worked over the intersections of the weave. Counted cross-stitch is worked with a blunt tapestry needle and cotton floss embroidery thread, with the fabric held between embroidery hoops. Because of the simplicity of the stitch, counted cross-stitch is an excellent choice for creating a sampler of your own design.

Candlewicking. Candlewicking is a form of embroidery that had its origins in colonial America. The thread used in candlewicking is similar to the cotton used in the wicks of candles. Both candlewicking thread and the background fabric are usually white. French knots and satin stitches are used most often in creating a variety of designs. One of the most popular candlewicking designs is the pineapple, a sign of welcome in colonial homes.

Crewelwork. Crewelwork is stitched with two-ply wool (wool with two strands twisted together) on a sturdy fabric. The earliest historical reference to crewelwork is to that done

STRAIGHT STITCH

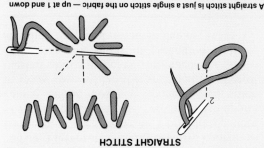

A straight stitch is just a single stitch on the fabric — up at 1 and down at 2. It is best worked in a hoop. The value of the stitch is the variety of designs a series of them can form. In A (above), they might be a row of grass, while in B they might form the spokes of a wheel or the petals of a flower.

SPLIT STITCH

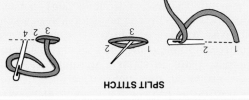

The split stitch does just what its name says it does. Each stitch splits the one before it. A hoop is not necessary. Working from left to right, bring the needle up at 1 and down at 2. Bring the needle back up at 3, midway between 1 and 2, splitting the existing stitch with the tip of the needle. Split stitch is a good outlining stitch as well as a good stitch for filling.

BACKSTITCH

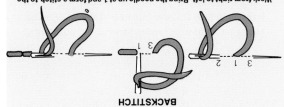

Work from right to left. Bring the needle up at 1 and form a stitch to the right by inserting it at 2. Bring the needle back out at 3 and insert it back at 1 again. Backstitch need not be worked in a hoop. Take care to keep the length of the stitches even. The distance between 1 and 2 should be the same as between 3 and 1.

CROSS STITCH
Work should be in a hoop.

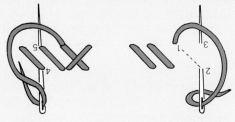

Work should be in a hoop. Bring the needle up at 1 and down at 2. Bring the needle up again at 3 and down at 4. If working on a printed pattern, the X's should follow the pattern. If doing counted cross-stitch, each X will represent a square on the graph pattern.

When doing an entire row of cross-stitch, it is best to do all of the bottom halves of the stitches first. Then continue back across the row with top halves. In working any cross-stitch pattern, be sure that the top halves of the crosses all slant in the same direction.

STEM STITCH

Stem stitch is widely used to outline crewel embroideries. It is not necessary to work in a hoop. Working from left to right, bring the needle up at 1 and down at 2. Bring it back up again at 3, keeping the spaces between 1 and 3 and 3 and 2 equal. In pulling the needle up at 3, be sure to keep the loop that is going to become the stitch against the fabric. Do not let the needle pass through the loop.

LAZY DAISY STITCH

The lazy daisy stitch is really a group of single chain stitches worked in a circular pattern to look like the petals of a flower. Bring the needle up at 1 and re-insert it at 1, leaving a loop on top of the fabric. Bring the needle up at 2, catching the loop, and put the needle back through the fabric at 3, catching the loop. Bring it up at the next inside point on the circle and continue until all petals have been worked.

CHAIN STITCH

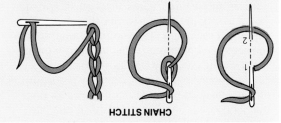

Chain stitch is easiest worked in a hoop. Bring the needle up at 1 and, leaving a loop on top of the fabric, re-insert it at 1. Bring the needle back up at 2, catching the loop under the tip of the needle. Pull the thread through and begin again, re-inserting the needle at 2. Chain stitches may be worked from right to left or up and down and make excellent stitches for outlining or filling.

FRENCH KNOT

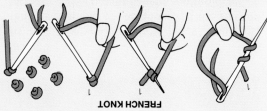

A French knot makes a lovely center for a flower. With work in a hoop, bring the needle up through the fabric, wrap the thread twice around the needle and pull it tight so that the wrapped thread moves down against the fabric. Insert the needle very close to point 1 and, holding the thread tight, pull it through to the back of the fabric.

SATIN STITCH

The satin stitch is a series of straight stitches placed closely side by side. Working with a hoop, from left to right, go up at 1 and down at 2. Bring the needle back out again at 3, right next to 1, taking care to keep the edge of the stitching even. Satin stitch can be used to fill in almost any shape.

For many centuries embroidery has been used to decorate military uniforms, ceremonial robes, and other clothing. This colorful monkey, part of a South American cloak, was made in Peru in the 1400's.

by the Hebrews in biblical times. The most famous example of crewelwork is the Bayeux tapestry, a linen wall hanging embroidered in France in the 1000's, which depicts the history of the Norman Conquest of England. English crewelwork patterns began to evolve in the 1600's. The craft was widely practiced in England and in America between the 1600's and 1800's. Its popularity was revived in the 1960's.

Crewelwork—or crewel, as it is often called—uses the basic embroidery stitches but relies more on filler stitches and less on outlining. One of the most versatile stitches in crewelwork is the **stem stitch**, which can be used as an outline or to fill an area by working rows closely side by side. One of the most popular crewelwork designs is called the Tree of Life.

▶NEEDLEPOINT

Needlepoint is a form of embroidery that is worked on an open-mesh base called a canvas. Needlepoint is durable, so it can be used for pillows, rugs, and upholstery. The craft, which closely resembles woven tapestry, dates back to the 1500's in Europe. It has seen a steady revival of popularity since the 1960's.

Materials

Needlepoint may be worked in any one or more of a number of yarns or threads, depending on the desired effect. The main requirement for needlepoint yarn is that it be strong enough to withstand passing through the canvas again and again. Three-strand Persian yarn is a popular and versatile yarn used for needlepoint because the three strands may be separated to use one, two, or three threads according to the mesh size of the canvas. Tapestry yarn is a single thick strand.

Most canvas is made of cotton or linen that has been stiffened. Molded plastic mesh with seven or ten meshes has recently been developed. This is an excellent choice for beginners because it needs no blocking, or shaping, afterward and does not need to be hemmed. It can be used for small three-dimensional objects, such as boxes or mobiles.

Needlepoint is worked with tapestry needles that have large eyes to accommodate yarn and blunt points to slide through the holes easily without splitting the threads. The needles range in size from size 13, for very heavy rug yarn, to size 26, which is appropriate for fine work. The perfect size needle should slip through the fabric easily yet it should be large enough to protect the yarn as it goes through the fabric.

Stitches

Needlepoint canvas may be worked in any embroidery stitch, but the square mesh is most suitable for repeat geometric patterns. Traditionally, needlepoint consists of slanting stitches, called **tent stitches**, that are worked across the intersections of the canvas mesh. When tent stitches are worked in horizontal rows, taking each stitch with the needle upright, it results in a series of small vertical stitches on the reverse. This kind of tent stitch is called **half cross-stitch**. It is often used for rugs and is worked on special large-scale rug canvas. Tent stitch is called "Continental" stitch when it is worked in horizontal rows with a slanting needle. It produces slanting stitches on both the top and underside. Tent stitch may also be worked in diagonal lines across the canvas, resulting in an attractive basket-weave pattern on the underside.

The **Florentine stitch**, usually known as **Bargello**, is used to create a bricklike pattern of long vertical stitches on the needlepoint canvas. In the most usual pattern, each stitch in every row is placed a specified number of meshes above or below the preceding stitch. This creates a series of ascending and descending lines that resemble flames.

▶ QUILTING

Quilting is stitching a sandwich of two layers of fabric together with padding in between. It was originally used to make garments that would give warmth and protection or comfort. Soldiers wore quilted shirts and suits under their armor in the Middle Ages.

During the 1600's and 1700's, quilted jackets and caps and even petticoats were popular items of clothing. But by the 1800's, quilting was used mostly to make coverlets for beds.

During frontier days in the United States, bed quilts were a necessity. Scraps of fabric were joined in patchwork patterns, then padded and quilted for warmth. Patchwork patterns were passed from one generation to the next. Some of these patterns, which are still popular today, are the Wedding Ring and Double Wedding Ring, the Flower Garden, the Log Cabin, and the Dresden Plate.

Making a Quilt

There are two main steps in making a quilt. First, the quilt top is made by joining patchwork pieces. Alternatively, larger patchwork designs may be joined and then embroidered or appliquéd. Sometimes, irregularly shaped pieces that are not cut according to a pattern are sewn down with decorative edging stitches on a muslin backing to make a "crazy quilt."

The quilt top may be made of cotton, silk, or a synthetic fabric. The padding between the layers of fabric may be cotton batting, carded wool, or a synthetic filler material. When all the squares that make up the top have been sewn together, the top is stretched on a large frame with the padding and the bottom fabric placed carefully beneath it.

The second step is the actual quilting. The quilting pattern is lightly traced on the quilt top. It may be simple or elaborate. The layers of fabric and padding are sewn together with small, even-running stitches, following the pattern indicated. The stitching may form designs such as feathers, flowers, or leaves.

▶ APPLIQUÉ

Appliqué is made by sewing one piece of material that has been cut to form a design onto a larger piece of material. The edges of the piece to be appliquéd to the background material are turned under and attached with tiny, almost invisible stitches or with a decorative embroidery stitch. Appliqué may be

The students of P.S. 48 in Queens, New York, appliquéd this wall hanging. It features Peter, the main character of several picture books by Ezra Jack Keats.

used to decorate clothing and quilt tops or to make pictures. Any fabric may be used for appliqué, but cotton and other soft fabrics are usually the best to work with because they fold neatly and the needle passes through them easily.

▶ ENJOYING NEEDLECRAFT

The enjoyment of doing needlecraft as an expression of creativity is great indeed. Whether an item is produced for personal use, for a gift, or for a craftshow, it represents many hours of labor and love.

Materials, equipment, and instructions for all kinds of needlecraft are available in needle-craft shops, general craft shops, and in many department stores. Kits for projects that include all necessary materials, as well as books about each craft, are also available to help the beginner gain the skills of a fine needlecrafter.

ERICA WILSON
Author, *Erica Wilson's For the Baby,*
Erica Wilson's Brides Book
President, Erica Wilson's Needle Works, Inc.

See also KNITTING; NEEDLES; SEWING.

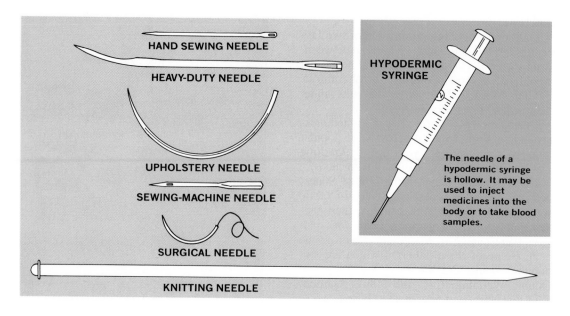

HAND SEWING NEEDLE

HEAVY-DUTY NEEDLE

HYPODERMIC SYRINGE

UPHOLSTERY NEEDLE

SEWING-MACHINE NEEDLE

SURGICAL NEEDLE

KNITTING NEEDLE

The needle of a hypodermic syringe is hollow. It may be used to inject medicines into the body or to take blood samples.

NEEDLES

Most needles are small, slender pieces of steel with a sharp point at one end and an eye, or hole, at the other, through which thread is passed.

Needles probably developed from the awl, a sharp-pointed instrument for piercing holes in soft materials. The first needles were made of bone or horn. Iron and bronze needles were used by the ancient Romans. Steel needles were perfected in the 1800's.

Different Kinds of Needles

There are many kinds of needles in everyday use. Some of these are hand sewing needles, machine stitching needles, knitting needles, and surgical needles.

Hand Sewing Needles. Needles for hand sewing include not only needles as small as those commonly used in every household but also large heavy-duty needles such as the straight and curved needles used by sailmakers and upholsterers.

Machine Needles. Special needles are made for the various uses of home sewing machines and industrial sewing machines. Machine needles are unusual in having the eye and the point at the same end of the needle. Very small machine needles are used for sewing lightweight textiles, larger needles for sewing fur and velvet, and even larger ones for sewing heavy materials like leather and canvas.

Surgical Needles. There are two kinds of needles used by surgeons to sew up wounds. One kind has an eye and can be rethreaded and used again. The other has the thread attached to the needle. It can be used only once.

Knitting Needles. There are both hand and machine varieties of knitting needles. Hand knitting needles are long and have no eyes. Needles used for machine knitting come in many sizes and shapes.

How a Hand Sewing Needle Is Made

Needles are made from a long steel wire. The wire is cut into lengths that are two needles long. They become pointed at both ends as they roll over a grindstone on the way through the machine. The center of the double-length needle is then slightly flattened, and the eyes are punched out. The double needles are broken apart between the heads. The heads are ground to the required shape. The needles are then tempered (toughened) by being heated red hot and then dipped in cold oil. Tempering discolors the needles, so they are given a polishing and a plating of nickel to make them smooth and resistant to rusting. The shiny, perfect needles are then packaged for sale.

Reviewed by W. S. SHEE
Scovill Manufacturing Company

NEGATIVE NUMBERS. See ALGEBRA; NUMBERS AND NUMBER SYSTEMS.

NEHRU, JAWAHARLAL (1889–1964)

Jawaharlal Nehru, India's first prime minister, was born on November 14, 1889, at Allahabad, in northern India. The son of a wealthy lawyer, Nehru received his early education at home. At the age of 15 he was sent to England. There he attended Harrow, a boys' school, and Cambridge University. After further studies he received his law degree and was admitted to the British bar. He returned to India in 1912.

Nehru's father, Motilal Nehru, was very active in the Indian National Congress, a political party working for India's independence from Britain. Through his father, Nehru became involved in the independence movement and met Mohandas Gandhi, the major force behind the drive for independence.

Through Gandhi the wealthy Nehru became interested in the problems of India's poor. He gradually gave up his law career and began to travel among the peasant villages, supporting the farmers' demands for improved social and economic conditions. Nehru was elected general secretary of the Indian National Congress in 1923. He became president of the party in 1929 and was re-elected to that post four times. In their struggle for freedom, the Indian nationalists adopted Gandhi's policy of nonviolent resistance to the British Government.

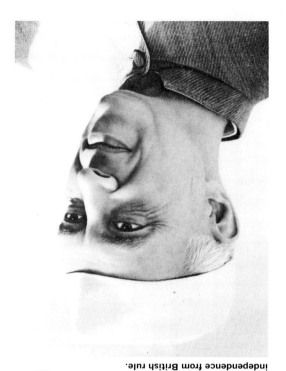

Jawaharlal Nehru, who served as prime minister of India from 1947 until 1964, helped lead the Indian struggle for independence from British rule.

Gandhi believed that the way to get the British out of India was not to fight them but to refuse to support them. When the British passed a law the Indians did not like, they should disobey it but should do so peacefully. The arrest of many people for civil disobedience would arouse sympathy for the Indian cause and make it harder for the British to rule. Nehru helped organize many nonviolent demonstrations. He was arrested many times and spent a total of about ten years in prison for his opposition to British rule. During these years he wrote several books about his work.

The independence movement affected all of Nehru's family. His wife, Kamala, whom he married in 1916, was also sent to prison. So were his parents, both of his sisters, and his daughter, Indira Gandhi, who later became prime minister of India.

After World War II ended in 1945, Nehru helped draw up the plans for independence. The Muslims in India wanted religious freedom as well as freedom from the British. Nehru and most other Indian leaders wanted the Muslims to remain in India. But they finally decided that the only way to avoid civil war was to divide British India into two countries based on religion—mostly Hindu India and mostly Muslim Pakistan.

When India gained independence in 1947, Nehru became his country's first prime minister. He held this post until his death. As prime minister, Nehru never forgot the promises he had made to India's poor during the fight for freedom. New schools and hospitals were built. Agricultural production was increased, and new industries were established. Nehru outlawed any form of discrimination based on the traditional caste system in public places and government employment.

Nehru opposed the use of violence in international relations. He worked to unite the new nations of Africa and Asia into a powerful force for peace, siding with neither the Communist countries nor the democracies of Western Europe and the United States.

Nehru died in New Delhi on May 27, 1964. As the leader of the world's largest democracy, in terms of population, he gained world respect and the love of the Indian people.

ROBERT I. CRANE
Syracuse University

See also GANDHI, MOHANDAS KARAMCHAND; INDIA.

NELSON, HORATIO, LORD (1758–1805)

Horatio Nelson was England's most famous admiral. Trafalgar Square in London is named after his greatest victory, and from the top of a lofty column, his statue surveys the city.

Nelson was born on September 29, 1758, at Burnham Thorpe rectory in Norfolk. He went to sea at the age of 12. Nelson was short, slight, and never strong, and life was hard in the old wooden sailing ships. But he resolved to "brave every danger" to win fame. By the time he was 20, he had seen service in the Arctic and the East and West Indies and had been promoted to captain. In 1787, in the West Indies, he married Mrs. Frances Nisbet, a widow. They returned to England, where he remained for five uneventful years.

Then, in 1793, war broke out between Great Britain and France. Most of Europe was subdued by Napoleon's armies, and England's freedom depended on its navy. Nelson was given command of the 64-gun *Agamemnon* and was sent to blockade France's Mediterranean ports so that the French fleet could not break out into the Atlantic. In 1794, while leading an attack on the island of Corsica,

Admiral Horatio Nelson was one of England's greatest heroes, even in his own lifetime. His flagship, the *Victory*, is preserved at Portsmouth, England.

Nelson lost the sight in one eye. Nevertheless, he remained in the Mediterranean and played an important part in the victory against France's ally Spain off Cape St. Vincent in February, 1797. He was knighted and promoted to rear admiral. In July he was wounded again, and his arm had to be amputated. This time he went home to England to recuperate, but soon he was back in the Mediterranean.

In 1798, Napoleon slipped by Nelson's squadron and invaded Egypt. After a desperate search, Nelson found Napoleon's fleet in Aboukir Bay at the mouth of the Nile, and in a brilliant and daring attack destroyed it. For this victory—which forced Napoleon to give up the idea of conquering Egypt—he was made Baron Nelson of the Nile.

Nelson was in Naples when he fell in love with Lady Emma Hamilton, wife of Sir William Hamilton, the British ambassador. Their love affair became one of the most famous in history. Later, Nelson parted from his wife and settled in England with Emma.

In 1801, Nelson was promoted to vice-admiral and appointed second-in-command of a squadron aimed against Napoleon's northern allies. During the bombardment of Copenhagen, Denmark, Nelson's cautious commander-in-chief, Admiral Sir Hyde Parker, signaled him to break off the action. When told of this, Nelson—raising his telescope to his blind eye—remarked that he could see no such signal. He continued the attack and forced the Danes to surrender. For this victory he was made a viscount.

In 1803, Nelson was given command of the Mediterranean fleet. His most important task was to destroy the French fleet so that Napoleon could not invade England as he planned. On October 21, 1805, Nelson found the combined Spanish and French fleets off Spain's Cape Trafalgar and attacked. During the fighting he was mortally wounded by a musket ball on the quarterdeck of the flagship *Victory* and died several hours later. But the French and Spanish were so severely defeated that all fear of invasion was over. Nelson's body was brought to England and buried, amid great mourning, in St. Paul's Cathedral. His victory is still celebrated on Trafalgar Day.

DOROTHY MARSHALL
Author, *Eighteenth Century England*

NEON AND OTHER NOBLE GASES

If you have ever been out at night in a large town or city, you probably have seen colored lights on stores and advertising signs. These are called neon lights, named for the gas, neon, that many of them contain. But not all of them are lighted by glowing neon gas. Other gases—such as helium, argon, krypton, and xenon—are also used in the lights.

Each of these gases gives out a different-colored light when electricity is sent through it. The color of light given out by the gas will vary, depending on such things as temperature, pressure, and electric voltage. Neon gives out red-orange light; argon gives out a reddish blue light. The light from helium is white, yellow, or sometimes violet; from krypton it is yellow, green, or pale violet; and from xenon, either blue or blue-green.

These gases form a family of elements known as the **noble** (sometimes called **inert**) **gases.** A sixth gas, radon, is also included in this group. Radon is a radioactive gas formed by the nuclear reactions of radium, thorium, and other radioactive elements.

The noble gases were once thought to be chemically inert—that is, scientists believed that these elements were totally incapable of combining with other elements to form compounds. We now know that these gases are not completely inactive but instead have a very low degree of reactivity. Chemists are able to prepare compounds of krypton and xenon with fluorine and compounds of xenon with oxygen under special laboratory conditions.

Sometimes the noble gases are called the rare gases, though some of them are far more abundant than many other elements. Which-ever name is used, their most important characteristic is that they are all relatively inactive chemically. They form no chemical compounds under normal conditions.

▸ USES OF NOBLE GASES

Besides providing colored light for signs, noble gases have a variety of other uses. Neon is used in the sodium-vapor lamps that light highways, in automobile spark plug testers, and in many electric tube devices.

Helium, the lightest noble gas, is used in balloons, blimps, and dirigibles. It has replaced hydrogen for this purpose because it is safe—it will not burn or explode. A non-flammable mixture of hydrogen and helium is also used. Helium is one of the noble gases used to protect metals that cannot be exposed to air when they are being welded. Welded joints may not be strong unless clean metal, free from oxygen compounds, is joined. The electronics industry uses helium in this way in manufacturing transistors.

Argon is also used as a protective gaseous shielding around metals that are being welded. One of the chief uses of argon, however, is in electric light bulbs. The argon slows down the evaporation of the tungsten filament in the bulb when it gets hot.

Krypton and xenon, although very rare gases, are widely used in photographic equipment, especially in flashbulbs. Both gases give a brilliant flash of light when electricity is sent through them. Such lamps may last for 10,000 flashes. Like argon, krypton slows down the evaporation of the filament in electric light bulbs. The bright lamps that light airport runways may be filled with krypton. Krypton-85 is a radioactive type of krypton gas that serves as a tracer gas in checking pipelines and other equipment for leaks. The radioactive gas can be detected by a Geiger counter and followed through the pipeline.

Xenon is often used in electron tubes. It can be made into a good conductor of electricity if its pressure is reduced and a high enough electric voltage is used. The noble gases do not conduct electricity at ordinary pressures.

Because of its radioactivity, radon is especially useful in the treatment of cancer and in biological research.

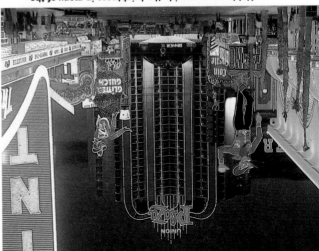

Noble gases provide the brightness in many of the glowing lights that illuminate the downtown area of many cities. These lights are usually called neon lights.

BASIC FACTS ABOUT THE NOBLE GASES

	NEON	ARGON	HELIUM	KRYPTON	XENON	RADON
Chemical Symbol	Ne	Ar	He	Kr	Xe	Rn
Atomic weight	20.179	39.948	4.0026	83.80	131.30	222
Percent in air	0.0018	0.93	0.0005	0.0001	0.000008	0
Uses	In neon signs, plug testers, glow lamps	In electric light bulbs; atmosphere for welding	Filler for airships and balloons; in welding	In photographic lights, Geiger counter tubes, airport lights	In photographic lights, electron tubes	Medical treatment and research
Color given out by gas when excited by electricity	Red-orange	Reddish blue	White, yellow, or violet	Yellow, green, or violet	Blue, blue-green	

HOW NOBLE GASES ARE OBTAINED

The chief source of the noble gases is ordinary air (except for helium, which is obtained from natural gas). The gases are mixed in the air together with oxygen, nitrogen, carbon dioxide, and other substances.

To obtain noble gases, ordinary air is first liquefied. Each gas is then removed from the air one at a time. This is done by chilling the air to a very low temperature, about $-330°F$ ($-200°C$), which liquefies it. The liquid air is then piped into tall towers and slowly heated. As each gas reaches its boiling point, it boils off from the liquid air as a gas. Each gas has a different boiling point and can thus be drawn off separately. This method of separation is known as fractional distillation. You can read more about this process in the article Dis-TILLATION in Volume D.

The Problem of Radon

Radon occurs naturally in the ground, especially near uranium deposits. (Uranium slowly breaks down to form radium.) In some regions, radon seeps into homes, where—if ventilation is poor—it accumulates and poses a health hazard to the occupants. In high concentrations, radon greatly increases a person's chances of developing lung cancer, but researchers are not sure exactly what levels of exposure are dangerous. Changes in construction practices plus repairs to existing homes may help prevent harmful accumulations of this radioactive gas. Special tests can determine if harmful levels have been reached.

DISCOVERY OF THE NOBLE GASES

Unlike some elements that have been known for hundreds of years, the noble gases were not discovered until the end of the 1800's. They escaped the notice of scientists for a long time for several reasons. For one, the gases make up only a tiny fraction of the Earth's atmosphere. Argon, the most plentiful noble gas, is 0.9 percent of the atmosphere, but it was difficult to find because it is inactive chemically. In fact, the name "argon" was chosen because of its chemical inertness. Its name comes from the Greek word for "lazy." The other noble gases are found in much smaller quantities in the air. Xenon makes up less than 1 part in 10 million parts of air.

Another reason that the noble gases were unknown for a long period is that they have no color, except when they give off colored light as an electric current goes through them. In addition, they have no odor or taste, and they do not burn. Unlike most other elements, they are not found combined with other substances in nature.

The most important work in discovering and isolating the noble gases (except radon) was done by the British chemists Sir William Ramsay and Lord Rayleigh. Argon was discovered by them in 1894. Helium was isolated from uranium ore by Ramsay in 1895. However, evidence of its existence in space was found earlier by astronomers studying light from the sun during the solar eclipse of 1868. Helium is the only element that was discovered in space before it was discovered on Earth.

Neon, krypton, and xenon were isolated in 1898 by Ramsay and Morris William Travers. Radon was isolated in 1900. Since that time the noble gases have become important in many areas of industry.

Reviewed by Elbert C. Weaver
Phillips Academy
Author, *Chemistry for Our Times*

See also Gases; Helium.

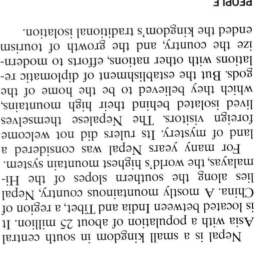

Terraced fields of rice, grain, and other crops are a common sight in the Kathmandu Valley, Nepal's most fertile and heavily populated region.

NEPAL

Nepal is a small kingdom in south central Asia with a population of about 25 million. It is located between India and Tibet, a region of China. A mostly mountainous country, Nepal lies along the southern slopes of the Himalayas, the world's highest mountain system. For many years Nepal was considered a land of mystery. Its rulers did not welcome foreign visitors. The Nepalese themselves lived isolated behind their high mountains, which they believed to be the home of the gods. But the establishment of diplomatic relations with other nations, efforts to modernize the country, and the growth of tourism ended the kingdom's traditional isolation.

▶ **PEOPLE**

The Nepalese are a varied people, who belong to two main ethnic divisions. More than half are descended from people of northern India. Most of the rest are of Mongolian ancestry, the descendants of people from Tibet.

The largest of Nepal's many ethnic communities are the Newars, who live in the central Kathmandu (Katmandu) Valley. Others include the Magars and Gurungs, who live in the west; the Kirantis and Limbus in the east; and the Sherpas, who live in the high mountain valleys of the Himalayas in the north.

The hardy Sherpas have traditionally served as guides and porters for mountain-climbing expeditions. In 1953, Tenzing Norgay, a Sherpa, and Edmund Hillary, a New Zealander, became the first people to reach the summit of Mount Everest, the world's highest mountain. Mount Everest lies on Nepal's border with Tibet. See the separate article on Mount Everest in Volume E.

Another ethnic group that draws from several ethnic communities is the Gorkha (or Gurkha). Members of this group are professional soldiers who have long served in the British and Indian armies. Their name comes from the state of Gorkha, whose ruler founded the first unified Nepalese kingdom in the 1700's.

Language. The official language of the country is Nepali, which is related to Hindi, the chief language of northern India. Many other Indo-Aryan languages are

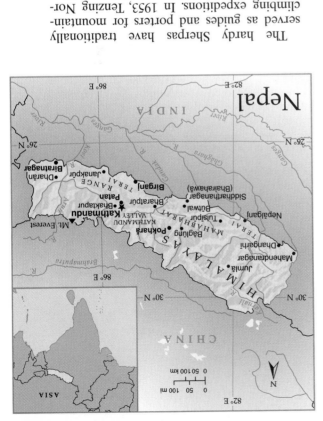

Nepal

The yak, a type of long-haired ox, is used in Nepal for food and transportation. Yaks are especially well suited to the country's colder, mountainous areas.

spoken, as well as languages belonging to the Tibeto-Burman family.

Religion. Most Nepalese are Hindus. A minority are Buddhists. Their two religions exist side by side and have intermingled to some extent. Religious ceremonies and festivals are often shared by both religions. Nepal also has a number of Muslims.

Way of Life. Most people live in the countryside, earning their living by farming and raising livestock. Only about 14 percent live in cities or towns. A traditional Nepalese house is constructed of sun-dried mud brick or stone, with a thatched or shingled roof. Rice is the staple food and is usually eaten with mixed vegetables and occasionally some fish or chicken. Tea is the most popular drink.

Clothing is varied. Nepalese women usually wear blouses with saris (long, draped garments of brightly colored material). Men traditionally wear tight trousers and loose robes that reach to the knees. However, they have recently adopted Western-style clothing.

Education. Free primary education was first introduced in 1975 to reduce the large number of people who could not read or write. About two-thirds of Nepalese children between the ages of 6 and 11 now attend school. Nepal has two major universities, Tribhuvan University and Kathmandu University, both located in Kathmandu.

▶ **LAND**

Nepal has several distinct geographical regions. The southern part of the country,

known as the Terai, makes up about one-quarter of Nepal's land area. It consists of a low plain, which is an extension of the great plain of northern India; dense jungles; and swamps. Important grain crops are grown in the settled areas of the plains. The jungles, which are inhabited by elephants, tigers, rhinoceroses, and other wildlife, are valuable natural areas and a source of timber.

North of the Terai is a region of broad valleys, hills, and mountains, including the lower ranges of the Himalayas. The heart of the region is the Kathmandu Valley, where Nepal's capital, Kathmandu, and other chief cities are located. It is the most fertile and heavily populated part of the country. In the far north, along the Tibetan border, are the towering peaks of the Himalayas. Eight of the world's ten highest mountains are located in this area. For more information on the Himalayas, see the article in Volume H.

Rivers. Nepal's river systems run from north to south, cutting through the mountain ranges. The three major rivers, the Kosi, Gandak, and Karnali, originate in Tibet and flow into the Ganges River system in India.

Climate. Nepal's climate varies widely according to region and elevation. In the Himalayas, winters are long and extremely cold, with heavy snowfall. The Kathmandu Valley has a temperate climate. Temperatures in the city of Kathmandu range from about 36 to 64°F (2 to 18°C) in winter and about 68 to 84°F (20 to 29°C) in summer. The Terai is subtropical, with a warm, humid climate. During the monsoon season, from June to Sep-

FACTS and figures

KINGDOM OF NEPAL is the official name of the country.

LOCATION: South central Asia.

AREA: 54,362 sq mi (140,797 km²).

POPULATION: 20,800,000 (estimate).

CAPITAL AND LARGEST CITY: Kathmandu.

MAJOR LANGUAGE: Nepali (official).

MAJOR RELIGIOUS GROUPS: Hindu, Buddhist.

GOVERNMENT: Constitutional monarchy. **Head of state**—king. **Head of government**—prime minister.

CHIEF PRODUCTS: Agricultural—Rice, corn, wheat, sugarcane, livestock. **Manufactured**—cotton textiles, jute products (burlap sacks, twine).

MONETARY UNIT: Nepalese rupee (1 rupee = 100 paisa).

tember, rainfall is considerable. In 2002 the heaviest monsoon season in more than thirty years caused extensive flash floods and landslides. More than 500 people were killed and thousands more were forced from their homes.

Natural Resources. In addition to timber, natural resources include quartz, lignite, copper, cobalt, and iron ore.

▶ ECONOMY

Agriculture and Forestry. Nepal is one of Asia's poorest countries. Although most people are farmers, less than 20 percent of Nepal's land is suitable for farming. Rice, corn, and wheat are the chief food crops. Rice is also exported. The main commercial crops are jute (used to make burlap sacks and twine), sugarcane, and tobacco.

The Nepalese raise a variety of livestock, including cows, yaks (long-haired oxen), water buffalo, sheep, goats, and chickens. Some provide food, while others are used as work animals or for transportation. The long-haired yak is especially suited to the cold mountainous areas. About 40 percent of the land remains forested and provides wood for cooking and heating and timber for export.

Industry. Industry in Nepal is limited. The chief manufactured goods are cotton textiles; jute products; refined sugar and other processed agricultural products; timber; paper, and other forest products; construction materials; and wood and metal handicrafts.

Transportation. Because of the rugged, mountainous terrain, transportation within Nepal is often difficult. Some parts of the country can be reached only by airplane or by the use of pack animals and guides over mountain trails. Roads now connect Kathmandu with Tibet and India.

▶ MAJOR CITIES

Kathmandu (Katmandu) is Nepal's commercial and cultural center, as well as its capital and largest city. It has an elevation of about 4,500 feet (1,370 meters) and a population of approximately 715,000. Kathmandu dates from at least the 700's, although it was probably founded much earlier. The city is noted for its many temples and religious shrines. Near Durbar Square in the old part of the city are the royal palace, several Hindu temples, museums, and bazaars.

Biratnagar is Nepal's second largest city. It has a population of about 222,000 and is growing rapidly as the result of migration from India and the Nepalese hills.

Patan, the third largest city, lies just a few miles from Kathmandu and is almost a suburb of the capital. It has a population of about 200,000. Patan itself is a former capital of one of the early Nepalese states.

Industry in Nepal includes the manufacture of handicrafts and textiles, which are often sold by street vendors.

Kathmandu, Nepal's largest city, became the nation's capital in the late 1700's. It is famous for its many temples and religious shrines.

▶ **HISTORY AND GOVERNMENT**

The Newars are thought to have lived in the region that is now Nepal since the A.D. 300's. Until the second half of the 1700's, this region consisted of small, mainly independent states. In 1769 the ruler of the state of Gorkha, Prithvi Narayan Shah, created the first unified Nepalese kingdom by conquering states in the Kathmandu Valley. He established his capital at Kathmandu and founded the dynasty that still rules.

By 1814 the Nepalese had moved into northern India. This created conflict with the British, who were extending their control over India. In the resulting 1814–16 war with Britain, Nepal was defeated.

The Rana Family. The period following the war with Britain was marked by a struggle for power between Nepal's kings and several of its noble families. In 1846, Jung Bahadur Rana seized control of the country, which he governed as prime minister. Although Nepal's kings continued to occupy the throne, they became figureheads. Real political power was in the hands of the Rana family, whose members governed as hereditary prime ministers for more than a century.

Restoration of Royal Authority. Dissatisfaction with the Ranas eventually led to an armed revolt that overthrew the family's long rule in 1951. Royal authority was restored to King Tribhuwan. Efforts to find a suitable form of representative government proved difficult for Tribhuwan and his son, Mahendra, who came to the throne in 1955. Nepal's first elected government took office under a constitution in 1959 but was soon dismissed by King Mahendra as unworkable.

Mahendra issued a new constitution in 1962 to establish a more traditional form of government based on *panchayats*, or councils. These ranged from the traditional village *panchayats*, elected directly by the people, up to national *panchayats*, elected by councils.

Mahendra was succeeded in 1972 by his eldest son, Birendra. In 1980, following student demonstrations for more democratic elections, King Birendra called for a national vote on the issue. The people voted to keep the *panchayat* system in place, but with reforms.

The king's modest reforms did little to appease the people, however. Widespread protests forced him to agree to a new constitution in 1990. It provided for a multiparty political system, with a two-house legislature. It also provided for a government headed by a prime minister.

In 2001, a tragedy occurred when Crown Prince Dipendra shot and killed several family members, including his parents, before killing himself. His uncle, Prince Gyanendra, was named king.

Recent Events. Since 1996, more than 10,000 people have been killed in a nationwide conflict in which Maoist rebels have tried to do away with the monarchy and establish a Communist republic. In 2002, King Gyanendra violated the nation's constitution by dismissing the prime minister. Legislative elections were suspended indefinitely and parliament was dissolved. In 2003, the government and the rebels agreed to a cease-fire. But talks broke down and the rebels called for a general workers' strike, which further undermined Nepal's already weakened economy. Maoist guerrilla fighters later stepped up their attacks, using bombs and blockades to force concessions from the government.

In 2005, the king assumed all powers with the help of the military, citing the government's failure to stop the insurgency and its general inefficiency. He declared a state of emergency and suspended fundamental civil liberties, including freedom of speech and freedom of the press. Parliamentary elections were postponed until 2007.

Reviewed by DAVID ZURICK
Eastern Kentucky University

NEPHRITIS. See DISEASES (Descriptions of Some Diseases).

NEPTUNE

The planet Neptune, the smallest of the four giant planets in the solar system, is so far away that very little was known about it until recently. In 1989, the planetary space probe *Voyager 2* flew past Neptune, revealing some remarkable facts about the planet and its moons. Among the things discovered is that this planet, named after the Roman god of the sea, has a thick atmosphere that completely covers a vast, strange ocean.

The Discovery of Neptune

The story of Neptune's discovery goes back to 1781 when the astronomer William Herschel found a tiny starry object while surveying the night sky. At first he thought it was a comet, but other astronomers soon realized that Herschel had discovered a new planet. They called this planet Uranus.

As astronomers tried to calculate the orbit of Uranus, they found that the planet was not always in the place their calculations said it should be—sometimes it went too fast and other times too slow. They began to wonder if the movement of Uranus was influenced by the gravity of some unknown planet.

In 1843, an English astronomer named John Couch Adams and a French astronomer named Urbain Leverrier began trying to calculate the location of such an unknown planet. By 1845, Adams had finished his calculations. He sent his predictions on the planet's location to Sir George Airy, the Astronomer Royal of England, but Airy did not try to find the planet. Leverrier sent his predictions, which were similar to those of Adams, to the Berlin Observatory in Germany. There, two German astronomers, Johann Galle and Heinrich D'Arrest, located the planet Neptune very near where Leverrier predicted it would be. Today, historians give credit for the discovery of Neptune to both Adams and Leverrier.

Neptune's Revolution and Rotation

Neptune, usually the eighth planet from the sun (see the Wonder Question accompanying this article), revolves around the sun once every 165 years in a huge elliptical (oval-shaped) orbit about 30 times greater than the Earth's orbit. Neptune's magnetic field rotates once in about 16 hours—the

length of the planet's "day." The rate of rotation of the visible features in Neptune's atmosphere varies greatly depending on the features' latitudes.

A Dim and Distant World

Neptune is about 2.8 billion miles (4.5 billion kilometers) from the sun. Because Neptune is so distant, it receives only about $\frac{1}{900}$ as much sunlight as Earth. This is why Neptune cannot be seen from Earth without using a telescope. The less sunlight reflected off a planet, the dimmer the planet appears from Earth. Also, although Neptune's diameter is about four times greater than Earth's, its great distance makes it appear very tiny even when viewed through large telescopes. It is no wonder no one discovered the planet until Adams and Leverrier told astronomers where to look.

The Blue Gas Giant

The gas giants—Neptune, Jupiter, Saturn, and Uranus—are very different from Earth, which has a rocky crust with an interior of molten rock. Neptune has a deep, thick atmosphere of hydrogen and helium, along with traces of methane gas. Far below is an ocean of water, methane, and ammonia.

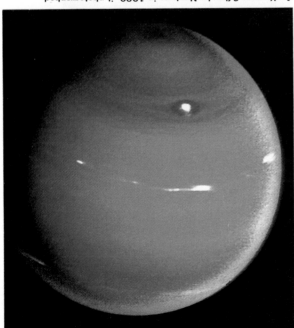

As *Voyager 2* flew by Neptune in 1989, it photographed the red haze and white clouds high above the planet's atmosphere. Methane gas in the atmosphere makes the planet appear blue.

The Composition of Neptune

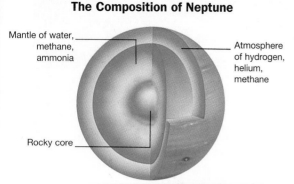

Mantle of water, methane, ammonia

Atmosphere of hydrogen, helium, methane

Rocky core

Neptune

Position in the solar system	Eighth planet from the sun
Distance from the sun (average)	2,800,000,000 miles (4,500,000,000 kilometers)
Revolution around the sun	165 Earth years
Diameter	30,800 miles (49,600 kilometers)
	4 times the diameter of Earth
Mass	103 sextillion tons
	About 17 times the mass of Earth
Density	1.8 grams per cubic centimeter
Rotation on its axis	Magnetic field: 16 hours 5 minutes; Features: vary according to latitude
Tilt of rotational axis	28.3°
Natural satellites known	13
Rings known	4
Surface	No surface; Neptune is a gas giant
Atmosphere	Hydrogen, helium, methane
Temperature (upper atmosphere)	–355°F (–215°C)
Symbol	♆
In mythology	Neptune, Roman god of the sea

Neptune is also different from the other gas giant planets. About 10 percent of Neptune's mass is made up of hydrogen and helium gases. The other 90 percent of its mass consists mostly of the heavier elements such as carbon, nitrogen, and oxygen. In contrast, Jupiter's mass is about 96 percent hydrogen and helium.

Neptune appears blue because of the methane gas in its atmosphere. Sunlight is made up of a spectrum of colors that are absorbed by some materials and reflected by others. Methane absorbs the reddish colors in the spectrum. When sunlight shines through methane gas, the reddish colors are absorbed and the bluish colors are reflected, making the planet appear blue. Thin, wispy clouds floating in the upper atmosphere are above most of the methane, so they appear white. The temperature in the upper atmosphere of Neptune is a frigid

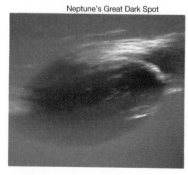

Neptune's Great Dark Spot

–355°F (–215°C). From there the atmosphere extends thousands of miles toward the planet's interior. The deeper you go, the warmer it gets. When the pressure of its atmosphere is about the same as the atmospheric pressure at the Earth's surface, the temperature on Neptune is high enough for methane to form clouds.

Below the clouds the pressure and temperature of the atmosphere gradually rise. Neptune has no solid surface. Its atmosphere extends downward for thousands of miles. Astronomers think that below the atmosphere, at a depth of about 6,000 miles (10,000 kilometers), is an ocean unlike any on Earth. It is made up of water, methane, and ammonia, and its surface temperature may be as hot as 4500°F (2500°C). At the center of Neptune may be a rocky core about the size of Earth. The temperature at the core may reach 15,000°F (8000°C).

The Great Dark Spot and "Scooter"

When *Voyager 2* approached Neptune, its cameras spotted the Great Dark Spot, believed to be an immense storm system about the size of Earth. Several smaller dark spots were seen, as well as an unusual white cloud called Scooter. Scooter moved at a different speed from the rest of Neptune's cloud cover, making it appear to "scoot" around the planet. Scooter was believed to be the top of a plume of warm gas similar to a thunder-

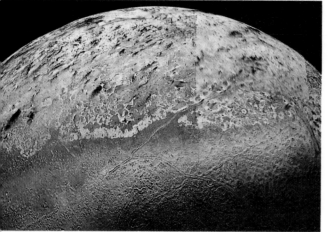

This composite image of Neptune's moon Triton shows the frozen surface of its large polar cap, which is probably made up of nitrogen ice.

storm on Earth. As the warm gas rises, it cools and the methane in it condenses, forming a white cloud. Observations by the Hubble Space Telescope in the 1990's failed to find the Great Dark Spot.

Triton—A World of Ice Volcanoes

Triton, Neptune's largest moon, or satellite, is very unusual. Slightly smaller than the Earth's moon, Triton is about 1,700 miles (2,700 kilometers) in diameter, and it circles Neptune once every 5 days and 20 hours. Most satellites orbit their planet in the same direction as the planet's rotation. But Triton circles Neptune in the opposite direction. Some scientists think that Triton's orbit is different because it was once a separate planet that was captured by Neptune's gravity.

Among Triton's other unusual features are ice volcanoes on its surface that eject frozen nitrogen, dust particles, and other materials from Triton's interior, which is quite warm. This warmth is caused by friction from tides in Triton's interior that result from Neptune's gravitational pull on it. Images from *Voyager 2* show eruptions blasting material from Triton's interior as much as 5 miles (8 kilometers) into space. Despite its interior warmth, the surface of Triton is bitterly cold—about -391°F (-235°C). In fact, it is the coldest planetary satellite known. Only the planet Pluto is likely to be colder.

Parts of Triton's surface are wrinkled. Other areas look like frozen lakes, which astronomers think are places where frozen water has erupted from inside Triton and then frozen as hard as rock. Much of Triton's surface is covered with fresh white snow. This snow cannot be ice formed from water because Triton's surface is too cold. Instead, scientists think the snow consists of crystals of nitrogen that have frozen out of the atmosphere. Sunlight reflecting off Triton's icy surface makes it one of the whitest objects in the solar system.

Triton is also unusual because it has a thin atmosphere consisting mostly of nitrogen gas. While most satellites are too small to hold an atmosphere, Triton is so cold that even its weak gravitational force can hold its nitrogen atmosphere for billions of years.

Neptune's Other Satellites and Its Rings
In addition to Triton, Neptune has twelve other moons: Naiad, Thalassa, Despina, Galatea, Larissa, Proteus, Nereid, and five others not yet named. The smallest moon, discovered by Mauna Kea Observatory in 2003, is only about 24 miles (38 kilometers) in diameter. This moon is also Neptune's most distant, orbiting about 30 million miles (48 million kilometers) away from the planet.

Some of Neptune's other satellites were discovered when astronomers studying pictures from *Voyager 2* noticed tiny specks of light very close to the planet. The largest of these is about 250 miles (400 kilometers) in diameter, and the smallest is about 30 miles

WONDER QUESTION

What is the outermost planet in the solar system?

Although Pluto is the ninth planet from the sun, it is sometimes but not always the outermost planet. Neptune and Pluto actually take turns being the outermost planet because of the shapes of their orbits. The orbits of all the planets are elliptical, or oval shaped, but Pluto's orbit is more elliptical than any of the others'. Therefore, Pluto's distance from the sun varies greatly as it travels in its orbit. Neptune's orbit, however, is almost a perfect circle, so it stays at a nearly constant distance from the sun. When Pluto's orbit brings it closest to the sun, it is actually closer to the sun than Neptune is, so Neptune becomes the outermost planet.

Because of their orbits, between 1979 and 1999 Neptune was farther from the sun than Pluto. In 1999, Pluto regained its status as the outermost planet. That will change in 2231, when Neptune will become the outermost planet again.

Cameras on board *Voyager 2* were the first to discover Neptune's mysterious rings. Arc sections in the outermost ring can be seen in this detail.

(50 kilometers) in diameter. More satellites may be discovered in the future by ground-based or orbital telescopes or by space probes.

The *Voyager 2* spacecraft also discovered four thin rings around the planet. Each ring is composed of billions of pieces of material ranging in size from fine bits of sand and dust to objects as large as boulders. These rings may be debris blasted off the small innermost satellites by meteorites, or they may be bits and pieces of another satellite that broke up long ago. Unlike most planetary rings, which appear smooth and uniform, Neptune's outermost ring has three bright arcs. Scientists believe the moon Galatea, which orbits just inside the ring, causes these arcs. A complex interaction between the moon's gravity and the ring causes light-reflecting ice in the ring to clump together in certain parts. This interaction also affects the moon's orbit.

The one, brief exploration of Neptune by *Voyager 2* certainly helped to expand our knowledge about it, but there is much that still remains a mystery. The next visit—perhaps around the year 2030 or later—will no doubt reveal much more about the beautiful blue planet near the edge of the solar system.

RICHARD BERRY
Author, *Discover the Stars*

See also PLANETS; SATELLITES; SOLAR SYSTEM.

NERO (37–68)

Nero Claudius Caesar Drusus Germanicus became emperor of the Roman Empire when he was 17. His reign is considered one of the cruelest in Roman history.

Nero was born in Antium, Italy, in A.D. 37. After the death of his father, Nero's scheming mother, Agrippina, married the emperor Claudius. She convinced Claudius to adopt Nero, making the boy next in line to the throne. In the year 53, Nero married Claudius' daughter Octavia. Agrippina then arranged the murder of Claudius, and in 54, Nero was crowned.

For the first few years of his reign Nero ruled wisely. Under the influence of Seneca and Burrus, his learned advisers, the new emperor made important changes in the government. His subjects respected him.

Soon, however, Nero turned to violence and plotted against people he thought were a threat. Britannicus, son of Claudius and the rightful heir to the throne, was poisoned. Agrippina sought greater power, and Nero finally arranged for her murder. Burrus died, and Seneca was removed. Nero divorced Octavia to marry the crafty, shrewd Poppaea. Octavia was banished and later put to death.

In the year 64 a great fire broke out in Rome. Flames raged for almost ten days, and most of the city was destroyed. Rumors suggested that Nero himself had caused the fire in order to rebuild Rome according to his own plan, but many historians believe that the tale has no basis in fact. Legend says that he amused himself by playing his lyre (a stringed instrument) while thousands died in a city reduced to ashes. Today, if a person fails to do his duty in an emergency, we say that he or she "fiddles while Rome burns."

Nero's plans for rebuilding were lavish, and his subjects were heavily taxed. He erected a magnificent palace called the Golden House. According to some stories, Nero accused the Christians of starting the fire. In an excess of violence Rome's Christian inhabitants became victims of cruel tortures.

In the year 68 a successful revolt against the emperor was staged under the leadership of Galba. The senate sentenced Nero to death and proclaimed Galba emperor. But Nero did not await his end at the hands of others. On June 9, he stabbed himself to death.

Reviewed by KENNETH S. COOPER
George Peabody College

NERVOUS SYSTEM

Every minute of every day a constant flood of electrical messages flows through your body. Some messages carry information about the world around you: what your eyes see, what your ears hear, what you taste, smell, and touch in your environment. Other messages are involved in the workings of the body: movements of your hands or feet or mouth, the flow of blood, the digestion of food, the elimination of wastes, and all the other processes that are a part of living. Still other messages deal with ideas, thoughts, and feelings. Without this constant flow of messages, the human body would not function.

The body's message-carrying network is the nervous system. It is something like a complicated telephone system. The central switchboard is the brain and spinal cord. Here incoming messages are sorted out and stored or sent on to new destinations. Outgoing messages are routed to the appropriate parts of the body.

Messages are carried along a network of **nerves** that branch and crisscross through every part of the body. Each of these nerves is a bundle of many tiny, threadlike nerve cells, called **neurons.** The neurons are bound together in a sheath of tissue something like the insulation that surrounds a telephone wire. All together, there are billions of neurons in a human body.

Information reaches the nervous system through specialized sense organs that gather information from the world outside us. Cells in the eyes are sensitive to light reflections. The ears are sound funnels that gather sound waves. The nose and mouth contain chemical sensors that we use to smell and taste. Specialized structures in the skin give us sensations of touch and pressure, heat and cold, as well as pain sensations that warn us of danger. All the information gathered by the sense organs would be meaningless if it were not carried to the brain, where it is interpreted. Our eyes may gather patterns of light reflections, but these must be sorted out in the vision center at the back of the brain for us to "see." Other specialized brain centers are concerned with the senses of hearing, taste, smell, and touch. You can read more about the senses in the article BODY, HUMAN (The Sense Organs) in Volume B.

Other centers in the brain are concerned with outgoing messages, with coordinating and controlling movements, and with various chemical processes of the body. Large areas of the brain are involved in thinking and feeling, in processing and storing memories, and in forming the personality that makes each person unique.

The nervous system receives, interprets, and responds to information from both inside and outside the body. The brain and spinal cord coordinate these functions.

Brain
Cranial nerves
Spinal cord
Spinal nerves

The human nervous system is divided into two main parts: the **central nervous system** and the **peripheral nervous system.** One reason for these names is obvious from a diagram of the nervous system: The brain and spinal cord, which make up the central nervous system, have a central position, in the head and down the length of the body. The branching network of nerves that make up the peripheral nervous system links the brain and spinal cord with all other parts of the body, carrying messages to and from the outside, or periphery. But the brain and spinal cord are central in more than just their position. They are the processing centers for all incoming messages and are the central sources for messages sent out to the organs and body parts on the periphery.

The Central Nervous System

The brain, a wrinkled, jellylike mass, is actually a combination of several structures. Hidden inside is the **brain stem,** smoothly joined to the top of the spinal cord. It contains centers that control the most basic functions of life. For example, one part of the brain stem, called the medulla oblongata, controls breathing, heartbeat rate, swallowing, and vomiting.

Above and to the front of the brain stem are structures called the **thalamus** and **hypothalamus.** The thalamus helps screen information and determine what is important enough to be sent to the higher (thinking) parts of the brain. The hypothalamus contains a variety of control centers that relate to such areas as composition of the blood, feelings of hunger or thirst, and strong emotions such as anger, fear, or pleasure.

A structure at the back of the brain, the **cerebellum,** helps to control and co-ordinate movements. The largest part of the brain, the **cerebrum,** also known as the cerebral cortex, is the thinking part of the brain. You can read more about the structure and many functions of the brain in the BRAIN article in Volume B.

Also part of the central nervous system is the spinal cord. It is a long, slender cord of nerves that runs down through the neck and back, protected by being inside the hollow, jointed, bony column of the spine. The spinal cord acts as a processing center for incoming messages carried to it by the peripheral nerves. Some, but not all, of these messages are relayed up to the brain.

The spinal cord responds to some messages directly, without involving the brain. The spinal cord is the central link in **reflex actions,** responses to incoming messages that occur very quickly, without conscious thought. If you touch a hot stove, for example, you jerk your hand back immediately, automatically, without thinking about it. Only later, when you are already out of danger and the messages have had time to be relayed to the brain, processed, and understood, do you feel the pain and realize that you might have been badly burned if you had not reacted so quickly. Some reflex actions protect us from danger; others make it simpler to do routine tasks like tying shoes or walking.

The Peripheral Nervous System

There are two main types of peripheral nerves: **Sensory nerves** carry messages to the central nervous system; **motor nerves** carry messages from the central nervous system to other parts of the body. Some messages carried by motor nerves act on muscle cells and produce movements. Others may have different effects, such as stimulating cells in a gland to secrete (release) a particular chemical.

Twelve pairs of peripheral nerves branch out from the underside of the brain. They are called **cranial nerves.** Some of them are sensory, such as the olfactory nerves (concerned with smell), the optic nerves (vision), and the acoustic nerves (hearing and balance). Others are motor, such as the oculomotor and trochlear nerves involved in eye movements and the hypoglossal nerves that control the tongue movements. Some cranial nerves are mixed, which means they contain both sensory and motor nerve cells. An important one is the vagus nerve, which helps control the heart, breathing, and the work of many organs.

There are 31 pairs of **spinal nerves** that branch off from the spinal cord. Each of these peripheral nerves is mixed, containing both sensory fibers that carry messages to the spinal cord and motor fibers that carry messages from it. They are linked together in complex networks called **plexuses** so that each part of the skin or muscles is linked with more than one spinal nerve. This arrangement provides for finer coordination and also provides a backup system. If one spinal nerve is damaged, the body part that it serves will not lose all its sensations or ability to move.

The Autonomic Nervous System

One part of the peripheral nervous system is organized into a special system concerned with the workings of internal organs such as the heart, lungs, stomach, and kidneys. This is the autonomic nervous system, so called because it works independently. The autonomic nerves are all motor nerves, and they produce effects such as causing the blood vessels to widen or narrow and speeding or slowing the heartbeat or breathing rate. Like spinal nerves, the autonomic nerves may be linked into branching networks called plexuses. The best known is the solar plexus, which has powerful effects on the heart, lungs, and arteries.

There are two main divisions of the autonomic system: the **parasympathetic** and **sympathetic. Parasympathetic** nerves are concerned with keeping the body running smoothly under normal conditions; sympathetic nerves are involved with preparing for emergencies, such as providing extra energy in case the person has to fight or run away. Most organs have both sympathetic and parasympathetic nerves, and they produce opposite effects. *Sympathetic* messages, for example, tend to narrow blood vessels, while parasympathetic messages widen them.

Actually, the nerves of the autonomic system are not completely independent; their action can be affected by messages from sensory nerves and control centers in the central nervous system. Their effects are closely tied in with the emotions: When a person turns pale with fear or has a ''sinking feeling in the stomach'' or breaks out in a cold sweat, these are effects of the autonomic system. Normally we have no conscious awareness or control of the working of the autonomic system. However, some people are able to learn to control some autonomic functions, such as slowing down the heartbeat rate or lowering the blood pressure, using techniques such as meditation or biofeedback.

▶ THE NEURON

Nerves are made up of many single nerve cells, called neurons. Like other body cells, most neurons are too small to be seen without a microscope, yet some of the nerve cells in the body are as much as 3 feet (1 meter) long. A typical neuron has three main parts. Branching out from the cell body are thread-like **dendrites.** (Their name literally means ''treelike.'') There is also a long, slender **axon,** which ends in branches so that it looks a bit like a rope with an unraveled end. In some neurons the axon is wrapped in a sheath of fatty substance called **myelin.** Those nerves look shiny white, while nerves without a my-elin sheath are gray. (The ''gray matter'' of the brain is made up of unmyelinated nerve cells.) Peripheral nerve cells are wrapped in an outer sheath, called the **neurilemma,** made up of living cells wrapped around the nerve fiber like a jelly roll.

Transmission Along the Nerve

A certain kind of electrical process is involved in the transmission of messages along nerve fibers. Movements of tiny charged chemical particles, called ions, produce changes in the electrical state, or condition, of the membrane that surrounds the neuron. This causes a tiny current to flow along the neuron. (Because of the role of the charged chemical particles, we say that the current is created electrochemically.)

The tiny current in a nerve cell moves much more slowly than the current in a telephone line, for example. An electric current travels along a wire at a speed of 186,000 miles (300,000 kilometers) per second, while messages travel along a neuron at a speed of only about 390 feet (119 meters) per second. In addition, messages flow along neurons in only one direction—from dendrites to the cell body and then out along the axon.

Neurons are linked together into chains and networks, but they are not actually joined. Between the ends of the axon of one neuron and the dendrites or cell body of the next is a tiny gap called a **synapse.** When a nerve impulse

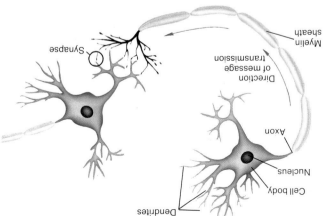

Nerve cells, called neurons, transmit messages through-out the body. Most neurons have many branching den-drites, a large cell body, and a long, insulated axon.

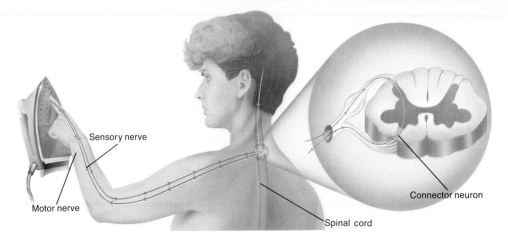

An important feature of the nervous system is the reflex arc, which helps protect us from injury. If a person touches a hot iron, for example, nerve messages travel up the arm to the spinal cord, where motor nerves are stimulated almost immediately, moving the hand away from danger.

Sensory nerve

Motor nerve

Connector neuron

Spinal cord

travels through a neuron and reaches the end of its axon, special chemicals, such as acetylcholine, are released. These chemical messengers are carried through the fluid in the synapse to the next nerve cell, where they start off new electrochemical reactions and continue the transmission of the message.

Repair of Nerve Damage

Some kinds of body cells—for example, blood cells and skin cells—are continually dying and being replaced by new cells. But this does not generally happen with nerve cells. You already have virtually all the nerve cells that your body will ever form. If the cell body of one of them is damaged, it will die and be lost forever. But a damaged axon of a neuron can be replaced; it regrows at a rate of about 1/10 of an inch (2.5 millimeters) a day. In 1998, researchers discovered that at least one part of the adult human brain involved with learning (the hippocampus) can produce new nerve cells.

Normally, peripheral nerve cells can regenerate after damage much more easily than neurons in the central nervous system. That is why damage to the spinal cord may result in permanent paralysis: When the connections to the spinal nerves are broken, the messages that tell the muscles to move can no longer be transmitted. Researchers have been working on ways to stimulate regeneration in damaged neurons of the central nervous system. This may prevent paralysis after a spinal injury.

▶ A TRIP ALONG THE NERVOUS SYSTEM PATHWAYS

Your fingers touch a hot iron! Before you have time to think about it, you pull your hand away from the hot surface. Let us follow the sequence of nerve messages to find out how you were able to react so quickly.

The hot iron damaged some cells in your fingertips. These cells released chemicals that stimulated the dendrites of sensory nerves in your skin. Along the membrane surrounding the threadlike dendrites, sodium and potassium ions began to flow into and out of the cell, causing a series of tiny electrochemical reactions. The reactions moved along the dendrites, past the cell bodies of the sensory neurons, and along their threadlike axons.

The pain message traveled all the way up your arm to your spinal cord in just a tiny fraction of a second. There the message crossed synapses to connector neurons in the cord, which sent the message on to motor neurons. The nerve message stimulated the muscle cells to contract so that your hand moved away from danger. You can see how this works in the diagram above.

For conscious actions, the nerve sequences are much more complicated, and they operate a bit more slowly. For example, imagine you are reading a page of Braille. You move your fingers over the patterns of raised dots that form the letters. Touch receptors in your skin send messages along nerve cells leading up your arm to the spinal cord. The messages are relayed farther, up the spinal cord to the brain. Areas of the brain that interpret touch sensations are stimulated, and you realize that the patterns can be formed into words. Other parts of the brain consider the meaning of the words and compare them to your memories so you understand what you are reading.

ALVIN SILVERSTEIN
College of Staten Island, CUNY
VIRGINIA SILVERSTEIN
Coauthors, *The Nervous System;*
World of the Brain

NETHERLANDS

The Netherlands is a small nation of twelve provinces situated in northwestern Europe, on the coast of the North Sea. Its popular name, Holland, is actually the name of a historical province, now divided into North and South Holland, that has long been the political and economic center of the country.

The Netherlands is one of the most densely populated nations in Europe and in the world. Its people call themselves Netherlanders or Hollanders. In English they are known as the Dutch.

"Netherlands" means "low countries." The name is appropriate, for nearly one-quarter of the country, in fact, lies below sea level, and almost half its people now live

Clockwise from right: Wooden shoes, called clogs, are the most distinctive feature of the traditional Dutch costume. Tulips and other flowers are grown for export. Windmills, once used to pump water away from the land, are now preserved as national treasures.

on land that has been reclaimed from the sea. "God made the world, but the Dutch made Holland" is an old proverb with much truth.

▶ **PEOPLE**

The Dutch are mostly descendants of Germanic peoples who settled in the region in ancient times. But the Netherlands has also been a place of refuge for immigrants from many lands. Among them were Jews who were expelled from Spain and Portugal in the 1500's and persecuted in Germany in the 1900's. More recent immigrants have come from former Dutch colonies that are now the nations of Indonesia and Suriname.

Language. Dutch, the chief language of the Netherlands, is a form of Low German, which was spoken in northern regions. It was first spoken by the Franks, a Germanic people who migrated from the east and set-

Above: Porters at the Alkmaar Cheese Market use shoulder barrows to carry large wheels of cheese, such as Gouda and Edam, which are enjoyed worldwide.
Right: Bicycles are a common form of transportation on narrow Dutch streets.

tled there in the 300's. Dutch is related to both modern German and English.

In the northern province of Friesland, Frisian is accepted as an official language along with standard Dutch. Frisian is the Germanic language closest to English. The Dutch are also taught to speak English.

Religion. The Netherlands is about equally divided between Roman Catholics and Protestants. Catholics tend to live in the south, while Protestants live mainly in the north and west. The country's single largest Protestant sect is the Dutch Reformed Church. The Netherlands is also home to lesser numbers of Jews and Muslims. The Dutch have a long tradition of religious tolerance, and freedom of worship is guaranteed under the constitution.

Education. Dutch schools are government-supported, and children are required to attend from the age of 4 to 16. After primary school, they may continue to one of several kinds of secondary schools, depending on ability. These provide students with a general or vocational (trade) education or prepare them for a university. Leiden University, the country's oldest, was founded in 1575.

Food and Drink. The Dutch are a hospitable and home-loving people. Dutch food is simple and hearty. Such cheeses as Gouda and Edam (named for the towns where they are produced) are enjoyed throughout the world. A typical winter dish is *erwtensoep*, which is a thick pea soup. Indonesian foods are especially popular. Fish, especially salted herring, is an important part of the Dutch diet. The Dutch are also known for their wide variety of excellent lagers and ales.

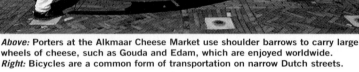

FACTS and figures

KINGDOM OF THE NETHERLANDS (Koninkrijk der Nederlanden) is the official name of the country.

LOCATION: Northwestern Europe.

AREA: 16,033 sq mi (41,526 km²).

POPULATION: 16,100,000 (estimate).

CAPITAL AND LARGEST CITY: Amsterdam.

MAJOR LANGUAGES: Dutch, Frisian (both official).

MAJOR RELIGIOUS GROUPS: Roman Catholic, Protestant.

GOVERNMENT: Constitutional monarchy. **Head of state**—monarch. **Head of government**—prime minister. **Legislature**—Staten Generaal (States General), consisting of the First Chamber and Second Chamber. **Seat of Government**—The Hague.

CHIEF PRODUCTS: Agricultural—wheat, flax, oats, potatoes, sugar beets, fruits, vegetables, livestock, dairy products (milk, cheese, butter), flowers and flower bulbs. **Manufactured**—processed foods and other agricultural produce, metal and engineering products, electrical machinery and equipment, chemicals, microelectronics. **Mineral**—natural gas, petroleum, salt.

MONETARY UNIT: Euro (1 euro = 100 cents).

▶ LAND

The Netherlands is bordered by Germany on the east, Belgium on the south, and the North Sea on the west and north.

Land Regions. The land can be divided into three regions: a narrow area of sand dunes running along the North Sea coast; the western lowlands; and the slightly higher eastern uplands. The western lowlands, where most of the people live in cities very close to each other, lie below sea level. The region is protected against the encroaching sea by the dunes and by dikes and dams. The eastern uplands have a gently rolling landscape. The highest elevations are in Limburg province in the southeast.

Lakes, Rivers, and Canals. Lakes dot the landscape in the north. Rivers wind across the land to the North Sea, and canals link various parts of the country. The western delta area is formed by its three biggest rivers—the Rijn (Rhine), with its numerous branches; the Maas (Meuse); and the Schelde. Its many rivers and canals create one of the densest network of waterways in the world.

Reclaiming the Land from the Sea. The western region of the Netherlands was once a great swamp, separated from the North Sea only by the narrow strip of dunes. The Dutch have greatly increased their amount of land by draining this region. Dikes were built around the flooded areas, and the water was pumped out with windmills. The drained areas—called polders—now make up about one-third of the total land area. Today most drainage pumps are driven by electricity or diesel engines.

A massive reclamation project involved the Zuider Zee (South Sea). Formerly an inlet of the North Sea, it was closed off from the sea by a dam and transformed into a freshwater lake, now called the IJsselmeer (Lake IJssel). Five great polders were created in the area. After years of allowing the rain to remove the sea salt, they are now the site of prosperous farms.

The Delta Plan, the largest water-control project in world history, was completed in 1986. It consists of a series of dams placed between the islands that make up the province of Zeeland in the southwest.

Climate. The climate in the Netherlands is moderate. Summer temperatures average about 63°F (17°C) and winter temperatures about 34°F (1°C). Periods of rain are frequent. About 30 inches (760 millimeters) of rain falls during the year.

Natural Resources. The Netherlands has limited natural resources, although it has one of the world's largest deposits of natural gas. Petroleum is mined in the North Sea.

▶ ECONOMY

Farming, fishing, shipping, and trade have traditionally been the main Dutch economic activities. Manufacturing now plays a dominant role in the economy. Banking and other service industries are also vital. The Netherlands was an original member of the European Economic Community, formed in 1957 and now called the European Union (EU).

Netherlands

Services. The service industries combined account for more than 70 percent of the economy and employ more than 70 percent of the workforce. From government services to tourism, banking, and business and personal services, the Netherlands has one of the strongest service economies in the EU.

Manufacturing. Manufacturing makes up about 26 percent of the economy and employs 23 percent of the workforce. The chief manufactured goods are processed foods, metal and engineering products, electrical machinery and equipment, chemicals, petroleum products, and microelectronics.

Agriculture and Fishing. Dutch farms are usually small, and only about 4 percent of the workforce is engaged in agriculture. But the farms are extensively cultivated with mechanical equipment and produce a surplus for export. Chief crops include wheat, flax (used to make linen), oats, potatoes, sugar beets, vegetables, and fruits. Fresh flowers and flower bulbs—mainly tulips, hyacinths, and narcissus—are also grown in large numbers and exported around the world. Dairy farming, however, is the most important part of the agricultural economy. Much of the land is used to graze dairy cows. The Netherlands is famous for such dairy products as cheeses, milk, and butter. Cattle and other livestock are also raised for meat.

The Dutch fishing industry has existed for centuries and still contributes to the economy. The primary catch is herring, mackerel, cod, haddock, and eels.

Trade. The country's location on the North Sea has made it a natural trade center. Not only does the Netherlands trade with many nations around the world, but its ships carry goods going to and from countries along the Rhine River. Its most important trading partners are Belgium, the United Kingdom, Germany, the United States, France, and Italy.

Transportation. The Netherlands maintains 1,744 miles (2,808 kilometers) of railways, which link all the major cities. The country also maintains 72,360 miles (116,500 kilome-

The Dutch economy is one of the strongest in Europe. *Clockwise from left:* Dairy farming and fishing are important agricultural activities. Rotterdam-Europoort is the largest and busiest port in the world.

▶ MAJOR CITIES

Amsterdam is the official capital and largest city of the Netherlands. It has a population of about 735,000 and is the center of the country's commerce, banking, and industry. See the article AMSTERDAM in Volume A.

The Hague ('s Gravenhage), with a population of 465,000, is situated about 30 miles (48 kilometers) south of Amsterdam. It is the seat of the Netherlands government and the site of the International Court of Justice, an organ of the United Nations.

Rotterdam, with a population of about 600,000 is the country's second largest city. Rotterdam-Europoort is the world's largest port and the gateway through which much of western Europe's shipping passes.

Other notable Dutch cities include **Haarlem**, a city of flower markets; **Groningen**, a market center in the north; **Eindhoven**, an industrial center; and the old university cities of **Leiden** and **Utrecht**.

▶ CULTURAL HISTORY

In the early 1500's, humanism—an intellectual movement that grew out of the Renaissance period—spread from Italy into northern Europe. Desiderius Erasmus, a Dutch scholar and priest, became the leading humanist in the north. His writings upheld the values of Christianity while challenging the practices of Catholic church leaders.

About this time, the Netherlands began producing great works of art, an achievement that continues to this day. Among the most famous of the Dutch masters are Hieronymus Bosch, Rembrandt van Rijn, Frans Hals, Jan Vermeer, Pieter de Hooch, Jacob van Ruisdael, Vincent van Gogh, Piet Mondrian, and M. C. Escher.

Fine art collections hang in several world-renowned museums. They include the Rijksmuseum (National Museum) and the Van Gogh Museum in Amsterdam, the Mauritshuis in The Hague, and the Kröller-Müller Museum in Otterlo, near Arnhem. The Stedelijk (Municipal) Museum, in Amsterdam, is devoted chiefly to modern art.

There are striking modern sculptures in many cities, particularly Amsterdam and Rotterdam. Utrecht and Amsterdam have statues dedicated to Anne Frank, the German-Dutch Jewish girl who died in a concentration camp during World War II and whose diary, published after her death, made her world famous. The Netherlands also supports several concert halls, including The Hague Philharmonic, the Netherlands Chamber Orchestra, and the Amsterdam Royal Concertgebouw, which is considered one of the best symphony orchestras in the world.

For more information on the arts in the Netherlands, see the articles DUTCH AND

ters) of highway. International airports are located in Amsterdam and Rotterdam.

Dutch traders and seafarers once made their nation a leading world power. Ports and harbors are located in Amsterdam, Delfzijl, Dordrecht, Eemshaven, Groningen, Haarlem, IJmuiden, Maastricht, Rotterdam, Terneuzen, Utrecht, and Vlissingen.

Communication. About 60 radio stations and 20 television stations are broadcast in the Netherlands.

Cellular telephone use is on the rise, and more than 9 million Internet users are serviced by more than 50 Internet service providers (ISP's). The country's foremost daily newspaper, *De Telegraaf*, is published in Amsterdam.

In wintertime, people can walk or skate on the frozen Keizersgracht, one of the many canals in Amsterdam, the official capital and largest city of the Netherlands.

The Dutch scholar Desiderius Erasmus was a leading figure of the Northern Renaissance.

FLEMISH ART, DUTCH AND FLEMISH MUSIC, and biographies of individual artists in the appropriate volumes.

▶ GOVERNMENT

The Kingdom of the Netherlands is a constitutional monarchy. The royal family belongs to the House of Orange-Nassau, founded by William I, Count of Nassau and Prince of Orange, in the 1500's. All Dutch monarchs in the 1900's were queens. Queen Wilhelmina reigned from 1890 to 1948. Queen Juliana reigned from 1948 to 1980. The present queen, Beatrix, came to the throne in 1980. The monarch serves as head of state, but the actual leadership of the government rests with the Council of Ministers, headed by a prime minister.

The legislative body, the Staten Generaal (States General), is composed of two chambers. The 75 members of the Eerste Kamer (First Chamber) are elected by the twelve provincial councils to 4-year terms. The 150 members of the Tweede Kamer (Second Chamber) are elected directly by the people to 4-year terms.

The prime minister and other members of the cabinet are appointed by the monarch from political parties with a majority in the States General. The Council of State, headed by the monarch, serves as an advisory body.

Overseas Territories. The Netherlands Antilles, also known as the Dutch West Indies, is a federation of islands in the Caribbean Sea that are self-governing parts of the Kingdom of the Netherlands. The Antilles islands associated with the Netherlands include Bonaire, Curaçao, Saba, St. Eustatius, and the southern portion of St. Martin. The island of Aruba, once part of the Netherlands Antilles, broke away from the federation in 1986 and became an autonomous member of the Kingdom of the Netherlands.

▶ HISTORY

The peoples that lived in the area of the Netherlands—Frisians, Batavi, Belgae—came under Roman rule in the 1st century B.C. and later became a part of the Frankish empire under Charlemagne. After Charlemagne died in 814, his empire was split up. Through marriage, inheritance, and war, the French dukes of Burgundy united most of the Low Countries (including what are now the Netherlands and Belgium) beginning in the 1300's.

Habsburg and Spanish Rule. In 1477, Mary of Burgundy married Maximilian of Habsburg, who was later elected Holy Roman emperor. Their son Philip took as his wife

A self-portrait (1887) of the Dutch postimpressionist painter Vincent van Gogh.

Joanna of Castile (known as Joan the Mad), the future queen of Spain. The emperor Charles V, a son of Philip and Joanna, inherited all the Habsburg possessions, including the Low Countries, Spain, and Austria. When Charles abdicated (gave up the throne) in 1555, he left Spain and the Low Countries to his eldest son, King Philip II of Spain.

The Dutch Revolt. A revolt against King Philip's rule broke out in the Low Countries in 1566. It was sparked by opposition to his efforts to suppress Protestantism, which had won many supporters, and by his policies, which favored Spain. The leader of the rebellion was William I, Count of Nassau and Prince of Orange (known as William the Silent), the greatest nobleman in the Low Countries. Armies sent by Philip were able to put down the rebellion in the southern part of the Low Countries (present-day Belgium), but the rebels held out in the north.

The Dutch Republic. In 1579 the northerners formed an alliance called the Union of Utrecht, and in 1581 they declared their independence from Philip II. After William the Silent was assassinated in 1584, the northern provinces won their independence as the Dutch Republic. But except for the Twelve

Years' Truce (1609–21), the war continued until Spain recognized Dutch independence in 1648 at the end of the Thirty Years' War. Leadership of the country remained largely with William the Silent's descendants, as stadholders (governors) of the republic.

The Golden Age. In the 1600's, the republic entered an era of great prosperity, power, and artistic achievement. It was Europe's leading commercial nation and its greatest sea power. The Dutch soon established settlements and colonies around the world—in the Dutch East Indies (present-day Indonesia) and other parts of Asia, Africa, South America, the Caribbean, and North America. On Manhattan Island they founded New Amsterdam, which later became New York City. Science, art, and literature flourished, along with commerce.

Decline and Invasion. By the end of the century, Dutch power had begun a slow decline, following wars with England and France. Relations with England improved under the stadholder William III, who, as husband of the English queen Mary II, became king of England in 1688. He ruled England jointly with his wife, while keeping his office of stadholder in the Netherlands.

The economic and political strength of the Netherlands declined further in the 1700's. In 1795, during the French Revolution, French troops occupied the country, which was renamed the Batavian Republic. In 1806 the French emperor Napoleon I made his brother Louis king of Holland and then absorbed it into the French Empire.

Kingdom of the Netherlands. After the Dutch defeated Napoleon in 1813, the Netherlands regained its independence, becoming a constitutional monarchy under the House of Orange. It was united with Belgium in 1815, but after a revolt by the Belgians in 1830–31, Belgium became a separate nation. With the adoption of a liberal constitution in 1848, political power passed from the

Queen Beatrix, shown here with her son Prince Willem-Alexander, has ruled the Netherlands since 1980.

monarch to the legislators in the States General.

The Netherlands remained neutral in World War I (1914–18) and World War II (1939–45). Nevertheless, the country was invaded by Nazi Germany in 1940. There was much suffering and destruction, and the last months of the war were marked by near-famine in the cities. More than 100,000 Dutch Jews were killed by the Nazis.

After the war, with aid from the United States under the Marshall Plan, the Dutch people rebuilt their country and its economy. The Netherlands East Indies, its richest colony, became independent as the Republic of Indonesia in 1949. They retained control of Irian Jaya (now Papua), on the island of New Guinea, until 1962. The former colony of Dutch Guiana in South America won its independence as the Republic of Suriname in 1975.

The Netherlands formed an economic union with Belgium and Luxembourg (called Benelux) in 1948. It was one of the original members of the European Economic Community, or Common Market, created in 1957. **Recent Events.** In the 1970's, the mining of petroleum in the North Sea and natural gas in the northern province of Groningen began providing the Netherlands with additional sources of income, which enabled the Dutch government to improve and expand its social welfare services. These benefits, which include national health care and social security, are among the most generous in Europe.

ANTHONY SAS
University of South Carolina
Reviewed by JOHAN P. SNAPPER
University of California, Berkeley

NETHERLANDS, ART OF THE. See DUTCH AND FLEMISH ART.

NETHERLANDS, MUSIC OF THE. See DUTCH AND FLEMISH MUSIC.

NEUHARTH, ALLEN. See JOURNALISM (Profiles).

NEUTRALITY. See INTERNATIONAL RELATIONS.

NEUTRON STARS. See PULSARS; STARS.

NEVADA

Nevada, located in the western region of the United States, is named for the Sierra Nevada, a mountain range that lies between Nevada and California. In Spanish, the word Nevada means "snow-clad" or "snowy."

In the mid-1800's, Nevada was considered little more than an obstacle blocking the western route to the gold mines of California. Then in 1859, silver ore was discovered near the site of what is now Virginia City. Suddenly, Nevada's population exploded with miners, prospectors, and speculators who came to exploit the fabulous silver and gold deposits, known as the Comstock Lode. Nevada became the richest silver-mining area in the world and was later nicknamed the Silver State.

In 1864, toward the end of the Civil War, Nevada achieved statehood to add weight to the Union side. Consequently, the state slogan is Battle Born.

State flag

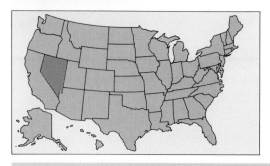

Nevada is a mountain state that is situated on a vast, high plateau dominated by numerous mountain ranges running north and south. It was once noted that from the sky, these mountains looked like an "army of caterpillars crawling toward Mexico." The basins between the mountains contain lakes or dry lake beds. Several areas are known for hot springs and geysers. The few rivers that do exist are used to irrigate the scant lowlands, where sheep and cattle graze.

Nevada is the driest state in the nation. Although it is typically known for an inhospitable terrain of rocky canyons and hot, sandy deserts, the landscape also includes occasional grassy valleys as well as snow-capped mountain peaks. Some of the mountains are covered with forests of pine, while others have scanty piñon and juniper groves that need little water to survive. The creosote bush—a tall, slender-trunked shrub with glossy leaves—grows in southern Nevada. When it blooms in the spring, its bright lemon yellow flowers richly color the landscape. Sagebrush is so abundant, Nevada is often called the Sagebrush State.

Nevada is the seventh largest of the fifty states, and more than 85 percent of the land is owned by the federal government. Much of this land has been set aside for use as national forests, military ranges and bases, and reservations for Nevada's Native American

population. Roughly 80 percent of Nevada's population lives on just 4 percent of the land, in and around the state's two major cities—Reno and Las Vegas.

Tourism is by far Nevada's most important industry. Every year Nevada draws nearly 30 million visitors, most of whom head for Reno or Las Vegas, where gambling casinos are open 24 hours a day. Las Vegas, with its added lure of world-class resort hotels and nightclub entertainment, is known as the Entertainment Capital of the World. Those who prefer more tranquil recreational activity can go camping in Nevada's state parks or enjoy the solitude of the high desert country. Still others prefer the winter sports activities found in the mountain resorts or the special annual events sponsored across the state. Among the most popular are the Reno Rodeo and the National Rodeo Finals in Las Vegas, the Cowboy Poetry Gathering in Elko, Kit Carson Days in Carson City, Frontier Days in Lovelock, and the Basque festivals in Reno and Elko.

▶THE LAND

Nevada is the most westerly of the mountain states. When most people think of Nevada, they think of a wide stretch of desert with few

Flowering cacti create a colorful spectacle in the dry, rocky landscape of Nevada's Lake Mead National Recreation Area. Glittering lights on the Las Vegas Strip welcome millions of tourists annually to the gambling capital of the West. Wild horses called mustangs roam Nevada's Basin and Range region.

FACTS AND FIGURES

Location: Western United States; bordered on the north by Oregon and Idaho, on the east by Utah and Arizona, on the south by Arizona and California, and on the west by California.

Area: 110,567 sq mi (286,367 km2); rank, 7th.

Population: 1,998,257 (2000 census); rank, 35th.

Elevation: Highest—Boundary Peak, 13,140 ft (4,005 m) on the California border; lowest—470 ft (143 m) on the Colorado River in Clark County.

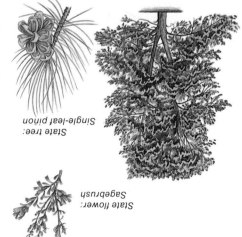

State tree: Single-leaf pinon

State flower: Sagebrush

Capital: Carson City.

Statehood: October 31, 1864; 36th state.

State Motto: All for our country.

State Song: "Home Means Nevada."

Nickname: Silver State; Sagebrush State.

Abbreviations: NV; Nev.

State bird: Mountain bluebird

surface landmarks. However, in addition to its desert lands, Nevada contains snowcapped mountains and some grassy valleys.

Land Regions

Most of Nevada lies within a large natural region of the western United States known as the Basin and Range. Small parts of other natural regions extend into the state, including the Columbia Plateau in the northeast and the Sierra Nevada in the west.

The Basin and Range is an enormous region that covers most of Nevada and, indeed, much of the western United States. In Nevada, the Basin and Range can be divided into two parts: the Great Basin and the Sonoran Desert. Both are mountainous desert areas.

The Sonoran Desert occupies a small area in the extreme southern tip of Nevada. The Great Basin extends from the Wasatch Range in central Utah to the Sierra Nevada in California. It contains a series of short, rugged mountain ranges that have flat basins between them. The higher ranges include the Ruby Mountains in the northeast, the Toiyabe Range in central

Nevada, and the White Mountains in the southwest. Boundary Peak in the White Mountains is the highest point in the state. It rises 13,140 feet (4,005 meters) above sea level. The basins between the ranges are generally flat and dry. The centers of the basins are called sinks. Sometimes they are occupied by shallow salty lakes. When these lakes dry up, the mud usually makes a smooth, hard surface. It is said that the surface is sometimes so hard that horses' hooves clatter as on a paved road.

The Columbia Plateau is another large region of the western United States, but only a small portion of it extends into northeastern Nevada from Idaho. This plateau region is made up of thick sheets of lava. In some places steep-walled canyons cut into the surface of the land, but in other places, the surface is flat to rolling.

The Sierra Nevada, the mountain range from which Nevada takes its name, actually lies mostly within the boundaries of the state of California. Only a few spurs of the Sierra Nevada—such as the Carson Range—extend into Nevada. In general, the mountains in this region are rugged and steep sided. At the base of the mountains are numerous hot springs.

Rivers and Lakes

Many of Nevada's basins have no permanent lakes or streams, especially in the drier central and southern parts of the state. Temporary lakes may form in these basins when rain flows down from the mountains.

Melting snow from the higher mountains provides the main source of water for Nevada's permanent rivers and streams. The Humboldt River is Nevada's longest permanent river. It rises in the northeast and flows westward across the state. Other permanent waterways are the Truckee, the Carson, and the Walker rivers in western Nevada and the Reese River in the central part of the state. The Colorado River, flowing southward to the Gulf of Mexico, forms much of Nevada's boundary with Arizona in the southeast.

Western Nevada has a number of natural lakes. Beautiful Pyramid Lake is fed by the Truckee River. Lake Tahoe, on the border be-

Nevada is the driest state in the nation. High temperatures bake the desert sands of the Basin and Range region, which covers most of the state.

tween Nevada and California, is surrounded by the forested slopes of the Sierra Nevada. Walker Lake is situated at the outflow point of the Walker River.

Nevada and Arizona share Lake Mead, the largest artificial lake by volume in the United States. It was created by Hoover Dam on the Colorado River. Davis Dam, on the Colorado River below Hoover Dam, forms Lake Mohave. The dams provide hydroelectric power. The lakes are part of a national recreation area. Most of the towns and smaller cities in Nevada obtain their water from wells. Las Vegas now gets most of its water from the Colorado River. Reno uses the Truckee River.

Climate

Nevada's annual rainfall is only 4 inches (100 millimeters), although some of its highest mountain peaks may receive up to 60 inches (152 centimeters) of snow. Storms traveling eastward from the Pacific Coast drop most of their rain and snow before they reach Nevada. The little rain or snow that does fall comes chiefly in winter and spring.

Nevada's dry and sunny climate is characterized by wide fluctuations in daily temperatures. Summertime temperatures depend on both latitude and elevation. Northern areas generally are cooler than southern areas. Higher elevations are cooler than lower elevations. Average July temperatures range from 86°F (30°C) in the south to 71°F (22°C) in the northwest. Winters in the western and central areas are fairly cold. Winters in the north and northeast are somewhat longer and colder but with much sunny weather. January temperatures in the northwest average 30°F (−1°C). Winters in the south are short, mild, and generally sunny. January temperatures there average 43°F (6°C).

In most parts of northern and central Nevada, frosts often begin in late September and continue into the early part of May. As a result there is a relatively short season for the growing of crops. Most of the agricultural areas

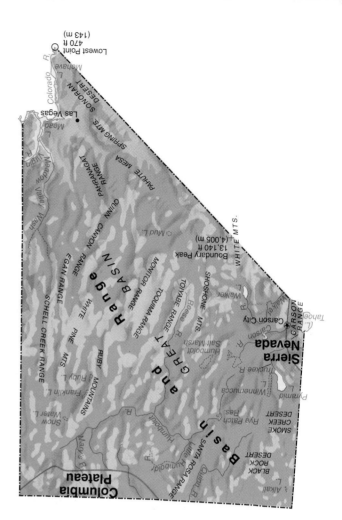

NEVADA Landforms

⊛ State capital
● Largest city
+ Highest point
○ Lowest point
— Landform boundary

0 20 40 60 80 100 mi
0 20 40 60 80 100 km

15,000 ft (4,500 m)
6,000 ft (1,800 m)
3,000 ft (900 m)
1,500 ft (450 m)
600 ft (180 m)
300 ft (90 m)
Sea Level
Below

Lake Tahoe is a popular resort area shared by Nevada and California. Formed by ancient glaciers, it is one of the deepest lakes on the North American continent.

Places of Interest

Nevada State Railroad Museum, Carson City

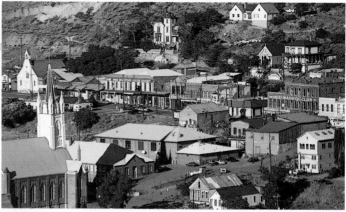

Virginia City

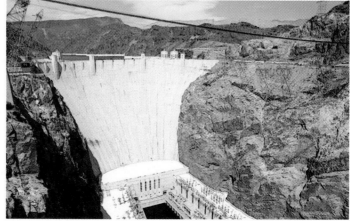

Hoover Dam

One of Nevada's slogans is "Recreation Unlimited." Ghost towns and resort cities, national and state recreation areas, and a variety of natural wonders attract millions of visitors each year.

Berlin-Ichthyosaur State Park, east of Gabbs, contains the silver-mining ghost town of Berlin. Also nearby are fossil remains of ancient sea-dwelling dinosaurs that once lived there.

Cathedral Gorge State Park, near Pioche, is known for towering cliffs that enclose a long, narrow valley. Wind and water have carved the cliffs into fantastic shapes, with some resembling cathedral spires or skyscrapers. Others seem to be likenesses of people or animals.

Fort Churchill Historical State Monument, northeast of Carson City, preserves the ruins of the first military post in Nevada, built in 1860. For a brief period the fort served as a station for the Pony Express and the telegraph. It was abandoned in 1871.

Lake Mead National Recreation Area, shared by Nevada and Arizona, extends about 240 miles (385 kilometers) along both sides of the Colorado River. This part of the Nevada-Arizona border includes Lake Mead and Lake Mohave. Along these lakes are many recreation centers, where people can camp, swim, water-ski, sail, and fish. The area includes **Hoover Dam**, an achievement of engineering. Elevators take visitors deep into the 726-foot (221-meter) dam to see the power plant at the base. Hoover Dam was completed in 1936. For a time it was known as Boulder Dam.

Las Vegas Strip, the major traffic artery running through Las Vegas, is lined with many of the world's most famous resort hotels and casinos. Flashing lights and neon signs give this avenue a unique and festive atmosphere.

Lehman Caves National Monument includes an area of caverns on the eastern flank of Wheeler Peak in eastern Nevada. The underground chambers and tunnels contain tall limestone columns and interesting formations. The national monument and Wheeler Peak, which is the second highest point in Nevada, are in the heart of Wheeler Peak Scenic Area.

Nevada State Railroad Museum, in Carson City, displays memorabilia from the Virginia & Truckee Railroad.

Pyramid Lake, Nevada's largest natural lake, is located on an Indian reservation northeast of Reno. When John C. Frémont first came across the lake in 1844, he named it for the pyramid-shaped rock that rises above the water. An island in the lake, Anaho Island, is a federal bird refuge. It is known for its sparkling blue waters in a desert setting.

Valley of Fire State Park is located in a scenic basin in the Lake Mead area. The park gets its name from red sandstone cliffs and rocks that have been eroded into strange shapes. At sunset the whole area takes on a reddish hue. Some of the rocks have carvings made by prehistoric peoples. There are also some petrified remains of ancient forest trees.

Virginia City, northeast of Carson City, is perhaps the most famous old mining town in the world. It was settled in 1859, when silver was discovered in the Comstock Lode. For the next 30 years its mines produced nearly $750 million worth of silver and gold. After the mines were exhausted, most of the people abandoned the city. Some of the buildings decayed, but many houses, saloons, banks, and stores remain.

State Recreation Areas. Numerous national forests, national and state parks, historic monuments, and other recreation areas make Nevada an interesting state to visit. For more information, write to the Nevada Commission on Tourism, P.O. Box 30032, Reno, Nevada 89520.

Left: Desert primroses beautify the land near Lake Mohave in southeastern Nevada.
Right: Turquoise, a popular blue-green gemstone, is mined throughout the state.

Plant and Animal Life

Nevada has a wide variety of plants and animals. Much of southern Nevada is covered by two kinds of shrub, creosote bush and burrowed. Blackbrush, mesquite, and Joshua trees are also plentiful. Various species of pine, including the single-leaf piñon, the state tree, dominate the state's woodlands. At elevations above 5,000 feet (1,500 meters) in central and western Nevada, the ever-present plant is sagebrush, with its dull green, sage-scented leaves. Among the most common wildflowers are Indian paintbrush, desert lilies, and violets.

Nevada's animal life includes wild horses, white-tailed and mule deer, pronghorn antelope, bighorn sheep, mountain lions, bobcats, elk, coyotes, rabbits, and porcupines. The state's leading game birds are sage grouse, chukar partridge, pheasant, quail, geese, and ducks. Snakes and lizards thrive in the hot desert climates. Nevada's lakes and rivers support trout, char, salmon, whitefish, suckers, and bass.

Natural Resources

Metal ores have long been Nevada's most important mineral resource. The state has been known through the years for its gold and silver as well as for copper, iron, molybdenum, mercury, and tungsten.

Nonmetallic minerals that are mined in Nevada include barite, sand and gravel, limestone, gypsum, marble, sandstone, magnesite, and diatomite. Some petroleum is found in east central Nevada.

Nevada lacks other significant natural resources. There are some pockets of fertile grazing lands and productive soils in the valleys. Natural reservoirs of hot water beneath the land are potential sources of solar and geothermal energy. Only about 12 percent of Nevada is naturally forested. The most common trees are piñon and juniper, which are cut for fence posts and firewood.

have between 100 and 140 frost-free days. Southern Nevada has a much longer growing season. There, most areas at lower elevations have 200 or more days free of frost.

Pyramid Lake, named for its striking rock formation, is a remnant of Lake Lahontan, an immense glacial lake that covered much of western Nevada thousands of years ago.

Families can enjoy a wide variety of outdoor activities in Nevada. Rodeos (*above*) are a particularly popular form of western entertainment. Major rodeo events are held in Reno (in June) and in Las Vegas (in December).

▶ **PEOPLE**

In recent decades, Nevada's population has grown more rapidly than any other state's. Most of Nevada's nearly 2 million residents live in Clark County, where Las Vegas is located, and in Washoe County, where Reno is located. Vast areas of the state have almost no permanent population.

Prior to the discovery of gold and silver in 1859, about 10,000 Native Americans resided in what is now Nevada. Then miners, teamsters, artisans, and businesspeople crowded into mining towns, and farmers came to the river valleys to produce food for the townspeople. By 1870, Nevada's population exceeded 40,000.

About half of the newcomers were born in foreign countries. Many were Irish, Canadian, English, German, Scottish, or Welsh. In the early 1900's, people came from eastern and southern Europe as well as from Mexico to work in the copper mines and mills. Basques from the Pyrenees mountain regions of France and Spain came to herd sheep, while Italians and Portuguese came to farm. After

World War II ended in 1945, most of the newcomers came from other states, particularly from other western states.

Today about 85 percent of Nevadans are of European or Mexican ancestry. About 7 percent are African Americans. The remaining 8 percent are mostly Native Americans, Asians, and Pacific Islanders. Nevada's Native American population is made up of Shoshoni, Washo, Goshute, and northern and southern Paiute. Many live on the seven reservations and smaller Indian colonies set aside for their use by the federal government. Most of these are located in northern Nevada.

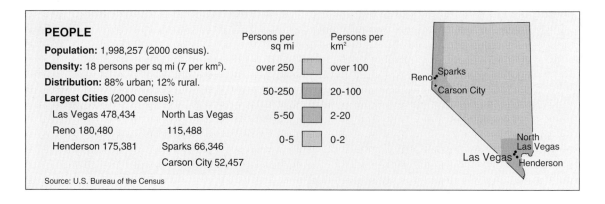

PEOPLE

Population: 1,998,257 (2000 census).

Density: 18 persons per sq mi (7 per km²).

Distribution: 88% urban; 12% rural.

Largest Cities (2000 census):

Las Vegas 478,434	North Las Vegas
Reno 180,480	115,488
Henderson 175,381	Sparks 66,346
	Carson City 52,457

Source: U.S. Bureau of the Census

Persons per sq mi	Persons per km²
over 250	over 100
50-250	20-100
5-50	2-20
0-5	0-2

Education

When Nevada became a territory in 1861, the laws provided for a public school system supported by county taxation. School districts were established after Nevada became a state in 1864. The larger towns were able to maintain schools, but many rural districts lacked money and teachers. A law of 1907 provided for a state superintendent of public instruction as well as a new district system. Today, although few in number, the public schools provide good facilities and instruction.

The University of Nevada was established at Elko in 1874 and moved to Reno in 1885. It has long been known for its mining division, the Mackay School of Mines, and for its renowned Desert Research Institute. A second branch campus was established in 1955 in Las Vegas. Various community colleges are located in Carson City, Elko, Sparks, and North Las Vegas.

The University of Nevada has two campuses offering four-year programs. The larger campus, in Las Vegas (below), enrolls more than 10,000 students annually.

Libraries and Museums

The cities and some of the larger towns in Nevada have public libraries. The Nevada State Library in Carson City contains more than 300,000 books and government documents, including a valuable law collection. The library of the Nevada Historical Society in Reno contains important historical records. The libraries of the University of Nevada have large general and special collections.

Nevada has several interesting museums. The Nevada State Museum in Carson City is located in a historic building that once was used by the United States Mint. Tunnels beneath the building contain mining exhibits. Natural history and Native American artifacts also are on display. The Nevada Historical Society Museum in Reno contains pioneer clothing and furnishings, primitive paintings, Indian baskets, cattle brands, and other items of historical interest. The museum of the Mackay School of Mines, also in Reno, has extensive mineral and rock collections. Exhibits there also show the history of mining in the state. The Las Vegas Museum of Natural History features animated dinosaur exhibits. The Lost City Museum in Overton features the culture of the ancient Pueblo Indians who once lived in the area.

Native American powwows, such as this one held in Carson City, provide a forum for Nevada's native peoples to display their cultural traditions.

▶ECONOMY

Until the mid-1900's, mining and agriculture were Nevada's chief sources of income. However, ever since gambling was legalized in the state in 1931, vacationers have poured into the state by the millions, making tourism Nevada's number one industry.

Services

About half of Nevada's workforce is employed in tourist-related services, and more than 80 percent of the state's annual revenues are generated by the services provided to tourists. Such services include the operation of hotels, motels, restaurants, gambling casinos, nightclubs, and other entertainment, amusement, and recreation centers, including ski resorts, hunting and fishing areas, and facilities for boating and waterskiing. The federal government, which staffs Nevada's national parks and military installations, is also a major employer.

Manufacturing

Nevada is one of the least industrialized states in the nation. Manufacturing accounts for relatively little of the state's overall economy. Nevada once was concerned chiefly with the processing of minerals and of agricultural products. Today's factories manufacture electronic and computer equipment, such as gaming machines for use in casinos, neon signs, building materials, construction equipment, printed materials, and food products.

Agriculture

About one-tenth of the land area of Nevada is dedicated to ranching and farming. The main agricultural areas are in the northern and western counties, which have the best grazing lands and the most water for irrigation. The chief agricultural products of the state are cattle and calves, milk, hay, alfalfa, potatoes, and sheep and lambs.

Below: Sheep graze on Nevada's rangelands. *Right:* Slot machines are a popular casino game. Players deposit coins and pull the lever, hoping to "hit the jackpot."

PRODUCTS AND INDUSTRIES

Manufacturing: Electronic and computer equipment, building materials, construction equipment, printed materials, food products.

Agriculture: Cattle and calves, milk, hay, alfalfa, potatoes, sheep and lambs.

Minerals: Gold, barite, diatomite, petroleum, sand and gravel, mercury, gypsum, clays, stone, silver.

Services: Wholesale and retail trade; finance, insurance, and real estate; business, social, and personal services; transportation, communication, and utilities; government.

*Gross state product is the total value of goods and services produced in a year.

Percentage of Gross State Product* by Industry

Agriculture 1%
Manufacturing 4%
Mining 6%
Construction 6%
Transportation, communication, and utilities 9%
Government 10%
Wholesale and retail trade 13%
Finance, insurance, and real estate 16%
Business, social, and personal services 35%

Source: U.S. Bureau of Economic Analysis

The long growing season in the extreme southern part of the state enables farmers there to grow cotton and a variety of fruits and vege-tables. Special products of other areas include cantaloupes, grown in the Fallon area, and po-tatoes, grown near Winnemucca.

Mining and Construction

Nevada leads the nation in the production of several valuable minerals, including gold, silver, barite, and mercury. Most of the gold, which accounts for two-thirds of the nation's total production, is mined in the north and central parts of the state. Silver is more plenti-ful in the southwest. Nevada is also a leading producer of diatomite, a chalky substance used in filters. Gemstones, especially turquoise and fire opals, also are mined throughout the state.

Nevada has a steady construction industry. In addition to the building and repair of roads, bridges, and dams, new tourist facilities, such as hotels, restaurants, and the like, are con-stantly under construction or renovation.

Transportation

Despite its large size and relatively small population, Nevada's state road system is ex-cellent, and major federal highways cross the state in both east and west and north and south directions.

Railroads came to Nevada in 1868, when the Central Pacific Railroad was built eastward through the Humboldt Valley. The Central Pa-cific Railroad accelerated economic develop-ment and created such communities as Reno, Wadsworth, and Elko. It also enabled ranchers and the lumber industry to develop markets outside the state. Today Nevada's most im-portant railroads are the Union Pacific and the Southern Pacific, which serve mainly as carriers of freight. The major airports are Reno-Cannon, serving Reno, and McCarran International in Las Vegas.

Communication

Nevada's first newspaper, the *Territorial Enterprise*, was first published in Genoa in 1858. The two newspapers with the largest circulations today are the *Las Vegas Review-Journal* and the *Reno Gazette-Journal*. Some of the larger towns also have dailies. There are more than half a dozen television stations and more than 60 radio stations in the state.

◀ CITIES

Nevada has limited numbers of cities and towns. Las Vegas and Reno are by far the largest cities. About 80 percent of the state's total population lives in either of these two metropolitan areas.

Carson City, Nevada's capital city, is located in Eagle Valley, near Lake Tahoe in western Nevada. Founded in 1858, the city was named in honor of Kit Carson, who guided John C. Frémont through that section of the Great Basin on an expedition in 1844. In 1861 it was named the capital of the Nevada Territory. It became the permanent capital when Nevada achieved statehood in 1864.

The original capitol building, built in the 1870's, is one of the city's many points of interest. Others include the Nevada State Mu-seum, the Nevada State Library, and a number of handsome Victorian houses.

Las Vegas, Nevada's largest city, is one of the most popular tourist centers in the world, known for its nightclubs, gambling casinos, and resort hotels. More than half the employed people of Las Vegas serve the needs of tour-ists. Las Vegas is also the home of the Univer-sity of Nevada at Las Vegas.

Las Vegas was once a stop on the Old Span-ish Trail between Santa Fe and Los Angeles. The Mormons settled on the site of the present city in 1855 but moved away two years later. Only ranches and a small settlement remained. Growth became more rapid after the San Pedro, Los Angeles & Salt Lake Railroad fin-ished construction in 1905. The population in-creased again in the 1930's when the city served as construction headquarters for the Hoover Dam.

Reno, which lies at the foot of the Sierra Nevada, is the principal city of western Nevada. It was the state's largest city until Las Vegas surpassed it in the 1950's.

Nevada's state capitol building in Carson City has a silver dome. Carson City was the capital of the Nevada Territory before it became the state capital in 1864.

Reno is located on the Truckee River at the foot of the Sierra Nevada in western Nevada. It was the largest city in the state until the 1950's, when Las Vegas surpassed it in population. Reno is the principal trading center for northwestern Nevada. It is also a tourist center, known for its gambling casinos and resort hotels. Winter sports are enjoyed on nearby Mount Rose and Slide Mountain and in the Lake Tahoe area. Products manufactured in Reno include building materials, processed foods, and communications equipment. The University of Nevada at Reno is located north of the business district.

Reno was the site of Paiute and Washo Indian communities. Pioneers founded the city in 1868 when it became a stop on the Central Pacific Railroad line. They named it in honor of Jesse Lee Reno, a Union general, who was killed in a Civil War battle.

▶ **GOVERNMENT**

The constitution of Nevada was adopted in 1864, less than two months before Nevada achieved statehood. Today the state is governed under the basic terms of this constitution, which has since been amended.

The constitution created an executive branch headed by a governor and lieutenant governor. Other elected executive branch officials include a secretary of state, treasurer, and attorney general. The legislative branch of

GOVERNMENT

State Government

Governor: 4-year term
State senators: 21; 4-year terms
State representatives: 42;
   2-year terms
Number of counties: 16 plus 1
   independent city (Carson City)

Federal Government

U.S. senators: 2
U.S. representatives: 3
Number of electoral votes: 5

For the name of the current governor, see STATE GOVERNMENTS in Volume S. For the names of current U.S. senators and representatives, see UNITED STATES, CONGRESS OF THE in Volume U-V.

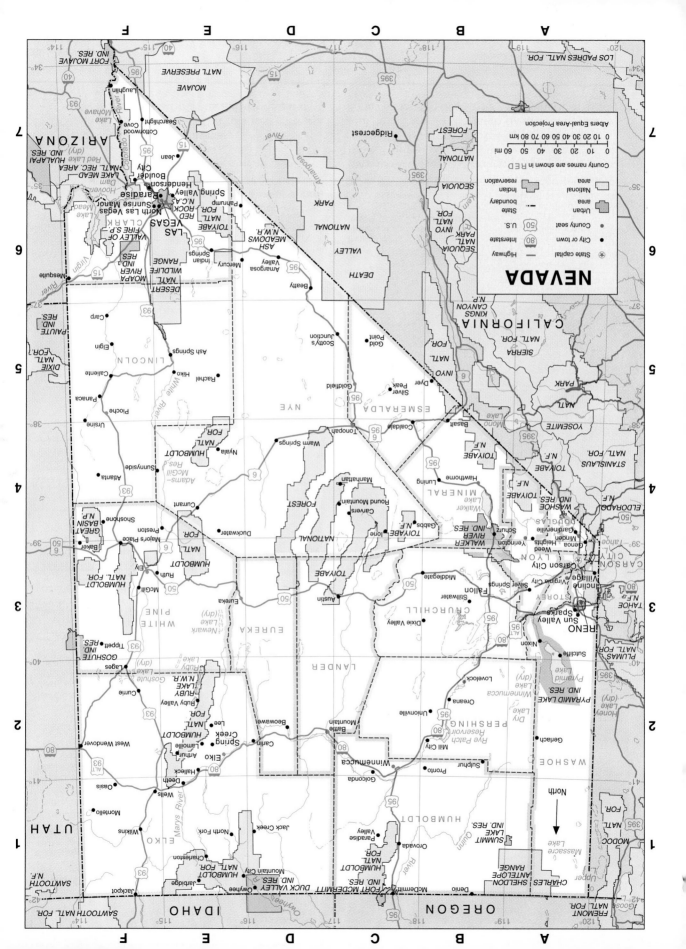

NEVADA

Albers Equal-Area Projection

County names are shown in RED

⊛ State capital		Highway	
● City or town	80 Interstate		National area
● County seat	50 U.S.	State boundary	Urban area
			Indian reservation

Famous People

Sarah Winnemucca Hopkins (1844?–91) (Indian name: Tocmetone, meaning "shell flower") was born near Lovelock. The daughter of the Paiute chief Winnemucca and the granddaughter of the chief Truckee, she served as an Indian interpreter for the U.S. Army during the Bannock War of 1878. Later she became the leading advocate for the rights of Nevada's native population. She wrote a best-selling book, *Life Among the Piutes* [sic] (1883), in which she described the suffering imposed on the Indians by the white settlers. She also tried, but was unsuccessful, in negotiating the return of Paiute lands to her people. In 1883 she established a school for Indian children in Lovelock, but white hostility forced her to settle in Montana, where she died.

Howard Robard Hughes (1905–76), born in Houston, Texas, was a businessman, aviator, and movie producer, who at one time owned RKO Studios, Hughes Aircraft Company, and a controlling interest in Trans-World Airlines (TWA). During World War II, Hughes built a prototype war plane, the *Spruce Goose*, with the largest wingspan ever attempted. The

Howard Hughes

plane, which was flown only once, strengthened Hughes's reputation as an eccentric millionaire. In the 1950's, he retreated to Las Vegas, where he owned substantial interests in casinos and nightclubs. His fame grew even more in his later years due to the mystery surrounding his whereabouts, business dealings, and his reportedly bizarre personal habits. Although it has been said he was worth billions, he left no legally valid will when he died.

John William Mackay (1831–1902) was the most famous of the Comstock mine owners. Born in Dublin, Ireland, he immigrated with his family to the United States in 1840. As a boy, Mackay worked in a shipyard in New York City. In 1851 he went to California as a miner. From there he joined the rush to Virginia City. He grew fabulously wealthy when a rich deposit of ore, known as the Big Bonanza, was discovered in 1873 in mines that he owned with James C. Flood, Wil-

---

the government is made up of a senate and an assembly. Members meet in regular sessions in January of odd-numbered years. Special legislative sessions may be called by the governor. The judicial branch of the state government is headed by the Nevada Supreme Court. Below it are the district courts and the municipal and justice courts.

▶ **HISTORY**

Nevada has been inhabited for at least 13,000 years. The earliest natives were the Northern and Southern Paiute, Shoshoni, Washo, and Goshute Indian groups. These prehistoric peoples were big-game hunters, who largely depended on mammoth, bison, and other large mammals for their food. With the eventual extinction of big game, these early native peoples had to rely even more on gathering roots, plants, and seeds; hunting smaller animals; and fishing.

Exploration and Settlement

In the 1500's, Spain claimed a vast territory in the New World that included present-day

Petroglyphs, the artistic legacy of Nevada's earliest native inhabitants, decorate stone cave walls in Valley of Fire State Park, Nevada's largest state park.

Nevada. Some historians believe the Spanish may have explored Nevada, but there are no records of such expeditions.

The first recorded expedition in Nevada took place in 1826, after the territory had come under Mexican rule. An American fur trader named Jedediah Smith traveled along the Colorado River border of Nevada on his way to California. On the return trip in 1827, he used a route through central Nevada.

The Canadian trapper Peter Skene Ogden probably entered northeastern Nevada in 1825. In 1828 he discovered the river now known as the Humboldt. Other explorations were made by Joseph Walker in 1833-34 and by John C. Frémont in 1843-44 and 1845-46. During this period, traders from Santa Fe, New Mexico, traveled through southern Nevada on their way to California.

In 1848 the area that is now Nevada was included in lands ceded to the United States by Mexico at the end of the Mexican War. That same year, gold was discovered in California. By 1849, a rush of gold seekers called the forty-niners crossed Nevada on their way to California. Mormons from Utah and other settlers established trading posts to supply the travelers with animals and food. A post in the Carson Valley called Mormon Station (which was renamed Genoa in 1855) became the first permanent settlement in Nevada. Most of present-day Nevada became part of Utah Territory in 1850. In 1855 a mission was established by the Mormons in Las Vegas Valley.

The Nevada Territory

In 1859 rich silver and gold deposits, known as the Comstock Lode, were discovered near present-day Virginia City. Nevada developed rapidly as Virginia City and other mining centers grew up. Roads were built between these centers and over the mountains to California. In 1861, Congress separated Nevada from Utah and established the Nevada Territory with Carson City as the capital.

Statehood

Shortly after Nevada became a territory, the nation was plunged into civil war between the slaves states and the antislavery states. Nevada did not yet have the required population for statehood, but the Union needed additional an-tislavery states to support President Abraham Lincoln and his war policies, his bid for a second term, and his efforts to pass an anti-slavery amendment to the Constitution. In

---

liam S. O'Brien, and James G. Fair. Later, Mackay moved to New York and turned to other financial undertakings. His wife and son were major benefactors of the University of Nevada.

Patrick Anthony McCarran (1876-1954), born on a ranch near Reno, was a powerful U.S. senator who for many years controlled Nevada politics. One of the state's leading attorneys, he served as associate justice (1913-17) and chief justice (1917-18) of the Nevada Supreme Court. In 1932 he was elected to the U.S. Senate, where he served until his death. In 1950, while chairman of the Senate Judiciary Committee, McCarran sponsored the Internal Security Act (1950). Otherwise known as the McCarran Act, the new law sought to eliminate the alleged Communist threat in the United States during the Cold War era.

William Morris Stewart (1827-1909), born in Galen, New York, came to Nevada in 1859 to practice law. Before that time, he had attended college in the East and had worked as a miner in California. He had also practiced law in California and served as attorney general of that state. In Nevada he was active in the organization of the territorial government and was elected to the U.S. Senate in 1864. Stewart was a specialist in mining law. He was always interested in the problems of miners and sponsored legislation in their favor. He is known especially as the author of the 15th Amendment to the U.S. Constitution, which guaranteed the voting rights of African American men.

Wovoka (1856?-1932), born in Lyon County, was known among whites as Jack Wilson. He was a prophet of the Paiute Indians and founder of the Ghost Dance religion among the Basin and Plains Indians. Between 1887 and 1889, Wovoka claimed he had visions in which he was instructed to teach the Indian peoples a sacred dance to be performed at regular intervals. If they did so, supposedly in the spring the Great Spirit would return and raise the dead; a flood would wipe out the white community; and the bison would return to the plains. Then the Indians could resume the lives they had once known, before the whites had invaded their lands. Attempts by the U.S. government to suppress the Ghost Dance, which had spread to other tribes, led to the Indian massacre at Wounded Knee, South Dakota, in 1890.

Sarah Winnemucca Hopkins

Wovoka

In 1931, Nevada legalized gambling. The state also boasted the most relaxed divorce laws in the nation. Someone once said, "If you can't do it at home, go to Nevada."

1863 a convention met at Carson City to draft a state constitution. A second draft was approved by the voters. In order to meet the filing deadline, the entire document was telegraphed to Washington, D.C., at a staggering cost of $3,416.77. On October 31, 1864, President Lincoln proclaimed Nevada the 36th state of the Union.

By 1868 a railroad, the Central Pacific, was completed across the northern part of the state. Nevada prospered while it was profitable to mine silver, but the price of silver soon declined. During the 1880's many mines closed, and thousands of people left Nevada.

In the early 1900's, new mineral deposits were discovered at Tonopah, Goldfield, and several other places. During the period 1900 to 1910, the population of Nevada almost doubled, but by 1918, many of the mines again had closed. By this time interest was shifting from silver and gold to other forms of mineral wealth, such as copper, lead, and zinc. Farming and ranching areas made important advances. Dams were built to store water for irrigation, and more land was cultivated. Reno, Elko, Las Vegas, Fallon, and other towns grew rapidly.

Modern Times

The modern era in Nevada began in the 1930's with the construction of Hoover Dam and the development of an improved system of roads. Tourist travel became significant for the first time.

Another important development was the increase of United States government activities in Nevada. Several naval and air force installations were established after 1941 when the United States entered World War II. Nuclear testing, which began in Nevada in 1951, was later restricted to underground sites.

Tourism developed steadily through the late 1900's, and there is little doubt that trade and the service industries will continue to be important as the state's population grows. Among the most important issues facing Nevadans today are the conservation of its resources and control of air and water pollution. The federal government, which owns most of Nevada's land, has taken measures to help conserve Nevada's resources. For example, to improve the condition of the rangelands, the U.S. Forest Service and the U.S. Bureau of Land Management have reduced the number of animals that they will allow to graze on a range, and at the same time, they have raised the grazing fees that they charge the ranchers. In addition, the state is continually seeking ways to increase Nevada's water supplies and to use them more efficiently.

EARL W. KERSTEN
University of Nevada at Reno
Reviewed by PHILLIP I. EARL
Curator of History, Nevada Historical Society

NEVELSON, LOUISE (1900–1988)

When she was a child, Louise Nevelson knew she wanted to be a sculptor, and she worked toward that goal until she achieved it. She was born Louise Berliawsky on September 23, 1900, in Kiev, Russia. In 1905 she and her family moved to Rockland, Maine. After graduating from high school, she married Charles Nevelson and moved to New York City, where she lived the rest of her life. Nevelson traveled widely and studied at the Art Students League in New York City. She wrote poetry, performed in plays, and studied philosophy and religion. None of these activities interfered with her work as a sculptor, yet many years passed before she earned the reputation that she deserved.

During the mid-1950's, she began to gather together old wooden spindles, spools, parts of furniture, sticks, and other everyday wooden objects. With these Nevelson created her famous assemblages, which she framed within boxlike compartments of varying sizes. She then painted each assemblage flat black or sometimes flat white or gold. Finally, by piling boxes of the same color against the wall, she produced gigantic and strikingly beautiful relief sculptures unlike anything other artists had ever done. She had created order out of disorder, and unity and visual beauty out of cast-aside junk. Pictures of assemblages by Nevelson can be found in SCULPTURE in Volume S and UNITED STATES, ART AND ARCHITECTURE OF THE in Volume U-V.

Later in her career, Nevelson also produced plastic and metal sculptures. These have been shown in major museum collections. In addition, many of her large-scale works have been installed in public locations both in the United States and abroad. One of her best-known works is the Chapel of the Good Shepherd (1977) in St. Peter's Lutheran Church in New York City. In 1978, as a tribute to her, a public square on New York City's Wall Street was named the Nevelson Square. She died on April 17, 1988, in New York City.

HOWARD E. WOODEN
Director Emeritus
The Wichita Art Museum

NEWARK. See New Jersey (Cities).

NEWBERY, JOHN (1713–1767)

John Newbery was the first person to make children's books an important part of publishing. He was born in Waltham St. Lawrence, England, in 1713. His father was a farmer. Newbery's only schooling was in the village school, but he loved to read and soon had a wide knowledge of literature.

In 1730, Newbery went to Reading and found a job as assistant to William Carnan, the editor of the newspaper *The Reading Mercury*. When Carnan died in 1737, he left a share of the business to Newbery, who later married Carnan's widow. After touring England to sell books, Newbery began publishing books in Reading in 1740. He moved to London in 1744 and set up a shop, The Bible and Sun, where he sold medicines and books.

Newbery published newspapers and magazines and some of England's best writers wrote for him, including Samuel Johnson and Oliver Goldsmith. Goldsmith describes Newbery in *The Vicar of Wakefield* as "a red-faced, good-natured little man who was always in a hurry."

Newbery's first children's book, *A Little Pretty Pocket-Book*, was one of the first to both amuse and instruct children. It taught the alphabet in a song, gave directions for games, and listed rules for children's behavior.

Newbery printed many books for children in his Juvenile Library. These tiny volumes were bound in flowered and gilt paper. Some of them were single stories, like *The History of Little Goody Two-Shoes*. He started *The Lilliputian Magazine*, a magazine that contained stories, folk and fairy tales, "jests," songs, and riddles. Newbery probably wrote or planned some of the stories himself.

John Newbery died on December 22, 1767. His name lives on in the Newbery Medal, given each year to the book judged the most distinguished contribution to American literature for children.

Reviewed by JEAN KARL
Author, *From Childhood to Childhood: Children's Books and Their Creators*

See also CALDECOTT AND NEWBERY MEDALS; CHILDREN'S LITERATURE.

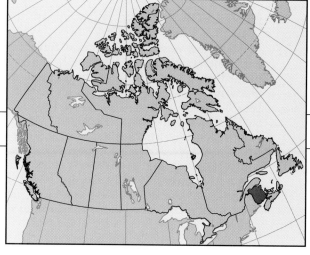

NEW BRUNSWICK

The lion on New Brunswick's flag (above) and coat of arms (opposite page) recalls the province's traditional ties with England. The galley reflects shipping and shipbuilding, two historical economic activities. The provincial bird is the black-capped chickadee (right), and the provincial flower is the purple violet (opposite page).

New Brunswick is one of the four Atlantic Provinces of Canada. The other three are Nova Scotia, Prince Edward Island, and Newfoundland and Labrador. New Brunswick's rich farmlands and vast forests, its beautiful beaches, rivers, and lakes, and its deep valleys and rolling hills have given it the nickname Picture Province.

▶ THE LAND

New Brunswick is shaped roughly like a rectangle. It measures about 160 miles (260 kilometers) from east to west and about 200 miles (320 kilometers) from north to south.

New Brunswick is bounded on the north by the province of Quebec and Chaleur Bay. East of New Brunswick are the Gulf of St. Lawrence and the Northumberland Strait. The strait separates New Brunswick from Prince Edward Island. On its southeastern shore, New Brunswick is joined to Nova Scotia by the Isthmus of Chignecto. To the south lies the Bay of Fundy, which juts in from the Atlantic Ocean between New Brunswick and Nova Scotia. To the west of New Brunswick is the state of Maine in the United States.

The northwestern interior of New Brunswick is very hilly. Most of the mountains are more than 2,000 feet (600 meters) high. Mount Carleton is the highest point in the province. In southern New Brunswick there is also a hilly area, north of the Bay of Fundy. Most of these hilly regions are made up of rocks that are only slowly worn down by stream erosion. But in several places, the rivers have carved out long, deep valleys.

Some of these valleys have rich soils that are excellent for farming.

In the east the rocky surface is softer, and it has been worn down to form a wide lowland stretching from Chaleur Bay to Northumberland Strait.

The Coastline

The coastline is very irregular, with many bays and coves. These often make good harbors. On the east coast, in the Gulf of St. Lawrence, there are important ports in Chaleur Bay and in Miramichi Bay. The Bay of Fundy coast in the south also has some excellent harbors. The east coast of New Brunswick has some fine sandy beaches. The other coasts are generally rugged.

Along the south coast, in the Bay of Fundy, are the highest tides in the world—rising as much as 50 feet (15 meters) at times. When the high tides are flowing, a line of moving water called a tidal bore can be seen. Twice a day the tidal bore advances up the Petitcodiac River near the city of Moncton. At low tide, ships in some of the south coast harbors are left sitting on the bottom. Throughout this area, shiny, wet mud flats are exposed during low tide.

Rivers and Lakes

New Brunswick has many rivers and lakes. In the north the Restigouche River flows along part of the Quebec border, emptying into Chaleur Bay. The river has cut a long, deep valley through the mountains. The Nepisiguit River flows eastward from Mount

The Bay of New Brunswick's southern coast, has the highest tides in the world. At low tide, huge rock formations stand out in Hopewell Rocks Provincial Park. The sandstone rocks were carved by the tides over thousands of years. At high tide, the rocks are partially submerged.

Climate

The climate of New Brunswick is typical of eastern Canada. The coldest places in winter and the warmest in summer are inland. Coastal areas are neither as cold nor as warm.

Cold air masses from the heart of Canada sometimes bring extremely low temperatures in winter. Very low temperatures in January and February are common in such inland places as Edmundston and Woodstock. Mild air masses from the south keep the province's southern coast warmer. But the east coast is almost as cold in winter as the inland areas because of ice covering the Gulf of St. Lawrence.

The annual rainfall in New Brunswick varies from north to south. The average

Carleton into Nepisiguit Bay, an inlet of Chaleur Bay. A third river, the Miramichi, flows eastward from the western mountains to the Gulf of St. Lawrence.

The St. John is the longest river in New Brunswick. It starts in Maine and flows in a generally southward direction through New Brunswick, reaching the sea near the city of Saint John on the Bay of Fundy. The valley of the St. John River is noted for its beauty. The St. John River provides the major source of electric power, with a series of six hydroelectric dams.

All of New Brunswick was covered by ice during the Great Ice Age. Much of the land was worn down as the ice moved across it from the north. When the ice melted, a great deal of sand, gravel, and clay was deposited on the land. This material blocked the rivers and caused the formation of thousands of lakes. New Brunswick's largest lake, Grand Lake, is really a widening of the St. John

River. Other large lakes include Oromocto Lake, Magaguadavic Lake, and the Chiputneticook lakes.

FACTS AND FIGURES

Location: Eastern Canada. **Latitude**—44°37' N to 48°03' N. **Longitude**—63°46' W to 69°03' W.

Joined Canadian Confederation: July 1, 1867, as one of the four original provinces.

Population: 729,498 (2001 census). **Rank among provinces**—8th.

Capital: Fredericton, pop. 47,560 (2001 census).

Largest City: Saint John, pop. 69,661 (2001 census).

Physical Features: Area—28,150 sq mi (72,908 km²). **Rank among provinces**—8th.
Rivers—St. John, Kennebecasis, Miramichi, Upsalquitch, Restigouche, Magaguadavic, St. Croix, Nepisiguit, Petitcodiac, Tobique.
Lakes—Grand, Chiputneticook, Oromocto, Magaguadavic. **Highest point**—2,690 ft (820m), Mt. Carleton.

Government: Self-governing province.
Titular head of government—lieutenant governor, appointed by the governor-general in council. **Actual head of government**—premier, leader of the majority in the legislature. **Provincial representation in federal parliament**—10 appointed senators; 10 elected member(s) of the House of Commons. **Voting age for provincial elections**—18.

Provincial Bird: Black-capped chickadee.
Provincial Flower: Purple violet.
Provincial Motto: *Spem reduxit* (Hope restored).

Industries and Products: Oil refining; sugar refining; shipbuilding; pulp and paper production; fish and fish products; dairy products; agriculture; mining.

amount each year is 35 inches (900 millimeters). Snowfall is abundant throughout most of the province. Lighter amounts are near the Bay of Fundy coastline and heaviest amounts are in the northeast. Yearly average snowfall ranges from less than 79 inches (200 centimeters) to 158 inches (400 centimeters).

Natural Resources

One of New Brunswick's greatest natural resources is its forests, which cover about 85 percent of the land area. Roughly half of this forested land is owned by the province. Other important resources are a wide variety of minerals, including zinc, silver, lead, potash, limestone, and coal.

Most of the forests in northern New Brunswick consist of coniferous trees, including balsam fir, spruce, and white pine. There are also some deciduous trees, such as maple and birch. The southern forests are a mixture of coniferous and deciduous trees.

New Brunswick's forests are the home of many animals, such as deer, moose, black bears, beavers, and rabbits. There are also game birds, such as partridges, as well as migrating ducks and geese. The rivers and lakes provide fishing for Atlantic salmon, bass, pike, and trout. Herring, mackerel, smelt, and lobsters are found in offshore waters.

▶ THE PEOPLE AND THEIR WORK

In New Brunswick, both English and French are the official languages. French is spoken widely.

Many people live in towns along the coast and along the St. John River valley. The important farming region around the town of Sussex, between Moncton and Fredericton, is also well populated. But very few people live in the vast central region of the province.

A little more than 40 percent of the people of New Brunswick are of British origin, many descended from Loyalists who emigrated from the United States at the time of the American Revolution. The rest are mostly of French ancestry. Of the more than 17,000 native peoples, métis (people of mixed Indian and European ancestry) number some 4,500. There are nine Micmac and six Maliseet communities in the province.

Industries and Products

Services are the biggest industry in New Brunswick, followed by manufacturing. Other major industries—mining, forestry, agriculture, and fishing—are based mainly on the province's natural resources.

Services. Service industries contribute heavily to New Brunswick's economy. Leading service activities are finance, insurance, and real estate and government. These are followed by business, social, and personal services, including education and health care, and retail trade. Other services in New Brunswick include transportation and wholesale trade.

Manufacturing. New Brunswick's most important industries in terms of value of factory shipments are the production of petroleum products and lead smelting. Other major contributors are the pulp, paper, and wood industries and the food processing industry.

Among New Brunswick's leading food products are fish and potato products. Other manufactures in the province include beverages, fabricated metal

The northwestern interior of New Brunswick has many hilly regions, such as this scenic and rural farming area in New Denmark.

products, nonmetallic minerals, print materials, and chemical products.

Construction. The construction industry employs many people in New Brunswick and contributes greatly to the economy. Factories and pulp and paper mills are currently upgrading their facilities and equipment, and energy sources are constantly being modernized to maintain an efficient system.

Mining. The mining industry has benefited from the development of base metals, zinc, silver, lead, and copper. Zinc is the largest mining product. Production of potash occurs at two mines near Sussex. Other commercially mined minerals are coal, limestone, antimony, tin, and gold.

Forest Industries. The forests of New Brunswick provide the raw materials for lumber, panel products, pulp, paper, and paperboard. Mills for lumber production are located throughout the province. Pulp and paper product mills are located at Edmundston, Nackawic, Saint John, Rothesay, St. George, Miramichi, Bathurst, Dalhousie, and Atholville. Forest products account for nearly half of New Brunswick's exports.

Agriculture. Farming is practiced in many settlements in the St. John River valley and around the north and east coast. The main crop in the hills of the upper valley is potatoes. Most of the potatoes are exported to the United States and other parts of the world. Apples are grown on the hillsides of the middle part of the valley, and vegetables are grown on the fertile soils of the lowlands along the river. A dairy industry is centered in the gently rolling country around Sussex. The northeast and southwest of the province have a thriving blueberry industry.

Fishing and Aquaculture. Commercial fishing is of great importance to New Brunswick's economy. More than 50 species of fish and shellfish are caught each year. Lobster is the most significant catch. This is followed by snow crab, herring, and scallops. Fishing is concentrated mainly in the Bay of Fundy, the Northumberland Strait, and the Chaleur Bay. Small boats and large draggers and seiners fish inshore waters and offshore banks. Large fish are brought to port for processing. There are more than 150 fish processing plants in the province.

Aquaculture, or fish farming, is rapidly growing in importance for the provincial economy, with the main cultivated species being the Atlantic salmon.

A paper and pulp mill operates in Saint John. This industry is a major contributor to the economy, and many mills are located throughout the province.

Transportation and Communication

Good paved roads connect all the cities and towns of New Brunswick. Gravel roads serve the logging areas in the sparsely populated central region. The Trans-Canada Highway runs from the Nova Scotia border west to the province of Quebec. This highway passes through Moncton, Sussex, Fredericton, and Edmundston.

Canadian National Railways operates a railroad running from Halifax, Nova Scotia, to Moncton and ending in Montreal, Quebec. Airline service is available throughout the province. Major airports are located in Saint John, Moncton, and Fredericton.

Major ferry services connect Saint John across the Bay of Fundy to Digby, Nova Scotia, and Cape Tormentine across the Northumberland Strait to Borden, Prince Edward Island. Another important ferry link connects Blacks Harbour to Grand Manan in the Bay of Fundy. There is also a ferry service from Letete to Deer Island.

Saint John is an important port, used for receiving imports to Canada and for exporting Canadian goods. It is an ice-free port, with modern container facilities.

The province has 5 daily and 19 weekly newspapers. The *Moncton Times-Transcript* is the largest single daily. The *Telegraph-Journal* and evening *Times-Globe* of Saint John have

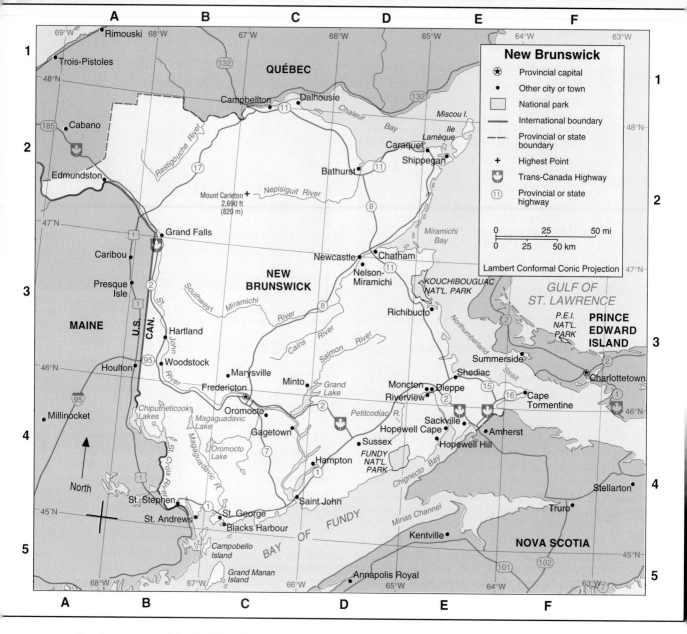

the largest combined daily circulation. The Fredericton *Daily Gleaner* serves the capital city region. The French language *L'Acadie Nouvelle*, published in Caraquet, serves the Acadian population of the province.

The province is serviced by both radio and television. There is cable television service in most areas. The use of fiber optics has made New Brunswick the leader in Canadian telecommunications and the headquarters of national and international call centers.

▶ **EDUCATION**

New Brunswick has a free public education system, with classes conducted in both French and English. There has been consolidation of rural schools into large regional facilities.

The New Brunswick Community College System offers trade and technical courses at nine campuses throughout the province. The University of New Brunswick, with campuses at Fredericton and Saint John, is the largest university in the province. In 1973, the New Brunswick Teachers College became part of the university's campus at Fredericton. Moncton is the home of the University of Moncton, the largest French-language university in Atlantic Canada. It has affiliated colleges in Edmundston and Shippegan. Other universities in the province include Mount Allison

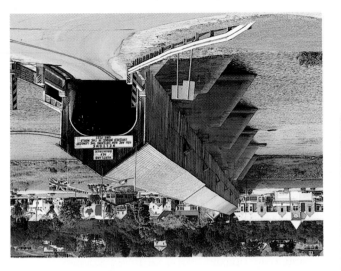

Above: Autumn comes to the Fredericton campus of the University of New Brunswick, the largest university in the province. *Right:* The Hartland Covered Bridge is considered to be the world's longest covered bridge.

University in Sackville and St. Thomas University in Fredericton.

All the main cities and towns and some of the smaller centers of New Brunswick have public libraries. Specialized libraries include the legislative library and the provincial archives in Fredericton and the New Brunswick Museum Archives in Saint John. Libraries provide services in English or French or both depending on the location.

New Brunswick Museum, in Saint John, was Canada's first museum. It has exhibits of pioneer life and natural history, as well as an art gallery. The Beaverbrook Art Gallery, in Fredericton, houses an important art collection donated to the province by Lord Beaverbrook. It features exhibitions of New Brunswick, Canadian, and international historical and contemporary art. Miramichi Natural History Museum, in Chatham, features historical artifacts and natural history exhibits. A number of local museums are located throughout the province.

▶ PLACES OF INTEREST

New Brunswick has a wide variety of interesting places to visit. These include national parks and historic sites, museums and art galleries, and places of scenic beauty.

Acadian Village, in Caraquet near Bathurst, is a re-created Acadian settlement of the period 1780–1880.

Carleton Martello Tower National Historic Site, in Saint John, has harbor fortifications that were built during the War of 1812.

Fort Beauséjour National Historic Park, near Sackville, includes a French fort dating from the 1700's.

Fundy National Park, between Moncton and Saint John, has many recreational facilities.

Hartland Covered Bridge, on the St. John River at Hartland, is 1,282 feet (391 meters) long. It is thought to be the world's longest covered bridge.

Kings Landing Historical Settlement, at Prince William near Fredericton, is a re-created Loyalist settlement of 1790–1870.

Loyalist House, in Saint John, is a home from the Loyalist period built and furnished in the Georgian style.

Magnetic Hill, outside Moncton, gives motorists the feeling of coasting uphill, when

Saint John, New Brunswick's largest city, is an important center for manufacturing. Located at the mouth of the St. John River, it is also a major port.

they are really driving downhill. This effect is due to an optical illusion.

Reversing Falls, at the mouth of the St. John River at Saint John, are produced by the powerful tides of the Bay of Fundy. Twice a day the rising tides force the water upstream.

Roosevelt Campobello International Park, in the Bay of Fundy, is on Campobello Island—the site of U.S. president Franklin D. Roosevelt's summer home.

St. Andrews, on the Bay of Fundy, was founded in 1784. It is one of New Brunswick's oldest towns.

▶ CITIES

Saint John, the largest city in New Brunswick, has a population of about 123,000. It is located at the mouth of the St. John River and is an important port that is able to handle large cargoes. Saint John is the site of North America's first deepwater terminal for oil tankers. Major industries include oil refining and the production of electric power, sugar production, and pulp and paper production.

Moncton is the second largest city in the province, located in the center of the Maritime Provinces—New Brunswick, Prince Edward Island, and Nova Scotia. It has about 118,000 people in its greater metropolitan area and is an important transportation and telecommunications center.

Fredericton, with a population of about 48,000, is the capital city of New Brunswick. It is located inland, on the north and south banks of the St. John River. It is a city of stately homes, history, fine arts and crafts, and theater. It is home to one of the oldest universities in North America and the site of Canada's first astronomical observatory, built in 1851.

▶ GOVERNMENT

The government of New Brunswick consists of a lieutenant governor, an executive council, and a legislative assembly. There is also a judiciary made up of a supreme court and other courts. The lieutenant governor is appointed by the governor-general of Canada and serves as the titular, or honorary, head of the province. The actual head of government is the premier. The premier is the leader of the majority party in the legislative assembly and chairman of the executive council, which acts as the cabinet. The legislative assembly makes the laws in the province. Its members are elected by the people. Elections must be held every five years but may be held more often.

▶ HISTORY

For thousands of years before the arrival of European explorers, the Micmac and Maliseet peoples, speakers of Eastern Algonkian languages, were well established in present-day New Brunswick. The Micmac territory covered the area from Gaspé to Cape Breton, including northern and eastern New Brunswick. The Maliseets lived along the St. John River and its tributaries. The rivers were important for transportation as well as food for these native peoples.

New Brunswick was visited by the French explorer Jacques Cartier in 1534. The first European settlement was made in 1604 by Samuel de Champlain and Pierre du Gua, Sieur de Monts, on the island of St. Croix at the mouth of the St. Croix River. But the settlement fared badly, and in 1605 it was transferred across the Bay of Fundy to Port Royal (now Annapolis Royal) in present-day Nova Scotia. In 1631 the French fur trader Charles La Tour established a fort and fur-trading post on the site of the city of Saint John.

French settlements spread gradually throughout the coastal areas, and the whole region, which included Nova Scotia and Prince Edward Island, was known as Acadia.

In 1713, under the Treaty of Utrecht, France lost possession of Acadia to Britain. But the struggle continued between the French and British over New Brunswick. The Treaty of Paris in 1763 ended the Seven Years' War between the two countries and gave Britain possession of the region. New Brunswick became part of Nova Scotia. During the 1760's some settlers from New England arrived in New Brunswick. In 1783,

following the American Revolution, thousands of American colonists who had remained loyal to Britain emigrated to New Brunswick. These emigrants, known as Loyalists, settled in the St. John River valley and in other parts of southern New Brunswick. Some of the original French settlers, the Acadians, had been driven out by the British but later returned. They were concentrated mainly on the east coast and in towns bordering on Quebec. Largely through the influence of the Loyalists, New Brunswick became a separate province in 1784.

In the first part of the 1800's, thousands of settlers went to New Brunswick from Britain. During this period New Brunswick's economy, built mainly on lumbering, fishing, and shipbuilding, flourished.

The boundary between Maine and New Brunswick had never been clearly defined, and there were many disputes over territory that was claimed by both sides. In 1839 the so-called Aroostook War broke out over disputed land in the Aroostook River valley. The militia was called out, but there was no real fighting. A truce was declared between the two sides, and in 1842 the boundary between New Brunswick and Maine was settled by the Webster-Ashburton Treaty.

By 1854, New Brunswick was granted responsible government (self-government) from Britain. In 1867, under the leadership of Samuel L. Tilley, New Brunswick joined with Nova Scotia, Quebec, and Ontario to form the Canadian Confederation.

The completion of the national railway systems in the later 1800's linked New Brunswick with cities throughout Canada and encouraged the rise of manufacturing towns in the province. However, these developments weakened the traditional lumbering, fishing, and shipbuilding economy, which had always relied on international markets. By the 1900's, even manufacturing was weakened by the declining political influence of the Maritime Provinces.

Nevertheless, today New Brunswick has found markets for its products. New mineral resources, the development of hydroelectric and nuclear power, and the rapid adjustment to technical breakthroughs in telecommunications give great hope for the future.

GARY T. WHITEFORD
University of New Brunswick

IMPORTANT DATES

2000 B.C.	Ancestors of present-day Micmacs lived along the Miramichi River.
A.D. 1534	Jacques Cartier explored New Brunswick.
1604	First European settlement established by Samuel de Champlain and Pierre du Gua, Sieur de Monts, on St. Croix Island.
1631	Charles La Tour established a fort and fur-trading post on site of Saint John.
1713	France gave up to Britain its claims to Acadia under the Treaty of Utrecht.
1783	United Empire Loyalists began to arrive in New Brunswick; 7,000 people land at Parrtown (Saint John).
1784	The province of New Brunswick is established, separating from Nova Scotia.
1785	Saint John becomes Canada's first incorporated city.
1820	The Bank of New Brunswick is established as the first chartered bank in Canada.
1842	Boundary between New Brunswick and Maine settled by the Webster-Ashburton Treaty.
1867	New Brunswick joined Canadian Confederation.
1890	Canadian Pacific Railway connected Moncton and Montreal.
1953	Large mineral deposits found near Newcastle.
1968	Mactaquac Dam, on the St. John River near Fredericton, completed.
1969	New Brunswick became first province to proclaim itself officially bilingual.
1974	Kouchibouguac National Park established on the Northumberland Strait.
1993	Equality between New Brunswick's English- and French-speaking communities is written into Canadian law.

During the Great Depression of the 1930's, New Deal programs initiated by President Franklin Roosevelt provided jobs to millions of desperate Americans, such as these Civilian Conservation Corps workers. The New Deal marked the first time the U.S. government assumed responsibility for the public welfare and the regulation of the economy.

NEW DEAL

When Franklin D. Roosevelt accepted the Democratic nomination for president of the United States in 1932, he pledged to create ". . . a new deal for the American people." The New Deal became the term that described all of Roosevelt's later efforts to help the tens of millions of people who had lost their homes, their jobs, and their savings during the Great Depression of the 1930's—a time when few government programs existed to help the needy.

The Hundred Days

The first of two waves of New Deal legislation came during the first one hundred days of Roosevelt's administration. Immediately after taking office on March 4, 1933, the president and his personal group of advisers (known as the "Brain Trust") worked closely with congressional leaders. They quickly established several agencies to curb the economic downswing by pumping federal funds into the economy. The Federal Emergency Relief Administration (FERA) provided funds outright to the needy, whereas the Civilian Conservation Corps (CCC), the Public Works Administration (PWA), and the Tennessee Valley Authority (TVA) put millions of unemployed to work on public projects. The Federal Deposit Insurance Corporation (FDIC) protected depositors in the event of bank failures; the National Recovery Administration (NRA) regulated prices and wages and promoted fair business competition; and the Agricultural Adjustment Administration (AAA) tried to help farmers by reducing excess production and increasing farm prices.

The Second New Deal

A second wave of legislation, which some call the Second New Deal, was approved in 1935 and included three major acts of Congress. The Works Progress Administration (WPA) (later called the Work Projects Administration) put more than 8 million people to work building roads, dams, bridges, and other public facilities. It also sponsored artists, writers, musicians, and actors. The National Labor Relations Act (the Wagner Act) supported the right of labor to engage in collective bargaining with employers. The Social Security Act established a federal old-age pension program and a joint federal and state system to provide unemployment insurance.

The New Deal Loses Support

Roosevelt's second term (1937–41) produced rising conflict and opposition. Many bitterly opposed his rash effort in 1937 to "pack" the Supreme Court with pro-New Deal justices because it had declared both the AAA and the NRA unconstitutional. Others blamed the New Deal for what they feared was a rising tide of labor radicalism, as manifested in the "sit-down" strikes of 1936–37. Especially damaging to the president's standing was the onset of a sharp recession in late 1937. With the exception of the Fair Labor Standards Act of 1938, which set minimum-wage as well as maximum-hour standards for workers, Congress gave little further support to Roosevelt's New Deal efforts.

JAMES T. PATTERSON
Brown University

See also ROOSEVELT, FRANKLIN D.

NEW DELHI. See DELHI.

NEW ENGLAND

New England is one of the oldest and most distinctive regions of the United States. Its six states, located in the northeastern corner of the country, are Maine, New Hampshire, Vermont, Massachusetts, Rhode Island, and Connecticut. The region received its name from Captain John Smith, who mapped much of the coast after a voyage of exploration in 1614. The name became permanent, especially as a result of its use throughout the 1600's by the English Puritan settlers of Massachusetts.

Together, the six states make up a region slightly smaller than the state of Washington. While its area is less than 2 percent of that of the United States, it holds more than 5 percent of the nation's people. Although relatively small, New England is a region of striking geographic diversity. The landscape includes a vast forest wilderness, rugged mountain ranges, more than 6,000 miles (9,660 kilometers) of varied Atlantic shoreline (including bays and inlets), rural farmland, small villages and towns, sprawling suburbs, and several large commercial and industrial cities.

In literature, education, and as well as in commerce and industry, New England has exerted a strong influence on the nation despite its relatively small size. The birthplace of five presidents, it has provided a model for local democracy with the town meeting form of government. The ideal of an educated citizenry has long been important in New England, and many of the country's oldest and most prestigious colleges and universities are located there.

The region was inhabited originally by several tribes of Algonkian-speaking peoples, who still maintain a small organized tribal presence here and there throughout the region. The first English settlers set up coastal fishing and trading stations in the early 1600's, mostly in New Hampshire and Maine. The famous Pilgrims, a group of English Separatists and their fellow passengers on the tiny *Mayflower*, began their community at Plymouth in 1620. Plymouth was soon overshadowed in numbers and importance by the Puritan colony of Massachusetts Bay, centered at Boston beginning in 1630. Eventually the Plymouth colony became part of Massachusetts. It was largely from Massachusetts Bay that English settlement spread into the rest of the region.

While the population of New England was mainly of English descent during the colonial and Revolutionary periods, today's New Englanders are noted for their ethnic and racial diversity. At various times during the 1800's and 1900's, beginning with Irish and French-Canadian arrivals before the Civil War, new peoples have come to live and work. These have included Europeans, African-Americans, Hispanic Americans, and Asians.

For the first century and a half after European settlement, the economy of coastal New England depended mainly on fishing, ship-building, and ocean trade, and the economy of the interior depended primarily on farming. Gradually during the 1800's, farming was largely replaced by manufacturing, especially of textiles. In recent decades, electronics and other high-technology manufacturing have supplanted textiles, and tourism and recreation have become important elements in the economy of every New England state. Current regional issues include balancing the need to maintain New England's resources and natural beauty with the pressures of population and economic development. Another challenge is maintaining jobs in the face of a shift away from defense activities, which have long helped sustain the New England economy.

CHARLES E. CLARK
University of New Hampshire

NEW ENGLAND

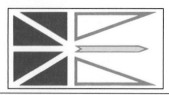

NEWFOUNDLAND AND LABRADOR

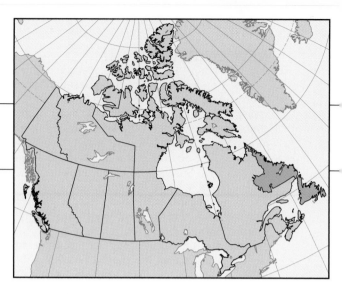

Newfoundland and Labrador's flag (above) was adopted by the provincial legislature in 1980. The coat of arms (opposite page) was granted by the king of England in 1637. The lions and unicorns on the shield are symbols of England, while the two supporting figures represent Newfoundland and Labrador's native peoples. The provincial bird is the puffin (right), and the provincial flower is the pitcher plant (opposite page).

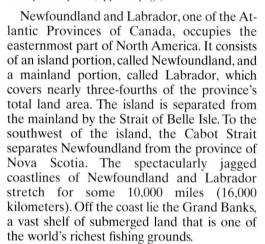

Newfoundland and Labrador, one of the Atlantic Provinces of Canada, occupies the easternmost part of North America. It consists of an island portion, called Newfoundland, and a mainland portion, called Labrador, which covers nearly three-fourths of the province's total land area. The island is separated from the mainland by the Strait of Belle Isle. To the southwest of the island, the Cabot Strait separates Newfoundland from the province of Nova Scotia. The spectacularly jagged coastlines of Newfoundland and Labrador stretch for some 10,000 miles (16,000 kilometers). Off the coast lie the Grand Banks, a vast shelf of submerged land that is one of the world's richest fishing grounds.

▶ THE LAND

The island of Newfoundland has a roughly triangular shape. It is part of a geographical region of North America called the **Appalachian Highlands**. On the western side of the island, the land rises abruptly to a mountain ridge with a maximum height of about 2,600 feet (800 meters). This ridge, the Long Range Mountains, forms the edge of a rolling plain that slopes away toward the east to elevations of a few hundred feet or less. The interior of the island is dotted with thousands of lakes and ponds. Hundreds of brooks and rivers break through the rugged coastal terrain to reach the sea.

Labrador is part of the land region known as the **Canadian Shield**. This region consists of low, rocky hills, many lakes, and glacial deposits of coarse gravel and sand. Labrador's

coastline is deeply indented with fjords, bays, and inlets, and its coastal waters are strewn with hundreds of islands. Magnificent wild rivers flow from the interior to enter the Labrador Sea. The Torngat Mountains in eastern Labrador have the highest elevations in Canada's eastern mainland. Some of the glaciated peaks and ridges are more than 5,000 feet (1,500 meters) high.

Climate

Newfoundland and Labrador has cold, though not severe, winters and warm to cool summers. A major influence is the very cold Arctic current that flows south past the coast, bringing drift ice and icebergs in season, chilling the winds, and delaying the arrival of spring. Average July temperatures range from 44°F (7°C) in northern Labrador to 60°F (15°C) in the southern part of Newfoundland. January temperatures range from 20°F (–7°C) on the southern coast of the island to 10°F (–12°C) on the coast of Labrador. In western Labrador it is not uncommon for winter temperatures to fall below –40°F (–40°C).

Annual precipitation varies from 55 inches (1,397 millimeters) in the southeast to 17 inches (432 millimeters) in the north. Snowfall represents about half the total precipitation in the north and about 20 percent of the total in the south.

Natural Resources

The extensive fishing grounds lying off the coast are the reason for Newfoundland and Labrador's existence as a settled community,

Approximately half the total population of the province live in some 1,000 tiny coastal villages, called **outports**. However, there is a trend toward urbanization, and the number of outports is constantly declining as towns and cities grow. The largest city in the province is the capital, St. John's, on the southeast coast of Newfoundland. This city is the center of New-foundland and Labrador's only metropolitan area, which also includes the city of Mount Pearl. Corner Brook, on the west coast, is the second largest city. The remainder of the urban population is distributed among fewer than 20 towns of 3,000 to 12,000 inhabitants. The interior of Newfoundland is virtually uninhabited and so is the greater part of Labrador. Most of Labrador's population is concentrated in the mining towns of Labrador City and Wabush and in Happy Valley-Goose Bay, an administrative and communications center.

Industries and Products

Newfoundland and Labrador's economy, once largely dependent on fishing, now also relies on other industries, including services, manufacturing, and mining.

Services. Service industries contribute heavily to the provincial economy and employ many people. Leading service activities are business, social, and personal services, includ-ing education, ocean research, health care, and services related to tourism. Other services in-clude government, wholesale and retail trade, financial services, and transportation, commu-nication, and utilities.

and fish remain one of its most vital resources. The most important fish is cod, but many others have commercial value, including halibut, haddock, pollack, redfish, sole, flounder, plaice, salmon, herring, mackerel, and tuna. Crab, lobster, shrimp, and squid also are commercially important.

Newfoundland and Labrador is rich in minerals. Iron is particularly abundant, and there are also deposits of gold, copper, asbestos, feldspar, talc, gypsum, and uranium. Very large reserves of oil have been discovered beneath the ocean floor in the Grand Banks, and enormous reserves of natu-ral gas have been found off the coast of Labrador.

Forests cover about one-third of the province. About half of the forest is productive. Much of the wood is unsuitable for saw milling but is ideal for the production of high-quality pulp. Commercially, the most im-portant trees are black spruce, balsam fir, and birch.

► THE PEOPLE AND THEIR WORK

About 95 percent of Newfoundlanders and Labradorians are of British origin. Most descended from people who came from southwestern Ireland and from the English counties of Devon, Dorset, and Somerset and settled the island in the 1600's, 1700's, and 1800's. Native peoples—the Inuit of northern Labrador, the Innu of the mid-Labrador coast, and the Micmac of Newfoundland's south coast—make up less than half of 1 percent of the total population.

FACTS AND FIGURES

Location: Eastern Canada, consisting of Newfoundland island and Labrador.

Newfoundland island: **Latitude**—46°37′ N to 51°38′ N. **Longitude**—52°38′ W to 59°25′ W. **Labrador**: **Latitude**—51°25′ N to 60°18′ N. **Longitude**—55°38′ W to 67°44′ W.

Joined Canadian Confederation: March 31, 1949, as the 10th province.

Population: 512,930 (2001 census). **Rank among provinces**—9th.

Capital and Largest City: St. John's, pop. 99,182 (2001 census).

Physical Features: **Area**—Newfoundland island, 43,359 sq mi (112,299 km²); Labrador, 112,826 sq mi (292,218 km²). **Rank among provinces**—7th. **Rivers**—Exploits, Gander, Humber (Newfound-land island); Churchill, Eagle, Naskaupi (Labrador). **Lakes**—Grand, Meelpaeg, Gander (Newfoundland island): Attikamagen, Lobstick, Melville (Labrador). **Highest point**—5,232 ft (1,595 m), in Torngat Mountains, northern Labrador.

Industries and Products: Fish; pulp and paper; mining; electricity.

Government: Self-governing province. **Titular head of government**—lieutenant governor, appointed by the governor-general in council. **Actual head of government**—premier, leader of the majority in the legislature. **Provincial representation in federal parliament**—6 appointed senators; 7 elected member(s) of the House of Commons. **Voting age for provincial elections**—19.

Provincial Bird: Puffin.

Provincial Flower: Pitcher plant.

Provincial Motto: *Quaerite prime regnum Dei* (Seek ye first the kingdom of God).

Above: The Torngat Mountains rise behind an ice-laden fjord in northern Labrador. **Left:** About half of all Newfoundlanders and Labradorians live in small coastal villages called outports.

Fishing Industry. For more than 400 years, fishing was the mainstay of the economy. Today, even though fish stocks have been severely depleted, more than 50,000 men and women are engaged in the catching, processing, and marketing of fish products. The United States is the principal importer of these products, but other markets in Europe and Asia are developing rapidly.

Manufacturing. Of Newfoundland and Labrador's manufactured products, processed foods—particularly fish products—rank first in importance. Codfish, both frozen and salted, is the leading fish product. Small food-processing plants produce bread, soft drinks, and other items.

Second in importance among manufactured goods are paper products. Three large paper mills at Grand Falls-Windsor, Stephenville, and Corner Brook export large quantities of newsprint.

Mining. Huge reserves of iron in western Labrador supply about 60 percent of Canada's total iron production. Once-important lead, zinc, copper, and fluorspar mines have been closed, but gold mining on the island has assumed growing importance. Asbestos and talc are also produced for export, while gypsum is mined to produce plasterboard. Since the 1990's, oil and gas production have increased at Hibernia, Terra Nova, and other off-shore fields.

Energy. Hydroelectric power generated from the province's numerous rivers and streams provides most of its electrical energy. One of the largest plants in the Western Hemisphere is located at Churchill Falls. Most of its production is exported to the province of Quebec.

Right: Logs trucked from a provincial forest are floated downriver for processing. *Below:* Fishing, long a mainstay of the economy, remains important.

Transportation and Communication

Rocky terrain and countless rivers and streams make road building in the province both difficult and expensive. Nevertheless, paved roads now link almost all communities on the island. The Newfoundland section of the Trans-Canada Highway runs from St. John's to Port aux Basques. From Port aux Basques and from Argentia, large car, truck, and passenger ferries provide connections to the North American road network.

In Labrador, a few communities in the south are linked by road and served by a car ferry to the island. The Trans-Labrador Highway links Happy Valley-Goose Bay with Quebec. But most coastal villages still depend on boats or airplanes for transportation services.

National and regional airlines provide service from airports at St. John's, Gander, Deer Lake, Stephenville, Wabush, and Happy Valley-Goose Bay, as well as from many smaller community landing strips.

Three daily newspapers are published in the province, while most of the larger towns have weekly papers. Radio service is provided by a number of public and private stations. Microwave, cable, and satellite technologies give access to television.

▶ EDUCATION

Primary and secondary education is free and is required of all children between the ages of 6 and 16. Most schools are operated by religious groups even though they are funded by the province. In 2001, the provincial government began sponsoring pre-kindergarten literacy programs.

Post-secondary education, while not free, is heavily supported by the government: students pay no more than 15 percent of the actual costs. The province has one university, Memorial University of Newfoundland, in St. John's, several community colleges, and two major technical colleges.

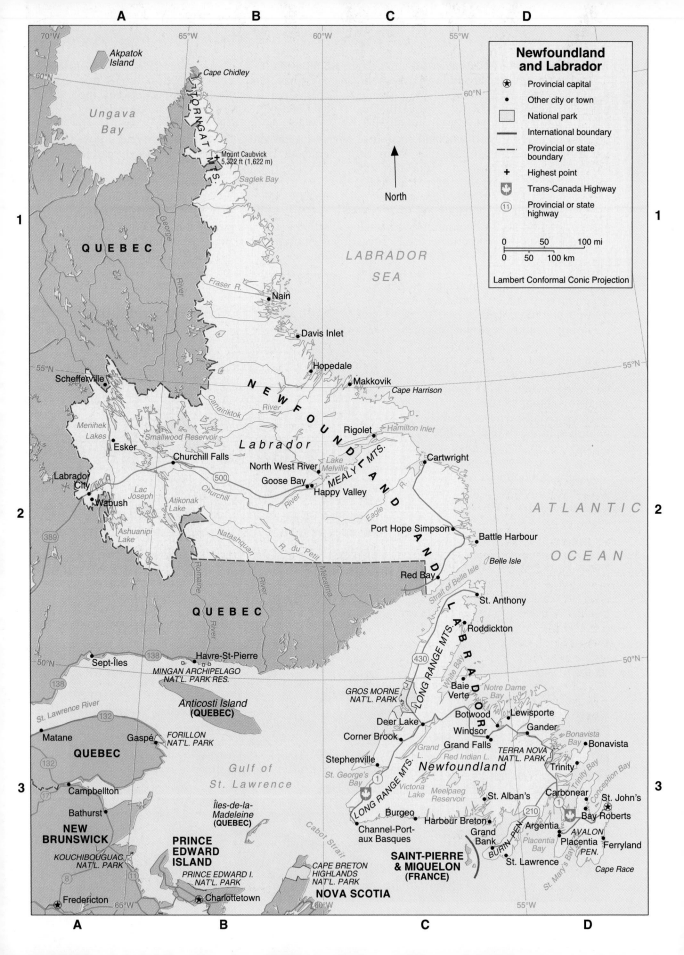

Puffins congregate on Gull Island, part of Witless Bay Islands Ecological Reserve.

PLACES OF INTEREST

Castle Hill National Historic Site overlooks the beautiful old town of Placentia, established in 1662 by the French as their administrative capital on Newfoundland island.

Gros Morne National Park is located on the west coast of the island. With its mountains, spectacular fjords, and splendid seascapes, the park offers some of the most impressive scenery in eastern North America.

L'Anse aux Meadows, at the northern tip of Newfoundland island, is the only authenticated Viking site in North America and dates from about A.D. 1000. A replica of the original settlement has been constructed on the site.

Red Bay, on the south coast of Labrador, is a fascinating archaeological site where the beautifully preserved wreck of the *San Juan,* a Basque whaler lost in 1565, has been discovered.

Saint Pierre and Miquelon, two small islands lying 8 miles (13 kilometers) off Newfoundland's southern coast, are part of France.

Signal Hill National Historic Site looms over the narrow entrance to the harbor of St. John's. It is the site at which Italian inventor Guglielmo Marconi received the first transatlantic radio signal. It is also the site of the last battle of the Seven Years' War (1756–63). Museums and displays introduce visitors to the history of the entire province.

Witless Bay Islands Ecological Reserve, south of St. John's, is a group of rocky islands where nesting colonies of thousands of sea birds—including the puffin, the provincial bird—can be observed.

Provincial parks are located throughout the province. Most are wilderness parks but provide basic camping facilities.

CITIES

St. John's is Newfoundland and Labrador's capital and largest city. Established in the early 1500's as a fishing village, it is one of the oldest settlements in North America. It is situated on the steep slopes of an excellent harbor on the eastern side of the Avalon Peninsula. This location has made the city a shipping center and a port of call for European fishing boats.

INDEX TO NEWFOUNDLAND AND LABRADOR MAP

St. John's is also the provincial center of industry, commerce, and education.

Corner Brook, the second largest city, is the only major settlement on the island's western coast. It has a large paper mill that produces newsprint, as well as cement and plasterboard plants. Located at the mouth of the Humber River, Corner Brook is also an excellent port and a center of fishing and fisheries.

Other settlements are small and are usually dependent on a single industry. Among the more important of these communities are **Grand Falls-Windsor**, **Gander**, **Stephenville**, **Lewisporte**, **Springdale**, **Harbour Grace**, and **Port aux Basques**. **Bonavista** is the largest fishing outport on the northeast coast.

▶ GOVERNMENT

Newfoundland and Labrador is a self-governing province with a unicameral (one-body) legislature called the House of Assembly. The assembly is composed of 48 members who are elected by the people. Elections must be held at least once every five years. The voting age in provincial elections is 19.

The province is administered by a lieutenant governor, who is appointed by the governor-general of Canada, but the actual head of government is the premier (prime minister). The premier chooses a cabinet, called the Executive Council, from among the elected members of the assembly, to advise in the fields of economics; social policies; intergovernmental affairs; treasury issues; and women's policies.

IMPORTANT DATES	
About 1000	Leif Ericson explored the coast of Newfoundland. Norse settlement established at L'Anse aux Meadows.
1497	John Cabot, exploring for the king of England, reached the island of Newfoundland and discovered its rich offshore fishing grounds.
1583	Sir Humphrey Gilbert proclaimed English sovereignty over Newfoundland.
1610	John Guy established the first colony in Newfoundland.
1634	Government by Fishing Admirals established.
1662	The first permanent French colony founded at Placentia.
1713	Treaty of Utrecht established British sovereignty over Newfoundland.
1729	Henry Osborne appointed Newfoundland's first royal governor.
1763	By the Treaty of Paris, all of Newfoundland, including Labrador, ceded to Great Britain.
1824	Newfoundland recognized as a British colony.
1832	The colony was granted the right to elect a general assembly.
1855	Great Britain granted Newfoundland self-government; first prime minister of Newfoundland elected.
1866	First successful transatlantic telegraph cable was laid from Valentia, Ireland, to Heart's Content.
1898	First railway across the entire island completed.
1901	First transatlantic wireless message received at Signal Hill.
1927	Labrador-Quebec boundary determined.
1934	Self-government suspended because of financial crisis.
1949	Newfoundland (along with Labrador) entered Canadian Confederation as the tenth province.
1966	First paved all-weather highway across the island completed.
1974	Churchill Falls hydroelectric power project in Labrador completed.
1979	The federal government granted Newfoundland control of its offshore oil and gas reserves.
1991	Due to depletion of stocks, a two-year moratorium was declared on the harvesting of northern cod.
1999	Newfoundland celebrated its 50th anniversary as a Canadian province.
2001	A constitutional amendment officially changed the province's name to Newfoundland and Labrador.

St. John's, Newfoundland and Labrador's capital and largest city, is a center of government, commerce, and education. Its excellent harbor has made the city a leading port.

◀ HISTORY

Native peoples lived in Newfoundland and Labrador for thousands of years before the arrival of the first Europeans. Viking explorers sailed its waters as early as A.D. 1000, establishing a temporary settlement at L'Anse aux Meadows. European fishermen had probably reached the coast of Newfoundland before 1497, when the explorer John Cabot arrived and claimed the land for England.

France and England sought to establish colonies, but the French were expelled in 1713, leaving the English in sole possession. Settlements continued to grow, and soon England appointed a naval governor. France attempted to reassert its claims during the Seven Years' War (1756–63), but British sovereignty was acknowledged under the Treaty of Paris (1763). France was given the islands of Saint Pierre and Miquelon as a base for its fishing fleets.

In 1824, Newfoundland was granted official status as a colony. In 1832 it was granted representative government, and 23 years later, in 1855, the right to full self-government was attained. In 1927 a border dispute with Quebec was settled, and Labrador became part of the colony of Newfoundland. (In 2001 the province was officially renamed Newfoundland and Labrador.) In 1931, Newfoundland became a member of the British Commonwealth, with the same status as Canada and other British dominions.

Newfoundland suffered severe economic losses during the Great Depression of the 1930's. Deeply in debt, it requested aid from Britain, thereby surrendering its political independence and accepting rule by a commission and a British governor. The construction of four U.S. military bases in Newfoundland during World War II (1939–45) and a growing demand for the region's resources led to an economic boom. Newfoundlanders were given the chance to decide democratically on their form of government. In a referendum held in 1948 they chose union with Canada. On March 31, 1949, Newfoundland, long known as Britain's oldest colony, became Canada's tenth province.

The economy advanced rapidly throughout the 1950's and 1960's. Modern pulp and paper mills, fish-processing plants, and iron-mining operations in western Labrador all contributed to economic growth. But the effects of a national recession in the late 1970's and early 1980's were compounded in Newfoundland by a rapid decline in fish stocks. This led to high unemployment rates, and many younger Newfoundlanders left the province in search of work. The development of offshore deposits of oil and natural gas offered the prospect of economic expansion in the 1990's, while hope remained that careful conservation would allow fish stocks to rebuild. The economy remained depressed as the jobless rate reached 17 percent by the end of the century.

LESLIE HARRIS
Author, *A Short History
of Newfoundland and Labrador*

Viking explorers reached Newfoundland Island about A.D. 1000. A replica of their settlement at L'Anse aux Meadows displays a Viking boat and a building of earth and timbers.

A boat travels past a fishing village in Papua, the western half of the island of New Guinea. Most of the island's people live in rural areas and consider themselves villagers.

NEW GUINEA

New Guinea is an island located in the southwestern Pacific Ocean, north of Australia and just south of the equator. With an area of about 342,000 square miles (885,780 square kilometers), it is the second largest island in the world (only Greenland is larger).

Politically, New Guinea is divided in half: Papua (formerly known as Irian Jaya), a province of Indonesia, is on the western half of the island. Papua New Guinea, an independent nation that includes several smaller islands, occupies the eastern half.

▶ PEOPLE

New Guinea has a population of nearly 8 million. Most are Melanesians (a Pacific island people). There are also people of European and Asian ancestry. Indonesian authorities have encouraged people to relocate to Papua from other Indonesian islands.

Language and Religion. More than 800 different languages are spoken on the island. Many people in Papua New Guinea speak Melanesian pidgin (a mixture of several languages) as a common tongue, while English is used in business and government. In Papua, Bahasa Indonesia has replaced Dutch as the language of government.

Traditionally, Melanesians practiced animism (the belief that spirits reside in all objects). Christianity was introduced by missionaries. Islam is practiced by many recent immigrants to Papua.

Way of Life. About 10 percent of the population lives in urban settlements, and urban influences have spread to rural areas. But most New Guineans consider themselves villagers. Villages are typically located in fertile valleys and consist of houses made of logs and thatch. For rituals and ceremonial occasions, many villagers wear traditional clothing made from animal skins and adorned with feathers and shells. Most villagers grow some of their own food and raise pigs and cassowaries (ostrich-like birds). But increasingly they supplement their diet with rice and canned meat and fish.

▶ LAND

New Guinea is about 1,500 miles (2,400 kilometers) long and 500 miles (800 kilometers) wide. It is shaped like a giant bird with its head facing the islands of Indonesia in the west and its tail drooping to the Coral Sea in the southeast. Most of the coast is fringed by coral reefs and swamps; towns are situated on the few deepwater harbors.

New Guinea's central mountain range is studded with high cliffs. The highest point on the island is Puncak Jaya, in Papua, which rises 16,535 feet (5,040 meters) above sea level. The fertile, grassy plateaus among the mountains are hard to reach by land. Thick jungles lie in many of the lower regions, and travel is made difficult by wide and often fast-flowing rivers. Major rivers include the Sepik, the Fly, and the Remu, all in Papua New Guinea.

Climate. New Guinea lies in the tropics, and at sea level the average temperature is between 70 and 90°F (21 and 32°C). The central highlands have much cooler and wetter conditions. From May through October, New Guinea is cooled by the southeast trade winds. At other times there are frequent, heavy rains—in some places more than 100 inches (2,500 millimeters) a year.

Wildlife. Native animals include wallabies and tree kangaroos, as well as snakes, crocodiles, and giant fruit-eating bats. Birds of paradise are still hunted for their beautiful feathers, but in Papua New Guinea, laws have been enacted to protect endangered species.

Natural Resources. New Guinea has some of the world's richest deposits of copper and gold ore. Attempts are being made to exploit natural gas and oil resources in Papua New Guinea. The forests of New Guinea contain many hardwood trees, but forests are disappearing at a rapid rate due to over-logging.

▶ **ECONOMY**

Mining operations dominate the economy, accounting for more than 70 percent of export earnings. But most New Guineans earn their living from agriculture, growing coffee, cocoa, and coconuts as cash crops. The plantations of the colonial era have mostly disappeared, although large-scale production of sugar and palm oil is still carried out. Most manufactured goods are imported.

▶ **CITIES AND TOWNS**

Port Moresby, the capital of Papua New Guinea, and Jayapura, Papua's provincial capital, are centers of commerce and government. Each has some 20,000 residents. Mining camps have sometimes grown into towns—for example, at Porgera.

▶ **HISTORY**

The first humans arrived on New Guinea at least 40,000 years ago, over a land bridge that once linked the island with Asia. More recently (5,000 to 8,000 years ago), Melanesian settlers reached the island by canoe. In the 1500's, Portuguese and Spanish explorers discovered New Guinea while seeking the Spice Islands but did not settle there. In 1828, the Dutch claimed the western half of the island to use as a base for trading and exploration but did little to develop it.

Missionaries from Europe began work on the island as early as 1858; European presence increased in the 1870's and 1880's. German plantations in the northeast, and in 1884 the German government proclaimed a protectorate. The British did the same in the southeast. In 1906 the British protectorate became the Territory of Papua, under the Australian government.

The Australians took over German New Guinea at the start of World War I (1914–18). Later, they administered it as the Territory of New Guinea, first under a mandate from the League of Nations (1920) and then as a United Nations trust territory. In 1949, it was joined with the Territory of Papua. The Territory of Papua and New Guinea became self-governing in 1973 and, along with several neighboring islands, became the independent nation of Papua New Guinea in 1975. However, it remains dependent on Australia for economic support.

In 1963, control of western New Guinea passed from the Dutch to Indonesia, which made it a province and, in 1973, gave it the name Irian Jaya. In 2002, Indonesia passed a law that was supposed to grant more local power to the province, which was officially renamed Papua.

A. GROVE DAY
University of Hawaii
Reviewed by DONALD DENOON
The Australian National University

See also INDONESIA; PAPUA NEW GUINEA.

New Guinea

NEW HAMPSHIRE

New Hampshire received its name from Captain John Mason, an English merchant who was the first European to hold title to much of the land. In 1622, Mason and another merchant, Sir Ferdinando Gorges, were granted a large tract of land in New England. They divided their holdings in 1629. Gorges called his share Maine, while Mason named his after his home county of Hampshire, England. In modern times, New Hampshire has been nicknamed the Granite State because of the massive deposits of that rock underlying much of the state. New Hampshire granite has provided the material for some of the most impressive monuments and buildings in the United States. Some like to extend the meaning of the nickname to include the people of the state, who in popular legend are often portrayed as durable and unchanging.

State flag

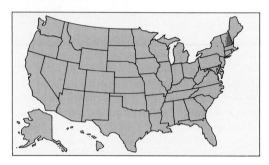

New Hampshire is one of the six New England states, wedged between its northern New England neighbors of Vermont and Maine in the northeastern corner of the United States. It is bordered on the north by Canada and on the south by Massachusetts. Although it is one of the smallest states in the nation, New Hampshire is a place of great diversity with a rich and interesting history.

New Hampshire is widely known for its recreational attractions. In the summer tourists and seasonal residents flock to its lakes, mountains, and seashore. Spectacular autumn foliage draws visitors in October. There are year-round opportunities for fishing and hunting, and the skiing season extends from December into early spring. Many New Hampshire residents make their living providing goods and services to tourists, skiers, and "summer people."

As one of the 13 original states, New Hampshire had an especially significant role: It was the ninth and therefore decisive state to ratify the Federal Constitution in 1788. Twice during the 1900's, New Hampshire has been the site of important world events. In 1905, President Theodore Roosevelt mediated the end of the Russo-Japanese War at a peace conference held in Portsmouth. In 1944, near the end of World War II, delegates from 44 nations met at Bretton Woods in the White Mountains for the United Nations Monetary and Financial Conference, which helped establish postwar economic stability. Since the 1950's, national attention has been focused every four years on the New Hampshire presidential primary election, which by state law must be held earlier than that of any other state. From 1952 until 1992, no candidate was elected president without first winning the New Hampshire primary.

▶ LAND

New Hampshire is a mountainous land, containing many of the highest elevations in the northeastern part of the United States.

Land Regions

New Hampshire has three land regions— the New England Upland, the White Mountains, and the Seaboard Lowland.

The New England Upland occupies most of the southern half of New Hampshire. It is a region of rounded hills separated by deep valleys and studded with many beautiful lakes. Rising above the hills are scattered mountains or groups of mountains called monadnocks. They are made up of very hard rock that resists erosion. The name "monadnock" comes from Mount Monadnock, which is located in the southwestern part of the state. This area is often called the Monadnock Region.

Opposite page, clockwise from left: **Snowshoers enjoy a wintry view of Squam Lake. The rock formation called the Old Man of the Mountain collapsed in 2003 but remains a state landmark. Blazing fall foliage is one of the state's most famous attractions.**

FACTS AND FIGURES

Location: Northeastern United States; bordered on the north by Canada (Quebec), on the east by Maine, on the southeast by the Atlantic Ocean, on the south by Massachusetts, and on the west by Vermont.

Area: 9,283 sq mi (24,044 km²); rank, 44th.

Population: 1,235,786 (2000 census); rank, 41st.

Elevation: Highest—Mt. Washington, 6,288 ft (1,917 m); lowest—sea level.

Capital: Concord.

Statehood: June 21, 1788; 9th state.

State Motto: Live free or die.

State Song: "Old New Hampshire."

Nicknames: Granite State (official); Primary State.

Abbreviations: NH; N.H.

State bird: Purple finch

State tree: White birch

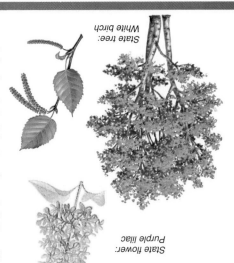

State flower: Purple lilac

Left: Mount Adams is a peak in the Presidential Range of the White Mountains, in northern New Hampshire. *Above:* A covered bridge spans the Connecticut River at Cornish. The river forms the state's western boundary.

The White Mountains Region, a part of the Appalachian system, covers the northern half of New Hampshire. The mountains cross the state from southwest to northeast and extend into Maine. They are the highest and most rugged in the northeastern United States. They are made up of several ranges including the Presidential Range, the Franconia Mountains, and the Sandwich Range. The peaks in the Presidential Range include Mount Washington, the highest point in the Northeast. Scenic mountain passes called notches separate the ranges.

The Seaboard Lowland is the coastal border of New Hampshire. It is made up of rolling plains and scattered low hills. At the Maine border, this region is only about 20 miles (30 kilometers) wide, but it widens to nearly 50 miles (80 kilometers) where it passes into Massachusetts. The short coastline is made up of sandy beaches separated by rocky promontories. An interesting feature of the Seaboard Lowland is a large tidal estuary, Great Bay, which drains into the Piscataqua River. Off the Atlantic coast are the Isles of Shoals, a group of rocky islands. The three southernmost islands—Star, White, and Lunging islands—belong to New Hampshire. The rest belong to Maine.

Rivers, Lakes, and Coastal Waters

The Connecticut River, New Hampshire's longest river, has its source in the three Connecticut Lakes in the northern part of the state. It forms the western boundary with Vermont. Central New Hampshire is drained by the Merrimack River and its tributaries. The Androscoggin and the Saco are the major rivers in the north. The Salmon Falls and the Piscataqua rivers in the south form part of the Maine–New Hampshire boundary. The Connecticut, Merrimack, and Androscoggin rivers have been an important source of waterpower.

New Hampshire has more than 1,000 lakes and ponds. The major lake area is around Lake Winnipesaukee in the foothills of the White Mountains. This lake is one of the loveliest in the nation. Its shoreline is deeply indented with bays and coves. Scores of wooded islands rise from its clear waters. Nearby are Squam, Ossipee, Newfound, and Winnisquam lakes. Lake Sunapee is to the southwest. The Connecticut Lakes are in the far north. A series of dams on these lakes and farther down the Connecticut River produces electric power for the New England power system.

New Hampshire's general coastline on the Atlantic Ocean is 13 miles (21 kilometers) long. The tidal shoreline, including indentations, measures 131 miles (211 kilometers).

Climate

New Hampshire has short, cool summers and long, cold winters. The presence of the

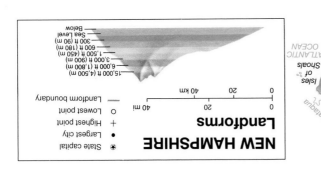

Plant and Animal Life

Woodlands occupy 84 percent of the total area of the state. The kinds of forests vary greatly from area to area. Oak, hickory, and white pine are the most numerous trees in the southern part of the state. Northern New Hampshire is covered by forests that include birch, beech, sugar maple, and white pine. At high elevations and in the extreme north, there are many spruce and fir trees. The white pine has always been the state's most important forest resource.

Native shrubs include juniper, yew, and wild blackberry, raspberry, and blueberry bushes. Wildflowers grow in profusion in fields and forests. Among the most common varieties are goldenrod, wild aster, black-eyed Susan, daisies, and paintbrush. Rare alpine flowers grow above the timberline in the Presidential and Franconia ranges of the White Mountains.

Deer, moose, bears, bobcats, foxes, raccoons, porcupines, and snowshoe rabbits are among the many inhabitants of the forest. Ruffed grouse, pheasant, duck, and woodcock are the chief game birds.

The state's lakes, ponds, and streams are well stocked with fish—landlocked salmon, trout, bass, pickerel, whitefish, and perch. Marine life found in the ocean and in Great Bay includes herring, mackerel, lobsters, clams, and crabs.

Natural Resources

New Hampshire's most valuable natural resources include its forests and rivers and its beautiful recreation areas—mountains, lakes, and seashore.

The state is attempting to conserve its valuable forests by encouraging what is called selective cutting. This means removing timber that is ready for harvesting without damaging the young, growing trees. The state is also trying to curb water pollution. Standards for water quality have been set for every stream, pond, lake, and reservoir.

sea in the southeast and of mountains in the north and west produces many local variations in climate.

The average January temperature in Concord is 21°F (−6°C), and the average July temperature is 70°F (21°C). The high mountains are the coolest areas, in both winter and summer. The frost-free growing season is 142 days, from May to September.

Precipitation usually falls evenly throughout the year. In Concord the average annual precipitation (including melted snow) is 36 inches (914 millimeters). Average annual snowfall ranges from about 50 inches (127 centimeters) on the coast to more than 100 inches (254 centimeters) in the mountains.

New Hampshire offers ample opportunities for outdoor recreation. *Above:* A canoeist and passenger glide along a tranquil lake. *Right:* Spectacular views reward a family of hikers after a challenging climb.

Most of the soils are filled with rocks and are poor or only moderately fertile. Scattered areas of more fertile soils are found in the Connecticut and the Merrimack river valleys and on the plains of the seacoast region.

The most common minerals in the state are sand, gravel, and stone—mainly granite. There are also deposits of clay, mica, and feldspar.

▶ PEOPLE

Of the more than 1 million people living in New Hampshire, slightly more than half reside in towns or cities of 2,500 or more. About one third of all residents live in the state's 13 incorporated cities.

American Indian names for lakes and other physical features are reminders of New Hampshire's first people. More than 2,000 Native Americans live in the state today.

The earliest European settlers of New Hampshire came from the British Isles by way of Massachusetts. Their "Yankee" descendants still form a significant part of the state's population. Immigrants from Quebec added a large French-Canadian component in the 1800's. Between 1880 and 1920 the mix of peoples was enriched still further by the arrival of newcomers from southern and eastern Europe. New Hampshire is home to a relatively small number of African-Americans and a small but growing number of Hispanic and Asian peoples.

Education

In 1647, when New Hampshire was still a part of Massachusetts, a law was passed requiring all communities of at least 50 people

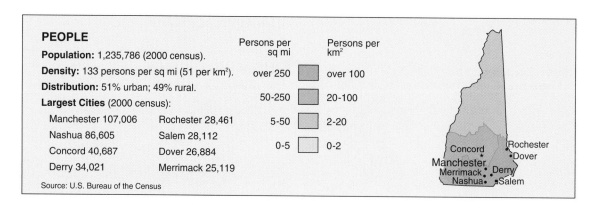

PEOPLE

Population: 1,235,786 (2000 census).

Density: 133 persons per sq mi (51 per km²).

Distribution: 51% urban; 49% rural.

Largest Cities (2000 census):

Manchester 107,006	Rochester 28,461
Nashua 86,605	Salem 28,112
Concord 40,687	Dover 26,884
Derry 34,021	Merrimack 25,119

Source: U.S. Bureau of the Census

Persons per sq mi	Persons per km²
over 250	over 100
50-250	20-100
5-50	2-20
0-5	0-2

Concord
Rochester
Manchester
Dover
Merrimack
Derry
Nashua
Salem

to maintain a school. This was the start of public education in New Hampshire.

The largest institution of higher learning is the University of New Hampshire at Durham, chartered in 1866 as the New Hampshire College of Agriculture and the Mechanic Arts. The university is now part of a state university system that also includes Plymouth State College and Keene State College (which began as teachers' colleges), the University of New Hampshire at Manchester, and the School for Lifelong Learning.

Dartmouth College in Hanover is the oldest and best-known institution of higher learning in the state. It was chartered in 1769 under the authority of King George III of England.

Other private colleges in New Hampshire include St. Anselm College, Notre Dame College, and New Hampshire College, in Manchester; Daniel Webster College and Rivier College, both in Nashua; New England College in Henniker; Franklin Pierce College in Rindge; Nathaniel Hawthorne College in Antrim; and Colby-Sawyer College in New London. Franklin Pierce Law Center is located in Concord.

One of the state's many private preparatory schools, the Phillips Exeter Academy in Exeter, was founded in 1781. Another, St. Paul's School in Concord, was founded in 1856.

Libraries, Museums, and the Arts

The first free public library supported by public funds in the United States was established in Peterborough in 1833. Today more than 200 communities in New Hampshire have public libraries. The state library sends bookmobiles to all ten counties. The New Hampshire Historical Society in Concord maintains both a library and a museum. Included in the library collections are the personal papers of Daniel Webster, Franklin Pierce, and other famous people of New Hampshire. Baker Memorial Library at Dartmouth College is noted for its many collections, which range from New Hampshire history to movie scripts.

Major art galleries include the Hopkins Center and Hood Museum of Art at Dartmouth College, the Currier Gallery of Art in Manchester, and the Lamont Art Gallery of the Phillips Exeter Academy.

The New Hampshire Symphony Orchestra is based in Manchester. The state has long been home to several well-known summer the-

Dartmouth College, in Hanover, is a distinguished institute of higher learning. Founded in 1769, it is one of the oldest colleges in the United States.

ater companies. Both resident and visiting companies perform in theaters in Portsmouth, at Dartmouth College and the University of New Hampshire, and at several other schools.

▶ ECONOMY

New Hampshire's traditional industries—forestry, farming, commercial, fishing, quarrying, and the once-great textile industry—make up only a small part of the economy today. What is most striking about the state's economy in modern times is its great diversity.

Services

Service occupations employ nearly 75 percent of New Hampshire's work force and provide about 70 percent of the gross state product (GSP)—the total value of goods and services produced in a year. Leading service activities are business, social, and personal services, especially those associated with tourism, such as restaurants and lodging. Finance, insurance, and real estate are also important, as are wholesale and retail trade. Other service industries are transportation, communication, and utilities and government.

A cozy inn is an inviting place to spend a winter weekend. New Hampshire draws vacationers year-round, and tourism contributes heavily to the state economy.

Manufacturing

Only about 20 percent of New Hampshire's workers are employed by manufacturing companies. Nevertheless, manufacturing provides the largest payroll and, after services, the largest contribution to the GSP of any major economic activity. The most important products manufactured in the state are machinery and electronics equipment—particularly computers and scientific instruments—and rubber and plastic products.

The manufacture of paper and paper products, a heavy contributor to the state's economy since the late 1800's, remains of great importance. So do other products of New Hampshire's forests, such as lumber.

The other great traditional industries of New Hampshire are the manufacture of textiles, clothing, and shoes. All these survive, but have declined markedly since the end of World War II.

Agriculture

In 1860 about 65 percent of New Hampshire was covered by farms. Today only about 10 percent of the land is in farms, and most of this is woodland.

The most important kinds of farming in New Hampshire are dairying and the raising of poultry. The products of these farms have large markets in cities and towns. Animal feed is shipped in from the Midwest. A little more than half the milk from the dairy farms is used in nearby cities. The rest is shippped to Boston and other cities in Massachusetts. Most of the poultry farms produce eggs for large markets in the state and around Boston.

Other products are important locally. Livestock—chiefly cattle—are raised in the Connecticut Valley and elsewhere. Hardy fruits, such as apples, are grown in the central and southern parts of the state. Special products include maple sap for sugar and syrup, blueberries, and nursery products, such as flowers, shrubs, and forest seedlings.

Mining and Construction

Most of the mining in the state is really quarrying. Granite once was quarried in large quantities at Concord and other towns and still forms a small part of New Hampshire's export economy.

The rapid expansion of New Hampshire's population between 1960 and 1990 created a large demand for the construction of new housing, especially in the southern part of the state. This great demand was diminished at the very end of the 1980's. Today construction projects employ less than 5 percent of the state's workers.

Transportation

One of New Hampshire's earliest roads was a cart road from Concord to Haverhill, Massachusetts. It was opened in 1727. As the state

---

PRODUCTS AND INDUSTRIES

Manufacturing: Machinery, electronics equipment, paper products, rubber and plastic products.

Agriculture: Milk, apples, eggs, cattle, maple sugar and syrup.

Minerals: Sand and gravel, granite.

Services: Wholesale and retail trade; finance, insurance, and real estate; business, social, and personal services; transportation, communication, and utilities; government.

*Gross state product is the total value of goods and services produced in a year.

Percentage of Gross State Product* by Industry

- Manufacturing — 24%
- Construction 4%
- Government — 8%
- Transportation, communication, and utilities — 8%
- Wholesale and retail trade — 16%
- Business, social, and personal services — 20%
- Finance, insurance, and real estate — 20%
- Agriculture contributes less than 1%.

Source: U.S. Bureau of Economic Analysis

developed, the need for better roads led to the building of turnpikes, or toll roads. Today New Hampshire has a good network of highways, including three modern toll roads—the New Hampshire Turnpike along the seacoast, the Spaulding Turnpike from Portsmouth to Union, and the Everett Turnpike from Nashua to Concord. Parts of the interstate highway system cross the state, linking Boston, Portland, New York, and Montreal.

Most of the major railroad lines of New Hampshire were in operation before the Civil War. The first of the early lines began operation from Lowell, Massachusetts, to Nashua in 1838. But the role of railroads in the state has decreased greatly. Rail service today is limited to a few main lines carrying long-haul freight through New Hampshire. A few branch lines remain to serve major industries.

There are about 25 small airports throughout the state. A few provide commercial air-

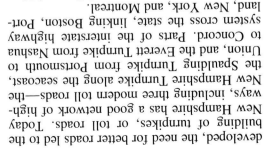

line service; the most important of these is in Manchester. The former Pease Air Force Base in Portsmouth and Newington is being developed for civilian purposes, including commercial air service.

Portsmouth is New Hampshire's only seaport. It handles chiefly bulk cargoes—petroleum, gypsum, coal—coming into the state.

Communication

The *New Hampshire Gazette*, which began publication in Portsmouth in 1756, was New Hampshire's first newspaper. Today the state has more than 30 newspapers, including 10 dailies. The largest are the *Union Leader* and the *New Hampshire Sunday News*, both published in Manchester. There are about 50 radio stations and 8 television stations.

► CITIES

Most of New Hampshire's urban population live in relatively small communities. Only two cities have more than 50,000 residents. Most towns and cities have fewer than 25,000.

Concord, the capital of New Hampshire and its third largest city, is located on the Merrimack River. The community was settled in the late 1720's. Early names given to it were Penacook and Rumford. In 1765 the town was renamed Concord.

Today Concord is an industrial and commercial city as well as the political center of the state. The State House is constructed partly from Concord granite.

Manchester, the largest city in the state, is also located on the Merrimack River. It was first settled in 1722. The town was known as

Above: The excellent deepwater harbor at Portsmouth can accommodate large cargo ships. Situated at the mouth of the Piscataqua River, Portsmouth is New Hampshire's only seaport. *Right:* Manchester is the largest city in the state and a leading industrial center. Its manufactures, once dominated by textiles, now include machinery and electronics equipment.

Places of Interest

The Flume, Franconia Notch

Strawbery Banke, Portsmouth

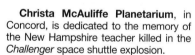
Christa McAuliffe Planetarium, Concord

Mount Washington Cog Railway

Christa McAuliffe Planetarium, in Concord, is dedicated to the memory of the New Hampshire teacher killed in the *Challenger* space shuttle explosion.

The Flume, in Franconia Notch, is a deep gorge some 800 feet (244 meters) long. Visitors can walk through the flume on a path along its towering rock walls.

Franklin Pierce Homestead, in Hillsboro, was the family home of the 14th president of the United States. The house, which was built in 1804, contains furnishings of the period.

Hampton Beach, on the New Hampshire seacoast, is a popular recreation spot for both residents and visitors from out of state. Its wide, sandy beach is considered one of the best in the Northeast.

Lake Winnipesaukee is the largest lake in the state. Swimming, boating, and fishing are among the recreational activities enjoyed by the lake's many visitors.

Mount Washington, in the White Mountains, is the highest peak in the Northeast. Scenic hiking trails lead to the summit, as does an auto road open from mid-May to mid-October. A cog railway, completed in 1869, runs from Crawford Notch to the peak of Mount Washington. Steam-powered trains make the 3-mile trip several times a day in summer.

Old Man of the Mountain, in Franconia Notch, was a natural granite rock formation that was the subject of a story by Nathaniel Hawthorne, "The Great Stone Face." Although it collapsed in 2003, the image remains a famous state symbol and appears on the New Hampshire state quarter.

Saint-Gaudens National Historic Site, in Cornish, is a memorial to the sculptor Augustus Saint-Gaudens. It preserves his home, Aspet, and his workshop, studio, and gardens.

Shaker Village, in Canterbury, was settled in 1792 by members of a religious community called Shakers. Shaker buildings, furniture, and crafts, all highly regarded today for their construction and design, are on display at the village.

Strawbery Banke, in Portsmouth, is an outdoor museum showing changing life in a waterfront neighborhood from the 1690's to the 1950's. The site was first settled in 1631. Tours of historic buildings, archaeological exhibits, and special events explore various periods in the neighborhood's long history.

State Recreation Areas. New Hampshire has numerous state parks and forests, as well as ten restored or protected historic sites. For information, write to the Department of Resources and Economic Development, Division of Travel and Tourism Development, P.O. Box 1856, Concord, New Hampshire 03302.

▶ **GOVERNMENT**

New Hampshire's present state constitution was adopted in 1784 and amended in 1793.

The governor is the chief executive officer of the state. An elected executive council advises the governor and shares most of the governor's powers. The state legislature is called the General Court. It is made up of the Senate and the House of Representatives. The General Court elects the secretary of state and the state treasurer.

The judicial branch of the state government includes a supreme court and a superior court system. Each county has a probate judge.

▶ **HISTORY**

The earliest inhabitants of what is now New Hampshire were Algonkian-speaking peoples, who practiced hunting and agriculture. The two most important tribes were the Penna-cooks and the Sokokis. There were probably fewer than 4,000 Native Americans in the area when the first Europeans arrived; few Native Americans remained in New Hampshire after about 1700.

Exploration and Settlement

It seems certain that Europeans saw the New Hampshire seacoast well before the first

Harrytown, as Tyngstown, and then as Derry-field. In 1810 it was given its present name for the industrial city of Manchester in England. During the 1800's, Manchester became a leading textile center. The most important mills were those of the Amoskeag Manufacturing Company, or Amoskeag Mills. The textile industry has lost its primary importance, but textiles are still manufactured.

Nashua is located where the Merrimack and the Nashua rivers join near the Massachusetts border. It is a manufacturing center and the second largest city in New Hampshire. The town grew up on the site of an early fur-trading post. During the first half of the 1800's, Nashua became an important textile center. Today electronics equipment, machinery, and tools are also produced.

Rochester, an industrial city in the southeastern part of the state, was originally part of the town of Dover, one of the state's oldest settlements. Rochester was settled slowly because of the Indian Wars, but it had grown into a booming community by about 1800. It was incorporated as a city in 1891. Since 1874, Rochester has been the site of a popular annual agricultural fair.

Portsmouth, a commercial center and New Hampshire's only seaport, is located at the mouth of the Piscataqua River opposite Kittery, Maine. It was incorporated as a town in 1653. In colonial times, Portsmouth was the seat of the provincial government. For many years it was an important shipbuilding center and port. The Treaty of Portsmouth, ending the Russo-Japanese War, was signed at Portsmouth Naval Base in 1905.

Berlin, in the northern part of the state, is known as the City That Trees Built because of its paper and lumber industry. It is also the home of the first ski club to be organized in the United States.

The State House, in Concord, is the home of state government. It is built of Concord granite, a fine-grained white stone mined in local quarries.

GOVERNMENT

State Government
Governor: 2-year term
State senators: 24; 2-year terms
State representatives: 400;
2-year terms
Number of counties: 10

Federal Government
U.S. senators: 2
U.S. representatives: 2
Number of electoral votes: 4

For the name of the current governor, see STATE GOVERNMENTS in Volume 5. For the names of current U.S. senators and representatives, see UNITED STATES, CONGRESS OF THE in Volume U-V.

recorded visit, by two English ships under the command of Martin Pring, in 1603. Seafarers from western England had discovered the rich western Atlantic fishing grounds many decades earlier. In 1605 the French explorer Samuel de Champlain sailed along the New Hampshire coast and made the first recorded sighting of the Isles of Shoals. English explorer Captain John Smith visited the same area nine years later.

The first permanent settlement was made at Odiorne's Point, in what is now the town of Rye, in 1623. A second settlement was established several years later up the Piscataqua River, in present-day Dover. Both settlements were mainly fishing and trading stations. The Odiorne's Point settlement was later relocated, becoming the nucleus of the present-day city of Portsmouth. Two other towns were established in southern New Hampshire by settlers from Massachusetts—Exeter in 1638 and Hampton in 1639.

All four of New Hampshire's original towns were affected by two wars that took place between France and England from 1689 to 1697 and from 1702 to 1713. During these wars, most of the Indians of Canada and northern New England sided with France, raiding the frontier settlements of New England.

Early Political and Economic Development

At first the four New Hampshire towns were separate settlements under no central colonial government, although the settlers of Hampton claimed to be within the jurisdiction of Massachusetts. In 1641, with the consent of the residents, the government of Massachusetts assumed authority over the settlements in New Hampshire. In 1680, England declared New Hampshire a separate royal province. But disputes over boundaries and jurisdiction continued for many years.

In 1740, when the boundary with Massachusetts was finally resolved, New Hampshire began a period of great prosperity. Settlement of the interior increased, and farming flourished there. Much of the wealth of the province during these years was based on the export of lumber products from the port of Portsmouth. Especially valuable were huge New Hampshire white pines, used as masts for British warships.

One of the first events of the American Revolution took place in New Hampshire on December 14 and 15, 1774, four months before the battles of Lexington and Concord. A mob of 400 people raided Fort William and Mary in Portsmouth Harbor, carrying off its powder and weapons. The royal governor, John Wentworth, lost his authority and left the province the following June. New Hampshire formed a revolutionary government and, on January 5, 1776, became the first colony to adopt a state constitution. On June 21, 1788, New Hampshire became the ninth state to join the Union.

INDEX TO NEW HAMPSHIRE MAP

• County Seat   Counties in parentheses   ★ State Capital

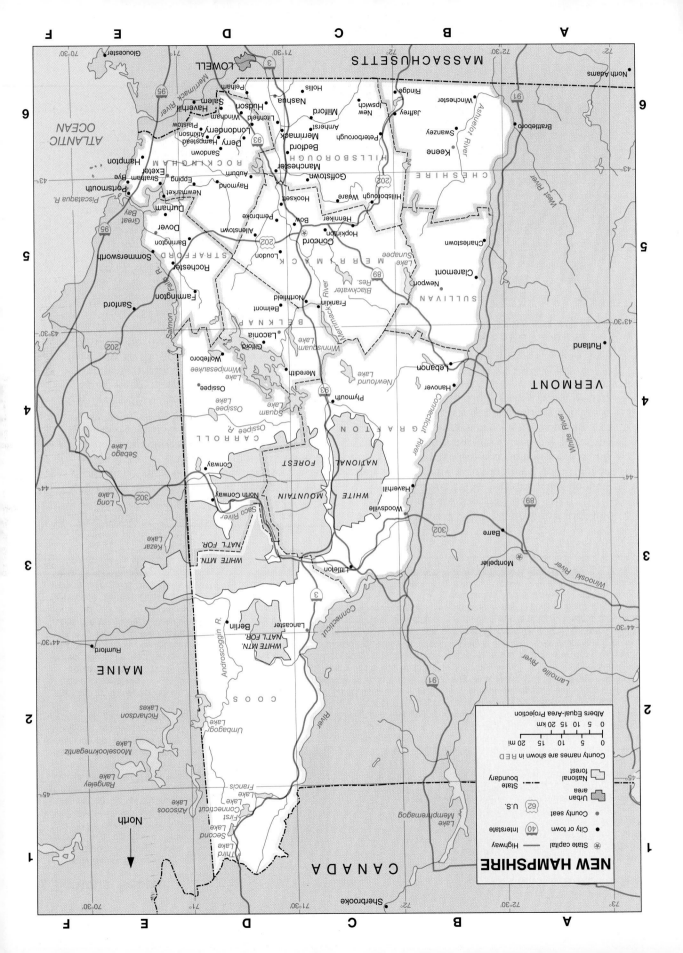

NEW HAMPSHIRE

	Highway	State capital
⌂40 Interstate	⑥2 U.S.	● County seat
● City or town		

Urban area
National forest
State boundary

County names are shown in RED

0 5 10 15 20 mi
0 5 10 15 20 km
Albers Equal-Area Projection

North

Famous People

Amy Marcy Beach (1867–1944), born in Henniker, was a pianist and composer. She made her debut as a pianist in Boston in 1883 and thereafter performed widely in the United States and Europe. Her *Gaelic Symphony* (1896) was the first published symphonic work composed by an American woman. Her other compositions include an opera, works for piano, and numerous songs. She was the cofounder (1923) and first president of the Association of American Women Composers.

Josiah Bartlett (1729–95) was a noted physician and Revolutionary War patriot. He practiced medicine in Kingston. A delegate to the Continental Congress, he was one of New Hampshire's three signers of the Declaration of Independence. Bartlett later served as chief justice (1788–90) and governor (1790–94) of New Hampshire.

Horace Greeley

Franklin Pierce

Robert Frost (1874–1963) was one of America's leading modern poets. Though born in California, he is identified mainly with New Hampshire, where he spent many years of his life. Most of his poems are concerned with life in rural New England, including those in the collection *New Hampshire* (1923), for which he received one of his four Pulitzer prizes. A biography of Frost appears in Volume F.

Horace Greeley (1811–72), born in Amherst, was an influential newspaper publisher. He founded the *New York Tribune* in 1841 and edited it until his death. His editorials attacked slavery and championed many other progressive causes, helping to shape public opinion in the years before and during the Civil War. One contained the widely quoted phrase, "Go West, young man." Greeley was an unsuccessful candidate for president of the United States in 1872.

Sarah Josepha Hale (1788–1879), a native of Newport, was a well-known editor and writer. She is remembered today as the author of the nursery rhyme "Mary's Lamb," first published in her book *Poems for Our Children* (1830). Active in humanitarian causes, she also edited *Godey's Lady's Book* and other women's magazines and wrote several novels, including *Northwood: A Tale of New England* (1827).

The 1800's

The Revolutionary War, and later the War of 1812, damaged New Hampshire's importance as a center of trade and commerce. The seacoast region lost its importance in the economic and political life of the state. In 1808 the state capital was moved inland to Concord.

In the decades before the Civil War (1861–65), New Hampshire agriculture changed. Small family farms were replaced by large commercial farms that sent livestock and produce to the Boston market. This same period also saw the rise of textile mills and shoe factories, which provided employment for the first wave of French-Canadian immigrants.

The chief influence on state politics between 1840 and 1860 was the debate over slavery. A key national figure was New Hampshire-born Daniel Webster. As U.S. senator from Massachusetts, Webster attempted to resolve the growing differences between the North and South. The 1852 presidential election was won by another New Hampshirite, Franklin Pierce, who also sought to appease both sides of the slavery issue.

More than 30,000 New Hampshire soldiers fought on the Union side in the Civil War. Because many men died in the war and because of a movement westward in search of better farmlands, New Hampshire's population declined between 1860 and 1870.

From 1870 to 1900, however, the population grew rapidly as immigrants from Canada and Europe arrived to take jobs in textile and paper mills, shoe factories, and the forest industry. The Amoskeag mill complex in Manchester became the largest producer of cloth in the world. During these same years, rail traffic increased. The grand hotels of

A photograph taken about 1912 shows a worker at a Manchester textile mill. New Hampshire was long a leading producer of cotton and wool cloth.

the White Mountains and the New Hampshire shore became fashionable summer retreats.

Modern Times

A strong Progressive movement arose in the early 1900's, bringing about political reforms. The Society for the Protection of New Hampshire Forests was founded in 1901 and fulfilled its first great goal, the creation of the White Mountain National Forest, in 1911.

Increasing competition from southern states and a series of labor disputes caused a severe decline in cotton and wool manufacturing following World War I (1914-18). Governor John P. Winant led the state through the Great Depression of the 1930's. Winant served as American ambassador to Great Britain during World War II (1939-45). Two New Hampshire women also gained national status—Mildred McAfee Horton as commander of Women in the Naval Service and Ruth Cheney Streeter as commander of the Marine Corps Women's Reserve.

During the post-World War II years, the state government, along with private development corporations, successfully attracted new businesses, such as the electronics industry, to New Hampshire. Tourism became more important than ever to the economy.

From the 1950's through the 1980's, as the national economy flourished, New Hampshire was one of the fastest growing states in the nation. In those years its population more than doubled. The national economic downturn of the later 1980's and early 1990's affected New Hampshire greatly, resulting in a loss of population as people looked elsewhere for jobs.

The dramatic changes of the second half of the 1900's have affected the state in many ways. Most of the economic prosperity and population growth occurred in the southern part of the state, leading to a perception of "two New Hampshires"—one "new," the other traditional and more rural. Bitter controversies have arisen over various industrial projects, notably the nuclear-powered generating plant at Seabrook, which began supplying electricity in 1990. There has been a continuous debate over the state's unusual policy of collecting neither a state income tax nor a sales tax. These are but some of the signs of New Hampshire's modern struggle to understand and express its identity under the pressure of intense and rapid change.

WILLIAM H. WALLACE
University of New Hampshire

Reviewed by CHARLES E. CLARK
University of New Hampshire

Sharon Christa McAuliffe (1948-86), a popular science teacher at Concord High School, was selected by the National Aeronautics and Space Administration in 1985 to be the first private citizen in space. Her participation in the flight of the space shuttle *Challenger* drew enormous national attention. This only served to deepen the country's shock and grief when *Challenger* exploded just seconds into its flight on January 28, 1986, killing all seven crew members.

Franklin Pierce (1804-69), born in Hillsboro, was the 14th president of the United States. He practiced law in Concord and served as both a congressman and a U.S. senator from New Hampshire before being elected president in 1852. A biography of Pierce can be found in Volume P.

Augustus Saint-Gaudens (1848-1907), a sculptor born in Ireland and raised in New York City, moved to Cornish in 1884. There he created some of his greatest sculptures, and his studio became the center of a renowned artists' colony. The most famous of his many notable works is probably the *Adams Memorial*, in Rock Creek Cemetery, Washington, D.C. Others include the

Sharon Christa McAuliffe

Shaw Memorial, on Boston Common; *General William Tecumseh Sherman*, in New York City's Central Park; and two important statues of Abraham Lincoln in Chicago.

Alan B. Shepard, Jr. (1923-98), of East Derry, was the first American to fly in space. As a Navy test pilot, he was one of the original seven men chosen by the National Aeronautics and Space Administration to train as astronauts. He made the first American manned suborbital flight on May 5, 1961, aboard the *Freedom 7*. In 1971, as commander of *Apollo 14*, he became the fifth man to walk on the moon.

Daniel Webster (1782-1852), born in Salisbury (now Franklin), was a leading American statesman famed for his abilities as an orator (eloquent public speaker). A graduate of Dartmouth College, he practiced law and began his political career in New Hampshire. A biography of Webster appears in Volume W-X-Y-Z.

NEW JERSEY

New Jersey was named for Jersey, the largest British island in the English Channel. James, the Duke of York, younger brother of King Charles II, bestowed the name in 1664 to honor George Carteret of Jersey, a major supporter of Charles' restoration to the English throne in 1660. New Jersey's nickname, the Garden State, began with early European settlers. Pleased with the fertile soil, they wrote home to praise the "garden spot." Slightly changed, the nickname has endured.

State flag

Midway between Philadelphia and New York City and halfway from Boston to Washington, D.C., New Jersey is the crossroads of the Middle Atlantic States. It is bordered by New York on the north and northeast and by Pennsylvania and Delaware on the west. Ninety percent of New Jersey's boundaries are water. The Delaware River forms the entire western boundary, and the Hudson River forms the northeastern boundary with New York. The state owes its historical, economic, and transportation vitality to these two rivers. The Atlantic Ocean and Delaware Bay lie to the east and south.

Busy is the word for modern New Jersey. The fifth smallest state in size, it is first in population density and urbanization, ninth in total population, ninth in value of industrial production, and first in density of research facilities. Despite the busy pace, large areas of tranquility exist. Low-lying mountains in the northwest are largely preserved in state parks or forests. The Pinelands National Reserve, the first such reserve in the nation, protects the Pine Barrens, a vast forested area covering some 1 million acres (400,000 hectares) in southern New Jersey.

The state's seacoast, known to residents as the Jersey Shore, often is associated only with summer crowds or year-round activity in the casinos of Atlantic City, one of the country's leading resorts. However, serenity can be found at Sandy Hook, part of the Gateway National Recreational Area, and at Island Beach State Park, where public use and environmental protection are carefully balanced.

New Jersey has been a meeting place for both human and plant life. People from many nations began intermingling in New Jersey long before the American Revolution; today, more than 100 ethnic groups exist within the state. Botanically, the Pine Barrens is where north meets south. Plants of northern Canada, such as the bearberry, grow side by side with wild orchids normally found only in the Carolinas or Georgia.

New Jersey's historical roots date back more than 10,000 years. European settlement began as early as 1630. No state played a more central role in the American Revolution. Today, as much of the United States moves from suburban or rural status to urban, New Jersey is deep in the study of problems relating to this population shift.

▶ LAND

The key to New Jersey is its geographical diversity. Geographers divide the state into four sections, one of which has two important subdivisions.

Land Regions

Northern New Jersey's land regions—the Appalachian Ridge and Valley, the Highlands, and the Piedmont—cross the state in a southwest to northeast pattern. Starting with the state's top altitude, 1,803 feet (550 meters) above sea level at High Point in the extreme northwestern area, the regions decline toward sea level at Newark.

Opposite page, clockwise from left: **The glitter of Atlantic City's casinos attracts thousands of tourists annually. Many New Jerseyans commute to New York City via the George Washington Bridge. A tranquil stretch of the Jersey Shore at Island Beach State Park.**

FACTS AND FIGURES

Location: Middle Atlantic region of the United States; bordered on the north and northeast by New York, on the east by the Atlantic Ocean, on the south by Delaware Bay, and on the west by Delaware and Pennsylvania.

Area: 8,215 sq mi (21,277 km²); rank, 46th.

Population: 8,414,350 (2000 census); rank, 9th.

Elevation: *Highest*—1,803 ft (550 m) at High Point; *lowest*—sea level.

Capital: Trenton.

Statehood: December 18, 1787; 3rd state.

State Motto: *Liberty and prosperity.*

State Song: None.

Nickname: Garden State.

Abbreviations: NJ; N.J.

State bird: Eastern goldfinch

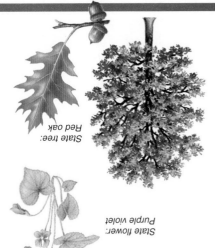

State tree: Red oak

State flower: Purple violet

Above: The Delaware Water Gap is a deep river valley that cuts through the Kittatinny Mountains. *Right:* In southern New Jersey's fertile farming region, a young farmer's stack of blueberry crates gets out of hand.

The Appalachian Ridge and Valley Region occupies the upper northwest portion of the state. It includes the Kittatinny Mountains, which are part of the Appalachian Mountain chain. Layers of rock in the region were folded, lifted up, then compressed during millions of years of geological time.

One of the region's most scenic spots is the Delaware Water Gap, a deep valley formed where the Delaware River passes through the Kittatinny Mountains. Over hundreds of years, the river relentlessly wore through some 1,200 feet (366 meters) of hard rock, from mountaintop to present-day river bed.

The Highlands (also called the New England Upland) are a continuous series of declining hills south and east of the Appalachian Ridge and Valley Region. The Highlands consist of many broad ridges with flat or rounded tops, separated by narrow valleys. The state's oldest rocks are found here, along with most of its lakes and some of its finest scenery.

The Piedmont consists of foothills that slope gently southeastward from the Highlands. Overlaying parts of the Piedmont, from Paterson to Far Hills, are ridges of hard volcanic rock. These include the Watchung Mountains. The Palisades, spectacular cliffs on the west bank of the Hudson River, were formed by the same lava flows that created the Watchungs about 100 million years ago.

The Coastal Plain is composed of two important subregions. The inner Coastal Plain is flat land broken by frequent low slopes. Colonial farmers first sought out the region because of its fertile, well-drained soil. Today it is the state's center of population, industry, culture, and higher education. It often is called the City Belt or the Corridor.

The outer Coastal Plain occupies the southeastern third of the state. It includes the Jersey Shore, the Pine Barrens, and the intensely farmed fertile soil along the lower Delaware River.

Rivers, Lakes, and Coastal Waters

The most vital New Jersey rivers are the Delaware and Hudson, shared as boundaries with other states. The longest internal rivers, the Raritan and the Passaic, drain the Highlands and the Piedmont.

Fast-moving streams also flow into the Delaware River from the mountains and highlands. Only one river, the Wallkill, flows north. It empties into the Hudson River at Kingston, New York. Southern New Jersey streams that move through flatlands and marshes are slow-moving and winding.

Except for Lake Hopatcong, which is about 7 miles (11 kilometers) long, New Jersey's lakes are small. Nearly all the state's lakes are man-made. Several large reservoirs conserve water for urban areas. Two, Round Valley and Spruce Run, combine water storage with public recreational areas. A giant underground reservoir, the Cohansey Aquifer, lies beneath the sandy surface of the Pine Barrens. Reliable estimates indicate that 17 trillion gallons (64 trillion liters) of water are contained in this aquifer.

New Jersey's seacoast, 127 miles (204 kilometers) from Sandy Hook to Cape May, includes some of the finest sandy beaches in the world. Numerous bays and inlets dot the coastline, but there are no harbors suitable for large ships.

Climate

New Jersey has four well-defined seasons. Summers are generally hot and humid, winters quite cold. Spring and fall feature pleasant temperatures and generally clear skies. Annual precipitation averages 45 inches (1,143 millimeters). Temperatures can rise above 100°F (38°C) in summer, but the average July temperature is about 75°F (24°C). Average January temperatures range from 24°F (-4°C) in Sussex County to 34°F (1°C) in Atlantic City and Cape May. Lows of -34°F (-37°C) and -36°F (-38°C) have been recorded.

Temperatures vary markedly from north to south. Farmers in southern New Jersey enjoy an average of 55 to 60 more growing days than farmers in the Kittatinny Mountains. This is the major reason for the large vegetable farms in the southern part of the state.

Plant and Animal Life

Despite its intense urbanization, New Jersey is still about 40 percent forested. Northern trees are hardwoods, including maple, oak, hickory, sycamore, beech, and poplar. Pine Barrens trees are mostly pine and scrub oak.

More than 4,000 wildflowers have been identified in the state, including more than 25 rare wild orchids. Most of the latter are in the Pine Barrens, although the pink lady's slipper

Left: The beach at Wildwood is one of many popular vacation spots along the New Jersey shore. *Below:* A father and son enjoy the unusual experience of touching and observing a shark during a visit to the New Jersey State Aquarium in Camden.

Opposite page: Blair Hall and Tower is one of the many historic buildings at Princeton University. Founded in 1746, Princeton is the nation's fourth oldest university.

is found throughout the state. Daisies, asters, Queen Anne's lace, and goldenrod adorn nearly all roadsides in season.

About 110 kinds of mammals are native to New Jersey. The most common are the cottontail rabbit, raccoon, opossum, skunk, red and gray fox, white-tailed deer, and black bear.

Natural Resources

The most productive resource is the state's variety of rich soils, ranging from sandy loam to deep, black "muckland" left by glaciers in some northern counties.

Sand and gravel are key resources in a state committed to development. Nearly every county has substantial rock quarries or sand pits. Stone, particularly limestone and traprock, is a vital mineral resource.

Iron ore ruled as the state's premier resource for more than 200 years. Some 600 million tons of iron ore are still underground in Morris, Hunterdon, Sussex, and Passaic counties. Zinc deposits are found in Sussex County.

State agencies regulate the use of water resources, state lands, the shoreline, wildlife areas, and wetlands. Most such activities are coordinated by the state department of environmental protection. Since 1961, voters have approved a series of five "Green Acres" land preservation bills, authorizing $600 million for the purchase of privately owned land by the state.

▶ PEOPLE

About 90 percent of New Jersey's 8.4 million people live in urban areas. Major new state and interstate highways have drawn people outward from the old cities. As those people have moved, they have created new heavily populated areas in Middlesex, Monmouth, Ocean, Camden, and Mercer counties. Major growth has been in Ocean County, where population has increased 700 percent since 1940, with most of that increase centered in communities for retired persons.

New Jersey has always attracted many different kinds of people. No colony had a greater variety of national groups in colonial days. Since then, several streams of immigrants have come to the state. The greatest influx, between 1890 and 1910, brought people mainly from southern and eastern Europe. By 1920, New Jersey had the highest percentage of immigrants in the nation.

New Jersey's African American population, present since colonial times, increased during the two world wars, when wartime industries drew workers from southern states. Growing numbers of Asian and Hispanic people have settled in the state in recent years.

Education

The first school in New Jersey was a church-sponsored academy established in 1682 in Bergen, now Jersey City. Public school education began in 1817. The first tax-supported schools appeared in 1829, and public education became required by law in 1875. Today public education is the costliest item in state and municipal budgets.

Higher public education centers on Rutgers, The State University, founded in 1766 as Queens College. The main campus is in New Brunswick, with other campuses in Newark and Camden. State colleges are located in Glassboro, Jersey City, Mahwah, Montclair, Pomona, Trenton, Union, and Wayne. The University of Medicine and Dentistry, in New Brunswick and Newark, and the New Jersey Institute of Technology, in Newark, are also state-supported. Eighteen of the 21 counties have public two-year community colleges.

Princeton University in Princeton, the fourth oldest university in the United States, was founded in 1746. Originally called the College of New Jersey, it became Princeton University in 1896. Much of the university's modern intellectual reputation is credited to Woodrow Wilson, president of Princeton from 1902 to 1910. Princeton also is home to the internationally known Institute for Advanced Study, established in 1933.

Other private universities are Drew University, in Madison; Seton Hall, in South Orange; and Fairleigh Dickinson, with locations in Rutherford, Teaneck, Madison, and Hackensack. Private colleges include Bloomfield College, in Bloomfield; Rider College, in Lawrenceville; St. Peter's College, in Jersey City; Monmouth College, in West Long Branch; Upsala College, in East Orange; and Stevens Institute of Technology, in Hoboken.

Libraries, Museums, and the Arts

New Jersey's first regular library service started in Trenton in 1750. Today the state has more than 300 public libraries, linked by a computer system that broadens book borrowing through interlibrary loans. The New Jersey State Library is the core of the program. Newark Public Library, founded in 1888, is recognized as one of the nation's finest small-city libraries. Rutgers University's varied collections are widely used by state residents.

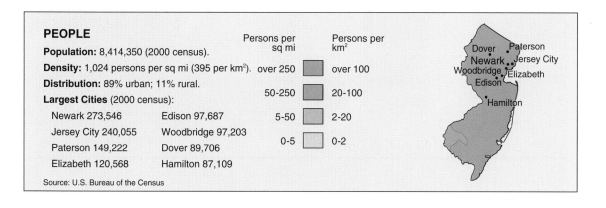

PEOPLE

Population: 8,414,350 (2000 census).

Density: 1,024 persons per sq mi (395 per km²).

Distribution: 89% urban; 11% rural.

Largest Cities (2000 census):

Newark 273,546	Edison 97,687
Jersey City 240,055	Woodbridge 97,203
Paterson 149,222	Dover 89,706
Elizabeth 120,568	Hamilton 87,109

Source: U.S. Bureau of the Census

Persons per sq mi	Persons per km²
over 250	over 100
50-250	20-100
5-50	2-20
0-5	0-2

The New Jersey State Museum in Trenton is known to nearly every New Jersey student. Hundreds of school groups each year tour the exhibits of Native Americans, birds and mammals, geology, art, history, and science. The Newark Museum contains important examples of American art as well as one of the nation's finest collections of Tibetan artifacts. The Montclair Art Museum is a major museum of painting and sculpture. The Morris Museum in Morristown has emerged as an important arts center for northwestern New Jersey. The New Jersey Historical Society in Newark has a fine collection of items related to New Jersey history.

The New Jersey Performing Arts Center in Newark plays host to dance and music performances for people of all ages. It is the home of the State Opera. Many popular and classical stars perform during the summer at the PNC Bank Arts Center in Holmdel. Dramas and musicals are staged at the Paper Mill Playhouse in Millburn. The State Theatre in New Brunswick is housed in a renovated vaudeville theater from the 1920's.

Sports

Two New Jersey professional teams—the Nets (basketball) and the Devils (hockey)—compete in the Continental Airlines Arena at the Meadowlands Sports Complex in East Rutherford. The New York area's major-league football teams, the Jets and the Giants, play all home games in the Meadowlands' Giants Stadium. Seton Hall University has a top-ranked men's basketball team, which plays its home games at the Continental Airlines Arena. The Rutgers University women's basketball team is nationally ranked.

▶ ECONOMY

New Jersey's people earn their livings in varied ways. They work in trade and service occupations of many kinds, including those that serve ever-growing numbers of tourists; in manufacturing plants; in transportation and construction; in the professions; in agriculture; and in government.

Services

Finance, insurance, and real estate are leading service industries, contributing heavily to the gross state product—the total value of goods and services produced in the state in a year. The headquarters of Prudential Financial, a leading insurance and investment firm, are in Newark.

Business, social, and personal services employ large numbers of New Jerseyans. These occupations include research, health care, and services related to tourism. There are more than 600 research laboratories within the state. Major areas of research are electronics (including television), chemicals, pharmaceuticals, and scientific instruments.

Wholesale and retail trade are vital service activities. Wholesale trade includes the distribution of products entering the state through the ports at Newark, Elizabeth, and Camden. Retail trade takes place mainly in large malls,

The chemical industry is a vital part of the New Jersey economy. Chemical plants such as this one produce paints, plastics, and other industrial and consumer products.

the centers for clothing, fast foods, books, and gifts. Retail trade in many small towns has declined because of mall competition.

Other service industries include government and transportation, communication, and utilities. Public Service Enterprise Group, a large utility company, is headquartered in Newark.

Manufacturing

The nature of New Jersey manufacturing has changed dramatically since the mid-1900's. It still can be said that New Jersey firms make some of nearly everything manufactured in the United States. However, many of the large manufacturing plants that formerly existed in the state have disappeared, either because the companies have moved elsewhere or because their product is no longer made.

More than 500,000 men and women work in manufacturing. Slightly more than one fifth of them are employed by makers of chemical products, including pharmaceuticals and plastics. New Jersey has held its strong position in areas important for the future, such as electronics equipment, scientific instruments, and fabricated metals.

Agriculture

Agriculture struggles to stay important in the Garden State. Increasing property values tempt farmers to sell their acres to developers. Still, farms remain in nearly every county—some 8,000 in all. Orchards in the southern part of the state make New Jersey fifth among all states in peach production. Cranberry harvests rank third nationally, and blueberries rank second. About 50,000 acres (20,000 hectares) of farmland, mostly in southern New Jersey, produce a wide array of vegetables. Greenhouse and nursery products are the leading agricultural income producers.

Agriculture in northern New Jersey consists mainly of dairy and chicken farming. New

A worker at a pharmaceutical plant scoops into a sea of pills. New Jersey is a leading producer of medicinal drugs and a center of pharmaceutical research.

Jersey hens produce about a half million eggs annually.

The New Jersey Agricultural Experiment Station at Rutgers University in New Brunswick is one reason for the state's continuing farming success. It is a leader in soil research and development of new varieties of fruits and vegetables.

Mining and Construction

Nonmetallic minerals, chiefly stone, make up New Jersey's mineral production. New Jersey is one of the nation's leading producers of crushed traprock, a hard stone of volcanic origin. In the town of Limestone, near Newton, limestone is mined and processed for crushed stone, for agricultural lime, and for uses in the poultry industry. Sand and gravel are mined throughout the state. Some clay is still mined in Middlesex County.

From the 1960's to the mid-1980's, the construction of homes, malls, and office buildings

---

PRODUCTS AND INDUSTRIES

Manufacturing: Chemicals, pharmaceuticals, plastics, processed foods, electrical and electronics equipment, transportation equipment, nonelectrical machinery.

Agriculture: Greenhouse and nursery products, dairy products, eggs, blueberries, peaches.

Minerals: Stone, sand and gravel.

Services: Wholesale and retail trade; finance, insurance, and real estate; business, social, and personal services; transportation, communication, and utilities; government.

*Gross state product is the total value of goods and services produced in a year.

Percentage of Gross State Product* by Industry

Finance, insurance, and real estate — 21%
Business, social, and personal services — 20%
Manufacturing — 18%
Wholesale and retail trade — 17%
Transportation, communication, and utilities — 9%
Government — 9%
Agriculture 1%
Construction 5%

Source: U.S. Bureau of Economic Analysis

Places of Interest

Boardwalk, Atlantic City

Six Flags Great Adventure, Jackson

Giants Stadium, Meadowlands Sports Complex

Sandy Hook Light, Gateway National Recreation Area

Atlantic City, on the Jersey Shore, had its beginnings as an ocean resort in the 1850's. The introduction of casino gambling in 1976 helped to make it one of the country's leading tourist destinations. Atlantic City also has a famous boardwalk and a popular convention center.

Cape May, at the southern tip of New Jersey, is one of the oldest seaside resorts in the United States. The town contains some of the finest, best-maintained Victorian homes in the nation.

Delaware Water Gap National Recreation Area protects about 35 miles (56 kilometers) of mostly unspoiled land along both the New Jersey and Pennsylvania sides of the Delaware River. It includes the scenic Delaware Water Gap, where the river cuts through the Kittatinny Mountains.

Edison National Historic Site, in West Orange, preserves the building and equipment used by Thomas Edison for many of his experiments. His home, Glenmont, is also on the site.

Gateway National Recreation Area spans Sandy Hook Peninsula in New Jersey and also includes sections on Staten Island and Long Island in New York. A notable landmark of the area is Sandy Hook Light, said to be the oldest lighthouse in the United States in continuous use (since 1764).

Meadowlands Sports Complex, near East Rutherford, has a track for horse racing, a stadium for football and soccer, and an arena for hockey, basketball, and concerts.

Morristown National Historical Park, in and near Morristown, preserves places where the Continental Army spent two winters during the American Revolution, in 1777 and 1779–80. Ford Mansion, which served as General Washington's headquarters, is in the park.

New Jersey State Aquarium, on the Delaware River in Camden, is one of the largest and newest aquariums in the eastern United States.

Pinelands National Reserve, the first such reserve ever established, covers about 1 million acres (400,000 hectares) in southern New Jersey. Historically known as the Pine Barrens, the area includes pine forests, marshes, and cedar swamps and is home to many rare plant and animal species.

Six Flags Great Adventure, in Jackson, features a drive-through safari park, where visitors can see wild animals roaming free. There is also a theme park with exciting rides.

Statue of Liberty National Monument is shared with New York. The article LIBERTY, STATUE OF, in Volume L, describes this famous monument. The statue can be reached by boat ride from Liberty State Park in Jersey City.

State Recreation Areas. New Jersey maintains numerous state parks, state forests (with recreation areas), and historic areas. One site, Palisades Interstate Park, is maintained jointly by New Jersey and New York. For more information, write to the Division of Parks and Forestry, 501 East State Street, CN 404, Trenton, New Jersey 08625.

created a demand for construction workers and materials. About 170,000 men and women worked in construction in 1987. In the following five years, more than 65,000 of those workers lost their jobs.

Transportation

New Jersey's location between two busy harbors always has made transportation supremely important. The nation's first steamboat ran from Burlington to Philadelphia in 1786. The state's first railroad, the Camden and Amboy, started operations in 1833. Today, highways dominate. More than 90 percent of New Jersey's workers commute to their jobs, mostly in automobiles. Few rail lines connect today's residential areas with scattered offices, industrial plants, and malls.

The New Jersey Turnpike, finished across New Jersey in the 1950's, links New York and Philadelphia. The Garden State Parkway, completed in 1954, traverses eastern New Jersey from the New York State border to Cape May. Bridges at Camden and elsewhere carry motorists across the Delaware River. Bridges and tunnels connect northern New Jersey with New York City.

Passenger trains serve commuters traveling to Philadelphia and New York City, and freight trains transport products throughout New Jersey and neighboring states.

New Jersey has some of the nation's busiest ports. The ports at Newark, Hoboken, and Elizabeth are part of the Port Authority of New York and New Jersey, which handles much of the export and import business of the United States. Newark Airport, adjacent to the Elizabeth and Newark ports, is one of the nation's busiest air facilities. It is maintained by the Port Authority. The Camden-Philadelphia port handles most Delaware River shipping, although the river is navigable to Trenton.

Communication

New Jersey's first newspaper was established by Isaac Collins of Burlington in 1777. Today, 22 daily newspapers and more than 200 other papers are published throughout the state. The Newark *Star-Ledger* is by far the largest newspaper in the state. New Jersey has more than 80 radio stations and 12 television stations. WNET, a station of the national Public Broadcasting Service, has its headquarters in Newark, although most of its programming originates in New York City. The state has its own public television network, with stations in Montclair, Trenton, New Brunswick, and Camden. Several radio and television stations in New York and Philadelphia also serve New Jersey audiences.

▶CITIES

About 75 percent of all New Jerseyans still live within a 30-mile (48-kilometer) -wide corridor between Bergen and Camden counties. New Jersey's old cities—Newark, Jersey City, Paterson, Elizabeth, Trenton, and Camden—were known traditionally as the Big Six. All of them have experienced rapid population drops or stagnation in the past 25 years.

Port Elizabeth is a center of container shipping for the Port of New York and New Jersey. Incoming goods leave the port by truck for delivery throughout the northeast.

People moving out of old cities have unintentionally created new population centers. According to the 2000 census, two such centers, Edison and Woodbridge townships, were ranked fifth and sixth in population, displacing Trenton and Camden. Such townships are not usually thought of as cities because they have no downtown areas, only malls, housing developments, and new office buildings.

Trenton is located at the head of navigation on the Delaware River. It was named for William Trent, a Philadelphia merchant who bought land there in 1714. Trenton served briefly as the United States capital when Congress met there in 1784, and it has been New Jersey's capital since 1790. It once was known for its large rubber, pottery, iron, and wire-rope factories. The gold-domed state capitol is a downtown landmark; nearby is the New Jersey Cultural Center. Revolutionary War sites are located in and near the city.

Newark was founded in 1666 by Robert Treat and other settlers from Connecticut. Today it is New Jersey's largest city and the state's financial and business center. Newark Airport and Port Newark make the city a transportation hub. A higher-education complex covers much of the inner city and includes the Newark campus of Rutgers University. The New Jersey Performing Arts Center, completed in 1997, gave the city a major economic and cultural boost.

Top: Newark is New Jersey's largest city and center of finance and business. One of the oldest of the major U.S. cities, it has undergone extensive urban renewal. *Above:* Old brick row houses and wrought-iron fences lend charm to a neighborhood in Jersey City.

Jersey City owes its prominence to its location directly across the Hudson River from New York City. It has been the eastern terminal for many national railroad systems since about 1840. The city also has deepwater harbor facilities and major highways to help carry its industrial products to national and international markets. Its waterfront is being revived with new high-rise office buildings and renovation of many old structures.

Paterson lies near the 70-foot (21-meter) Great Falls of the Passaic River. The town was founded there in 1791 by Alexander Hamilton and others as the first planned industrial city in the United States. Waterpower from the falls was used to spin cotton. Later, Paterson became a center for the making of railroad locomotives, the production of silk, and the assembly of airplane motors. Modern manufactures include chemicals and electronics equipment. Great Falls Historic District preserves much of the old center around the falls.

Elizabeth, settled in 1664, was the first New Jersey town founded by English-speaking people. It was briefly New Jersey's capital when the colonial legislature met there in 1688. Modern Elizabeth's prosperity is based on its large port, one of the world's largest shipping points for preloaded freight containers.

Camden was founded in 1681, a year before Philadelphia, its neighbor across the Delaware River. Starting as a landing for ferryboats crossing the Delaware, Camden later became the entry point for railroads coming into New Jersey. It was a center of shipbuilding, soup canning, and the manufacture of sound equipment. Today, much industry has left, and railroads are of minor importance. Camden is the site of the New Jersey State Aquarium and a campus of Rutgers University. Two bridges link Camden and Philadelphia.

▶GOVERNMENT

New Jersey's first state government dates from July 2, 1776, two days before the Declaration of Independence was adopted. The second constitution was approved in 1844. The present state constitution was adopted in 1947. It divides powers of government among executive, legislative, and judicial branches.

The executive branch is headed by the governor, who is elected by the people. The governor appoints, with the consent of the Senate, many other state officials, including the sec-

The gold-domed state capitol building in Trenton is the headquarters of state government. Trenton has been the capital of New Jersey since 1790.

retary of state, the attorney general, and the treasurer. The legislative branch is made up of the Senate and General Assembly. The members meet each year, beginning on the second Tuesday in January. The governor reports to the legislature at the beginning of each regular session and keeps it informed of the needs of the state. The judicial branch is made up of the state Supreme Court, the Superior Court, county courts, and lesser courts of limited power. The Supreme Court makes the rules governing all courts in the state.

▶HISTORY

Indian peoples reached what is now New Jersey about 10,000 years ago. The Indians about whom most is known are the Delaware (also called Lenni-Lenape or Lenape), who probably arrived about 600 years ago. They built their settlements on streams, lakes, and bays. They were an agricultural people, but they also gathered wild plants, fished, and hunted. Some tribes spent the summers at the seashore, gathering shellfish. They ate the flesh and used the shells for ornaments and wampum (money).

GOVERNMENT

State Government
Governor: 4-year term
State senators: 40; 4-year terms
State representatives: 80;
  2-year terms
Number of counties: 21

Federal Government
U.S. senators: 2
U.S. representatives: 13
Number of electoral votes: 15

For the name of the current governor, see STATE GOVERNMENTS in Volume S. For the names of current U.S. senators and representatives, see UNITED STATES, CONGRESS OF THE in Volume U-V.

European exploration disrupted the Indian way of life. Giovanni da Verrazano, an Italian navigator exploring for France, sailed along the New Jersey coast in 1524. In 1609, Henry Hudson, an Englishman sailing for the Dutch, explored the coast and entered Newark Bay. Dutch fur traders quickly followed, perhaps within a year. Dutch explorer Cornelius Mey sailed around the southern tip of New Jersey in 1620; Cape May was later named for him.

Swedish settlers arrived on the Delaware River in 1638. Faced with competition for the fur trade, the Dutch drove the Swedes from the area in 1653. Dutch settlers established the first permanent town, Bergen, in 1660 in what is now Hudson County and spread out along the Hackensack and Raritan rivers. The English began their main attempts at settlement in the 1660's, buying land from the Lenape.

Pressure from colonial settlements weakened the Lenape. Many died of European diseases. Others left to live in other colonies. The few who remained by 1758 were given a reservation at Brotherton, now Indian Mills, in Burlington County. It was abandoned in 1802.

English Settlement

In 1664, the Dutch surrendered their claims to England. That year, the Duke of York granted the land between the Hudson and Delaware rivers to Lord John Berkeley and Sir George Carteret. In the meantime, the governor of New York, unaware of the Duke's grant, encouraged people from Long Island and New England to settle in New Jersey.

The Dutch recaptured the area in 1674, only to have New Jersey retaken by the English in 1675. Shortly after, New Jersey was split into two parts, known as East Jersey and West Jersey. In 1702 the two parts were united as a royal province under the governor of New York. Finally, in 1738, New Jersey became a separate province, with Lewis Morris as its first royal governor.

The Revolution and Statehood

New Jersey joined the other American colonies in the War for Independence against Great Britain. New Jersey's position between New York and Philadelphia made it the site of many battles and skirmishes. The Battle of

INDEX TO NEW JERSEY MAP

• County Seat   Counties in parentheses   ★ State Capital

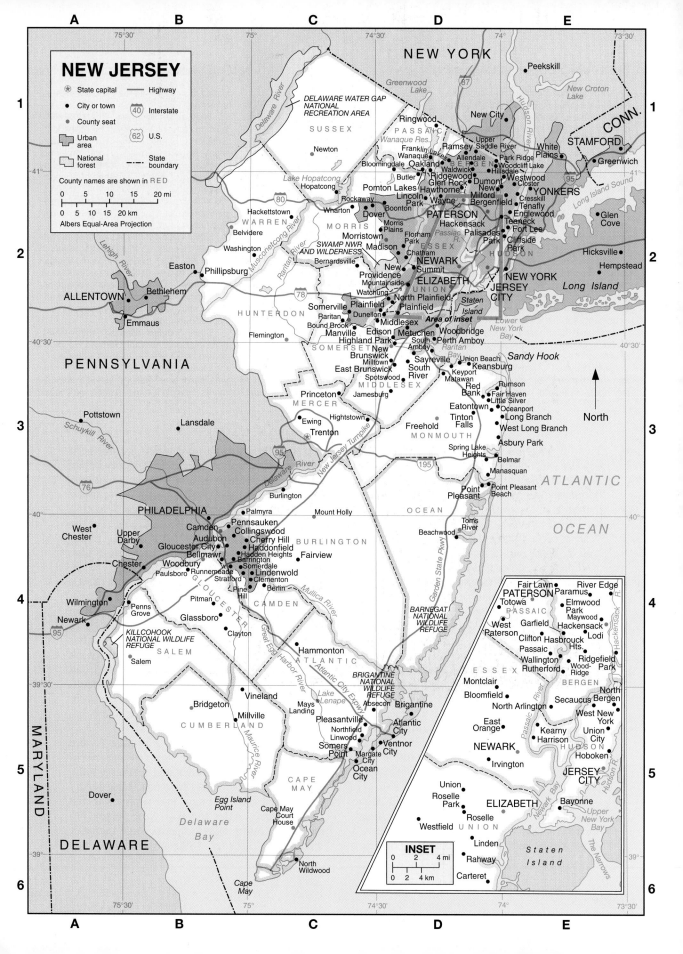

NEW JERSEY

Legend:
- ✳ State capital
- ● City or town
- ● County seat
- Urban area
- National forest
- — Highway
- ⟨40⟩ Interstate
- ⟨62⟩ U.S.
- —·—·— State boundary

County names are shown in RED

0   5   10   15   20 mi
0 5 10 15 20 km
Albers Equal-Area Projection

NEW YORK

PENNSYLVANIA

MARYLAND

DELAWARE

CONN.

ATLANTIC OCEAN

North

Counties and places

SUSSEX, PASSAIC, BERGEN, WARREN, MORRIS, ESSEX, HUDSON, UNION, HUNTERDON, SOMERSET, MIDDLESEX, MERCER, MONMOUTH, BURLINGTON, OCEAN, CAMDEN, GLOUCESTER, SALEM, ATLANTIC, CUMBERLAND, CAPE MAY

INSET

0   2   4 mi
0 2 4 km

PATERSON, PASSAIC, ESSEX, NEWARK, BERGEN, HUDSON, UNION, ELIZABETH, JERSEY CITY

Famous People

Many famous people have links with New Jersey. Aaron Burr (1756–1836), a Revolutionary War hero and a vice president of the United States, was born in Newark. The famous duel in which Burr shot and killed his political rival, Alexander Hamilton, took place at Weehawken in 1804. Grover Cleveland (1837–1908), the 22nd and 24th U.S. president, was born in Caldwell. Woodrow Wilson (1856–1924), born in Virginia, was president of Princeton University (1902–10) and governor of New Jersey (1911–13) before becoming the 28th U.S. president.

Although they were not born in New Jersey, Revolutionary War leader William Livingston (1723–90), inventor Thomas Edison (1847–1931), and scientist Albert Einstein (1879–1955) did much of their important work while living in the state. Biographies of all these figures can be found in the appropriate volumes of this encyclopedia.

Seth Boyden (1788–1870), inventor and manufacturer, did much to promote Newark's industrial growth after he

Woodrow Wilson when he was president of Princeton

moved there from Massachusetts. He developed and manufactured the first patent leather ever produced in the United States. Boyden also made stationary steam engines and railroad locomotives, grew giant strawberries, and invented a hatforming machine. Thomas Edison

called Boyden "one of America's great inventors."

William J. Brennan, Jr. (1906–97), born in Newark, was a justice of the U.S. Supreme Court (1956–90). He wrote many important majority opinions and cast consistently liberal votes on such issues as civil rights, freedom of speech, and criminal law. Prior to his appointment to the U.S. Supreme Court, Brennan served as a judge on the New Jersey Supreme Court (1952–56).

Hetty Green (1834–1916) was a Wall Street financier and the richest woman of her day. Born in New Bedford, Massachusetts, to a strict Quaker family, Green was known for her eccentric behavior. She spent her later years in Hoboken, where she saved money by living in rundown boardinghouses.

Clara Louise Maass (1876–1901), head nurse at Newark German Hospital, served as an army nurse in Cuba during the Spanish-American War. In 1901, she was the only woman volunteer in experiments to control the spread of yellow

---

Trenton, in 1776, was an important early victory for the Americans. Other major battles include the Battle of Princeton (1777) and the Battle of Monmouth (1778). General Washington and his army spent three winters in New Jersey, two of them in Morristown.

New Jersey declared its independence on July 2, 1776, two days before the Declaration of Independence was adopted. William Livingston was elected the state's first governor.

New Jersey delegates to the Constitutional Convention of 1787 proposed that all states, regardless of size, have equal representation within the government. Although this proposal, called the New Jersey Plan, was not adopted, it led to the creation of a two-house legislature. One house, the Senate, has equal representation for each state. The other, the House of Representatives, has representation according to size of the population. On December 18, 1787, New Jersey became the third state to ratify the U.S. Constitution.

The 1800's

New Jersey's industrial development began early. The first ironworks in New Jersey opened in Shrewsbury in 1676. Within 25 years forges and furnaces sprang up in many

areas of the state, particularly in the northern counties. Zinc mining in Sussex County began in the early 1800's at Franklin and Ogdensburg. In 1791, Alexander Hamilton founded the Society for Useful Manufactures, selecting the falls of the Passaic River as the site for the industrial city of Paterson. Camden, Elizabeth, Jersey City, Newark, and Trenton also became centers of industry.

Transportation developments in the 1830's aided New Jersey's growth. The Morris Canal between Phillipsburg and Newark, opened in 1831, connected industrial New Jersey with Pennsylvania coal mining areas. Another canal joined Bordentown and New Brunswick in 1834. The Camden and Amboy Railroad started running from South Amboy to Bordentown in 1833, and more railroads soon were built linking other New Jersey cities. New settlements rose beside the railroads.

In 1860, the state's leading products were ironware, food and drink, textiles and clothing, carriages, and leather and leather goods. During the Civil War (1861–65), New Jersey contributed men, money, and supplies to the Union cause. After the war New Jersey became ever more industrialized. Huge factories were built, and by 1890 railroads reached

fever. She died after being bitten several times by infected mosquitoes. The Clara Maass Medical Center in Belleville, formerly the Newark German Hospital, was named in her honor.

William Paterson (1745–1806), Irish-born statesman, grew up in New Jersey. He graduated from the College of New Jersey (now Princeton University) and then studied law. As a delegate to the Constitutional Convention of 1787, he proposed the New Jersey Plan, which led to equal state representation in the U.S. Senate. He was governor of New Jersey (1790–93) and a member of the U.S. Supreme Court (1793–1806). The city of Paterson was named in his honor.

Paul Robeson (1898–1976), born in Princeton, gained fame as an actor and singer. He graduated

Clara Louise Maass

at the top of his class from Rutgers University, where he had been named an all-American football player. He earned his law degree from Columbia University, then became a noted stage and screen actor before turning to an international career as a concert singer. Robeson was active in movements for racial equality and other causes. He published his autobiography, *Here I Stand*, in 1958.

Frank Sinatra (1915–98), a singer and actor, was born in Hoboken. He gained fame as a band vocalist in the early

Paul Robeson

1940's and soon became a successful solo artist. His vocal techniques made him a leading interpreter of popular songs. Sinatra also acted in films, winning an Academy Award for his performance in *From Here to Eternity* (1953).

James Still (1812–85), a lifelong resident of the Pine Barrens, gained respect and affection throughout southern New Jersey as the "Black Doctor of the Pines." Though he had no formal training, he made his own medicines using local herbs and treated Pinelands people with great skill for some 30 years.

Patience Wright (1725–86), born into a Quaker home in Bordentown, was a sculptor in wax and the first American to win recognition as a sculptor. She traveled to England in 1772 and became a favorite in the court of England's King George III.

nearly every town. An important new industry began when railroads reached the Jersey Shore. By the late 1800's the shore, long considered worthless, had become one of the state's most valuable areas as the railroads carried swarms of vacationers to the seaside.

Faced with agricultural products brought from western states, mainly wheat and beef, the state's farmers began specializing, turning to dairying, truck farming, and chicken ranges. Thomas Edison established the nation's first industrial research laboratory at Menlo Park in 1876, launching New Jersey's rise to prominence as a research center.

The 1900's

Research led the way throughout much of the 1900's, particularly in pharmaceuticals, chemicals, and electronics. These industries helped New Jersey take a major role as a military supplier in World War I and World War II. Such research giants as RCA, Merck, Johnson & Johnson, Hoffmann-La Roche, and CIBA established facilities in the state. The transistor, central to miniaturization in everything from computers to space exploration, was patented by scientists at Bell Laboratories in Murray Hill in 1947.

Since 1970, the state's rapid growth has led to serious problems. Deteriorating conditions in cities caused many industries to move to suburban and rural areas, creating problems in both the cities and the new locations. The moves have swallowed considerable amounts of farmland, and, in some cases, have threatened wetlands. As commuters rely more heavily on automobiles, wider highways have been built, creating ever-worsening traffic and pollution problems. Northeastern New Jersey has experienced serious water shortages.

New Jersey's people have fought back in determined efforts to solve these problems. Many multimillion-dollar proposals to improve the environment have been approved by voters. Government agencies have tackled such problems as finding jobs for workers laid off when factories close their doors. New Jersey, as the most densely populated and most urbanized of all states, has in essence become a huge laboratory in which to study the problems and opportunities of urbanization as that trend spreads across the nation.

JOHN T. CUNNINGHAM
Author, *New Jersey: America's Main Road*

NEWMAN, PAUL. See MOTION PICTURES (Profiles: Movie Stars).

NEW MEXICO

New Mexico was named in the mid-1500's by Spanish conquistadors, the first Europeans to explore the American Southwest. Venturing north out of Mexico, a land they had already colonized, the Spanish dreamed of finding a "new" Mexico to conquer, a rich land where they imagined endless quantities of gold and other treasure would be theirs for the taking.

Today's New Mexicans call their state the Land of Enchantment, a nickname that aptly defines the bewitching charm of this hypnotic land, with its deep blue skies, golden sunshine, open spaces, and ever-changing landscapes. The name was chosen in 1921 by the state's bureau of tourism, which hoped to entice visitors to this then little-known but fascinating part of the country.

State flag

New Mexico is a southwestern state. It borders four other states—Arizona, Colorado, Oklahoma, and Texas—and one foreign country, Mexico. New Mexico's northwest corner belongs to what is known as the Four Corners area. This is the only place in the nation where four states—Utah, Colorado, New Mexico, and Arizona—meet at a single point.

New Mexico's cultural diversity stands as a part of its living history. Native Americans, the region's original inhabitants, maintain a strong presence in New Mexico's various Indian communities and on Pueblo, Navajo, and Apache reservations. More than 40 percent of the population claims Hispanic heritage.

When the Spanish settled in north-central New Mexico in 1598, they established the second permanent European settlement, after St. Augustine, Florida, in what is now the United States. They colonized New Mexico nine years before the English settled Jamestown and ten years before the French settled Quebec. The Spanish ruled New Mexico for more than 200 years, until 1821, when the region came under the rule of an independent Mexico. Then, in 1848, the United States acquired the territory by the Treaty of Guadalupe Hidalgo.

New Mexico is the nation's fifth largest state in area, and except for its southwest corner, it is nearly square in shape. Despite its large size, New Mexico ranks only 36th in population, and more than one-third of the people live in or around Albuquerque, which

is by far the state's largest city. Santa Fe, the nation's oldest capital city, has served as a regional seat of government for 400 years.

A state since 1912, New Mexico's population and economic growth were at first comparatively slow. But with the United States' participation (1941–45) in World War II, New Mexico became a principal center for nuclear energy research and the development of nuclear weapons.

Services, notably research and development and tourism, are the leading industries. At the same time, the availability of dry land encourages extensive ranching, and diverse mineral deposits make New Mexico a major mining center. Still, its modest population, scarcity of water, and great distance from major commercial centers have discouraged the development of large-scale industries.

▶ LAND

In general, New Mexico slopes down from north to south and from west to east. More than half the state lies between 5,000 and 10,000 feet (1,524 and 3,048 meters) above sea level—a relatively high elevation.

Land Regions

New Mexico's land surface includes four distinct and widely varied land regions.

New Mexico's fascinating character is shaped by its ever-changing landscapes and unique blending of many cultures, including Hispanic and Native American. At Christmastime, Santa Fe dazzles in the festive glow of traditional Mexican luminaria. Pueblo, Navajo, and Apache arts and crafts preserve native traditions.

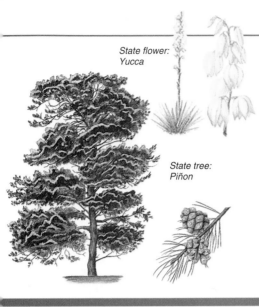

State flower:
Yucca

State tree:
Piñon

FACTS AND FIGURES

Location: Southwestern United States; bordered on the north by Colorado, on the east by Oklahoma and Texas, on the south by Texas and Mexico, and on the west by Arizona.

Area: 121,598 sq mi (314,939 km²); rank, 5th.

Population: 1,819,046 (2000 census); rank, 36th.

Elevation: *Highest*—13,161 ft (4,011 m) at Wheeler Peak; *lowest*—2,817 ft (859 m) at Red Bluff Reservoir.

Capital: Santa Fe.

Statehood: January 6, 1912; 47th state.

State Motto: *Crescit Eundo* ("It grows as it goes").

State Song: "O Fair New Mexico."

Nickname: Land of Enchantment.

Abbreviations: NM; N. Mex.

State bird:
Roadrunner

New Mexico's landscape is strikingly varied. The Sangre de Cristo Mountains (*left*) in the north-central part of the state are a southern range of the Rocky Mountains. They stand in marked contrast to the Llano Estacado (*below*), the dry, flat plain that lies to the east of the Pecos Valley.

The Great Plains cover the eastern third of the state. This part of New Mexico contains two important river valleys: The valley of the Canadian River is deep, with many **mesas** (flat-topped hills), canyons, and cliffs; that of the Pecos River is much smoother and contains flat plains as well as rocky canyons. To the east of the Pecos Valley is a level plain called the Llano Estacado or Staked Plain. It is some of the earth's flattest land.

The Rocky Mountains extend southward from Colorado into north-central New Mexico. This mountain region is divided by the valley of the Rio Grande. To the east of the river is a high and rugged mountain range that the Spaniards named the Sangre de Cristo, meaning "blood of Christ." These mountains extend to a point just south of Santa Fe. Wheeler Peak, New Mexico's highest point, lies in this range. To the west of the Rio Grande lie the Jemez Mountains.

The Colorado Plateau covers the northwestern part of the state. An elevated area of mostly level land, it is an area where the Colorado River and its tributaries have dug through layers of rock to form deep canyons.

The Basin and Range Province is the state's largest land region. It blankets the southwestern, central, and south-central portions of the state. This province is dotted with isolated mountain ranges separated by broad, flat desert valleys, or drainage basins. These basins, most notably the Rio Grande Valley, support most of the state's population.

Rivers and Lakes

A large, landlocked state, New Mexico has only about 250 square miles (647 square kilometers) of surface water. Its five most important rivers supply most of the state's water.

New Mexico's most important river is the Rio Grande, the third longest river in the United States. Measuring a total length of 1,885 miles (3,033 kilometers) from its headwaters in Colorado to its mouth at the Gulf of Mexico, the Rio Grande runs 470 miles (756 kilometers) southward through the center of New Mexico. The Pecos River, the state's second longest river, flows from north-central

New Mexico through the Great Plains region and into the Rio Grande in west Texas. A third important river, the Canadian River, rises near the Colorado border and cuts through the northeastern corner of New Mexico.

To the west of these three rivers is the **continental divide**, a fold in the earth's surface that separates North America's eastern rivers (which drain into the Atlantic Ocean) from its western rivers (which drain into the Pacific Ocean). The two important rivers in New Mexico on the west side of the continental divide are the San Juan and the Gila rivers, both tributaries of the Colorado River.

New Mexico's few natural lakes are mostly high-altitude lakes in the mountain region. Its reservoirs, or artificial lakes, have been created by building dams on the state's rivers. Chief among these reservoirs are the Elephant Butte, the Conchas, and the Navajo (shared with Colorado). They provide farmers with an even flow of irrigation water and serve as recreation areas for fishing and boating.

Climate

New Mexico has a dry, sunny climate. Temperatures vary widely throughout the state due to the differences in elevation. However, the normal average temperature in Albuquerque is 35°F (2°C) in January and 79°F (26°C) in July. Precipitation from rain and snow averages only 15 inches (381 millimeters) a year. The mountains receive more than the average amount, while the Basin and Range Province receives less than the average. Some of the lowest lying areas receive fewer than 10 inches (254 millimeters) of yearly rainfall, making them nearly true deserts. Three fourths of New Mexico's precipitation falls between June and September during the growing season. The remainder comes mostly during the winter, at which time rain falls in the lower elevations and snow falls in the higher elevations. Mountain snow feeds the streams and rivers in the spring.

Plant and Animal Life

At the highest elevations, New Mexican terrain supports very few plants or animals. However, at levels between 8,500 and 12,500 feet (2,591 and 3,810 meters) are spruces, firs, and aspens, along with animals and birds that make

their homes in mountain forests. At a level between 7,000 and 9,000 feet (2,134 and 2,743 meters) lies a major timber zone, rich in Ponderosa pine, that shelters mountain lions, bears, and elk.

Three fourths of the state lies between 5,000 and 7,000 feet (1,524 and 2,134 meters). Native to this level are junipers, piñons, blue grama grass, and sagebrush. Deer, coyotes, antelope, and prairie dogs are abundant.

Below 5,000 feet (1,524 meters), mesquite, cactus, creosote, and black grama grass grow, sustaining desert fox, rabbits, bats, kangaroo rats, squirrels, and a variety of reptiles. The cutthroat trout, the official state fish, inhabits high mountain waters. The yucca, the official state plant, is a cactus type found in the Basin and Range Province.

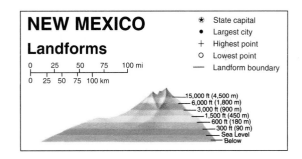

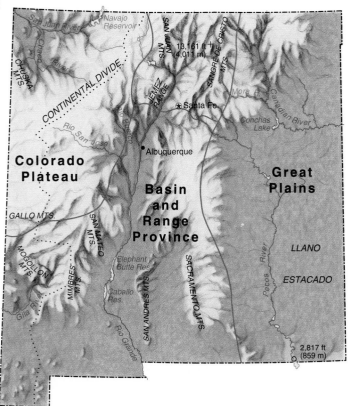

The people of New Mexico represent many cultures. Less than half the population claims northern European heritage (*left*). Among the fifty states, New Mexico has the highest percentage of both Hispanic Americans and Native American Indians. The Spanish have maintained a strong presence in New Mexico since 1598; various Indian groups have thrived there for more than 10,000 years.

Natural Resources

One-fourth of New Mexico's land surface is covered with forest and woodlands. The state has approximately 30 essential minerals, including abundant quantities of uranium, perlite, potash, copper, pumice, and molybdenum. New Mexico also contains oil and natural gas reserves in the northwest plateau region and in the southern third of the eastern plains. Extensive coal reserves are found throughout the state.

▶ PEOPLE

New Mexico's population reflects the multicultural stages of its long history. Native Americans had lived there for thousands of years when Spanish adventurers first explored the region in the mid-1500's, then conquered it. For 250 years thereafter, New Mexico was a colony of Spain, then Mexico.

Three significant periods of immigration to New Mexico occurred after the territory was acquired by the United States in 1848. Settlers came to the area from other parts of the United States as well as from foreign countries. The first major wave of immigration occurred during the 1850's, New Mexico's first decade as an American territory. The second occurred after 1879 when the railroads arrived, bringing laborers to work in the booming mining industries and to farm the eastern plains. The third came after 1945, following World War II. New Mexico became a primary defense and nuclear-research center, opening many employment opportunities.

Hispanics account for 42 percent of the population, reflecting the state's early Spanish influence. About 10 percent claim Indian ancestry; many live on one of New Mexico's 24 Indian reservations, including 19 Pueblo, 3 Navajo, and 2 Apache reservations. Blacks make up about 2 percent of the population. Non-Hispanic whites make up the largest single group of New Mexicans. Increasing numbers of recent newcomers to the state have come from Mexico and from Central and South America.

Education

New Mexico offers free public education to all children between the ages of 5 and 18. State laws guarantee equal funding for each student. State-supported institutions of higher learning include the University of New Mexico in Albuquerque, the New Mexico Institute of Mining and Technology in Socorro, New Mexico State University in Las Cruces, and Western New Mexico University in Silver City, all founded in the late 1800's. Since that time, several other regional universities and two-year college programs have been created by the state. There are several private colleges and universities, among them the College of Santa Fe and St. John's College, both in Santa Fe, and the College of the Southwest in Hobbs.

Libraries, Museums, and the Arts

Although New Mexico established its first public library only after 1900, today many cities and towns across the state have public library facilities. All of the state universities house extensive collections of books concerning the Southwest, as do the Museum of New Mexico and the New Mexico State Library.

Santa Fe is home to the four branches of the Museum of New Mexico, each with its own focus: New Mexico history; Indian arts and culture; international folk art; and the fine arts. Albuquerque is home to the New Mexico Museum of Natural History, the Fine Arts Museum, and the Maxwell Museum of Anthropology. Alamogordo has the Space Center museum, featuring the International Space Hall of Fame. Los Alamos highlights its Bradbury Science Hall and Museum and

The Santa Fe Opera House, located in the foothills of the Sangre de Cristo Mountains, is one of the nation's most spectacular performing arts centers.

the County Historical Museum, which presents a history of the Manhattan Project—the development of the atomic bomb.

The art of New Mexico also reflects the state's diverse population, and the state has an unusually high proportion of artists among its residents. Painters, writers, folk artists, and performing artists have long made New Mexico their home. The state supports a wide variety of performing arts, particularly music. The Santa Fe Opera, begun in 1957, is perhaps the state's most widely known attraction. It is situated in a delightful open-air theater in the foothills of the Sangre de Cristo Mountains.

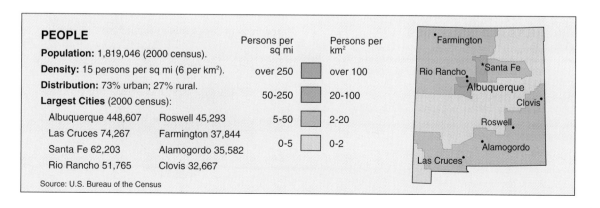

PEOPLE

Population: 1,819,046 (2000 census).

Density: 15 persons per sq mi (6 per km²).

Distribution: 73% urban; 27% rural.

Largest Cities (2000 census):

City	Population	City	Population
Albuquerque	448,607	Roswell	45,293
Las Cruces	74,267	Farmington	37,844
Santa Fe	62,203	Alamogordo	35,582
Rio Rancho	51,765	Clovis	32,667

Source: U.S. Bureau of the Census

Persons per sq mi	Persons per km²
over 250	over 100
50-250	20-100
5-50	2-20
0-5	0-2

Farmington
Rio Rancho
*Santa Fe
Albuquerque
Clovis
Roswell
Alamogordo
Las Cruces

▶ ECONOMY

New Mexico's economy has undergone tremendous change since World War II. Once agriculture and mining were the main contributors to the gross state product (GSP)—the total value of goods and services produced in a year. However, today the service industries completely dominate the economy.

Services

New Mexico's service industries employ approximately 85 percent of the state's entire work force. Tourism, business, legal, health, and other personal services lead in employment, followed closely by government. The federal government, in addition to state and local government services, contributes greatly to New Mexico's GSP through its funding of defense research and development at Los Alamos National Laboratory and Sandia National Laboratories. Other services in order of importance are finance, insurance, and real estate; wholesale and retail trade; and transportation, communication, and utilities.

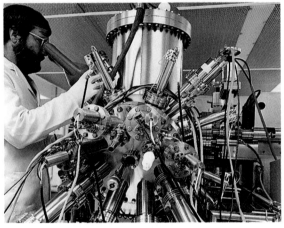

Manufacturing

Historically, manufacturing has played a small role in the economy of New Mexico. Heavy industry is almost nonexistent. Early manufacturing involved processing the state's minerals and agricultural produce. Petroleum refining and food processing were most important. Today major manufacturers produce

---

PRODUCTS AND INDUSTRIES

Manufacturing: Electronic equipment, analytical instruments, transportation equipment, printed materials, processed foods, lumber and wood products.

Agriculture: Cattle, dairy products, hay, chili peppers, pecans, cotton, potatoes, onions, wheat.

Minerals: Natural gas, petroleum, copper, coal, potash, sand and gravel, perlite.

Services: Wholesale and retail trade; finance, insurance, and real estate; business, social, and personal services; transportation, communication, and utilities; government.

*Gross state product is the total value of goods and services produced in a year.

Percentage of Gross State Product* by Industry

- Government — 20%
- Business, social, and personal services — 20%
- Finance, insurance, and real estate — 16%
- Wholesale and retail trade — 12%
- Transportation, communication, and utilities — 12%
- Manufacturing — 8%
- Agriculture 4%
- Construction 4%
- Mining 4%

Source: U.S. Bureau of Economic Analysis

Although cattle ranching (*left*) is New Mexico's most profitable agricultural enterprise, the service industries, which include research and development, make up the largest segment of the economy. Among the state's scientific research centers are Sandia National Laboratories (*below left*) and the National Radio Astronomy Observatory, which operates the powerful Very Large Array radio telescope (*right*).

electronic equipment, analytical instruments, transportation equipment, printed materials, processed foods, lumber and wood products, and clothing. New Mexico also is famous for its arts and crafts, particularly Indian-made rugs, jewelry, pottery, and baskets.

Agriculture

Because New Mexico's climate is so dry, more than 35 million acres (14 million hectares) of its agricultural land is used as rangeland. Most ranching takes place on the eastern plains. There are almost as many cattle in New Mexico as people. Cash receipts for cattle and dairy products account for two thirds of New Mexico's farm earnings.

Cash crops make up the remainder of agricultural output. Chief among these are hay, chili peppers, and pecans. Other important crops are cotton, potatoes, onions, and wheat. Of the land in crop production, more than half must be irrigated.

Mining and Construction

The production of natural gas and crude petroleum are the state's leading mining activities. Some coal is mined in the northwest and is used to generate electricity. Also mined are copper, potash, and perlite. New Mexico also was a primary producer of uranium and molybdenum, but mining of these has stopped. Construction of roads, bridges, and buildings is ongoing and of equal economic importance to mining.

Transportation and Communication

The first road in New Mexico was *El Camino Real* (Spanish for "the Royal Road"). It linked Santa Fe with Vera Cruz, Mexico. In 1821 the opening of the Santa Fe Trail connected New Mexico with Missouri.

New Mexico began building its modern road system about 1920. Today, three interstate highways cross the state north to south and east to west, covering more than 1,000 miles (1,600 kilometers).

The Atchison, Topeka, and Santa Fe Railway came to New Mexico in 1879. Today's railroads still provide both commercial and passenger service. AMTRAK's Southwest Limited and Sunset Limited stop in New Mexico. Bus services link small towns with a central terminus in Albuquerque. Major air carriers fly in and out of the Albuquerque International Airport.

New Mexicans support approximately 20 daily newspapers. The *Albuquerque Journal* enjoys the widest circulation, followed by the *Albuquerque Tribune*. There are more than 100 radio stations. Most of populated New Mexico has television through direct or translator broadcasts or through cable services.

▶ CITIES

More than seven in ten New Mexicans live in urban areas, which are defined as communities with more than 2,500 people. Albuquerque, with a population approaching 450,000, is New Mexico's largest city. It is more than six times larger than either Las Cruces or Santa Fe, the state's second and third largest cities, respectively.

Santa Fe, the state capital, was founded about 1610 by Governor Pedro de Peralta. It is the oldest capital city in the United States, and for 85 years it was the only European settlement in New Mexico. In the 1800's it was the last stop on the Santa Fe Trail. Today it is home to major historical and art museums, the old Palace of the Governors, and notable churches.

Places of Interest

White Sands National Monument, near Alamogordo

Taos Pueblo, in Taos

The Big Room, Carlsbad Caverns National Park, near Carlsbad

Chaco Culture National Historical Park, near Farmington

New Mexico is filled with places of scenic and historic interest, ranging from the pre-Columbian cliff dwellings of the Anasazi Indians and many present-day pueblos and reservations to the site of the explosion of the first atomic bomb.

Bandelier National Monument, located in Frijoles Canyon near Los Alamos, features the remarkable cliff dwellings that the Anasazi occupied between A.D. 1200 and 1500 after abandoning such sites as Chaco Canyon. The site was named for the archaeologist Adolph Bandelier (1840–1914), who lived among the Pueblo Indians (1880–86).

Capulin Volcano National Monument, near Raton, is an almost perfect volcanic cinder cone. It rises 1,000 feet (305 meters) above the plains. The cone of this inactive volcano is 10,000 years old. It was formed in the last great period of volcanic activity in western North America.

Carlsbad Caverns National Park, near Carlsbad, is New Mexico's most visited tourist attraction and the state's only national park. It is made up of a series of connected underground caverns. The largest of these, the Big Room, is one of the largest single limestone chambers in the world. It is as high as a 22-story build-

ing, and its floor area could contain 14 football fields. It has always been a popular summer home for bats; in the evenings as many as 5,000 bats a minute fly into the caverns' main opening.

Chaco Culture National Historical Park, located in a canyon near Farmington, preserves fascinating remains of Anasazi culture. Most notable among the various ruins is the communal dwelling *Pueblo Bonito*, meaning "Pretty Town." The four-story complex, completed about A.D. 1130, contained more than 650 well-plastered rooms and housed perhaps as many as 1,200 people.

Fort Union National Monument, in Watrous, preserves the site of three U.S. forts that provided supplies and safe haven to travelers along the Santa Fe Trail. A large array of wagon wheel ruts still can be seen along this stop on the Santa Fe National Historic Trail.

Lincoln State Monument, in Lincoln, is the Old Lincoln County Courthouse, from which the outlaw Billy the Kid made a famous jailbreak on April 28, 1881.

Palace of the Governors State Monument, in Santa Fe, was built in 1610 and served as the office and residence of New Mexico's governors. It is the oldest continuously used public structure in the

United States. Today it houses the history branch of the Museum of New Mexico, highlighting 400 years of European presence in the Southwest.

Smokey Bear Historical State Park, in Lincoln National Forest at Capitan, was dedicated in 1979 to the mascot of forest fire prevention. Rescued as a cub from a fire in Lincoln National Forest, Smokey was moved to the National Zoo, where he became a national symbol. After his death in 1976, he was buried here.

Taos Pueblo, in Taos, is one of the most frequently visited of New Mexico's 24 reservations.

Trinity Site, on the White Sands Missile Range, is opened twice a year to those who wish to visit the site of the first successful atomic bomb test.

White Sands National Monument, near Alamogordo, contains the world's largest gypsum dunes. The glistening white gypsum dissolves off the surrounding mountains and washes into the basin below.

State Parks. For more information on New Mexico's 45 state parks and other places of interest, contact the New Mexico State Tourism Department, 491 Old Santa Fe Trail, Santa Fe, N.Mex. 87503.

Albuquerque, located in central New Mexico on the Rio Grande, is New Mexico's largest city and the state's primary manufacturing center.

Albuquerque and its surrounding metropolitan area is home to more than one-third of the state's population. Founded in 1706, it grew rapidly after 1879 when the Atchison, Topeka, and Santa Fe Railway came through. The population surged again with World War II and the establishment of military bases and Sandia National Laboratories. Old Town, the site of the original settlement, is still a major attraction. The University of New Mexico is located near the center of the city.

Las Cruces, meaning "the crosses," also became an important town after the arrival of the railway in 1881. Located in the Mesilla Valley, Las Cruces today is a rapidly growing city. It is the center of a major farming area and home to New Mexico State University.

Santa Fe has had four state capitol buildings in its 400-year history. The current structure (*right*) was completed in 1966.

▶ **GOVERNMENT**

New Mexico entered the Union in 1912 under a constitution written in 1910. Although it has been amended many times, the 1910 constitution remains in effect today.

New Mexico's executive branch is led by a governor and a lieutenant governor. Both are elected to 4-year terms; they may serve no more than two consecutive terms. The attor-

GOVERNMENT

State Government
Governor: 4-year term
State senators: 42; 4-year terms
State representatives: 70;
2-year terms
Number of counties: 33

Federal Government
U.S. senators: 2
U.S. representatives: 3
Number of electoral votes: 5

For the name of the current governor, see STATE GOVERNMENTS in Volume S. For the names of current U.S. senators and representatives, see UNITED STATES, CONGRESS OF THE in Volume U-V.

ney general, secretary of state, treasurer, and auditor are also elected statewide.

The legislature has two houses. Senators serve 4-year terms, and members of the House of Representatives serve 2-year terms. The state legislature meets for 30 days during even-numbered years and 60 days during odd-numbered years.

The judicial branch of government is similar to the federal court system. There is a state supreme court, a court of appeals, and district courts. Judges are appointed by the governor and serve 4- to 8-year terms.

New Mexico's 33 counties are governed by commissions that have both executive and legislative powers. Towns and cities have either a mayor and council or a commission and manager. Also at the local level are Indian tribal governments. Pueblo governments have governors and councils. Non-Pueblo tribes have presidents or chairmen and councils. Tribal governments may also have their own police forces and court systems.

▶ HISTORY

New Mexico's earliest people were big-game hunters. They first came to the region more than 10,000 years ago and stayed until the climate became so hot and dry that the big game disappeared. Later desert dwellers moved into the area, about 6000 B.C. For 3,000 years these hunters and gatherers roamed for food, but once they learned to grow corn, squash, and the red kidney bean and to make pottery, they started to settle more permanent villages.

Early Indian Cultures

From the early settlers emerged the Mogollon, who lived in west-central New Mexico, and also the Anasazi, who lived to the north. During the height of their culture (A.D. 1050–1300), some Anasazi built pueblos, or multi-storied stone apartment houses, while others created great cliff dwellings. The Anasazi built their largest pueblos on the floor of Chaco Canyon in northwestern New Mexico.

The descendants of the Anasazi, whom we now know as the Pueblo Indians, began to develop their culture about 1450, mostly in the Rio Grande Valley. They built multistoried pueblos and farmed. Also in the area were the Navajo, who learned farming from the Pueblos, and the Apaches.

Exploration and Colonization

The voyages of Christopher Columbus brought the Spanish to the Americas, where they claimed vast territories for Spain, including Mexico.

In 1539 the Spanish embarked on their first expedition from Mexico into the American Southwest, including New Mexico, where

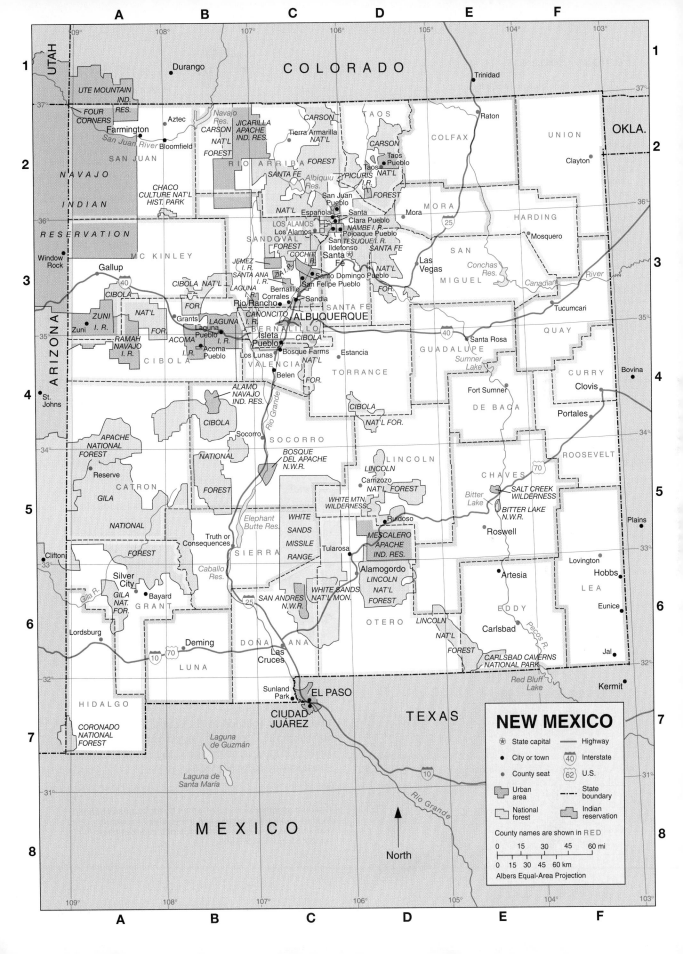

Famous People

Billy the Kid (**Henry McCarty**, also known as **William H. Bonney**) (1859–81) became famous as a result of the Lincoln County range wars (1878–81). Arrested for fighting on the side of the newcomers to Lincoln County, Billy the Kid was tried and convicted in April 1881 for the murder of Lincoln's sheriff and was sentenced to death. On April 28 he killed his two guards and escaped from the Lincoln County Courthouse. Entering Fort Sumner on July 13, he was shot and killed by Lincoln's new sheriff, Pat Garrett, just after midnight.

Christopher (Kit) Carson (1809–68) was born in Kentucky but settled in Taos in 1826. Carson stayed on to become a trapper, hunter, and scout. In 1843 he married Josefa Jaramillo, a member of a prominent Taos family. During the Civil War, Carson commanded one of the territory's two volunteer regiments. In 1862 he was ordered to defeat the Mescalero Apache and the Navajo. (A biography of Kit Carson appears in Volume C.)

Dennis Chavez (1888–1962), born in Los Chavez, was the first Hispanic to serve in the U.S. Senate. A Democrat, he did much to further the development of New Mexico and establish the Fair Employment Practices Commission to aid minorities.

Francisco Vásquez de Coronado (1510?–54), born in Spain, headed the first major European expedition into New Mexico. (A biography of Francisco Coronado appears in Volume C.)

Pat (Patrick Floyd) Garrett (1850–1908), born in Alabama, was a buffalo hunter, cowboy, horse rancher, Texas Ranger, and sheriff of Lincoln County, New Mexico. In July 1881, he tracked down and killed escaped outlaw Billy the Kid. Garrett wrote *The Authentic Life of Billy the Kid* and was later murdered under mysterious circumstances.

Billy the Kid

Robert Hutchings Goddard (1882–1945), born in Worcester, Massachusetts, moved to Mescalero Ranch near Roswell in 1930, where he built and tested liquid-fueled rockets. Goddard's research led to 214 patents. Although the U.S. Armed Forces neglected to use this knowledge during World War II, German scientists used Goddard's ideas to build the deadly V-2 rockets that bombed London in 1944. The U.S. later used Goddard's research to build booster rockets for missiles and spacecraft. In 1959, years after his death, the United States acknowledged Goddard's achievements by awarding him the Congressional Medal.

John Baptist Lamy (la-ME) (1814–88), born in Lempdes, France, arrived in New Mexico in

they hoped to find the Seven Cities of Cíbola, a land of legendary wealth. Instead they encountered only the pueblo villages of the Zuñi Indians and claimed the land for Spain. A second expedition (1540–42), headed by Francisco Vásquez de Coronado, also failed to find the riches they sought.

In 1598, Don Juan de Oñate founded the first Spanish settlement in north-central New Mexico, near present-day Española. But the settlers' conflicts with the Acoma Indians, their failure to find gold, and Oñate's strict rule caused many of them to abandon the colony.

The Pueblo Revolt

In 1609 the king of Spain made New Mexico a royal colony and replaced Oñate with a new governor, Pedro de Peralta, who soon founded a new capital at Santa Fe. For the next seventy years, Franciscan missionaries worked to suppress the Pueblo religions and convert the Indians to the Catholic faith. But in 1680 the Pueblos, united under a leader named Popé, attacked the Spanish and forced them out of New Mexico.

Spanish governors brought Roman Catholic missionaries to New Mexico to Christianize the Native Americans. The Indians tried to overthrow colonial rule but were finally conquered in 1696.

Robert H. Goddard

the building of many parochial (church-sponsored) schools to educate New Mexico's children in the absence of free public schools. His life is the subject of author Willa Cather's book, *Death Comes for the Archbishop* (1927).

Georgia O'Keeffe (1887–1986) was born in Sun Prairie, Wisconsin, but settled in New Mexico in 1946. O'Keeffe's New Mexico paintings established her as one of America's greatest modern-day artists. (A biography of Georgia O'Keeffe appears in Volume O.)

Popé (po-PAY) (?–1688?) (Indian name: Po-png, meaning "Pumpkin Mountain") was born in San Juan Pueblo. A medicine man and religious leader, Popé was considered a devil worshiper by the Spanish missionary priests and was arrested in 1673. After his

Georgia O'Keeffe

release he moved to Taos Pueblo and organized a rebellion. He led the successful Pueblo Revolt of 1680, which drove the Spaniards out of New Mexico. It was the only time, anywhere, that Native Americans succeeded in driving out their conquerors.

Robert (Bobby) Unser (1934–) and **Al Unser, Sr.** (1939–), both born in Albuquerque, are members of one of America's most famous families of racing car drivers. The two brothers won countless races, including the most prestigious, the Indianapolis 500, a total of seven times: Al, Sr., is one of three four-time winners (1970, 1971, 1978, and 1987) and Bobby is a three-time winner (1968, 1975, and 1981). Also winning the Indianapolis 500, in 1992 and 1994, was Al's son, **Al Unser, Jr.**

1851. As the Catholic bishop (1853–75) and later archbishop (1875–88) of Santa Fe, Lamy oversaw the building of 45 new churches and St. Michael's, a Catholic college in Santa Fe. He also encouraged

---

Spanish and Mexican Rule

The Indians' victory was short-lived; by 1696 the Spanish had regained control over the Rio Grande Pueblos. Throughout the 1700's, Spanish communities adapted to the isolated frontier land, blending Spanish culture with the local traditions.

In 1821 Mexico declared its independence from Spain, and New Mexico became part of independent Mexico. Outside trade began at once. Many traders brought goods from the United States into New Mexico by way of the Santa Fe Trail. Anglo-American mountain men also arrived to trap beaver in the northern mountains near Taos.

In 1846 a war broke out between the United States and Mexico; U.S. commander Stephen W. Kearny marched his army into New Mexico and claimed the entire region for the United States. The claim became official in 1848, when the Treaty of Guadalupe Hidalgo ended the Mexican War and ceded New Mexico to the United States.

U.S. Territory

In 1850, the territory of New Mexico was created. The original territory included all of present-day New Mexico and Arizona and parts of Colorado and Nevada.

Two Civil War battles were fought there in 1862. The second battle, at Glorieta Pass near Las Vegas, stopped the Confederate advance on Fort Union. This defeat forced the Confederacy to abandon New Mexico and its plans for controlling the West.

Between 1862 and 1864, Union commander Kit Carson of the 1st New Mexico Volunteers was ordered to round up the Navajo and Apache Indians, who had been attacking settlements in New Mexico. The Indians were detained far from their homelands and were later placed on reservations.

A general lack of law and order plagued the frontier settlers. New Mexico's particular struggle was characterized by the Lincoln County range wars (1878–81), which involved the notorious outlaw Billy the Kid.

New Mexico began to change once the railroads came into service. The trains carried local products to national markets and brought many newcomers to the territory. New Mexico's population grew and new towns were established. Farming, cattle and sheep raising, and mining prospered.

During World War II, the atomic bomb was developed at Los Alamos, New Mexico, by a team of scientists headed by J. Robert Oppenheimer. The first successful test (*left*) took place at White Sands Proving Grounds on July 16, 1945. A few weeks later, U.S. forces dropped atomic bombs on the Japanese cities of Hiroshima and Nagasaki, forcing Japan to surrender.

Statehood

In 1912 New Mexico became the 47th state. When the United States entered World War I five years later, New Mexico had the nation's highest per capita volunteer rate.

The Taos Society of Artists was formed in 1912, and by the 1920's several art colonies had grown up in both Santa Fe and Taos. Novelists, poets, and painters advanced their distinctive style and started attracting attention to the southwestern culture.

Most New Mexicans prospered until the Great Depression of the 1930's. During that terrible decade, the farmers and ranchers within the Dust Bowl on the eastern plains and the villagers of northern New Mexico suffered food shortages and other hardships. Prosperity did not return until after 1941, when the United States entered World War II.

World War II

During World War II, New Mexicans fought all over the world against the Germans, Japanese, and their allies. In 1942, 3,000 New Mexicans were among those forced by the Japanese to take part in the Bataan Death March in the Philippines; only half of them survived. Navajo soldiers, some from New Mexico, aided American intelligence efforts by coding secret messages in the Navajo language that the Japanese could not decipher.

During the war, American scientists working on the Manhattan Project developed the first atomic weapons. One of their major re-search centers was the Atomic Research Laboratory, now called the Los Alamos National Laboratory, in the Jemez Mountains in north-central New Mexico. It was at White Sands Proving Grounds that the first atomic bomb was exploded on July 16, 1945.

Modern New Mexico

Since the end of World War II, New Mexico has seen both its economy and population grow. At the same time, Indian and Hispanic New Mexicans have remained on the lands of their ancestors, at times fighting to protect their land and traditions.

In the 1960's many Hispanic New Mexicans in the north joined the *Alianza Federal de Mercedes* (the Federal Alliance of Land Grants) to battle the U.S. government for land grant titles. They claimed that millions of acres had been illegally taken from their ancestors by the ranchers and the U.S. Forest Service. The *Alianza* failed to win any land grants for the villagers, but it exposed the problems of northern New Mexicans.

In 1970, after a separate battle with the forest service, the Indians of Taos Pueblo got Congress to set aside Blue Lake and 48,000 acres (19,440 hectares) of the Carson National Forest for their sole use. Events like these continually remind New Mexicans of their multicultural identity.

CALVIN A. ROBERTS
SUSAN A. ROBERTS
Coauthors, *New Mexico*

NEW ORLEANS

New Orleans, Louisiana, is one of the most colorful and interesting cities in the United States. Established in 1718 as the capital of France's Mississippi Valley colony, it retains a dazzling style and distinct atmosphere that reflects its early European heritage. In 2005, Hurricane Katrina struck the Gulf Coast and Mississippi Delta, and New Orleans suffered the worst natural disaster in the history of the United States. In his response to the crisis, U.S. president George W. Bush assured the country, "There is no way to imagine America without New Orleans, and this great city will rise again."

With a population of approximately 485,000, New Orleans is Louisiana's largest city. Its greater metropolitan area contains more than 1 million people. Descendants of the original French and Spanish settlers are known as Creoles. There are also many Cajuns (Acadians), descendants of the French-speaking people who fled to the area, driven from their homes in Nova Scotia by the British during the French and Indian War (1756–63).

New Orleans, one of the world's great port cities, is situated on the Mississippi River, about 110 miles (180 kilometers) upriver from the Gulf of Mexico. Lake Pontchartrain forms its northern border. The climate is subtropical, with hot, humid summers and mild winters. Annual rainfall is approximately 60 inches (1,520 millimeters), accounting for the lush abundance of the city's trees and flowers.

Oil and gas production, the port, and tourism are the mainstays of New Orleans' economy. Also a major convention center, New Orleans attracts as many as 9 million visitors a year. The 1984 Louisiana World Exposition (World's Fair), held in New Orleans, stimulated renewal of the riverfront area. It now includes a world-class aquarium, a mile-long recreation park, and a riverside retail shopping center.

New Orleans is generally acknowledged as the birthplace of jazz, and every spring it hosts the International Jazz and Heritage Festival, drawing mammoth crowds. The city is also recognized for its rollicking Mardi Gras festival, one of the world's most famous carnivals, held during the weeks before the Christian observance of Lent.

Places of Interest. New Orleans is known for its fine restaurants, specializing in Creole and spicy Cajun cuisine. Nightclubs and bars play jazz and other music at all hours on Bourbon Street, the city's most famous promenade. Streetcars clang along the oak tree-shaded St. Charles Avenue and along the edge of the French Quarter, the oldest section of the city. Otherwise known as the Vieux Carré (French for "Old Square"), the French Quarter reflects both French and Spanish influences in architecture.

The French Quarter's most famous landmark is Jackson Square, named for General (later U.S. president) Andrew Jackson. Jackson Square contains several

A jazz musician entertains tourists on Bourbon Street in New Orleans. Many of the city's residences have ornamental balconies overlooking the narrow streets.

buildings of historical interest: the lovely St. Louis Cathedral; the Cabildo, once the seat of Spanish governors; and the Presbytère, which was used as a courthouse. The Cabildo and Presbytère are now branches of the Louisiana State Museum.

Classic revival architecture adds elegance to homes in the Garden District, which lies some 2 miles (3 kilometers) upriver from Canal Street. Many of its handsome homes were built before the Civil War (1861–65).

The city has dozens of neighborhood parks and two particularly large ones. City Park, covering 1,550 acres (620 hectares), contains a regionally acclaimed children's playland and the New Orleans Museum of Art. Audubon Park, covering 285 acres (114 hectares), boasts a top-rated zoo.

Six universities operate within city limits—the University of New Orleans, Tulane, Loyola, Xavier, Southern, and Dillard. There are also two colleges, Delgado and Holy Cross. The university and public libraries are supplemented by the Historic New Orleans Collection, a research organization.

Early History. New Orleans was founded in 1718 by Jean-Baptiste Le Moyne, Sieur de Bienville, a governor of what was then the French colony of Louisiana. The city was named after Philippe, the Duke of Orléans, regent to the young King Louis XV. Bienville picked the site for the city at a graceful crescent in the Mississippi River. New Orleans, for this reason, is often called the Crescent City. The location assured its future success as a world seaport.

New Orleans remained under French rule until 1763, when Spain acquired the region by treaty. Spain then ruled it until 1803, when France regained possession. But the following year, the French sold the land to the United States as part of the Louisiana Purchase.

On January 7, 1815, General Andrew Jackson—unaware that a treaty ending the War of 1812 had already been signed—famously led his troops to victory against the British at the Battle of New Orleans at nearby Chalmette.

Hurricane Katrina. The possibility of a catastrophic flood has always concerned the residents of New Orleans. This is because the city is situated on a bed of silt that lies at least 6 feet (2 meters) below sea level between the Mississippi River and Lake Pontchartrain. It was thought the city would be suitably protected by a system of levees built to keep the river and lake from overflowing. However, these levees were not strong enough to withstand the fury of Katrina, which hit the Gulf Coast and Mississippi Delta as a Category 3 hurricane on August 29, 2005.

As many as 100,000—about 20 percent of the city's residents—failed to evacuate the city, as they were either unable or unwilling to leave. Those who could sought shelter in the city's convention center and Superdome football stadium.

The hurricane made landfall at 6:30 A.M. on Monday, August 29, near Grand Isle, about 100 miles (160 kilometers) south of New Orleans. The constant battering force of high winds and water levels caused four major breaks in the local levees. Water from Lake Pontchartrain began pouring in, flooding at least 80 percent of the city.

The people who had stayed in New Orleans were trapped for days before significant help arrived. Those who had not found shelter were stranded on rooftops and highway overpasses. Hundreds more drowned. Violent crime and looting became widespread, and panic ensued. Local police, firefighters, and medical teams were overwhelmed.

Outside relief services eventually came to the rescue. National Guard helicopters began airlifting survivors off rooftops. Meanwhile, help poured in from around the nation as well as from dozens of foreign countries. However, federal, state, and local agencies came under attack for responding too slowly to the crisis. The Federal Emergency Management Agency (FEMA), a branch of the U.S. Department of Homeland Security, was particularly faulted.

It was estimated that it would take years for New Orleans to recover from Hurricane Katrina, and no one could predict how much of the original city could be saved. U.S. troops were expected to spend several months repairing the levees and pumping the water from the streets. The impact on the economy and the environment—in addition to the human toll—was impossible to estimate.

WALTER G. COWAN
Coauthor, *New Orleans, Yesterday and Today*

See also CARNIVALS; JACKSON, ANDREW (The Battle of New Orleans); LOUISIANA PURCHASE.

NEWPORT. See RHODE ISLAND (Cities; Places of Interest).

Reading the newspaper is one of the best ways to keep up with current events. In addition to the news itself, newspapers contain a wide range of other useful information, including sports, reviews, travel tips, advice, opinion, and the comics. Young and old alike can find something to read in the newspaper!

NEWSPAPERS

Newspapers are one of the oldest ways to get news to many people. Only the town crier and the publicly posted notice are older. A newspaper is so familiar that a definition may not seem necessary. Even the word "newspaper" conveys an idea of what it is—a paper on which news of general interest is printed and circulated.

What is news? It might be defined simply as important new events. However, it is not always easy to decide just how important an event is. Two inches of snowfall might be "news" in Miami, Florida, while in Minneapolis, Minnesota, it probably would not be.

What makes an event important in one city but not in another? In Miami, snowfall is very rare. It could stop traffic and everything else in the city. People who had never seen it in their lives might go outdoors to see and feel the snowflakes. Such an event would doubtless be covered on the front page of the newspaper there. In Minneapolis, where snow falls frequently and heavily in the winter, two inches might not be reported in any way other than as a weather statistic for the area.

What if two inches of snow fell in Miami on the same day that war was declared in the Middle East? Which would be the more important story? What if the war involved Americans? Would that make its news value more important to Miamians than the snowfall?

In most communities, newspapers try to take into account people's differing viewpoints about what is newsworthy. In the example given, both stories would probably be printed. Snow in Miami might even be news in Minneapolis! However, there is always a question about how much newspaper space should be given to any story, as well as where it should be placed. The length of the article and its location might vary with the situation.

As you can see, deciding on what news stories go into each issue of the newspaper is not simple. So many events happen every day in each town, city, and state—and throughout the United States and the world—that newspaper editors must constantly make choices about what news to print.

▶ BEYOND THE NEWS

Publishing the news is not the only role of newspapers in informing the public. Advertisements, which bring in the income necessary for publishing, are a major feature of newspapers. They usually occupy more space in an issue of a newspaper than the news does.

Newspapers also contain editorials, which are opinions about all sorts of topics of interest to readers. Editorials may discuss which candidate to vote for, or whether a proposed highway will help the people more than it hurts the environment, or whether a politician who is accused of wrongdoing is honest. Editorials are usually printed in a different format than the regular news and are given the same placement in each issue of the newspaper to help readers identify them.

One of the most popular kinds of editorial is the editorial cartoon, a daily drawing that usually pokes fun at someone or something currently in the news. A good political cartoon can say in one drawing and a few words what an editorial might take 1,000 words to say—and it can make us laugh in the bargain!

Many newspapers carry the writings of several columnists. Columnists are people who are experts in certain fields, or writers whose opinions are well known and respected. Most newspapers try to pick columnists with differing opinions, so that the reader will get a range of views about important issues.

Most newspapers also publish letters from their readers on the editorial page. In this way, the thoughts and ideas of interested citizens may also be known, as well as those of the publisher, writers, and public officials.

Students work on the layout of their high school newspaper. A job on a student newspaper provides valuable insights into how newspapers function.

Opinion may appear in other parts of the newspaper in addition to the editorial page. Sports predictions, movie reviews, analyses of business trends, and travel suggestions all are expressions of opinions. In fact, opinion can appear any place, even in the comics. With practice, the reader learns to tell the difference between news and opinion. It is an important distinction to make.

Newspapers also print a great deal of other information: feature articles or columns on such topics as travel, gardening, hobbies, business, science, religion, entertainment, and the arts; weather predictions; horoscopes; television schedules; advice columns; sports scores; stock prices; and the comics. Each newspaper has an index, usually on page 1 or 2, to help readers find their way through the maze of information in that day's paper.

Newspapers differ greatly in content and quality. An interesting way to compare news-

WONDER QUESTION

Is the news truth?

When a writer on the newspaper is told to "cover," or write about, an event, he or she is expected to report it fairly and truthfully. However, newswriters seldom witness the events they are covering and must draw their information from others, preferably those who did see or experience them. Sometimes they must evaluate or interpret what they hear. Can they be sure of writing the truth? It may be difficult, especially when the people they interview do not agree on the facts of what happened.

Sometimes newspapers are accused of not telling the truth, even those that have tried to build a reputation for honesty. Where does the truth lie? Readers can check other sources, such as television, radio, books, and newsmagazines, but must ultimately decide for themselves. When making a judgment, it helps to understand the difference between news and opinion and to be skeptical of early news reports.

Have you ever seen a newspaper headline that you doubted? How does one identify those newspapers that maintain a policy of truthful reporting? Over time, a newspaper can gain a reputation for truthful newswriting and for making opinion clearly recognizable by its placement and treatment. Every newspaper must earn that reputation, and keep it, through consistent performance.

papers is to request 10 to 20 papers from cities all over the country for one specific day—perhaps the day after national elections, the Fourth of July, or the Super Bowl. Then compare what each puts on the front page, how and where it expresses opinion, what non-news features it carries, how much and what kind of advertising it has. In today's world of easily available information, newspapers must compete to keep their readers. Judge for yourself how good a job each newspaper you receive is doing.

▶ **KINDS OF NEWSPAPERS**

The earliest American newspapers began as weeklies; that is, they were published once a week. The success of many led them to become dailies, especially in large cities. There are still a large number of weeklies in smaller communities, or serving special needs in larger ones. Most weeklies handle local news, although they may carry national and state news that affects local people.

Many kinds of newspapers are published. Some are geared to the interests of a particular community or group; others have a national or international focus.

Most major U.S. cities have one or more large dailies. Major U.S. dailies include the *Los Angeles Times*, *Washington Post*, *Miami Herald*, *Des Moines Register*, *Seattle Times*, *Louisville Journal*, *Chicago Tribune*, *New York Times*, *Christian Science Monitor*, *Wall Street Journal*, and *USA Today*. The last four have national circulations.

Newspapers of many kinds appear around the world today. The idea of a free press fostered in the United States by the U.S. Constitution is shared by other countries as well.

(See the article FIRST AMENDMENT FREEDOMS in Volume F.) But in many parts of the world the press is controlled by the government.

The following are some of the most important newspapers of the world. In Canada, leading papers include the English-language *Toronto Globe and Mail* and the French-language *La Presse*. Major Latin American newspapers include *La Prensa* and *La Nación* of Argentina; *O Estado de São Paulo* of Brazil; and *Excélsior* of Mexico. In Europe, leading newspapers include *The Times*, *The Guardian*, and the *Daily Telegraph* of Great Britain; *Le Monde* and *Le Figaro* of France; *La Stampa* and *Corriere della Sera* of Italy; *Frankfurter Allgemeine*, *Die Welt*, and *Süddeutsche Zeitung* of Germany; and *Izvestia* of Russia. (Russia's leading Communist newspaper, *Pravda*, ceased publication in 1996.) Asian newspapers include *Renmin Ribao* of China; *Asahi Shimbun* and *Mainichi Shimbun* of Japan; and the *Times of India* and *Navbharat Times* of India. Among newspapers of Africa and the Middle East are the *Daily Graphic* of Ghana; *The Standard* of Kenya; *The Times of Zambia* of Zambia; and *Al-Ahram* of Egypt.

▶ **HOW NEWSPAPERS FUNCTION**

The organization that publishes a newspaper has a chief executive called the publisher (who often is also the owner). Those reporting to the publisher are the top editor and the news and editorial staff; the graphics editor, artists, and photographers; the production manager and press operators; the advertising manager and staff; the circulation manager and staff; and the business manager and staff. Larger newspapers may also have human resources and marketing departments.

Editorial Department

Gathering the News. Reporters find the news, usually after the editor has assigned

Reporters gather the news by a variety of means. Press conferences and interviews are ways to obtain newsworthy statements from important figures.

them specific stories to cover. Reporters may also hear about a story through contact with other people. Often, officials "leak" information to the press—giving it to reporters in secret, as a way of getting the news out while appearing to remain silent.

A **beat reporter** holds a long-term assignment in one specific area, or beat. For example, a police reporter follows crime reports and arrests; an education reporter follows school issues; another reporter might cover everything having to do with the city council. The advantage of beat reporters to the editor is that they get to know people who may help them find new stories. A **general assignment reporter** covers news events that do not fall into a particular beat. General assignment reporters may also help beat reporters if several stories on a beat break at the same time.

In addition to their local reporters, most newspapers use other methods to gather news. Large dailies often open offices, or **news bureaus**, in cities other than their own, in order to cover the news there. For example, *The New York Times* operates a bureau in Washington, D.C., because much news of interest to New Yorkers comes from the nation's capital. Furthermore, the *Times* has many readers in Washington as well as in New York.

Smaller newspapers may also want to cover news outside their local areas but lack the money to support news bureaus in other cities. They can obtain coverage through **wire services**. Wire services are organizations that collect, write, and distribute news to participating newspapers seeking broader news coverage. Text and graphics are transmitted over a teletype system, by computer modem, or via satellite. Even large newspapers use the wire services, since it would cost too much to maintain news bureaus in every city.

Syndicates are organizations that sell and distribute to newspapers popular features such as comics, columns, and editorial cartoons. You might find the same comic strip, sold by a syndicate, running in hundreds of newspapers on the same day. Through syndicates, many newspapers can carry the work of well-known writers and artists that one newspaper alone could not pay for on a daily basis.

Writing and Editing. Editors have the difficult job of deciding what news will be covered in each issue of the newspaper. An editor also

The newsroom of a large daily newspaper is a busy place. Stories are written on computers, with last-minute information sometimes taken by telephone.

plans the length of all the stories and features and decides where they will be placed in the newspaper.

In some cases, news stories are written by the reporters themselves. In other cases, editorial staff members called **rewriters** take information from reporters, often by telephone, and work this information into a news story.

When a reporter or rewriter completes a story, a copy editor reads and corrects it for accuracy, grammar, and spelling. The editor may also shorten a story if it is too long or if more space is needed for other news. Shortening is made easier by the journalistic practice of putting the most important information at the beginning of an article and the least important information at the end. With this "inverse pyramid" method of writing, an article can be shortened quickly by cutting paragraphs from the bottom.

At a large paper, the top editor may have any number of subeditors to help with the job of editing. Some papers have a separate editor for each section—for example, news, business, sports, style, food, and health. A small newspaper, on the other hand, may be headed by one person, who is both publisher and editor. The editorial staff may consist only of the editor and several reporters.

WONDER QUESTION

What is a press release?

A press release is a document used by civic groups, corporations, promoters, advertising agencies, and government offices, as well as by private citizens, to get news to the newspaper. Anyone can write a press release and send it to the newspaper. Persons who write press releases must understand that the paper may or may not use them, depending on the volume of other news available at the time it is received. Most of the time, the paper will print press release information if it is of interest to the general public.

If you write a press release, be sure to provide enough information. For guidance, follow the journalist's method of writing a story. Remember the five W's and the H: Who, What, When, Where, Why, and How. Who did or is doing what? When are they doing it and where? Why are they doing it and how? Do not worry too much about style—the paper will do any rewriting that may be necessary.

Graphics and Page Design

Graphics, or illustrations, have assumed a role of great importance in the job of communicating news. Newspapers obtain photographs and drawings from staff and freelance photographers and artists. They also buy photographs and drawings from wire services. Today, many newspaper illustrations are printed in color, with a quality approaching that of magazines.

Assembling all the stories, illustrations, and advertisements that make up a single newspaper edition is a huge task. It is easier than it once was, however, because of computers. For many years, all the letters and other characters that make up the text of a story were set into metal type. In a more recent process called phototypesetting, photographic images of the letters were created. (You can read more about typesetting in the article PRINTING in Volume P.) The typeset text was then put into position on the page along with illustrations.

At some newspapers, such as this small weekly, pages are pasted up by hand. Increasingly, however, some or all of a paper's page design is done on computers.

Today, reporters writing their stories on computers produce copy that is in the correct type style and ready for page design. At most newspapers, pages are designed on computers. Artwork is created electronically and fitted into the computerized page design. Typically, the newspaper's computers print out pages containing everything except photographs and advertisements, which are pasted into spaces left for them. The pages are then

Monitored by press operators, rolls of newsprint speed through a printing press. In the United States alone, some 60 million newspapers are printed each day.

photographed, and the resulting film is used to make metal plates for the printing press.

Through the use of computerized photography, some newspapers have eliminated even the final pasteup process. They design and print the entire contents of each page on computer. This process, called **pagination**, will be used by more and more newspapers in the future.

Printing the Newspaper

Each day's newspaper must be "put to bed" by a specific time, or deadline, in order to be delivered to readers on time. For newspapers publishing morning editions, that time may be late at night or just after midnight. For newspapers published in the afternoon, deadline will be sometime in the morning. Tensions rise, computer keyboards click, and news decisions that editors must make become more critical as the deadline approaches.

When an edition has been put to bed, the press operators swing into action to turn paper and ink into the finished product. Modern newspapers are printed on rotary presses, which use curved printing plates. The printing method most often used today is offset lithography, or offset. More information on offset lithography and rotary printing presses can be found in the article PRINTING.

Newsprint, the paper on which newspapers are printed, has been developed to provide a printable surface at low cost. It is lighter in weight than most magazine paper, and its surface is not as smooth.

When the huge presses are turned on, they begin to hum and then roar as huge rolls of paper are picked up automatically and fed through faster than the eye can follow, coming out at the other end printed and folded, with sections in the right order. Press operators constantly adjust the machinery throughout the press run to make the print clearer and the color brighter.

Recycling. Newspapers use a lot of paper. Newspapers and government are working to see that old newspapers are recycled—collected and used to create new newsprint. Recycling will have an impact on newspaper printing costs in the future. Paper mills in the United States and Canada are in the process of adapting their production equipment to produce newsprint from used newspapers as well as from lumber. The newspaper industry has also sponsored research for an agricultural source of newsprint fiber that would be more readily renewable than the tree pulp currently in use.

Old newspapers are collected for recycling. They will be used to create new newsprint. Government and the newspaper industry work together to promote recycling.

Advertising

Newspapers are ideal for advertising because they reach so many people, because they provide space for details about the product or service for sale, and because advertising information can be referred to whenever the reader chooses.

The advertisements in the newspaper pay for at least 75 percent of the cost of publishing it. Money earned from selling copies of the newspaper represents no more than 25 percent of a newspaper's income, only enough to pay for printing it. This makes the advertising department of a newspaper vitally important. The people working in this department sell ads, write and prepare advertising copy, send bills to advertisers, and promote the use of the newspaper as a medium for advertising.

There are generally two kinds of newspaper advertisements: display ads and classifieds. Display ads use photographs, text, and eye-catching graphics to draw attention to a product. They can be quite large, perhaps even a full page. Display ads are used by businesses to bring their products and services to the attention of potential consumers. Classified ads are smaller and shorter advertisements, intended to communicate briefly and to cost as little as possible. They are called "classified" because they are grouped together in categories where readers can find a particular product or service they want. Classifieds are used by smaller businesses and private citizens to sell services and such items as new and used equipment, furniture, and vehicles, supplies, produce, and animals.

Circulation

The circulation department is in charge of selling the newspaper and distributing it. This is a huge task at larger newspapers, where hundreds of thousands of copies must get to the right people at the right time every day. Circulation managers and their staffs must be good at sales, service, and keeping track of

numbers. No matter what the weather, the circulation department packages the copies of the newspaper and puts them on fleets of trucks. The trucks drop them at newsstands, automatic dispensing machines, and spots where carriers pick them up and deliver them to individual homes. In the United States alone, some 60 million newspapers are circulated each day.

Business Operations

Newspapers are in business for profit. Like other corporations, a newspaper must pay bills

Newspapers are taken by truck to newsstands, vending machines, and pickup sites for carriers. Circulation is an important part of the newspaper business.

and taxes, hire and pay employees, evaluate employee performance, buy and maintain office equipment, collect payments from advertisers and subscribers, keep records of income and expenses, and control its operating costs. In short, it must operate as efficiently and effectively as possible.

A large newspaper may employ quite a few people just to carry out these management tasks. In addition to general business administrators, a number of business specialists, including accountants, marketing experts, and promotion personnel, may be employed at a sizable newspaper.

An example of a promotional operation is the Newspaper in Education program, which distributes newspapers to schools to use as teaching tools. Newspapers sponsor this program not just as a public service but also to encourage readership, attract would-be journalists to the field, and increase their circulation as the students they are now reaching become adults.

►HISTORY OF NEWSPAPERS

In ancient Rome, handwritten notices called *Acta Diurna* ("Acts of the Day") were posted in public places to inform citizens of battles, election results, Senate actions, and other news. Newsletters were also sent by courier from the capital to the far reaches of the empire about events in Rome. Then, as now, the use of written news was tied to literacy. Only the educated, who knew how to read, might be informed.

Left: An early issue of the *Boston Gazette*, one of the first regularly published American newspapers. *Below:* Sensational newspaper reporting of the late 1800's is typified by this 1898 front page of William Randolph Hearst's *New York Journal* reporting the sinking of the U.S. warship *Maine.*

The development of printing made mass communication possible; public education, which taught people to read, made it a reality. Block printing was used in China as early as the A.D. 600's. In Europe, letterpress printing with movable type was invented by Johann Gutenberg in Germany in the mid-1400's. Newspapers began to appear in Europe by the 1500's—in Italy in 1566, Germany in 1594, Holland in 1616, and Sweden in 1624. The first English newspaper, the *Weekly Newes*, began publication in London in 1622.

Newspapers in the United States

The first newspaper in the American colonies was published in 1690, but it was suppressed by the colonial government after the first issue. America's first regularly published newspaper, the *Boston News-Letter*, appeared in 1704 and continued publication for 72 years. Benjamin Franklin began publishing the *Pennsylvania Gazette* weekly in Philadelphia in 1729. Franklin was one of the first American editors to use illustrations in a newspaper. They were printed using woodcut blocks.

By the time of the Revolutionary War, there were more than 30 American newspapers. By 1800 the number had grown to 235, of which 24 were dailies. Newspapers at this time expressed the views of their owners, who usually were leaders of political parties, rather than offering objective news coverage.

Beginning in the 1830's, the first metropolitan, mass-circulation papers were founded. One of the keys to their success was their low price—one cent per issue. The first successful penny paper was the *New York Sun*, founded in 1833. It covered such items as crimes, fires, accidents, and human interest stories and was read by thousands of people. Other newspapers that started as penny papers were the *New York Herald*, the *New York Tribune*, and *The New York Times*. In the late 1800's, newspaper reporting focused increasingly on scandals, disasters, and other sensational news, especially in the papers of Joseph Pulitzer and William Randolph Hearst. Photography and photoengraving were developed for newspaper use about 1890, making it possible to print photographs and line drawings along with news articles.

In the first half of the 1900's, newspapers grew in number and power. Since the 1950's newspapers have been forced to compete with radio and television, which offer more entertainment and can report news almost as it happens. *USA Today*, which started publishing in 1982 as the first nationwide daily newspaper, launched a revolution in newspaper design with its use of color illustrations.

The number of daily newspapers in the United States dropped in the last half of the 1900's. Many of the remaining papers belong to newspaper groups or chains, corporations that own several newspapers. Major chains include Gannett, Scripps-Howard, and Newhouse. Most cities and towns have one newspaper today, rather than several competing ones. Newspapers remain a profitable business, however, and are expected to hold a place in the ever-changing array of information resources.

Recent Developments

The effect of modern technology has been strongly felt in the newspaper world. Many newspapers now have call-in services that allow readers to deliver "talking" letters to the editor, hear a selection from a recently reviewed tape or CD, or learn the score of a late game. Computer services and networks provide file copies of stories that have been published in the best-known newspapers.

Computers have also changed the way departments in the newspaper are organized. Rather than hand-carrying the story through several different departments from reporter to editor to layout artist to typesetter to proofreader, newspapers now place most of those people together in the newsroom. The story is shifted electronically from computer to computer, sometimes without being put on paper until it is printed in that day's newspaper.

There are other new developments under way that promise further widespread change. One field that will doubtless affect the collection and distribution of news is telecommunications—the global transmission of information at high speed via satellite, telephone lines, microwave links, and fiber-optic cables. Digital computers already exchange data via high-speed modems over telephone lines and satellite links. Most corporations and many private citizens subscribe to computer information services that transmit by these means.

Electronic versions of some newspapers are available to personal computer users. *Below:* A close-up look at a screen of the *Chicago Tribune*'s on-line service shows that users can read the entire text of the day's paper or use the menu to select a specific feature.

As newspaper readers become more computer literate and better equipped, it has become possible to distribute newspapers to readers via computer. Some of these personal-computer newspaper services offer more than just the text of the day's newspaper. They may also allow the user to look up past articles and communicate by computer with reporters and fellow readers. Other features include access to classified advertisements and electronic "bulletin boards" that post local news and information. What other new technology will be adopted by newspapers, and which will be accepted by the public for commercial use? It remains to be seen.

JUDITH D. HINES
Journalism Education Fellow
The Freedom Forum

NEW TESTAMENT. See BIBLE.

NEWTON, ISAAC (1642–1727)

Isaac Newton was one of the greatest scientists of all time. He is best-known for his discovery of the law of universal gravitation and the laws of motion. Much of modern science is based on the understanding and use of his laws.

Isaac Newton was born on Christmas Day, 1642, in the small English town of Woolsthorpe. His father, a farmer, died shortly before Isaac was born. When the boy was 3 years old, his mother remarried and moved to another town. Isaac stayed on at the farm in Woolsthorpe with his grandmother. After attending small country schools, he was sent at the age of 12 to the Kings School in the nearby town of Grantham.

▶ STUDENT DAYS

At first Isaac was a poor student. He cared little for schoolwork, preferring to paint, make kites, write in his notebooks, or invent toys. He made no friends. Silent and dreamy, he was at the bottom of his class. Oddly, it was a savage kick by a school bully that caused Newton's great mind to awaken. The mild, dreamy boy flew into a rage and beat the other boy thoroughly. Isaac determined to beat the bully in schoolwork as well. Soon Isaac was at the head of his class.

In 1656 Newton's stepfather died. His mother returned to Woolsthorpe to take care of the farm left by Newton's father. But she could not manage the farm by herself. Isaac was taken out of school and brought home to help her.

As a farmer, Newton proved to be a dismal failure. He neglected the necessary chores and thought only of books to study and mechanical things to make. There are many stories about him at that time that show how absent-minded he was becoming. One day while he was leading a horse, the animal slipped its bridle and ran away. Isaac continued walking home with the empty bridle in his hand, unaware that the horse was gone.

When an idea got into Newton's head, he could think of nothing else. Once, during a storm, his mother sent him to shut the barn doors to keep them from being torn off. Half an hour later she went to see what was keeping the boy so long. He had forgotten all about the barn doors. They were ripped off their hinges, and Newton was jumping again and again from an open window to the ground. Each time, he marked the spot where he landed. Newton was trying to measure the force of the wind. When the gusts were strong, his jumps were longer than when the wind was weaker.

Realizing that her son was simply not suited to farm life, Newton's mother sent him back to Kings School. He graduated in 1661.

When he was 18 years old, Newton went to Trinity College in Cambridge University. He quickly proved to his teachers that he was no ordinary student. He read all the books he could get, especially those on mathematics and physics. These interested him most. His professors were amazed to find that Newton knew about certain subjects even before he was taught. The young man had mastered the subjects by himself.

In 1665, when Newton was only 22 years old, he worked out a basic formula in mathematics that has been used ever since. Today it is called the binomial theorem.

That same year, 1665, Isaac Newton graduated from Trinity College. He wanted to stay on at the university to continue his studies. But the plague, the Black Death, had broken out in England. The university was closed and the students sent home, for fear the plague would strike at Cambridge. Newton then returned to Woolsthorpe.

Fear of the plague kept Newton close to the farm for the next 18 months. Almost always alone, he spent his time thinking out mathematical problems. In those 18 months he laid the foundation for his life's work. During that time he hit upon a new mathematical tool that he called fluxions or flowing quantities. Today it is called the calculus.

One day in 1665 Newton was sitting in the garden in Woolsthorpe, thinking about the moon. While he was wondering about the force that kept the moon moving around the earth, he saw an apple fall from a tree. This set him thinking about falling objects. Why did they fall down and not up? It must be because the earth was attracting all objects to itself. The same force that made the apple fall downward must also be attracting the moon and helping to keep it in orbit.

From these thoughts Newton began to work out the law concerning attraction between all objects in the universe. The law is called the law of universal gravitation.

▶ EXPERIMENTS WITH LIGHT

While at Woolsthorpe, Newton began experimenting with light. He succeeded in showing that a beam of sunlight is made up of bands of colors from red to violet, as in a rainbow. He called these bands the spectrum.

After the plague ended, Newton returned to Cambridge and continued working on light and color. This work led him to the discovery of the reflecting telescope. Most modern telescopes, such as that on Mount Palomar in California, are based on Newton's telescope.

In recognition of his work in mathematics and optics (the science of light) Newton was appointed professor of mathematics at Trinity College in 1669. Early in 1672 he was elected a member of the Royal Society.

▶ THE RIDDLE OF GRAVITATION

Although Newton experimented mostly with optics during these years at Trinity College, his mind always returned to the problem of gravitation. He was trying to calculate the exact amount of force that objects exert on each other. Rather than spending time with people, he spent his time working. He made very few friends and became more absentminded than ever.

Finally, he completed the mathematics of the law of gravitation. Using this law, Newton in 1682 proved mathematically one of the laws of planetary motion. This law had been figured out by the German astronomer Johannes Kepler in the early 1600's. Kepler's law stated that a planet's orbit around the sun had to be in the shape of an ellipse. But he had not been able to show mathematical proof of this.

Because he was a shy man who cared little for fame, Newton put these and other calculations away in a drawer instead of making them public. But his few friends knew of the brilliant work he was doing. At last they persuaded Newton to write a book in which he would explain his work on planetary motion, gravitation, and other matters.

▶ NEWTON'S FAMOUS BOOK

In 1685 Newton plunged into this gigantic task. He drove himself mercilessly, scarcely

Isaac Newton studying the spectrum of sunlight.

eating or sleeping. As he walked in his garden a thought might suddenly occur to him. He would rush upstairs to his room to jot it down, not even sitting down to write.

Newton's book *The Mathematical Principles of Natural Philosophy* appeared in 1687. It was written in Latin, the language in which most scientific books were written at that time. Newton's book is usually called the *Principia,* after its Latin title. Many scientists think it is the most important scientific book ever written. It contains Newton's famous three laws of motion. It also contains his law of universal gravitation. This law does not only apply to heavenly bodies. It also explains why a baseball drops from your hand to the ground and why a particle of dust settles on a bookshelf.

During later years Newton served his country in Parliament, as well as in other ways. In 1703 he was elected president of the Royal Society, and in 1705 he was knighted by Queen Anne.

Isaac Newton died in 1727. He was buried in Westminster Abbey, among the great men of England. His statue stands today in the hall of Trinity College, Cambridge University.

DAVID C. KNIGHT
Author, *Isaac Newton, Mastermind of Modern Science*

See also GRAVITY AND GRAVITATION; LIGHT; MOTION.

NEWTS. See AMPHIBIANS

恭賀新禧

Chinese

Left: A person dressed in a colorful dragon costume parades past onlookers as they celebrate the Chinese New Year in New York City. The Chinese celebrate two New Year's Days—the first on January 1, the second sometime between January 21 and February 19. *Far left and right:* The greeting "Happy New Year" is illustrated in nine different languages.

NEW YEAR CELEBRATIONS AROUND THE WORLD

Welcoming the new year is one of the world's oldest and most widely celebrated customs. In many places people stay up late to see the old year out and the new year in. Almost everywhere in the world church bells ring, horns toot, whistles blow, sirens shriek. London's Trafalgar Square and New York City's Times Square swarm with crowds of happy, noisy people. The hullabaloo expresses people's high spirits at holiday time.

New Year's Day is a time for entertaining, visiting, and gift-giving. Schools, offices, and businesses are closed. Churches hold services on New Year's Eve and New Year's Day. Because it marks the beginning of the year, New Year's Day is thought of as a good time to make New Year's resolutions—the resolve to do better in the year just beginning than you did in the year just ended.

No festival has ever been observed on so many different dates or in so many ways. Ancient Greeks began their new year with the new moon after June 21. Before the time of Julius Caesar the Roman new year started on March 1. In most European countries during the Middle Ages the new year began on March 25, the day of the Feast of the Annunciation.

In most Christian countries the new year begins on January 1. This custom started during the 1500's, when the calendar now in general use was introduced. January, the first month of the year, was named after Janus, the Roman god of gates or doors.

Other countries and religions observe New Year's Day on different dates, according to the calendars they use. The Chinese celebrate two New Year's Days. One is on January 1. The other is a much more festive celebration. It takes place on the New Year's Day calculated according to the Chinese lunar calendar, which is based on the movement of the moon. This second celebration may occur any time between January 21 and February 19. Indonesia also has two New Year celebrations—the official one on January 1 and another on the Islamic New Year, whose date varies from year to year. The Russian Orthodox Church observes the New Year according to the Julian calendar, which places the day on January 14. The Jewish New Year, Rosh Hashanah, is celebrated about the time of the autumnal equinox at the end of September or the beginning of October. In Vietnam the new year usually begins in February. Iran celebrates New Year's Day on March 21. Each of the religious groups in India has its own date for the beginning of the year. One Hindu New Year, Baisakhi, comes sometime in April or May. The people in Morocco observe the beginning of the year on the tenth day of Muharram, the first month of the Islamic year. The Koreans celebrate their New Year the first three days in January.

Old New Year's Customs

The ancient Romans sent each other little gifts as good-luck tokens on New Year's Day —numbers, indicating the date, which were dipped in gold, or a small coin. Every good citizen was also expected to give his emperor a gift. At first the gifts were simple, but as time went on they became more costly. Later the English kings and queens followed the

Happy New Year

Roman custom of expecting New Year's gifts from their subjects. They received fine clothing, jewels, food, and money. In time this custom became a burden to the people, and it was stopped.

The ancient Persians sent one another gifts of eggs on the New Year. The druids, priests of Britain and Gaul, gave out branches of the sacred mistletoe on the holiday. The mistletoe was believed to protect against sicknesses, demons, and witches. In some parts of Germany children gave their teachers small gifts on New Year's Day. This custom may have come from the Roman practice of paying teachers on the first day of the new year.

The New Year's card has been used in China for more than a thousand years. It carried only the name of the visitor who came to call, but no greeting or message. The caller extended good wishes in person.

Beginning with medieval times, the wassail bowl was an important part of the English Christmas and New Year's celebrations. The bowl was filled with punch of spiced wine or ale. Wassail comes from the Anglo-Saxon *wes hāl*, which means "be whole" or "be well." Wassailing went on everywhere in England— in the royal palace, in monasteries, and in private homes. It still continues today in the custom of friends wishing each other good health on the New Year over a glass of wine.

Happy New Year Around the World

The idea of a "clean start" for the new year means exactly that in many places. In part of the Balkans, the people sprinkle themselves, their houses, and their yards with freshly drawn well water. People in Morocco observe the same practice. The people in Madagascar and Myanmar pour water on their heads on New Year's Day. Throughout the Orient, where the New Year is the most joyful and important festival of the year, the clean start applies to many things. All debts must be paid at the end of the old year. Houses are thoroughly cleaned. People dress in their newest and best clothes. In China the New Year's holiday may go on for many days. Much time is spent preparing special foods. Feasts, fireworks, visiting, and the exchange of gifts are enjoyed. Children receive red envelopes containing gifts of money from their relatives and friends. The Japanese New Year is equally cheerful. Homes are decorated with pine branches and bamboo, symbols of long life.

People in the United States observe the holiday by going to church and giving and attending parties on New Year's Eve. It is a time for hospitality, and many people hold open-house receptions for their friends and families on New Year's Day.

Iran's New Year's Day, which falls in March, celebrates not only the beginning of the new year according to the solar calendar, but also *bahar,* "the beginning of spring."

In many European countries—Italy, Portugal, and the Netherlands, among others—families start the new year by first attending church services. Then they pay calls on friends and relatives. Italian boys and girls receive gifts of money on New Year's Day. In parts of Italy sprigs of mistletoe are hung over the doorways for luck.

In Scotland and parts of England the first person to cross the threshold of the home after the old year has passed is called the "first-footer." If the first-footer is a dark-haired man, he is believed to bring good luck to the household. He is even more welcome when he brings food and drink to wish his hosts a happy New Year!

Reviewed by LAVINIA DOBLER
Author, *Customs and Holidays Around the World*

See also CALENDAR; HOLIDAYS; PARADES; RELIGIOUS HOLIDAYS.

NEW YORK

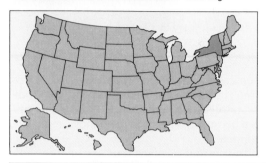

State flag

In 1664, British troops in North America seized the Dutch colony of New Netherland, including its prized settlement, New Amsterdam, at the mouth of the Hudson River. Both the colony and the settlement were renamed New York in honor of James, Duke of York, the brother of England's King Charles II.

More than a century later, after the United States had won its independence from England, New York City briefly served as the capital (1785–90) of the new republic. While delivering a speech there in 1785, General George Washington declared, "I pray that Heaven may bestow its choicest blessing on your city . . . and that your state, at the present seat of empire, may set such examples of wisdom and liberality as shall have a tendency to strengthen and give permanency to the Union. . . ." Many historians believe that this is the origin of New York's official nickname, the Empire State.

New York is a Middle Atlantic state, located in the northeastern United States. Its southernmost region is dominated by the magnificence of New York City, the nation's largest city and one of the world's foremost centers of commerce, trade, finance, tourism, and culture. Picturesque upstate New York is far less hurried, from the lovely lakes and forestlands of the Adirondack Mountains in the northeast, to the spectacular cascades of Niagara Falls in the west, to the craggy beauty of the Catskill Mountains in the southeast.

While New York City represents the pulse of the state's economy, agriculture flourishes in the Hudson and Mohawk valleys, and manufacturing thrives in the cities of Buffalo, Rochester, and Syracuse. Government drives the economy at Albany, the state's capital and oldest permanent European settlement.

Ever since its founding as a Dutch colony in 1624, New York has held a preeminent position in North America. Transcontinental commerce and trade immediately flourished at the site of its great ice-free harbor of the Atlan-

Clockwise from left: The Empire State Building is a cherished New York City landmark. Niagara Falls is one of North America's greatest natural wonders. Many upstate New Yorkers enjoy outdoor recreational activities. The Catskill Mountains display spectacular colors in the fall.

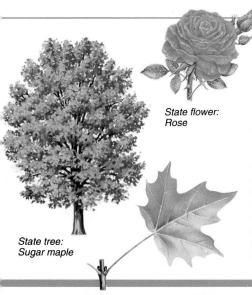

State flower:
Rose

State tree:
Sugar maple

FACTS AND FIGURES

Location: Northeastern United States; bordered on the north by Canada (Ontario and Quebec) and Lake Ontario, on the east by Vermont, Massachusetts, and Connecticut, on the south by New Jersey and Pennsylvania, and on the west by Pennsylvania, Lake Erie, Canada (Ontario), and Lake Ontario.

Area: 53,989 sq mi (139,833 km²); rank, 27th.

Population: 18,976,457 (2000 census); rank, 3rd.

Elevation: *Highest*—5,344 ft (1,629 m) at Mount Marcy; *lowest*—sea level, along the Atlantic Ocean.

Capital: Albany.

Statehood: July 26, 1788; 11th state.

State Motto: *Excelsior* ("Ever upward").

State Song: "I Love New York."

Nickname: Empire State.

Abbreviations: NY; N.Y.

State bird:
Bluebird

Right: Vineyards surround Keuka Lake, one of the eleven finger-shaped lakes in the Allegheny Plateau region of central New York. *Below:* Long Island's Montauk Point, the state's easternmost location, juts into the Atlantic Ocean. Its stone lighthouse was commissioned by President George Washington in 1795.

tic Ocean, where the towering city of New York now stands. Once New York had established itself as an economic stronghold, prosperity quickly spread inland, by way of the Hudson and Mohawk rivers, straight to the heartland of the continent.

Throughout the 1800's, New York remained a leader in transportation, social legislation, and economic opportunity. New York City, the primary point of entry for millions of European immigrants, was considered the Gateway to the New World. The Statue of Liberty, erected in New York Harbor in 1886, became an internationally recognized symbol of hope and the American dream.

From 1820 until 1970, New York lived up to its reputation as the Empire State, ranking first among the states in population and in the value of its economy. Today it is outranked only by California and Texas in population and only by California in economy. The energetic people of New York have built a prosperous community almost without equal on the globe.

▶ LAND

New York is the only state to border both the Atlantic Ocean and the Great Lakes. Its Atlantic coastline measures 127 miles (204 kilometers) long; its entire shoreline, including all of its islands and bays, measures 1,850 miles (2,977 kilometers).

Land Regions

The land surface of New York is divided almost equally into lowlands, mountains, and eroded plateaus.

The Coastal Plain, covering Staten Island and Long Island in the southeast, is a gently sloping lowland with some hilly areas. Long Island's northern shore has steep-sided bays and narrow peninsulas called necks. Its southern shore is lined with beaches.

The New England Upland covers a slice of eastern New York State from New York City to just south of Lake George. The region also includes the Taconic Mountains and the Hudson Highlands.

The Adirondack Upland in the northeast is noted for its beautiful Adirondack Mountains, forests, and clear, blue lakes. Mount Marcy, New York's highest point, is located here.

The Allegheny Plateau, the northern portion of the Appalachian Plateau, extends through most of southwestern New York. Its rolling hills and valleys and famous slender lakes, notably the Finger Lakes, were formed by ancient glaciers. The plateau rises to the east to the rugged and heavily forested Catskill Mountains, where water has carved deep gorges into the mountains. The Catskills were immortalized in Washington Irving's tale "Rip Van Winkle."

The Hudson-Mohawk Lowland, covering much of the Hudson and the Mohawk river valleys, is a fertile farming region. It is often called the Gateway to the West because the two rivers provide the only natural transportation route through the Adirondacks.

The St. Lawrence-Champlain Lowland rims the northern reaches of the Adirondacks. Its alternately hilly and flat landscape is moderately fertile. The scenic Lake Champlain and Thousand Islands belong to this region.

The Erie-Ontario Lowland, often called the Great Lakes Lowland, is a fertile plain off the shores of Lakes Erie and Ontario. Oval-shaped hills called drumlins occasionally interrupt the flatness of the land.

The Tug Hill Plateau in central New York is broad, elevated, and flat-topped, with poor soil, sluggish streams, and a rocky terrain.

Rivers, Lakes, and Coastal Waters

The most important waterway in New York is the Hudson River. It begins in tiny Lake Tear of the Clouds in the Adirondacks and flows more than 300 miles (483 kilometers) toward New York City and the Atlantic Ocean. It is navigable for oceangoing ships as far north as Albany. The Mohawk River is the Hudson's largest tributary. It begins in central New York and flows south and southeast for about 140 miles (225 kilometers) to join the Hudson at Cohoes.

The Genesee, Oswego, and Black rivers flow into Lake Ontario. The Niagara River, which connects Lake Erie to Lake Ontario, and the St. Lawrence River, which connects Lake Ontario to the Atlantic Ocean, form part of the U.S.-Canadian border.

Lake Champlain (which New York shares with Vermont and Quebec) and most of the rivers of northern New York drain into the St. Lawrence River. Four important rivers—the Delaware, the Susquehanna, the Allegheny, and the Hudson—drain southern New York.

Within New York there are more than 2,000 lakes, ponds, and reservoirs. The largest body of water entirely within the state is Oneida Lake. Other well-known natural lakes are Lake Placid and Lake George in the Adirondacks and the Finger Lakes in the Allegheny Plateau. Parts of Lake Erie and Lake Ontario are included within New York's boundaries.

Climate

New York's most severe climates are found in the Adirondacks. New York City has a much milder climate because it is adjacent to

The round, forested peaks of the Adirondack Mountains extend from northeastern New York into southern Canada.

Places of Interest

Kayaking in the Adirondacks

Sagamore Hill National Historic Site, near Oyster Bay

The Metropolitan Museum of Art, in New York City

New York offers almost matchless attractions to visitors. The state's seashore, mountains, and inland lakes are famous for their beauty, while New York City's skyscrapers, theaters, and museums are among the most famous in the world.

Corning Glass Center, in Corning, has displays covering the history and art of glass. It also includes a library on glass, the Hall of Science and Industry, and the Steuben factory, where fine crystal is blown and engraved by hand.

Eleanor Roosevelt National Historic Site, in Hyde Park, preserves Mrs. Roosevelt's Val-Kill estate, which the first lady used as her personal retreat.

Federal Hall National Memorial, in New York City, is the site of Federal Hall, the first capitol of the United States. George Washington was inaugurated as president there in 1789.

Fire Island National Seashore, a barrier island off the south shore of Long Island, is a national wilderness area and popular beach resort.

Fort Ticonderoga, located between Lake George and Lake Champlain, was begun by the French in 1755 and named Fort Carillon. The British captured it four years later and renamed it Ticonderoga.

Gateway National Recreation Area, shared by New York and New Jersey, preserves beaches and marshlands in the New York Harbor area.

George Eastman House, in Rochester, is the home of the noted inventor of photographic equipment. The house is now a museum of art and photography. An adjoining theater shows movies from the past.

General Grant National Memorial, in New York City, includes the tombs of President and Mrs. Grant.

Home of Franklin D. Roosevelt National Historic Site, in Hyde Park, is the birthplace, home, and grave site of the 32nd president of the United States. Nearby is the Franklin D. Roosevelt Library and Museum, containing the president's papers, his personal book collection, and collections on naval and New York colonial history.

Martin Van Buren National Historic Site, in Kinderhook, was the home of the eighth president of the United States from the time he left office in 1841 until his death in 1862.

National Baseball Hall of Fame and Museum, in Cooperstown, contains more than eight thousand pieces of memorabilia and commemorates some of the game's greatest players.

New York City is one of the world's great cultural centers. Articles on three of its famous landmarks, **Lincoln Center for the Performing Arts**, the **Metropolitan Museum of Art**, and the **Statue of Liberty**, appear in volumes L, M, and S re-spectively. For a description of the city's numerous other attractions, see the article NEW YORK CITY in this volume.

Niagara Falls, near the city of Niagara Falls, is one of the world's most spectacular natural wonders. An article on Niagara Falls appears in Volume N.

Sagamore Hill National Historic Site, near Oyster Bay, was the home of President Theodore Roosevelt after 1885.

Saratoga National Historic Park, in Stillwater, commemorates the American victory over the British in 1777 during the Revolutionary War.

Saratoga Performing Arts Center, south of Saratoga Springs, offers programs in music and dance during the summer months.

Women's Rights National Historical Park, in Seneca Falls, is the site of the first women's rights national convention (1848) and the home of suffragist Elizabeth Cady Stanton, who helped organize that first convention.

State Park Areas. New York has more than 140 state parks. Adirondack State Park, the largest park in the nation, is more than three times larger than Yellowstone National Park. The state parks contain many campsites, forest preserves, and skiing areas. For more information, contact the Office of Parks, Recreation, and Historic Preservation, Albany, New York 12238.

the relatively warm waters of the Atlantic Ocean. January temperatures average 14°F (−10°C) in the Adirondacks and 30°F (−1°C) along the coast. July temperatures average 66°F (19°C) in the Adirondacks and 74°F (23°C) along the coast. Annual precipitation in the form of rain and snow also varies. The Adirondacks receive the most, approximately 58 inches (1,470 millimeters), and New York City and Long Island receive less than 15 inches (380 millimeters). The growing season ranges from about 100 days in the Adirondacks to 180 to 200 days on Long Island.

Plant and Animal Life

More than half of New York is covered with forests. About one sixth of the forestlands—approximately 3 million acres (1.2 million hectares)—are in forest preserves or in state parks and wetlands. The most common evergreens are cedar, spruce, hemlock, balsam, and pine. The most common deciduous trees are oak, maple, hickory, ash, tulip, and beech. Shrubs, which grow in abundance, include mountain laurel, rhododendron, wild roses, witch hazel, spice bush, wild azalea, alder, and sumac.

Wildlife abounds in New York's forests and mountains. Bears and wildcats can be seen, as well as foxes, raccoons, porcupines, and other small mammals. Deer are quite numerous. Common birds include crows, mourning doves, house sparrows, blue jays, cardinals, woodpeckers, robins, owls, and bluebirds. Among the game fish caught in the rivers and lakes are trout, bass,

muskellunge, and pike. Saltwater fish and shellfish include bluefish, bass, flounder, clams, scallops, and crabs.

Natural Resources

The richest soils in New York are found in the Mohawk and the Genesee river valleys. The rugged parts of the plateaus and mountainous areas usually have thin, rocky soils. The state is endowed with such nonmetals as granite, marble, slate, salt, gypsum, emery, garnet, and talc; such metals as iron ore, titanium, and zinc; and small amounts of petroleum and natural gas. Wood from New York's forests is used mainly for lumber and fuel and for making furniture, paper, cardboard, and fence posts.

New York's many lakes and rivers provide residents with a large supply of fresh water. Its many swift streams supply waterpower, and giant hydroelectric plants have been built at Niagara Falls and at the rapids of the St. Lawrence River below Ogdensburg. These and many other plants produce vast quantities of electric power.

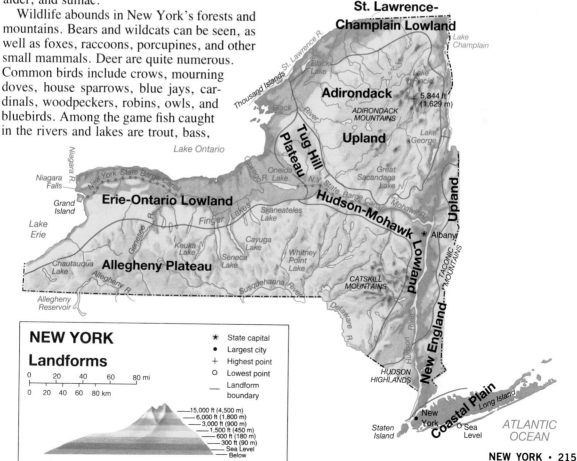

NEW YORK · 215

ing about 1820, New York began taking in significant numbers of German and Irish immigrants. After 1880, the source of emigration shifted to southern and eastern Europe, with Italians and Jews making up the largest proportion of newcomers. In the 1920's national quotas reduced immigration, but in the 1960's the laws were relaxed, and New York again

Above: New York City's multicultural atmosphere attracts immigrants from all over the world. *Right:* Cadets celebrate graduation day at the United States Military Academy at West Point.

▶ PEOPLE

More than 85 percent of New York's residents live in urban areas. Most of them are in a population belt covering Long Island, the Hudson Valley, from New York City to Albany, and the Mohawk Valley, from Albany to Buffalo. From 1820 until 1970, New York was the most populous state in the nation. In 2000, with a population of almost 19 million, it ranked third behind California and Texas.

The Dutch were the first Europeans to settle in New York. After English forces seized their colony, New Amsterdam, in 1664, English, Welsh, Scotch-Irish, Germans, and blacks began to arrive in large numbers. Indeed, in 1775 more African Americans lived in New York than in any other northern state. Start-

became a magnet for foreigners. In the early 1990's, the largest numbers of newcomers were from the Dominican Republic, Russia, China, Guyana, Jamaica, and Mexico.

New York's African American population averages 16 percent, but the percentages are higher in the cities. Approximately 15 percent claim Hispanic origin. Very few Indians still

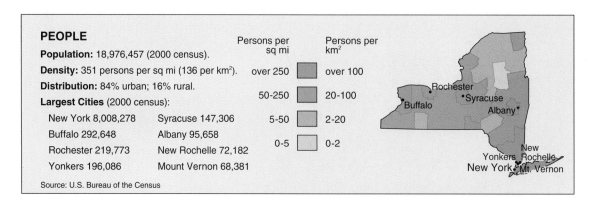

PEOPLE

Population: 18,976,457 (2000 census).

Density: 351 persons per sq mi (136 per km²).

Distribution: 84% urban; 16% rural.

Largest Cities (2000 census):

New York 8,008,278	Syracuse 147,306
Buffalo 292,648	Albany 95,658
Rochester 219,773	New Rochelle 72,182
Yonkers 196,086	Mount Vernon 68,381

Source: U.S. Bureau of the Census

Persons per sq mi	Persons per km²
over 250	over 100
50-250	20-100
5-50	2-20
0-5	0-2

reside in New York. Today they make up less than half a percent of the population.

Education

During colonial times there were few free public schools in New York, so many children attended religious or private schools. Public school districts were organized after the first public school law was passed in 1812.

In 1948 the existing public institutions of higher education (except for those in New York City) were reorganized as the State University of New York (SUNY), with major campuses at Albany, Binghamton, Buffalo, and Stony Brook. The City University of New York (CUNY) public system has multiple campuses in New York City.

Numerous private colleges and universities are located throughout the state. Columbia University, founded as King's College in 1754 in New York City, is the state's oldest and wealthiest institution of higher education. Also in New York City are Barnard College, which is part of Columbia University, Cooper Union, Fordham University, New York University, the Juilliard School of Music, St. John's University, and Yeshiva University.

Elsewhere in the state are Cornell University in Ithaca, the University of Rochester in Rochester, Union College in Schenectady, Syracuse University in Syracuse, Hamilton College in Clinton, Colgate University in Hamilton, Sarah Lawrence College in Bronxville, Vassar College in Poughkeepsie, Skidmore College in Saratoga Springs, and Rensselaer Polytechnic Institute in Troy. Also in New York are the United States Military Academy at West Point, where U.S. Army officers are trained, and the United States Merchant Marine Academy at Kings Point.

Libraries, Museums, and the Arts

Every county in the state is served by a public library. The New York Public Library in New York City is the largest in the state and one of the largest in the nation. Columbia, Cornell, the University of Rochester, and the New York State Library in Albany also have substantial library holdings. The Franklin D. Roosevelt Library at Hyde Park contains the president's papers and special collections on naval and New York colonial history.

New York City contains dozens of the world's most famous museums, including the Metropolitan Museum of Art, the American Museum of Natural History, and the Museum of Modern Art. Lincoln Center for the Performing Arts, a seven-building complex, houses the New York Philharmonic Orchestra, the Metropolitan Opera, the New York City Ballet, and the New York City Opera, all world-renowned institutions.

Notable museums elsewhere in the state include the Buffalo Museum of Science and the Albright-Knox Art Gallery in Buffalo, the Albany Museum of History and Art and the New York State Museum in Albany, the Remington Art Museum in Ogdensburg, the Shaker Museum in Old Chatham, the Corning Museum of Glass in Corning, and the Fenimore House near Cooperstown. Also in Cooperstown are the National Baseball Hall of Fame and Museum, the Cooperstown Indian Museum, and the Farmers' Museum.

Left: The Buffalo Bills, of the National Football League, play at Rich Stadium in Orchard Park, near Buffalo. New York's two other professional football teams—the New York Giants and the New York Jets—play at Giants Stadium in the Meadowlands Sports Complex, just across the state line in New Jersey.

Sports

The modern game of baseball began in New York City and in nearby Hoboken, New Jersey, in the 1840's. Today New York has two major league baseball teams, the New York Yankees and the New York Mets. New York has three National Football League teams—the Buffalo Bills, the New York Jets, and the New York Giants—and three National Hockey League teams—the Buffalo Sabres, the New York Islanders, and the New York Rangers. Basketball fans root for the New York Knickerbockers (the Knicks) and the New York Liberty women's team. Golf was first played in America in Westchester County, and New York City has long been the home of the United States Open tennis championship. The annual New York City Marathon attracts long-distance runners from around the world.

▶ ECONOMY

Ever since the Dutch established a trading post at the southern tip of Manhattan in 1625, New York has been a powerful economic force in North America. Today, among the fifty states, only California has a stronger economy.

Services

New York service industries account for approximately 80 percent of employment. Of particular importance is New York City, a global center of insurance and real estate, wholesale and retail trade, tourism, and advertising. Wall Street, in the heart of New York's financial district, is considered the financial center of the world. It is home to the American Stock Exchange and the New York Stock Exchange, which handles about 90 percent of all of the securities trading in the United States. Also contributing to the services category are transportation, communication, utilities, and government.

Manufacturing

New York, a leader in manufacturing since before the Civil War, is noted for both the value and the variety of its products. New York City is the nation's largest publisher of books, magazines, and other printed materials. Statewide, other important manufactures include scientific instruments, machinery, chemicals, electrical equipment, processed foods, clothing, cameras and film, electric appliances, medicines, and aircraft.

Agriculture

Dairy farming, particularly in the St. Lawrence Valley, is the major agricultural activity in New York. Milk is its most important product. Beef production is another leading source of farm income. Apple orchards are found throughout the Hudson and the Champlain valleys. Grapes are grown east of Lake Erie and in the Finger Lakes region. Other important sources of agricultural income are hay, corn, and greenhouse products.

New York City is headquarters for many of the world's largest department stores (*left*) and is home to the New York Stock Exchange (*right*), the world's leading marketplace for the trading of stocks and bonds.

Mining and Construction

Stone and sand and gravel are quarried in various parts of New York and are used mainly as building materials. Salt from the Allegheny Plateau is used in making chemicals. New York ranks high among the states in production of zinc. Its talc and wollastonite are used in making ceramics and paints, and its garnet and emery are used to make sandpaper. Construction and repair of buildings, roads, and bridges contribute significantly to the state's economy.

Transportation

New York's first hard-surfaced road was built in 1797 and connected Albany and Schenectady. The state's first railroad began operation between Albany and Schenectady in 1831. Today New York has nearly 110,000 miles (177,028 kilometers) of roadways and is served by approximately 30 railroads. In addition, New York City has one of the world's largest subway systems.

Between 1840 and 1950, New York City's port was the busiest in the world. Other important ports are at Albany, Buffalo, Ogdensburg, Oswego, and Rochester. New York's inland waterway system remains one of the nation's busiest. It includes the New York State Barge Canal System, an important system of waterways connecting the Hudson River with Lake Erie, and the St. Lawrence Seaway, joining the Great Lakes to the Atlantic Ocean.

New York has approximately 500 airports, heliports, and seaplane bases. Two of the world's busiest airfields are New York City's John F. Kennedy International and La Guardia International airports.

Communication

New York's first newspaper, the *New York Gazette*, was founded in 1725 by William

The printing and publishing of newspapers, books, and magazines are the state's most important manufacturing industries.

Bradford. Today about 90 daily newspapers are published in the state; two in particular, *The New York Times* and *The Wall Street Journal*, are world-renowned. Others include the *New York Post*, the *Buffalo News*, the *Rochester Democrat-Chronicle*, and the *Syracuse Post Standard*. Foreign-language newspapers—Spanish, Italian, Polish, Yiddish, and others—also are numerous. In addition, two of the nation's most popular weekly news magazines, *Time* and *Newsweek*, are published in New York City.

New York has approximately 280 radio stations and more than 40 television stations. New York City also is headquarters of the nation's three major television networks.

PRODUCTS AND INDUSTRIES

Manufacturing: Printed materials, scientific instruments, machinery, chemicals, electrical equipment, processed foods, clothing, photographic products.

Agriculture: Dairy products, greenhouse products, cattle, apples.

Minerals: Crushed stone, sand and gravel, salt, zinc, talc, wollastonite, garnet, emery.

Services: Wholesale and retail trade; finance, insurance, and real estate; business, social, and personal services; transportation, communication, and utilities; government.

Percentage of Gross State Product* by Industry

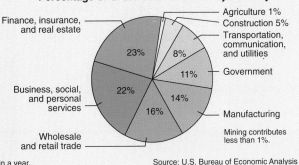

- Finance, insurance, and real estate — 23%
- Business, social, and personal services — 22%
- Wholesale and retail trade — 16%
- Manufacturing — 14%
- Government — 11%
- Transportation, communication, and utilities — 8%
- Agriculture 1%
- Construction 5%
- Mining contributes less than 1%.

*Gross state product is the total value of goods and services produced in a year.

Source: U.S. Bureau of Economic Analysis

New York City is one of the world's most populous and densely built cities. This view shows the top of the famous Chrysler Building, looking out across the borough of Queens.

▶ **CITIES**

New York's major cities are located on its waterways. The two largest, New York City and Buffalo, both are major ports.

Albany, the state's capital and oldest permanent European settlement, is located on the Hudson River in the east-central part of the state. Founded as Fort Orange by the Dutch in 1624, the colony remained under Dutch administration until the British took control in 1664 and named it for their king's brother, James, the duke of both Albany and York.

Albany has been the seat of state government since 1797. The city grew as a commercial center after the Erie Canal opened in 1825; today it is a major shipping center, and the tri-city area of Albany-Schenectady-Troy supports high-technology industries and is a major manufacturer of electronic equipment. Other local industries produce pharmaceuticals, textiles, and meat products.

Rochester is a port city on Lake Ontario. It is also the headquarters of several large companies, including Xerox and Eastman Kodak.

New York City, the largest city in the United States, is one of the largest, wealthiest, and most influential cities in the world. For more information, see the article on New York City following this article.

Buffalo, New York's second largest city, is located at the foot of Lake Erie on the Niagara River, not far from Niagara Falls. Buffalo was first settled by the French in 1758. The present city was laid out in 1803.

Today Buffalo is a leading inland port city, and its Buffalo Customs District handles much of the trade between the United States and Canada. It is also a major industrial center, producing chemicals, machinery, paper, and printed materials. Buffalo is home to a branch of the State University of New York and several other colleges. It is also noted for the Buffalo Philharmonic Orchestra and several excellent museums and libraries.

Rochester, the state's third largest city, is located at the mouth of the Genesee River on Lake Ontario. Founded by businessman Nathaniel Rochester in 1812, the city today is known for the manufacture of optical goods, cameras, photographic supplies, and computer equipment. The University of Rochester includes the famous Eastman School of Music.

State government office buildings surround the Nelson A. Rockefeller Empire State Plaza in the heart of Albany. The capitol building (in the background) was designed in the French Renaissance style and completed in 1898. Other buildings in the complex include the state library, the state museum, a convention center, and a performing arts center.

GOVERNMENT

State Government
Governor: 4-year term
State senators: 61; 2-year terms
State representatives: 150;
  2-year terms
Number of counties: 62

Federal Government
U.S. senators: 2
U.S. representatives: 29
Number of electoral votes: 31

For the name of the current governor, see STATE GOVERNMENTS in Volume S. For the names of current U.S. senators and representatives, see UNITED STATES, CONGRESS OF THE in Volume U-V.

▶ **GOVERNMENT**

New York's first state constitution was adopted in 1777. The present constitution, which dates from 1894, has been amended more than 180 times.

The governor is the state's chief executive officer. Other elected officers are the lieutenant governor, comptroller, and attorney general. Each is elected to a 4-year term.

The legislature is made up of two houses, the Senate and the Assembly. Members are elected to 2-year terms and meet annually.

The Court of Appeals is New York's highest judicial body, followed by the appellate division of the state supreme court, the supreme court, and city and county courts.

▶ **HISTORY**

New York's first known inhabitants came to the region as long as 12,000 years ago. They were the ancestors of the Iroquoian and Algonkian-speaking tribes that the early European settlers encountered in the 1600's.

The Algonkians included the Delaware, or Lenni-Lenape, and the Mahican (or Mohican). The five Iroquois tribes that lived in central and western New York were the Mohawk, Oneida, Onondaga, Cayuga, and Seneca. By the late 1500's they had formed the League of the Iroquois, which the Tuscarora joined in 1722.

European Exploration

Giovanni da Verrazano, an Italian navigator in the service of France, sailed into New York Bay in 1524. Nearly a century later, in 1609, the French explorer Samuel de Champlain came into the New York region from Canada and discovered the lake that now bears his name. That same year, Henry Hudson sailed his ship the *Half Moon* from the Atlantic Ocean up the river that now bears his name. The Dutch, recognizing the opportunity for fur-trading profits, soon sent trading vessels into the Hudson Valley. In 1614 a temporary fort and trading post, Fort Nassau, was built on an island south of Albany.

Early Settlement

In 1621, the Dutch government chartered the Dutch West India Company and authorized it to colonize in America. In 1624 the Dutch settled a wide region they called New Netherland that included most of present-day New York, Connecticut, New Jersey, Delaware, and Pennsylvania; they established their first settlement at Fort Orange (now Albany). That same year they built a fort on Nut Island (now Governors Island) in Upper New York

Bay, but they moved it the following year to the southern tip of Manhattan Island and renamed it New Amsterdam. This little town later became the giant city of New York. New Netherland prospered under the most famous of its governors—the hot-tempered peg-legged Peter Stuyvesant, who administered the colony from 1647 until 1664.

English Rule

The British had long been interested in New Netherland. They coveted the settlement at the mouth of the Hudson River and resented the presence of a Dutch outpost between the English colonies of Virginia and Massachusetts. In 1664, King Charles II sent warships to seize New Netherland. The Dutch, who were outgunned, were forced to surrender. New Amsterdam was soon renamed New York City, and Fort Orange became Albany.

After 1689, France became England's major rival in North America. The French and their Indian allies frequently attacked New York frontier settlements. During the French and Indian War (1754–63), several major battles were waged in New York, at forts Niagara, Oswego, Ticonderoga, William Henry, and Crown Point. The French finally surrendered their claims after the British won a decisive victory at Quebec in 1759.

New York prospered during the period of British control. Settlements grew up along the Hudson north of Albany and westward through the Mohawk Valley. The colony produced and exported large quantities of meat, flour, and lumber to the West Indies and furs and naval supplies to the British Isles. But eventually the British Parliament began to impose taxes that many of the colonists considered illegal, and in 1775 the Revolutionary War broke out.

The Revolutionary War and Statehood

On July 9, 1776, the Provincial Congress met in White Plains and ratified America's Declaration of Independence. The following year, three important battles of the war took place in New York—the First and Second Battles of Freeman's Farm and the Battle of Saratoga, in which the British suffered their first major defeat. That same year, the people of New York adopted a state constitution and elected George Clinton to the first of his seven terms as governor.

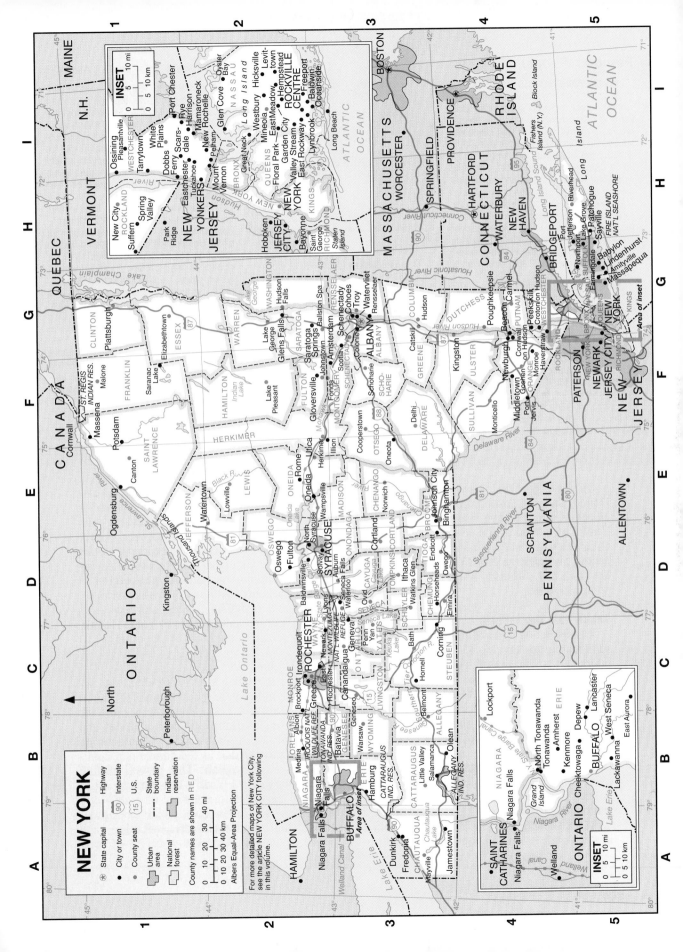

Famous People

Lucille Ball (1911–89), known as the Queen of Comedy, was one of the world's most beloved television stars. Born in Jamestown, she began her career as a model and later had moderate success in Hollywood films. In the 1950's she and her husband Desi Arnaz (1917–86), a Cuban-born bandleader, achieved world stardom with the phenomenal success of their first television series, *I Love Lucy* (1951–57). Constantly shown in reruns around the world, it remains one of the most popular situation comedies ever produced. After their divorce in 1960, Ball produced and starred in two other series, *The Lucy Show* (1962–68) and *Here's Lucy* (1968–74).

Mathew B. Brady (1823?–96), born in Warren County, is remembered for his photographic documentation of the Civil War (1861–65). The photo stills that he and his assistants took while traveling with the Union armies provide fascinating and invaluable information about the conflict. In addition to his battlefield shots, Brady took approximately one third of the known photographs of President Abraham Lincoln. His negatives are preserved in the National Archives and the Library of Congress.

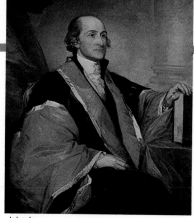

John Jay

George Clinton (1739–1812), born in Little Britain, was known as the "father of the state." New York's first governor, he served a total of seven terms (1777–95 and 1801–04). He also served as vice president of the United States (1805–12) under Presidents Thomas Jefferson and James Madison. His nephew, **De Witt Clinton** (1769–1828), born in Little Britain, was the chief sponsor of the Erie Canal. He also served in the state legislature (1779–1802), in the U.S. Senate (1802–03), as mayor of New York City (1803–15), and as governor of New York (1817–21 and 1825–28).

Thomas Cole (1801–48), born in Lancashire, England, was the first important landscape artist in the United States and the founder of the Hudson River School of painting. Influenced by the English artist J.M.W. Turner, Cole's paintings focused on the unspoiled and idyllic beauty of northeastern America, particularly the forests, mountains, and rivers of New York's Hudson Valley.

Edward Henry Harriman (1848–1909), born in Hempstead, was a Wall Street financier and a powerful railroad executive of the Union Pacific and Southern Pacific railroads. His battle with James J. Hill for control of the Northern Pacific Railroad, which caused a national financial panic in 1901, made him a symbol of corporate greed. His son, **W(illiam) Averell Harriman** (1891–1986), born in New York City, was a leading statesman of the 1900's. During World War II he coordinated President Franklin D. Roosevelt's Lend-Lease program to equip Great Britain with war materials. Under President Harry S. Truman, he served as ambassador to the Soviet Union (1943–46); secretary of commerce (1946–48); and chief administrator of the Marshall Plan (1948–52). He then served one term as governor of New

On July 26, 1788, New York ratified the United States Constitution and became the eleventh state. For five years (1785–90) New York City served as the new nation's capital. Great tracts of land were opened to settlers in central and western New York, and by 1820 the state had surpassed Virginia as the most populous state.

Reform and Development

Transportation breakthroughs contributed significantly to New York's progress. Robert Fulton's first successful commercial steamship, the *Clermont*, made its maiden voyage up the Hudson River in 1807. The Erie Canal, which opened in 1825, marked a major engineering achievement and opened up the Great Lakes to international commerce. As canal commerce boomed, many of the small settlements along the canal grew into important cities. By the 1850's, roads and railroads linked New York City to western New York and beyond to Chicago.

At the same time, New York led the nation in social legislation and population growth. In 1817 it became one of the first states to pass an antislavery law (effective in 1827), and in 1848 it was the first state to guarantee a married woman's right to own property. At the same time, New York City became the chief gateway for European immigrants escaping poverty, famine, or political persecution in their homelands. Millions of Irish, Germans, Scandinavians, Italians, Poles, and Jews from eastern Europe entered New York Harbor, seeking refuge in the Land of Opportunity.

The Civil War

During the Civil War (1861–65), the demand for military supplies stimulated manufacturing in New York. The state became the Union Army's leading supplier of troops and war materials. After the war, manufacturing continued to expand, as did commerce, banking, and transportation. This growth created many jobs in New York's fast-growing cities but also gave rise to a variety of evils—city slums, political corruption, unfair labor practices, ethnic and racial discrimination, and waste of natural resources. Several of New

York (1955–58). Later, as undersecretary of state for political affairs (1963–65), he helped negotiate the 1963 Nuclear Test Ban Treaty, and as an ambassador-at-large he headed the U.S. delegation (1968–69) to Paris to discuss ending the Vietnam War. Averell's wife, **Pamela Digby Churchill Hayward Harriman** (1920–97), born in Farnborough, England, helped rebuild the Democratic Party in the 1980's and was a major fundraiser for Bill Clinton's 1992 presidential campaign. From 1993 until her death, she served as the nation's first female ambassador to France.

Arthur Miller (1915–2005), born in New York City, was a leading American playwright. Many critics consider his Pulitzer Prize-winning *Death of a Salesman* (1949) one of the greatest American dramas of the 1900's. *The Crucible* (1953), a play about the Salem witch hunts of 1692, won an Antoinette Perry (Tony) Award. *After the Fall* (1964) includes a thinly disguised representation of Miller's unhappy marriage to the actress Marilyn Monroe. Publications include *The Theater Essays of Arthur Miller* (1978) and his autobiography, *Timebends: A Life* (1987).

Franklin and Eleanor Roosevelt

Consult the Index to find more information in *The New Book of Knowledge* about the following people who were either born in New York or are otherwise associated with the state. Also see the article NEW YORK CITY following this article.

ARTHUR, Chester A.	HUGHES, Charles Evans	SHERMAN, James S.
ASTOR, John Jacob	JAY, John	SMITH, Joseph
BRANT, Joseph	LIVINGSTON FAMILY	SPAHN, Warren
BROWN, Marcia	McENROE, John	STANTON, Elizabeth Cady
BURROUGHS, John	MORRIS, Gouverneur	STEINMETZ, Charles P.
CLEVELAND, Grover	MORTON, Levi P.	STUYVESANT, Peter
COOPER, James Fenimore	MOSES, Grandma	TEKAKWITHA, Kateri
CORLISS, George H.	POLLOCK, Jackson	TOMPKINS, Daniel D.
DOUGLASS, Frederick	PULLMAN, George	TRUTH, Sojourner
EASTMAN, George	ROCKEFELLER, John D.	TUBMAN, Harriet
ERVING, Julius	ROCKEFELLER, Nelson A.	VAN BUREN, Martin
FERRARO, Geraldine	ROOSEVELT, Eleanor	VANDERBILT FAMILY
FILLMORE, Millard	ROOSEVELT, Franklin D.	WESTINGHOUSE, George
GOULD, Jay	ROOSEVELT, Theodore	WHEELER, William A.
HAMILTON, Alexander	SANGER, Margaret	WHITE, E. B.
HIAWATHA	SEWARD, William H.	WHITMAN, Walt
HUDSON, Henry	SHERIDAN, Philip H.	WILLARD, Frances

York's more progressive governors, including future presidents Grover Cleveland and Theodore Roosevelt, initiated reform measures to fight corruption and improve living and working conditions for laborers.

New York Leads the Nation

World War I (1914–18) further stimulated New York's economy. Afterward, Governors Alfred E. Smith and Franklin D. Roosevelt continued to press for government reforms. Governor Herbert H. Lehman supported relief efforts during the Great Depression of the 1930's.

After the United States entered World War II in 1941, New York again became a leader in the production of war materials. New York City became the nation's major port of embarkation for troops going to Europe to fight Nazi Germany.

Under the governorship of Thomas E. Dewey (1943–55), New York made a smooth transition from wartime production to a prosperous peacetime economy. In 1952, New York City became the seat of international government with the opening of the United Nations' permanent headquarters. The opening of the St. Lawrence Seaway in 1959 further stimulated commerce in northern New York, as did the opening of one of the world's largest hydroelectric plants near Niagara Falls in 1961.

In the following decades, succeeding governors continued efforts to improve New York's health, educational, and recreational services and to control pollution and protect the environment. But the state suffered major setbacks in the 1970's. It lost many manufacturing jobs, the population declined, and for the first time New York City faced bankruptcy. However, the state's economy rebounded in the 1980's and 1990's, and today New York's gross state product is larger than any other state's except California.

JAMES A. FROST
Coauthor, *New York: The Empire State*
Reviewed by KENNETH T. JACKSON
Columbia University

See also ERIE CANAL; NEW YORK CITY; NIAGARA FALLS; SAINT LAWRENCE RIVER AND SEAWAY.

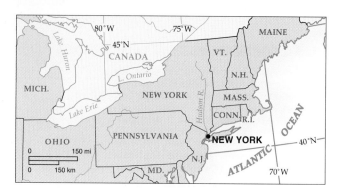

New York City's skyline is famous for its skyscrapers, including the Chrysler Building (foreground) and the Empire State Building (background).

NEW YORK CITY

No city in the United States commands more attention than New York City. With a population of more than 8 million, it is by far the nation's most populous city as well as its predominant center of culture and communications. New York is also a primary center of world finance. New York has the nation's greatest urban mass-transit system and its biggest school system. It claims the most millionaires and the most poor people. It attracts the greatest number of immigrants. And its population is so diverse that no racial or ethnic group can claim a majority.

New York City is made up of five separate districts called boroughs. They are Manhattan, Queens, Brooklyn, the Bronx, and Staten Island. Manhattan, the smallest and most densely populated of the five, is the hub of a megalopolis that sprawls deep into New York State's Hudson Valley and into the satellite cities of New Jersey and Connecticut.

Every year about 20 million Americans and more than 5 million foreigners visit Manhattan. Its chief attractions include the Statue of Liberty, the Empire State Building, the Metropolitan Museum of Art, Radio City Music Hall, Times Square, and its famous Broadway theaters. Another landmark, the famous New York City skyline, was tragically altered on September 11, 2001, when its two tallest skyscrapers—the twin towers of the World Trade Center—were destroyed in the worst terrorist attack ever to take place on American soil.

▶ LAND

New York City is located at the southeastern tip of New York State, where the Hudson River courses south to join the Atlantic Ocean in lower New York Bay. It covers nearly 322 square miles (834 square kilometers) of generally flat, sea-level terrain. The expansive natural harbor, broad beaches, gentle terrain, and temperate climate provide natural strategic advantages that New Yorkers have exploited for hundreds of years.

Islands

New York is a city of islands linked by bridges, tunnels, and ferries. Only the Bronx and a sliver of Manhattan belong to the mainland. Brooklyn and Queens compose the western end of Long Island. Staten Island is the only borough that stands alone.

Waterways

The Hudson River, which flows between Manhattan and New Jersey before widening into New York Bay, is the region's biggest river. The East River, which separates Manhattan and Queens, connects the Atlantic Ocean to Long Island Sound. It is not a true river but a tidal basin or strait.

Climate

New York City has a temperate climate. Summers can be hot and muggy; winters are generally frigid and damp. Temperatures average around 32°F (0°C) in January and 77°F (25°C) in July. Waterways remain navigable throughout the winter, and beaches are cooled by ocean breezes in summer. Precipitation averages 47 inches (1,194 millimeters) a year.

▶ THE FIVE BOROUGHS

Most of what is now New York City was consolidated as Greater New York in 1898.

Manhattan, founded by the Dutch in 1625 as New Amsterdam, is frequently referred to as "the city," even by residents of the other boroughs. The smallest in area, covering only 23 square miles (60 square kilometers), it is also the most congested. Manhattan is home to the stock exchanges, the city's daily newspapers, the seat of city government, and most of the major cultural institutions.

Brooklyn, founded as the Dutch village of Breuckelen, is a major seaport and center of manufacturing. The borough with the most residents, Brooklyn by itself would be one of the nation's most populous cities. Known as the borough of churches and homes, its 71 square miles (184 square kilometers) has many recreational areas, such as Coney Island and Prospect Park.

Queens, covering 108 square miles (280 square kilometers), is the largest borough in area. Rows upon rows of single-family houses have given Queens a distinctly residential, al-

New York City Marathon runners cross the Verrazano-Narrows Bridge from Staten Island (in the background) to Brooklyn. At 4,260 feet (1,298 meters), the bridge is the longest suspension span in North America.

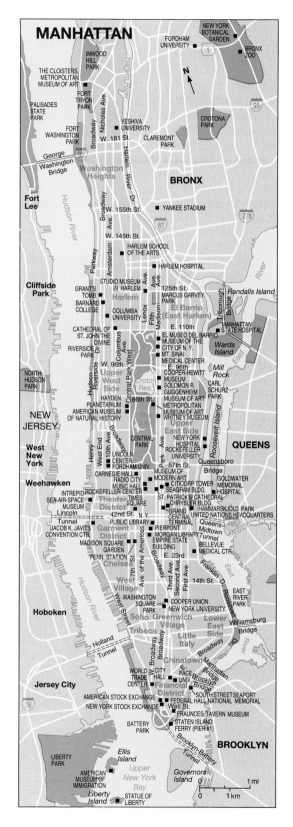

most suburban, character. Queens has been described as the most diverse county in the country, with roughly equal proportions of blacks, Hispanics, and non-Hispanic whites.

The Bronx, named for Jonas Bronck, an early Dutch settler, is the only borough on the mainland. Covering 41 square miles (106 square kilometers), it is primarily a residential district, with many high-rise apartment buildings.

Staten Island, known as Richmond until 1975, covers 64 square miles (166 square kilometers). Ferry service once provided the island's only major link to the rest of the city, but the opening of the Verrazano-Narrows Bridge in 1964 sparked an explosion of residential development.

▶ **PEOPLE**

Since 1625, when the Dutch first settled among the Native Americans in lower Manhattan, New York has been a multicultural community. Over three centuries, periodic waves of immigrants have made New York the model for the term "melting pot."

Dutch settlers were closely followed by the English. In the 1800's came millions of Irish, Germans, Italians, eastern Europeans (many of them Jews), Puerto Ricans, Latin Americans, Caribbean blacks, and Asians. They were joined largely during the 1900's by American-born blacks migrating from the South. More recent surges in immigration from Asia and Latin America are approaching the record levels set in the early 1900's. Today, with a population of more than 8 million, New York City contains about 42 percent of the population of New York State.

Education and Libraries

A million students are enrolled in the city's public school system, which includes high schools that specialize in science and other subjects. In cooperation with the state, the city also offers unusual opportunities for higher education through the government-financed City University of New York (CUNY), which includes nine senior colleges, a technical college, graduate schools of medicine and law, and seven two-year community colleges. Private institutions include Columbia University, New York University, Barnard College, Fordham University, Cooper Union,

the New School for Social Research, Pace University, and Yeshiva University.

The New York Public Library, headquartered on Fifth Avenue in Manhattan, has more than 80 branches. Specialized collections are also maintained at such places as the New York Public Library for the Performing Arts at Lincoln Center, the New-York Historical Society, the Pierpont Morgan Library, the Library for the Blind and Physi-

New York City attracts people from all over the world. Many ethnic groups, such as Chinese Americans (*below*) and Italian Americans (*right*), take pride in maintaining aspects of their cultural heritages. The intermingling of races and nationalities (*below right*) has given the city a distinctive multicultural character.

cally Handicapped, and the Schomburg Center for Research in Black Culture.

Housing and Architecture

A scarcity of land in desirable locations has made New York City famous for its skyscrapers. More offices and apartments are stacked atop one another in New York than any-

where else in the United States. The city's tallest and most renowned skyscrapers are in Manhattan. They include the Empire State Building, the Chrysler Building, Rockefeller Center, and the Citicorp Building.

New York has been primarily a city of renters since the 1800's, when the number of multiple dwellings increased. In the 1980's, clusters of apartment buildings that had been abandoned were transformed by the city into housing for the poor and the homeless. Today several hundred thousand New Yorkers live in publicly funded housing projects.

Museums

All over the city, museums large and small celebrate the arts and sciences. A section along Fifth Avenue is known as Museum Mile. It encompasses the Museum of the City of New York, the Solomon R. Guggenheim Museum, the Cooper-Hewitt Museum, El Museo Del Barrio, and the Metropolitan Museum of Art, the largest museum in the United States. Other notable museums include the Cloisters, a branch of the Metropolitan; the Museum of Modern Art; the Whitney Museum of American Art; the Asia Society Galleries; the Studio Museum in Harlem; the Museum of Television and Radio; the American Museum of the Moving Image; the Museum of Broadcasting; the American Museum of Natural History and the Hayden Planetarium; the New York Hall of Science; the Intrepid Sea-Air-Space Museum; the New York Aquarium; the South Street Seaport Museum; the Statue of Liberty National Monument; the Theodore Roosevelt Birthplace National Historic Site; Federal Hall National Memorial; and the Fraunces Tavern Museum. Other special sites include the world-renowned Bronx Zoo/Wildlife Conservation Park and various other zoos and botanical gardens.

New York City is the nation's most populous city, and housing is always in demand. Many residents live in high-rise apartment buildings, such as these in the Bronx (*left*). The city's many homeless people (*below*) seek shelter wherever they can.

Theater, Music, and Dance

New York has been called America's cultural capital. Broadway, the name of a major avenue, and the side streets off Times Square include a theater district known throughout the world for its plays and musical productions. Actors in off-Broadway productions often perform experimental theater.

The numerous resident companies of Lincoln Center for the Performing Arts host

Manhattan's Central Park (*above*) provides refuge from the hectic pace of the city. Times Square (*right*), in the heart of the theater district, is one of the world's busiest crossroads.

the world famous New York Philharmonic Orchestra, the Metropolitan Opera, the New York City Ballet, and the Big Apple Circus. Carnegie Hall, one of the world's premier concert auditoriums, celebrated its centennial in 1991. Dozens of other New York performing groups—from the Alvin Ailey, Joffrey, and Martha Graham dance companies to the Boys Choir of Harlem—are internationally renowned.

Parks

New York City's Parks Department presides over about 1,500 parks, playgrounds, malls, squares, and other public spaces. Pelham Bay Park in the Bronx, covering 2,764 acres (1,119 hectares), is by far the city's largest, although Manhattan's Central Park is the best known. Designed by Frederick Law Olmsted in the mid-1800's, it was the first formally planned park in the United States. Occupying 840 acres (340 hectares), Central Park offers a charming zoo, a carousel, landscaped walkways, restaurants, and boating.

Although New York is the model of urban America, the city surprisingly contains several popular public beaches, including Coney Island in Brooklyn, the Rockaways in Queens, and Orchard Beach in the Bronx.

Sports

For spectators and participants alike, New York City offers a wide variety of professional and amateur sports. Baseball fans can choose between the American League Yankees, who play at Yankee Stadium in the Bronx, and the National League Mets, who play at Shea Stadium in Queens. The Giants and Jets of the National Football League include New York in their team names, but their home stadium, the Meadowlands Sports Complex, lies across the Hudson River in New Jersey.

Manhattan's Madison Square Garden, the city's largest indoor sports arena, is home to the New York Knickerbockers (the Knicks) of the National Basketball Association, the New York Liberty of the Women's National Basketball Association, and the New York Rangers of the National Hockey League. The Garden also hosts a variety of track meets, boxing and tennis matches, rodeos, and dog and cat shows. The annual United States Open tennis tournament is held at the National Tennis Center in Flushing Meadow, Queens. Central Park marks the finish line of the annual New York City Marathon. Cricket, soccer, bocce, and other games compete with baseball, basketball, handball, and stickball in the city's playgrounds and streets.

Famous People

William F. Buckley, Jr. (1925–), born in New York City, established himself as the leading intellectual voice of American conservative thought with his book *God and Man at Yale* (1951). In 1955 he founded the *National Review*, a magazine of conservative political commentary, which he headed until 2004. Known for his sharp wit and debating ability, Buckley hosted the television interview program *Firing Line* (1966–99) and has written a syndicated newspaper column called "On the Right" since 1962.

Shirley St. Hill Chisholm (1924–2005), born in Brooklyn, was the first African American woman elected to the U.S. House of Representatives (1969–83). A fiery orator and an advocate for minorities' and women's rights, she was a candidate for president in the 1972 Democratic primary.

Rudolph W. Giuliani (1944–), born in Brooklyn, was New York City's 107th mayor (1994–2001). During his two terms, Giuliani, a Republican, reduced crime, cut welfare rolls in half, and cleaned up the city's landmarks and subways. Some of the tactics he used to improve city life, such as aggressive police action, angered many minority groups. But following the September 11, 2001, terrorist attacks on the World Trade Center,

Shirley Chisholm

Rudolph Giuliani

Giuliani exhibited such outstanding leadership and support that he became known as America's Mayor. He later established a consulting firm and wrote a best-selling book, *Leadership* (2002).

Henry Robinson Luce (1898–1967), born in Tengchow, China, cofounded *Time,* a weekly newsmagazine, which first appeared in 1923. It was followed by *Fortune* (1930), *Life* (1936), and *Sports Illustrated* (1954). He also founded and published Time-Life books. His wife, **Clare Boothe Luce** (1903–87), a noted editor, playwright, and politician, was born in New York City. She served as a U.S. representative (1943–47) from Connecticut and as ambassador to Italy (1953–57). She was the first American woman to hold a major diplomatic post.

Robert Moses (1888–1981), born in New Haven, Connecticut, became known as New York's master builder. A politician involved in a variety of public works commissions (1913–63), he helped to create such landmarks as Lincoln Center for the Performing Arts, the United Nations headquarters, Shea Stadium, the Long Island parkway system, Jones Beach, and the Triborough and Verrazano-Narrows bridges.

J(ulius) Robert Oppenheimer (1904–67), born in New York City, was one of the nation's most influential physicists. As director of the Los Alamos Laboratory (1943–45) in New Mexico, he led the team that developed the world's first atomic bombs, which were used on Japan to end World War II. But he later opposed the development of the hydrogen bomb.

▶ ECONOMY

New York was once the leading manufacturing city in the United States, but manufacturing declined as industry shifted to the suburbs. However, while New York has lost factory jobs, it has increased its number of office workers.

Services

New York has been transformed since World War II into a service economy. Health services have emerged as the largest service employer, followed by business services (such as advertising), wholesale trade, banking, social services, finance, insurance, and real estate. The New York Stock Exchange, the American Stock Exchange, and commodities exchanges—all located in lower Manhattan and known collectively as Wall Street—handle the vast majority of stocks and bonds traded in the United States. Millions of tourists and the jobs they generate also drive the city's economy.

Manufacturing

Together, all the people employed in manufacturing continue to predominate compared to any one of the individual service sectors. In the city, the apparel (clothing) industry is the largest, followed by printing and publishing. Hundreds of small firms make everything from metal products to pickles. But the number of factory jobs has declined dramatically as a result of automation and of cheaper production costs for goods made elsewhere in the United States or overseas.

Transportation

New York City was once the nation's leading hub of railroad, bus, shipping, and air travel, but its dominance in transportation has eroded in recent years. Cruise and cargo traffic has shifted to other ports, although one passenger ship terminal remains. Nevertheless, the John F. Kennedy International and La Guardia International airports, both located in Queens, rank among the world's

In 1953 the Atomic Energy Commission (AEC), questioning his patriotism, declared him a security risk and suspended him from his position as chairman. In 1963, as a belated apology, he received the prestigious Enrico Fermi Award, for his contributions to theoretical physics.

Jacob August Riis (1849–1914), born in Denmark, was a journalist and author. Through his photographs, newspaper articles, and books, including *How the Other Half Lives* (1890), Riis exposed the squalid conditions of the immigrant poor and advocated child-labor laws and other social welfare legislation. He was known as the great emancipator of the slums.

Carl Edward Sagan (1934–96), born in New York City, was a scientist, astronomer, and educator who popularized scientific topics and his ideas of life's origins and evolution. Among his best-selling books are *The Dragons of Eden* (1977), winner of the 1978 Pulitzer Prize, and *Cosmos* (1980), based on his acclaimed public television series.

William Marcy Tweed (1823–78), born in New York City, headed Tammany Hall, once a powerful Democratic political organization. Known as Boss Tweed, he and other city politicians, called the Tweed Ring, swindled millions of dollars from the city treasury. Charged with corruption in 1871, Tweed was convicted of fraud and spent his final years in prison.

Robert Moses

Fiorello La Guardia

Consult the Index to find more information in *The New Book of Knowledge* about the following people who were either born in New York City or are otherwise associated with it:

ABDUL-JABBAR, Kareem	GEHRIG, Lou	MELVILLE, Herman
ALLEN, Woody	GERSHWIN, George	MORGAN, John Pierpont
BALDWIN, James	GIBSON, Althea	NAST, Thomas
BEECHER, Henry Ward	GREELEY, Horace	NEVELSON, Louise
BERLIN, Irving	HAYES, Helen	O'NEILL, Eugene
BERNSTEIN, Leonard	HOWE, Julia Ward	PEALE, Norman Vincent
BERRA, Yogi	HUGHES, Langston	POWELL, Adam Clayton, Jr.
BLACKWELL, Elizabeth	IRVING, Washington	POWELL, Colin
BOAS, Franz	JAMES, William	QUEEN, Ellery
BOGART, Humphrey	JOHNSON, James Weldon	RUTH, Babe
BROWN, Margaret Wise	KOUFAX, Sandy	SALK, Jonas
CAGNEY, James	LA GUARDIA, Fiorello	SCORSESE, Martin
CALLAS, Maria	LANGMUIR, Irving	SENDAK, Maurice
COOPER, Peter	L'ENGLE, Madeleine	SILLS, Beverly
COPLAND, Aaron	LIPPMANN, Walter	THURBER, James
DE NIRO, Robert	MALCOLM X	TOSCANINI, Arturo
DEWEY, John	MANTLE, Mickey	VERRAZANO, Giovanni da
DiMAGGIO, Joe	MARX BROTHERS	WARHOL, Andy
DODGE, Mary Mapes	MCCORD, David	WHARTON, Edith
FEYNMAN, Richard P.	MEANY, George	ZENGER, John Peter

busiest. Grand Central Terminal, more commonly known as Grand Central Station, was once one of the busiest rail links to other cities. It is now largely used as a commuter terminal for residents of the northern suburbs. Pennsylvania Station is the center for noncommuter train service, although it also services commuters. Hundreds of buses converge daily on New York's immense Port Authority bus terminal.

Dozens of bridges connect the city's five boroughs and outlying regions. Perhaps the most splendid is the Brooklyn Bridge, connecting Brooklyn to lower Manhattan. The Verrazano-Narrows Bridge, connecting Staten Island and Brooklyn, is the longest suspension span in North America. Other notable bridges are the George Washington Bridge, connecting Manhattan with New Jersey; the Triborough Bridge, linking Manhattan, the Bronx, and Queens; and the Throgs Neck and Bronx-Whitestone bridges, connecting the Bronx and Queens.

New York also has many important tunnels. The Brooklyn-Battery Tunnel, connecting lower Manhattan and Brooklyn, is the second longest tunnel in the United States. Others of note are the Lincoln and Holland tunnels, connecting Manhattan and New Jersey, and the Queens-Midtown Tunnel, connecting midtown Manhattan and Queens.

New York City is also home to one of the nation's oldest subways. It is made up of three separate underground railway systems—the Interborough Rapid Transit (IRT), the Independent Subway (IND), and the Brooklyn-Manhattan Transit Company (BMT). Many people like to get around the city on foot; but to travel great distances or to save time, most prefer to take the subway, a city bus, or one of the many thousands of taxicabs that cruise the city's 6,000 miles (9,660 kilometers) of streets. Also, ferry service among the boroughs has expanded as traffic on the roads, tunnels, and bridges has become increasingly congested.

Thousands were killed when the twin towers of the World Trade Center, two of the world's tallest buildings, were destroyed by terrorists on September 11, 2001.

Communication

Radio and television are among the city's leading employers. Many of the nation's major television networks are headquartered in New York, as are a wide variety of important news and literary magazines. The city also publishes two of the nation's most celebrated newspapers, *The New York Times* and *The Wall Street Journal*, and is headquarters for the Associated Press news wire service.

▶ GOVERNMENT

New York City has a complicated system of government. It is one city, but it includes five counties that double as boroughs. The city employs about 200,000 people; it runs its own hospitals, schools, and transit systems; and it is New York's largest landlord. Its 41,000-member police force is larger than some nations' standing armies.

The city is run by a mayor, who is elected to a 4-year term. Other elected officials include five borough presidents, 51 city council members, a comptroller, and a public advocate, who heads the City Council. The City Charter, revised in the early 1990's, increased the powers of the mayor and expanded the number of city districts from 35 to 51.

▶ HISTORY

New York had been long settled by various Indian tribes when Italian explorer Giovanni da Verrazano sailed into New York Bay in 1524. Henry Hudson, sailing for the Dutch in 1609, explored the river that now bears his name. By 1624 the Dutch West India Company had established a colony there called New Netherland. Its primary settlement, New Amsterdam, was founded on the southern tip of Manhattan the following year. Legend has it that Peter Minuit, the colony's first governor, bought the island of Manhattan from the Indians for about $24 of trinkets, beads, and knives. In 1664, the Dutch surrendered their colony to the English, who renamed it New York in honor of their king's brother, the Duke of York. After the Revolutionary War (1775–83), it briefly served as the capital (1785–90) of the new nation.

From the beginning, New York grew by staggering proportions. Its strategic location as a port fueled its development as a trading and financial center. By the mid-1800's, the first waves of immigrants and the Industrial Revolution further transformed New York and assured its place as the nation's largest city. But with growth also came problems of overcrowding, crime, pollution, and racial tensions. In 1975, financial demands for services stretched the city's limited resources and brought New York to the brink of bankruptcy, but the city rebounded in the 1980's.

In 1993, a car bomb exploded at the World Trade Center, killing six people. Terrorists linked to the Saudi-born guerrilla leader Osama bin Laden were tried and found guilty. But the horror of 1993 was eclipsed by the calamity that took place on September 11, 2001. Terrorists, again linked to bin Laden, hijacked two U.S. commercial airplanes and crashed them into the twin towers of the World Trade Center. Both buildings collapsed, and the death toll reached into the thousands, providing the greatest challenge yet to the resiliency of the city's inhabitants.

SAM ROBERTS
Urban Affairs Columnist
The New York Times

See also LIBERTY, STATUE OF; LINCOLN CENTER FOR THE PERFORMING ARTS; METROPOLITAN MUSEUM OF ART.

NEW ZEALAND

New Zealand is a nation in the South Pacific Ocean, consisting of two main islands and several smaller ones. It is situated about 1,200 miles (1,930 kilometers) southeast of Australia. Its first inhabitants, the Maori, came from Polynesia in the A.D. 1200's. Some tribes called their new home Aotearoa, or the "land of the long white cloud," because of a strange-looking cloud formation they saw as they approached the islands. Today, in poem and legend, the Maori recall the courage of their ancestors, who made the long voyage over stormy seas without charts or instruments.

The first Europeans to see the islands were Dutch sea captain Abel Tasman in 1642 and British navigator Captain James Cook in 1769. The country was named for the Dutch province of Zeeland.

▶ PEOPLE

Most New Zealanders are of British descent. Nearly three-fourths of the population lives on the North Island, and one-fourth on the larger South Island.

The Maori population, numbering about 600,000, is growing faster than the European population and makes up approximately 16 percent of the inhabitants. Some Maori live in villages on the North Island, where they preserve their traditional language, chants, and dances.

Clockwise from above: **A New Zealand shepherd. A Maori woman in traditional dress. A scenic view of Milford Sound in Fiordland National Park.**

Their intricately carved meeting-houses and wooden figures are distinctive expressions of their art, and there is a major effort to keep this art alive.

The Maori have been giving up their traditional ways for a long time, and now over 85 percent live in towns and cities. As a result, the Maori are experiencing great economic and social changes.

Language and Religion. Both English and Maori are official languages of New Zealand. Maori is spoken on most official occasions, but it remains threatened as a language of everyday use. Only about 10 percent of Maori speak it fluently, despite the establishment in the 1980's of *kohanga reo*—schools that immerse young children in the Maori language. Although Maori is taught in some schools, it is not compulsory.

The major religious organizations of New Zealand are the Church of England, the Presbyterian Church, the Roman Catholic Church, and the Methodist Church.

Education and Libraries. Almost everyone in New Zealand can read and write. The government provides free education for children from ages

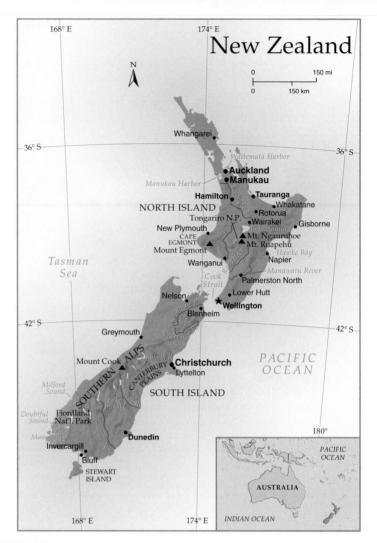

FACTS and figures

NEW ZEALAND is the official name of the country.
LOCATION: South Pacific Ocean.
AREA: 103,737 sq mi (268,680 km²).
POPULATION: 4,000,000 (estimate).
CAPITAL: Wellington.
LARGEST CITY: Auckland (metropolitan area).
MAJOR LANGUAGE: English, Maori (both official).
MAJOR RELIGIOUS GROUPS: Protestant, Roman Catholic.
GOVERNMENT: Constitutional monarchy (dominion within the Commonwealth of Nations). **Head of state**—British monarch, represented by a governor-general. **Head of government**—prime minister. **Legislature**—House of Representatives.
CHIEF PRODUCTS: Agricultural—wheat, barley, potatoes, pulses, fruits, vegetables, wool, beef, dairy products, fish. **Manufactured**—processed foods, wood and paper products, textiles. **Mineral**—coal, natural gas, iron ore.
MONETARY UNIT: New Zealand dollar (1 dollar = 100 cents).

3 to 19. Education is compulsory for children between the ages of 6 and 16, but most enter school by the age of 5.

The main universities are the University of Auckland; Victoria University at Wellington, the capital; Massey University at Palmerston North; the University of Canterbury at Christchurch; and the University of Otago at Dunedin.

The country has an extensive library system. Major research libraries include the Auckland Public Library; the Alexander Turnbull Library and the National Library of New Zealand, both in Wellington; and the Hocken Library in Dunedin.

Home Life. New Zealanders enjoy a relatively high standard of living, although few have great wealth. The majority of families still live in one-story wooden homes. Most families have an automobile and many have modern

home appliances. But poverty is increasing, especially among those with limited education.

Sports and Recreation. New Zealanders enjoy the outdoors, and people of all ages take part in sports. Favorite activities are camping, boating, hunting, and fishing. Horse racing draws crowds to racetracks. Rugby is the leading sport. Other team sports are soccer, cricket, basketball, and field hockey. The country's long-distance runners have set world records. In 1953, New Zealander Edmund Hillary and his Sherpa guide Tenzing Norgay became the first persons to climb Mount Everest, the world's highest peak. Hillary was later knighted for his accomplishment.

▶ **LAND**

New Zealand is in a region of the Pacific Ocean where earthquakes are common. In 1931, an earthquake at Napier on Hawke Bay caused 255 deaths. Small earthshocks occur often in several parts of the country, but major earthquakes so far have occurred in relatively unpopulated areas.

Land Regions. New Zealand is made up of two large islands and some small outlying islands. Its two large islands, the North Island and the South Island, are separated by Cook Strait. The smaller Stewart Island is south of South Island. The Chatham Islands lie about 400 miles (644 kilometers) to the east.

On the North Island, Ruapehu, Tongariro, and Ngauruhoe are active volcanoes in Tongariro National Park. Mount Egmont, a dormant volcano, is on the western coast. There are geysers and hot springs at Rotorua.

On the South Island, the Southern Alps form a backbone of sharp peaks with snowfields and glaciers along the island's western part. Tasman, Franz Joseph, and Fox glaciers are three of the most scenic. Mount Cook, the highest peak in New Zealand, rises 12,349 feet (3,764 meters) and is located in the Southern Alps. The Maori called it Aorangi— "the cloud piercer." In the southwest the mountains rise directly from the sea, and there are a number of inlets, or fjords. This area has been set aside as Fiordland National Park. Near the head of Milford Sound are the spectacular Sutherland Falls.

A geothermal power station at Wairakei uses steam from underground hot springs to generate electricity. High-pressure steam is piped to turbines from wells that have been drilled deep into the hot ground.

Rivers and Lakes. The rivers of New Zealand are short and fast-flowing and provide important sources of energy. Only in a few places can they be used for navigation. The Waikato is the longest. It flows through the center of the North Island to the Tasman Sea. It both feeds and drains Lake Taupo, the country's largest lake. The Rangitikei, Wanganui, and Manawatu are other North Island rivers. The Clutha is the longest river in the South Island. Like the Waitaki, Rakaia, and Clarence, it flows into the Pacific Ocean. The Wairau flows into Cook Strait. The lakes of this island were formed by glaciers that scooped out valleys or dammed them with rock and gravel deposits.

Climate. Its position in the belt of westerly winds gives New Zealand a climate similar to that of the northwestern coast of North America. Summers are mild. Winters are cool and rather stormy. Temperatures do not often fall below freezing in the lowlands. The pastures stay green all year. The uplands of both main islands have permanent snowfields, providing fine ski areas. The greatest variation in rainfall occurs on the South Island. More than 300 inches (7,600 millimeters) fall in Fiordland each year. Rainfall east of the mountains can be as little as 15 inches (380 millimeters).

Natural Resources. When Europeans first came to New Zealand, forests covered more than half the country. Today, only about a quarter of the area is forested. Much of the timber was cut or burned to clear land for pastures and crops. This, along with grazing by too many sheep and damage caused by rabbits, reduced the productivity of the land. Much has been done in recent years to improve the situation. But soil erosion is still a problem in hilly parts of the country.

New Zealand has outlawed the building of nuclear power plants, and hydroelectricity remains the major source of local energy. Hydroelectric power is provided by several New Zealand river systems. The Waikato River is the chief source of hydroelectric power on the North Island. The country's largest hydroelectric station is on the South Island—underground turbines draw water from Lake Manapouri and discharge it into Doubtful Sound. The power networks of the island are linked by submarine cable across Cook Strait.

Coal is New Zealand's most valuable mineral. About one-third of it comes from around Greymouth on the South Island. Natural gas has been found on the North Island south of Cape Edgemont, but this energy source will soon be exhausted. Nearly all the nation's petroleum must be imported, although there are hopes of finding deposits in the natural gas fields. Sand, gravel, and limestone deposits are found in many parts of the country. Iron is found in the sands of the North Island beaches. Ilmenite sands on the South Island's west coast are a source of titanium.

The kiwi is a flightless bird found only in New Zealand. A road sign *(right)* tells drivers to watch out for the bird.

Because of New Zealand's isolated location, unusual kinds of birds and reptiles abound. The country is rich in bird life. Some birds that could not fly were able to exist in New Zealand because they had no natural enemies. The best-known living example is the kiwi, a bird with no tail and only stumps for wings. An unusual New Zealand animal is the tuatara.

NEXT **8** km

This reptile has been called a living fossil because it is a relative of the dinosaurs. New Zealand once had no native land mammals except bats. The European settlers brought goats, pigs, rabbits, weasels, deer, and opossums. They have become pests, destroying both forests and grasslands, because there are no natural enemies to keep them in check.

Fish and shellfish abound in the waters around New Zealand. Whales and seals were taken in large numbers off the coasts in the 1800's. But both sperm whales and southern right whales have recovered greatly in recent years. Protected fur seals have also recovered and are a common sight on the coasts of the cooler South Island.

▶ ECONOMY

Although New Zealand is an agricultural country, only about 7 percent of the workers are actually engaged in farming. But many others are involved in the processing and trade of farm products. More and more people today work in the nation's growing service industries.

Services. Since the 1920's, the majority of New Zealanders have worked in service industries. Traditionally, the transportation sector and the government have been major service employers. However, the tourism industry—including restaurants and other food suppliers—is becoming a major employer.

Manufacturing. New Zealand's main exports come from the nation's farms—wool, meat, butter, cheese, and hides and skins. Many people process farm products in dairy factories, canneries, breweries, and meat-refrigerating plants. Sawmilling is an important industry where logging is carried on in the forests.

Most of New Zealand's heavy machinery must be imported. But woolen goods, carpets, clothing, shoes, furniture, electrical appliances, and computer software are manufactured. Imported petroleum is refined by an oil refinery at Whangarei. An aluminum smelter at Bluff uses hydroelectricity to refine ore that is imported from Australia.

Agriculture and Fishing. Livestock raising is the basis of the economy. The country has over 40 million sheep and 10 million cattle. Pasture grasses are the main crop grown on most farms. There are also many dairy farms, especially in the Waikato Valley, around New Plymouth, and northeast of Wellington; there are an increasing number in the drier parts of the South Island. On the South Island the large sheep ranches are called runs. The main breed of sheep on these runs is the merino, which produces fine wool. Beef cattle are raised in many parts of the country.

On the lowland plains some farms grow such crops as wheat, barley, and potatoes. The Canterbury Plains are the leading wheat-

Sheep are rounded up on a New Zealand farm. Livestock raising is the basis of the country's economy.

growing area. Hops are grown near Nelson on the South Island. New Zealand's apple orchards produce enough for a large export market. A rapidly increasing number of vineyards produce high-quality wine grapes.

Since the 1970's, fishing has grown into a major industry, contributing about 5 percent of export earnings. Since 1992, half of New Zealand's catch has been granted to Maori, but tribes have still not agreed about how this income should be shared. Aquaculture (fish farming) has flourished in recent years, with mussel and oyster farms increasing along the coast.

Mining. New Zealand's coal is used to generate steam, make gas, provide fuel for

Wellington (*left*), New Zealand's capital, stands on high hills above one of the world's deepest harbors. A streetcar in Christchurch (*above*), the largest city on the South Island.

homes and factories, and produce electricity. Sand and gravel, used for road building and concrete construction, ranks second to coal in value. Limestone is used to make fertilizer and cement. South of Auckland, steel is made from nearby iron sand.

Transportation. Passengers and goods move within the country on modern systems of transportation. Ships travel between the main ports, and ferries run across Cook Strait. Railroads and paved highways connect the major towns and cities of both islands. Air New Zealand operates airline services within the country and to several overseas nations.

Communication. New Zealand has modern telephone, telegraph, and radio services reaching all settled parts of the country. International telephone cables, radio-telephone, and communications satellites connect with Australia, North America, and the rest of the world. There are about nine television stations and 418 radio stations. Cities and large towns have their own daily newspapers. Among the most widely read include the *New Zealand Herald*, *The Press*, and the *Sunday Star Times*.

▶ **MAJOR CITIES**

Over 85 percent of New Zealand's people live in towns and cities, and the proportion of urban population is increasing.

Wellington, the capital of New Zealand—and the southernmost national capital in the world—stands on hills surrounding Port Nicholson at the south end of the North Island. The city's population is over 300,000. Its harbor is the sunken crater of an ancient volcano. Cable cars run from the business district up to Victoria University.

Auckland, located at the north end of the North Island, is the largest urban center in New Zealand. It has a population of about 1.1 million. The city has two harbors, Waitemata on the Pacific side and Manukau on the Tasman Sea. A bridge spans Waitemata Harbor, connecting the main city with the suburbs. Auckland is the first and last port of call for many ships from abroad.

Christchurch, with a population of over 300,000, is the largest city on the South Island. Its parks remind many visitors of England. The city is noted for the large number of bicycles used by its residents. Rail and automobile tunnels through the Port Hills connect Christchurch to its port at Lyttelton.

▶ **CULTURAL HERITAGE**

The National Symphony Orchestra gives concerts throughout the country. There are also opera and ballet companies, as well as many art galleries and museums. Among the best-known New Zealand-born writers are Katherine Mansfield, Dame Ngaio Marsh, Sylvia Ashton Warner, and Janet Frame. Frances Hodgkins and Colin McCahon were talented painters. Opera stars Kiri Te Kanawa and Donald McIntyre are widely acclaimed. Movie director Peter Jackson has raised the profile of New Zealand's film industry with the success of *The Lord of the Rings* trilogy.

▶ GOVERNMENT

New Zealand is a dominion (self-governing state) in the Commonwealth of Nations. A governor-general representing the British monarch is appointed on the advice of the New Zealand government. The House of Representatives, the only house in the legislative branch of government, is the lawmaking body. Five of its members are Maori, who are elected by Maori voters. Every citizen over 18 years of age may vote. Women have had the right to vote since 1893. National elections are held at least every three years. The leader of the party that wins the majority of seats in an election becomes the prime minister. The prime minister and the cabinet carry out the executive functions of the government. The Court of Appeal is the highest court in the judicial branch of the government. Judges are appointed by the governor-general.

▶ HISTORY

Eastern Polynesians voyaged to New Zealand about A.D. 1200. After about 1400, rough seas prevented return voyages to Polynesia, and a distinctive Maori culture emerged. The rising population placed pressure on resources. By 1500, Maori had hunted the

A Maori man creates an intricate wooden carving. A major effort has been made to keep this distinctive Maori art alive.

moa and 40 other bird species to extinction. Fire used for hunting and clearing forests for crops destroyed nearly half the existing forest area. After 1500, the Maori managed their resources much more carefully. Although Maori spoke one language, tribal divisions made them vulnerable to colonization. The clan remained the most important unit of social organization. There were about 100,000 Maori and over 50 major tribes by the time Europeans arrived in 1769.

Early Development. Not long after Captain James Cook reached New Zealand in 1769, whaling and sealing stations were established along the coasts. Soon trade in timber and fibers began. In 1814, Samuel Marsden, who was born in England, arrived from Australia with the first missionaries. In 1840, Captain William Hobson claimed New Zealand for the British. The Treaty of Waitangi, signed with the Maori in the same year, made New Zealand a British colony and guaranteed the Maori ownership of their lands. In spite of this guarantee, most of the land later fell into the hands of Europeans.

Colonization. Colonists were settled at Wellington by the New Zealand Company under the direction of Edward Gibbon Wakefield. About this time, sheepherders began to take over grasslands of the South Island. Other settlements grew up at Nelson, New Plymouth, and Wanganui. The Free Church of Scotland founded Dunedin in 1848. In 1850 the Canterbury Pilgrims of the Church of England arrived at Christchurch.

By an act of the British Parliament in 1852, New Zealand achieved the status of a self-governing colony, which took effect in 1853. Between 1860 and 1870, a series of Maori uprisings occurred on the North Island as a result of land disputes. During this time gold was discovered in the North Island and around Greymouth, attracting gold seekers.

The first shipment of refrigerated cargo from Dunedin in 1882 marked the beginning of the valuable meat trade and encouraged the growth of sheep and dairy farming. In the years that followed, prime ministers Richard Seddon and William Massey were key leaders in developing New Zealand's political and economic life.

New Zealand was a pioneer in public welfare and social security legislation. Old age pensions began in 1898. Since then the government has provided pensions for widows and the blind, as well as children's allowances for every family. There are also payments in case of sickness or unemployment.

The Path to Independence. In 1907, New Zealand became a dominion in the British Empire. It is now a member of the Commonwealth of Nations, an association of independent countries with a common British connection. The government usually consults with other members of the Commonwealth, but New Zealand is free to make its own foreign policy. It fought alongside other Commonwealth nations in World War I and World War II. It sent troops to aid the United Nations forces in the Korean War, fought in the Vietnam War, and assisted the United States and United Nations in the Gulf War and the reconstruction of Afghanistan and Iraq.

New Zealand has several Pacific island dependencies. It administers the Tokelau Islands and handles foreign affairs and defense for the self-governing Cook Islands and Niue.

In spite of its distance from the main world centers, New Zealand plays an active role in world affairs. It has ties with its South Pacific neighbors and with nations of Southeast and East Asia, as well as with Britain and other Commonwealth countries.

New Zealand joined the ANZUS defense alliance with Australia and the United States in 1951. But when a nuclear-powered U.S. Navy destroyer was denied permission to visit in 1985, the United States suspended its defense obligations to New Zealand.

David Lange of the Labour Party (LP) served as prime minister from 1984 to 1989. He was succeeded by the leader of the National Party (NP), Jim Bolger, who served from 1990 to 1997. That year, NP leader Jenny Shipley became New Zealand's first woman prime minister. She was succeeded by the LP leader, Helen Clark, in 2000. Clark was re-elected in 2002.

At first Clark's government was popular. But complaints from the NP leadership that New Zealand's native people have received an unfair percentage of government assistance have affected voters. This along with a weakening economy threatened the current government's standing.

Reviewed by Dr. Tom Brooking
University of Otago

NIACIN. See Vitamins and Minerals.

NIAGARA FALLS

Niagara Falls is located in the Niagara River, approximately halfway between Lake Erie and Lake Ontario, about 16 miles (26 kilometers) northwest of Buffalo, New York. The Niagara River, which flows out of Lake Erie, begins its 36-mile (58-kilometer) journey quietly, but soon turns into a rampaging stream. About midway on its course, the swift water surges forward and plunges over the edge of a high cliff to form the falls. So spectacular are these foaming torrents of water that Niagara has become one of the most famous tourist attractions on the North American continent. More than 10 million people visit the falls every year, and they are a favorite spot for honeymooners.

Actually, Niagara Falls consists of three waterfalls—the Horseshoe (or Canadian) Falls, the American Falls, and the Bridal Veil (or Luna) Falls. The international border between Canada and the United States passes through the Horseshoe Falls close to the United States side of the river. Goat Island separates the Horseshoe Falls from the American and Bridal Veil Falls and is joined to the mainland by footbridges. Below the falls, several bridges cross the river and connect the cities of Niagara Falls, New York, and Niagara Falls, Ontario. Public parks and hydroelectric power stations have been built on both sides of the falls.

Niagara's waters are one of the world's greatest sources of hydroelectric power. The major hydroelectric installation on the United States side of the river is the Robert Moses Niagara Power Plant. Four Canadian installations are located on the Niagara River. These are the Rankine (Canadian Niagara) and Ontario power generating stations and two Sir Adam Beck stations. Power plants on both sides of the falls harness the falls' power to produce nearly 4.5 million kilowatts of electricity. More water is diverted for electricity during the night, so that the full natural flow of water can be viewed during daylight hours.

About 90 percent of Niagara's waters, or as much as 41 million gallons, flows over the deeply curved Horseshoe Falls every minute. These falls, the wider of the two, are about 175 feet (53 meters) high and about 2,500 feet (762 meters) wide. At the base the water rises in a constant, cloudlike mist. Although the American Falls are a bit higher, they are only 1,000 feet (305 meters) wide.

Behind the small Bridal Veil Falls, on the United States side of the river, there was a deep cavity cut by the swirling water into the

Niagara Falls actually consists of three waterfalls: the American Falls (far left), the small Bridal Veil Falls (middle), and the wide, deeply curved Horseshoe, or Canadian, Falls (right).

solid rock. Called the Cave of the Winds, this huge cavity was some 75 feet by 100 feet (23 meters by 30 meters). From 1834 to 1920, people walked into the cavity. Since 1920, people have been permitted to walk only to the base of the falls. The ceiling of the cave was blasted away in 1955.

How the Falls Came to Be. Niagara Falls is considered by geologists to be quite young—it is perhaps no more than 12,300 years old. In the Ice Age, glaciers covered all of what became known as the Niagara region. As the glacial ice melted, Lake Erie was formed. The overflow from the lake found an outlet to the north and became a river. As the river flowed northward, it spilled over an escarpment (cliff) near what is now the town of Lewiston, New York. The escarpment, topped by a hard layer of dolostone created the original Niagara Falls. Since then the falls have been cut back by the powerful force of the water. They are now some 7 miles (11 kilometers) upstream from their original location. But the hard dolostone at the top of the falls is not easily eroded. Instead, the water spills over the ledge and strikes the riverbed below. There the swirling currents eat away the underlying softer limestone, sandstone, and shale. This weakens the dolostone cap rock and causes it to break off. As a result, the falls cut back, or retreat, upstream. The rate of retreat is uneven, because the sandstone, limestone, and shale vary in hardness, and the amount of water going over the falls changes.

History. The first account of Niagara Falls appeared in 1697. It was written by the French missionary Father Louis Hennepin, who had seen the falls in 1678 while on an expedition to the New World with the explorer Robert Cavelier, Sieur de La Salle. The falls cut across the inland water route followed by early French explorers and missionaries, so they used the Native American portage, or overland route, around the falls. In time, missions, forts, and trading posts were built nearby. Many historical events took place nearby, including the battle at Lundy's Lane during the War of 1812.

By 1881 Jacob Schoellkopf had built the first water-powered electric generator on the Niagara River. Numerous industries have located in the Niagara area because of cheap and abundant power. Tourism is the fastest-growing industry, however. Many new attractions were constructed in the 1980's and 1990's, including aquariums and theme parks.

Parks, Recreation, and Education. Close by is the New York State Reservation at Niagara Falls. This is the oldest state park in the United States. Fort Niagara State Park is about 14 miles (23 kilometers) away; Old Fort Niagara, built in 1726, is located there. At the falls there are viewing platforms on both sides of the river. Sightseeing boats and helicopters take visitors on excursions around the falls. At night, colored searchlights illuminate the plunging waters and turn Niagara Falls into a kaleidoscope of changing colors. Nearby is the Niagara Gorge Discovery Center, a museum of the natural history of the falls. Overlooking the gorge a few miles from the falls is Niagara University, a private Catholic institution founded in 1856.

Reviewed by PAUL GROMOSIAK
Niagara Falls Historian

See also WATERFALLS; WATERPOWER.

NICARAGUA

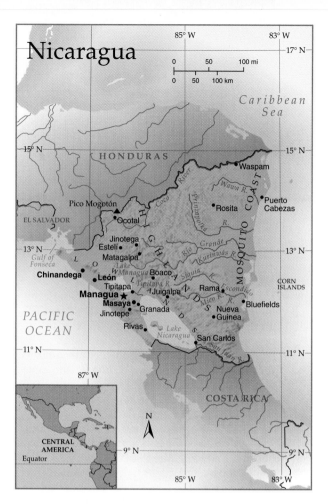

Nicaragua is the largest country in area in Central America. Lying between the Pacific Ocean and the Caribbean Sea, an arm of the Atlantic Ocean, it is a land that has known little peace. Dictatorships, foreign intervention, and civil wars have marked much of its history.

▶ PEOPLE

Nicaraguans can be divided into four ethnic groups. About 70 percent are mestizos, or people of mixed European and Indian descent. About 17 percent are of pure Spanish ancestry, and about 5 percent are Indians, mostly from the Miskito (or Mosquito) group. The rest are blacks, descendants of immigrants from the West Indies.

Approximately 40 percent of Nicaraguans live in the country's cities and towns. The Pacific coastal region, where the largest cities are located, is the most densely populated area. Most of the Indians and blacks live on the Atlantic Coast, along the Caribbean Sea. This region has long been known as the Mosquito Coast.

Language and Religion. Spanish is the official language. However, English and native languages spoken on the Atlantic Coast are the official languages in that region. Most Nicaraguans are Roman Catholic, but there is a rapidly growing number of Evangelical Protestants.

Education. In the past, many families were too poor to pay for their children's schooling. Primary and secondary education became free and compulsory for all children in 1979. Nicaragua has several universities. The largest is the National Autonomous University of Nicaragua, in Managua, the capital.

▶ LAND

Land Regions. Nicaragua has three distinct landforms: the Atlantic Coast, the central highlands, and the Pacific lowlands.

The Atlantic Coast lies along the Caribbean Sea. It is a wide, flat plain with many swamps and tropical rain forests. The coastline is dotted with bays, lagoons, and sandy beaches.

The highlands form the backbone of Nicaragua. Two mountain ranges run down the center of the country, reaching altitudes of up to 6,560 feet (2,000 meters). The higher mountains are in the north and the lower ranges lie farther south. The fertile highlands contain lush forests as well as most of the minerals found in Nicaragua. The country's highest point, Pico Mogotón, is in the northwest, near the border of Honduras. It has an elevation of 6,898 feet (2,102 meters).

The Nicaraguan lowlands stretch along the Pacific coast and slant across the country to the valley of the San Juan River and the Caribbean Sea. In the northwest the lowland region is bordered by a string of more than 20 volcanoes, many of them still active. Volcanic ash has made the soil very fertile. The lowlands have numerous river valleys and two large lakes, Nicaragua and Managua.

Rivers and Lakes. Lake Nicaragua is one of the largest bodies of fresh water in the Americas. It is the world's only inland lake in which there are sharks. Lake Nicaragua is linked to Lake Managua by the Tipitapa River, and to the Caribbean Sea by the San Juan River. Two of the country's chief rivers are the Grande and the Escondido.

Climate. Nicaragua's climate is tropical. It is hot and humid, with temperatures averaging about 80°F (27°C) year-round. The Atlantic Coast is the wettest region in Central America. It receives an average of about 100 inches (2,500 millimeters) of rainfall a year.

Natural Resources. Nicaragua's most important natural resources are its fertile soil, forests, and mineral deposits. Among Central American countries, Nicaragua is second only to Honduras in its mineral resources. Gold is the most important mineral export. There are also deposits of silver, copper, tungsten, lead, and zinc.

Much of Nicaragua's land is made up of rugged mountains, forests, and large lakes. Mombacho, an extinct volcano, towers over Lake Nicaragua, the largest lake in Central America. The lake is part of a long-considered canal route across Nicaragua.

A ruined tank in Managua, the capital of Nicaragua, is a reminder of the civil wars that have marked much of the country's recent history.

► ECONOMY

Nicaragua is one of the poorest countries in the Western Hemisphere. Recent civil wars, inflation, and a massive foreign debt have devastated its economy. But economic reforms introduced in the 1990's have helped reduce inflation and foreign debt, and the rapid expansion of the tourist industry has boosted economic growth.

The economy is based largely on agriculture and cattle raising. Coffee, cotton, tobacco, bananas, and sugarcane are the leading commercial crops. The most important food crops are rice, corn, and sesame seeds. Nicaragua is the leading cattle-raising country in Central America. Much of the cattle grazing is carried out on the Atlantic Coast. Other important agricultural products include pork, poultry, and dairy products.

Service industries account for about 45 percent of Nicaragua's economy. Services related to tourism are especially significant.

The country is still covered with vast areas of forest. The rain forests of the Atlantic Coast yield such valuable woods as mahogany and rosewood.

Fishing is also important, particularly in the waters off the Caribbean coast. Fish are caught for domestic consumption, and shrimp are processed for export.

Industries include food and beverage processing, petroleum refining and distribution, and the manufacture of chemicals, machinery, metal products, textiles, clothing, and shoes.

► MAJOR CITIES

Managua, the capital and largest city, has a population of about 1.5 million and lies on the shore of Lake Managua. It has often suffered earthquake damage. **León**, the second largest city, was once the Spanish colonial capital of Nicaragua. Its Metropolitan Cathedral is the largest cathedral in Central America. **Chinandega**, the third largest city, is a center of industry and trade.

► GOVERNMENT

Nicaragua is a republic. A president serves as chief of state and head of government. The president and vice president are elected by popular vote for a maximum of two nonconsecutive 5-year terms. Nicaragua's legislative body is the National Assembly, with 93 seats. Its members are elected by proportional representation to serve 5-year terms with no limits on re-election.

► HISTORY

Christopher Columbus landed in Nicaragua in 1502. At this time, Nicaragua was inhabited by numerous Indian groups. Spanish colonization began in the 1520's, and Spanish rule lasted for nearly 300 years.

Independence. Nicaragua and the other Spanish colonies in Central America declared their independence in 1821. After briefly joining with Mexico, they formed their own federation, the United Provinces of Central America. But political rivalries soon broke up the federation, and Nicaragua became an independent republic in 1838.

After independence two political groups, the Liberals and Conservatives, struggled for control of the country. In 1855, William Walker, an American, was invited to Nicaragua by the Liberals. Helped by U.S. business leaders, Walker made himself president of Nicaragua. But after re-introducing slavery and declaring English the official language, he was driven from the country. Although Walker had acted without the official approval of the U.S. government, many Nicaraguans felt his actions showed the desire of the United States to dominate their country.

Conservative Rule. In 1863 the Conservatives came to power and ruled for thirty years, although the struggle between the two parties continued. For many years the United States had been interested in building a canal across Nicaragua, linking the Atlantic and Pacific oceans. This made Nicaragua important to the United States. (A canal was eventually built across Panama.) In 1912, U.S. Marines were sent to Nicaragua to put down a revolt and protect U.S. interests. They remained for 13 years, during which U.S. officials administered almost all state functions in Nicaragua. The Marines left in 1925 but returned the next year, after civil war erupted between the Conservatives and Liberals. One Liberal general, Augusto César Sandino, waged a guerrilla war, refusing to lay down arms until the United States agreed to end its military presence there. The Marines withdrew in 1933.

The Somozas. When the Marines withdrew, they left behind a legally elected government and a National Guard, trained by the United States, to maintain peace. However, the National Guard commander, Anastasio Somoza García, used the guard to seize control of the country. He ordered Sandino's assassination in 1934 and was elected president in 1936 after the previous president resigned and fled the country.

Somoza restored peace, but he banned political opposition and was criticized for governing for his own profit. He was assassinated in 1956 and was succeeded by his son Luis Somoza Debayle. Anastasio Somoza Debayle, a brother of Luis, became president in 1967. Like other members of his family, he acquired great wealth from his office. Opposition to his rule led to civil war in 1978. The anti-Somoza rebels were called Sandinistas, after the guerrilla hero Sandino. The war destroyed cities and industries and made it impossible to plant or harvest crops. Anastasio Somoza Debayle resigned in 1979 and was later assassinated.

The Sandinista Government. The victorious Sandinistas formed a government led by a junta (council). They nationalized (brought under government control) much of the country's economic activity. They also began a program of land redistribution.

Some praised the Sandinistas' efforts at reform. They pointed to improvements in health care, a literacy program, and land redistribution. Others noted the collectivization of agriculture and seizure of businesses. They charged that the Sandinistas employed Communist methods, which restricted civil liberties and the country's economic growth.

In the 1980's a new civil war broke out between the Sandinistas and opponents of the government (called contras) who were aided by the United States. Feeling threatened by the United States, the Sandinistas expanded the army and obtained tanks and helicopters

Wearing the sash of office, Violeta Barrios de Chamorro celebrated her inauguration as president of Nicaragua in 1990. Mrs. Chamorro, leader of the United Opposition (UNO) had defeated former president Daniel Ortega Saavedra (*right*), the Sandinista leader, in the presidential election. The Sandinistas had held power in Nicaragua since 1979.

from the Soviet Union. Nicaragua now had a larger army than any of its neighbors. Other Central American nations became alarmed and accused Nicaragua of aiding leftist rebels in neighboring El Salvador.

Elections in 1984 installed Daniel Ortega Saavedra, a Sandinista commander, as president. Opponents charged that the Sandinistas had controlled the campaign and the election. Meanwhile, Nicaragua's economy remained in crisis, due to mismanagement, contra attacks, shortages of goods caused by the expense of the huge army, and a U.S. trade embargo.

Regional Peace Accord. An agreement signed by Ortega and four other Central American presidents in August 1987 led to new elections in Nicaragua in 1990 under United Nations supervision. Violeta Barrios de Chamorro led the United Opposition (UNO), a group of 14 political parties, in defeating Ortega. The U.S. embargo was then lifted and the contras were disbanded.

Under Chamorro, peace was restored, but not prosperity. Constitutional changes barred Chamorro from running for re-election. She was succeeded in 1996 by José Arnoldo Alemán Lacayo of the Liberal Party, a member of the UNO coalition.

In 2001, Ortega made another bid for the presidency but was defeated by Enrique Bolaños Geyer. In 2003, ex-president Alemán was convicted of embezzlement and fraud.

The Sandanistas and the Liberals remain the country's two largest political parties. The Bolaños government's efforts to eliminate corruption have often put it at odds with the Liberal Party, which remains under Alemán's control, thus forcing it to rely on Sandinista support to carry out its political goals.

Reviewed by JULIET HOOKER
University of Texas

NICHOLAS

Nicholas was the name of two emperors of Russia who sought to maintain the absolute rule of the Russian monarchy.

Nicholas I (1796–1855) reigned as emperor from 1825 to 1855. He came to the throne at the moment a revolt led by aristocratic army officers (known as the Decembrists) was taking place. He crushed the revolt but lived with the fear of further rebellion throughout his long reign.

To clamp down on dissent, Nicholas created a secret political police, which supervised all branches of the government, censored books and newspapers, and spied on ordinary citizens as well as suspected revolutionaries. Believing that certain kinds of education were a threat to social order, he decreed that universities and secondary schools reduce instruction in history and social thought and increase the time devoted to mathematics, ancient languages, and religion.

Throughout his reign, Nicholas I sought territorial gains against the declining Turkish Ottoman Empire to ensure Russian control of the Black Sea. This led him into the disastrous Crimean War (1853–56) opposed by Britain and France. He pursued a more successful campaign in Central Asia, which re-

Emperor Nicholas I ruled Russia from 1825 to 1855.

sulted in Russia's acquiring a vast region, including what is now Kazakhstan.

Nicholas I never addressed the great social problems of his time, particularly the question of serfdom, in which many peasants (called serfs) were bound by law to the land, and his reign is remembered chiefly for its harshness. See the article on the Crimean War in Volume C.

Nicholas II (1868–1918), the last Russian emperor, reigned from 1894 to 1917. He ascended the throne with the firm belief that he was obliged to preserve absolute rule by the monarchy. As a result, he turned his back on the reform tradition of some earlier emperors and tried to govern in the rigid style of his great grandfather, Nicholas I.

Nicholas II dreamed of making Russia the dominant power in Asia by expanding its influence in China and Korea. This policy conflicted with Japan's ambitions in the region and led to the Russo-Japanese War (1904–05). Russia's humiliating defeat in the war worsened a revolutionary situation. Following riots and violent workers' strikes, Nicholas reluctantly issued the October Manifesto (1905), which provided for an elected legislature (the Duma) and made the emperor a constitutional monarch. But Nicholas never really accepted this change.

With the outbreak of World War I in 1914, Nicholas was occupied as commander of the army and left almost all responsibility for government in the hands of his wife, Empress Alexandra. Because of the ill health of the young heir to the throne, Alexis, the empress had come under the powerful influence of the shadowy faith healer Rasputin, creating a national scandal that weakened the government. This, combined with the heavy losses in the war and increasing discontent at home, led to a revolution in February 1917, which forced Nicholas to give up the throne. A Provisional Government was established, but it fell, in October 1917, to the Bolsheviks (later renamed Communists). In July 1918 the Bolsheviks executed Nicholas and his family at Ekaterinburg in Siberia.

PETER CZAP, JR.
Amherst College

See also RUSSIA (History: Revolution).

NICHOLSON, JACK. See MOTION PICTURES (Profiles: Movie Stars).

NICKEL

Nickel is one of the most useful of metals. It is strong and tough. It is silver-white in color and takes a bright polish. Nickel can be easily shaped. Pure nickel can be used in making coins or as a plating to protect and beautify countless objects. However, it is most useful when combined with other metals in mixtures called **alloys**. Nickel gives an alloy more strength and toughness. It also helps it to resist corrosion.

Ore. The ore from which nickel comes was first named in medieval times. In a copper and cobalt mine, German miners found a red ore they thought was a new kind of copper. They were mining for material to be used in coloring pottery. But the new kind of "copper" ruined the pottery-coloring materials. The new ore also made the miners ill. They feared that evil spirits or even Old Nick (the devil) was in the ore. They began to call it *Kupfer Nickel* (Old Nick's copper). The ore material that changed the color of the pottery glaze was nickel. But the material that made the miners ill was arsenic.

In 1751 a Swedish scientist, Axel Cronstedt, identified nickel as a separate metal. He named the metal nickel because he got it from the *Kupfer Nickel* ore. Nickel is a plentiful element. But not much of it was used because there was no good method of separating the nickel from other materials in the ores in which it was found. It was also difficult to find ore deposits large enough to be mined for profit.

Then, in the 1800's, rich deposits of nickel ores were found in New Caledonia and in the Sudbury District of Ontario, Canada. Processes were developed to produce nickel in large quantities.

Uses. The first commercial products made from these large amounts of nickel were

---

BASIC FACTS ABOUT NICKEL

CHEMICAL SYMBOL: Ni.

ATOMIC WEIGHT: 58.71.

SPECIFIC GRAVITY: 8.9 (nearly 9 times as heavy as water).

COLOR: Silvery white.

PROPERTIES: Harder than iron; takes a brilliant polish; easily shaped; magnetic at ordinary temperatures; alloys easily with other common metals.

OCCURRENCE: Found mixed with several other metals (such as iron, cobalt, copper, and many others) in various sulfide and oxide ores.

CHIEF SOURCES: Canada (largest producer), New Caledonia, and Cuba.

electroplated silverware and coins. The United States 5-cent piece is an alloy of 25 percent nickel and 75 percent copper. The Canadian 5-cent piece is made of nickel-plated steel. Nickel also is used in coins of many other countries, either alloyed or in pure form.

In the late 1800's it was discovered that steel became stronger, tougher, and longer lasting when small amounts of nickel were added. Nickel steels were first used for construction and weapons. Soon they were used in automobiles, trains, aircraft, and many kinds of machinery. Today, almost half of all the nickel produced is used to make stainless and heat-resisting steels. Products made of nickel stainless steel are strong and easy to care for, and they will not rust. They include pots and pans, kitchen sinks, and important parts of chemical plants.

In 1905, nickel-copper alloys were developed. Nickel alloys are valuable because of such characteristics as corrosion resistance, strength, and high electrical resistance. Soon many other alloys were being developed— nickel-iron alloys and nickel-chromium alloys, for example. Nickel is now used in more than 3,000 alloys.

Alloys containing nickel are valuable for jet engines and for rockets and satellites that travel into space. Many parts of nuclear reactors and other power plants are made from nickel alloys. Nickel-cadmium batteries are used in cordless appliances and communications satellites. Nickel chemicals are used in many products, from paint to lubricating oil. Nickel also is used to speed the chemical processes of turning oils to solid fats.

Reviewed by J. Scott Weaver
Columbia University

NICKNAMES. See Names and Nicknames.

NICOLET, Jean (1598–1642)

Jean Nicolet, the discoverer of Lake Michigan, was born in the French seaport of Cherbourg in 1598. At the age of 20 he went to New France (Canada) to work in the fur trade with Samuel de Champlain. Champlain sent Nicolet to live among the Indians, to learn their language and encourage them to sell furs to the French. Nicolet spent two years with the Algonkin Indians on Allumette Island in the Ottawa River. The river was the main fur-trade route between the Great Lakes and Quebec.

Life among the Indians was very hard. One winter Nicolet had nothing but bark to eat for several weeks. But he learned the Algonkian language and became an interpreter for the French fur traders. During the next eight or nine years, he lived among the Nipissing Indians, who made him a member of their tribe and their council.

In 1633, Nicolet returned to Quebec to work as a clerk and interpreter for the Company of One Hundred Associates, which had taken control of the fur trade. The next year he was put in charge of the company's post at Trois Rivières on the St. Lawrence River. In 1637, Nicolet married Marguerite Couillard.

About 1634, Nicolet started west in the hope of reaching the rich land of China—the dream of explorers since Columbus. To impress the Chinese, he carried in his canoe a ceremonial robe made of fine linen and decorated with colored figures of flowers and birds. Of course, Nicolet met Indians instead. But he did discover Lake Michigan and crossed it to Green Bay, becoming the first European to see what is now Wisconsin.

At Green Bay Nicolet discovered the Fox River, and the Indians there told him of a great water to the west. Nicolet thought they meant the Pacific Ocean. He journeyed on a short time but then turned back. If he had continued his route for three more days, he would have been the first European to reach the headwaters of the Mississippi River.

In 1642, Nicolet was called to Trois Rivières to try to save an Iroquois prisoner whom the Algonkins wanted to torture to death. While he was on the way, his canoe was upset in a storm, and he was drowned in the St. Lawrence River. Today a lake, a river, a town, and a county in the province of Quebec are named Nicolet in his honor.

A statue of Jean Nicolet now stands overlooking the waters of Green Bay, commemorating the arrival of Europeans to the area.

John S. Moir
University of Toronto

NIGER

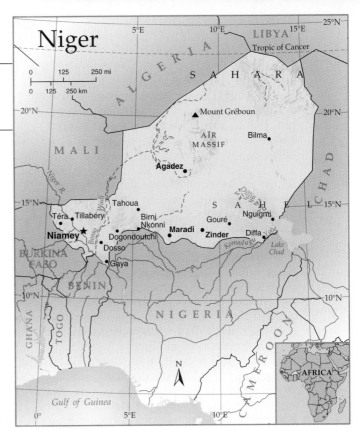

Niger is an enormous but thinly populated nation of West Africa. It lies at the southern edge of the Sahara, the great desert of northern Africa. It is a very poor country, largely because the landscape is mostly desert or semidesert. Niger takes its name from the Niger River, which flows through the southwestern part of the country.

▶ PEOPLE

Most Nigerians live in the south, between the Niger River and Lake Chad, where rainfall is sufficient for growing crops. The two main ethnic groups of this region are the Hausa and the Djerma. Other groups include the Fulani, who herd cattle just to the north, and the Tuareg, a nomadic people, who travel widely over the northern desert region seeking pasture for their camels, cattle, and goats.

Niamey, the capital of Niger, is a modern city that has grown up amid the traditional homes and farms of the Djerma people of the southwest.

Language. French is Niger's official language, but more than half the population speaks Hausa. Other native languages include Djerma, Fulani, Mansa, Zarma, and Tuareg.

Religion. Muslims make up 95 percent of Niger's population. There are small minorities of Christians and followers of traditional African religions.

Education. Niger is a poor country, and education suffers as a result. School attendance is low, only approximately 30 percent. The literacy rate (ability to read and write) is even lower, about 14 percent.

▶ LAND

Much of northern Niger is covered by rolling sand dunes. It is true desert, receiving less than 4 inches (100 millimeters) of rain a year. A surprisingly green mountainous region, known as the Aïr, rises in the north central part of the country. Mount Gréboun, Niger's highest point, at 6,376 feet (1,943 meters), is located there. In southern Niger there is a grassy steppe, or plain, which receives low to moderate rainfall. Crops can be grown there, but the sandy soil does not retain much moisture.

ECONOMY

Niger's economy is based on agriculture and livestock raising, which employ most of the population, and the production of uranium, the country's most important mineral. Livestock products include meat, milk, and hides and skins, which are used to make leather goods. There is little industry, except for the processing of agricultural and livestock products and the manufacture of cement, bricks, and textiles.

MAJOR CITIES

Niamey, the capital, is the only large city in Niger. Its population is approximately 675,000. Niamey is a busy commercial port city, situated on the Niger River in the southwestern part of the country. It grew considerably after the 1970's when uranium mining became an important industry.

Zinder, with a population of about 171,000, is Niger's second largest city. It once served as the colonial capital and was very important to trade between Agadez and Kano, Nigeria. Today it contains many beautiful examples of Hausa architecture.

Agadez, the chief town of the Tuareg people, has a population of about 77,000. Traditionally the city was an important stop on the caravan route across the Sahara. Like Niamey, Agadez's population grew significantly in the 1970's because of expanded uranium production and an influx of drought refugees.

HISTORY AND GOVERNMENT

Western Niger was once part of the Mali kingdom. The east was ruled by various Hausa states and the kingdom of Kanem-Borno. In the 1800's, much of the region became part of the Fulani Empire.

Niger was explored by Mungo Park of Scotland in the 1790's and by Heinrich Barth of Germany in the 1850's. By the end of the 1800's, France ruled the south. In 1906 it took control of the Aïr. The Colony of Niger was created in 1922. In 1958, Niger became a self-governing member of the French Community. It gained full independence in 1960.

Niger was severely affected by the great Sahel drought that lasted from the late 1960's to 1974. Animal herds and harvests were drastically reduced, and as many as one-quarter of the people died from famine. Hamani Diori, who had been president since independence, was accused of mishandling the economy, and in 1974 he was overthrown in a military coup. A government headed by a Supreme Military Council was formed to run the country. Lieutenant Colonel General Seyni Kountché, the coup leader, headed the council until his death in 1987.

Recent History. A new constitution was approved in 1993 and has since been amended twice. It provides for a president, elected by the people for a 5-year term, and a legislature, the National Assembly, whose members are also elected for five years.

Elections for a new president, held in 1993, resulted in a victory for Mahamane Ousmane. But he was overthrown in 1996 in a coup led by Colonel Ibrahim Bare Mainassara. Mainassara claimed victory in presidential elections held later that year, although the election results were denounced by the opposition. Mainassara was assassinated in 1999. Civilian rule was restored later that year under a newly elected president, Tandja Mamadou, a retired army colonel. Mamadou was re-elected in 2004.

R. J. HARRISON-CHURCH
Author, *West Africa*

Reviewed by CASSANDRA VENEY
Illinois State University

FACTS and figures

REPUBLIC OF NIGER (République du Niger) is the official name of the country.

LOCATION: West Africa.

AREA: 489,189 sq mi (1,267,000 km²).

POPULATION: 11,700,000 (estimate).

CAPITAL AND LARGEST CITY: Niamey.

MAJOR LANGUAGES: French (official), Hausa, Djerma.

MAJOR RELIGIOUS GROUPS: Muslim, traditional African.

GOVERNMENT: Republic. **Head of state and government**—president. **Legislature**—National Assembly.

CHIEF PRODUCTS: Agricultural—cowpeas, cotton, peanuts, millet, sorghum, cassava, rice, livestock. **Manufactured**—cement, bricks, textiles, processed foods. **Mineral**—uranium, coal, iron ore, tin, phosphates, gold.

MONETARY UNIT: African Financial Community (CFA) franc (1 CFA franc = 100 centimes).

NIGERIA

Nigeria, situated in West Africa, is one of Africa's most populous nations. It takes its name from the Niger River, which flows through the heart of the country. Often called Africa's Giant, it is more than twice the size of the state of California. Although several African countries are larger in area, few are as rich in natural resources, particularly oil.

▶ PEOPLE

The people of Nigeria belong to more than 250 different ethnic groups, each with its own language, history, and customs. About half are members of three such groups—the Hausa, the Yoruba, and the Igbo (Ibo).

The Hausa, the largest group north of the Niger and Benue rivers, once ruled several powerful states in the region. Almost all Hausa are Muslims. Other large groups in the north include the Fulani, Kanuri, and Tiv.

The Yoruba are the largest group southwest of the Niger River. They established large city-states long before the first Europeans arrived in the 1400's. These states were particularly strong in the 1700's and 1800's.

Instead of forming kingdoms, the Igbo of the southeast lived in large family groups or villages, often separated by dense forests. Most of them became Christians after the Europeans arrived. Other important groups in southern Nigeria include the Edo (Beni), the Ijaw, and the Ibibio-Efik.

Language. English is the official language of Nigeria, but most Nigerians speak their own ethnic languages within their communi-

Above: The Yoruba make up the largest ethnic group in southern Nigeria. About half of the Yoruba are Christians. *Left:* The Hausa, most of whom are Muslim, live in villages in the north.

Vendors sell clothing at a market in Lagos. Women in southern Nigeria typically wear wrapped headpieces and skirts fashioned of brightly colored cloth.

confined to their home compounds, according to Islamic tradition. Both trading and farming are carried on by men. Herding is the historic occupation of the Fulani people.

The oil boom and the spread of education are changing traditional ways of life all over the country. Young men and women flock to the cities to seek wage-earning jobs and a more dynamic society.

Dress. In the north, men often wear embroidered garments called *rigas*. Women cover their heads with flowing cloths and often wear loose tunics over long cloths wrapped like skirts. In the southwest, men wear long, loose robes called *agbadas* and floppy cloth caps. Women wear wide, loose-sleeved blouses, bright headpieces, and long wrapped skirts. Babies often ride on their mothers' backs in cloth slings. In the east, men wear shorter, tunic-style robes, and women dress in wrapped

ties. Among the most commonly spoken are Hausa, Yoruba, and Igbo (Ibo).

Religion. The population in the north is predominantly Muslim, while Christians make up a majority in the south. In many places, Christians join in the celebrations at the end of Ramadan (the Muslim month of fasting), and Muslims share in the festivities of the Christian holiday Easter. About 10 percent of the people follow traditional African religions based on the worship of many gods and spirits. But people of all faiths take part in ceremonies associated with the traditional religions and culture.

Education. Education is free and compulsory for Nigerian children from age 6 to 15. Education beyond elementary and middle school is taught in English. There is a charge to attend secondary schools and institutions of higher learning. Nigeria has more than 30 colleges and universities. The largest is the University of Ibadan.

Way of Life. In southern Nigeria, women have long planted and tended the crops and run the local markets. Men clear the fields and harvest forest products, while children often help their mothers. In the far north, some Hausa women are

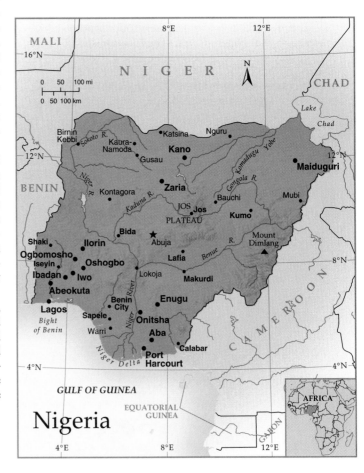

Nigeria

FEDERAL REPUBLIC OF NIGERIA is the official name of the country.

LOCATION: West Africa.

AREA: 356,667 sq mi (923,768 km²).

POPULATION: 123,000,000 (estimate).

CAPITAL: Abuja.

LARGEST CITY: Lagos.

MAJOR LANGUAGES: English (official), Hausa, Yoruba, Igbo (Ibo), numerous other African languages.

MAJOR RELIGIOUS GROUPS: Muslim, Christian, traditional African religions.

GOVERNMENT: Republic. **Head of state and government**—president. **Legislature**—National Assembly, consisting of a senate and house of representatives.

CHIEF PRODUCTS: **Agricultural**—cacao, peanuts, palm oil, corn, rice, sorghum, millet, cassava, yams, rubber, livestock, timber, fish. **Manufactured**—processed foods, textiles, wood products, rubber products, cement and other construction materials, footwear, chemicals, fertilizer, printing, ceramics, steel. **Mineral**—crude oil, coal, tin, columbite.

MONETARY UNIT: Naira (1 naira = 100 kobo).

skirts and fitted blouses. But many men also wear western pants and shirts.

▶ LAND

Land Regions. The huge delta of the Niger River and other coastal regions in Nigeria are dotted with swamps and creeks. Stretching northward from the coast is a tropical forest that covers about one-third of the country. The southwestern forest area is the source of Nigeria's cocoa production. As one moves north, vegetation becomes more sparse. Beyond the forest is the rolling grassland, or savanna. Grain and cotton are grown on the Northern High Plains. The only highlands are the Jos Plateau and low mountain ranges in the east. At 6,698 feet (2,042 meters), Mount Dimlang, in the Shebshi Mountains, is Nigeria's highest peak.

Rivers, Lakes, and Coastal Waters. Nigeria is situated on the Gulf of Guinea, an arm of the Atlantic Ocean. The chief rivers are the Niger and the Benue. Lake Chad, in northern Nigeria, was once a significant body of water. But as northern Nigeria has become increasingly arid, it has drastically decreased in size.

Climate. Nigeria has a tropical climate, with a rainy season extending from May to October. The amount of rainfall each year varies from more than 130 inches (3,300 millimeters) along the coast to less than 25 inches (635 millimeters) along the northern border. The south has high humidity most of the time and temperatures of 68–86°F (20–30°C) all year. The northern part of the country is less humid than the south, although the north can sometimes be quite hot. In December and January, the harmattan, a dry wind carrying dust and sand, blows in from the Sahara desert of northern Africa.

Natural Resources. The country's greatest resource by far is its huge reserves of high-quality oil in the Niger Delta and offshore. Iron ore deposits are found in the area where the Niger and Benue rivers meet. Large amounts of tin and columbite (a mineral used in making certain kinds of steel) are found in the central part of the country. Other notable minerals include coal, lead, and zinc. Nigeria's tropical forest is an important natural resource. Soils throughout the country are moderately fertile, depending on rainfall.

Jebba is one of many villages situated along the shores of the Niger River, Nigeria's chief inland waterway. The surrounding Niger Delta is the country's most fertile region.

An oil tanker takes on cargo at an industrial port on the Niger River. Nigeria is among the world's leading exporters of oil.

▶ ECONOMY

Oil dominates Nigeria's economy. It makes up about 95 percent of its export revenues and more than two-thirds of its total revenue, which has been used to develop manufacturing, modern roadways, electricity, and educational institutions.

Services. Services form a large segment of Nigeria's economy. Millions of Nigerian men and women are employed by hotels, restaurants, banks, and the like. Government-related services, such as education, utilities, and civil services, employ many people.

Manufacturing. Nigeria's leading industrial activities are the production of food, textiles, rubber products, cement and other construction materials, footwear, chemicals, fertilizer, and printed materials. The fishing industry is also important. Nigeria's forests provide timber and other wood products.

Agriculture. Agriculture employs more than half of Nigeria's population. Major food crops include cacao, peanuts, palm oil, corn, rice, sorghum, millet, cassava (a starchy root), and yams. Cocoa and palm oil are the largest agricultural exports. Cattle and other livestock are raised in the north.

Although agricultural output has increased, the amount required to feed Nigeria's people exceeds what can be grown. The government has tried to stimulate food production by teaching modern agricultural techniques, encouraging the use of fertilizers, and building irrigation systems. But some food, such as wheat, must be imported.

▶ MAJOR CITIES

Abuja, Nigeria's capital, was built in 1991 specifically to replace Lagos as the nation's seat of government. It was thought that its location in the center of the country would make it more of a symbol of national unity. The city has an estimated population of 380,000.

Lagos is Nigeria's largest city and chief port. It has a population of more than 1 million in the city proper and about 4 million in its metropolitan area. Lagos occupies part of the mainland and several islands in the Gulf of Guinea. A cosmopolitan city, it is crowded and busy, with modern skyscrapers competing for space with more traditional buildings.

Lagos is one of Africa's largest cities and busiest ports south of the Sahara. It lies along the Gulf of Guinea, an arm of the Atlantic Ocean.

Ibadan, Nigeria's second largest city, is a vibrant center of Yoruba culture and commerce. It is home to the University of Ibadan.

▶ CULTURAL HERITAGE

Art. Clay figures from Nok, an ancient culture in central Nigeria, are among the earliest known examples of African sculpture. Even more famous are the cast-metal Ifé heads—large, naturalistic portraits of Yoruba rulers made between the 1100's and the 1400's. Bronze plaques and statues of rulers, warriors, and animals from Benin, a Yoruba kingdom in the western Niger Delta, are world-renowned. So are the intricate wood carvings still made in many parts of the country. The leatherwork of northern Nigeria is also well known. For centuries it has been transported across the Sahara to be sold as Moroccan leather. Other Nigerian art forms that are still practiced include the making of beautiful pottery, metalwork, and handwoven textiles. For more information, see the article AFRICA, ART AND ARCHITECTURE OF in Volume A.

Literature. Several Nigerian authors writing in English have won international acclaim. Among the best known are the novelist Chinua Achebe and the poet and playwright Wole Soyinka, winner of the 1986 Nobel Prize for literature. For more information, see the article AFRICA, LITERATURE OF in Volume A.

▶ GOVERNMENT

Nigeria's most recent constitution was adopted in 1999. The country is a federation of a national government and 36 states, formed largely according to ethnic groups. Each state has a governor and its own two-house legislature. The federal government is headed by a president, who is elected by popular vote. The federal legislature, the National Assembly, is made up of a 360-member house of representatives and a 109-member

Above: About 1,000 years ago, artists in the kingdom of Ifé in the Niger Delta began using cast-metal techniques to produce lifelike sculptures in bronze.

senate (three senators per state). Nigeria also has an independent court system and electoral commission.

▶ HISTORY

The savanna has been inhabited by farming people for thousands of years. The region's earliest known civilization is that of Nok, which dates back to 500 B.C. After that time, several great empires developed in what is now Nigeria.

The Great Empires. Kanem-Borno, the oldest organized state in what is now Nigeria, had appeared by A.D. 900 and was centered near Lake Chad. Its rulers were the first Nigerians to adopt Islam, in the 1000's.

In later centuries the Hausa developed states west of Kanem-Borno. In the southwest, just north of the forest, some Yoruba peoples were organized into the Ifé kingdom, ruled by a divine king, as early as A.D. 1000.

The most politically powerful Yoruba kingdom was that of Oyo. This kingdom dissolved in the late 1700's, weakened by war and the slave trade. The Yoruba then moved southward, dividing into several competing states.

The most powerful forest kingdom of the 1400's was Benin, in the western Niger Delta. It was also weakened by wars and the slave trade. It was taken over by the British in 1897.

In the early 1800's, the Fulani empire emerged out of religious warfare in northern Nigeria. Uthman Dan Fodio, a devout Fulani Muslim scholar, led the conquest of the Hausa states. He appointed Fulani emirs to rule over the conquered Hausa states. By the late 1800's, this empire began dividing into smaller states.

The Europeans in Nigeria. The first Europeans reached the area in the 1400's, when Portuguese explorers encountered the wealthy and powerful kingdom of Benin. Various European countries soon struggled for control of the local slave trade. Hundreds of thousands of slaves were sent to the Americas from this area, known to Europeans as the Slave Coast.

The British gradually gained control of what is now Nigeria, first creating the colony of Lagos in 1861. They conquered Benin and fought their way inland, often against fierce resitance. In 1914 the British formed the Colony and Protectorate of Nigeria and governed it indirectly through traditional rulers.

After World War II, Nigerians began to demand self-government. In 1946, Britain divided the colony into three regions—the Northern Region (with a Hausa-Fulani majority), the Western Region (where the Yoruba dominated), and the Eastern Region (predominantly Igbo).

In 1967, the Igbo of Nigeria's Eastern Region established the short-lived independent Republic of Biafra. An ensuing civil war claimed the lives of nearly 1 million civilians, chiefly from malnutrition.

Independence and Civil War. On October 1, 1960, Nigeria became an independent federation of three regions. The following year, part of the western Cameroons also became part of Nigeria. In 1963 the Mid-Western Region was created.

Nigeria's history since independence has been stormy. Until 1966 it had a parliamentary government. But some Nigerians felt deprived of political power. That year the central government was overthrown in a military coup, and the country's first prime minister, Sir Abubakar Tafawa Balewa, was murdered. General Johnson Aguiyi-Ironsi, an Igbo army commander, assumed control of the government. In a countercoup that same year, Aguiyi-Ironsi was killed, and Colonel Yakubu Gowon, a northerner, became head of a military government.

In the ethnic violence that followed, thousands of Igbo living in the north were killed. Many others fled to their traditional homeland in the Eastern Region. In 1967 the Eastern Region seceded from Nigeria and proclaimed itself the independent Republic of Biafra. Civil war raged there until 1970, when Biafra surrendered.

In 1975, Gowon was overthrown in another military coup, and the new government sought to create democratic institutions. Elections in 1979 returned the government to civilian democratic rule.

In the early 1980's, the world's oversupply of oil created serious economic problems for Nigeria. As oil revenues fell, development projects were canceled and many workers were dismissed. With exports reduced, imports fell sharply, including food and medicine. People's real earnings fell by 50 to 80 percent, and many Nigerians became impoverished. The government's inability to solve the country's economic problems led to military takeovers in 1983 and 1985.

Recent History. In 1985, General Ibrahim Babangida, the army chief of staff, became head of a military government. But in 1993, he interfered with the results of a presidential election, which caused widespread protests. Babangida was then replaced by another military leader, General Sani Abacha.

Abacha ruled with violence, incompetence, and corruption and tried to crush Nigeria's democratic movement. When he died in 1998, General Abdulsalam Abubakar was named president. In 1999 a new civilian government, headed by President Olusegun Obasanjo, took office.

In 2003, Obasanjo was accused of manipulating the election results that had returned him to power. Meanwhile, the country faced another crisis when striking oil workers seized four offshore rigs and held one hundred foreign workers hostage to their demands.

JEAN HERSKOVITS
State University of New York, Purchase

Reviewed by JON KRAUS
State University of New York, Fredonia

NIGHTINGALE, FLORENCE (1820–1910)

Florence Nightingale, an Englishwoman, was the founder of modern nursing and a pioneer in hygiene and sanitation. She was born on May 12, 1820, in Florence, Italy, the younger of two daughters. Florence was brought up in great luxury in England and was tutored by her father in English literature, history, philosophy, and several languages. In 1837, at age 17, she wrote that she had heard the voice of God calling her to service. Several years later, she decided this had been a call to nurse the sick.

Her family strongly opposed this choice. Nursing was considered unsuitable for a lady, and Florence was expected to devote herself instead to a husband, family, and social activities. She did not want this kind of life, however, and refused to marry.

In 1851, Nightingale traveled to Kaiserswerth, Germany, to gain nursing experience and soon became an expert on hospital administration. In 1853 she took her first post—managing a small hospital for women on Harley Street in London (later called the Florence Nightingale Hospital for Gentlewomen). She revolutionized the hospital's administration by emphasizing training for nurses and better patient care.

In 1854, shortly after the Crimean War broke out (between Russia, Britain, France, the Turkish Ottoman Empire, and Sardinia), news reached London of the terrible state of hospitals in the Russian Crimea (a peninsula in the Black Sea). Because Nightingale had been so successful with her hospital in London, Sidney Herbert, war secretary for the British government, asked her to recruit nurses to care for war victims. On October 21, 1854, she and 38 nurses sailed for the Crimea. There they found more than 5,000 wounded and sick soldiers in so-called hospitals: bare, unsanitary buildings with no facilities for medical care.

After Nightingale's assignment was reported in the British press, readers of the *London Times* raised funds to help her with her work. At first she made improvements in the patients' meals. She then equipped the hospitals and made them sanitary, and also inspected each ward daily. Although she encountered resistance from those who did not want a woman involved with such matters, she eventually triumphed and saved many lives.

When Nightingale returned to England in 1856, she was hailed as a heroine but refused all honors and went into seclusion. Although many believed she had died, she had actually come home to continue her work for the soldiers. She believed that personal popularity would create prejudices against her in the government. Quietly, unknown to the public, she worked for army reform. In this she was encouraged by Queen Victoria and helped by Sidney Herbert. For the first time, army living conditions were scientifically examined and stricter health and sanitary measures were adopted. In 1858, Nightingale published a lengthy report on army hospitals. She also published many other works, including a short book for the general public on basic nursing care.

Florence Nightingale's study of army hospitals led her to work with civilian hospitals and public health. In 1860, with donated money, she opened the Nightingale Training School for Nurses at St. Thomas's Hospital, London. This was the beginning of modern nursing. Women all over the world were increasingly drawn to the nursing profession, particularly in the United States during the Civil War (1861–65).

Although Nightingale became an invalid due to illness contracted during the war, she continued working for several more years and assisted the British War Office. She drew up regulations, reported on plans for new barracks, and reviewed papers on sanitation. In 1907 she became the first woman to receive the British Order of Merit. She died in London at age 90 on August 13, 1910.

CECIL WOODHAM-SMITH
Author, *Florence Nightingale*

Feluccas (light boats used since ancient times) sail on the Nile River near Aswan, Egypt. The Nile is the world's longest river and a birthplace of western civilization.

NILE RIVER

The Nile River, in Africa, is the longest river in the world and a birthplace of western civilization. It is also one of the world's most important rivers. For thousands of years the people living along the Nile depended on it to water the desert land and make it fertile. Although the Nile is usually thought of as most important to Egypt, it is also vital to Sudan, Ethiopia, and other east African countries.

▶ **THE COURSE OF THE NILE**

The Nile has a total length of over 4,100 miles (6,600 kilometers). Its main branches are the comparatively quiet White Nile and the torrential Blue Nile.

The White Nile starts at Lake Victoria, the Nile River's largest source, located on the border of Uganda, Tanzania, and Kenya at an elevation of over 3,700 feet (1,130 meters). It flows through steep canyons into swampy Lake Kyoga. From this lake the river again flows through canyons and huge broken rocks. At Kabalega (formerly Murchison) Falls, it plunges 130 feet (40 meters) into Lake Albert, on the border between Uganda and the Democratic Republic of Congo.

After leaving Lake Albert, the White Nile gradually broadens and is known at different points by different names. Some 250 miles (400 kilometers) later it reaches a vast swamp in southern Sudan called the Sudd. Here the river divides into many small, sluggish channels. Since the region is hot year-round, much of the White Nile's water is lost there by evaporation. As the river flows northward, it passes through land that eventually turns into desert near Khartoum.

The Blue Nile begins at Lake Tana, high on the Ethiopian plateau. It leaves Lake Tana by flowing over a series of rapids until it drops into a deep gorge. Farther downstream, after leaving the plateau, the river proceeds more slowly to its meeting with the White Nile.

During the flood season in late summer and autumn, the Blue Nile contributes approximately two-thirds of the total volume of the Nile, while the White Nile usually furnishes less than about one-fifth of the total. It is the Blue Nile that deposits most of the fertile mud along the banks of the river and causes most of the seasonal floods.

The White Nile and the Blue Nile join at Khartoum, the capital city of Sudan. North of Khartoum the Nile receives waters from another key tributary, the Atbara River, which contributes approximately one-fifth of the total volume of the Nile. During the rainy seasons in the spring and summer, the Atbara floods the shores. In the dry winter, it is hardly more than a series of muddy pools.

For the rest of its journey northward to the Mediterranean Sea, the Nile flows through the desert. It is bordered by the Libyan Desert on the west and the Nubian and Arabian deserts on the east. These deserts are all part of the Sahara, a vast desert region that covers large parts of northern Africa. In this dry land, wadis (desert valleys through which temporary streams flow) carry small amounts of water to the Nile during the infrequent rainfalls. In Egypt, the river enriches a strip of desert land about 10 to 15 miles (15 to 25 kilometers) wide.

Between Cairo (Egypt's capital) and the sea, the Nile divides into two main branches (the Damietta and Rosetta) that flow through a fan-shaped area of land called the Nile Delta. A **delta** is built up over millions of years by deposits of silt (fine soil particles) or sand at the mouth of a river. The Nile Delta is about 135 miles (220 kilometers) wide.

▶ HOW PEOPLE USE THE NILE

The Nile irrigates about 2 million acres (800,000 hectares) of land in Sudan. The Gezira, the vast flood plain in Sudan between the White Nile and the Blue Nile, has seen much economic development in recent years under an irrigation project that opened up the land to crop raising. With irrigation, the deep, fertile soils of this area are ideal for the growing of cotton, grain, peanuts, and vegetables. In addition, large numbers of sheep and cattle are raised in the area. A number of canal projects have been proposed to help drain the swampy Sudd area, but only one was begun and it was never finished.

The Nile also irrigates about 6 million acres (2.4 million hectares) of land in Egypt. The fertile strip of land along the Nile is densely populated in both the Nile Valley and the Nile Delta. More than 95 percent of Egypt's population lives in the valley and the delta. Much of the delta marshland has been drained and irrigated to form a huge garden oasis. Cotton, rice, corn, wheat, and other crops are grown on these lands.

In the past, Egyptian farmers (known as fellahin) depended on the rise and fall of the Nile and on primitive irrigation methods. The situation changed with the creation of the Aswan High Dam in southern Egypt, completed in 1971. Lake Nasser, an artificial lake, was formed behind the dam to store surplus floodwater for use throughout the year. Today much more land can be farmed year-round, and hydroelectric power plants in the city of Aswan provide electricity for much of Egypt's agriculture and industry. However, because the river no longer overflows its banks, the Nile Valley is much less fertile and Egypt must now import fertilizer.

▶ THE HISTORIC NILE

The Nile was one of the great highways of the ancient world. The ruins of forts used by invaders stand along its banks today.

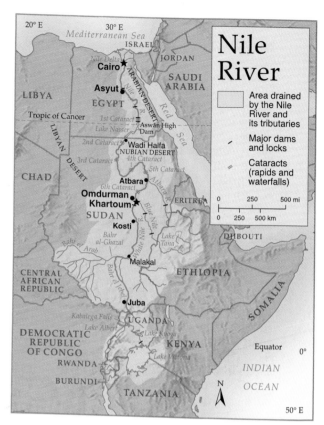

Nile River

▢ Area drained by the Nile River and its tributaries

⌐ Major dams and locks

≈ Cataracts (rapids and waterfalls)

For centuries the ancient Egyptians bathed in the Nile, drank its waters, told legends about it, and built tombs and temples near its shores. The pyramids on the western bank of the Nile at Giza served as tombs for the ancient Egyptian pharaohs. The temples of Abu-Simbel, Medinet Habu, and Deir el-Bahri were built near the Nile.

When the Nile rose during the flood season, religious festivals were held in honor of the goddess Isis. The Egyptians thought the river rose because Isis had dropped a tear. During some historic periods, a human sacrifice was offered to the Nile. Even today, the time when the Nile starts to rise in June is called the Night of the Drop.

The Nile continues to be an essential part of the lives of 70 million Egyptians and millions of others in Sudan and other African countries.

JAMES MATTHAI
Murray State University
Reviewed by Dr. IRA M. SHESKIN
University of Miami

NIMITZ, CHESTER. See WORLD WAR II (Profiles: Allied Powers).

NITROGEN

Nitrogen is a chemical element. It has the chemical symbol N, an atomic number of 7, and an atomic weight of 14.007. The element nitrogen is all around us. Nitrogen gas makes up 78 percent of the volume of air. Nitrogen gas is composed of molecules, each one of which contains two nitrogen atoms. Elemental nitrogen gas is represented by the symbol N_2.

Nitrogen gas is colorless and odorless. It is also quite unreactive, because the bond between the two atoms that make up its molecules is very strong. Yet, if enough energy is available to break the bond, nitrogen will react. Lightning contains more than enough energy to break the bond. When lightning flashes, it heats up the surrounding air and causes nitrogen to react with oxygen to form compounds containing both of these elements. There are also some bacteria that are capable of using nitrogen gas to form nitrogen compounds. Such bacteria are called **nitrogen-fixing** bacteria.

All living organisms need nitrogen in order to grow. Nitrogen atoms are contained in body molecules such as proteins and deoxyribonucleic acid (DNA). Animals get nitrogen from the foods they eat. Plants cannot use the nitrogen gas in the air, so they must use nitrogen compounds in the soil. Some of these compounds are provided by nitrogen-fixing bacteria. Others come from decayed plant material or animal wastes.

Modern agriculture often requires more nitrogen in the soil than is available from either of these natural sources, so nitrogen compounds from industrial sources are added. These sources often contain nitrogen salts, which are mined from deposits in various parts of the world. A common synthetic fertilizer is ammonia, which is made up of nitrogen and hydrogen.

Ammonia gas is the most important industrial compound of nitrogen. Over 15 million tons of ammonia gas is made each year in the United States. It is made by the Haber process, in which nitrogen gas and hydrogen gas are combined at a very high temperature and pressure using a **catalyst** to speed up the reaction. Liquefied ammonia is applied directly to farm fields as a fertilizer. Ammonia is also used to prepare many other chemical compounds. Ammonia burns to form oxides of nitrogen, and these are used to make nitric acid and nitrogen salts. Ammonia is also used in converting petroleum into other products, including plastics, such as nylon; cosmetics; and pharmaceuticals.

Some nitrogen compounds are quite unstable and decompose rapidly, releasing a great deal of energy. Examples include nitroglycerine, which is used in dynamite, and trinitrotoluene, also called TNT. Another unstable nitrogen compound is sodium azide, which forms nitrogen gas when it decomposes. It is used to inflate automobile air bags.

Elemental nitrogen gas is separated from the air by chilling air until it becomes a liquid and then allowing the liquid air to boil (become a gas again). The nitrogen boils off before oxygen and is collected, providing nearly pure nitrogen. Nitrogen boils at -321°F (-196°C), so liquid nitrogen is very cold. Because it is so cold and unreactive, it is used as a refrigerant for transporting perishable items, for freeze-drying foods, and for long-term preservation of biological specimens.

Although it is all around us, nitrogen was not identified as a distinct component of air until 1772, when German-Swedish chemist Carl Scheele and Scottish chemist Daniel Rutherford each discovered it independently. French chemist Antoine Lavoisier was the first to recognize nitrogen as an element. He called it *azote*, meaning "without life." However, in 1790 it was called nitrogen by French scientist Jean Chaptal, to indicate that it was a component of niter (a nitrogen salt), and this is the name that has endured.

RODNEY SCHREINER
BASSAM SHAKHASHIRI
University of Wisconsin, Madison

See also ELEMENTS, CHEMICAL.

FACTS ABOUT NITROGEN

Chemical Symbol: N

Atomic Number: 7

Atomic Weight: 14.007

Density: 1.25 grams per liter (gas); 0.808 gram per cubic centimeter (liquid).

Properties: Colorless gas at room temperature.

Occurrence: Makes up 78 percent of the Earth's atmosphere.

RICHARD M. NIXON (1913–1994)

37th President of the United States

FACTS ABOUT NIXON

Birthplace: Yorba Linda, California
Religion: Quaker
College Attended: Whittier College,
 Whittier, California; Duke
 University Law School, Durham,
 North Carolina
Occupation: Lawyer
Married: Thelma Catherine
 (Patricia) Ryan
Children: Patricia (Tricia), Julie
Political Party: Republican
Office Held Before Becoming President: Vice
 President
President Who Preceded
 Him: Lyndon B. Johnson
Age on Becoming
 President: 56
Years in the Presidency:
 1969–1974 (resigned from
 office, August 9, 1974)
Vice President: Spiro T.
 Agnew; Gerald R. Ford
President Who Succeeded
 Him: Gerald R. Ford
Age at Death: 81
Burial Place: Yorba Linda,
 California

RING OUR

DURING NIXON'S PRESIDENCY

Below left: U.S. *Apollo II* astronauts
Neil A. Armstrong and Edwin E.
(Buzz) Aldrin, Jr., made the first
manned landing on the moon
(1969). *Left:* Protests against the
Vietnam War erupted on many U.S.
college campuses. Congress established the U.S. Postal Service as an
independent government agency (1970). The
U.S. Supreme Court ruled the busing could be
used to achieve school desegregation (1971).
The 26th Amendment to the Constitution,
lowering the voting age to 18, was ratified
(1971). *Below:* Nixon's visit to the People's
Republic of China (1972) was the first by a
U.S. president. The Vietnam War cease-fire
agreement was signed in Paris (1973). Nixon
became the first U.S. president to resign
(1974), as a result of the Watergate scandal.

NIXON, RICHARD MILHOUS. Richard M.
Nixon's political career was marked by extraordinary contradictions. Many people believed that his career had come to an end in
1960, after he narrowly lost the presidential
election to John F. Kennedy. Two years later,
in 1962, he again suffered defeat, this time in
the race for governor of California, and Nixon
himself announced that his days in politics
were over. However, a combination of events
pushed him to the political forefront once
more, and his election as president in 1968
was one of the most remarkable political
comebacks of modern times.

Nixon brought with him to the presidency
a lifetime of political experience, sometimes
controversial, as a congressman, senator, and
vice president. His achievements as president,
particularly in foreign affairs, were significant, and they won him election to a second
term in 1972. But his accomplishments were
overshadowed by his role in the Watergate
scandal, which forced him to resign from office in 1974, the only U.S. president to do so.

► EARLY LIFE

Richard Milhous Nixon was born on January 9, 1913, in Yorba Linda, California. He
was the second of five sons of Francis and
Hannah Milhous Nixon. His parents were serious, hardworking Quakers, who ran a small
lemon farm. When Richard was 9, the farm
failed and the family moved to Whittier, California, where his father operated a combination general store and gas station. The Nixons
had little money, and the boys helped out by
pumping gas, working in the store, and doing
various odd jobs.

Nixon attended local public schools and, at
17, entered Whittier College, a small Quaker
institution. There he excelled in debating and
won a college public-speaking contest. He
also won his first election, as president of the
student body. A good student, he graduated
second in his class in 1934 and received a
scholarship to Duke University Law School.

► LAW, MARRIAGE, AND WAR YEARS

Nixon graduated from Duke with his law

At Whittier College, Nixon played on the football team (wearing number 12), excelled in debating, and served as president of the student body.

degree in 1937. But, unable to find the kind of work he wanted, he returned home and joined a Whittier law firm.

At a community theater tryout in Whittier, Nixon met Thelma Catherine Ryan, known as Patricia, or Pat, who taught shorthand and typing at a local high school. They were married in 1940 and had two daughters, Patricia (Tricia) and Julie. Julie later married David Eisenhower, grandson of former president Dwight D. Eisenhower. Tricia married Edward Cox.

With the entry of the United States into World War II in 1941, Nixon went to work for the Office of Price Administration in Washington, D.C. In 1942 he joined the Navy and was commissioned a lieutenant (junior grade). He served mainly in naval air transport in the South Pacific, and by the war's end in 1945, he had achieved the rank of lieutenant commander.

▶CONGRESSMAN AND SENATOR

After his discharge from the Navy in early 1946, Nixon ran as a Republican for a seat in the U.S. House of Representatives from California. Although given little chance to win, he defeated a veteran Democratic congressman, Jerry Voorhis, by waging the kind of hard, aggressive campaign that became a Nixon characteristic. After winning re-election in 1948, he was appointed to the House Un-American Activities Committee. That year the committee began its investigation of Alger

Hiss, a U.S. State Department official who was accused of passing secret documents to a Soviet spy ring. Nixon gained fame for his role in the case, in which Hiss was convicted of perjury, or lying under oath.

In 1950, Nixon ran for the U.S. Senate. In what was called one of the roughest, most bitter campaigns in political history, he accused his Democratic opponent, Helen Gahagan Douglas, of ignoring the threat of Communist subversion and defeated her by a wide margin.

By 1952, Nixon had become a nationally known figure. He had attracted the attention not only of the voters but also of Dwight D. Eisenhower. When Eisenhower was nominated by the Republicans for the presidency that year, he asked that Nixon be made his vice-presidential running mate.

Nixon's rising career received a temporary setback when he was accused of having improperly accepted campaign contributions from wealthy Californians. Amid demands from his opponents that he leave the race, Nixon delivered an emotional speech defending himself. Known as the Checkers speech, because of his reference in it to his dog, Checkers, it was received favorably by the public, and Eisenhower kept him as his vice-presidential candidate.

▶VICE PRESIDENT

The Eisenhower-Nixon ticket was swept into office in the Republican landslide of 1952. Nixon received the vice-presidential nomination again in 1956, easily winning re-election with Eisenhower.

During Nixon's eight years in the office, he altered the traditional role of the vice president from a passive figurehead to an active participant in the business of government. He served

---

IMPORTANT DATES IN THE LIFE OF RICHARD M. NIXON

1913	Born in Yorba Linda, California, January 9.
1934	Graduated from Whittier College.
1937	Graduated from Duke University Law School.
1940	Married Thelma Catherine (Patricia) Ryan.
1942– **1946**	Served in the United States Navy.
1947– **1951**	Served in the U.S. House of Representatives.
1951– **1953**	Served in the U.S. Senate.
1953– **1961**	Vice president of the United States.
1969– **1974**	37th president of the United States (resigned the presidency, August 9, 1974).
1994	Died in New York City, April 22.

as "acting" president during President Eisenhower's three illnesses and visited 56 countries and five continents as the president's personal representative.

Two of these visits were particularly notable. In 1958, while in Caracas, Venezuela, on a goodwill tour of Latin America, he became the object of violent anti-U.S. demonstrations. In 1959, he was in Moscow to open a U.S. exhibition of home equipment. There he engaged in a sharp debate—the famous "kitchen" debate—with the leader of the Soviet Union, Nikita Khrushchev, over the merits of the free-enterprise and Communist systems.

▶ THE 1960 CAMPAIGN

With Eisenhower's second term coming to an end, Nixon was the overwhelming choice of his party for the presidency in 1960. His Democratic opponent was the young Senator John F. Kennedy of Massachusetts. Campaigning at top speed for nine weeks, Nixon drove himself, his staff, and his wife, Pat, who accompanied him, to the edge of exhaustion. The campaign was unique for the four television debates between Kennedy and Nixon, which played a crucial part in what proved to be one of the closest elections in U.S. history. Kennedy won 303 electoral votes to Nixon's 219, but Kennedy's margin of victory in the popular vote was only about two-tenths of 1 percent.

At a U.S. home equipment exhibition in Moscow in 1959, Vice President Nixon engaged in the famous "kitchen" debate with Soviet leader Nikita Khrushchev.

▶ FROM DEFEAT TO THE PRESIDENCY

Following his defeat, Nixon returned to California and practiced law in Los Angeles. He won the Republican nomination for governor of California in 1962, but after losing the election by a wide margin, he told reporters that he was leaving the political arena. He moved to New York, where he became a partner in a prominent law firm. But he also kept a close eye on the course of Republican politics.

Two occurrences were to restore him once again to the top of his party. The first was the shattering defeat of conservative Republican

During the 1952 campaign, Nixon, then a vice-presidential candidate, relaxed with his wife Pat, daughters Patricia and Julie, and family dog Checkers.

The 1960 presidential campaign was the first in which the candidates debated on television. Nixon was defeated by his Democratic opponent, John F. Kennedy.

Barry Goldwater by Lyndon B. Johnson in the 1964 election. The second was Nixon's successful campaigning on behalf of Republican candidates for Congress, who won an increased number of seats in 1966 elections.

Announcing his candidacy for the 1968 presidential nomination, Nixon proceeded to win most of the state primary elections he entered. He thus accumulated so much strength among the delegates at the Republican Convention that his nomination was a foregone conclusion. His vice-presidential running mate was Governor Spiro T. Agnew of Maryland. Their Democratic opponents in the 1968 election were Lyndon Johnson's vice president, Hubert H. Humphrey of Minnesota, who was running for president, and Senator Edmund S. Muskie of Maine, for vice president. Nixon won 301 electoral votes to Humphrey's 191. Governor George C. Wallace of Alabama, running on the American Independent Party, won 46 electoral votes. The popular vote, again, was exceedingly close.

▶ HIS FIRST TERM

As he took office as president in 1969, Nixon was faced with a number of problems, both abroad and at home. These included the war in Vietnam, and the opposition of many Americans to the war; the economy; and the continuing struggle over civil rights.

The Vietnam War. Probably the most difficult issue was the Vietnam War. Peace talks had begun in Paris in 1968 but showed little sign of success. In 1969, Nixon announced a policy of gradual withdrawal of U.S. forces from Vietnam, accompanied by "Vietnamization" of the conflict, under which South Vietnam would be responsible for its defense against Communist North Vietnam and its guerrilla allies in the South.

The president's plan was criticized by some, but it was generally approved of by most Americans. However, a military strike by U.S. and South Vietnamese troops against North Vietnamese bases in Cambodia in 1970 led to widespread protests, particularly on university campuses. The most serious incident took place at Kent State University in Ohio, where four students were killed and others wounded when national guardsmen fired into a group of demonstrators.

Meanwhile, the Vietnam conflict continued, at times escalating. In 1971 it spilled over into neighboring Laos. Although the last U.S. ground combat troops departed from Vietnam in 1972, the signing of a cease-fire would not take place until Nixon's second term of office.

China and the Soviet Union. Among Nixon's foreign policy aims was improved relations with the People's Republic of China, with whom the United States had long been at odds. He eased trade restrictions with China and, in 1972, made a historic trip to that country. It was the first visit by a U.S. president since a Communist government had come to power on the mainland of China in 1949, and it marked the beginning of a new era in relations between the two countries.

The China visit was followed by one to the Soviet Union, where Nixon signed an arms-limitation agreement, negotiated earlier, with the Soviet leader Leonid Brezhnev. The Soviet government also agreed to purchase large amounts of U.S. wheat.

Major Legislation. Nixon's domestic program had mixed results. His plan for a national welfare system that would provide a minimum standard of payment to the needy failed to gain congressional approval. More favorably received was his proposal, in 1969, for a change in the Selective Service System to allow for a lottery-based military draft. (The draft itself would be abolished in 1973, replaced by an all-volunteer armed forces.)

Nixon rebounded from his 1960 defeat to win election as president in 1968. He is seen here with his vice-presidential running mate, Spiro T. Agnew of Maryland.

Nixon was greeted by Chairman Mao Zedong on his historic visit to Communist China in 1972. The visit marked a new era in U.S.-Chinese relations.

Congress established the U.S. Postal Service in 1970 as an independent government agency. It also passed a measure the same year lowering the voting age to 18 in federal elections. Ratification of the 26th Amendment to the Constitution in 1971 made 18 the legal voting age in all elections. The administration's project for a supersonic transport (SST) was defeated after lengthy debate in 1971. But one of Nixon's major pieces of legislation, a revenue-sharing plan to provide federal funds for state and local governments, was finally approved in 1972. Congress also passed the Equal Rights Amendment (ERA) in 1972, but it would fail to gain approval by the states.

The Economy and the Supreme Court. Nixon took a number of steps to try to improve the nation's economy, which was gripped by high rates of inflation and unemployment. These included a temporary freeze on wages and prices and a devaluation of the dollar, or the lowering of its value in relation to other world currencies. By 1972 the economic climate had improved somewhat.

The U.S. Supreme Court handed down two important decisions on civil rights issues during Nixon's presidency. In 1969 it declared that segregated schools must be desegregated "at once," and in 1971, it upheld the busing of students to achieve racial balance. The busing issue was controversial, and critics of the administration accused it of purposely slowing efforts at integration.

Nixon twice suffered rebuffs by the Senate on nominations to the Supreme Court in 1970. Three of his candidates for associate justice

were eventually approved—Lewis F. Powell, Jr., Harry Blackmun, and William Rehnquist. Warren Burger was named chief justice.

Moon Landing. Perhaps the most widely followed event of 1969 was the *Apollo II* spaceflight, which carried two U.S. astronauts, Neil A. Armstrong and Edwin E. (Buzz) Aldrin, Jr., to the first manned landing on the moon. See the article on Space Exploration and Travel in Volume S.

The 1972 Election. Nixon easily won renomination in 1972, with Agnew again his vice-presidential running mate. Their Democratic opponents were Senator George S. McGovern of South Dakota, for president, and R. Sargent Shriver, former director of the Peace Corps, for vice president. The result was an overwhelming victory for Nixon, who received 520 electoral votes to 17 for McGovern.

▶ **SECOND TERM**

Cease-Fire in Vietnam. The Paris peace talks resulted in a cease-fire agreement in Vietnam in early 1973. Henry Kissinger, the president's adviser, had helped negotiate the agreement and was appointed secretary of state soon after. Although the agreement effectively ended the participation of U.S. troops in the war, it did not end the conflict. South Vietnam would later fall to a victorious North, and the country would be united under Communist rule. See the article on Henry Kissinger in Volume J-K and the article on the Vietnam War in Volume U-V.

Middle East War. Later in 1973, war again erupted in the Middle East between Israel and its neighbors Egypt and Syria. Since the United States had traditionally supported Israel and the Soviet Union the Arab states, this fourth Arab-Israeli war threatened the new détente, or easing of relations, between the two superpowers. Nevertheless, U.S. and Soviet representatives were able to work out an agreement, through the United Nations, to end the fighting.

Because of its support of Israel, however, the United States became the major target of an oil embargo by the Arab oil-producing nations. The embargo, by halting oil shipments, produced an energy crisis in the United States and other Western nations and hampered efforts to improve the national economy.

The Watergate Scandal. The event that would bring down the Nixon presidency

President Nixon announced his resignation from office in 1974, as a result of the Watergate scandal. Pat Nixon and daughter Tricia stand behind him.

occurred in 1972, some months before the election. Five men had been caught breaking into the headquarters of the Democratic National Committee in the Watergate building in Washington, D.C. Arrested and brought to trial, they were revealed to be employees of Nixon's re-election committee. Nixon would be charged not with having authorized the break-in but with attempting to cover it up.

In 1973 a special Senate committee was formed in response to the Watergate affair and accusations of campaign irregularities. A special prosecutor, Archibald Cox, was named to investigate the matter. Nixon asserted that he had no knowledge of a cover-up attempt, but he refused to turn over White House tape recordings to the committee. He later dismissed Cox as special prosecutor. Now under great pressure, which included calls for his impeachment, or formal charges of misconduct, Nixon agreed to turn over the tapes. A new special prosecutor, Leon Jaworski, was chosen, as the House of Representatives began an inquiry on impeachment.

In his later years, Nixon became an unofficial political adviser. In 1993, the year before his death, he was invited to the White House by President Bill Clinton.

Resignation of Agnew. The Nixon administration was further jolted by a federal grand jury investigation of Vice President Spiro T. Agnew. It ended with Agnew's resignation in October 1973 and his plea of no contest to a tax-evasion charge. Nixon named Congressman Gerald R. Ford of Michigan to replace him as vice president.

Nixon's Resignation and Pardon. In 1974 the special prosecutor requested more tapes from the president. Nixon refused, claiming executive privilege. The question was decided by the Supreme Court, which ruled unanimously that the president must surrender the tapes. After months of hearings, the House Judiciary Committee voted to recommend three articles of impeachment against the president. Additional tapes revealed that Nixon had ordered the Federal Bureau of Investigation (FBI) to limit its investigation of the affair. With the release of this incriminating information, impeachment by the House of Representatives and trial by the Senate were certain.

On August 8, 1974, Nixon announced that he would resign from the presidency, effective the following day. He admitted no criminal wrongdoing. Vice President Ford was sworn in as president to succeed him. On September 8, 1974, Ford granted Nixon "a full, free, and absolute pardon" for all offenses he might have committed against the United States.

▶ **LATER YEARS**

After leaving office, Nixon returned to California, to the family home in San Clemente. He would later establish residences in New York and New Jersey. The former president spent much time writing an account of his political life. *RN: The Memoirs of Richard Nixon* was published in 1978. Other books on political and world affairs followed. In 1990, the Richard Nixon Library and Birthplace was opened in Yorba Linda, California.

In his later years, Nixon gained appreciation as an elder statesman. He revisited China and traveled to the former Soviet Union. He died in New York City on April 22, 1994, and was buried in Yorba Linda, next to his wife, Pat, who had died in 1993.

ROBERT B. SEMPLE, JR.
The New York Times Washington Bureau

See also WATERGATE.

NOBEL, ALFRED BERNHARD
(1833–1896)

Alfred Nobel, a Swedish inventor, left most of his fortune to establish a fund for the Nobel Prizes, annual awards honoring outstanding achievement in six fields.

Alfred Bernhard Nobel is noted as the founder of the Nobel Prizes. He invented dynamite and other powerful explosives and amassed a fortune in manufacturing these substances and in other business enterprises.

Nobel was born on October 21, 1833, in Stockholm, Sweden. He was educated in Russia, France, and the United States. He was fluent in five languages and had a great interest in literature. Nobel traveled widely, then returned to work in his father's factory in St. Petersburg, Russia.

Later, in Sweden, Nobel began to experiment with explosives. In 1867, he received a patent for dynamite. About 1875 he produced an even more powerful explosive called blasting gelatin. In all, Nobel held more than 100 patents.

In his will, Nobel left $9.2 million to set up a fund for the Nobel Prizes. The prizes are awards given each year for the most important work in six categories—physics, chemistry, physiology or medicine, literature, peace, and economics.

The Royal Swedish Academy of Sciences gives the awards in physics, chemistry, and economics. The Karolinska Institutet awards the prize in physiology or medicine. The Swedish Academy awards the prize in literature. The Norwegian Nobel Committee gives the prize for peace.

Presentation ceremonies are held on December 10, the anniversary of Nobel's death. The Nobel Foundation in Stockholm supervises the awarding of the prizes. The peace prize is awarded in Oslo, Norway. The other prizes are presented in Stockholm. Each Nobel Prize winner receives a gold medal, a diploma, and prize money.

Reviewed by Swedish Information Service

NOBEL PRIZES

 PHYSIOLOGY OR MEDICINE

1901 Emil von Behring (Germany) for his work on serum therapy.

1902 Sir Ronald Ross (Great Britain) for his work on malaria.

1903 Niels Ryberg Finsen (Denmark) for his contributions to the treatment of diseases with concentrated light radiation.

1904 Ivan Petrovich Pavlov (Russia) for his work on the physiology of digestion.

1905 Robert Koch (Germany) for his work on tuberculosis.

1906 Camillo Golgi (Italy) and Santiago Ramón y Cajal (Spain) for their work on the structure of the nervous system.

1907 Charles Louis Alphonse Laveran (France) for his studies of the role of protozoa in causing diseases.

1908 Paul Ehrlich (Germany) and Élie Metchnikoff (Russia) for their work on immunity.

1909 Emil Theodor Kocher (Switzerland) for his work on the physiology, pathology, and surgery of the thyroid gland.

1910 Albrecht Kossel (Germany) for his work on proteins.

1911 Allvar Gullstrand (Sweden) for his work on the dioptrics of the eye.

1912 Alexis Carrel (United States) for his work on vascular suture and the transplantation of blood vessels and organs.

1913 Charles Robert Richet (France) for his work on anaphylaxis.

1914 Robert Bárány (Hungary) for his work on the physiology and pathology of the vestibular apparatus.

1915–18 No award.

1919 Jules Bordet (Belgium) for his discoveries relating to immunity.

1920 August Krogh (Denmark) for his discovery of the capillary motor regulating mechanism.

1921 No award.

1922 Archibald V. Hill (Great Britain) for his discovery relating to the production of heat in the muscle, and Otto Meyerhof (Germany) for his discovery of the relationship between oxygen and the metabolism of lactic acid.

1923 Frederick Grant Banting and John J. R. Macleod (Canada) for their discovery of insulin.

1924 Willem Einthoven (the Netherlands) for his invention of the electrocardiograph.

1925 No award.

1926 Johannes Fibiger (Denmark) for his discovery of the Spiroptera carcinoma.

1927 Julius Wagner-Jauregg (Austria) for his discovery of malaria inoculation as a treatment for dementia paralytica.

1928 Charles Nicolle (France) for his work on typhus.

1929 Sir Frederick Gowland Hopkins (Great Britain) for his discovery of the growth-stimulating vitamins, and Christiaan Eijkman (the Netherlands) for his discovery of the antineuritic vitamins.

1930 Karl Landsteiner (Austria) for his discovery of human blood groups.

1931 Otto H. Warburg (Germany) for his discovery of the respiratory enzyme.

1932 Sir Charles Scott Sherrington and Edgar D. Adrian (Great Britain) for their discoveries regarding the function of neurons.

1933 Thomas H. Morgan (United States) for his discoveries concerning the role played by the chromosome in heredity.

1934 George Minot, William P. Murphy, and George H. Whipple (United States) for their work with liver therapy for anemia.

1935 Hans Spemann (Germany) for his discovery of the organizer effect in embryonic development.

1936 Sir Henry Hallett Dale (Great Britain) and Otto Loewi (Austria) for their discoveries in the chemical transmission of nerve impulses.

1937 Albert Szent-Györgyi von Nagyrapolt (Hungary) for his discoveries in connection with biological combustion processes, vitamin C, and the catalysis of fumaric acid.

1938 Corneille Heymans (Belgium) for his discovery of the role of the sinus and aortic mechanisms in the regulation of respiration.

1939 Gerhard Domagk (Germany) for his discovery of the antibacterial effects of prontosil.

1940–42 No award.

1943 Edward A. Doisy (United States) for his discovery of the chemical nature of vitamin K, and Henrik Dam (Denmark) for his discovery of vitamin K.

1944 Joseph Erlanger and Herbert Gasser (United States) for their discoveries relating to the functions of single nerve fibers.

1945 Sir Alexander Fleming, Ernest B. Chain, and Sir Howard W. Florey (Great Britain) for their discovery of penicillin.

1946 Hermann Joseph Muller (United States) for the discovery of the production of mutations by X-ray irradiation.

1947 Carl F. Cori and Gerty Cori (United States) for their discovery of the course of catalytic conversion of glycogen, and Bernardo Houssay (Argentina) for his discovery of the role of the hormone of the anterior pituitary lobe in the metabolism of sugar.

1948 Paul Mueller (Switzerland) for his discovery of the effectiveness of DDT.

1949 Walter R. Hess (Switzerland) for his discovery of the function of the interbrain, and Antonio Egas Moniz (Portugal) for his discovery of leucotomy as a treatment for certain psychoses.

1950 Philip S. Hench and Edward C. Kendall (United States) and Tadeus Reichstein (Switzerland) for their discoveries of adrenal cortex hormones.

1951 Max Theiler (South Africa) for his discoveries concerning yellow fever.

1952 Selman A. Waksman (United States) for his discovery of streptomycin.

1953 Fritz Albert Lipmann (United States) for his discovery of coenzyme A, and Hans Adolf Krebs (Great Britain) for his discovery of the citric-acid cycle.

1954 John F. Enders, Thomas H. Weller, and Frederick C. Robbins (United States) for their studies of poliomyelitis viruses.

1955 Hugo Theorell (Sweden) for his studies of oxidation enzymes.

1956 Dickinson W. Richards and Andre F. Cournand (United States) and Werner Forssmann (West Germany) for their discoveries concerning heart catheterization.

1957 Daniel Bovet (Italy) for his development of antihistamines.

1958 George Wells Beadle and Edward Lawrie Tatum (United States) for their discovery of the chemical action of genes, and Joshua Lederberg (United States) for his studies of genetic recombination.

1959 Arthur Kornberg and Severo Ochoa (United States) for their work in biological synthesis of ribonucleic acid and deoxyribonucleic acid.

1960 Sir Macfarlane Burnet (Australia) and Peter B. Medawar (Great Britain) for their discovery of acquired immunological tolerance.

1961 Georg von Bekesy (United States) for his discoveries of the physical mechanism of stimulation within the cochlea.

1962 Francis H. C. Crick and Maurice H. F. Wilkins (Great Britain) and James D. Watson (United States) for their discoveries of the molecular structure of nucleic acids.

1963 Alan L. Hodgkin and Andrew F. Huxley (Great Britain) and Sir John Eccles (Australia) for their research on nerve cells.

1964 Feodor Lynen (West Germany) and Konrad Bloch (United States) for their work on cholesterol and fatty acid metabolism.

1965 François Jacob, Jacques Monod, and André Lwoff (France) for their discovery of regulatory genes that control activity of other genes.

1966 Charles B. Huggins (United States) for his discoveries in hormonal treatment of prostate cancer, and Francis P. Rous (United States) for his discovery of tumor-producing viruses.

1967 George Wald and Haldan Keffer Hartline (United States) and Ragnar Granit (Sweden) for their discoveries concerning vision.

1968 Robert W. Holley, H. Gobind Khorana, and Marshall W. Nirenberg (United States) for their work on the genetic code in bacteria.

1969 Max Delbruck, Alfred D. Hershey, and Salvador E. Luria (United States) for their discoveries concerning viruses.

1970 Julius Axelrod (United States), Sir Bernard Katz (Great Britain), and Ulf von Euler (Sweden) for their independent research in the chemistry of nerve transmission.

1971 Earl W. Sutherland (United States) for his discoveries concerning the action of hormones.

1972 Gerald M. Edelman (United States) and Rodney R. Porter (Great Britain) for their research on the chemical structure of antibodies.

1973 Karl von Frisch and Konrad Lorenz (Austria) and Nikolaas Tinbergen (the Netherlands) for their work in ethology.

1974 Albert Claude and Christian René de Duve (Belgium) and George Emil Palade (United States) for their research in cell biology.
1975 David Baltimore and Howard Temin (United States) and Renato Dulbecco (Great Britain) for their work on tumor viruses and cell genetics.
1976 Baruch S. Blumberg and D. Carleton Gajdusek (United States) for their independent studies of infectious diseases.
1977 Rosalyn S. Yalow, Roger C. L. Guillemin, and Andrew V. Schally (United States) for their independent studies in body chemistry.
1978 Daniel Nathans and Hamilton Smith (United States) and Werner Arber (Switzerland) for their work in genetics.
1979 Allan MacLeod Cormack (United States) and Godfrey Newbold Hounsfield (Britain) for their development of the CAT scan.
1980 George D. Snell and Baruj Benacerraf (United States) and Jean Dausset (France) for their independent research in immunology.
1981 Roger W. Sperry and David H. Hubel (United States) and Torsten N. Wiesel (Sweden) for their research on the human brain.
1982 Sune Bergstrom and Bengt Samuelsson (Sweden) and John R. Vane (Great Britain) for their discoveries in controlling prostaglandins.
1983 Barbara McClintock (United States) for her discoveries in plant genetics.
1984 Cesar Milstein (Argentina), Georges J. F. Köhler (West Germany), and Niels K. Jerne (Denmark) for their research in immunology.
1985 Michael S. Brown and Joseph L. Goldstein (United States) for their research in metabolism.
1986 Rita Levi-Montalcini and Stanley Cohen (United States) for their research in cell growth and tissue development.
1987 Susumu Tonegawa (Japan) for his work on immunological defenses against disease.
1988 Sir James Black (Britain) and Gertrude B. Elion and George H. Hitchings (United States) for their development of drugs.
1989 Harold E. Varmus and J. Michael Bishop (United States) for discovering a collection of normal genes that can cause cancer.
1990 Joseph E. Murray and E. Donnall Thomas (United States) for organ and tissue transplants.
1991 Erwin Neher and Bert Sakmann (Germany) for their discoveries in basic cell functions.
1992 Edmond H. Fischer and Edwin G. Krebs (United States) for a discovery about cell proteins made in the 1950's.
1993 Phillip A. Sharp and Richard J. Roberts (United States) for their discovery of split genes.
1994 Alfred G. Gilman and Martin Rodbell (United States) for their discovery of G-proteins in the human body.
1995 Edward B. Lewis and Eric F. Wieschaus (United States) and Christiane Nusslein-Volhard (Germany) for discovering how genes control the structural development of the body.
1996 Peter C. Doherty (Australia) and Rolf M. Zinkernagel (Switzerland) for their discoveries about the immune system of the human body.

1997 Stanley B. Prusiner (United States) for his discovery of prions, proteins that have been linked to fatal brain diseases.
1998 Robert F. Furchgott, Louis J. Ignarro, and Ferid Murad (United States) for discovering that the human body uses the gas nitric oxide to relax blood vessels.
1999 Günter Blobel (Germany) for his discovery of how proteins find their way around in cells.
2000 Paul Greengard and Eric R. Kandel (United States) and Arvid Carlsson (Sweden) for their discoveries about communication between nerve cells in the brain.
2001 Tim Hunt and Paul Nurse (Great Britain) and Leland Hartwell (United States) for their cancer research.
2002 Sydney Brenner and John E. Sulston (Great Britain) and H. Robert Horvitz (United States) for identifying genes that regulate organ development and cell death.
2003 Paul Lauterbur (United States) and Peter Mansfield (Great Britain) for developing magnetic resonance imaging (MRI).
2004 Linda B. Buck and Richard Axel (United States) for their research on the sense of smell.
2005 Barry J. Marshall and J. Robin Warren (Australia) for linking bacterial infection to ulcers of the stomach and intestines.

LITERATURE

1901 René Sully Prudhomme (France), poems.
1902 Christian Matthias Theodor Mommsen (Germany), historical writings.
1903 Bjørnstjerne Bjørnson (Norway), poems.
1904 Frédéric Mistral (France), poems; and José Echegaray y Eizaguirre (Spain), dramas.
1905 Henryk Sienkiewicz (Poland), novels.
1906 Giosuè Carducci (Italy), poems.
1907 Rudyard Kipling (Great Britain), stories, novels, and poems.
1908 Rudolf Christoph Eucken (Germany), philosophic writings.
1909 Selma Lagerlöf (Sweden), novels.
1910 Paul von Heyse (Germany), poems, novels, dramas, and stories.
1911 Maurice Maeterlinck (Belgium), dramas.
1912 Gerhart Hauptmann (Germany), dramas.
1913 Rabindranath Tagore (India), poems.
1914 No award.
1915 Romain Rolland (France), novels.
1916 Verner von Heidenstam (Sweden), poems.
1917 Karl Adolph Gjellerup (Denmark), poems; and Henrik Pontoppidan (Denmark), novels and short stories.
1918 No award.
1919 Carl Spitteler (Switzerland), epic writings.
1920 Knut Hamsun (Norway), novels.
1921 Anatole France (France), stories, novels, and essays.
1922 Jacinto Benavente y Martínez (Spain), dramas.
1923 William Butler Yeats (Ireland), poems.
1924 Wladyslaw Reymont (Poland), novels.

1925 George Bernard Shaw (Great Britain), dramas.
1926 Grazia Deledda (Italy), novels.
1927 Henri Bergson (France), philosophic writings.
1928 Sigrid Undset (Norway), novels.
1929 Thomas Mann (Germany), novels.
1930 Sinclair Lewis (United States), novels.
1931 Erik A. Karlfeldt (Sweden), poems.
1932 John Galsworthy (Great Britain), novels.
1933 Ivan Bunin (Russia), stories and novels.
1934 Luigi Pirandello (Italy), dramas.
1935 No award.
1936 Eugene O'Neill (United States), dramas.
1937 Robert Martin Du Gard (France), novels.
1938 Pearl Buck (United States), novels.
1939 Frans Eemil Sillanpää (Finland), novels.
1940–43 No award.
1944 Johannes V. Jensen (Denmark), novels and poems.
1945 Gabriela Mistral (Chile), poems.
1946 Hermann Hesse (Switzerland), novels.
1947 André Gide (France), novels.
1948 T. S. Eliot (Great Britain), poems.
1949 William Faulkner (United States), novels.
1950 Bertrand Russell (Great Britain), philosophic writings.
1951 Pär Lagerkvist (Sweden), novels.
1952 François Mauriac (France), novels.
1953 Sir Winston Churchill (Great Britain), historical writings.
1954 Ernest Hemingway (United States), novels and stories.
1955 Halldór K. Laxness (Iceland), novels.
1956 Juan Ramón Jiménez (Spain), poems.
1957 Albert Camus (France), novels and philosophic writings.
1958 Boris Pasternak (Soviet Union), poems and novels.
1959 Salvatore Quasimodo (Italy), poems.
1960 Saint-John Perse (France), poems.
1961 Ivo Andrić (Yugoslavia), novels.
1962 John Steinbeck (United States), novels.
1963 Giorgos Seferis (Greece), poems.
1964 Jean-Paul Sartre (France), novels and philosophic writings.
1965 Mikhail Sholokov (Soviet Union), novels.
1966 Shmuel Yosef Agnon (Israel), stories and novels; and Nelly Sachs (Sweden), poems.
1967 Miguel Angel Asturias (Guatemala), novels and poems.
1968 Yasunari Kawabata (Japan), novels.
1969 Samuel Beckett (Ireland), dramas and poems.
1970 Aleksandr Isaevich Solzhenitsyn (Soviet Union), novels.
1971 Pablo Neruda (Chile), poems.
1972 Heinrich Böll (West Germany) for aiding postwar revival of German literature.
1973 Patrick White (Australia), novels.
1974 Harry Edmund Martinson (Sweden), novels and poems; and Eyvind Johnson (Sweden), novels.
1975 Eugenio Montale (Italy), poems.
1976 Saul Bellow (United States), novels.
1977 Vicente Aleixandre (Spain), poems.
1978 Isaac Bashevis Singer (United States), novels and stories, written in Yiddish.
1979 Odysseus Elytis (Greece), poems.
1980 Czeslaw Milosz (United States), poetry, prose, and essays, written in Polish and English.
1981 Elias Canetti (Great Britain), fiction, drama, and nonfiction, written in German.

1982 Gabriel García Márquez (Colombia), novels and short stories.
1983 William Golding (Great Britain), novels.
1984 Jaroslav Seifert (Czechoslovakia), poems.
1985 Claude Simon (France), novels.
1986 Wole Soyinka (Nigeria), poems.
1987 Joseph Brodsky (Soviet Union), poems, written in Russian and English.
1988 Naguib Mahfouz (Egypt), novels, short stories, and dramas.
1989 Camilo José Cela (Spain), novels.
1990 Octavio Paz (Mexico), verse and social essays.
1991 Nadine Gordimer (South Africa), stories and novels concerning apartheid.
1992 Derek Walcott (West Indies), poems and dramas about the Caribbean.
1993 Toni Morrison (United States), novels about the lives of African Americans.
1994 Kenzaburo Oe (Japan), novels about life in Japan.
1995 Seamus Heaney (Ireland), poems.
1996 Wislawa Szymborksa (Poland), poems.
1997 Dario Fo (Italy), dramas.
1998 José Saramago (Portugal), novels.
1999 Günter Grass (Germany), novels.
2000 Gao Xingjian (China), novels and dramas.
2001 V. S. Naipaul (Great Britain), novels and essays.
2002 Imre Kertesz (Hungary), novels about the Holocaust.
2003 J. M. Coetzee (South Africa), novels.
2004 Elfriede Jelinek (Austria), novels and plays.
2005 Harold Pinter (Great Britain), plays.

 PEACE

1901 Jean Henri Dunant (Switzerland), founder, Red Cross; and Frédéric Passy (France), founder and president, first French peace society.
1902 Élie Ducommun (Switzerland), honorary secretary, Permanent International Peace Bureau, and Charles Albert Gobat (Switzerland), secretary-general, Inter-Parliamentary Union.
1903 Sir William R. Cremer (Great Britain), secretary, International Arbitration League.
1904 Institute of International Law.
1905 Bertha von Suttner (Austria), honorary president, Permanent International Peace Bureau.
1906 Theodore Roosevelt, president, United States of America.
1907 Ernesto T. Moneta (Italy), president, Lombard League of Peace, and Louis Renault (France), professor of international law.
1908 Klas Pontus Arnoldson (Sweden), founder, Swedish Peace and Arbitration League, and Fredrik Bajer (Denmark), honorary president, Permanent International Peace Bureau.
1909 Auguste M. F. Beernaert (Belgium), member, International Court of Arbitration at The Hague, and Paul d'Estournelles de Constant (France), founder, Committee for the Defense of National Interests and International Conciliation.
1910 Permanent International Peace Bureau, Bern, Switzerland.
1911 Tobias M. C. Asser (the Netherlands), originator of conferences on international law, and Alfred H.

Fried (Austria), founder, *Die Friedenswarte*, a peace publication.

1912 Elihu Root (United States), originator of various treaties of arbitration.

1913 Henri Lafontaine (Belgium), president, Permanent International Peace Bureau.

1914–16 No award.

1917 International Committee of the Red Cross, Geneva, Switzerland.

1918 No award.

1919 Woodrow Wilson, president, United States of America; advocate, League of Nations.

1920 Léon Bourgeois (France), president, Council of the League of Nations.

1921 Karl Hjalmar Branting (Sweden), delegate, Council of the League of Nations, and Christian Louis Lange (Norway), secretary-general, Inter-Parliamentary Union.

1922 Fridtjof Nansen (Norway), delegate, League of Nations; originator of the Nansen passports for refugees.

1923–24 No award.

1925 Sir Austen Chamberlain (Great Britain), an originator of the Locarno Pacts, and Charles G. Dawes (United States), chairman, Allied Reparation Commission.

1926 Aristide Briand (France), an originator of the Kellogg-Briand Pact and the Locarno Pacts, and Gustav Stresemann (Germany), an originator of the Locarno Pacts.

1927 Ferdinand Buisson (France), founder and president, League for Human Rights, and Ludwig Quidde (Germany), a participant in various peace conferences.

1928 No award.

1929 Frank Billings Kellogg (United States), an originator of the Kellogg-Briand Pact.

1930 Nathan Söderblom (Sweden), a leader in the ecumenical movement.

1931 Jane Addams (United States), international president, Women's International League for Peace and Freedom, and Nicholas Murray Butler (United States), a promoter of the Kellogg-Briand Pact.

1932 No award.

1933 Sir Norman Angell (Great Britain), member, Executive Committee of the League of Nations and National Peace Council.

1934 Arthur Henderson (Great Britain), president, Disarmament Conference, 1932.

1935 Carl von Ossietzky (Germany), journalist, for promoting world disarmament.

1936 Carlos Saavedra Lamas (Argentina), president, League of Nations; a mediator in a conflict between Paraguay and Bolivia.

1937 Viscount Cecil of Chelwood (Great Britain), founder and president, International Peace Campaign.

1938 Nansen International Office for Refugees, Geneva, Switzerland, a relief organization.

1939–43 No award.

1944 International Committee of the Red Cross, Geneva, Switzerland.

1945 Cordell Hull (United States), prominent participant in originating the United Nations.

1946 Emily G. Balch (United States), honorary international president, Women's International League for Peace and Freedom, and John R. Mott (United States), chairman, International Missionary Council, and president, World Alliance of the YMCA.

1947 American Friends' Service Committee, Washington, D.C., and Friends' Service Council, London.

1948 No award.

1949 John, Lord Boyd Orr of Brechin (Great Britain), organizer and director, General Food and Agricultural Organization; president, National Peace Council and World Union of Peace Organizations.

1950 Ralph Bunche (United States), United Nations mediator in Palestine, 1948.

1951 Léon Jouhaux (France), president, Trade Union Confederation.

1952 Albert Schweitzer (France), missionary surgeon and founder of Lambaréné Hospital, French Equatorial Africa (now Gabon).

1953 George C. Marshall (United States), originator of the Marshall Plan.

1954 Office of the United Nations High Commissioner for Refugees, an international relief organization.

1955–56 No award.

1957 Lester B. Pearson (Canada), president, 7th session of the UN General Assembly.

1958 Georges Pire (Belgium), Dominican priest; a leader of organization for refugees "l'Europe du Coeur au Service du Monde."

1959 Philip J. Noel-Baker (Great Britain), worker for international peace and cooperation.

1960 Albert John Luthuli (South Africa), former president of the African National Congress.

1961 Dag Hammarskjöld (Sweden), late secretary-general of the United Nations.

1962 Linus C. Pauling (United States), 1954 Nobel laureate in chemistry; an opponent of nuclear arms testing.

1963 International Committee of the Red Cross and the League of Red Cross Societies.

1964 Martin Luther King, Jr. (United States), a leader of the civil rights movement in the United States.

1965 United Nations Children's Fund (UNICEF).

1966–67 No award.

1968 René Cassin (France), a pioneer in world peace efforts.

1969 International Labour Organisation for their fight against poverty and unemployment.

1970 Norman E. Borlaug (United States) for research yielding new strains of wheat and rice that may help solve world hunger.

1971 Willy Brandt (West Germany) for his efforts to ease the tensions between East and West Europe.

1972 No award.

1973 Henry Kissinger (United States) and Le Duc Tho (North Vietnam) for negotiating Vietnam cease-fire. (Le Duc Tho refused the prize.)

1974 Eisaku Sato (Japan) for attempts to stop the spread of nuclear weapons, and Seán MacBride (Ireland) for human-rights work.

1975 Andrei Sakharov (Soviet Union) for his dedication to the cause of human rights.

1976 Mairead Corrigan and Betty Williams (Northern Ireland) for their efforts toward peace in Northern Ireland.

1977 Amnesty International, London.

1978 Anwar el-Sadat (Egypt) and Menachem Begin (Israel) for their peacemaking efforts in the Middle East.

1979 Mother Teresa (Albania) for her work among the poor of India.

1980 Adolfo Pérez Esquivel (Argentina) for promoting human rights in Latin America.

1981 Office of the United Nations High Commissioner for Refugees.

1982 Alva Myrdal (Sweden) and Alfonso García Robles (Mexico) for their efforts to promote disarmament.

1983 Lech Walesa (Poland) for his contribution toward workers' rights.

1984 Desmond Tutu (South Africa), Anglican bishop, for his nonviolent efforts to end apartheid.

1985 International Physicians for the Prevention of Nuclear War.

1986 Elie Wiesel (United States), Holocaust survivor, for bearing witness against forgetfulness.

1987 Oscar Arias Sanchez, president of Costa Rica, for regional peace plan for Central America.

1988 United Nations peacekeeping forces.

1989 The Dalai Lama, Tenzin Gyatso (Tibet), for nonviolent efforts to free Tibet from Chinese rule.

1990 Mikhail S. Gorbachev, president of the Soviet Union, for his promotion of international peace and efforts to end the cold war.

1991 Aung San Suu Kyi (Myanmar) for her nonviolent struggle for democracy and human rights.

1992 Rigoberta Menchú (Guatemala) for her work for social justice.

1993 F. W. de Klerk, president of South Africa, and Nelson Mandela, president of the African National Congress (South Africa), for their work together to end apartheid and advance racial equality in South Africa.

1994 Yitzhak Rabin, prime minister of Israel, Shimon Peres, foreign minister of Israel, and Yasir Arafat, chairman of the Palestine Liberation Organization, for their efforts to create peace in the Middle East.

1995 Joseph Rotblat (Great Britain) for his leadership of a campaign to eliminate nuclear weapons.

1996 José Ramos-Horta and Bishop Carlos Ximenes Belo (East Timor) for their work to create independence in East Timor.

1997 The International Campaign to Ban Landmines, and Jody Williams, coordinator (United States).

1998 John Hume and David Trimble (Northern Ireland) for their efforts to bring peace to their country.

1999 Médecins Sans Frontières (Doctors Without Borders) for its international humanitarian work.

2000 Kim Dae Jung (South Korea) for his promotion of democracy and human rights and his efforts toward closer ties with North Korea.

2001 The United Nations and its secretary-general Kofi Annan for their continued efforts toward world peace and prosperity.

2002 Jimmy Carter, former president, United States of America, for his efforts to promote world peace, human rights, and economic progress.

2003 Shirin Ebadi (Iran) for promoting democracy and the rights of women and children in Iran.

2004 Wangari Maathai (Kenya) for her environmental work.

2005 The International Atomic Energy Agency (IAEA) and its director general Mohamed El Baradei (Egypt) for his efforts to reduce the spread of nuclear weapons through diplomacy.

PHYSICS

1901 Wilhelm C. Roentgen (Germany) for discovery of X-rays.

1902 Hendrik Antoon Lorentz and Pieter Zeeman (the Netherlands) for research on the influence of magnetism on light.

1903 Antoine Henri Becquerel (France) for discovery of spontaneous radioactivity, and Marie Curie and Pierre Curie (France) for study of radium.

1904 Lord Rayleigh (Great Britain) for studies of densities of gases and discovery of argon.

1905 Philipp Lenard (Germany) for his work on cathode rays.

1906 Joseph John Thomson (Great Britain) for his studies of electrical conduction by gases.

1907 Albert A. Michelson (United States) for developments in measuring the speed of light.

1908 Gabriel Lippmann (France) for his work in color photography.

1909 Guglielmo Marconi (Italy) and Karl Ferdinand Braun (Germany) for development of wireless telegraphy.

1910 Johannes Diderik van der Waals (the Netherlands) for his work with liquids and gases.

1911 Wilhelm Wien (Germany) for his discoveries regarding the radiation of heat.

1912 Nils Dalén (Sweden), invention of automatic gas regulators for lighthouses and buoys.

1913 Heike Kamerlingh Onnes (the Netherlands) for his production of liquid helium.

1914 Max von Laue (Germany) for discoveries of X-ray diffraction by crystals.

1915 Sir William Henry Bragg and William L. Bragg (Great Britain) for their studies of crystal structure by X-rays.

1916 No award.

1917 Charles Barkla (Great Britain) for discovery of radiation of X-rays by elements.

1918 Max Planck (Germany) for the quantum theory of light.

1919 Johannes Stark (Germany) for discovery of the Doppler effect in canal rays and the splitting of spectral lines in electric fields.

1920 Charles E. Guillaume (France) for discovery of anomalies in nickel-steel alloys.

1921 Albert Einstein (Germany) for his work in theoretical physics and for discovery of the law of the photoelectric effect.

1922 Niels Bohr (Denmark), automatic studies.

1923 Robert A. Millikan (United States) for work on the elementary charge of electricity and the photoelectric effect.

1924 Karl M. G. Siegbahn (Sweden) for discoveries and research in X-ray spectroscopy.

1925 James Franck and Gustav Hertz (Germany) for their discovery of laws governing the impact of an electron upon an atom.

1926 Jean Baptiste Perrin (France) for work on the structure of matter and discovery of sedimentation equilibrium.

1927 Arthur H. Compton (United States) for discovery of the Compton effect, and Charles T. R. Wilson

(Great Britain) for a method of tracing the paths of ions.

1928 Owen W. Richardson (Great Britain) for work on the thermionic principle and for discovery of the Richardson law.

1929 Louis Victor de Broglie (France) for discovery of the wave nature of electrons.

1930 Sir Chandrasekhara Venkata Raman (India) for work on the scattering of light and discovery of the Raman effect.

1931 No award.

1932 Werner Heisenberg (Germany) for the creation of quantum mechanics.

1933 Paul Dirac (Great Britain) and Erwin Schrödinger (Austria) for discovery of new forms of atomic theory.

1934 No award.

1935 James Chadwick (Great Britain) for discovery of the neutron.

1936 Carl David Anderson (United States) for discovery of the positron, and Victor F. Hess (Austria) for discovery of cosmic radiation.

1937 Clinton Davisson (United States) and George Thomson (Great Britain) for their discovery of the diffraction of electrons by crystals.

1938 Enrico Fermi (Italy) for discoveries of new radioactive elements.

1939 Ernest O. Lawrence (United States) for invention of the cyclotron.

1940–42 No award.

1943 Otto Stern (United States) for development of the molecular ray method and discovery of the magnetic moment of the proton.

1944 Isidor Isaac Rabi (United States) for a method of recording the magnetic properties of atomic nuclei.

1945 Wolfgang Pauli (Austria) for discovery of the exclusion principle.

1946 Percy Williams Bridgman (United States) for research in high-pressure physics.

1947 Sir Edward V. Appleton (Great Britain) for study of the physics of the atmosphere.

1948 Patrick M. S. Blackett (Great Britain) for development of the Wilson cloud chamber method and discoveries in nuclear physics and cosmic radiation.

1949 Hideki Yukawa (Japan) for discovery of mesons.

1950 Cecil Frank Powell (Great Britain) for a photographic method of studying nuclear processes and for work with mesons.

1951 Sir John D. Cockcroft (Great Britain) and Ernest T. S. Walton (Ireland) for their work on the transmutation of atomic nuclei.

1952 Felix Bloch and Edward Mills Purcell (United States) for development of nuclear magnetic precision measurements.

1953 Frits Zernike (the Netherlands) for invention of the phase contrast microscope.

1954 Max Born (Great Britain) for research in quantum mechanics, and Walther Bothe (West Germany) for coincidence method.

1955 Willis E. Lamb (United States) for discoveries on the structure of the hydrogen spectrum, and Polykarp Kusch (United States) for determining the magnetic moment of the electron.

1956 William Shockley, Walter H. Brattain, and John Bardeen (United States) for research on semiconductors and invention of transistor.

1957 Chen Ning Yang and Tsung Dao Lee (China) for disproving the parity laws.

1958 Pavel A. Cherenkov, Ilya M. Frank, and Igor Y. Tamm (Soviet Union) for their discovery of the Cherenkov effect.

1959 Emilio Segrè and Owen Chamberlain (United States) for discovery of the antiproton.

1960 Donald A. Glaser (United States) for invention of the bubble chamber.

1961 Robert Hofstadter (United States) for studies of atomic nuclei and the structure of nucleons, and Rudolf L. Mössbauer (West Germany) for research in gamma radiation and discovery of the Mössbauer effect.

1962 Lev Davidovich Landau (Soviet Union) for theories concerning condensed matter.

1963 Eugene P. Wigner and Maria Goeppert-Mayer (United States) and Hans D. Jensen (West Germany) for their research on the structure of the nucleus of the atom.

1964 Charles H. Townes (United States) and Aleksandr Prochorov and Nikolai Basov (Soviet Union) for quantum electronics.

1965 Richard P. Feynman and Julian S. Schwinger (United States) and Shinichiro Tomonaga (Japan) for work in quantum electrodynamics.

1966 Alfred Kastler (France) for his method of studying atomic structure by the use of radiation.

1967 Hans Albrecht Bethe (United States) for his theoretical work on nuclear reactions.

1968 Luis W. Alvarez (United States) for contributions to the physics of subatomic particles and techniques for their detection.

1969 Murray Gell-Mann (United States) for his work in the classification of elementary particles and their interactions.

1970 Louis E. F. Néel (France) for research in magnetism, and Hannes O. G. Alfvén (Sweden) for work in magnetohydrodynamics.

1971 Dennis Gabor (Great Britain) for invention of holography.

1972 John Bardeen, Leon N. Cooper, and John R. Schrieffer (United States) for research on superconductivity in ultra-cold metals.

1973 Leo Esaki (Japan), Ivar Giaever (United States), and Brian D. Josephson (Great Britain) for work in the behavior of electrons in solids.

1974 Sir Martin Ryle and Antony Hewish (Great Britain) for work in radio astrophysics.

1975 James Rainwater (United States) and Aage N. Bohr and Ben R. Mottelson (Denmark) for their contributions to nuclear physics.

1976 Burton Richter and Samuel C. C. Ting (United States) for their discovery of a subatomic particle known as psi or J.

1977 Philip W. Anderson and John H. Van Vleck (United States) and Sir Nevill F. Mott (Great Britain) for their work in electronics.

1978 Arno Penzias and Robert Wilson (United States) for their discovery of background radiation, and Piotr Kapitsa (Soviet Union) for his work in low-temperature physics.

1979 Steven Weinberg and Sheldon L. Glashow (United States) and Abdus Salam (Pakistan) for their work on the Weinberg-Salam Theory of Weak Interactions.

1980 James W. Cronin and Val L. Fitch (United States) for their discoveries concerning the symmetry of subatomic particles.

1981 Nicolaas Bloembergen and Arthur L. Schawlow (United States) for their work in laser spectroscopy, and Kai M. Siegbahn (Sweden) for his work in electron spectroscopy.

1982 Kenneth G. Wilson (United States) for analyzing basic changes in matter under the influence of pressure and temperature.

1983 Subrahmanyan Chandrasekhar and William A. Fowler (United States) for their work on what happens as stars age.

1984 Carlo Rubbia (Italy) and Simon van der Meer (the Netherlands) for their discovery of three subatomic particles.

1985 Klaus von Klitzing (West Germany) for discoveries in electronics and computers.

1986 Ernst Ruska (West Germany) for his contributions to electron microscopy, and Gerd Binnig (West Germany) and Heinrich Rohrer (Switzerland) for their work on a new type of electron microscope.

1987 Karl Alex Muller (Switzerland) and J. Georg Bednorz (West Germany) for their work on superconductivity.

1988 Leon M. Lederman, Melvin Schwartz, and Jack Steinberger (United States) for studies involving neutrinos.

1989 Norman F. Ramsey (United States) for work leading to development of the atomic clock, and Hans G. Dehmelt (United States) and Wolfgang Paul (West Germany) for methods to isolate atoms and subatomic particles.

1990 Richard E. Taylor (Canada) and Jerome I. Friedman and Henry W. Kendall (United States) for confirming the existence of quarks.

1991 Pierre-Gilles de Gennes (France) for discoveries about the ordering of molecules in various substances.

1992 George Charpak (France) for the invention of a particle detector.

1993 Joseph H. Taylor and Russell A. Hulse (United States) for their discovery of the binary pulsar and evidence of gravitational waves.

1994 Clifford G. Shull (United States) and Bertram N. Brockhouse (Canada) for developing neutron spectroscopy.

1995 Martin L. Perl and Frederick Reines (United States) for their discoveries of two subatomic particles, the tau and the neutrino.

1996 David M. Lee, Robert C. Richardson, and Douglas D. Osheroff (United States) for their discovery of superfluidity in helium-3.

1997 Steven Chu and William D. Phillips (United States) and Claude Cohen-Tannoudji (France) for developing a method to trap atoms.

1998 Robert B. Laughlin and Daniel C. Tsui (United States) and Horst L. Stormer (Germany) for discovering that electrons in strong magnetic fields can form new types of particles, with fractions of charges.

1999 Gerardus 't Hooft and Martinus J. G. Veltman (the Netherlands) for mathematically predicting properties of subatomic particles.

2000 Zhores I. Alferov (Russia) and Herbert Kroemer and Jack St. Clair Kilby (United States) for their contributions to modern information technology.

2001 Eric Cornell and Carl Wieman (United States) and Wolfgang Ketterle (Germany) for creating a new form of matter.

2002 Guisseppe Giacconi (United States) for his contributions to X-ray astronomy, and Raymond Davis, Jr. (United States) and Masatoshi Koshiba (Japan) for their method of detecting neutrinos.

2003 Alexei Abrikosov and Anthony Leggett (United States) and Vitaly Ginzburg (Russia) for their theories about superconductivity and superfluidity.

2004 David J. Gross, H. David Politzer, and Frank Wilczek (United States) for explaining the force binding particles inside an atom's nucleus.

2005 John L. Hall and Roy J. Glauber (United States) and Theodor W. Haensch (Germany) for applying modern quantum physics to the study of optics.

CHEMISTRY

1901 Jacobus Henricus van't Hoff (the Netherlands) for discovery of the laws of chemical dynamics and osmotic pressure.

1902 Emil Fischer (Germany) for his work on sugar and purine syntheses.

1903 Svante August Arrhenius (Sweden) for the electrolytic theory of dissociation.

1904 Sir William Ramsay (Great Britain) for discovery of the inert (noble) gases.

1905 Adolf von Baeyer (Germany) for work on organic dyes and hydroaromatic compounds.

1906 Henri Moissan (France) for isolating flourine and developing the electric furnace.

1907 Eduard Buchner (Germany) for his biochemical research and discovery of cell-free fermentation.

1908 Ernest Rutherford (Great Britain) for his studies of the disintegration of elements and the chemistry of radioactive substances.

1909 Wilhelm Ostwald (Germany) for his work on catalysis and investigations of chemical equilibria and rates of reaction.

1910 Otto Wallach (Germany) for his work on alicyclic compounds.

1911 Marie Curie (France) for her discovery of radium and polonium.

1912 Victor Grignard (France) for discovery of the Grignard reagent, and Paul Sabatier (France) for a way to hydrogenate organic compounds.

1913 Alfred Werner (Switzerland) for his work on the linkage of atoms in molecules.

1914 Theodore W. Richards (United States) for determining atomic weights of many elements.

1915 Richard Willstätter (Germany) for research on chlorophyll and other plant pigments.

1916–17 No award.

1918 Fritz Haber (Germany) for the synthesis of ammonia from nitrogen and hydrogen.

1919 No award.

1920 Walther Herman Nernst (Germany) for his work in thermochemistry.

1921 Frederick Soddy (Great Britain) for studies of radioactive substances and of the origin and nature of isotopes.

1922 Francis W. Aston (Great Britain) for discovering isotopes in non-radioactive elements and for stating the whole-number rule.

1923 Fritz Pregl (Austria) for the method of microanalysis of organic substances.

1924 No award.

1925 Richard Zsigmondy (Germany) for studies and methods in colloid chemistry.

1926 Theodor Svedberg (Sweden) for work on disperse systems.

1927 Heinrich O. Wieland (Germany) for studies of bile acids and related subjects.

1928 Adolf Windaus (Germany) for studies of sterols and their connection with vitamins.

1929 Arthur Harden (Great Britain) and Hans August Simon von Euler-Chelpin (Sweden) for their investigations of the fermentation of sugar and fermentative enzymes.

1930 Hans Fischer (Germany) for studies of chlorophyll and for the synthesis of hemin.

1931 Karl Bosch and Friedrich Bergius (Germany) for their development of chemical high-pressure methods.

1932 Irving Langmuir (United States) for discoveries and studies in surface chemistry.

1933 No award.

1934 Harold C. Urey (United States) for discovery of heavy hydrogen.

1935 Irène Joliot-Curie and Frédéric Joliot (France) for their synthesis of new radioactive elements.

1936 Peter J. W. Debye (Germany) for investigations of dipole moments and of the diffraction of X-rays and electrons in gases.

1937 Walter N. Haworth (Great Britain) for investigations of carbohydrates and vitamin C, and Paul Karrer (Switzerland) for investigations of carotenoids, flavin, and vitamins.

1938 Richard Kuhn (Germany) for work on carotenoids and vitamins.

1939 Adolph Butenandt (Germany) for his work on sex hormones, and Leopold Ruzicka (Switzerland) for his work on polymethylenes and higher terpenes.

1940–42 No award.

1943 Georg von Hevesy (Hungary) for work on the use of isotopes as tracers.

1944 Otto Hahn (Germany) for discovery of the fission of heavy nuclei.

1945 Artturi Virtanen (Finland) for a fodder preservation method.

1946 James A. Sumner (United States) for discovering that enzymes can be crystallized, and Wendell M. Stanley and John H. Northrop (United States) for preparation of enzymes and virus proteins in a pure form.

1947 Sir Robert Robinson (Great Britain) for studies of plant products.

1948 Arne Tiselius (Sweden) for discoveries in the complex nature of serum proteins.

1949 William Francis Giauque (United States) for work in chemical thermodynamics.

1950 Kurt Alder and Otto Diels (West Germany) for developing a method of synthesizing organic compounds of the diene group.

1951 Edwin M. McMillan and Glenn T. Seaborg (United States) for their discoveries in the chemistry of transuranium elements.

1952 Archer J. P. Martin and Richard Synge (Great Britain) for their invention of partition chromatography.

1953 Hermann Staudinger (West Germany) for discoveries in macromolecular chemistry.

1954 Linus C. Pauling (United States) for research into the chemical bond.

1955 Vincent du Vigneaud (United States) for work on sulfur compounds and for the first synthesis of a polypeptide hormone.

1956 Sir Cyril Hinshelwood (Great Britain) and Nikolai N. Semenov (Soviet Union) for their research in chemical reactions.

1957 Sir Alexander Todd (Great Britain) for work on nucleotides and nucleotide coenzymes.

1958 Frederick Sanger (Great Britain) for work on insulin and other proteins.

1959 Jaroslav Heyrovský (Czechoslovakia) for discovery and development of the polarographic method of analysis.

1960 Willard F. Libby (United States) for a method of carbon-14 dating.

1961 Melvin Calvin (United States) for research on carbon-dioxide assimilation in plants.

1962 John Cowdery Kendrew and Max Ferdinand Perutz (Great Britain) for their studies of globular proteins.

1963 Giulio Natta (Italy) and Karl Ziegler (West Germany) for their research in plastics.

1964 Dorothy C. Hodgkin (Great Britain) for determining the atomic structures of biochemical compounds.

1965 Robert B. Woodward (United States) for his work in synthesizing chlorophyll.

1966 Robert S. Mulliken (United States) for his work concerning chemical bonds that hold atoms together in a molecule.

1967 Ronald George Wreyford Norrish and George Porter (Great Britain) and Manfred Eigen (West Germany) for contributions toward understanding very fast chemical reactions.

1968 Lars Onsager (United States) for his work in thermodynamics.

1969 Odd Hassel (Norway) and Derek H. R. Barton (Great Britain) for work on three-dimensional orientation of molecules.

1970 Luis F. Leloir (Argentina) for his work on the chemical processes in which body sugar is broken down into simple carbohydrates.

1971 Gerhard Herzberg (Canada) for his research in the structure of the molecule.

1972 Christian Boehmer Anfinsen, Stanford Moore, and William H. Stein (United States) for their research on ribonuclease.

1973 Ernst Otto Fischer (West Germany) and Geoffrey Wilkinson (Great Britain) for their work on merging organic and metallic atoms.

1974 Paul J. Flory (United States) for work in macromolecules.

1975 John W. Cornforth (Great Britain) for his study of enzymes, and Vladimir Prelog (Switzerland) for developing systematic rules concerning molecular structure.

1976 William N. Lipscomb, Jr. (United States) for his studies of boranes.

1977 Ilya Prigogine (Belgium) for work in the field of thermodynamics.

1978 Peter Mitchell (Great Britain) for his theory of bioenergetics.

1979 Herbert C. Brown (United States) and Georg Wittig (West Germany) for helping to develop substances that have made possible the mass production of important chemicals.

1980 Walter Gilbert and Paul Berg (United States) and Frederick Sanger (Great Britain) for methods to map the structure and function of DNA.

1981 Kenichi Fukui (Japan) and Roald Hoffmann (United States) applying theories of quantum mechanics to predict the course of chemical reactions.

1982 Aaron Klug (Great Britain) for researching the structure of nucleic acid-protein complexes.

1983 Henry Taube (United States) for discovering the basic mechanism of chemical reactions.

1984 R. Bruce Merrifield (United States) for his research into the uses of proteins.

1985 Herbert A. Hauptman and Jerome Karle (United States) for research on the structure of crystals and crystal molecules.

1986 Dudley R. Herschbach and Yuan T. Lee (United States) and John C. Polanyi (Canada) for their study of how molecules form new substances.

1987 Jean-Marie Lehn (France), Donald J. Cram and Charles J. Pedersen (United States) for pioneering work in supramolecular chemistry.

1988 Johann Deisenhofer, Robert Huber, and Hartmut Michel (West Germany) for studies on proteins involved in photosynthesis.

1989 Thomas R. Cech and Sidney Altman (United States) for discovering that RNA aids chemical reaction in cells.

1990 Elias James Corey (United States) for his retrosynthetic analysis technique.

1991 Richard R. Ernst (Switzerland) for refinements in nuclear magnetic resonance spectroscopy.

1992 Rudolf A. Marcus (United States) for achieving a way to predict certain interactions between molecules in solution.

1993 Kary B. Mullis (United States) for a technique to copy gene fragments, and Michael Smith (Canada) for a method of splicing components onto gene molecules.

1994 George A. Olah (United States) for his research on hydrocarbons.

1995 F. Sherwood Rowland and Mario Molina (United States) and Paul Crutzen (Germany) for identifying the chemical processes that damage Earth's ozone layer.

1996 Robert F. Curl, Jr., and Richard E. Smalley (United States) and Harold W. Kroto (Great Britain) for their discovery of fullerenes.

1997 Paul D. Boyer (United States) and John E. Walker (Great Britain) for showing how all living things make adenosine triphosphate, or ATP, an energy-storing molecule, and Jens C. Skou (Denmark) for discovering an enzyme involved in the chemistry of ATP.

1998 Walter Kohn and John Pople (United States) for developing practical ways of calculating how quantum mechanics affects the properties of molecules and chemical reactions.

1999 Ahmed H. Zewail (Egypt) for demonstrating that a rapid laser technique can show the movement of a molecule's atoms during chemical reaction.

2000 Alan J. Heeger and Alan G. MacDiarmid (United States) and Hideki Shirakawa (Japan) for discovering that plastic is capable of conducting electricity.

2001 William Knowles and Barry Sharpless (United States) and Ryoji Noyori (Japan) for research that helped develop affordable life-saving medications.

2002 John B. Fenn (United States), Koichi Tanaka (Japan), and Kurt Wuethrich (Switzerland) for procedures that identify and analyze proteins.

2003 Peter Agre and Roderick MacKinnon (United States) for their studies of channels in cell walls.

2004 Aaron Ciechanover and Avram Hershko (Israel) and Irwin Rose (United States) for discovering how cells kill unwanted proteins.

2005 Robert H. Grubbs and Richard R. Schrock (United States) and Yves Chauvin (France) for methods to produce drugs and plastics more efficiently and with less harzardous waste.

ECONOMICS

1969 Ragnar Frisch (Norway) and Jan Tinbergen (the Netherlands) for work in econometrics.

1970 Paul A. Samuelson (United States) for work in the scientific analysis of economic theory.

1971 Simon Kuznets (United States) for his concept of using a country's gross national product to determine its economic growth.

1972 Kenneth J. Arrow (United States) and John R. Hicks (Great Britain) for work on general economic equilibrium and welfare theories.

1973 Wassily Leontief (United States) for the "input-output" system of economic analysis.

1974 Gunnar Myrdal (Sweden) and Friedrich von Hayek (Austria) for analysis of the interdependence of economic, social, and institutional phenomena.

1975 Tjalling C. Koopmans (United States) and Leonid V. Kantorovich (Soviet Union) for their contributions to the theory of optimum allocation of resources.

1976 Milton Friedman (United States) for his theories on money.

1977 Bertil Ohlin (Sweden) and James E. Meade (Great Britain) for contributions to the theory of international trade.

1978 Herbert Simon (United States) for work on how economic organizations make decisions.

1979 Sir Arthur Lewis (St. Lucia) and Theodore W. Schultz (United States) for their work on the economic problems of poorer nations.

1980 Lawrence R. Klein (United States) for the creation of econometric models.

1981 James Tobin (United States) for his analyses of financial markets and their effect on how businesses and families use money.

1982 George J. Stigler (United States) for his studies of industrial structures, functioning of markets, and effects of public regulation.

1983 Gerard Debreu (United States) for his research on how prices balance supply with demand.

1984 Sir Richard Stone (Great Britain) for systems for measuring national economies.

1985 Franco Modigliani (United States) for analyses of saving patterns and financial markets.

1986 James McGill Buchanan (United States) for theories on keeping national budgets balanced.

1987 Robert M. Solow (United States) for contributions to the theory of economic growth.

1988 Maurice Allais (France) for theories on market behavior and efficient use of resources.

1989 Trygve Haavelmo (Norway) for work on methods for testing economic theories.

1990 Harry M. Markowitz, William F. Sharpe, and Merton H. Miller (United States) for evaluating the risks of investment.

1991 Ronald H. Coase (Great Britain) for analyzing the role of institutions in the economy.

1992 Gary S. Becker (United States) for his economic theories regarding human behavior.

1993 Robert W. Fogel and Douglass C. North (United States) for applying economic theory and quantitative measures to historical issues.

1994 John F. Nash and John C. Harsanyi (United States) and Reinhard Selten (Germany) for their work in game theory.

1995 Robert E. Lucas (United States) for his economic theories about how human behavior can affect economic models.

1996 James A. Mirrlees (Great Britain) and William Vickrey (United States) for their contributions to the economic theory of incentives in an area of microeconomics that deals with how information affects business decisions.

1997 Robert C. Merton and Myron S. Scholes (United States) for a formula that helps investors price and trade stock options.

1998 Amartya Sen (India) for his research on poverty and economics.

1999 Robert Mundell (Canada) for his work on financial policies and common market theory.

2000 James J. Heckman and Daniel L. McFadden (United States) for developing techniques to analyze the choices people make.

2001 Joseph Stiglitz, George Akerlof, and A. Michael Spence (United States) for their research into the faults of market systems.

2002 Daniel Kahneman and Vernon Smith (United States) for their studies in economic decision making.

2003 Robert Engle (United States) and Clive Granger (Great Britain) for their use of statistical methods for analyzing data.

2004 Finn E. Kydland (Norway) and Edward C. Prescott (United States) for their business cycle research.

2005 Robert J. Aumann (Israel/United States) and Thomas C. Schelling (United States) for using game theories to explain economic and political conflicts.

NOBLE GASES. See NEON AND OTHER NOBLE GASES.

NOISE

Noise is any sound that people find disagreeable or disturbing. Exposure to loud noise can damage hearing. But noise may be harmful even if it is not loud. Prolonged exposure to noise can cause a variety of problems, from increased blood pressure, insomnia, and fatigue to impaired memory and concentration.

Noise intensity is measured in units called **decibels**. The faintest sound that most people can hear—a whisper, for instance—is 0 decibels. Normal conversation at a distance of several feet is about 65 decibels, while shouting is approximately 85 decibels. Prolonged exposure (several hours a day for a long period of time) to noise over 85 decibels can eventually cause hearing loss. Very loud sounds of 120 decibels or more are painful to the ear and can cause immediate and permanent hearing loss.

Noise pollution is a growing problem. Many people are regularly exposed to high sound levels without realizing it. Traffic noise, loud music, car alarms, and the sounds of lawn mowers, power tools, and household appliances are part of our daily environment.

Although there is no way to escape noise pollution completely, noise control is possible. Most environmental noise regulations are established and carried out by local governments. These regulations range from planning housing and transportation systems with sound control in mind to banning leaf blowers and jet skis. In industrial settings, wearing ear-protection devices and adding mufflers to power tools can save workers' hearing and increase safety. Products to help control noise have also been developed, such as building materials that isolate and absorb sound. Electronic devices that emit soothing "white noise" (a mixture of different frequencies of sound waves that sounds like a gentle breeze) are often used to block out unwanted noise and promote relaxation.

Reviewed by ALICE H. SUTER
Consultant, industrial audiology and
community noise

See also EAR; ENVIRONMENT; SOUND AND ULTRASONICS.

NOMADS

Nomads are people who have no permanent homes but travel, instead, from place to place. They do so because they usually live in lands that will not support settled life. Nomads can be found in many parts of the world, particularly in the deserts and sparse grasslands of Africa and Asia. Some also live on the edge of the frozen Arctic region.

Most nomads are herders of livestock. The word "nomad" comes from a Greek word meaning "to pasture," or "feed on grass and other vegetation." Some nomads in parts of Africa and in the tropical rain forests of Southeast Asia get their food by hunting and by gathering wild plants. Some Gypsies in Europe and elsewhere are wandering traders, artisans, or fortune-tellers. However they earn their living, nomads traditionally move from place to place in search of food, work, or pasture for their animals.

Nomads live where it is too hot, too cold, or too dry to permit farming. But hardy plants and sparse grasses grow in some parts of these lands. Grazing animals can live if they keep moving in search of pasture, and people can live if they follow the animals. Nomadic herders move on when their flocks or herds have eaten all the pasture in one area. Or they may move from a drier place to a place where seasonal rains have caused grass to spring up.

Some nomads are part-time farmers, too. In deserts they live in villages or oases for a few months of the year and grow small crops. Then when rains bring grass, they begin the migration. Nomads may cover vast distances in their search for pasture for their livestock. Desert nomads of the Middle East often break camp and move every few days. The Sami of Lapland migrate in spring and fall. The men follow the reindeer from the forests and moss fields outside their winter homes to summer grazing lands near the Arctic Ocean.

Many nomads live in tents. Tents are easy to transport on the animals' backs when it is time to move. Nomads have a few dishes, cooking pots, and clothes. But these belongings, along with blankets or bedrolls, must also be packed. Nomads can have only as many possessions as their animals can carry or haul.

The nomads' animals supply many of the things a nomad family needs to live. Tents, blankets, clothes, and containers are made from the skin of the animals or are spun and woven from the hair. Animals are a source of milk, cheese, and sometimes meat, although the herder cannot often afford to kill an animal for food. Nomads sometimes use animal sinews for thread. At one time, knives were made from animal bones. Nomads are also traders, selling animals and animal products in order to buy food and other goods.

Nomads keep animals suited to the climate. Mongolian herds include yaks, a kind of hairy ox, as well as camels. Bedouins of the Arabian desert were long dependent on the camel, although they raise other animals, too.

Nomad children learn at an early age to help in herding the animals. But they cannot spend much time in school because their families wander. Sometimes teachers may travel with the nomads. Some nomads send their children away to school. Today many people who used to be nomads settle in towns, and in some places the nomadic way of life is disappearing.

Reviewed by DANIEL JACOBSON
Michigan State University

See also DESERTS; GYPSIES; LAPLAND.

Nomads in Mongolia use camels to transport their portable homes (yurts) and other belongings.

NONSENSE RHYMES

To begin with, "nonsense" is a two-faced word. First of all, it means "no sense," the opposite of sense. This kind of nonsense is of no value to anyone. But nonsense can also mean a kind of creative writing—usually verse but sometimes prose—that is written purely for fun. These two basic meanings of nonsense are quite distinct. If people say to you "That's nonsense," they mean that although you are using normal words, the idea those words express is silly or stupid without being funny. In short, they mean that you are making little or no sense when you should be. Very different is the nonsense of inspiration.

Nonsense stories and rhymes ignore rules of logic and common sense. Imaginary creatures and impossible situations are presented quite matter-of-factly. All of this makes nonsense delightful and highly amusing, though we may only partly understand it. The finest nonsense defies complete understanding. Being itself a work of the imagination, it asks imagination on the reader's part.

You do not read nonsense at a glance. You taste it, you savor it, you reread it. The English author Thomas De Quincey once said, "None but a man of extraordinary talent can write first-rate nonsense."

Several well-known examples of nonsense are included in this article. Read them slowly—and read them aloud so that you hear the sound of the words. For some reason, the sound of nonsense is closely related to the look of nonsense. Indeed, certain famous and difficult nonsense verses are only half appreciated if the words are not seen on the printed page. Real nonsense, then—the kind that goes into poems and stories—should be seen as well as heard.

▶ NONSENSE WORDS

Much good nonsense uses plain, ordinary words, but it uses them in an extraordinary way. Other nonsense uses words of the writer's own invention. Outstanding examples of this kind of nonsense rhyme are found in works by the English writer Lewis Carroll. In the poem "Jabberwocky," from *Through the Looking-Glass* (1872), Carroll invents names for totally imaginary creatures such as the Jabberwock and the Bandersnatch. He also creates words by putting existing words together in new ways; for example, "chortle" is a combination of "snort" and "chuckle." Many of these words have become part of our everyday language. A biography of Carroll, with an excerpt from his book *Alice in Wonderland* (1865), can be found in Volume C.

JABBERWOCKY

'Twas brillig, and the slithy toves
Did gyre and gimble in the wabe:
All mimsy were the borogoves,
And the mome raths outgrabe.

"Beware the Jabberwock, my son!
The jaws that bite, the claws that catch!
Beware the Jubjub bird, and shun
The frumious Bandersnatch!"

He took his vorpal sword in hand:
Long time the manxome foe he sought—
So rested he by the Tumtum tree,
And stood awhile in thought.

And, as in uffish thought he stood,
The Jabberwock, with eyes of flame,
Came whiffling through the tulgey wood,
And burbled as it came!

One, two! One, two! And through and through
The vorpal blade went snicker-snack!
He left it dead, and with its head
He went galumphing back.

"And hast thou slain the Jabberwock?
Come to my arms, my beamish boy!
O frabjous day! Callooh! Callay!"
He chortled in his joy.

'Twas brillig, and the slithy toves
Did gyre and gimble in the wabe:
All mimsy were the borogoves,
And the mome raths outgrabe.

LEWIS CARROLL

HABITS OF THE HIPPOPOTAMUS

The hippopotamus is strong
     And huge of head and broad of bustle;
The limbs on which he rolls along
     Are big with hippopotomuscle.

He does not greatly care for sweets
     Like ice cream, apple pie, or custard,
But takes to flavor what he eats
     A little hippopotomustard.

The hippopotamus is true
     To all his principles, and just;
He always tries his best to do
     The things one hippopotomust.

He never rides in trucks or trams,
     In taxicabs or omnibuses,
And so keeps out of traffic jams
     And other hippopotomusses.

ARTHUR GUITERMAN

JELLYFISH STEW

Jellyfish stew,
I'm loony for you,
I dearly adore you,
oh, truly I do,
you're creepy to see,
revolting to chew,
you slide down inside
with a hullabaloo.

You're soggy, you're smelly,
you taste like shampoo,
you bog down my belly
with oodles of goo,
yet I would glue noodles
and prunes to my shoe,
for one oozy spoonful
of jellyfish stew.

JACK PRELUTSKY

Edward Lear, another English writer, was also a master at creating nonsense words. One doubts at once if Lear's Tiniskoop-hills, Gromboolian plain, Twangum tree, or Chankly Bore exist or ever existed. But "scratchifaction" is clearly a combination of "scratch" and "satisfaction." Since most of us do scratch to relieve an itch, "scratchifaction" is a very satisfying word, all nonsense aside.

Writers since Carroll and Lear have invented nonsense words—scroobious, pilderpips, meloobious, Gulliby, Tickletoeteaser, and Anagazander, among many others. The curious spelling and twisted look of these words, as well as their sound, add to their charm. The wealth of unusual place-names in the world has also helped nonsense writers, and such real places as Antigonish and Passamaquoddy have found their way into nonsense verse.

▶ **LIMERICKS**

Without question, the most popular form of nonsense verse is the limerick, which Ed-

ELETELEPHONY

Once there was an elephant,
Who tried to use the telephant—
No! no! I mean an elephone
Who tried to use the telephone—
(Dear me! I am not certain quite
That even now I've got it right.)

Howe'er it was, he got his trunk
Entangled in the telephunk;
The more he tried to get it free,
The louder buzzed the telephee—
(I fear I'd better drop the song
Of elephop and telephong!)

LAURA E. RICHARDS

THE REASON FOR THE PELICAN

The reason for the pelican
Is difficult to see:
His beak is clearly larger
Than there's any need to be.

It's not to bail a boat with—
He doesn't own a boat.
Yet everywhere he takes himself
He has that beak to tote.

It's not to keep his wife in—
His wife has got one, too.
It's not a scoop for eating soup.
It's not an extra shoe.

It isn't quite for anything.
And yet you realize
It's really quite a splendid beak
In quite a splendid size.

JOHN CIARDI

ANTIGONISH

As I was going up the stair
I met a man who wasn't there!
He wasn't there again today!
I wish, I *wish* he'd stay away.

HUGHES MEARNS

ward Lear popularized, although he did not invent it.

The limerick consists of five lines, of which the last line always rhymes with the first two, and the third and fourth lines with each other. The rhyme words are frequently distorted or else combine two or three words into one. The limerick is somewhat flexible, however, in that lines one, two, and five may have from eight to eleven syllables each, and lines three and four may have from four or five to seven syllables.

The limerick looks easy to write, but it is not. In all literature, among thousands and thousands of limericks, there are probably not 200 genuine, flawless examples.

▶ HISTORY OF NONSENSE

Where did nonsense begin? No one knows for sure. There is much satire but little nonsense written in Latin and Greek. It is doubtful if any was created in the ancient cultures of Arabia, Persia, or India. On the other hand, there is strong evidence of nonsense

I wish that my room had a floor;
I don't care so much for a door,
    But this walking around
    Without touching the ground
Is getting to be such a bore!
                    GELETT BURGESS

There was a young lady of Woosester
Who usest to crow like a roosester;
    She usest to climb
    Two trees at a time,
But her sisester usest to boosest her.
                    ANONYMOUS

There was an old man with a beard,
Who said, "It is just as I feared—
    Two owls and a hen,
    Four larks and a wren
Have all built their nests in my beard!"
                    EDWARD LEAR

There was an old man of Peru
Who dreamed he was eating his shoe.
    He woke in the night
    In a terrible fright,
And found it was perfectly true.
                    ANONYMOUS

LIMERICKS

verse and prose in Europe—in Cervantes' *Don Quixote* (1605; 1615) and in Rostand's *Cyrano de Bergerac* (1897), for example. But there is a closer and earlier connection between the nonsense of the Norse countries and Scotland and England. Nonsense, as we know it, does not rove back much further than the 1600's. There is no nonsense in Chaucer, but the plays of Shakespeare are flecked with nonsense—Act IV, Scene 1 of *The Merry Wives of Windsor* (1600–01) is all nonsense.

But above all, the base of English and American nonsense verse is firmly rooted in nursery rhymes, tongue twisters, and counting-out rhymes. Most English-speaking people remember or recognize "Hickory, Dickory, Dock," "Mary, Mary, Quite Contrary," and "Sing a Song of Sixpence." Many people grow up chanting tongue twisters ("Peter Piper picked a peck of pickled peppers") or counting-out rhymes ("One for the money, two for the show …").

Besides Lear and Carroll, some other masters of nonsense are Sir W. S. Gilbert, L. Frank Baum, Hilaire Belloc, Laura E. Richards, James Thurber, and Dr. Seuss. Baum's *The Wonderful Wizard of Oz* (1900) and its sequels are nonsense in character if not in language. Thurber's fairy tales, including *The 13 Clocks* (1950) and *The Wonderful O* (1957), are sheer nonsense for those of any age. Other writers who have left a mark with nonsense prose are Stephen Leacock, Charles E. Carryl, Robert Benchley, Ring Lardner, Frank Sullivan, and A. A. Milne.

"Whatever the journey may be," said Walter de la Mare, "the wayfarer must bring to it at least as much as it offers." Bring yourself, then, to the reading of nonsense rhymes. They are worth the trip.

                    DAVID MCCORD
                    Author, *Take Sky*

See also TONGUE TWISTERS.

NORMANDY INVASION. See WORLD WAR II.

NORSEMEN. See VIKINGS.

NORSE MYTHOLOGY

Norse mythology is the mythology of the Scandinavian (Norse) peoples of the Middle Ages. It is also, in part, the mythology of the Germanic peoples of the same time, but the mythology survived longest and was best preserved in Scandinavia, particularly Iceland.

▶ SOURCES

The most important sources for Norse mythology are two books from Iceland. The *Poetic Edda* is a collection of oral poems about the Norse gods and heroes that was first written down in the 1200's. The *Prose Edda* was written by Snorri Sturluson, an Icelandic historian, sometime between 1220 and 1230. Snorri's book was written as a guide to the poetry of the **skalds**, court poets who used mythological images and stories in their verse. Snorri, a Christian, believed that the myths were not really about gods but about great people from ancient times, who were made into gods by later people.

Norse myths are also found in the first book of the *Heimskringla*, a history of the Norwegian kings written by Snorri; in Saxo Grammaticus's *Gesta Danorum*, a history of Denmark written in Latin some time in the 1200's; and in many of the skaldic poems.

Most of Scandinavia was converted to Christianity by the end of the 1100's. Our knowledge of Norse mythology is affected by the fact that the writers who preserved the old stories were Christian. Their writings do not explain pagan beliefs, and so we know very little about how the Norse worshiped their gods. Also, some of the poems and stories appear to have been influenced by Christianity, so the myths that we know may differ from those told by pre-Christian Norse people.

Some of the stories survived in folk beliefs and ballads until recent times. For example,

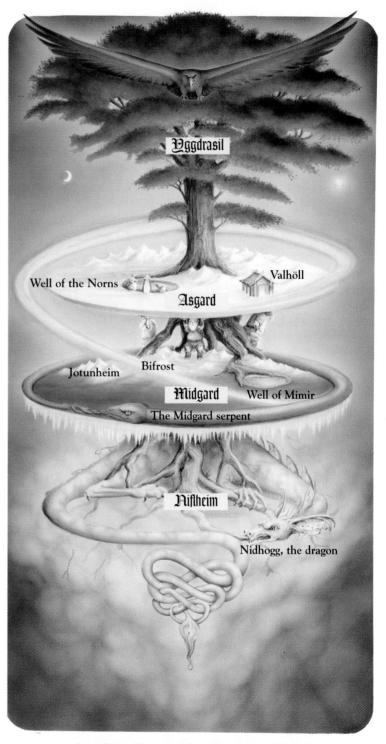

According to Norse mythology, the world is divided into separate realms, including Asgard, the home of the gods, and Midgard, the abode of humans. Yggdrasil, the World Tree, grows through all the realms.

ballads sung in the Faroe Islands have Norse gods and heroes as characters. Many of the stories about dwarfs, elves, trolls, and other supernatural creatures told in modern Scandinavia have their origins in Norse mythology.

▶ THE BEGINNING OF THE WORLD

In the beginning, say the *Prose Edda* and other sources, there were two regions: the fiery realm of Muspell in the south and the wintry realm of Niflheim in the north. In be-

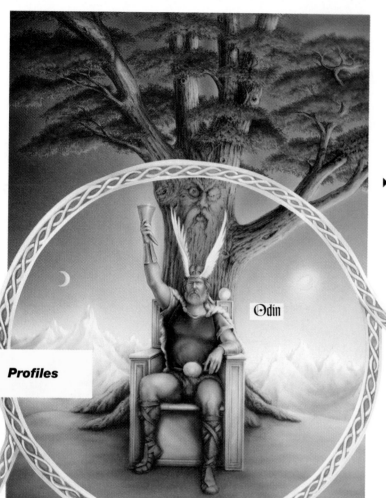

Odin

Profiles

and humans. Heimdall can hear grass grow and can see for more than 100 miles by day or night. He is said to need less sleep than a bird. When his horn is sounded, it can be heard throughout the world. He is Loki's greatest enemy, and the two kill one another at Ragnarok.

Loki is the strangest of the Norse gods. In many ways he is like the trickster in North American Indian folktales, a sociable character who gets the gods both into and out of trouble. He can change his shape to do mischief or help the gods. There is often a playful quality to Loki's behavior. He can be sarcastic and disrespectful of the gods, too, as in the poem called the *Lokasenna*, in which he recites all the gossip he knows about the gods. The gods punish Loki for the murder of Baldr, chaining him to three large rocks and causing a venomous snake to drip poison on him. Loki eventually breaks free from his bonds to lead the enemies of the gods against them in the battle at the end of the world.

Baldr was the most beautiful of the gods, beloved for his goodness. The most famous myth about Baldr is the story of his death. After Baldr had dreams foretelling his death, Frigg got pledges from all things on earth that they would never harm Baldr. But she neglected to ask one small plant, the mistletoe. The gods then made a game of throwing weapons at Baldr, because they knew they could not harm him. But Loki tricked the blind god Hoder into throwing a dart made of mistletoe at Baldr, which immediately struck and killed him. The gods, grief stricken at Baldr's death, asked Hel, goddess of the realm of the dead, to return him to the living. Hel said that if everything on earth would weep for Baldr, he could come back to life. All the earth mourned for Baldr except for one old hag, who the gods believed was Loki in disguise. Because she would not mourn, Baldr had to stay in the world of the dead. He would come back to life at the rebirth of the world after Ragnarok.

Freyja was an important Norse fertility goddess. She was the most beautiful of the goddesses and had a wonderful necklace known as the Brisingamen (the Brisings' necklace). Although there is a reference in a poem to Loki stealing the necklace, the story has not survived.

Freyr, like most of the Vanir, was associated with fertility. Horses were sometimes sacrificed to Freyr and eaten. Freyr once sat in the high seat of Odin, the seat that allowed Odin to see all the world. He saw a beautiful woman he wanted to marry. His servant Skirnir offered to make a journey to the woman and arrange the marriage in exchange for Freyr's sword. Freyr gave Skirnir his sword and for that reason does not have it to fight with at Ragnarok.

Heimdall is a mysterious god about whom little is known. He is the watchman of the gods and the guardian of Bifrost, the bridge between the realms of gods

Niord was the father of Freyr and Freyja. He was a god of sea, wind, and fire. Like Thor, he is appealed to when fair weather is needed for fishing and

Freyja

tween was an empty space called the Ginnungagap. Where the heat and cold met, a giant, Ymir, was created, who was the father of humans and giants. Next, a cow called Audhumla came into being, whose milk fed Ymir. As the cow licked the salty ice of Niflheim, a man came forth, who was called Buri.

Buri had a son called Bor, who was the father of the god Odin. Odin and his two brothers killed Ymir and created the world from his body. From Ymir's blood they made the seas, from his skin the land, and from his bones and teeth the rocks. From Ymir's skull they made the vault of the sky, which was supported by four dwarfs—Austri, Vestri, Sudri, and Nordri. The modern English words *east*, *west*, *south*, and *north* are related to these names.

The three sons of Bor also created the first man and woman, from two logs they found on the seashore. The first god gave them life, the second gave them consciousness, and the third gave them their senses. From this man, called Ask, and woman, called Embla, are descended the human race.

The world in Norse mythology is a flat circle surrounded by ocean. The *Prose Edda* tells us that Asgard, the home of the gods, Midgard, the home of humans, and Jotunheim, the home of the giants, are all in different parts of this circle. The abodes of the gods and humans are connected by the rainbow

sea voyages. Niord got his wife in this way: The giant Thiassi kidnapped the goddess Idunn, guardian of the apples that kept the gods young. With Loki's help, the gods trapped and killed Thiassi and so got Idunn and her apples back. But Thiassi's daughter Skadi put on her armor and came to the gods demanding payment for her father's death. The gods allowed her to choose one of them as her husband, but she could see only their feet when choosing. Skadi selected an attractive pair of feet, assuming that they must belong to Baldr, the handsomest of the gods, but they were Niord's feet. The couple agreed to alternate between their homes, spending nine nights in Niord's home by the sea and nine nights at Skadi's dwelling in the mountains. But each hated the other's home, and eventually they parted.

Odin is the most mysterious and powerful of the Norse gods. He is the oldest of the Æsir, and most of them are his children. He is one-eyed, having given an eye to drink from the well of Mimir in order to gain wisdom. He once allowed him-self to be hanged as a sacrifice so that he could gain knowledge from the dead. As a god of war, Odin often guarantees victory, but he is unpredictable, frequently withdrawing his protection from warriors at the height of a battle. Those who die are brought to Valhöll; they form the army that will fight for Odin at Ragnarok, the final battle. Odin is also the god of poetry and of runes, the characters of the ancient Germanic alphabet. His wife Frigg is said to know men's destinies.

Sif, Thor's wife, is known mainly through a story about the gifts dwarfs made for the gods. One morning Sif awoke to find that Loki had cut off her beautiful golden hair. Thor was about to kill him, but Loki promised to get the dwarfs to make hair of real gold for her. These dwarfs also made a ship for Freyr and a spear, called Gungnir, for Odin. Loki challenged them to make more things and wagered his head that they could not succeed. The dwarfs then made a boar with golden bristles, the gold ring Draupnir, and the hammer Mjollnir, which was to become Thor's weapon. Because Loki had distracted the dwarfs in order to win his bet, Mjollnir's handle was too short, though the gods judged it the most important of the gifts. Loki lost his wager, but the dwarfs did not cut off his head because he persuaded them that, although they had a right to his head, they could not touch his neck.

Thor is the second most powerful of the Norse gods. People appealed to him for protection and help in times of trouble—in famines and bad weather—and for guidance in making decisions. In the myths, Thor is often portrayed as rather stupid, though possessing immense physical strength, which he uses to protect the gods from the attacks of the giants. For example, when the gods discover that the mysterious smith they hired to build Valhöll is a giant, it is Thor who kills him. Thor's weapon is his hammer, Mjollnir, which is often stolen. In one story, a giant who has stolen the hammer will give it back only if he gets Freyja as his wife. Loki convinces Thor to disguise himself as Freyja in order to get his hammer back. The giant, who is even more stupid than Thor, does not recognize Thor in his disguise—even though Thor's great red beard is in plain view. Thor is able to get his hammer back and kill the giant with it.

Tyr is the bravest and most heroic of the gods according to the *Poetic Edda*. People prayed to him to bring them victory in battles. Many of the attributes of Tyr are like those of Odin, leading scholars to believe that Odin replaced Tyr as the main god in Norse mythology. The best-known story about Tyr is how he lost his hand. The gods wanted to leash the great wolf Fenrir but found he could break even the strongest chains. Finally, the dwarfs made a magic leash, and the gods tricked Fenrir into testing it. The leash was so slender that Fenrir was suspicious and would allow it to be put around his neck only if one of the gods would put his hand in Fenrir's mouth as a guarantee that they were telling the truth. Only Tyr would risk his hand. When Fenrir discovered that he had been tricked, he bit off Tyr's hand.

Amulet (protective charm) in the shape of Thor's short-handled hammer.

some of our modern English names for the days of the week come from Norse mythology? The names of the Norse gods as they are shown in this article have equivalent forms in Old English, the ancient form of the English we use today. In Old English, Tyr is Tiw, Odin is Woden, and Thor is Thunor. (The goddess Frigg has the same name in Old English as in Norse.) Several days of the week were named in honor of these gods and goddess.

The modern English word "Tuesday" comes from the Old English *Tiwesdæg* (Tiw's day). "Wednesday" is from *Wodnesdæg* (Woden's day), "Thursday" is from *Thunresdæg* (Thunor's day), and "Friday" is from *Frigesdæg* (Frigg's day).

Thus, although it was replaced long ago by other practices and beliefs, Norse mythology in one small way remains with us—literally—to this day.

bridge Bifrost, guarded by the god Heimdall. The Midgard serpent Iormungand surrounds it all with its body. Below the world is the realm of the dead, called Niflheim (or mistland or Hel), ruled by the goddess Hel.

At the center of the world is a great ash tree, Yggdrasil, whose roots reach through all the abodes of the gods and men. A mighty eagle perches at the top of the tree. At its base the gods hold their councils. Beneath one of the roots is the well of Mimir, which gives wisdom to whoever drinks from it. Beneath another is the well of the Norns, three maidens who control human destiny. Like everything else in the world of Norse mythology, Yggdrasil is doomed to die. Stags eat its leaves, while the dragon Nidhogg and other serpents tear at its roots. The Norns water Yggdrasil from their well each day, repairing the damage. But at the great battle (Ragnarok) at the end of the world, Yggdrasil will fall.

Dwarf

▶ GODS AND GODDESSES

Most of the Norse gods belong to two races: the **Æsir**, which include Odin and his wife Frigg, Thor, Thor's wife Sif, Tyr, Baldr, and Heimdall, and the **Vanir**, including Niord and his children Frevr and Frevia. The Æsir and the Vanir fought each other until they finally tired of the fighting and made peace.

Another god, Loki, is neither Æsir nor Vanir but is the son of giants. He is often at the center of the adventures of the gods. Loki's children are the wolf Fenrir, the Midgard serpent, and Hel, the goddess of the dead. The feature on pages 278 and 279 describes these gods and some of the best-known stories about them.

▶ OTHER SUPERNATURAL BEINGS

Other creatures inhabit the world besides gods and humans. They include elves, dwarfs, and giants, and Norns and Valkyries.

Elves are divided into two kinds. The light elves are a people of the sky and forests. They are talented musicians, and their music has supernatural powers. The dark elves live underground and often cause sickness or injuries to humans.

Dwarfs are secretive creatures who live underground. Expert metalworkers, they make the weapons, jewelry, and other treasures of the gods. Dwarfs sometimes have magical powers; for example, they are able to change their shape. If forced to make an object, they will put a curse on it, and their curses are very powerful.

Giants of Norse mythology are the main enemies of the gods, although they sometimes marry gods. While they are often portrayed as stupid, they can be intelligent and may possess magical powers. The giant Utgard-Loki, for example, is able to trick Thor into thinking the gigantic Midgard serpent is a common house cat. Giants can be dangerous foes, but the gods always win in the end.

Norns, three maidens who live by a well at the base of the ash tree Yggdrasil, can foretell the futures of all humans. Their names are Urdr (Fate), Verdandi (Being), and Skuld (Necessity). Other Norns visit humans, elves, and dwarfs when they are born and shape their destinies. Some of the Norns are descended from the Æsir, some from elves, and some from dwarfs.

Valkyries are divine maidens who gather the souls of the dead from the battlefield and escort them to Odin's enormous hall, called Valhöll (often called Valhalla). There the slain warriors fight during the day and feast at night until they are needed in Odin's army for the battle at Ragnarok.

▶ **HEROES**

The last part of the *Poetic Edda* tells the story, or saga, of the Volsung family and its great heroes Sigmund and Sigurd. The story is told more fully in a saga called the *Volsunga Saga*. Sigmund has a special destiny because he is the only person able to pull out a sword that has been thrust into a huge tree by Odin. The sword has magical properties, and with it Sigmund is victorious in all his battles. Finally, in one battle, Odin appears and shatters the sword, enabling Sigmund's enemies to kill him. Sigmund's son Sigurd inherits the pieces of the sword, which are welded back together when he comes of age. Sigurd kills a dragon with the sword and goes on to have many other adventures. In German legend, Sigurd is called Siegfried, and his story is told in the *Nibelungenlied*, a famous German epic of the Middle Ages.

▶ **THE END OF THE WORLD**

Norse mythology is unusual in depicting a world in which the gods are doomed to die in the end. The best version of this story is told in an extraordinary poem called *Völuspá* ("the prophecy of the seeress") from the *Poetic Edda*. It is in these final days that Loki and the great wolf Fenrir lead an army of giants against Asgard and the army of Odin. At Ragnarok, the terrible battle that follows, Thor kills the Midgard serpent but is killed by its venom. Heimdall and Loki kill each other. Odin is swallowed by Fenrir, though his son Vidar kills the wolf. Freyr, who is without his good sword, dies in the battle. In the end, the gods and giants are all slain, and the world is burned up by the fire giant Surtr. But a new world is born, repopulated by the descendants of the old gods and two humans who survive the apocalypse. Baldr returns from the dead, and life for the gods and men begins anew. Some scholars think that the Norse story of the end of the world and its rebirth was influenced by the Christian story of the apocalypse.

DAVID E. GAY
Folklore Institute, Indiana University

Ragnarok

NORTH AMERICA

North America is one of the two continents of the Western Hemisphere. (South America is the other.) It is bordered by the Pacific Ocean on the west; the Arctic Ocean on the north; the Atlantic Ocean, including the Caribbean Sea, on the east; and South America on the south.

North America is made up of three large countries and many smaller ones. The three largest countries, in order of area, are Canada, the United States, and Mexico. Belize, Costa Rica, El Salvador, Guatemala, Honduras, Nicaragua, and Panama are the nations forming Central America, which is generally considered part of North America. Numerous islands are also considered part of North America. These include Greenland, a vast territory of Denmark; and the islands of the Caribbean Sea, most of which are independent countries.

North America is the world's third largest continent in area, after Asia and Africa. It ranks fourth in population, after Asia, Europe, and Africa.

The first inhabitants of North America are thought to have arrived there from Asia some 40,000 years ago, crossing a land bridge, which then linked Siberia and Alaska, over what is now the Bering Strait. These people were the ancestors of the American Indians.

Vikings probably visited North America about A.D. 1000. But otherwise there was little known contact between North America and Europe until Christopher Columbus' voyage to the Caribbean in 1492. To Europeans, Columbus had discovered a new world. Over the next century and a half, a number of European nations founded settlements there. Spain, Britain, and France were the major European colonizers, although Dutch, Swedish, and other settlements were founded as well. The Spanish first established themselves in the Caribbean islands. They went on to conquer the great Indian civiliza-

The panorama of North America: *Below from left to right:* The lush, tropical coastline of Puerto Rico; a man from the Caribbean islands in carnival dress; the towering Rocky Mountains, which extend across much of western North America. *Opposite page, clockwise from left:* An overview of the junction of the Colorado and Green rivers in Utah; a parade in New York City's Chinatown; a polar bear and cub, whose habitat is the continent's far north; an expressway in Oakland, California; a sculpture of an Indian warrior, part of the ruins of the ancient Maya civilization at Chichén Itzá, Mexico.

tions of what are now Mexico and Central America, then expanded northward into parts of the present-day United States.

The chief French and British settlements were in what are now Canada and the United States, the French having founded fur-trading posts in the St. Lawrence Valley and explored the Great Lakes and the Mississippi River. The United States developed out of 13 separate British colonies lying along the eastern coast of North America. Britain, France, and the Netherlands also colonized islands in the Caribbean.

This European heritage is still evident in North America, especially in its languages and culture. North Americans, however, are a mixture of many different peoples—descendants of the original Indians, or native Americans; the first colonists; blacks brought from Africa as slaves; and immigrants from nearly every corner of the world. For more information on the history of North America, see the articles on the individual countries of the continent.

▶ THE LAND

On the map, North America looks roughly like a triangular kite, with Central America as its tail. It is widest in the north and narrowest at the Isthmus of Panama. Its greatest length from north to south is about 5,300 miles (8,500 kilometers). Its greatest width from east to west is about 4,000 miles (6,400 kilometers). In area, North America is about half the size of Asia. It is about twice as large as Europe.

The North American landscape is one of enormous variety, with great rivers, towering mountains, dense forests, rugged plateaus, and broad stretches of plains. It has areas of fertile soil and rich mineral resources. At the same time, some areas of the conti-

The enormously varied landscape of North America includes vast areas of open plains (*above*), which form the heartland of the United States and Canada; such forbidding deserts as Death Valley (*far left*), the lowest point on the continent; and the dense, tropical rain forests of Central America (*left*).

nent, particularly in northern Canada and Greenland, are too cold for cultivation, and others, especially in the southwestern United States and northern Mexico, are desert.

In all, about half of the United States is suitable for agriculture. Canada's farmland lies mainly in its southern region. In Mexico and Central America, much of the fertile land is limited to the narrow coastal plains, the plateaus, and the valleys lying between the mountains.

Geographical Features

Geographically, North America can be divided into a number of different regions. In this article, four major physical regions will be discussed: the North American Cordillera in the west, the Appalachian Highlands in the east, the Great Central Plain in the vast interior of the continent, and the Canadian Shield in the north and northeast.

The North American Cordillera. This is an extensive mountain system extending across most of western North America. The Rocky Mountains make up the greater part of the cordillera. It also includes the Alaska Range, the Coast Mountains, the Cascade Range, the Sierra Nevada, and the mountains of the Sierra Madre.

The Rocky Mountains span an area of about 3,000 miles (4,800 kilometers). The great ridge of the Rockies, known as the Continental Divide, separates river systems that flow to opposite sides of the continent. Many of the ranges in the Rockies are high and particularly rugged, with elevations that frequently exceed 14,000 feet (4,300 meters). See the article on the Rocky Mountains in Volume Q-R.

The Alaska Range stretches in a great arc through south central Alaska. Its major peak, Mount McKinley, which rises to 20,320 feet (6,194 meters), is the highest point in North

America. The Coast Mountains extend south from the Alaska Range and include Mounts Logan, St. Elias, Luciana, and King. The Cascade Range reaches from British Columbia to California, where it meets the Sierra Nevada. Both the Cascades and the Sierra Nevada are noted for their scenic beauty. Mount Whitney is the highest peak in the Sierras.

The Sierra Madre is the chief mountain system of Mexico. It includes the Sierra Madre Occidental, the Sierra Madre Oriental, and the Sierra Madre del Sur. These main ranges of the Sierra Madre enclose a great central plateau containing many smaller ranges and numerous depressions. South of Mexico City is an east-west line of lofty volcanoes, including Citlaltepetl (or Pico de Orizaba), which rises to 18,700 feet (5,700 meters) and is the highest in the Sierra Madre system.

The Appalachian Highlands. This region consists of a broad plateau with several mountain ranges. The plateau extends southwest from the Gulf of St. Lawrence to central Alabama. Much of the eastern part of the highlands is occupied by the Piedmont, an area of gently rolling to hilly land that descends eastward to the Atlantic Coastal Plain. Major ranges in the Appalachian Highlands include the Green Mountains in Vermont, the White Mountains in Maine and New Hampshire, and the Blue Ridge, which runs from southern Pennsylvania to northern Georgia.

The highest point in the Appalachians is Mount Mitchell, in North Carolina, which

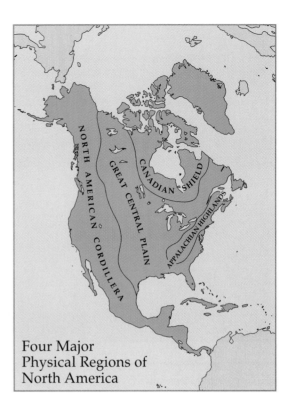

Four Major Physical Regions of North America

rises to 6,684 feet (2,037 meters). The western part of the highlands consists largely of a lower, rough plateau.

The Great Central Plain. This enormous plain lies between the cordillera on the west and the Appalachians on the east. A low ridge that extends from Newfoundland to the

Many of the islands of the Caribbean Sea, such as the U.S. Virgin Islands, seen here, are of volcanic origin. The sea takes its name from the Carib Indians.

One of the major waterways of North America, the Mississippi River flows across the central part of the United States, before emptying into the Gulf of Mexico.

Rocky Mountains divides it into northern and southern sections.

North of the ridge, the land slopes gradually to the north and northeast and is generally low and quite level. In the extreme northern portion, the land is swampy and consists of tundra, or frozen plain. To the south the central plain is further divided by the Mississippi River into two unequal regions. The eastern region is well watered and composed largely of low and level prairie. The western region is much drier and rises from the Mississippi to the foothills of the Rockies.

Stretching southward from Texas into Mexico is a coastal plain that borders the Gulf of Mexico. This Gulf Coastal Plain reaches its widest extent on the Yucatán Peninsula of Mexico.

The Canadian Shield. Extending over much of eastern and northern Canada is a distinct geological formation known as the Canadian Shield (or Laurentian Shield). Shaped roughly like a saucer, it surrounds Hudson Bay and the nearby lowlands. The Canadian Shield contains the oldest and hardest rocks in North America. Elevations are generally below 2,000 feet (600 meters) but may exceed 5,000 feet (1,500 meters) in Labrador. The action of glaciers has pockmarked the region with numerous lakes. It also has many bogs and swamps, called muskegs.

The Great Smoky Mountains (*above*) are part of the Appalachian Highlands region of North America. Beavertail cactus, century plant, brittlebush, and cholla (*left*) are typical desert vegetation found in the southwestern United States and northern Mexico.

North America has more lakes than any other continent. Patzcuaro, one of Mexico's highest lakes, lies at an elevation of 6,706 feet (2,044 meters) above sea level. The lake is within the homeland of the Tarascan Indians, who fish from simple dugouts employing traditional butterfly nets.

Rivers and Lakes

River Systems. North America has five great river systems: Arctic, Atlantic, Gulf, Pacific, and inland.

The chief rivers of the Arctic system are the Mackenzie, the Saskatchewan, and the Nelson. In the Atlantic system, the major river is the St. Lawrence, which drains the region of the Great Lakes. Other important rivers of this system are the Connecticut, Hudson, Susquehanna, James, and Potomac. The Gulf system includes the great Mississippi, with all its tributaries; the Rio Grande, which forms most of the boundary between the United States and Mexico; and the Colorado. See the article on the Mississippi in Volume M.

Of the streams flowing directly into the Pacific, the Columbia and the Frazer are the most important. The inland river system consists of largely intermittent streams that do not drain into the sea.

Lakes. North America has more lakes than any other continent. Most are found in the Great Central Plains. The five Great Lakes, four of which are shared by the United States and Canada, are the largest bodies of water in North America. Lake Superior, the largest of the Great Lakes, is the world's largest freshwater lake. Other major lakes, all in Canada, are Great Bear Lake, Great Slave Lake, Lake Athabasca, and Lake Winnipeg. See the article on the Great Lakes in Volume G.

The northeastern part of the continent has numerous smaller lakes, of which the best known are Lake Nipissing in Ontario, the Finger Lakes in New York, and Moosehead Lake in Maine. Great Salt Lake in Utah is the largest lake in western North America. Other western lakes—Lake Cheland in Washington, Crater Lake in Oregon, and Lake Tahoe in California—are noted for their beauty. Lake Chapala is the largest lake in Mexico; and Lake Nicaragua in Nicaragua is the largest of Central America's lakes.

Climate

Because of its size, the extent of its latitude, and the great differences in elevation,

North America's climate ranges from polar in the north to tropical in the south. In the extreme north, the seas remain frozen for much of the year.

The Great Central Plain is the continent's most productive agricultural region, yielding large quantities of wheat and other grains.

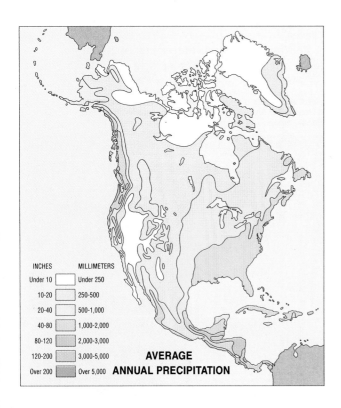

INCHES	MILLIMETERS	
Under 10		Under 250
10-20		250-500
20-40		500-1,000
40-80		1,000-2,000
80-120		2,000-3,000
120-200		3,000-5,000
Over 200		Over 5,000

AVERAGE ANNUAL PRECIPITATION

INDEX TO NORTH AMERICA PHYSICAL MAP

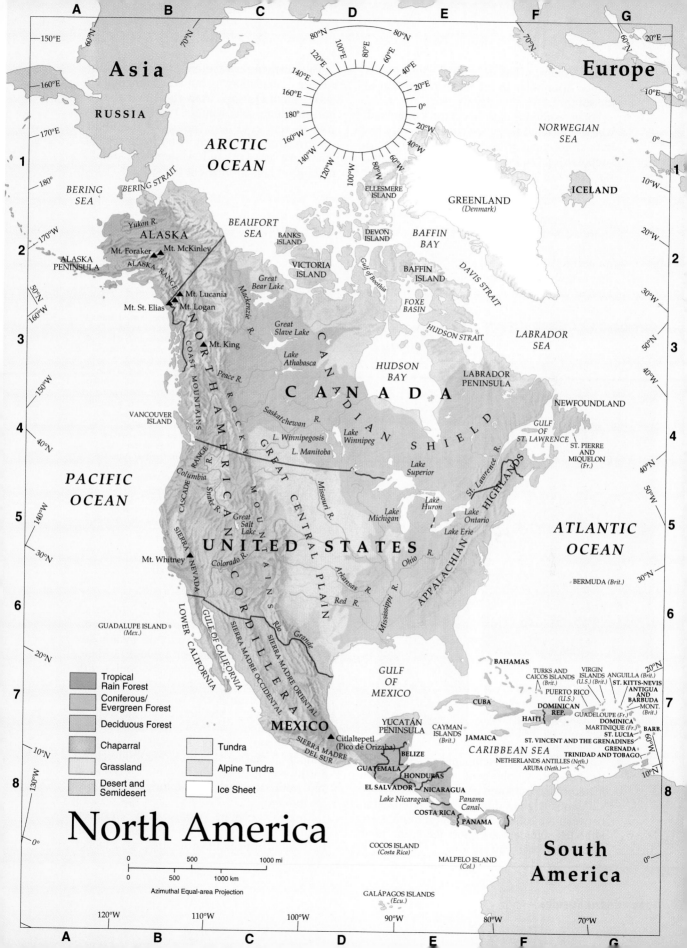

North America

Asia
RUSSIA

Europe

BERING
SEA

ARCTIC
OCEAN

NORWEGIAN
SEA

ICELAND

ELLESMERE
ISLAND

GREENLAND
(Denmark)

BEAUFORT
SEA

BANKS
ISLAND

DEVON
ISLAND

BAFFIN
BAY

Yukon R.
ALASKA

▲ Mt. Foraker ▲ Mt. McKinley
ALASKA RANGE

ALASKA
PENINSULA

VICTORIA
ISLAND

BAFFIN
ISLAND

DAVIS
STRAIT

Great
Bear Lake

Gulf of Boothia

▲ Mt. Lucania
Mt. St. Elias ▲ ▲ Mt. Logan

Mackenzie R.

Great
Slave Lake

FOXE
BASIN

HUDSON STRAIT

LABRADOR
SEA

▲ Mt. King

Lake
Athabasca

C A N A D I A N   S H I E L D

LABRADOR
PENINSULA

Peace R.

C A N A D A

Saskatchewan R.

HUDSON
BAY

NEWFOUNDLAND

VANCOUVER
ISLAND

L. Winnipegosis

Lake
Winnipeg

GULF OF
ST. LAWRENCE

ST. PIERRE
AND
MIQUELON
(Fr.)

L. Manitoba

Columbia R.

Lake
Superior

St. Lawrence R.

PACIFIC
OCEAN

Great
Salt Lake

Snake R.

Missouri R.

Lake
Huron

Lake
Michigan

Lake
Ontario
Lake Erie

ATLANTIC
OCEAN

Mt. Whitney ▲

Colorado R.

G R E A T   C E N T R A L   P L A I N

Arkansas R.

Ohio R.

APPALACHIAN

BERMUDA (Brit.)

U N I T E D   S T A T E S

Red R.

Mississippi R.

GUADALUPE ISLAND
(Mex.)

Rio Grande

GULF
OF
MEXICO

BAHAMAS

TURKS AND
CAICOS ISLANDS
(Brit.)

VIRGIN
ISLANDS
(U.S.) (Brit.)

ANGUILLA (Brit.)
ST. KITTS-NEVIS

ANTIGUA
AND
BARBUDA
(Brit.)

PUERTO RICO
(U.S.)

MEXICO

Citlaltepetl ▲
(Pico de Orizaba)

YUCATÁN
PENINSULA

CUBA

DOMINICAN
REP.

HAITI

CAYMAN
ISLANDS
(Brit.)

JAMAICA

GUADELOUPE (Fr.)
DOMINICA

MONT.
(Brit.)

MARTINIQUE (Fr.)
ST. LUCIA

BARB.

SIERRA MADRE
DEL SUR

BELIZE

ST. VINCENT AND THE GRENADINES

GRENADA

GUATEMALA

HONDURAS

CARIBBEAN SEA

NETHERLANDS ANTILLES (Neth.)
ARUBA (Neth.)

TRINIDAD AND TOBAGO

EL SALVADOR

NICARAGUA

Lake Nicaragua

Panama Canal

COSTA RICA

PANAMA

COCOS ISLAND
(Costa Rica)

MALPELO ISLAND
(Col.)

**South
America**

GALÁPAGOS ISLANDS
(Ecu.)

Legend

- Tropical Rain Forest
- Coniferous/ Evergreen Forest
- Deciduous Forest
- Chaparral
- Grassland
- Desert and Semidesert
- Tundra
- Alpine Tundra
- Ice Sheet

Scale

0 — 500 — 1000 mi
0 — 500 — 1000 km
Azimuthal Equal-area Projection

North America has a varied climate that ranges from polar in the north to tropical in the south.

Polar conditions exist in central Greenland, which is covered by an ice cap and where the temperature never rises above freezing. A subpolar, or tundra, climate is found in the far northern parts of Canada and most of Alaska. Winters here are long and severe, and summers are short. Snow remains on the ground for much of the year. See the article on Greenland in Volume G.

The northeastern United States and southeastern Canada have a humid continental climate. Summers vary from short and cool to hot and long, and winters from moderately cold to very cold. The climate of the southeastern United States is humid subtropical. Summers are hot and winters are usually mild. Rain falls throughout the year.

North America's wild animal life is as varied as its climate. The stately elk (*left*) makes its home just below the northern tundra. The bald eagle (*far left*) is also found mainly in the northern reaches of the continent, usually near water, since fish makes up a large part of its diet. The colorfully plumaged scarlet macaw (*below*) lives in the rain forests of Central America. The timber wolf (*opposite page*) once roamed over much of North America but is now limited to Canada and to Alaska and a few other areas of the United States.

The interior of North America has a continental climate, marked by hot summers and cold winters, with a wide range in temperature between the two seasons. A polar continental, or taiga, climate occurs just south of the subpolar region, with equally great differences of temperature between the coldest and warmest months. But although summers are short there, the hours of sunshine each day are long.

Most of the western interior of the continent either has a semi-desert climate, suitable mainly for cattle grazing, or is desert, where agriculture is possible only with large-scale irrigation. Coastal areas of central and southern California have a Mediterranean subtropical climate, with warm summers and cool winters. Rainfall is slight. A temperate marine climate is found along the northwestern coast, where rainfall is plentiful and both summer and winter temperatures are moderate.

Mexico's climate varies with elevation from temperate and dry to tropical and wet. Its rainfall ranges from as little as 2 inches

(50 millimeters) in the northern deserts to as much as 185 inches (4,700 millimeters) in the tropical lowlands along the southern coast. Tropical southern Mexico, Central America, and the Caribbean islands are influenced by the warm, moist trade winds, which provide the heavy rainfall.

Ocean currents also play an important role in determining North America's climate. The Japan Current has a warming effect on a large area of the Pacific Coast, extending from Oregon to Alaska. The Gulf Stream moderates the climate of the Caribbean islands as well as the continent's Atlantic Coast, and the cold Labrador Current produces a frigid climate along the eastern coast of Canada.

Natural Resources

North America has substantial natural resources, which have contributed to its economic development. These include fertile soils, vast expanses of forest, and a wide variety of minerals.

Soils. The continent has many different types of soils. Northern Canada and northern Alaska have tundra soils that are of little value for agriculture. Much of the rest of northern North America has glacial soils, which vary in quality. The northeastern

United States has chiefly gray-brown soils, which are only moderately fertile, but the southeast is an area of rich red and yellow soils. The central United States and Canada have fertile prairie soils. West of the prairie is a narrow band of black soils that are among the most fertile in the world.

Mountain soils are found mainly on the southern Pacific coast and alluvial soils in the northwest. Red desert soils cover much of northern Mexico, while the more fertile black and dark-gray soils occur in the much better watered areas of southern Mexico and Central America.

Vegetation. Vegetation varies with the climate and soils. The far north is a treeless region consisting chiefly of reindeer moss and a few hardy plants that mature during the brief Arctic summer. The Great Central Plain has vast areas of prairie, or open grassland. In the southwestern United States and northern Mexico, there are extensive growths of cactus, while the coastal areas of central and southern California are home to chaparral and other scrub vegetation.

Although many of the forests that once covered North America have been cut down, more than 1,000 varieties of trees remain. Of these, about 100 are of commercial importance. South of the frozen tundra, stretching across most of the continent, are forests of cone-bearing trees such as spruce, fir, hemlock, and pine. The most remarkable trees of the Pacific region are the sequoias, or giant

COUNTRIES OF NORTH AMERICA

Country	Capital
Antigua and Barbuda	St. John's
Bahamas	Nassau
Barbados	Bridgetown
Belize	Belmopan
Canada	Ottawa
Costa Rica	San José
Cuba	Havana
Dominica	Roseau
Dominican Republic	Santo Domingo
El Salvador	San Salvador
Grenada	St. George's
Guatemala	Guatemala City
Haiti	Port-au-Prince
Honduras	Tegucigalpa
Jamaica	Kingston
Mexico	Mexico City
Nicaragua	Managua
Panama	Panama City
St. Kitts and Nevis	Basseterre
St. Lucia	Castries
St. Vincent and the Grenadines	Kingstown
Trinidad and Tobago	Port of Spain
United States of America	Washington, D.C.

NONINDEPENDENT TERRITORIES OF NORTH AMERICA

Territory	Status
Anguilla	British dependency
Aruba	Self-governing territory of the Netherlands
Bermuda	British dependency
Cayman Islands	British dependency
Greenland	Province of Denmark
Guadeloupe	Overseas department of France
Martinique	Overseas department of France
Montserrat	British dependency
Netherlands Antilles	Self-governing territory of the Netherlands
Puerto Rico	Commonwealth of the United States
St. Pierre and Miquelon	Overseas department of France
Turks and Caicos Islands	British dependency
Virgin Islands (U.S.)	United States territory
Virgin Islands (British)	British dependency

redwoods, some of which are 300 feet (90 meters) tall and more than 3,000 years old.

In the eastern highlands, forests stretch as far as the Gulf of Mexico, pine and cypress making up the bulk of the tree varieties in the south. Near the Great Lakes, pine forests support a large pulpwood industry. Oak and pine are found in the highlands of Central America, and mahogany and other hardwoods in the tropical rain forests.

Animal Life. The northern tundra is home to musk oxen, caribou, and polar bears. Wolves, coyotes, elk, moose, different kinds of bears, and a great variety of birds and fish inhabit the great forest region to the south. Deer and pronghorn (incorrectly called antelope) roam the valleys of the western mountains, while bighorn sheep and Rocky Mountain goats live in the northern ranges.

Vast herds of bison once covered the great plains, but they were nearly wiped out by arriving settlers. Today, gophers and prairie dogs are more commonly found there. The eastern forests contain many kinds of birds as well as deer, squirrels, porcupines, beavers, and foxes. Alligators and opossums are typically found in the southern wetlands. Tropical Mexico and Central America have a wide variety of animal life, including brightly plumaged parrots and other birds, jaguars, ocelots, tapirs, and monkeys.

North America's surrounding waters are rich in food fish and valuable shellfish. Seals, walruses, and whales are found in the Arctic waters.

Minerals. North America has a wealth of mineral resources, including many on which modern industry depends.

The continent has about 18 percent of the world's coal reserves, most of which are found in the eastern United States. It has about 13 percent of the known reserves of petroleum and natural gas, the major fields being along the coast of the Gulf of Mexico, California, Alaska, and western Canada. More than 30 percent of the world's phosphate rock, used in making fertilizer, comes from North America, as does

about 6 percent of its iron ore, with the largest single deposits found in the Mesabi Range of Minnesota. Canada and Cuba are the world's leading producers of nickel, and Mexico is its chief exporter of silver. Jamaica is a major producer of bauxite, the principal ore of aluminum. Canada is the world's chief source of uranium, from which nuclear energy is obtained, and the United States ranks (along with Chile) as one of the world's two leading copper-producing nations. Other minerals are also found in significant quantities in North America. They include gold, cobalt, zinc, tungsten, molybdenum, and vanadium.

Water. Most of North America's supply of water is ample and relatively constant over long periods, but like other natural resources, it is often unevenly distributed. In the United States, for example, water is more plentiful in the east than the west, except for parts of the northwest. Much of Mexico is arid, while many of the smaller Caribbean islands have little underground water and few lakes and streams, and the people are dependent on rainfall for their drinking water. In addition, increased demand, changing use patterns, and

pollution have all affected the continent's water supply.

Mexico has complained that the increasing diversion of water for irrigation in the western part of the United States has adversely affected the quality of some of its major rivers. In some areas of the continent, chemical wastes from industry have leached into nearby waters, creating a threat to the supply of pure drinking water in the future.

Throughout the region, however, national and local governments, along with environmental groups, are making determined efforts to clean up polluted rivers and lakes. Greater re-use of water may be expected as demand increases. Much research has also been directed toward converting seawater into water

An Inuit fisherman (*right*) mends his nets in preparation for the next day's catch. North America's abundant mineral resources include large deposits of copper, usually produced from open pit mines, such as this one (*below*) in Utah.

suitable for irrigation and for municipal and industrial use. The chief obstacle has been the generally high cost of such conversion.

Energy

North America's rapid industrial growth was based to a great extent on the availability of large supplies of mineral fuels—coal, oil, and natural gas. But today such nonrenewable sources of energy (that is, those that cannot be replaced) are increasingly expensive to produce, and there is the possibility that one day they may run out altogether. A growing energy crisis has prompted the search for new deposits of mineral fuels and for new ways of extracting and utilizing the known deposits.

At the same time, there has been intensive research and development in the use of non-polluting, renewable forms of energy, such as solar power (derived from the sun), water and nuclear power, and the use of alcohol as a fuel.

North America is fortunate in having both large deposits of uranium for producing nuclear energy and numerous swift rivers that are a source of hydroelectric power. The great plains region can also supply the enormous amounts of grain that would be needed for the production of alcohol as a substitute fuel, especially for motor vehicles.

▶ **THE PEOPLE**

North America has slightly more than 8 percent of the world's population. The most populous countries of the continent are the United States, which has about 60 percent of its people, and Mexico, which has about 20 percent. The people are not evenly situated across the land, however, with some areas of dense population, others where few people live, and some that are completely uninhabited.

Distribution and Growth

In the United States, the greatest concentration of people is found along the Atlantic coast between Massachusetts and Virginia. There are also large population clusters in the Great Lakes region and on the Pacific coast, particularly between the California cities of Los Angeles and San Francisco. Parts of the western mountains and desert areas, the central plains, and Alaska are sparsely populated. Canada, although vast in area, has a relatively small population. Most of its people live in a belt of land stretching from coast to coast in the southern part of the country. Be-

cause of the cold, inhospitable climate, large areas of northern Canada have few or no permanent inhabitants.

Mexico's densest population is found on its central plateau, particularly in and around Mexico City, the capital, with smaller population clusters on the coastal plains. The pattern is the same for Central America, with populations tending to be concentrated on fertile plateaus and coastal areas. In the Caribbean, more than 80 percent of the people live on the four large islands of Cuba, Hispaniola (shared by Haiti and the Dominican Republic), Jamaica, and Puerto Rico.

In the United States, Canada, and Mexico, the great majority of the people are city dwellers. The level of urbanization varies in other parts of North America. In Haiti, for example, most of the people live in rural areas. But the trend is toward the increasing migration of the population from rural to urban areas. There has also been, particularly within the United States and Canada, a frequent movement of people from one urban section of the country to another, often for economic reasons.

In terms of population growth, Mexico and Central America are increasing in numbers of people at a rate about twice that of the United States and Canada. Mexico, which had one of the world's highest rates of population growth, has reduced its growth rate in recent years, although about one-half of its people are still under 20 years of age.

Ancestry

The United States is composed chiefly of people of European descent, originally British but later including immigrants from nearly every country of the world. Blacks make up a considerable minority, and Hispanics, mainly from Mexico and Cuba, represent an increasing percentage of the population. The United States also has a significant number of Asians, chiefly of Chinese and Japanese origin but also including people from Korea, South and Southeast Asia, and the Middle East. The Native American population remains relatively small.

Faces of North America: *Opposite page, from top:* An elderly man from Barbados in the Caribbean; a Mexican college student; a Pueblo Indian girl from New Mexico; an Idaho potato farmer; a Cuna Indian woman from Panama in traditional dress; a Chinese shopkeeper. *Clockwise from left:* A Hispanic taxicab driver from New Jersey; an Inuit boy with a prize salmon; a Canadian Mountie in ceremonial uniform; an African American schoolteacher.

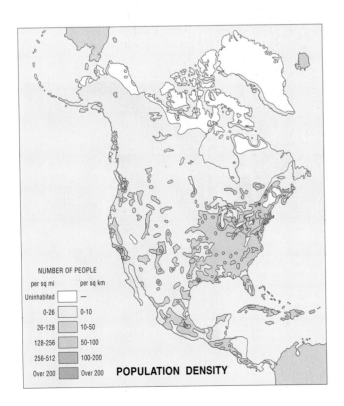

These Canadians enjoy a northern treat, maple syrup. Canada is the largest country of North America, but it has a relatively small population.

NUMBER OF PEOPLE

per sq mi	per sq km
Uninhabited	—
0-26	0-10
26-128	10-50
128-256	50-100
256-512	100-200
Over 200	Over 200

POPULATION DENSITY

INDEX TO
NORTH AMERICA POLITICAL MAP

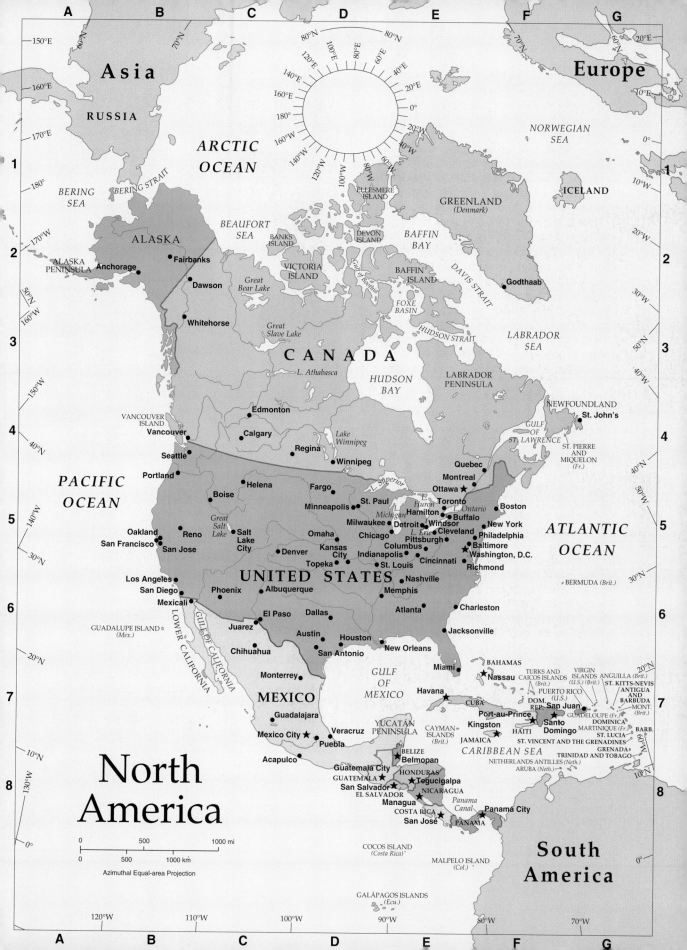

Most Canadians are of British ancestry, but there is a large and important French minority, chiefly in the province of Quebec. Canada has also attracted immigrants from many parts of the world.

People of Spanish and native Indian ancestry predominate in Mexico and Central America. The majority of Mexicans are mestizos, or of mixed European (mainly Spanish) and Indian descent. The racial makeup varies in Central America. In Costa Rica, for example, the people are largely of Spanish origin, while in Guatemala, Indians make up approximately half of the population. The population of the Caribbean islands is mixed. Most of the original Indian inhabitants died out, and the people today are mainly the descendants of the British, Spanish, French, and Dutch settlers, and of the Africans and East Indians who were brought to the islands to work the sugar plantations.

Language

English and Spanish are the most widely used languages of North America. Spanish is spoken in Mexico, Central America (except for Belize), Cuba, the Dominican Republic, and other former Spanish colonies in the Caribbean. English is the major language of the United States, although numerous other languages are spoken. English is also spoken in Belize and in other former British Caribbean colonies.

English and French are the official languages of Canada. French is spoken in Haiti and in the Caribbean islands of Guadeloupe and Martinique, and Dutch is the language of the Netherlands Antilles. To these can be added a variety of Indian and Inuit languages.

Religion

Most of the world's religions are represented in North America, but Christianity is the predominant faith. The people of Mexico, Central America, and the Spanish-speaking Caribbean islands are mainly Roman Catholics. Canada is about equally divided between Roman Catholics and Protestants. Protestants of various denominations make up the largest religious group in the United States, although there are also large numbers of Roman Catholics and a significant number of Jews. Immigration has also increased the Muslim, Hindu, and Buddhist populations.

The Independence Monument stands in the heart of Mexico City, Mexico's capital and major city and one of the world's largest and fastest-growing urban centers.

Education

Priests and missionaries who accompanied the European explorers and colonizers established the first schools in North America. The earliest public schools were founded in the 1600's in what would become the United States. The oldest university in North America, the Autonomous University of Santo Domingo in the Dominican Republic, dates from 1538, nearly a century before the founding of Harvard, the first university in the United States.

Education levels vary. Most of the people of the United States and Canada are literate (able to read and write), and Mexico has a literacy rate of about 90 percent. But in other parts of North America, literacy may be as low as 50 percent. The United States and Canada also have increasing percentages of students who go on to complete their secondary-school and college educations. However, many of the Central American countries suffer from shortages of schools and teachers, and often less than half of their children complete primary school.

This view of New York City's soaring skyline, with the Empire State Building prominent in the foreground, is seen from the Hudson River on the west side of Manhattan, one of the city's five boroughs.

▶ CITIES

In the United States and Canada, the population has long been urbanized, while in other parts of the continent, it is only in recent decades that many of the people have become largely city dwellers. In the United States, the main population shift has been from the older urban centers in the Northeast to those in the West, Southwest, and South. An east–west population shift has occured in Canada, where the movement has been chiefly away from the traditional urban areas in the provinces of Ontario and Quebec to those in Alberta and British Columbia.

Mexico City, the capital of Mexico, is the oldest major city on the North American continent, dating from the 1500's. With about one-quarter of Mexico's people, it is one of the world's most populous urban areas. New York, the most populous city in the United States, is also the center of a large metropolitan area. Originally founded by Dutch settlers (as New Amsterdam), it later came under British rule. Other major U.S. cities include Chicago, Los Angeles, Philadelphia, Houston, Detroit, Cleveland, Dallas, and San Diego. Baltimore and New Orleans are, along with New York, major U.S. ports. Washington, D.C., is the national capital. Canada's two major cities are Toronto and Montreal. Articles on each of these cities can be found in the appropriate volumes.

Most of Central America's major cities are found in its highland areas: Guatemala City, capital of Guatemala; San Salvador, capital of El Salvador; Tegucigalpa, Honduras' capital; and San José, capital of Costa Rica. The largest cities in the Caribbean islands are Havana, Cuba's capital; San Juan, the capital of

Two curved towers and a reflecting pool (*below*) highlight the distinctively modern City Hall in Toronto, one of Canada's two largest cities. A narrow side street in Quebec City (*right*) reflects the French-Canadian atmosphere of Quebec Province.

Puerto Rico; and Santo Domingo, the capital of the Dominican Republic.

▶ THE ECONOMY

Geography, climate, soils, and an abundance of natural resources have all contributed to the economic growth of North America. Economic development varies greatly across the continent, however. The United States, Canada, and, to a lesser extent, Mexico are highly industrialized, while in Central America and the Caribbean, agriculture is generally the most important sector of the economy.

Agriculture

The great interior plains of the United States and Canada are the most productive agricultural region of North America, providing enormous quantities of corn, wheat, soybeans, and other crops. Between them, the United States and Canada export more than half the world's supply of wheat. Hogs, beef cattle, and dairy cows are also raised in vast numbers. Cotton, tobacco, rice, and peanuts are grown in the southeastern United States, and citrus fruits and a variety of vegetables in California and Florida. Less than 3 percent of

the U.S. and Canadian workforce is directly engaged in agriculture, but productivity is quite high because farming is extensively mechanized.

By contrast, only about 12 percent of Mexico's land is suitable for farming, although nearly 25 percent of the labor force is employed in agriculture. Farms in the north are large and produce fruits and vegetables for export, while in the south, peasant farmers practice subsistence agriculture, growing basic food crops of corn and beans on small holdings. In much of Central America, the agricultural economy is based on the hacienda system of large estates and the production of such commercial crops as bananas and coffee. Sugarcane is a major cash crop in the Caribbean, particularly in Cuba and other large islands.

North America's surrounding waters abound in food fish, making commercial fishing (*below*) an important economic activity. Bananas, usually grown on large plantations (*right*), are the major cash crop of Central America.

Manufacturing and Service Industries

The United States is the dominant manufacturing nation of North America. Traditionally, its centers of heavy industry have been in the Northeast and in the cities around the Great Lakes region. But the South and Southwest (known as the Sunbelt for its warm climate) and Pacific coast are now important industrial areas as well. Textiles, once

Corn flows freely from a harvester (*above*). North America produces nearly half of the world's corn, chiefly in the United States and Mexico. Automobile bodies (*right*) are welded by robots at a U.S. assembly plant.

a leading industry in New England, are now produced mainly in the South. In all, manufacturing employs about 20 percent of the U.S. workforce. Chief manufactured goods include machinery, automobiles and other transportation equipment, processed foods and food products, chemicals, electric and electronic equipment, and fabricated metal products.

Manufacturing in Canada, which also engages about 20 percent of its labor force, is centered in the provinces of Ontario and Quebec. Pulp and paper products, motor vehicles, refined petroleum, and processed meat products are some of its major manufactured goods.

Mexico's industry has been boosted by its large petroleum deposits. About 11 percent of its labor force is employed in manufacturing, with processed foods, iron and steel, petrochemicals, synthetic fibers, and electrical equipment among the country's chief products. Most of Central America and the Caribbean are in the early stages of their industrial development.

Service industries represent one of the fastest-growing sectors of the U.S. and Canadian economies. These include tourism (a major source of income for much of North America), education, health care and social services, retail sales, financial services, real estate, advertising, and insurance.

Mining, Fishing, and Forestry

Its large and varied mineral deposits make mining one of North America's most important economic activities. For information on the continent's mineral production, see the section Natural Resources (Minerals).

Commercial fishing is carried out in four main offshore fishing grounds. The Grand Banks, off the northeastern coast of the

United States and the southeastern coast of Canada, are a source of cod, herring, flounder, lobster, and mackerel. The southern Atlantic is fished primarily for sardines, and the Gulf of Mexico for shrimp and oysters. Tuna, salmon, and other fish are found in the waters of the Pacific.

Canada has North America's most extensive area of forests, providing wood pulp, paper, timber, and other wood products. The United States relies for commercial purposes mainly on forested areas in the Pacific north-

IMPORTANT DATES

About 40,000 B.C.
Probable period of first migrations from Asia to North America.

A.D. 300–1400
Maya civilization flourished in Mexico and parts of Central America.

900's Toltec civilization rose in Mexico.

About 1000
Vikings reached North America.

1300's–1400's
Height of Aztec civilization in Mexico.

1492 Christopher Columbus made his first landing in the Americas.

1497 John Cabot reached the shores of Newfoundland and claimed it for England.

1513 Vasco Núñez de Balboa, at Panama, became the first European to see the Pacific Ocean.

1521 Conquest of Mexico accomplished by Spaniards under Hernando Cortés.

1534 French expedition led by Jacques Cartier reached Canada.

1535 Cartier explored the St. Lawrence River.

1605 The first permanent French settlement in Canada was established at Port Royal.

1607 Jamestown (Virginia), the first permanent English colony in North America, was founded.

1620 The Pilgrims landed at Plymouth (Massachusetts).

1682 The Louisiana Territory was claimed for France by Robert Cavelier, Sieur de La Salle.

About 1754–63
The French and Indian War was fought by Britain and France for control of North America, ending in a British victory.

1775–83 Period of the Revolutionary War between Britain and its American colonies.

1776 The Declaration of Independence was proclaimed by the 13 American colonies.

1787 The United States Constitutional Convention met in Philadelphia.

1803 The Louisiana Territory was purchased by the United States from France.

1804 Haiti won independence from France.

1812–14 The War of 1812 was fought between Britain and the United States.

1821 Mexico won independence from Spain.

1823 Five Central American provinces won independence from Spain.

1823–38 The United Provinces of Central America existed as a federation of states.

1823 Monroe Doctrine proclaimed, warning European powers against intervening in the Americas.

1861–65 Period of the U.S. Civil War.

1867 Canada was established as a dominion; Alaska was purchased from Russia by the United States.

1869 The first transcontinental railroad linked the eastern and western parts of the United States.

1890 The International Union of American Republics (Pan American Union) was formed.

1898 The Spanish-American War was won by the United States, which gained Puerto Rico, the Philippine Islands, and Guam.

1902 Cuba gained independence from Spain.

1914 The Panama Canal was opened.

1914–18 World War I was fought between the Allies and the Central Powers.

1929 Beginning of the Great Depression.

1931 Canada became an independent member of the British Commonwealth.

1939–45 World War II was fought between the Allies and the Axis Powers.

1945 The United Nations was founded at the San Francisco Conference.

1948 The Organization of American States adopted its charter and present name.

1951 The Organization of Central American States was founded.

1959 Alaska and Hawaii became the 49th and 50th states of the United States; Fidel Castro came to power following a revolution in Cuba.

1962 Trinidad and Tobago won its independence.

1966 Barbados gained independence.

1974 Grenada became independent.

1978 Dominica became independent.

1979 St. Lucia and St. Vincent and the Grenadines gained independence.

1981 Belize and Antigua and Barbuda became independent.

1982 Passage of the Canada Act of 1982 gave Canada full control of its constitution.

1983 St. Kitts and Nevis became independent.

1987 President Oscar Arias Sánchez of Costa Rica won the Nobel Peace Prize for his Central American peace plan.

1992 The United States, Canada, and Mexico signed the North American Free Trade Agreement (NAFTA).

1996 Leftist rebels and government leaders in Guatemala reached an accord aimed at ending 35 years of civil war.

1999 The United States transferred responsibility for the Panama Canal to Panama.

2001 On September 11, the worst terrorist attacks in the history of North America took place, killing more than 2,700 people in the United States.

An offshore oil rig (*above*) in the Gulf of Mexico, one of the continent's major oil-producing regions. Timber from Canadian forests (*right*) is floated downriver to sawmills.

west and the southeastern states, although it also imports timber and other forest products from Canada. Forests cover about 25 percent of Mexico. Less than one-third of this, however, is exploited commercially; the rest is maintained for protection against soil erosion. Central America's tropical rain forests include some valuable hardwoods, but these are often inaccessible.

Trade

The countries of North America are each other's major trading partners, although the United States far exceeds all the others in the total value of its trade. Generally, the trade relationship between the United States and other countries of the continent has been one in which the United States imports raw materials and specialty goods from those countries and exports manufactured products and foodstuffs to them.

There are especially strong commercial and investment ties between the United States, Canada, and Mexico, which created a free trade zone for their products under the North American Free Trade Agreement (NAFTA) in 1992–93. There are also regional organizations to promote trade among the countries of Central America and the Caribbean. See the article on the North American Free Trade Agreement (NAFTA) following this article.

Transportation

The United States and Canada have extensive transportation systems to serve their vast areas and far-flung populations. These include networks of highways, railroads, airlines, and inland waterways. The United States alone has almost 25,000 miles (40,000 kilometers) of navigable waterways, of which the largest and the most important is the Mississippi-

North America has an extensive transportation network to connect its vast areas and scattered populations. This is the Dallas/Fort Worth airport in Texas.

Missouri system. Commerce on the Great Lakes is of great importance to both Canada and the United States, and the St. Lawrence Seaway, shared by the two countries, enables oceangoing vessels to sail deep into the heart of the continent. The Atlantic and Pacific are among the world's most heavily trafficked oceans, and the Panama Canal, which connects the two oceans, is a vital international waterway. See the article on the Panama Canal in Volume P. An article on the Saint Lawrence River and Seaway can be found in Volume S.

Railroads, highways, and airlines link Mexico's major cities. The chief road system of Mexico and Central America is the Inter-American Highway, a part of the Pan American Highway extending southward from the U.S.-Canada border.

The North American Free Trade Agreement (NAFTA) was signed by the United States, Canada, and Mexico in 1992. Its aim was the elimination of tariffs and other trade barriers among the three countries.

▶ THE FUTURE

Although North America is rich in natural resources, its levels of economic development vary widely. Of the North American countries, the United States is the most fortunate in its climate, large areas of fertile land, and wealth of mineral resources, conditions that have helped make it an economic superpower. Its standard of living, along with that of Canada, ranks among the highest in the world.

Mexico and the nations of Central America and the Caribbean, less well endowed in terms of geography and natural resources, are much poorer. They also suffer from population pressures that have hampered their economic and social development. In addition, much of Central America has been torn by decades of civil war, while Mexico has seen a peasants' revolt in its southern province of Chiapas.

Still, there are reasons for optimism, especially since Central America seems to have achieved a measure of peace. It is in this southern region of North America, with its young population, that the future of the continent lies.

PAUL F. GRIFFIN
Western Oregon State College

Author, *Global Geography*

See also CARIBBEAN SEA AND ISLANDS; CENTRAL AMERICA; INDIANS, AMERICAN.

NORTH AMERICAN FREE TRADE AGREEMENT (NAFTA)

The North American Free Trade Agreement (NAFTA) is a trade pact, signed on December 17, 1992, linking the United States, Canada, and Mexico. Its aim is to create a regional common market by eliminating tariffs, or taxes on imports, and other trade barriers among the three countries. The framers of NAFTA drew on earlier trade agreements with similar aspirations, such as those that created the European Community (now the European Union). It also built on the 1989 free trade agreement between the United States and Canada, by adding Mexico as a third member.

The measure provoked stormy debate. Its supporters pointed to the economic benefits that would result from the creation of such a vast free trade zone, with more than 370 million people. Opposition arose chiefly from U.S. labor groups, who feared the loss of jobs, particularly to Mexico, where wages were much lower; and from those concerned that it might lead to lower environmental and safety standards. To meet these objections, several supplemental agreements were added, relating to labor and environmental issues, and the pact was ratified in 1993.

NAFTA officially went into force in 1994, but many of its key provisions, such as those on automobiles and some farm products, were not scheduled to go into effect for another 10 to 15 years.

ARTHUR CAMPBELL TURNER
University of California, Riverside

See also EUROPEAN UNION; TARIFF.

NORTH ATLANTIC TREATY ORGANIZATION (NATO)

The North Atlantic Treaty Organization (NATO) was formed by a group of nations in 1949 to provide mutual aid and a common defense in case of aggression in Western Europe by the Soviet Union and other members of the Communist bloc. The North Atlantic Treaty, which established NATO, was signed in Washington, D.C., on April 4, 1949. Belgium, Canada, Denmark, France, Iceland, Italy, Luxembourg, the Netherlands, Norway, Portugal, the United Kingdom, and the United States were the original members. Greece and Turkey joined in 1952, West Germany in 1955, Spain in 1982, and a reunited Germany in 1990. Poland, Hungary, and the Czech Republic joined in 1999. Bulgaria, Estonia, Latvia, Lithuania, Romania, Slovakia, and Slovenia joined in 2004.

The chief governing body is the North Atlantic Council. It is composed of permanent representatives of the member states, who sit in continuous session at NATO's headquarters near Brussels, Belgium. The chairman of the council is the secretary-general.

The Military Committee is the highest military authority of NATO. It is composed of the chiefs of staff—or their aides—of the member countries, plus a civilian representative for Iceland. NATO has three military commands—the European, Atlantic, and Channel Commands—plus the Canada–United States Regional Planning Group.

The European Command, the most important of the three, is headed by the Supreme Allied Commander, Europe. The European Command has four subcommands—for Northern, Central, and Southern Europe, and the Mediterranean.

In 1999, NATO celebrated its 50th anniversary with the addition of three new members. But festivities were overshadowed by the civil war in Yugoslavia. In March 1999, after failing to help negotiate a peace settlement, NATO began air strikes against the Serbs for the slaughter of ethnic Albanians in the province of Kosovo. In June, NATO ceased its attacks and installed peacekeeping forces throughout the region.

In 2003 the opposition of France, Germany, Belgium, and Luxembourg to the U.S.-led war in Iraq caused tensions within the alliance. But NATO agreed to expand its support of the U.S.-led campaign against terrorism, and it took command of peacekeeping troops in Afghanistan, the first such operation outside Europe in its history.

Reviewed by NORMAN D. PALMER
University of Pennsylvania

NORTH CAROLINA

North Carolina is part of what was once an enormous land grant known as the Province of Carolana, or the Land of Charles. It was named after England's King Charles I, who granted the region's first charter in 1629.

The origin of North Carolina's nickname, the Tar Heel State, is harder to determine. One story claims that during the Revolutionary War, North Carolina patriots dumped barrels of tar into a stream to choke the advance of British General Lord Cornwallis. Other stories are rooted in Civil War legend. One tells how a North Carolina regiment complained that they needed to put tar on the heels of other Confederates to make them stick better in the next battle. But a different story claims it was really the Carolinians who needed the tar on their heels.

North Carolina is located on the Atlantic Coast in the southeastern United States. Its scenery is dramatically varied and beautiful. To the east are the Outer Banks, a chain of narrow islands that stretches the length of the state's Atlantic coastline and includes Cape Hatteras and Cape Lookout national seashores. On the low, level shores of the mainland are old colonial towns and plantation houses surrounded by trees draped with Spanish moss. Farther inland are the broad agricultural lands on which bright-leaf tobacco, North Carolina's leading crop, is grown.

Centers of industry and education lie farther inland in the Piedmont region. Three Piedmont cities—Raleigh, Durham, and Chapel Hill—surround an area called the Research Triangle Park, a center for the development of science and industry. Each of these cities is also home to a major university. The Piedmont's factories turn out much of the nation's tobacco products and textiles. North Carolina's vast forests have spawned another important industry—the manufacture of wooden furniture.

The state's beautiful mountain region, located in the far west, includes parts of two famous national areas—the Blue Ridge Parkway and the Great Smoky Mountains National Park. The mountain region is sparsely populated. In some of the more isolated places, old customs and even old patterns of speech have been preserved.

State flag

▶ LAND

From east to west, North Carolina rises from the shores of the Atlantic Ocean to the tops of the Blue Ridge Mountains.

Land Regions

North Carolina's varied surface makes up three natural land regions. They are the Atlantic Coastal Plain, the Piedmont Plateau, and the Mountain Region.

The Atlantic Coastal Plain. About two fifths of the state lies on the Coastal Plain. This region contains four subdivisions—the Outer Banks, the Tidewater, the Inner Coastal Plain, and the Sandhills.

The Outer Banks are a chain of sandbars, or barrier islands, along the Atlantic Coast. Cape Hatteras, Cape Lookout, and Cape Fear are points where low, narrow banks jut out into the Atlantic Ocean. The area off the coast of Cape Hatteras is called the Graveyard of the Atlantic because its treacherous waters and shifting sandbars have caused so many shipwrecks. Between the Outer Banks and the mainland are broad stretches of water called sounds. The two largest are Pamlico Sound and Albemarle Sound.

North Carolina's landscape is as breathtaking as it is varied. The forested dunes of the central Sandhill country (*top left*) and the scenic lighthouse at Cape Hatteras on the Atlantic Ocean in the east (*top right*) stand in marked contrast to the stunning, broad vistas of the Blue Ridge Mountains in the west (*bottom*).

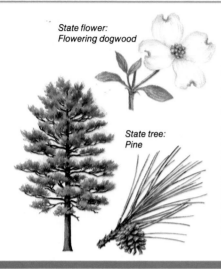

State flower:
Flowering dogwood

State tree:
Pine

FACTS AND FIGURES

Location: Southeastern United States; bordered on the north by Virginia, on the south by South Carolina and Georgia, on the east by the Atlantic Ocean, and on the west by Tennessee.

Area: 52,672 sq mi (136,421 km²); rank, 29th.

Population: 8,049,313 (2000 census); rank, 11th.

Elevation: *Highest*—6,684 ft (2,037 m) at Mount Mitchell; *lowest*—sea level along the Atlantic Ocean.

Capital: Raleigh.

Statehood: November 21, 1789; 12th state.

State Motto: *Esse Quam Videri* ("To be rather than to seem").

State Song: "The Old North State."

Nickname: Tar Heel State (official); Old North State.

Abbreviations: NC; N.C.

State bird:
Cardinal

Above: National wildlife refuges lie in the swamplands of the Tidewater region. *Right:* Bogue Sound separates the Outer Banks from the mainland.

The Tidewater is a low, swampy area along the coast of the mainland. One of the swamplands is the Great Dismal Swamp National Wildlife Refuge. Established in 1973, it covers about 750 square miles (1,940 square kilometers) in the northeastern part of the state. Rising above the Tidewater is a better-drained area called the Inner Coastal Plain. The sandy soils of this area are favorable for growing tobacco and cotton. The Sandhill country, an area of large forested dunes in the southwestern corner of the Atlantic Coastal Plain, is a popular winter resort area, also known for its peach orchards.

The Atlantic Coastal Plain extends westward to the Fall Line, where the soft coastal soil ends and the rockier hill country begins.

The Piedmont Plateau. The Piedmont, the "doorstep" to the Appalachian Mountains, is where most of North Carolina's people live. Forests and artificial lakes are scattered throughout the area, but the Piedmont is mostly composed of gently rolling hills. Its many swift streams are well-suited to the development of waterpower.

The Mountain Region. The western part of the state is covered by a system of mountain ranges belonging to the Appalachian chain. All of these ranges together are known as the Blue Ridge section. But in North Carolina the name "Blue Ridge" usually is given only to the narrow range that forms the eastern border of the mountain system. The western border is formed by a chain of ranges that reaches its highest elevations in the Great Smoky Mountains. Numerous cross ranges, like rungs on a ladder, connect the eastern and western border ranges.

Mount Mitchell, in the Black Mountains, at 6,684 feet (2,037 meters), is the highest peak east of the Mississippi River. The area has more than 200 peaks with elevations higher than 5,000 feet (1,500 meters). The mountains of North Carolina have few crags, bare cliffs, or rocky slopes. The summits are rounded, and forests grow at the highest elevations. In some areas there are rounded grassy summits known as "balds."

Rivers, Lakes, and Coastal Waters

The principal rivers of North Carolina flow in a southeasterly direction toward the Atlantic Ocean. The Roanoke, the Tar-Pamlico, and the Neuse rivers empty into the sounds. The Cape Fear River flows into the Atlantic. The Yadkin-Pee Dee and the Catawba rivers both flow into South Carolina before reaching the ocean. In the western part of the state are the Little Tennessee River and the French Broad River. They flow toward the Mississippi River and the Gulf of Mexico.

Most of the natural lakes in North Carolina are in the Coastal Plain region. Lake Mattamuskeet and Phelps Lake are the largest. Many others are located in shallow, egg-shaped depressions called Carolina Bays. There are many theories about the origins of these depressions. One of the most interesting suggests that showers of meteorites fell on the area a long time ago, creating thousands of shallow craters. Most of them are now marshy areas called bogs.

The grassy valleys that lie among the Great Smoky Mountains in the far western part of the state provide bountiful pastureland for farmers.

Most of the lakes in the highlands are artificial. Large dams on the major rivers have created reservoirs that are used for hydroelectric power, recreation, and flood control. Lake Norman on the Catawba River and Fontana Reservoir on the Little Tennessee River are the largest reservoirs that exist entirely within the state. The John H. Kerr Reservoir, shared with Virginia, is on the Roanoke River.

Climate

The climate in North Carolina varies greatly. Differences in elevation account for most of the variations in temperature. At almost any time of the year the average temperature along the coast is a good deal warmer than it is in the mountains. At Wilmington, on the Coastal Plain, temperatures average 47°F (8°C) in January and 70°F (21°C) in July. Charlotte, in the Piedmont, averages 43°F (6°C) in January and 79°F (26°C) in July. Asheville, in the mountains, averages 35°F (2°C) in January and 72°F (22°C) in July.

The total annual precipitation—rain and melted snow—varies from east to west. The Coastal Plain receives about 50 inches (1,520 millimeters) annually. About 47 inches (1,190 millimeters) fall on the Piedmont. The Mountain Region receives about 60 inches (1,520 millimeters), two thirds of which is snow.

Precipitation is fairly well distributed throughout the year, but it is heaviest during the summer. North Carolina's climate is generally good for agriculture. The growing season ranges from about four months in the high mountains to almost ten months on the Outer Banks. The state's generally temperate weather is occasionally interrupted by violent storms. Tornadoes may sweep through inland and hurricanes are almost a yearly hazard along the Atlantic Coast.

Plant and Animal Life

North Carolina has been called Nature's Sample Case because of the variety of natural resources found there.

More than half of North Carolina is covered by woods and forests. The high mountain areas contain spruce and balsam—species usually found in subarctic regions; yet palmettos and other subtropical trees and shrubs grow along the southern coast. In between are pines and a great variety of hardwoods, such as oak, hickory, walnut, maple, and ash. Common smaller plants found in the wild are

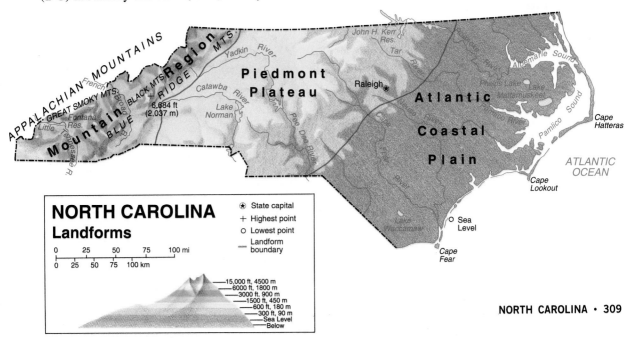

NORTH CAROLINA
Landforms

0   25   50   75   100 mi
0   25   50   75   100 km

✷ State capital
+ Highest point
○ Lowest point
— Landform boundary

15,000 ft, 4500 m
6000 ft, 1800 m
3000 ft, 900 m
1500 ft, 450 m
600 ft, 180 m
300 ft, 90 m
Sea Level
Below

rhododendrons, mountain laurels, sumacs, azaleas, Venus's-flytraps, dogwoods, camellias, redbuds, orchids, pitcher plants, and sundews.

Animals roam wild, especially in the woodlands. The most common mammals are black bears, deer, foxes, beavers, squirrels, opossums, raccoons, rabbits, otters, skunks, and minks. Dolphins can be found offshore in the Atlantic Ocean.

Birds found in the state include quail, ruffed grouse, wild turkeys, cardinals, wrens, mockingbirds, chickadees, woodpeckers, warblers, mourning doves, and woodcocks. Common snakes are copperheads, rattlesnakes, coral snakes, and water moccasins.

The rivers, lakes, and coastal waters supply a rich harvest of marlin, menhaden, sailfish, sturgeon, bluefish, bass, bluegill, crappie, sunfish, trout, and shad. Oysters, clams, shrimp, and turtles also are harvested.

Natural Resources

North Carolina's Department of Natural Resources and Community Development has various agencies that manage and protect the state's natural resources and environment. The Environmental Management Commission, for example, protects air and water resources. Other agencies are involved with fisheries and soil and other ground resources.

Forests. North Carolina is a leading lumber-producing state, and the forest resources are carefully used and monitored. The state ranks second in the nation in growing hardwood stock and eleventh in growing softwood stock.

Minerals. More than 300 different minerals, ranging from gold to sand, can be found in North Carolina. Gemstones, such as rubies, sapphires, emeralds, and even diamonds, have been found in the Piedmont and also in the mountains.

About 80 percent of the nation's lithium ore deposits are in North Carolina. Limestone and phosphate rock also are mined. The state ranks first in the nation for the mining of mica and second in clay, which is used to make bricks.

Soils. The best soils in North Carolina are the sandy, well-drained soils of the Coastal Plain. Many sections of the Piedmont also have good soils, but it is mostly made up of red clay. In the mountains the soils usually are rocky and thin.

▶ **PEOPLE**

When Spanish explorers first arrived in the North Carolina region in 1540, there were about 30,000 Native American Indians living there. Today about 95,000 Native Americans live in North Carolina, making up 1.2 percent of the total population.

The earliest colonists came directly from England. But North Carolina was settled largely by people from neighboring colonies, such as Virginia and Pennsylvania. Most were of English, Scottish, and German descent. The largest group of people who came directly from Europe were Scottish Highlanders, who settled in the upper Cape Fear Valley. Smaller groups included the French Huguenots and the Swiss.

More than half of the people of North Carolina live in rural areas, and nearly half of the state's population lives in the central Piedmont region.

Education

North Carolina's elementary and secondary public schools have an enrollment exceeding 1 million pupils. There are about 140 local school districts and 2,000 schools.

North Carolina was the first state to establish a state university. The University of North Carolina, chartered in 1789, opened its doors in 1795 at Chapel Hill. Today it has additional campuses in Asheville, Charlotte, Greensboro, and Wilmington and has an enrollment of more than 23,000. North Carolina State

About 6,000 members of the Eastern Cherokee Nation live and work on the Cherokee Indian Reservation, near the Great Smoky Mountains National Park.

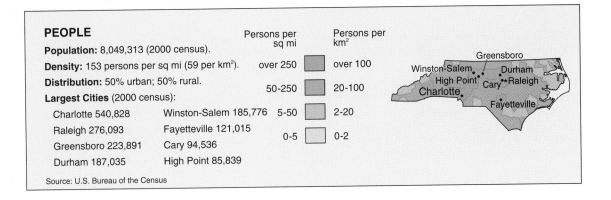

University at Raleigh was founded in 1887 and has an enrollment of more than 26,000.

Among the more than 30 universities and colleges in North Carolina are several distinguished private institutions. Among them are Duke University in Durham, Davidson College in Davidson, and Wake Forest University in Winston-Salem.

Libraries, Museums, and the Arts

The state's first public library was founded in 1700 by the Reverend Thomas Bray at St. Thomas Episcopal Church in Bath. Today the largest libraries are at Duke University in Durham and at the University of North Carolina at Chapel Hill. Both have extensive collections relating to Southern history. The Sondley Reference Library in Asheville includes collections on Indians of the Southeast, the Civil War, and natural history.

The North Carolina Museum of Art in Raleigh is one of the finest art museums in the South. Also in Raleigh is the North Carolina Museum of History, which chronicles the history of the state dating back to the 1500's.

The Mint Museum of Art in Charlotte is housed in a building that once was a branch of the U.S. Mint. (In the mid-1800's, North Carolina was the nation's largest producer of gold.) Also in Charlotte is the Nature Museum for children.

Located on the campus of the University of North Carolina at Chapel Hill are the William Hayes Ackland Memorial Art Center and the Morehead Planetarium (one of the nation's oldest and best known). The North Carolina Maritime Museum, with its nature and maritime exhibits, is located in Beaufort.

North Carolina is known for its historical pageants. Two well-known outdoor dramas

Left: The North Carolina Museum of Art in Raleigh contains an impressive collection of paintings by old masters. *Below:* College basketball fans enjoy the rivalry between Duke and Wake Forest, two of North Carolina's many fine universities.

are staged during the summer in western North Carolina. *Horn of the West,* the story of Daniel Boone and other pioneers, is presented at the town of Boone near the Blue Ridge Parkway and *Unto These Hills,* about the Cherokee, is performed in the town of Cherokee. *The Lost Colony,* a play about the earliest settlers, is staged every summer at Roanoke Island. It is the nation's oldest outdoor drama presentation still running.

North Carolina was one of the nation's first states to fund a symphony orchestra and also to found a state-supported school of the arts —the North Carolina School of the Arts in Winston-Salem. The North Carolina Symphony, located in Raleigh, performs throughout the state, especially in schools. Several of the larger cities support symphony orchestras and dance companies.

▶ ECONOMY

During colonial times, most North Carolinians were farmers, and tobacco was the major cash crop. The chief commercial activities were lumbering and the production of tar, pitch, rosin, and turpentine for shipbuilding.

Agriculture and lumbering are still major industries, and tobacco is still the leading crop, but today North Carolina is more of an industrial giant. The value of the state's manufactured goods far exceeds the value of its farm products, and the service industries are more important than agriculture and manufacturing combined.

Services

North Carolina's service industries produce about 62 percent of North Carolina's entire gross state product (GSP), the total value of goods and services the state produces in one year.

Wholesale and retail trade, or the buying and selling of industrial and personal goods, are the most profitable of all the service industries. Combined, they account for 16 percent of the state's total GSP. Charlotte and Raleigh are major wholesale trade centers in the state.

Financial services—banking, insurance, and real estate—are next in importance, accounting for 13 percent of the GSP. They are followed by government services (the maintenance of schools, hospitals, and military bases) which account for 12 percent.

Other types of services, such as business, legal, medical, tourist, recreational, community, social, and personal services combined account for another 12 percent of the GSP. Remaining service industries fall under the transportation and communication category.

Manufacturing

North Carolina is the leading manufacturing state in the Southeast. Manufacturing industries, most of which are centered in the Piedmont, account for 31 percent of the GSP.

Textiles are the state's most important manufactured product. North Carolina leads the nation—and indeed most foreign countries—in the production of clothing, hosiery, carpeting, synthetic fabrics, sheets, towels, and other textile products.

Tobacco products are the second most profitable manufacturing enterprise. North Carolina produces more tobacco products than any other state in the nation. About half of all the cigarettes produced in the United States come from Greensboro, Reidsville, and Winston-Salem. Chewing and pipe tobaccos also are processed in Winston-Salem.

Chemical products, including medicines, are third in importance followed by wood and paper products. Furniture manufacturing, another profitable industry, has prospered due to the state's abundant supply of hardwood. Most of the furniture comes from the Piedmont—High Point produces so much furniture, it has been called the Furniture Capital of the United States.

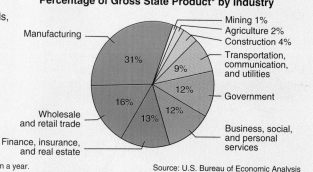

PRODUCTS AND INDUSTRIES

Manufacturing: Textiles, tobacco products, chemicals, wood and paper products, clothing, furniture, food products, electronics, non-electrical machinery.
Agriculture: Tobacco, broilers, hogs, turkeys, sweet potatoes, corn, soybeans, peanuts, apples, peaches, strawberries, watermelons, eggs, dairy products, beef cattle.
Minerals: Crushed stone, phosphate rock, sand and gravel, lithium, clay, mica, feldspar, gemstones.
Services: Wholesale and retail trade; finance, insurance, and real estate; business, social, and personal services; transportation, communication, and utilities; government.
*Gross state product is the total value of goods and services produced in a year.

Percentage of Gross State Product* by Industry

Manufacturing — 31%
Mining 1%
Agriculture 2%
Construction 4%
Transportation, communication, and utilities — 9%
Government — 12%
Business, social, and personal services — 12%
Finance, insurance, and real estate — 13%
Wholesale and retail trade — 16%

Source: U.S. Bureau of Economic Analysis

Tobacco farming (*left*) and textile manufacturing (*below*) are two of North Carolina's most profitable industries. The coastal waters of the Atlantic Ocean provide a bountiful harvest for commercial fisheries (*below left*).

Agriculture

Until the 1950's, agriculture was North Carolina's primary source of income, but today farm products account for only 2 percent of the GSP.

More than 10 million acres (4 million hectares) of North Carolina farmland are harvested annually. The farmers grow a variety of crops, but they are best known for their tobacco. North Carolina is the nation's leading producer of tobacco and also of sweet potatoes. Other important cash crops are corn, soybeans, peanuts, and fruit, such as apples, peaches, strawberries, and watermelons.

Poultry is another source of farm income, and North Carolina is the nation's leading producer of turkeys. Hogs, beef cattle, dairy products, and eggs are also produced in quantity. Fishing as an industry is declining, but commercial fisheries can still be found along the Atlantic Coast.

Transportation and Communication

North Carolina's first roads were Indian paths and water routes. The state began a road-building program in the 1850's that was so successful, North Carolina became known as the Good Roads State.

Today there are 25 railroad lines supplying freight service and passenger trains serving twelve cities. Air traffic is centered primarily in Raleigh-Durham and Greensboro, but there are about 350 airports in all. Harbors at Morehead City, Southport, and Wilmington are part of the Atlantic Intracoastal Waterway.

Some 50 daily newspapers are published in North Carolina. The *Charlotte Observer News* and the *News and Observer* of Raleigh have the largest circulations. More than 300 radio stations and 35 television stations broadcast across the state. The transportation and communication industries together account for 9 percent of the GSP.

Mining and Construction

Mining accounts for less than 1 percent of North Carolina's GSP. Phosphate rock, the state's leading mineral product, is mined for fertilizer. Lithium compounds also are of considerable value.

Crushed stone, sand, and gravel are mined for construction purposes. Construction accounts for 4 percent of the GSP.

Places of Interest

USS *North Carolina* Battleship Memorial, Wilmington

Wright Brothers National Memorial, near Kitty Hawk

Biltmore Estate, near Asheville

Swinging Bridge at Grandfather Mountain, near Linville

Biltmore Estate, located near Asheville, was the country estate of George W. Vanderbilt, a member of a family prominent in finance and transportation. The house, which was completed in 1895, contains art treasures collected from all over the world. Fifty-five rooms are open for viewing. The grounds measure 8,000 acres (14 hectares) and include formal gardens of roses and azaleas. The estate was the site of the first forestry school in the United States.

Blue Ridge Parkway is a scenic motorway connecting the Great Smoky Mountains National Park with the Shenandoah National park in Virginia. It follows the crest of the Blue Ridge Mountains and contains several recreation areas that have spectacular views.

Cape Hatteras National Seashore stretches along the Outer Banks and includes Bodie, Hatteras, and Ocracoke islands. The seashore is noted for its windswept dunes, beautiful wildflowers, wildlife, and many points of historical interest. Cape Hatteras lighthouse once warned ships away from the treacherous, shifting sand ridges of Diamond Shoals.

Carl Sandburg Home National Historic Site, at Flat Rock, preserves Connemara Farm, which was the home of the famous poet and Pulitzer prize-winning author for the last 22 years of his life. (A biography of Carl Sandburg appears in Volume S.)

Fort Raleigh National Historic Site, on Roanoke Island, preserves the site where English colonists made their first attempts to settle in America (in 1585 and 1587). This was the birthplace of Virginia Dare, the first English child born in the New World (August 18, 1587). The old fort has been excavated and partially restored.

Grandfather Mountain, near the town of Linville, is so named because the face of the mountain resembles that of an older man. Tourists can cross a mile-high (1.6 kilometer-high) swinging bridge that connects two crests. Also nearby are Linville Falls and Linville Caverns.

Great Smoky Mountains National Park covers a vast stretch of forest land. More than half the park lies in North Carolina. About 200 miles (320 kilometers) of the scenic Appalachian Trail runs through here. It is also the site of the **Cherokee Indian Reservation**, the home of the descendants of the Native Americans who escaped the infamous Trail of Tears relocation march to Oklahoma in the 1830's.

Old Salem, in Winston-Salem, preserves many of the buildings of the original village. Salem was established in 1766 by Moravians, a religious group from Pennsylvania. The town soon became a center of trade and culture in the Piedmont.

USS *North Carolina* Battleship Memorial features the 35,000-ton vessel that took part in all the major offensive battles in the Pacific during World War II. It is permanently anchored on the west bank of the Cape Fear River in Wilmington.

Wright Brothers National Memorial, on the Kill Devil Hills near Kitty Hawk, commemorates the first power-driven flight on December 17, 1903. The park includes a large monument, a museum, and reconstructions of the launching apparatus, the hangar, and the camp used by the pioneering aviators. (A biography of the Wright Brothers appears in Volume W.)

State Parks. North Carolina has more than two dozen state parks. For information, contact the Travel and Tourism Division, 430 North Salisbury Street, Raleigh, NC 27611.

Charlotte (*left*), North Carolina's largest city, is a major commerical and industrial center. Raleigh (*below*) is the state's capital and second largest city.

▶ CITIES

North Carolina has six cities with populations exceeding 100,000 each. These are Charlotte, Raleigh, Greensboro, Durham, Winston-Salem, and Fayetteville. All of them lie in the Piedmont region. Charlotte is located in the southwest, but all the others lie relatively near each other in the north central part of the state.

Charlotte, North Carolina's largest city and the heart of its textile industry, lies close to the South Carolina border. Settled in 1748 and chartered in 1768, the city was named in honor of Charlotte Sophia of Mecklenburg-Strelitz, the wife of King George III of England. In the late 1700's Charlotte became a gold-rush center. Today its tall buildings, large warehouses, and busy factories stand in evidence of its importance as a center of commerce and industry.

Raleigh is the state's capital and second largest city. The land on which the city is built was bought in 1788 by a group of legislators who wished to establish a permanent capital there. The city was named for Sir Walter Raleigh, who tried to establish North Carolina's first colony in the 1580's. Today Raleigh, the home of North Carolina State University, is an educational center as well as the center of the state's government. It also is a prominent research and development center for such industries as electronics and chemicals.

Greensboro, founded in 1808, was named in honor of Nathanael Greene, who commanded the colonial forces at the Battle of Guilford Courthouse during the Revolutionary War. Today Greensboro is an industrial center, important in the manufacture of textiles, tobacco products, machinery, and electronic components. Greensboro College, Guilford College, and a branch of the University of North Carolina are located there.

Durham is an important industrial and cultural center in the southeast. With Raleigh and Chapel Hill, it forms a metropolitan area of about 1 million people. The city was founded in 1853. In 1865, General Joseph E. Johnston surrendered his Confederate Army to Union forces just west of the city. Today Durham is the home of Duke University and North Carolina Central University.

Winston-Salem is one of the world's largest tobacco centers. It is also famous for its hosiery manufacturing, breweries and electronic products. The city actually is made up of two different towns—Salem, founded by Moravians in 1766, and Winston, founded in 1849. The two were formally joined in 1913. It is the site of Wake Forest University.

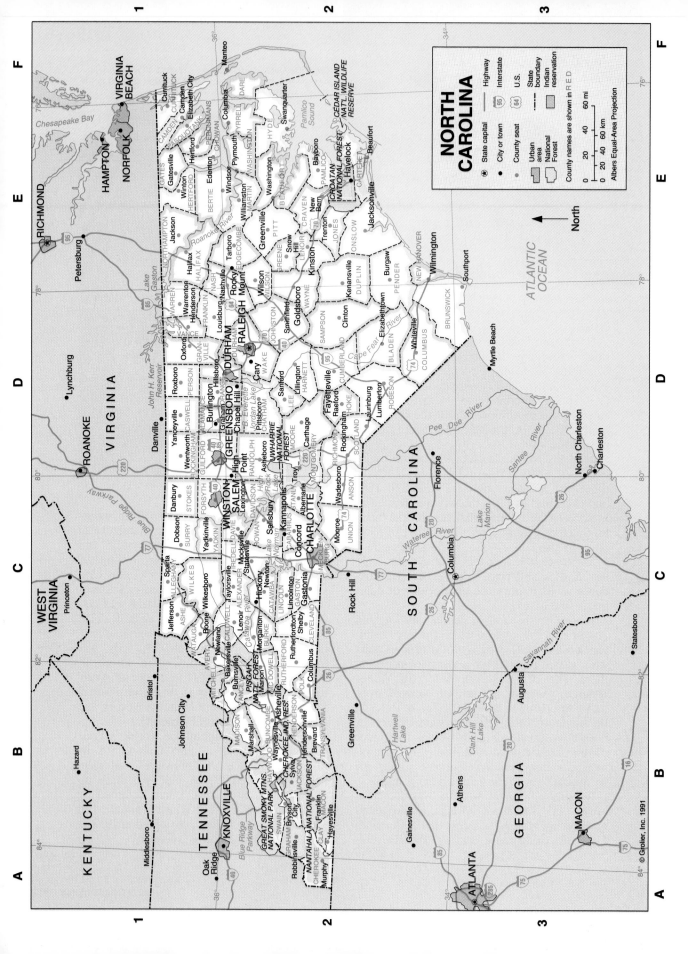

INDEX TO NORTH CAROLINA

• County Seat   Counties in parentheses   ★ State Capital

In 1788, North Carolina state legislators chose Raleigh as the site for a permanent state capital city. The capitol building shown above was completed in 1840.

▶ GOVERNMENT

The basic structure of North Carolina's government is similar to that of the other states. The legislative branch, known as the General Assembly, makes policies for dealing with the problems of government. The executive branch, headed by the governor, puts these policies into effect. The judicial branch interprets the law and settles disputes.

The General Assembly is made up of a senate and a house of representatives. Since 1974, the members have met yearly.

The governor, lieutenant governor, secretary of state, attorney general, auditor, treasurer, superintendent of public instruction, and commissioners of agriculture, insurance, and labor are elected by popular vote for 4-year terms. The state constitution does not give the governor as much power as many other state governors have. The North Carolina governor is the only governor who cannot veto (reject) laws passed by the legislature.

At the head of the court system is the state supreme court, with a chief justice and six associate justices. All are elected for 8-year terms. Below the supreme court are the superior courts and a network of district courts.

GOVERNMENT

State Government
Governor: 4-year term
State senators: 50; 2-year terms
State representatives: 120; 2-year terms
Number of counties: 100

Federal Government
U.S. senators: 2
U.S. representatives: 13
Number of electoral votes: 15

For the name of the current governor, see STATE GOVERNMENTS in Volume S. For the names of current U.S. senators and representatives, see UNITED STATES, CONGRESS OF THE in Volume U-V.

About ten thousand years before Spanish explorers set foot on North Carolina soil, Native Americans belonging to various tribes inhabited the land. They included the Cherokee in the west; the Pamlico and the Coree on the Coastal Plain; the Catawba, Cheraw, Keyauwee, and Waxhaw in the Piedmont; the Tuscarora both on the Coastal Plain and in the Piedmont; and the Hatteras (or Croatan) along the Atlantic Coast.

The Europeans Arrive

In 1524, Giovanni da Verrazano, an Italian explorer under contract to King Francis I of France, became the first European to sail by the North Carolina coast. It was the Spanish, however, who were the first to explore the area. In 1526 Lucas Vásquez de Ayllón tried to establish a colony near Cape Fear on the Carolina coast, but most of the settlers died of fever or starvation. Then in 1540, an expedition led by Hernando de Soto probably crossed the southwestern corner of North Carolina.

The Earliest Settlements

Although the Spanish were the first to explore North Carolina, the first colonies were established by the English. Sir Walter Raleigh, a favorite of Queen Elizabeth I, sponsored the first two expeditions, both of which proved unsuccessful. The first group of colonists landed on Roanoke Island in Pamlico Sound in 1585, but they returned to England the following year, unable to face sickness and starvation. The second group journeyed to Roanoke Island in 1587, with John White as their governor. A baby girl, named Virginia Dare, was born on the island and thus became the first English child born in the New World.

After only a few months, John White was forced to return to England for supplies. For the next several years, he was detained in Europe by a war with Spain. When he finally returned to Roanoke Island in 1590, all of the settlers had mysteriously disappeared.

To this day, no one knows what became of the "lost colony." Some people believe that the settlers died, but evidence suggests that they might have joined the Croatan Indians. In fact, many of today's Lumbee Indians, who are descended from the Croatans, have the same last names as some of the colonists who disappeared.

In 1629, King Charles I of England granted to Sir Robert Heath a broad stretch of land in the New World. The territory originally was called Carolana (which is Latin for "land of Charles"), but the name was later changed to Carolina. Heath failed to bring colonists into the territory, so his rights to it were declared void. In 1663, Charles II regranted the territory to eight government officials, who established Albemarle County in the northern part of the territory. In 1712, Carolina was formally separated into two distinct colonies—North Carolina and South Carolina—but the boundary line between them was not agreed upon until 1735. North Carolina became known as the "Old North State" to distinguish it from its southern neighbor.

The Revolutionary War Years (1775–81)

In the days before the Revolutionary War, North Carolinians agitated against the various taxes imposed on the colonies by the British. They also complained of dishonest practices in local government. On April 12, 1776, a provisional congress meeting in Halifax drew up the Halifax Resolves, authorizing the North Carolina delegation to the Continental Congress to vote for independence. The first state constitution was drawn up shortly thereafter and went into effect in January 1777.

One of the early battles of the Revolutionary War was fought at Moore's Creek Bridge near Currie on February 27, 1776. After that, little fighting occurred in North Carolina until the closing days of the war. Many North Carolinians, however, served directly under General George Washington in various campaigns elsewhere.

The fierce Battle of Guilford Courthouse on March 15, 1781, was the last important Revolutionary battle fought in North Carolina, and was one of the last of the war. American forces under General Nathanael Greene were attacked by the well-trained and superbly equipped army commanded by the British General Lord Cornwallis. After several hours of bitter fighting, General Greene gave the order for his troops to retreat. Cornwallis claimed victory, although losses were heavy on both sides. His army was so severely weakened that Cornwallis withdrew to Virginia. Several months later on October 19, 1781, he surrendered to General Washington at Yorktown and ended the war.

Statehood

On November 21, 1789, North Carolina ratified the United States Constitution and became the twelfth state of the Union. Several places served as temporary capital cities, including New Bern, Hillsborough, Smithfield, Halifax, Fayetteville, and Tarboro. Finally, in 1792, the state bought 1,000 acres (405 hectares) of land near the Wake County Courthouse to establish a permanent capital, and the new capital city of Raleigh was born.

Economic Development in the 1800's

North Carolina developed more slowly than its prosperous neighbors Virginia and South Carolina, chiefly because its transportation routes were inadequate. The state's major rivers, which served as highways of commerce, flow north and south. This made it difficult to transport goods from the east to the west. The farmers in the eastern part of the state, along the commercial corridor of the Atlantic seaboard, prospered the most.

After 1835, North Carolina's industry began to grow, due in part to a revision of the state's constitution that gave western North Carolinians greater representation in the state government. A network of wooden plank roads running east and west was built and the textile industry began to grow. When the railroads came in 1840, a new era of economic prosperity was assured.

Trail of Tears

The westward movement of North Carolina settlers eventually brought them into conflict with the Cherokee. Whites soon began spreading into territories that earlier treaties had guaranteed to the Indians. Instead of enforcing the treaties, the U.S. government decided to relocate the Indians.

In the 1830's thousands of Cherokee and members of other Indian nations, including Creek, Seminole, Choctaw, and Chickasaw, were forced to march more than 1,000 miles (1,600 kilometers) to a location west of the Mississippi River, in present-day Oklahoma. The route the Indians were forced to take became known as the Trail of Tears. About one thousand Cherokee escaped the roundup and hid in the hills of western North Carolina. Their leader, Tsali, was captured and executed, but his followers were allowed to remain. Their descendants still occupy the area.

Modern-day Civil War enthusiasts gather in Raleigh to re-enact famous battles. North Carolina lost more soldiers in that war than any other Confederate state.

The Last Southern State to Secede

Just before the Civil War began in 1861, North Carolina was divided over the issues of slavery and secession (withdrawal from the Union). Most western North Carolinians were pro-Union, but the easterners sympathized more with the Confederacy. However, most North Carolinians did not favor secession from the union, and only seceded after the April 1861 attack on Fort Sumter forced President Abraham Lincoln to call Union troops to arms. North Carolina was the last southern state to secede.

The Civil War (1861–65)

North Carolina was particularly hard hit by the Civil War. The Union Navy captured Cape Hatteras, Roanoke Island, and most of North Carolina's east coast. However, Union forces were not able to seize Wilmington, and that city became known as the Lifeline of the Confederacy.

On land, 84 battles and skirmishes were fought in North Carolina. The last one fought there took place at Bentonville (March 19–21, 1865) and was the bloodiest of all. The Confederates, under the command of General Joseph E. Johnston, were beaten by General William T. Sherman and his Union forces. After Sherman took Raleigh, Johnston surrendered to him on April 26.

By the end of the Civil War, North Carolina had suffered more casualties than any other state. About one fourth of all Confederate soldiers killed had come from North Carolina, even though North Carolina accounted for only one ninth of the population of the Southern states.

Famous People

John Coltrane (1926–67), a saxophonist and composer born in Hamlet, was one of the major innovators of modern jazz. He played with a number of top bands, gaining great fame as a member of a quintet led by Miles Davis. Coltrane formed his own quartet in 1960. He became known for his methods of improvisation and for his technical ability, which allowed him to play what has been described as "sheets of sound."

Elizabeth Hanford Dole (1936–), born in Salisbury, is a high-ranking figure in the Republican Party. She was the only woman appointed to two different cabinet posts, as secretary of transportation (1983–87) and secretary of labor (1989–90). In 1990 she left public office to become president of the American Red

Cross. She resigned in 1999 to pursue her own political ambitions. In 2000 she was briefly a candidate for president of the United States. In 2002 she was elected U.S. senator from North Carolina.

William Franklin (Billy) Graham, Jr. (1918–), was born in Charlotte. A Baptist minister, Graham is known all over the world for his large-scale evangelical crusades. Since 1949 his religious radio and television broadcasts have reached millions. Graham encourages his listeners to accept Jesus Christ as their savior. His many books include *Peace With God* and *How to Be Born Again*.

Billy Graham

Andrew Johnson (1808–75), 17th president of the United States, was born in Raleigh. As a young man, Johnson was apprenticed to a tailor, and he later established his own business at Carthage. In 1826, Johnson moved to Tennessee, where he began his political career. (A biography of Andrew Johnson appears in Volume J.)

Dolley Madison (1768–1849), born Dorothea Payne in Guilford County, was the wife of President James Madison and one of the most famous of all the first ladies. She acted as White House hostess of Thomas Jefferson, who was a widower, and for her own husband during

Reconstruction and After

Like all of the Confederate states after the war, North Carolina found itself in economic ruin and social turmoil. During the period of Reconstruction (1865–76), Union troops occupied and ruled the state. When North Carolina was readmitted to the Union in 1868, the state was controlled by the Republican Party, consisting mainly of newly arrived northerners (called carpetbaggers because of the type of bag in which they carried their belongings), blacks, and pro-Union Southern whites.

Still, the state grew, especially its industry. In 1880 a period of vast railroad expansion began. Cigarette manufacturing and textile mills boomed. By 1900 more than 7,200 factories employed 70,000 workers.

In agriculture, the postwar practice of sharecropping took hold. Poor tenant farmers, many of them black, would rent farmland, often paying a rent as high as two thirds of their annual yield to the landowners. This was the only way many of the newly freed blacks could earn a living. In addition, the institution of "Jim Crow" laws in the 1880's officially segregated blacks from white society.

Progress in Public Education

In the early 1900's, advancements were made in the state's educational system. During the administration of Governor Charles B. Aycock (1901–05), 1,200 new schools were built, the school term was lengthened, and several teachers' colleges were established.

First in Flight

On December 17, 1903, on an isolated beach near Kitty Hawk, Orville Wright, a bicycle maker from Ohio, made the first successful flight in a self-propelled airplane. Orville and his brother, Wilbur, had designed the kite-like plane themselves as well as the engine that propelled it. The flight lasted only 12 seconds, and the distance flown was less than half the length of a football field, but the impact of this event on human history is immeasurable. Today's North Carolina license plates bear the words "First in Flight" to commemorate the state's role in aviation history.

The 1920's and 1930's

After World War I ended in 1918, North Carolina experienced a period of great progress in communication, business, and higher education. In response to the booming economy, more than 6,000 miles (9,660 kilometers) of roads were built.

In the 1930's the Great Depression brought the state's economic expansion to a halt. Thousands of people lost their jobs as factories closed and farmers went bankrupt.

The 1940's and 1950's

World War II (1939–45) put an end to the Great Depression. After 1941, North Carolina's industries and agriculture boomed, producing goods for the U.S. Armed Forces. Textile industries produced everything from bandages to uniforms. Shipbuilders in Wil-

his two terms in office. During the British invasion of Washington, D.C., in 1814, she escaped to Virginia and is credited for saving various important state documents and a Gilbert Stuart portrait of George Washington.

Edward R. Murrow (1908–65) was born Egbert Roscoe Murrow in Greensboro. He became famous during World War II for his on-the-scene reporting of German bombing attacks on London. In the 1950's he broadcast television shows for the Columbia Broadcasting System (CBS), including *Person to Person* and *See It Now*, which is regarded as the model for modern documentary programming. Murrow repeatedly won the Peabody Award for

Dolley Madison

Thomas Wolfe

excellence in journalism. In 1964 he received the Medal of Freedom, the highest civilian honor.

James Knox Polk (1795–1849), 11th president of the United States, was born in Mecklenburg County. A monument near Pineville marks his birthplace. As a youngster, Polk moved with his parents to Tennessee, but he returned to North Carolina to attend college. In 1818 he

graduated from the University of North Carolina at the top of his class. (A biography of James K. Polk appears in Volume P.)

Thomas Clayton Wolfe (1900–1938), one of the great American novelists of the 1900's, was born in Asheville. In 1916 he entered the University of North Carolina and became a Carolina Playmaker. His first novel, *Look Homeward, Angel,* was based on his childhood in Asheville, where he grew up in a boardinghouse run by his mother. Wolfe also drew upon his North Carolina experiences to create the narratives for *The Web and the Rock* and *You Can't Go Home Again,* which were published after his sudden death following surgery.

---

mington launched ships for the navy, and several military bases were operating in the state, including Fort Bragg Military Reservation and Camp Lejeune Marine Corps Base.

After the war, industry began to surpass agriculture as the state's primary economic base. In 1959, research and development was furthered by Duke University, North Carolina State University, and the University of North Carolina. They combined their efforts and built the North Carolina Research Triangle Park, a complex of research laboratories near Durham, Raleigh, and Chapel Hill.

Civil Revolution in the 1960's

Although the University of North Carolina admitted its first black students in 1951, racial segregation persisted in North Carolina into the 1960's. In February 1960, four black college students staged a sit-down strike, or a "sit in," when they were refused service at a Greensboro lunch counter, announcing that they would not leave until they were either served or arrested. Other blacks in Greensboro then began a boycott of all the downtown stores, and by July they were being served alongside the whites. Protests such as these led to the Civil Rights Act of 1964, which put an end to legalized segregation in public places.

Integration of North Carolina's schools took place slowly, but without the degree of violence found in other southern states. By 1972 most of North Carolina's school districts had become racially integrated.

In 1960 a group of students, who had been refused service at a "whites only" lunch counter in Greensboro, staged a sit-down strike to protest racial segregation.

Recent Trends

Although limited supplies of coal and iron have prevented heavy industry from developing in North Carolina, its hydroelectric power, fertile soils, mild climate, good transportation facilities, and thriving labor force have combined to make it one of the most progressive and prosperous states in the nation. North Carolina today is a leader in industry, agriculture, and education, and the variety and abundance of its resources will ensure the state's continued growth in these key areas.

JOHN M. HOWELL
East Carolina University
Reviewed by Thomas G. Aylesworth
Author, *Let's Discover the States* Series

NORTH DAKOTA

North Dakota is the northern half of what was once called the Dakota Territory. Its name comes from the Sioux Indians, the region's original inhabitants, who called themselves Dakota or Lakota, their word for "friends" or "allies." Two of the state's many nicknames, the Sioux State and the Land of the Dakotas, honor this heritage. Others include the Peace Garden State, for the International Peace Garden that lies along the U.S.-Canadian border, and the state's official nickname, the Flickertail State, for the quick flickertail squirrels found all over North Dakota's prairies.

State flag

North Dakota lies in the midwestern United States, in the geographic center of the North American continent. It is a prairie state, yet only the eastern area is flat. The central area has a rolling landscape with many ridges, lakes, and wooded hills. The west is more rugged. Its fragmented landscape includes a region of eroded formations of sandstone, clay, and shale, known as the Badlands.

With fewer than 645,000 residents, North Dakota is one of the most thinly populated states. About half of its total population lives in rural areas; the other half lives in the state's small cities. Fewer than 95,000 North Dakotans live in Fargo, the largest city. Fewer than 56,000 live in Bismarck, the capital city.

North Dakota is primarily an agricultural state. It is the nation's leading producer of barley and sunflowers, and it competes with Kansas for the top spot in the production of wheat, North Dakota's most valuable crop. But north Dakota is unquestionably the nation's leading producer of durum wheat, a type used to make spaghetti and other pastas.

The first non-Indian explorers appeared in North Dakota in 1738. Since then four nations have claimed the region—France, Spain, Great Britain, and the United States. Thousands of homesteaders migrated to North Dakota in the 1870's, when the Northern Pacific Railroad cut through the frontier. They hunted the bison that grazed on the grass-covered prairies and fought bitterly with the Indians for possession of the land. North Dakota's Indians eventually were removed by the U.S. government to a handful of reservations. Four of these still exist today.

▶ **LAND**

North Dakota's surface has been etched and molded by the natural forces of wind, water, and especially ice. The last great continental ice sheet shaved down the highlands, filled in the lowlands, and changed or destroyed the courses of rivers and streams. It also left an uneven covering of broken and pulverized rock over most of the landscape.

Land Regions

North Dakota is divided into three distinct levels that rise toward the west like steps in a giant stairway. They are the Red River Valley, the Drift Prairie, and the Great Plains.

The Red River Valley. The lowest and most easterly level, the Red River Valley is North Dakota's most productive agricultural region. It is part of a larger region of the United States known as the Central Lowland. The Red River Valley is not a true river valley but the bed of an ancient lake, Lake Agassiz, that drained away about 10,000 years ago.

The Drift Prairie. The second level of the "stairway" also lies in the greater Central Lowland region. It is called the Drift Prairie because the land is composed of glacial deposits called drift. Most of this roll-

North Dakota's landscape varies greatly. *Opposite page, left:* In the east, the fertile plains of the Red River Valley support vast farmlands. *Bottom right:* In the west, the mysterious and rugged Badlands rise out of the Great Plains. *Top right:* Bison roam free in Theodore Roosevelt National Park.

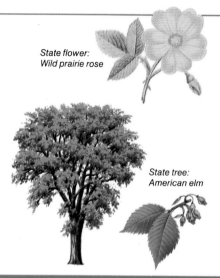

State flower:
Wild prairie rose

State tree:
American elm

FACTS AND FIGURES

Location: North central United States; bordered on the north by Canada (Manitoba and Saskatchewan), on the south by South Dakota, on the east by Minnesota, and on the west by Montana.

Area: 70,704 sq mi (183,123 km²); rank, 18th.

Population: 642,200 (2000 census); rank, 47th.

Elevation: *Highest*—3,506 ft (1,069 m) at White Butte; *lowest*—750 ft (229 m), in Pembina County.

Capital: Bismarck.

Statehood: November 2, 1889; 39th state.

State Motto: *Liberty and Union. Now and Forever. One and Inseparable.*

State Song: "North Dakota Hymn."

Nickname: Flickertail State (official); Sioux State; Peace Garden State; Rough Rider State; Land of the Dakotas.

Abbreviations: ND; N.D.; N. Dak.

State bird:
Western meadowlark

ing land is excellent for farming, especially for growing grains. Hundreds of lakes dot the landscape, and the ground is marked by moraines, or ridges of rocky glacial materials. The Turtle Mountains in the north make an area of wooded hill country that extends across the border into Canada.

The Great Plains. The highest and westernmost level is the Great Plains region, which, in North Dakota, is called the Missouri Plateau. The plateau begins at the Missouri Coteau, which is an escarpment (or hilly slope) that crosses the state diagonally, from the northwest to the southeast.

In the southwest lies a high, rolling plain called the Slope. Many buttes (flat-topped hills) rise abruptly from the Slope, including White Butte which, at 3,506 feet (1,069 meters), is the highest point in the state. The southwest also contains what many consider to be the most scenic part of North Dakota—the famous Badlands, which also extend into South Dakota. The name Badlands came from translating the Sioux words *Mako Shika*, meaning "land bad."

Long ago, the Badlands were made up of level layers of soft sandstone and shale. Running water and other natural forces carved these layers into a complex network of canyons, gullies, and buttes with many odd and fantastic forms.

In his book *Ranch Life and Hunting Trail*, Theodore Roosevelt described the Badlands in this way: "For a stretch of nearly 10 miles along the Little Missouri above my range . . . there are but three or four places where it is possible for a horseman to get out to the eastern prairie through the exceedingly broken country. . . . In such very bad ground the whole country seems to be one tangled chaos of canyonlike valleys, winding gullies and washouts with abrupt, unbroken sides, isolated peaks of sandstone, marl, or 'gumbo' clay, which rains turn into slippery glue."

Rivers and Lakes

North Dakota occupies part of a great divide that separates waters that flow in different directions. The Missouri River, which drains about 60 percent of the land toward the Gulf of Mexico, is the only river in the state that provides a reliable water supply. It has several tributaries, including the Little Missouri, the Knife, the Heart, and the Cannonball rivers. The Missouri River is joined by the Yellowstone River in the west and the James River in the southeast.

The rest of the land in North Dakota is drained by rivers that lead to Hudson Bay. These include the Souris River (which often is called the Mouse River because *souris* is the French word for "mouse"; the Red River of the North, simply called the Red River (which is formed by the joining of the Bois de Sioux

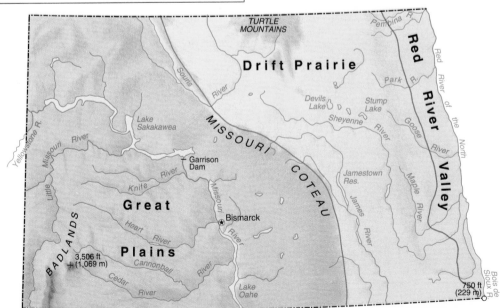

NORTH DAKOTA Landforms

☀ State capital
+ Highest point
○ Lowest point
— Landform boundary

0 20 40 60 mi
0 20 40 60 km

—15,000 ft, 4500 m
—6000 ft, 1800 m
—3000 ft, 900 m
—1500 ft, 450 m
—600 ft, 180 m
—300 ft, 90 m
—Sea Level
—Below

Left: The Red River of the North forms the North Dakota-Minnesota border and flows through one of the richest agricultural regions in the world. *Above:* Lake Sakakawea is a popular recreation area. The reservoir was formed when the Garrison Dam on the Missouri River was completed in 1960.

and Otter Tail rivers near Wahpeton); the Sheyenne (which is a tributary of the Red River that forms the state's border with Minnesota); and the Pembina; the Park; and the Goose rivers.

North Dakota's largest lakes have been created by dams. The great Garrison Dam—which is 2 miles (3 kilometers) long and 200 feet (60 meters) wide—created the reservoir known as Lake Sakakawea. The dams generate hydroelectric power for the state, and the reservoirs serve as popular recreational areas. Some of the state's larger, natural lakes include Devils Lake and Stump Lake in the northeast. Hundreds of smaller lakes dot the central countryside.

Climate

North Dakota, which lies in the center of the continent, lacks the moderating influence of the oceans. Summers are hot and winters are cold. In central North Dakota in January, the coldest month, temperatures average 7°F (−10°C). In July, the warmest month, temperatures average 70°F (21°C). Normal annual precipitation (from rain and melted snow) is 15.36 inches (390 millimeters).

Plant and Animal Life

North Dakota is part of the great "sea of grass" that once extended from the woodlands of the eastern United States to the forests of the Rocky Mountains. The Red River Valley is tall-grass country, decorated with wildflowers, including the wild prairie rose, the state flower.

Of the many kinds of animals that roam wild, the most common are white-tailed deer, mule deer, pronghorns, prairie dogs, badgers, bobcats, beavers, coyotes, foxes, lynxes, minks, muskrats, rabbits, raccoons, skunks, weasels, and flickertail squirrels. Wild game birds include ducks, grouse, Hungarian partridges, and pheasants. North Dakota's rivers and lakes support bass, carp, catfish, perch, trout, and walleyed pike.

Of the mere one percent of North Dakota that is forested, the most common trees are ash, aspen, bassswood, box elder, cottonwood, elm, oak, poplar, and willow.

Natural Resources

North Dakota's most valuable resources are its minerals. Conservation, especially of the soil, has been an important consideration since

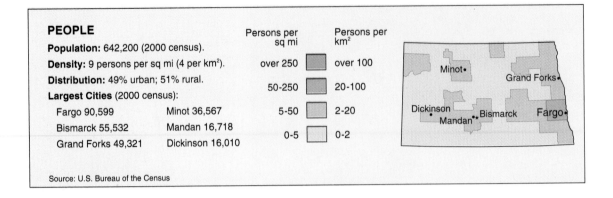

a ruinous drought in the 1930's temporarily destroyed the state's economy.

Soils. The Red River Valley contains some of the world's richest agricultural land. Its black soil is free of stones and enriched by a deep layer of humus, a dark brown or black organic matter formed by decomposed plant and animal remains.

Drift Prairie soils come from glacial deposits and are usually dark brown. They are highly productive, but often stony. The thinner soils of the unglaciated Great Plains have made grazing more important there than general farming.

Minerals. Western North Dakota is part of the Williston Basin, an enormous oil-rich region that covers several north-central states and part of Canada. Large amounts of natural gas also can be found, mixed in with the oil. The area also has immense salt deposits.

Thick beds of lignite, a very soft coal, underlie most of the western part of the state. North Dakota has the largest reserves of lignite coal in the whole country. Some of the coal beds in the Badlands have been slowly burning for centuries, ignited by spontaneous combustion or some other natural cause, such as lightning. Burning lignite bakes the surrounding clay and sand into a kind of natural brick called scoria.

The red color of scoria adds beauty to the landscape and is widely used as a form of gravel. Leonardite, another product of burning lignite, is used to make wood stain. Uranium and molybdenum also have been found in some lignite deposits.

Clay, sand, and gravel are abundant throughout the state. Large deposits of sodium sulfate can be found in the northwest; building stone is found in the southwest. Among the other minerals found in North Dakota are manganese, marl, and quartzite.

▶ **PEOPLE**

With fewer than 645,000 residents, North Dakota ranks only as the 47th most populous state in the union. The most densely populated section is the fertile Red River Valley.

Indians first settled on the plains thousands of years ago. Today about 30,000 Native Americans from a variety of tribes live in North Dakota: Mandan, Hidatsa, and Arikara live on the Fort Berthold Indian Reservation along Lake Sakakawea; Chippewa live on the Turtle Mountain Indian Reservation near Rolla; and Sioux live on the Totten Indian Reservation near Devils Lake and the Standing Rock Indian Reservation on the South Dakota border.

Most of the non-Indians who live in North Dakota are descended from immigrants who settled the area within the last 120 years. Farmers, lured by the promise of cheap and abundant land, came from Europe to clear the prairies. They came from Scandinavia (particularly Norway), Russia, Germany, Canada, and from elsewhere in the United States.

Education

Elementary and secondary education in North Dakota is administered by more than 300 public school districts and 100 private schools. About 45 schools are administered by the Bureau of Indian Affairs. The state also operates a variety of schools for the physically and mentally disabled.

Among the state's institutions of higher learning are the University of North Dakota in

Grand Forks, founded in 1883. It has an enrollment of about 12,000 students. North Dakota State University at Fargo, founded in 1890, has an enrollment of about 9,000 students. Other state universities are located in Dickinson, Mayville, Minot, and Valley City. Leading private colleges include Jamestown College in Jamestown and the University of Mary in Bismarck.

Libraries, Museums, and the Arts

North Dakota has about 80 public libraries, and traveling bookmobiles provide reading materials to many of the state's remote rural areas. The state's largest library is the Chester Fritz Library at the University of North Dakota.

One of the state's most prominent art museums is the E'Lan Art Gallery in Bismarck. It contains folk art and fine art, much of which was created by local artists. The Heritage Center, on the capitol grounds in Bismarck, contains the State Archives, the Research Library, and the State Museum, which has state history and geology exhibits and an impressive collection of Indian artifacts. A separate Indian museum, operated by the Hidatsa, Arikara, and Mandan tribes, is located in New Town.

The North Dakota Council on the Arts and the National Endowment for the Arts supports

North Dakota State University is in Fargo. Founded in 1890, its enrollment is second only to that of the University of North Dakota in Grand Forks.

community opera, theater, symphony, dance, and other performing art programs throughout the state. Two of the most popular attractions can be found in Medora in the Badlands—the Dakota Cowboy Poetry Gathering, held over Memorial Day weekend, and the Medora Musical, held nightly during the summer.

Below: Performers in the Medora Musical fondly recreate North Dakota's pioneer days. *Right:* Native North Dakotans include the Sioux Indians. *Below right:* Today's residents are mostly descended from Scandinavian and other northern European immigrants.

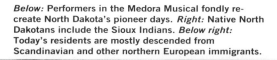

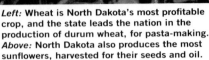

Left: Wheat is North Dakota's most profitable crop, and the state leads the nation in the production of durum wheat, for pasta-making. *Above:* North Dakota also produces the most sunflowers, harvested for their seeds and oil.

▶ECONOMY

Throughout its brief history, North Dakota has sold raw materials (mainly farm products) and bought manufactured goods from other places. Manufacturing, therefore, is less important here than it is in most other states. The majority of its workers are employed in the agricultural and service industries.

Services

Service industries account for about 68 percent of North Dakota's gross state product (GSP) (which is the total value of goods and services produced in the state in a year). Many industries fall within the services category. They include financial services, wholesale and retail trade, government services, personal services, and transportation, communication, and utilities.

Financial Services. The most significant of all the service categories, financial services include banking, insurance, and real estate. Financial services account for 17 percent of the total GSP, although they employ a mere 4 percent of the work force.

Wholesale and Retail Trade. Trade is the buying and selling of goods and services—such as in restaurants, stores, supermarkets, automobile dealerships, and the like. The money earned through trade in North Dakota is 16 percent of the total GSP, and related industries employ 23 percent of the work force.

Government Services. State schools, public hospitals, military bases, and Indian reservations all are maintained by government services. Together, the state, local, and federal government services in North Dakota earn 11 percent of the GSP and employ 22 percent of the work force.

Other Services. Dozens of other industries belong in the services category. These include health, legal, and other professional services; social services; community and recreational services; and personal services (dry cleaning, for example). Together they account for 13 percent of the GSP and employ 20 percent of the work force. These figures do not include transportation and communication, which are also service industries.

PRODUCTS AND INDUSTRIES

Manufacturing: Processed foods, farm and construction equipment, printed materials, petroleum products.

Agriculture: Spring wheat, durum wheat, barley, rye, flaxseed, sunflowers, oats, potatoes, pinto beans, honey, soybeans, sugar beets, hay, cattle, sheep, hogs, poultry, bees.

Minerals: Oil, lignite coal, clay, salt, limestone, construction sand and gravel, crushed stone.

Services: Wholesale and retail trade; finance, insurance, and real estate; business, social, and personal services; transportation, communication, and utilities; government.

*Gross state product is the total value of goods and services produced in a year.

Percentage of Gross State Product* by Industry

Finance, insurance, and real estate — 17%
Construction
Mining
5%
6%
Manufacturing — 6%
Transportation, communication, and utilities — 11%
Wholesale and retail trade — 16%
Government — 11%
Business, social, and personal services — 13%
Agriculture — 15%

Source: U.S. Bureau of Economic Analysis

Agriculture

Almost 21 million acres (9 million hectares) —or about half of the entire state of North Dakota—is given over to farming. Of all the states, North Dakota ranks third in overall agricultural productivity. North Dakota farmers grow many different crops, but they are best known for raising wheat and barley. Among the state's other important crops are rye, flaxseed, oats, hay, potatoes, pinto beans, soybeans, honey, sugar beets, and sunflowers.

North Dakota ranks about 35th in the nation in raising cattle, hogs, sheep, and poultry. All together, the farms of the state produce 15 percent of the GSP and employ 14 percent of the work force.

Manufacturing

Most of the manufacturing in North Dakota is related to agriculture, and the most important manufacturing enterprise is food processing. Breads, cereals, dairy products, potato chips, sunflower oil, honey, and table sugar are produced. Fertilizers and farm equipment, such as tractors, also are produced. Other important industries include the production of printed materials, petroleum products, and construction equipment. Manufacturing accounts for 6 percent of the GSP and employs 5 percent of the work force.

Transportation and Communication

Two railroad lines supply freight service through the state, and an Amtrak line provides passenger service between Fargo and Williston. North Dakota's network of roads includes two interstate highways, one running east to west and the other running north to south. There are more than 100 commercial airports, with the largest located in Fargo, Bismarck, Grand Forks, and Minot. Farmers and ranchers use hundreds of privately owned airstrips.

Dozens of daily, weekly, and semi-weekly newspapers are published in North Dakota, including four Indian newspapers. Of the state's ten daily newspapers, the Fargo *Forum* and the Bismarck *Tribune* have the largest circulations. Both papers have won Pulitzer prizes. Other media outlets include about 70 radio and 20 television stations.

The transportation and communications industries, along with utilities (such as gas and electric services), account for 11 percent of the GSP and employ 6 percent of the work force.

Mining and Construction

Most of North Dakota's mineral production is made up of fuels—petroleum, lignite coal, and natural gas. Nonfuel minerals include limestone, crushed stone, and sand and gravel for construction. Clay, which is abundant and easily mined, is used in the manufacture of bricks. Mining accounts for 6 percent of the GSP and employs 2 percent of the work force.

Construction is an ongoing process that occurs wherever roads, bridges, houses, office buildings, and stores are being built or repaired. Construction enterprises account for 5 percent of the GSP and employ 4 percent of the work force.

▶CITIES

About half of North Dakota's residents live in cities, although only four cities in the state have populations exceeding 25,000. These are Fargo, Bismarck, Grand Forks, and Minot.

Bismarck, the state's capital and second largest city, is located in a rich agricultural and mining area. A growing center for the coal and oil industries, Bismarck also is a retail and medical center.

Bismarck was founded in 1873 and was named after Otto von Bismarck, who was chancellor of Germany at the time. It was hoped that bestowing this honor would persuade the Germans to help finance the state's railroad construction. The scheme failed, but the name Bismarck stuck. Bismarck became the capital of the Dakota Territory in 1883 and of the state of North Dakota in 1889.

Fargo is North Dakota's most populous city. Located in the valley of the Red River of the North, it is an important industrial center and a transportation hub of the Northwest.

Fargo, North Dakota's largest city, is located in the eastern part of the state on the Red River of the North. It is the state's primary manufacturing and trade center and is the location of some of the nation's largest stockyards. Fargo also is an important regional medical center and the home of North Dakota State University, founded in 1890. In recent years, legalized gambling has boosted tourism in Fargo.

Fargo was settled in 1871 and named in honor of William George Fargo, who was a director of the Northern Pacific Railway and a founder of Wells, Fargo & Company, an early banking and transportation company.

Grand Forks is North Dakota's third largest city. It is located in the east and serves as a major trade center for the Red River Valley. Its main industries include potato processing, grain milling, and sugar refining. The University of North Dakota, which houses the official state art gallery, is located there, as is the state School for the Blind.

Early French explorers called Grand Forks "Les Grandes Fourches" because it is located at the fork of the Red River of the North and

GOVERNMENT

State Government
Governor: 4-year term
State senators: 53; 4-year terms
State representatives: 118;
2-year terms
Number of counties: 53

Federal Government
U.S. senators: 2
U.S. representatives: 1
Number of electoral votes: 3

For the name of the current governor, see STATE GOVERNMENTS in Volume S. For the names of current U.S. senators and representatives, see UNITED STATES, CONGRESS OF THE in Volume U-V.

Red Lake River. The railroads reached Grand Forks in 1880, and the city was incorporated the following year.

Minot, located in the oil-rich Williston Basin, is the agricultural trading center for the Souris River valley. It is surrounded by lignite strip mines. Minot was settled in 1886 as a tent town during the construction of the Northern Pacific Railroad. Minot State College is located there.

▶GOVERNMENT

North Dakota's constitution was adopted in 1889, the year of statehood. It provides for a government made up of three branches—legislative, executive, and judicial.

The Legislative Assembly represents the legislative, or law-making, branch. It is made up of two houses—a house of representatives and a senate. The house and senate hold sessions beginning in January of odd-numbered years.

The executive branch, headed by the state's governor, carries out the laws of the state. Other executive officials, in addition to the governor, also are elected by the people. These include the lieutenant governor, the attorney general, the secretary of state, the treasurer, the auditor, and the superintendent of public schools. The people also elect commissioners for agriculture, labor, insurance, taxation, and public service.

The judicial branch—the court system—is responsible for interpreting and applying the laws. There are three kinds of courts in the state: the state supreme court, the district courts, and the county courts. All state judges are elected by the people. The supreme court has five justices, and each is elected to a 10-year term; each of the state's 26 district judges is elected to a 6-year term; and each of the 53 county judges is elected to a 4-year term.

The state capitol in Bismarck, completed in 1934, is one of the nation's few legislative houses built in the form of a skyscraper.

Knife River Indian Villages

Fort Union Trading Post

Frontier Village

North Dakota contains dozens of historic sites that date back to the early days of settlement. It also contains many national wildlife refuges, in keeping with the conservationist spirit of Theodore Roosevelt, who spent much time in the state.

Bonanzaville, U.S.A., in West Fargo, is a pioneer village that brings to life the era of the huge bonanza farms, when agriculture first boomed in North Dakota. Reconstructed farmhouses, log cabins, a church, a school, general stores, and a railroad station give a flavor of what life was like there in the 1800's.

Camp Hancock State Historic Site, in Bismarck, contains part of a military camp, which was set up in 1872 by the U.S. Army to protect workers on the Northern Pacific Railroad. Attractions include an early Northern Pacific locomotive and one of Bismarck's oldest churches.

Chateau de Morès State Historic Site, near Medora, preserves the stately home of Antoine de Vallombrosa, Marquis de Morès, a wealthy French businessman who settled in North Dakota for several years in the 1880's. This 26-room, two-story home is filled with its original French furnishings.

Fort Abercrombie State Historic Site, near Abercrombie, is the site of the first U.S. military outpost established in North Dakota (1857). Its original stockade and blockhouse have been restored.

Fort Buford State Historic Site, southwest of Williston, was an important outpost during the Indian wars of the 1870's and 1880's. Now a museum with pioneer and cavalry artifacts, it is where Sitting Bull surrendered to U.S. troops in 1881.

Fort Lincoln State Park is located where the Heart and the Missouri rivers meet, south of Mandan. It preserves the former sites of Fort McKeen and Fort Abraham Lincoln. In 1876, Lieutenant Colonel George A. Custer set out from Fort Lincoln to fight the Battle of the Little Bighorn in Montana. The park contains reconstructed blockhouses and Indian earth lodges. Its museum displays Indian and U.S. military relics.

Fort Totten State Historic Site, a military post that dates from 1867, is located 13 miles (21 kilometers) southwest of Devils Lake on the Totten Indian Reservation. It is one of the best-preserved forts from the era of the Indian wars.

Fort Union Trading Post National Historic Site, near Williston, was built in 1829 by the American Fur Company, which was once owned by the fur tycoon John Jacob Astor. This was the largest, most influential trading post on the Upper Missouri River.

Frontier Village, near Jamestown, is home to "the world's largest bison," a huge 26-foot (8-meter) statue made from steel and concrete. Also on the grounds are restored buildings, including a railroad depot, a school, and a church.

Geographical Center Pioneer Village and Museum, near Rugby, marks the center of the North American continent. (The geographical center of the United States is in South Dakota.)

International Peace Garden, located on the North Dakota-Manitoba border north of Dunseith, serves as a symbol of the friendly relations between the United States and Canada. The park covers an area of 2,339 acres (947 hectares) and contains formal gardens, an amphitheater, a peace chapel, a bell tower, a floral clock, and an arboretum.

Knife River Indian Villages National Historic Site, near Stanton, preserves the remains of five villages of the Hidatsa, Arikara, and Mandan tribes. Members of the Lewis and Clark expedition wintered here in 1804–05. This is where they met and employed their Indian guide, Sacagawea.

Theodore Roosevelt National Park, located in the Badlands, was established in 1947 as a memorial to the conservationist president. The park's three sections encompass 70,374 acres (28,480 hectares) of spectacular scenery and include Roosevelt's Elkhorn Ranch.

Whitestone Battlefield State Historic Site, northwest of Ellendale, commemorates an 1863 battle between the U.S. Army and the Sioux.

Writing Rock, a giant boulder near Grenora, preserves pictures that the Indians carved in the stone.

State Parks. North Dakota has numerous national wildlife refuges and a dozen state parks. For more information about them, contact North Dakota Tourism Promotion, Liberty Memorial Building, 604 East Boulevard, Bismarck, N.D. 58505.

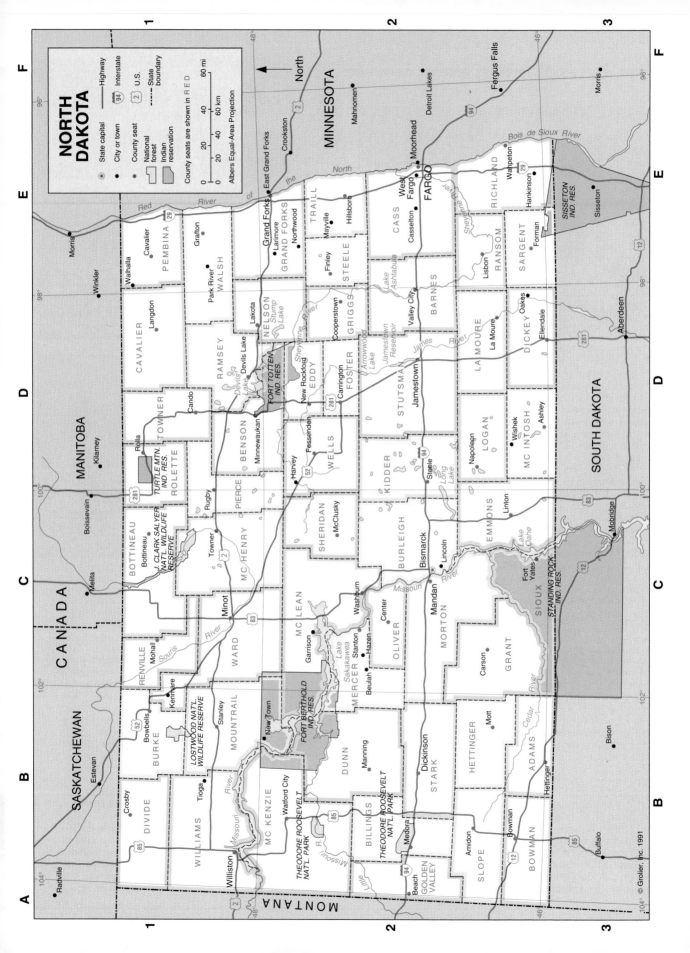

NORTH DAKOTA

Legend:
- ★ State capital
- • City or town
- ∘ County seat
- National forest
- Indian reservation
- Highway / Interstate
- 94 Interstate
- 2 U.S.
- ---- State boundary

County seats are shown in RED

60 mi
0 20 40 60 km
Albers Equal-Area Projection

North

CANADA

SASKATCHEWAN

MANITOBA

MONTANA

MINNESOTA

SOUTH DAKOTA

Radville
Estevan
Boissevain
Kilarney
Winkler
Morris

Crosby
Bowbells
Kenmare
Mohall
Bottineau
Rolla
Langdon
Cavalier
Walhalla
Grafton

DIVIDE
BURKE
RENVILLE
BOTTINEAU
ROLETTE
TOWNER
CAVALIER
PEMBINA

Williston
Tioga
Stanley
Minot
Towner
Rugby
Cando
Park River
WALSH

WILLIAMS
MOUNTRAIL
WARD
MC HENRY
PIERCE
BENSON
RAMSEY
NELSON
Lakota

Watford City
New Town
Garrison
Washburn
McClusky
Minnewaukan
Devils Lake
New Rockford
Grand Forks
East Grand Forks
Crookston
Northwood
Larimore

MC KENZIE
DUNN
MERCER
OLIVER
MC LEAN
SHERIDAN
WELLS
EDDY
FOSTER
GRIGGS
STEELE
TRAILL
GRAND FORKS

Theodore Roosevelt Natl. Park
Medora
Beach
Dickinson
Manning
Beulah
Hazen
Stanton
Center
Mandan
Bismarck
Lincoln
Steele
Carrington
Cooperstown
Finley
Hillsboro
Mayville

BILLINGS
GOLDEN VALLEY
STARK
MORTON
BURLEIGH
KIDDER
STUTSMAN
BARNES
CASS

Amidon
Mott
Carson
Fort Yates
Linton
Napoleon
Wishek
Ashley
Jamestown
Valley City
West Fargo
Casselton
FARGO
Moorhead

SLOPE
HETTINGER
GRANT
SIOUX
EMMONS
LOGAN
MC INTOSH
LA MOURE
DICKEY
RANSOM
SARGENT
RICHLAND

Bowman
Hettinger
Buffalo
Bison
Mobridge
Aberdeen
La Moure
Oakes
Ellendale
Lisbon
Forman
Oakes
Wahpeton
Hankinson
Sisseton

BOWMAN
ADAMS

Fergus Falls
Morris
Detroit Lakes
Mahnomen

Missouri River
Little Missouri River
Souris River
Red River of the North
Sheyenne River
James River
Lake Sakakawea
Lake Oahe
Devils Lake
Stump Lake
Lake Ashtabula
Jamestown Reservoir
Arrowwood Lake
Long Lake
Cedar River
Bois de Sioux River

FORT BERTHOLD IND. RES.
FORT TOTTEN IND. RES.
TURTLE MTN. IND. RES.
STANDING ROCK IND. RES.
SISSETON IND. RES.

THEODORE ROOSEVELT NATL. PARK
LOSTWOOD NATL. WILDLIFE RESERVE
J. CLARK SALYER NATL. WILDLIFE RESERVE

© Grolier, Inc. 1991

INDEX TO NORTH DAKOTA MAP

► HISTORY

About 10,000 years before Europeans settled in North America, a variety of Indian tribes lived peacefully on the land that is now North Dakota. The Mandan were probably the first to arrive, followed by the Hidatsa and the Arikara. The Chippewa later migrated to the Turtle Mountains, and the Cheyenne occupied the southeast for a time, but they were later driven out by the Sioux.

The Europeans Arrive

In 1682, French explorer René-Robert Cavelier, Sieur de la Salle, claimed for France all of the land in the Mississippi River system, including the lands surrounding the Missouri River. France also claimed the lands south of Canada's Hudson Bay. Together, both claims gave France sovereignty over most of the land in present-day North Dakota. Then in the 1700's, various parts of the North Dakota territory were given over to British and Spanish rule as well. The United States did not own all of North Dakota until 1818, the year Great Britain ceded to the United States all of the territory south of the 49th parallel, the present U.S.-Canadian border line.

Early Exploration

The first non-Indians to see North Dakota were probably led by Pierre Gaultier de Varennes, Sieur de la Vérendrye, a French explorer and fur trader from Canada. In 1768, Jonathan Carver, an American explorer and soldier, explored the Red River Valley. Then in 1797, David Thompson, an English geographer, mapped the Souris and Missouri rivers. In that same year, Charles Chaboillez established a fur-trading post at Pembina.

After the United States bought the Louisiana Territory in 1803, President Thomas Jefferson sent Meriwether Lewis and William Clark to explore the West. In October 1804, Lewis and Clark went up the Missouri River and into North Dakota. Near the present site of Stanton, they set up winter quarters at Fort Mandan, among the Mandan and Hidatsa Indians. There, for the first time, the United States flag was raised on Dakota soil.

Railroads hastened the settlement of North Dakota. In the early 1900's, "immigrant trains" brought in pioneers —mostly farmers—by the thousands.

Famous People

Maxwell Anderson (1888–1959), a playwright, lived in Jamestown and graduated from the University of North Dakota in 1911. He is best remembered for *What Price Glory?* (1924), about American soldiers in France during World War I; *Mary of Scotland* (1933); *Key Largo* (1939) and *Both Your Houses* (1933), a satire about Congress that won him the Pulitzer Prize for drama.

Louis L'Amour (1908–88), a prolific writer of Western frontier novels, was born near Jamestown. He was known for his talent for description and sympathetic treatment of minority groups. Some of his most famous books include *Hondo, The Daybreakers*, and *The Haunted Mesa*. Many have been made into films and television dramas.

Peggy Lee (1920–2002) was born Norma Deloris Engstrom in Jamestown. Considered one of the great jazz vocalists, Lee's sultry style was popular in the 1950's.

Manuel Lisa (1772–1820) was one of the most important American fur traders on the upper Missouri River. He established many trading posts, including Fort Manuel, which served the Knife River villages. Lisa became known for his fair treatment of Indian customers.

Roger Maris (1934–85), a major-league baseball outfielder, was born in Minnesota, but spent his youth in Fargo.

Marquis de Morès

He played most of his twelve-year career with the New York Yankees. A career .260 hitter, in 1961 he broke Babe Ruth's single-season home-run record with 61 homers. He was chosen MVP (most valuable player) in the American League in 1960 and 1961. He retired in 1968.

Eric Sevareid (1912–92), a writer, broadcast journalist, and reporter, was born in Velva. He established his reputation during World War II. He later became senior news analyst for CBS News. Among his books are *Not So Wild a Dream* and *This Is Eric Sevareid*.

Settlement Begins

In 1812, Scottish colonizer Thomas Douglas, Earl of Selkirk, brought a group of Scottish colonists from Canada to settle near the Pembina trading post. Most of Selkirk's settlers, or "Selkirkers" as they were called, moved when it was discovered Pembina was not on the Canadian side of the international border. But many other settlers remained, and Pembina grew into North Dakota's first permanent settlement. The state's first school was founded there in 1818.

The Dakota Territory

In 1861 the U.S. government formally organized the Dakota Territoy, and established the first territorial capital at Yankton (in present-day South Dakota).

The arrival of the settlers provoked the Indians, especially the Sioux, to defend their hunting grounds. Throughout the 1860's and 1870's, the U.S. Army pursued the Indians and forced them onto reservations. The Sioux continued to resist until 1881, when their leader, Sitting Bull, surrendered to U.S. troops at Fort Buford.

Agriculture Thrives

North Dakota was rapidly settled as soon as the railroads came, beginning in 1871. The first, the Northern Pacific Railroad, eventually stretched from Minnesota to Washington. It reached Fargo in 1872.

THEODORE ROOSEVELT IN THE BADLANDS

Of all the people associated with North Dakota, the most colorful was Theodore Roosevelt, 26th president of the United States. Roosevelt first visited the Dakota Territory in 1883 to hunt bison and other big game. He was captivated by the wide-open spaces and the rugged beauty of the Badlands. When his wife died tragically in 1884, the grieving young widower resigned from the New York state legislature and retreated to the Badlands to raise cattle. He established the Maltese Cross Ranch near Medora on the Little Missouri River, and later bought the Elkhorn Ranch. He rode the range, sometimes for sixteen hours a day, earning the grudging respect of the tough local cowboys and ranchers, who had dubbed him Old Four Eyes and the Dude from New York.

During the hard, bitter winter of 1886–87, most of the cattle in the Dakota Territory either froze or starved to death. Roosevelt's ranches failed, and he returned to New York to resume his political career. Years later, in 1898, Roosevelt recruited many of the men he had known in the Badlands to join his cavalry unit of Rough Riders during the Spanish-American War. That is why today North Dakota is sometimes called the Rough Rider State.

Clyfford Still (1904–80), born in Grandin, was a leader of the abstract expressionist movement in art. He began his career painting landscapes of western plateaus but changed over to the abstract style in the 1940's. He was famous for his large canvases, filled with brightly colored abstract shapes.

Era Bell Thompson (1906–86), a prominent journalist, grew up in Driscoll. From 1951 to 1970 she was co-managing editor of *Ebony* magazine. She traveled widely throughout Africa to research her book, *Africa, Land of My Fathers*.

Antoine de Vallombrosa, Marquis de Morès (1858–96), a wealthy French nobleman, was an early settler of the Badlands. Seeing endless business opportunities for cattle ranching in the Da-

kotas, he arrived in 1883 and founded a town he named Medora, after his wife. There he tried to build a meat-packing empire. When all of his business ventures failed, he returned to France in 1886.

Pierre Gaultier de Varennes, Sieur de la Vérendrye (1685–1749), a French-Canadian explorer and fur trader, led a group of men who were the first non-Indians to see what is now North Dakota. In 1731 he set out from Montreal with four companions to find a route to the Pacific Ocean. By 1738 he had reached the Dakotas, which he claimed for the king of France.

Roger Maris

Eric Sevareid

Lawrence Welk (1903–92), born near Strasburg, was one of the most popular entertainers of his time. He began his musical career as a solo accordionist and later formed a dance band. In 1950 he took his "champagne music" to television, appearing on *Cavalcade of Bands*. He later hosted the enormously popular *The Lawrence Welk Show*, which aired from 1955 until 1971.

In the 1870's, North Dakota began to establish its reputation as a farming region, and a new agricultural era began. Hundreds of enormous wheat farms were developed in the Red River Valley. They were called bonanza farms because they were so large and profitable. Some of them were as large as 60,000 acres (24,000 hectares) and employed hundreds of workers.

In the 1880's, many bonanza farms failed due to drought, plagues of grasshoppers, and falling wheat prices.

Statehood

In 1883, the capital of the Dakota Territory was moved from Yankton to Bismarck. In February 1889, Congress passed an act dividing the territory into two parts, and on November 2, President Benjamin Harrison signed documents admitting the two new states to the Union—North Dakota as the 39th and South Dakota as the 40th.

The Nonpartisan League

Pioneer farmers continued to face a variety of hardships, so in 1915 the farmers organized the Nonpartisan League. This political group was designed to give the farmers more control over the production and distribution of their produce and to prevent their exploitation by wealthy businessmen, who kept the freight rates, interest rates, and the price of grain artificially high.

World War II and Postwar Economic Developments

A terrible drought in the 1930's ruined the economy of North Dakota, and thousands of people fled the state. But agricultural prosperity returned in the early 1940's, and North Dakota farms contributed tremendous amounts of food to the nation and the world during World War II (1939–45).

When oil was discovered near Tioga in 1951, new industries developed in North Dakota. Garrison Dam on the Missouri River was completed in 1960, forming a reservoir for farm irrigation, flood control, and hydroelectric power. Air bases and missile sites, established in the 1960's, continued to boost the state's economy.

Recent Developments

North Dakota began developing its oil, coal, and natural gas reserves in the 1970's when an energy crisis occurred. The rate of fuel production slowed down, however, when oil prices dropped in the 1980's.

Efforts are now being made to attract a wider range of industry to North Dakota. But in the meantime, the state's prosperity will continue to depend on the profit of its agricultural industry.

BERNT L. WILLS
Author, *North Dakota*
Reviewed by THOMAS G. AYLESWORTH
Author, *Let's Discover the States* Series

NORTHERN IRELAND

Northern Ireland is one of four parts of the United Kingdom of Great Britain and Northern Ireland. It occupies about one-sixth of the total area of the island of Ireland. Belfast is the capital of Northern Ireland and its largest city.

For centuries, all of Ireland was governed by Great Britain. But in 1920, Britain partitioned (divided) the island in two. The much larger southern region eventually became the independent Republic of Ireland. The smaller northeastern region remained within the United Kingdom and became known as Northern Ireland.

Ever since partition, Northern Ireland has been the center of conflict between Unionists and Nationalists. The Unionists (or Loyalists) wish Northern Ireland to remain part of the United Kingdom. The Nationalists seek to unite it with the Republic of Ireland.

▶ PEOPLE

Northern Ireland's population of about 1.6 million is divided by religion, cultural differences, and political loyalties. Of the total population, about 50 percent is Protestant and 38 percent Roman Catholic. Most of the remaining 12 percent claims no religious affiliation. English is the official language.

The divisions between Protestants and Catholics have been deepened by segregation.

Belfast is the capital of Northern Ireland, a self-governing province of the United Kingdom. A port and industrial city, Belfast is one of the world's largest shipbuilding centers.

Protestants and Catholics live in different neighborhoods, go to different schools, and generally lead lives apart from each other.

▶ LAND

Northern Ireland covers approximately 5,450 square miles (14,120 square kilometers). It once included six of the nine counties of the ancient province of Ulster—Antrim, Armagh, Londonderry, Down, Fermanagh, and Tyrone. In 1974 these were reorganized into 26 districts.

The landscape is varied, with low, rugged mountains, deep valleys, rolling plains, numerous rivers and lakes, and coastal waters. The highest peak, Slieve Donard in the Mourne Mountains, has an elevation of 2,796 feet (852 meters). The major river is the Bann. Lough Neagh is the largest lake. The region has few mineral resources.

▶ ECONOMY

The northern region of Ireland once had highly developed industry based mainly on shipbuilding and the manufacture of linen. These have declined in importance and have been partly replaced by the production of textiles made from synthetic fibers. Engineering and aircraft construction are also important. Few new industries have developed due to the political instability of the region. Today, Northern Ireland is heavily dependent on financial aid from Britain.

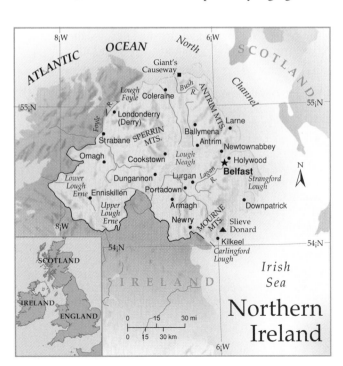

About 85 percent of the land in Northern Ireland is devoted to agriculture, but farming employs only about 10 percent of the workforce. The most important agricultural products are pigs, poultry, beef, and dairy products. Most other foods must be imported.

▶ HISTORY AND GOVERNMENT

Creation. When Ireland was partitioned by Britain in 1920, both parts were offered limited self-government under a regional parliament (legislature). This plan was accepted by the mostly Protestant Unionists in the north, who wished to remain within the United Kingdom; it was rejected by the mostly Catholic Nationalists in the south, who wanted the entire island to become an independent Irish nation. In 1921 a treaty with Britain divided the island, establishing Northern Ireland and the Irish Free State. The Irish Free State officially became independent as the Republic of Ireland in 1949.

Unionist Rule. From 1920 to 1972, Northern Ireland remained firmly in Unionist control. Protestants almost always voted for Unionist candidates, who regularly won a majority of seats in the regional parliament, eventually established at Stormont Castle outside Belfast. Unionists also controlled local governments, as many election districts were arranged to give them a majority. Catholics were thus systematically, but not illegally, prevented from gaining political power. They also faced discrimination in employment and public housing.

The Civil Rights Movement. Catholic resentment against the Unionist government resulted in the formation of a broad civil rights movement in the late 1960's. But a Protestant backlash led to open violence between the two communities. British troops were sent to the region in 1969 to restore order. Soon after, the Irish Republican Army (IRA), a Nationalist organization, began a campaign of guerrilla warfare. Its aim was to drive the British out of Northern Ireland and unite the province with the Republic of Ireland. Other militant groups, including pro-British groups, also carried out terrorist acts. As the bloodshed and violence escalated, the British government suspended the local parliament at Stormont in 1972 and took direct control.

Northern Ireland Today. British rule did not succeed in ending the violence, and compromise between Protestants and Catholics seemed impossible. Protestants refused to share power with Catholics because they feared Catholics would attempt to merge Northern Ireland with the Republic of Ireland. Catholics themselves were divided over whether to support the IRA or nonviolent Nationalist political parties.

In 1985 an agreement with Britain gave the Republic of Ireland an advisory role in Northern Ireland's affairs. A new framework for peace talks, introduced in 1995, was hampered by disagreements on disarming and by the IRA's resumption of bomb attacks in 1996. But peace talks resumed in 1997 when Sinn Fein, the IRA's political arm, agreed to a cease-fire. In 1998, a peace accord, known as the Good Friday Agreement, was overwhelmingly approved by voters in Northern Ireland and the Republic of Ireland. The peace agreement arranged to keep Northern Ireland within the United Kingdom while giving Catholics in Northern Ireland more political power. But in 2002, the fragile peace was disrupted when spying allegations were made against the IRA. Britain then suspended the power-sharing arrangement and re-imposed direct rule on Northern Ireland. In 2005, the IRA formally declared it would no longer use violence to further its cause.

JAMES S. DONNELLY, JR.
University of Wisconsin, Madison

See also IRELAND (History); UNITED KINGDOM.

NORTH KOREA. See KOREA, NORTH.
NORTH POLE. See ARCTIC.
NORTH SEA. See OCEANS AND SEAS OF THE WORLD.
NORTH STAR. See NAVIGATION.
NORTHWEST ORDINANCE. See WESTWARD MOVEMENT.

Mourners mark the anniversary of Bloody Sunday, a 1972 massacre in which more than a dozen peaceful demonstrators in Londonderry were killed by British troops.

NORTHWEST PASSAGE

The Northwest Passage is a route that connects the Atlantic and Pacific oceans by way of the icy Arctic waters of North America. For centuries European explorers who sought a faster trade route to Asia imagined that such a route must exist, and many devoted their lives to finding it.

The search for the fabled Northwest Passage, which began soon after Christopher Columbus' voyage of 1492, reveals tales of extraordinary courage and determination. When Columbus sailed westward across the Atlantic Ocean and landed on an island in the Bahamas, he believed he had reached Asia, his intended destination. The European explorers who followed him, however, soon realized that Columbus had not reached Asia at all, but had approached the shores of two unknown continents. At first they considered this New World little more than an obstacle in their journey to the Orient, and they immediately began looking for a way to sail through it.

The first attempts to find the Northwest Passage were made by John Cabot (1497) for Britain and Giovanni da Verrazano (1524) and Jacques Cartier (1534) for France. However, the British began the search in earnest after 1576, when Sir Martin Frobisher discovered what is now Baffin Island. About nine years later, John Davis explored the western coast

of Greenland and sailed into the strait that now bears his name.

In the 1600's, the search for the Northwest Passage centered around Hudson Bay, discovered by Henry Hudson in 1610. Then William Baffin explored Hudson Strait, Hudson Bay, and the shores of Baffin Bay between 1612 and 1616. Baffin sailed almost as far north as 78 degrees north latitude. This achievement was not equaled for another 200 years because after 1631 exploration efforts in the north focused on finding furs, which could be sold in Europe for enormous profit.

It was not until 1818 that Commander John Ross renewed Britain's search for a continuous westward route to the Pacific Ocean. Ross followed the course Baffin had taken some 200 years earlier, and he charted much of the coastline along the way.

The most famous voyage of this period, however, was Sir John Franklin's tragic expedition of 1845. Franklin and his men disappeared and dozens of rescue parties searched for them in the following years. Unfortunately, Franklin and his men were never found alive, but consequently, the rescue missions contributed about 6,000 miles (9,560 kilometers) of newly explored coastline to the map of Canada's Arctic Islands.

From 1850 to 1854, Captain Robert McClure traveled, partly by sea and partly by sled and on foot, from the Bering Sea eastward to

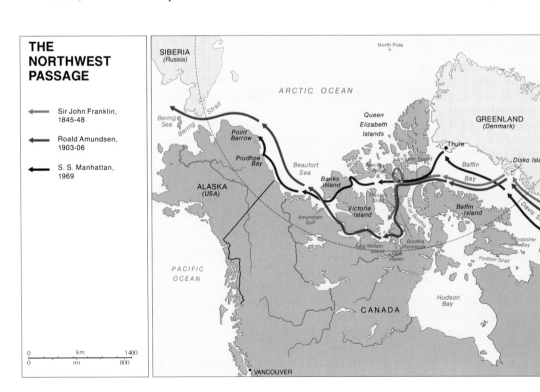

THE NORTHWEST PASSAGE

→ Sir John Franklin, 1845-48

→ Roald Amundsen, 1903-06

→ S. S. Manhattan, 1969

Profiles

Amundsen, Roald (1872–1928), Norwegian explorer, b. Borge. Amundsen achieved many firsts in exploration, including the first successful voyage through the Northwest Passage (1903–06). Then, concentrating his efforts on the other side of the world, he led an expedition to the South Pole. He reached the pole on December 14, 1911, beating the ill-fated British explorer, Robert Scott, by just five weeks. In 1920, Amundsen returned to the Arctic and completed a voyage through the Northeast Passage. He thus became the first person to sail both the Northwest and Northeast passages. In 1928, Amundsen disappeared in the Arctic while searching for Italian explorer Umberto Nobile.

Franklin, Sir John (1786–1847), British rear admiral, b. Lincolnshire. Franklin went in search of the Northwest Passage in 1845, having previously explored the mouth of the Coppermine River (1819) and other Arctic regions (1825–26). It is now known that Franklin discovered the passage on his third Arctic expedition, but he disappeared during the course of it. His ships, *Erebus* and *Terror*, were last seen in Baffin Bay in July 1845. Over the years, no fewer than forty expeditions were sent to find him. In 1859, a search party sponsored by Franklin's wife found a cairn (memorial of piled rocks) on King William Island, revealing Franklin had died on June 11, 1847. Others apparently had died trying to make it back on foot to the Canadian mainland. An earlier search expedition in 1850 had found the graves of three sailors on Beechey Island. More than a century later, in 1984, scientists examined two of the bodies. (See photo below.)

Frobisher, Sir Martin (1535–94), British navigator and explorer, b. Yorkshire. Frobisher made three voyages in search of the Northwest Passage. On his first voyage in 1576, he discovered what is now Frobisher Bay, an inlet in Baffin Island. He returned to England with some ore that was mistakenly identified as gold. Investors hoping to find more of the precious metal sponsored Frobisher's next two voyages (1577 and 1578). Frobisher did not find gold, but he did discover what later became known as the Hudson Strait. He went on to serve as vice admiral in Sir Francis Drake's 1585–86 expedition to the West Indies, and in 1588 he was knighted for fighting against the Spanish Armada. He was fatally wounded in 1594 while fighting the Spanish on the coast of France.

Ross, Sir John (1777–1856), British explorer, b. Wigtownshire, Scotland. From 1818 to 1834, he led several Arctic expeditions specifically to find the Northwest Passage, and an 1850 expedition to find Sir John

Roald Amundsen

Sir John Franklin

Franklin. John Ross explored Boothia Peninsula, the Gulf of Boothia, and King William Land. His nephew, **Sir James Clark Ross** (1800–1862), b. London, joined his uncle's 1829–33 expedition, during which he discovered the North Magnetic Pole. In 1848 he also commanded an unsuccessful, two-year expedition in search of Sir John Franklin. But James Clark Ross is best known for exploring Antarctica.

The body of John Torrington, a crew member of Sir John Franklin's ill-fated 1845 expedition, was found perfectly preserved in the Arctic permafrost.

the Atlantic. McClure's travels, along with the findings of the Franklin search expeditions, showed that no practical water route existed through the Arctic islands. The ice floes (sheets of floating ice) simply made the route impassable through much of the year.

The historic first crossing of the Northwest Passage by sea finally was made by a Norwegian explorer, Roald Amundsen, in a 47-ton herring boat named the *Gjoa*. Sailing east to west, Amundsen's three-year voyage (1903–06) ran through Lancaster Sound and then south and west to the Beaufort Sea and the Bering Strait.

The first successful west-to-east voyage was begun in 1940 by Henry A. Larsen of the Royal Canadian Mounted Police. He sailed from Vancouver, British Columbia, on the 80-ton schooner *St. Roch* and reached Halifax, Nova Scotia, two years later. In 1944, Larsen made the return voyage from Halifax to Vancouver, and the *St. Roch* distinguished itself as the first vessel to make the trip in a single season.

In 1960 the first undersea voyage was accomplished by the U.S. nuclear submarine *Seadragon*, and in 1969 the U.S. icebreaking oil tanker *Manhattan* became the first commercial vessel to break through.

More recent exploration has been aided by advancements in radar and aerial photography. Because of its treacherous conditions, however, the Northwest Passage has yet to become a commercially practical route between the Atlantic and Pacific oceans.

C. CECIL LINGARD
Director, *Canada Year Book*

See also EXPLORATION AND DISCOVERY.

NORTHWEST TERRITORIES

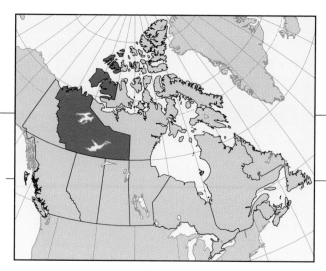

The Northwest Territories' location in the far north is reflected in its coat of arms (opposite page). It features two narwhals and an arctic fox, animals native to northern regions. The coat of arms also appears on the territorial flag (above). The territorial bird is the gyrfalcon (right), and the official flower is the mountain avens (opposite page).

The northern region of Canada known as the Northwest Territories makes up just over 12 percent of the country's total area. This vast region extends from the 60th parallel to the North Pole. While large in geographic size, the Northwest Territories contains few people. With only 8 persons per 100 square miles, the Northwest Territories is one of the most sparsely populated areas in the world.

Two other northern territories, the Yukon Territory, on the west, and the territory of Nunavut, on the east, border the Northwest Territories. Its southern boundary is the 60th parallel, which serves as the border with three Canadian provinces: British Columbia, Alberta, and Saskatchewan.

The second largest political unit in Canada, the Northwest Territories extends over a huge area that consists of a continental mainland and arctic islands situated in the Beaufort Sea of the Arctic Ocean. Banks Island is the largest of the islands, with an area of 27,310 square miles (70,033 square kilometers).

The process of creating provinces and territories from the Northwest Territories began in 1898, with the establishment of the Yukon Territory. In 1905, the provinces of Alberta and Saskatchewan were created. Manitoba, Ontario, and Quebec also received land from the Territories. The most recent division of the Territories occurred on April 1, 1999, when the territory of Nunavut was formed.

▶ THE LAND

The Northwest Territories can be divided into four geographic regions: the Interior Plains, the Cordillera, the Canadian Shield, and the Arctic Region. Each region has a distinct type of landform. The Interior Plains is an area of flat to gently rolling land. Most of the forested land and all the commercial petroleum deposits in the Northwest Territories lie within this region. The Mackenzie River, the second longest river in North America, flows across the Interior Plains to the Beaufort Sea. The Cordillera, which lies to the west of the Interior Plains, is a mountainous region that stretches northwest from the province of British Columbia. The Mackenzie and Richardson mountains are a major part of the Cordillera in the Northwest Territories. They form the boundary between the Yukon Territory and the Northwest Territories.

The Canadian Shield, a region of rugged and hilly terrain, lies to the east of the Interior Plains. Two large lakes, Great Bear Lake and Great Slave Lake, lie along the border between the two regions. Many minerals are found in the Canadian Shield, including gold and diamonds. The Arctic region is the most northerly geographic area. Much of the Arctic land is tundra—treeless plains that are covered by snow for much of the year.

▶ CLIMATE AND NATURAL RESOURCES

Because of its high latitude, the Northwest Territories has an extremely cold climate. Within the Northwest Territories, an arctic climatic zone is found on the islands in the Arctic Ocean and along the coast of the mainland. The arctic climate is characterized by extremely long, cold, and dark winters and

short summers. The average daily temperature of the warmest month does not exceed 50°F (10°C). During the winter, daily temperatures often drop to –40°F (–40°C) and lower for many weeks. While winters are generally clear and calm, arctic snowstorms often occur. Even with these storms, the annual precipitation is extremely low, in places less than 4 inches (10 centimeters) a year.

Over the remainder of the Northwest Territories, but particularly in the Mackenzie Valley, a subarctic climate occurs. Daily summer temperatures often exceed 60°F (16°C). Precipitation, while only about 8 inches (20 centimeters) per year, is higher than in the arctic climate.

The natural wealth of the Northwest Territories ranges from renewable resources, such as timber stands and wildlife, to such nonrenewable resources as diamonds, gold, and oil. Minerals are found in the Canadian Shield and oil and gas in the Interior Plain. Gold occurs in several places, but the most important deposits are near Yellowknife and at the Lupin mine located some 250 miles (400 kilometers) northwest of Yellowknife. Huge oil and gas reserves have been discovered in the Beaufort Sea and the Mackenzie Delta, but these deposits have not been developed because of the high cost of production and transportation to southern markets.

▶ **THE PEOPLE AND THEIR WORK**

The population of the Northwest Territories is just under 40,000. Native peoples make up approximately 50 percent of the population; included in this group are roughly 11,200 North American Indians, 4,000 Inuit, and 3,700 métis (people of mixed Indian and European ancestry). The majority of the rest of the people are of European origin.

A large majority of the people—all but about 2,000—live in small towns and villages along the shores of Great Slave Lake and the Mackenzie River. The rest of the Northwest Territories is very sparsely populated.

Industries and Products

About 80 percent of the labor force works in the service industries, which include both private firms and public agencies. Government—federal, territorial, and municipal—dominates the services, employing nearly half the labor force of the Northwest Territories. A growing tourist industry also provides some employment.

Mining employs about 15 percent of the workforce and contributes significantly to the economy. Leading minerals include gold and diamonds, mined near Yellowknife, and oil, produced at Norman Wells in the Mackenzie Valley. Other minerals include silver and tungsten.

Manufacturing, mainly of printed materials, employs less than 2 percent of the labor force. Inuit carvings and other native art have gained international recognition and are sold through local cooperatives.

Hunting and trapping were leading occupations in the past but have declined in importance. Commercial fishing is concentrated on Great Slave Lake.

Transportation and Communication

The vast size of the Northwest Territories makes both transportation and communica-

Yellowknife, on Great Slave Lake, is the capital of the Northwest Territories. With a population of some 17,000, it is by far the Territories' largest community.

tion more difficult and expensive than in more southerly regions of Canada. Air transportation is commonly used, especially in settlements beyond the road network. The centers lying along the Mackenzie River and Great Slave Lake have access to river transportation in the summer months. In fact, river barges serve about 80 percent of the communities while highways extend to just over half of the settlements. The highway system extends over some 1,400 miles (2,250 kilometers). Temporary roads add another 500 miles (800 kilometers) in the winter. Rail transportation ends at the river port of Hay River on the south shore of Great Slave Lake.

Several weekly newspapers are published in the Northwest Territories. Radio and television reception is available in most communities. Widespread use of computers by individuals, companies, and governments enables communication via e-mail and the World Wide Web.

▶ EDUCATION

The Department of Education of the territorial government is responsible for primary, secondary, and post-secondary education. High schools are located in Yellowknife, Hay River, Fort Smith, Inuvik, Fort Simpson, and

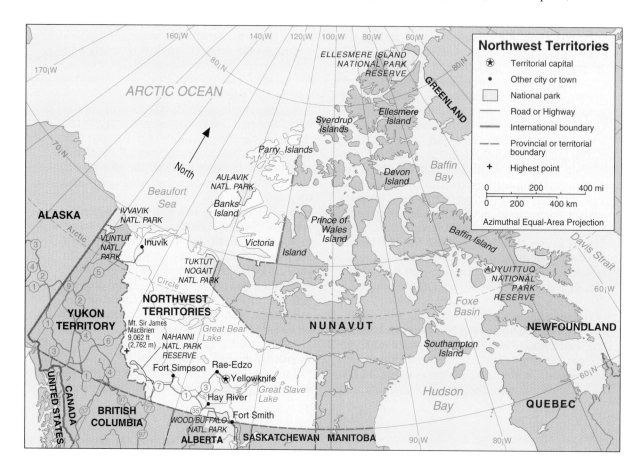

Norman Wells. Aurora College, with campuses in Fort Smith, Inuvik, and Yellowknife, provides post-secondary education classes and training programs. Students who attend provincial universities receive financial support from the territorial government.

▶ **PLACES OF INTEREST**

National parks are Nahanni (declared a U.N. World Heritage site in 1979); Wood Buffalo, which provides a wilderness area for buffalo; and Tuktut Nogait, situated along the Arctic coast.

Prince of Wales National Heritage Centre, in Yellowknife, has a museum and archives. The center is a resource for public information and research.

▶ **CITIES**

The Northwest Territories has approximately 35 communities, or small villages. Yellowknife, the capital and center of government, is the Territories' only city and its largest community. It is situated on Yellowknife Bay of Great Slave Lake and has a population of about 16,500. Other towns include Hay River, Inuvik, Fort Smith, Rae Edzo, and Fort Simpson.

▶ **GOVERNMENT**

Under the Canadian system, the federal government assigns political powers to the territorial government and appoints a commissioner, who, in the past, served as the chief executive officer. Today, actual political power rests with a legislative assembly of 19 elected members. An executive council, selected from the assembly, elects one of its members as premier. Legislative and taxation powers over education, health, housing, renewable resources, and social services have been assigned to the territorial government. There are no political parties in the Northwest Territories.

▶ **HISTORY**

Nomadic native peoples—the Inuit in the Arctic and the Dene in the subarctic—lived by hunting and fishing. The first known European explorers to visit the Northwest Territories were the Vikings, who sailed to the eastern Arctic about A.D. 1000. In 1576 the British explorer Martin Frobisher became the first of many Europeans to seek a northwest passage to Asia through the Arctic islands.

IMPORTANT DATES	
1870	Hudson's Bay Company and Great Britain transferred area of mainland Northwest Territories to Canada.
1880	Great Britain transferred Arctic islands to Canada.
1899	Treaty signed by Canada with Dene (Indians) of southwestern Northwest Territories.
1903	First voyage through the Northwest Passage begun by Roald Amundsen.
1919	Oil discovered at Norman Wells, on the Mackenzie River.
1922	Treaty signed by Canada with Dene (Indians) of the Mackenzie Valley.
1930	Radium and uranium discovered at Port Radium on Great Bear Lake.
1934	Gold discovered on Yellowknife Bay, Great Slave Lake.
1941	Canol Project to provide oil for Alaska from Norman Wells.
1948	The first road into the Northwest Territories was built from Grimshaw, Alberta, to Hay River.
1967	Yellowknife was named capital of the Northwest Territories, and commissioner and territorial government offices were moved there from Ottawa.
1984	Land claims agreement was reached between the Inuit of western Arctic and the Canadian government.
1998	Diamond production began.
1999	The Northwest Territories was divided into two territories.

Exploration of the interior was carried out mainly by fur traders such as Samuel Hearne, who crossed the Barren Lands in 1770–71, and Alexander Mackenzie, who followed the Mackenzie River to the Beaufort Sea in 1789.

Until 1870, the Northwest Territories was part of British North America. In that year the British government transferred lands formerly under the control of the Hudson's Bay Company to Canada. Over time, the size of the Northwest Territories diminished as some of its lands were transferred to five provinces. The most recent division occurred in 1999, when Nunavut was carved out of the eastern part of the Northwest Territories.

ROBERT M. BONE
Department of Geography
University of Saskatchewan

NORTH YEMEN. See YEMEN.

NORWAY

Norway is one of the Scandinavian nations of northern Europe. It occupies the western and northern parts of the Scandinavian Peninsula, which it shares with Sweden. Denmark, another Scandinavian country, lies just to the south and is part of the European mainland. While most of Norway borders on Sweden, it also borders Finland and Russia in the far north. (See the article SCANDINAVIA.)

▶ PEOPLE

The Norwegians are closely related to the neighboring Swedes and Danes as well as to the people of Iceland. Approximately 43,000 Sami (formerly called Lapps), the main ethnic minority, live in the far northern region of Norway called Lapland. Norway is one of the least densely populated countries of Europe. The majority of the population lives in towns

Clockwise from left: Cross-country skiing is one of the most popular outdoor activities enjoyed by Norwegians. A boy and girl in traditional dress. Fjords, or deep inlets of the sea formed by glaciers, characterize the Norwegian landscape.

and cities in the southeast and along the south and southwest coasts. Oslo, the capital, is located in the southeast.

Language and Religion. Norwegian is the official language of Norway. It is a Germanic language derived from Old Norse, and it has two forms: Bokmål (Book Language), which is most commonly used, and Nynorsk (New Norse). There are also small Sami- and Finnish-speaking minorities.

Most Norwegians belong to the Evangelical Lutheran Church, the state church. But all religions may be practiced freely.

Education and Libraries. By law, all Norwegian children must attend school from the age of 6

to 16. The basic elementary course consists of seven years of lower and three years of upper education. Students may then attend secondary schools that will train them for a job or prepare them for study at a university. There are about 36 institutions of higher learning. The country's oldest university, Oslo University, is located in the capital. Norway also has about 70 Folk High Schools, where teenagers, adults, and retirees can study a wide range of subjects. In addition, Norwegians benefit from a government-supported continuing education system and an extensive public library system. The National Library is located in Oslo.

Food and Drink. Fish is an important element in the Norwegian diet and forms part of the *koldtbord* (cold luncheon or dinner), a buffet of various cold dishes. Basic foods include meats, goat's milk cheese *(gjetost)*, and a thin, crispy, flat bread *(knekkebrød)*. Beer is often drunk with meals.

Sports and Recreation. Norwegians particularly enjoy outdoor activities. Skiing is a traditional sport, and Norwegians have won numerous Olympic medals in downhill and cross-country skiing and ski jumping. Holmenkollen, a famous ski jump and site of the 1952 Winter Olympic Games, overlooks Oslo. Norwegian Olympian Sonja Henie won three gold medals in figure skating (1928, 1932, and 1936). Soccer is a favorite summer sport. Hiking and fishing are also popular.

▶ **LAND**

Mountains and evergreen forests cover most of the land, which is also marked by numerous steep valleys, lakes, swift rivers, waterfalls, and glaciers—enormous, slow-moving sheets of ice. Norway's long coastline is indented by countless fjords—deep inlets of the sea lined by towering cliffs. The highest point in the country is Galdhøpiggen, which rises to 8,100 feet (2,469 meters) in the Jotunheimen mountain region of south central Norway.

The country extends from the Barents Sea, an arm of the Arctic Ocean, in the north to the North Sea and the Skagerrak channel in the south, a distance of more than 1,100 miles (1,770 kilometers). Nearly one-third of its land lies north of the Arctic Circle.

Land Regions. Norway's physical features divide it into five distinct regions: Østlandet (East Country), Sørlandet (South Country),

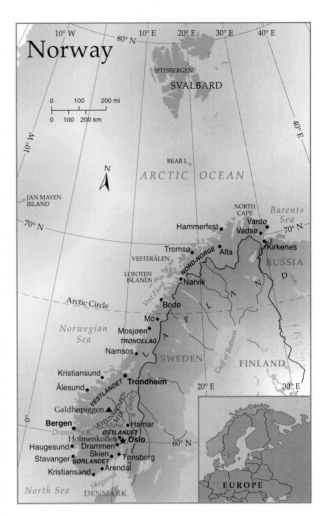

Vestlandet (West Country), all in South Norway; Trøndelag (the Trondheim region); and Nord-Norge (North Norway).

Østlandet, located in the southeast, is the most important agricultural region. Although it makes up less than 30 percent of the total area, its broad valleys provide nearly 50 percent of Norway's productive farmland. It is the home of about half the people; the site of the capital; and a center of commerce, industry, and education.

Sørlandet is the smallest region, with about 5 percent of Norway's area. Vestlandet, situated along the southwestern coast, is a land of snowcapped mountains, deep fjords, seaside towns, and tiny farms. It is Norway's second most populous region. Fishing and the raising of livestock are traditional occupations here, but have been replaced in economic importance by petroleum and natural gas production in offshore waters.

Left: An offshore oil rig operates in the North Sea, where most of Norway's petroleum and natural gas—its most important natural resources—are extracted.

Below: A worker unloads the day's catch from a fishing boat. Norway's long coastline makes fishing one of the nation's most important industries.

Trøndelag is a lowland region in central Norway with a considerable area of agricultural land. Nord-Norge is the long, narrow northern strip of Norway. It is the largest region, with about 35 percent of the total area, but has the second smallest population, after Sørlandet. Most of Norway's Sami live here, and fishing and iron mining are important.

Islands, Rivers, and Lakes. Norway's territory also includes Svalbard (formerly called Spitsbergen), a group of four large islands and over 100 smaller ones, plus Jan Mayen Island—all located in the Arctic Ocean. Off Norway's northwestern coast is the Lofoten island group, located in the Norwegian Sea. Most of Norway's west coast is dotted with thousands of islands. Norway's longest rivers are the Glåma and Dramselva. There are also many lakes, the largest of which is Mjøsa.

Climate. Norway has a moderate climate for a country situated so far north; the warm waters of the North Atlantic Drift bring in moist air from the southwest. Coastal areas are generally above freezing in the winter. But winter temperatures drop sharply inland, sometimes falling below 0°F (–18°C), and heavy snowfall is common. Summers are cool, and rainfall is considerable throughout the country. In the far north, during the summer, there is daylight 24 hours a day; the region is sometimes called the Land of the Midnight Sun. In the winter, the conditions are reversed and there is mostly darkness.

Natural Resources. Petroleum and natural gas, extracted mainly from the North Sea, are Norway's most important natural resources. Also important are its forests; fast-flowing rivers, a source of hydroelectric power; and fish. Iron ore and copper are the chief metallic mineral resources.

▶ **ECONOMY**

Oil and gas production, together with related products and services, make up about 40 percent of the country's economy. Oil and gas extraction made Norway rich, and this wealth helped broaden the economy, especially in the areas of high technology and research and development.

Services. Services account for about 65 percent of Norway's economy. Government is the largest service sector employer. Tourism is also important, especially the popular cruises of Norway's west coast fjords. Other services include wholesale and retail trade, finance, insurance, real estate, transportation, and communication.

Manufacturing. About one-fifth of the workforce is employed in various industries. After oil and natural gas, the leading exports are hydroelectric equipment, ships and oil platforms, office equipment, electronic products, paper and paper pulp, metals, and chemicals. Shipping and related activities have long been important to the Norwegian economy.

Agriculture, Forestry, and Fishing. Only about 3 percent of Norway's land is suitable for agriculture, with the raising of livestock the primary activity. Wheat, barley, and potatoes are grown for food. But much of the land is devoted to hay and other crops used as fodder (feed) for livestock. Meat and milk are the chief livestock products.

Norway's forests provide wood for pulp, paper, and lumber. Wood products account for about 6 percent of export income.

Most commercial fishing is carried out in the waters of North Norway. Cod, herring, and mackerel are the main varieties of fish caught; the salmon farms along the coast are also important. Whaling has a long tradition in Norway; each year a small number of minke whales are harvested, despite an international ban on commercial whaling.

Transportation. Ferries, an extensive rail system, and a huge road network help people get around Norway easily. In the late 1800's, a steamship service, the *Hurtigruten*, was established, linking the towns on Norway's west coast. Oslo Airport is Norway's main airport.

Communication. Norway is one of the most technologically advanced countries in the world. Cell phones and the Internet are

widely used, and satellite and cable television are available. There are more than 300 radio stations and about 200 newspapers.

▶ **MAJOR CITIES**

Oslo is Norway's capital and largest city, as well as its commercial, industrial, and cultural center. Situated on the Oslo Fjord, the city's population is about 513,000. Greater Oslo has a population of about 1 million. Oslo was founded in the 1000's. A fire destroyed most of the original city in 1624. It was rebuilt and renamed Christiania, a name it kept until 1925, when the name Oslo was restored. (See the article OSLO.)

Bergen, Norway's second largest city, is a port on the western coast and the cultural heart of the Vestlandet region. It has a

The Rådhus, or City Hall, overlooks Oslo's inner harbor. Oslo is Norway's capital and largest city.

population of about 200,000. During the Middle Ages, Bergen was a center of commerce, and it was Norway's largest city into the 1800's.

Tromsø, with a population of about 56,000, is the main city in northern Norway. Founded in the mid-1200's as a market and a trade town, it is now a research, education, and cultural center for the region and home to Tromsø University and important museums.

▶ CULTURAL HERITAGE

Norwegian cultural achievements have gained world renown. Literature and the arts receive generous government support.

The Leonardo Bridge, based on designs drawn up 500 years ago by Leonardo da Vinci, was built in 2001 in a small town near Oslo.

Norwegian playwright Henrik Ibsen was one of the founders of modern drama. The playwright and poet Bjørnstjerne Bjørnson, novelist Knut Hamsun, and novelist Sigrid Undset all won Nobel Prizes for literature.

The painter Edvard Munch was one of the most influential figures in modern expressionism. Gustav Vigeland was Norway's greatest sculptor. Many of his works are displayed in Frogner Park in Oslo.

Edvard Grieg was the first Norwegian composer to gain international fame. The soprano Kirsten Flagstad was known for her roles in the operas of Richard Wagner.

Norway has produced a number of great explorers. Among them are Fridtjof Nansen, who also won the Nobel Peace Prize in 1922 for his humanitarian work; Roald Amundsen, the first person to reach the South Pole, in 1911; and Thor Heyerdahl, who tried to prove that sea voyages played a key role in the spread of early civilizations.

For more information, see the article on Scandinavian literature and biographies of Grieg, Heyerdahl, and Ibsen.

▶ GOVERNMENT

Norway is a constitutional monarchy. The monarch is the head of state, but executive power is exercised through a cabinet, the State Council, headed by a prime minister. The State Council, although appointed by the monarch, must be approved by the Storting (the parliament, or legislature). The Storting is elected by the people every four years. After each election, it divides itself into two chambers. One quarter of its members form the Lagting; the rest make up the Odelsting. If the two chambers disagree on legislation, a two-thirds majority of the full Storting is required for its passage.

▶ HISTORY

Archaeological evidence points to the existence of people in Norway as early as 10,000 years ago. Agriculture arrived in the region about 5,000 years ago.

The Viking Age. During the Viking Age (about A.D. 800–1000), Norwegians and other Scandinavians had some influence on the rest of Europe. These Vikings were known for their trading and raiding, as well as for the settlements they established.

Impelled by the population growth and a shortage of land, Norwegian Vikings traveled to Great Britain, Ireland, France, and other parts of Europe. They settled Iceland and colonized Greenland. A descendant of Norwegian Vikings, Leif Ericson, led an expedition to what are now parts of eastern Canada about A.D. 1000.

Unification. In the late 800's, the unification of Norway from several small kingdoms into a medieval state began under King Harold (or Harald) I the Fairhaired. It was completed under King Olaf (or Olav) II Haraldsson, who died in 1030. Olaf II was also important in establishing Christianity in Norway, and as Saint Olaf he is Norway's patron saint.

Norway reached the height of its power in the 1200's under King Haakon IV Haakonsson. But by the mid-1300's, Norway had fallen into political and economic decline. This was caused mainly by civil war, the loss of control of its foreign trade to the German merchants of the Hanseatic League, and the ravages of a plague known as the Black Death, which killed between one-third and one-half of the population.

A relic of Norway's history is exhibited in the Viking Ship Museum in Oslo. Leif Ericson may have sailed to North America in such a ship.

Danish and Swedish Rule. After the last male descendant of King Harold I the Fairhaired died in 1319, Norway and Sweden were ruled jointly by a Swedish king. In 1380 Norway and Denmark were united, and in 1397 a union of Denmark, Norway, and Sweden was established. Sweden left the union in 1523, but Norway remained and gradually lost its independence to Danish control. This situation lasted until 1814, when a group of Norwegians drafted a constitution, selected a Danish prince as king, and declared the country's independence. However, Norway was forced to accept a dynastic union with Sweden—under which Norwegians still retained considerable political and economic autonomy. The government was based on a constitution that remains the basis of Norwegian government today.

Independence Regained. Problems plagued the Norwegian-Swedish union, and demands for independence grew stronger in the late 1800's. In 1905, by the agreement of both countries, the union was dissolved. A Danish prince, who took the name Haakon VII, was elected king of an independent Norway.

The 1900's. After independence, the development of Norwegian industry was emphasized, and important political and social advances were made. Norway was one of the first countries to give women the right to vote in municipal elections (in 1901) and in national elections (in 1913). It was a pioneer in social welfare measures that are now common in many countries, including medical and unemployment insurance, pensions for the elderly, and aid to the disabled and to children.

Norway remained neutral in World War I (1914–18) but was unable to do so through World War II (1939–45). In 1940 it was invaded and occupied by Nazi Germany. The Norwegian government went into exile in Britain but inspired a resistance movement in Norway. Norway was a founding member of the United Nations, whose first secretary-general, Trygve Lie, was a Norwegian. Norway was also one of the original members of the North American Treaty Organization (NATO).

Recent History. The 52-year reign of King Haakon VII ended with his death in 1957. He was succeeded by his son, Olaf V. The present king, Harold V, came to the throne in 1991.

Petroleum and natural gas, first discovered beneath Norwegian waters in the late 1960's, have been major exports since 1975; additional deposits were found in the 1980's. Oil and gas extraction have given Norwegians one of the highest standards of living in the world.

Norway's new wealth has also allowed the country to pursue an independent course in Europe. Twice—in 1972 and 1994—the country has voted against joining the European Union (EU). A recent problem, however, has been the growing number of political parties in Norway, which has made majority rule in parliament difficult to achieve.

Reviewed by BYRON J. NORDSTROM
Gustavus Adolphus College

See also ERICSON, LEIF; LAPLAND; VIKINGS.

NOSE. See BODY, HUMAN (The Respiratory System).

NOSEBLEED. See FIRST AID.

NOUN. See PARTS OF SPEECH.

NOVA SCOTIA

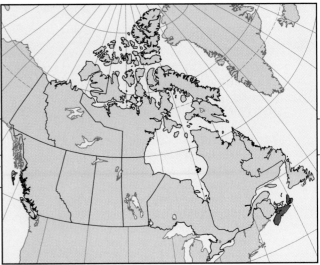

Nova Scotia's flag (above) and coat of arms (opposite page) recall the province's ties to Scotland. Both feature the cross of St. Andrew and the Scottish arms. The coat of arms also has a unicorn, symbolizing England, and an Indian, representing Nova Scotia's native people. The provincial bird is the osprey (right), and the provincial flower is the trailing arbutus (opposite page).

Nova Scotia is the most populous and the wealthiest of Canada's Atlantic Provinces (which also include New Brunswick, Prince Edward Island, and Newfoundland and Labrador). Nova Scotia means "New Scotland" in Latin. The name comes from the royal charter issued in 1621 by James I of England, granting lands to Sir William Alexander, who was a Scot. But for much of its earliest history, the area was known as Acadia—a name given it by the French, the first Europeans to settle the region.

▶ THE LAND

The province of Nova Scotia is divided into two major parts—the peninsula of Nova Scotia itself and a large island, Cape Breton Island. Together they jut out into the North Atlantic, guarding the approaches to the Gulf of St. Lawrence. The province is about 380 miles (610 kilometers) long. It is separated from the New Brunswick mainland by a narrow neck of land, the Isthmus of Chignecto.

South of the isthmus is the Bay of Fundy. To the north is the Northumberland Strait in the Gulf of St. Lawrence. The Northumberland Strait separates Nova Scotia from Prince Edward Island, and Cabot Strait separates it from the island of Newfoundland. The Atlantic Ocean lies to the east and south.

Between the peninsula and Cape Breton Island lies the Strait of Canso. The two main parts of the province were joined by a causeway in 1955. Smaller islands—including Sable Island—are located off Nova Scotia's Atlantic coast.

The Peninsula of Nova Scotia. The eastern and southern shores of the peninsula, on the Atlantic Ocean, are indented with hundreds of bays and coves. Many make fine harbors. The shores along the Northumberland Strait and the Bay of Fundy are straighter. There are few bays or coves, and good harbors are scarce. On the shores of the Northumberland Strait there are many fine sandy beaches. In Chignecto Bay and Minas Basin, which are parts of the Bay of Fundy, the tides are among the highest in the world. Their daily range is about 35 feet (10 meters).

Most of southern Nova Scotia consists of rough, hilly upland—part of the Atlantic Upland. The highest land in this part of the peninsula is about 700 feet (210 meters) high. The underlying rock is not easily worn down by the rivers and streams. The glaciers of the Ice Age scarred and scoured the land and deposited much gravelly material in the valleys. In this area are thousands of lakes and many short rivers. Along some of the river valleys and some coastal areas there are level lowlands. Some of these are suitable for farming, but most of the area is forested. The largest valley is the Annapolis Valley, which runs parallel to the Bay of Fundy. It is separated from the bay by a long, narrow ridge called North Mountain.

Northern Nova Scotia, in the area south of the Northumberland Strait, is very different. The rocks there are softer. The land has been worn down in many places to form a lowland, where the soils are good. On the Chignecto Isthmus are the steep Cobequid Mountains, as

FACTS AND FIGURES

Location: Eastern Canada. **Latitude**—42°25′ N to 47°15′ N. **Longitude**—59°40′ W to 66°25′ W.

Joined Canadian Confederation: July 1, 1867, as one of the four original provinces.

Population: 908,007 (2001 census). **Rank among provinces**—7th.

Capital and Largest City: Halifax, pop. 359,111 (metropolitan area; 2001 census).

Physical Features: Area—21,345 sq mi (55,284 km²). **Rank among provinces**—9th. **Rivers**—St. Marys, Mersey, Lahave, Musquodoboit, Annapolis, Margaree, Cornwallis. **Lakes**—Bras d'Or, Ainslie, Shubenacadie, Gaspereau, Sherbrooke, Malaga, Rossignol, Fishers. **Highest point**—1,747 ft (532 m), on Cape Breton Island.

Industries and Products: Coal, salt, and gypsum mining; iron and steel mills; pulp and paper; petroleum and coal products; transportation equipment; shipbuilding; automobile assembly; scallop, lobster, and cod fishing; livestock, dairy, fruit and berry farming; tourism.

Government: Self-governing province. **Titular head of government**—lieutenant governor, appointed by the governor-general in council. **Actual head of government**—premier, leader of the majority in the legislature. **Provincial representation in federal parliament**—10 appointed senators; 11 elected member(s) of the House of Commons. **Voting age for provincial elections**—18.

Provincial Bird: Osprey.

Provincial Flower: Trailing arbutus.

Provincial Motto: *Munit haec et altera vincit* (One defends and the other conquers).

---

well as level farmlands that have been reclaimed from the sea by dikes.

Cape Breton Island. This part of Nova Scotia is very hilly and, in places, mountainous. In the north, tablelands, or flat-topped mountains, rise directly out of the sea to heights of more than 1,000 feet (300 meters). North Barren, the highest point in the province, is there. The Bras d'Or Lakes occupy the center of the island. They are really part of the Atlantic.

Climate

Cold air masses from the heart of Canada and warm air masses from the Atlantic Ocean influence the climate of Nova Scotia. At times in winter it can be bitterly cold. But usually Nova Scotia has a mild winter climate, particularly on the south coast. There are many winter storms. Rain is common when mild air moves in from the south. Snow is common when cool air comes from the north.

The summer climate is pleasantly warm and sunny. Inland places are a bit warmer than coastal places. Summer temperatures of 75°F (24°C) are common.

The annual rainfall varies from about 40 inches (1,000 millimeters) in the northern interior to 55 inches (1,400 millimeters) in the south. Snowfall is usually about 70 inches (175 centimeters) in all areas. Fog often occurs along the south coast in spring and summer when warm air passes over cool coastal waters.

Drift ice covers most of the waters of the Gulf of St. Lawrence in late winter and spring. This ice sometimes blocks off ports in the north and on Cape Breton Island. The south coast and the Bay of Fundy are ice-free, and the ports there are open the year round.

Natural Resources

Nova Scotia has a variety of natural resources, including forests, minerals, fish, and wildlife. The best soils are found in the valleys and river bottoms.

Vegetation. Most of Nova Scotia is covered with forest. But some formerly forested areas have been cleared for agriculture. Some parts of the province are rocky barrens, and a few areas are covered with bogs and marshes.

The upland areas in the south have thin rocky soils, but they support forests. The forest growth is best on the hill slopes and in the valleys, where the soils are deeper. These forests are made up mainly of evergreen coniferous trees, such as spruce, fir, pine, and hemlock. There are also deciduous trees, such as maple, ash, tamarack, and alder.

The northern parts of the province have a different kind of forest, with bigger trees and better growth, because they have better soils and climate. The trees there are mostly deciduous. The commonest types are maple, birch, beech, ash, elm, and sometimes oak, basswood, and butternut. Conifers, such as spruce, fir, and pine, also grow there.

The coastal waters contain many seaweeds. One kind, called Irish moss, is gathered in great quantities. It is used in making ice cream, soaps, jellies, and cosmetics. Wild berries are gathered from barren and burned-out lands.

Left: Cape Breton Island, which forms the northeastern tip of Nova Scotia, has a rugged coastline and a forested interior. Its dramatic scenery makes it a popular tourist spot. *Above:* Peggy's Cove, near Halifax, is a picturesque example of the many sheltered bays that indent the province's Atlantic coast.

Minerals. Coal is Nova Scotia's most important mineral, followed by rock salt, gypsum, and sand and gravel. Barite, lead, zinc, gold, and tin are found in lesser quantities. There are deposits of oil and natural gas off the southern Atlantic coast.

Fish and Wildlife. The shallow coastal waters of Nova Scotia, known as banks, cover many thousands of square miles. Fish are plentiful. The Nova Scotia banks and the Newfoundland banks have been fished by many countries for hundreds of years.

Fur trading was important to the province's early settlers. Today beaver, moose, and deer are still found. Nova Scotia has a number of wildlife sanctuaries that protect these and other species.

▶ THE PEOPLE AND THEIR WORK

Most Nova Scotians live in communities scattered along the ocean coasts. About 45 percent of them live in rural areas. The rest live in the province's towns and cities. Nearly one third of the people live in the area of Halifax, the capital and largest city, and nearby Dartmouth. Population is also concentrated in the industrial Cape Breton area stretching from Sydney to Glace Bay.

More than 80 percent of Nova Scotians were born in the province. Most are of British origin, descended either from 18th-century immigrants from the American colonies or from people who arrived directly from Britain early in the 19th century. The Scottish are the most numerous, followed by the English and Irish. Smaller numbers of French, Germans, Dutch, and native peoples also live in the province.

More than one third of Nova Scotians are Roman Catholics. The other leading denominations are United Church of Canada, Anglican, Baptist, Presbyterian, and Lutheran. Because many of the early immigrants settled among people from their home countries—Scots in Cape Breton, French along the southwestern shore, Germans in Lunenburg—there is a great deal of cultural variety in the province. But traditional distinctions have been fading over the years. Today more than 90 percent of the people of Nova Scotia use English as their first language.

Industries and Products

Much of Nova Scotia's industry is based on its natural resources—its forests, minerals, and fish. But raw materials from abroad are also processed. Agriculture is limited, but it remains important.

Fishing and Fish Processing. Many of the first settlers came to Nova Scotia to fish. Fishing is still important, both along inshore waters and on the offshore banks. The most valuable species caught are lobster, scallop, cod, haddock, and herring. In the past, most fishing was done along the coast from small open boats or at sea from decked schooners. The most famous of the wooden schooners was the *Bluenose*, a five-time winner of international racing competitions. Today, small boats are still used for inshore fishing, especially lobster trapping. But more than half of the catch is made by the offshore fleet, headed by large factory ships. Factory ships catch fish and process them while still at sea.

The rest of the catch is brought ashore for processing in factories. Lunenburg, North Sydney, Canso, Halifax, and Riverport are all major processing centers. Old-fashioned salt curing has been replaced by freezing and canning, and modern transportation allows much of the catch to be sold live. The most important export market is the United States.

Mining. Extensive mining operations are carried out in Nova Scotia. Deep-pit mines, located mostly in Cape Breton, produce large quantities of bituminous, or soft, coal. Most of this fuel is used locally to manufacture steel and to generate electricity. Rock salt is mined in large-scale underground operations in the northeast part of the peninsula. Most of the salt is used in the region to help clear snow from winter roads. Nova Scotia's third major mineral, gypsum, is used abroad in the manufacture of building materials. The largest of the open-pit gypsum quarries are found near Windsor. Small quantities of other minerals such as lead, zinc, and tin are also mined.

Agriculture. Less than 10 percent of Nova Scotia is suitable for agriculture, but farming is active in areas such as the Annapolis Valley (famous for its apple orchards), the headwaters of the Bay of Fundy, and along the Northumberland Strait. The traditional family farm produced small quantities of many products. It is being replaced by large farm units that produce a few things in large quantity—dairy products, livestock, vegetables, or fruit and berries. Co-operative processing and marketing methods have given farmers a growing share of the local market and have enabled them to sell more abroad.

Forest Industries. Part of the annual tree harvest is sawed into lumber in dozens of small mills scattered across the province. But most of the wood goes to large factories for processing into paper and related products. Some of the major factories are located at Liverpool, Pictou, and Port Hawkesbury. These paper mills get most of their wood from land leased from the provincial government. Small, private woodlots provide the rest of the pulpwood.

Other Manufacturing. Manufacturing of all kinds is the most important part of Nova Scotia's economy. Besides the factories that process the province's own fish, agricultural produce, and wood, there are others that use imported materials. The province's leading manufacturer uses imported rubber to produce automobile tires. The steel plant at Sydney specializes in the production of railroad rails. Nova Scotia has one automobile assembly plant and two oil refineries. Several other plants turn out goods ranging from textiles to

Below: The fertile Annapolis River valley in western Nova Scotia is an important agricultural region. Its apple orchards and dairy farms are especially productive. *Right:* Fishermen empty a snow crab trap. Both small boats and large factory ships make up the province's fishing fleet.

beer. Traditionally, the manufacturers in Nova Scotia depended on selling their goods in central Canadian markets. But exports now go increasingly to the United States and other countries.

Tourism. More than a million people visit Nova Scotia in the summer. They are attracted by splendid scenery, numerous historic sites, and the opportunity for fishing, boating, hunting, and other recreational activities. Government and private campgrounds abound. Fairs, craft shows, concerts, and theaters offer lively diversion from early summer to late autumn.

Transportation and Communication

During winter, when the St. Lawrence Seaway is closed to navigation, Halifax operates as Canada's main Atlantic port. A greater volume of year-round traffic is now going to Halifax, thanks to containerization. This is a system using huge cargo boxes that can be moved quickly and cheaply from ship to railcar or truck through specially equipped ports. Container fleets now link Halifax by sea with Europe and Asia.

The rail line between Halifax and Montreal remains important, but branch railways in Nova Scotia are being phased out. In the 1960's and 1970's, a network of paved all-weather highways was built across the province. These roads now carry most of the people and goods moving from place to place. Car ferries link Nova Scotia with neighboring provinces and with Maine in the United States.

Nova Scotia has six daily newspapers. The first newspaper published in Canada was the Halifax *Gazette,* founded in 1752. Today the leading dailies are the *Chronicle-Herald* and

the *Mail Star,* of Halifax, and the Cape Breton *Post,* published in Sydney.

There are five television and 24 radio stations in the province, and most urban areas are serviced by cable television.

▶EDUCATION

Free and compulsory primary education has existed in Nova Scotia for more than a century. Fifty years ago, most people left school before the age of 15. But now a majority complete high school or vocational school. Since World War II, the scattered one-room schools have been replaced by centralized schools to which children are brought by bus. Segregation by religion and race has been largely eliminated.

At the university level, the 1960's brought large increases in students, as well as in costs.

Halifax, Nova Scotia's capital and largest city, is a center of government, education, and culture. Its excellent harbor, which opens onto the Atlantic Ocean, has made the city one of Canada's leading ports.

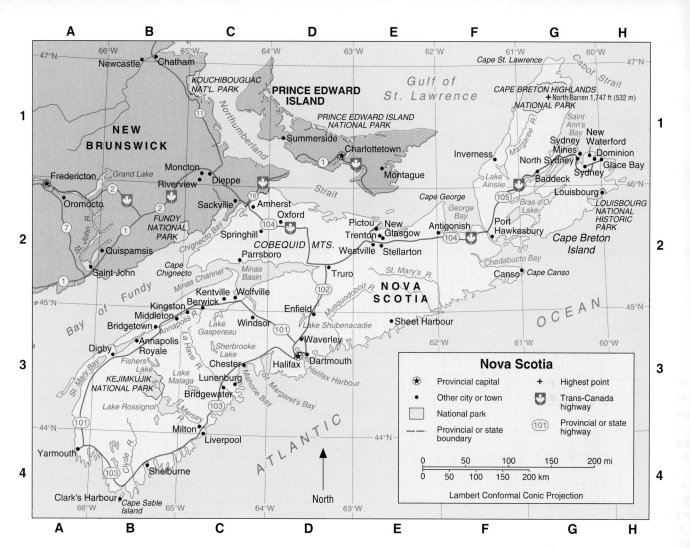

Private donations gave way to government grants as the major means of financing higher education. Nova Scotia now has several universities and colleges. The largest is Dalhousie University, in Halifax. Halifax is also the home of the University of King's College, Saint Mary's University, Mount Saint Vincent University, the Nova Scotia College of Art and Design, and the Technical University of Nova Scotia. Université Sainte-Anne is located in Church Point. Acadia University is in Wolfville, Saint Francis Xavier University is in Antigonish, and the University College of Cape Breton is in Sydney.

The Provincial Library, established in 1952, co-ordinates regional library services across the province. Bookmobiles travel to areas that do not have regular branches. Additional library facilities are provided by the universities, as well as by such government research centers as the Bedford Institute of

Oceanography in Dartmouth. The Library of the Public Archives in Halifax holds thousands of documents on the province's past.

▶**PLACES OF INTEREST**

Places of scenic beauty and historical sites abound in Nova Scotia. The drama of the Fundy tides can be best observed in the Cumberland and Minas basins. Peggy's Cove, near Halifax, is the most picturesque of the province's fishing villages. Lunenburg combines a living fishing tradition with unique wooden architecture dating from the 19th century. Halifax's harbor front is being rebuilt to give traditional architecture a modern use.

Much of Nova Scotia's scenery and many of its historic sites are preserved in national areas. Among them are the following:

Alexander Graham Bell Museum National Historic Park, in Baddeck, features exhibits and rec-

Young dancers demonstrate their talents at the Antigonish Highland Games, an annual festival of Scottish music, dance, and sports. The province's Scottish heritage plays an important role in its cultural life, especially in eastern Nova Scotia.

ords of Bell's inventions, which included the telephone.

Cape Breton Highlands National Park, on Cape Breton Island, is popular for its sports facilities and scenery. A scenic drive, the Cabot Trail, offers magnificent views of the mountains and the ocean.

Fort Anne National Historic Park, in Annapolis Royal, is the site of a French fort built to protect the early Acadian settlers.

Fortress of Louisbourg National Historical Park, on Cape Breton, is a stunning reproduction of an 18th-century French town and naval base.

Grand Pré National Historic Park, in the Annapolis Valley, marks the area of the main Acadian settlements in Nova Scotia. It was the setting of the poem "Evangeline," by Henry Wadsworth Longfellow.

Halifax Citadel National Historic Park, in Halifax, is the site of a fort built in 1749 and restored in 1828.

Kejimkujik National Park preserves a portion of the scenic lake country of southwestern Nova Scotia.

Maritime Museum of the Atlantic, in Halifax, celebrates Nova Scotia's long involvement with the sea.

Nova Scotia Museum of Industry, in Stellarton, tells the story of industrial production in Nova Scotia.

Port Royal Habitation National Historic Park, near Annapolis Royal, is a reconstruction of the first French settlement in Nova Scotia.

A rich array of artifacts from prehistory to the present are held by the Provincial Museum in Halifax. The museum also maintains a series of historic houses dating from the 18th and 19th centuries. An insight into the life of the past can be obtained by visiting Ross Farm, in Lunenburg County, and other restorations and museums.

▶**GOVERNMENT**

Nova Scotia's government is headed by the lieutenant governor, appointed by the federal government. But in practice, power is exercised by the premier and a cabinet drawn from the political party with the most members in the 52-seat House of Assembly. Assembly elections take place every five years or sooner, depending on political conditions. The assembly makes the laws of the province, within limits set by the Canadian constitution. The province's municipal institutions depend on the assembly for much of the money needed to run local services. There is also a judiciary made up of the Supreme Court and various other courts.

▶**HISTORY**

Human beings may have lived in Nova Scotia for as long as 10,000 years. When Europeans arrived, the area was thinly occupied by a people known as the Micmac. They lived as nomadic hunters and fishers. Claims that Vikings visited Nova Scotia in the 11th century —and Scots in the 14th century—are unconfirmed. John Cabot, on his famous voyage of 1497, may have sighted Nova Scotia. But historic records of discovery go back only to the early 1500's.

The first permanent European settlers in Nova Scotia were the French. In 1605, Pierre du Guast, Sieur de Monts, and Samuel de Champlain founded Port Royal (now Annapolis Royal). The French established farming settlements around the Bay of Fundy. They were able to farm the fertile tidal marshlands by building dikes to keep back the high tides. They called the whole area—which also included Prince Edward Island and New Brunswick—Acadia. These original French settlers and their descendants have been called Acadians ever since.

In 1621, Sir William Alexander received a charter to the territory from King James I of England (James VI of Scotland). In 1629 the Scots established two short-lived settlements in Nova Scotia.

Between 1613 and 1713 the British and French fought for control of the area, and it changed hands many times. Finally, in 1713, under the Treaty of Utrecht, the British received most of Nova Scotia. The French kept Cape Breton Island with a fortress at Louisbourg until 1758, when Louisbourg was captured by the British in the Seven Years' War.

Under British rule, Halifax was founded by Edward Cornwallis in 1749. During the Seven Years' War the Acadians, who refused to swear allegiance to Britain, were driven off their lands in Nova Scotia. They settled in other parts of Canada, in New England, and in the French colony of Louisiana. Some returned later to Nova Scotia and settled.

Around 1753 the first German settlers arrived at Lunenburg. English settlers from the New England colonies came to Nova Scotia in large numbers in the early 1760's, replacing the Acadians. They started coastal fishing settlements and began farming in the Annapolis Valley and on the northern lowlands along the Northumberland Strait. Scottish settlers came to Pictou in the 1770's.

The American Revolutionary War (1775–83) brought to Nova Scotia thousands of Loyalists, who refused to fight against Britain. During the first half of the 1800's, a new wave of settlers arrived, mainly from Scotland and Ireland. Most of them settled in northern Nova Scotia and on Cape Breton Island, which became part of Nova Scotia in 1820.

The Napoleonic Wars and, later, trade with Britain and the British West Indies led to economic growth in Nova Scotia. With prosperity came demands for political change. Joseph Howe, a Halifax newspaper editor, led a struggle for reform that ended in 1848, when Nova Scotia was granted responsible government. This meant that the province was more democratic and less closely controlled by Britain.

In 1867, Nova Scotia joined New Brunswick, Quebec, and Ontario to form the Confederation of Canada. The economy continued to expand largely because of Nova Scotia's large fleet of wooden sailing ships. But the fleet became obsolete (outdated) by the 1890's. This and other changes destroyed Nova Scotia's prosperity, and the province turned to industry. However, the 1920's brought widespread factory closings, and many people left the province.

Since then, Nova Scotia has searched for economic recovery. Federal spending and special efforts to revive coal and steel production have helped, and new industries have come to the province. The fisheries also offer hope for the future. Exploration for oil and gas is being carried on along the continental shelf.

The society of Nova Scotia is undergoing major changes. Thousands of people have left farming, fishing, mining, and forestry to find jobs in industry, government, and the professions. And more women are entering the job force than ever before. Government spending for health, education, and welfare has helped raise the standard of living.

DAVID A. SUTHERLAND
Dalhousie University

IMPORTANT DATES

1497 Possible discovery of Nova Scotia by John Cabot.

1605 Champlain and De Monts established the first settlement—Port Royal.

1621 Area named Nova Scotia under charter granted by King James I to Sir William Alexander.

1629 First British settlements established—Charlesfort and Rosemar.

1713 France lost mainland Nova Scotia to Great Britain under Treaty of Utrecht; French began building fortress of Louisbourg on Cape Breton Island.

1749 Halifax founded by Edward Cornwallis.

1752 First newspaper in Canada, the *Halifax Gazette*, founded.

1755 Expulsion of Acadians began.

1758 British captured Louisbourg.

1763 British gained Cape Breton Island under Peace of Paris ending Seven Years' War.

1769 Prince Edward Island separated from Nova Scotia.

1784 New Brunswick separated from Nova Scotia.

1820 Cape Breton Island annexed to Nova Scotia.

1848 Responsible government granted to Nova Scotia.

1867 Nova Scotia, Ontario, Quebec, and New Brunswick formed Canadian Confederation.

1876 Railway from Halifax to Quebec completed.

1917 Large section of Halifax destroyed by explosion of munitions ship in Halifax harbor.

1939–1945 Halifax became an important naval center and convoy assembly point during World War II.

1955 Causeway across the Strait of Canso completed, linking Cape Breton Island with Nova Scotia mainland; Angus L. Macdonald Bridge, connecting Halifax and Dartmouth, completed.

1967 Establishment of government ownership of the coal and steel industries.

1970 Environmental Pollution Act passed.

1986 Federal-provincial agreement signed on sharing of income from offshore mineral development.

NOVELS

Novels are long stories written in prose. They are works of fiction; that is, they are about imaginary people and events. A novelist may use facts in a story and base its characters on real people. But the main aspects of a novel are usually invented by the author.

A novel is longer than most other types of fiction. Most novels are book-length and have at least 40,000 words. But there are no set rules about the length of a novel. Novelists may write long books or short books.

Nor are there rules about the subject of a novel or the way the author presents the story. A novel can be about almost anything imaginable. It can be realistic or pure fantasy. A novelist's writing style may be dignified and formal, or it may be conversational and filled with slang expressions.

The novelist, then, has a great deal of freedom. But all novels have certain features in common. They have characters, a setting, a plot, and a theme.

The main characters in a novel may be rich or poor, good or evil, ordinary or highly unusual. But no matter what the characters are like, the reader must be convinced that they could actually exist. It is the job of the novelist to involve the reader in the lives of the characters. By revealing their appearance, actions, speech, and thoughts, the novelist makes the characters exist for the reader as real people.

The setting is where the action of the novel takes place. It may be a modern U.S. city, a 19th-century whaling ship, a distant planet far in the future, or any number of other times and places.

The plot, or plan of the novel, consists of a series of related events. Some novels present the events of the plot in chronological order, while others skip backward and forward in time. In most novels, the characters face a problem or conflict, and the plot is formed around the development of the problem and its solution.

The theme is the main idea of the novel. It may also be the author's comment on some aspect of human life: love, money, social class, or family relationships, for example.

▶BEGINNINGS OF THE NOVEL

The novel is the youngest of all the great forms of literature. Poetry and drama have

Cervantes' masterpiece, *Don Quixote*, is one of the earliest novels. Its plot revolves around the adventures of an idealistic knight and his loyal servant.

been created for thousands of years. But the novel did not become an established literary form until the 1700's. Many early works of literature resembled novels. In Greek and Roman times, long fictional stories, such as Longus' *Daphnis and Chloë*, Apuleius' *Golden Ass*, and Petronius' *Satyricon* had some similarities to the novels of today. In the Middle Ages, *The Decameron*, a collection of tales by the Italian writer Giovanni Boccaccio, and *Troilus and Criseyde*, a long poem of unhappy love by the English writer Geoffrey Chaucer, had many elements of the novel.

Some critics believe that the first true novel was *Don Quixote* (1605, 1615), by the Spaniard Miguel de Cervantes. It is in part a satire on the romances of chivalry that were popular at the time. These romances usually told of the fantastic adventures of a heroic knight. In its story of an idealistic man who has become confused from reading tales of chivalry, *Don Quixote* turns away from the purely imaginary world of the romances. Its realistic characters, well-constructed plot, and interest in human nature and the real world look forward to the themes and techniques of later novels.

English Novels

The novel became an established form of literature in England during the 1700's. Five writers in particular were central to the development of the English novel.

Daniel Defoe in *Moll Flanders* (1722) and *Robinson Crusoe* (1719) used a plain style to describe very ordinary, probable things. Even though Robinson Crusoe had the extraordinary experience of being shipwrecked on a desert island, Defoe tells mainly about ordinary things, such as how Crusoe learned to raise food for himself and how he built a house. Defoe was interested in practical questions of how people get along in the world.

Samuel Richardson wrote novels in the form of letters, such as *Pamela: or, Virtue Rewarded* (1740) and *Clarissa* (1748). He was more interested in feelings and personal relationships than in practical, everyday affairs. He explored the emotions of his heroines in great detail.

Henry Fielding thought that Richardson exaggerated emotion and began to write *Joseph Andrews* (1742) as a satire on *Pamela*. But the story soon turned into a masterful comic novel. Fielding's best-known novel, *Tom Jones* (1749), has a complicated but highly organized plot.

Tobias Smollett confirmed the popularity of the novel with his lively, humorous works *Roderick Random* (1746), *Peregrine Pickle* (1751), and *Humphrey Clinker* (1771). Laurence Sterne wrote *Tristram Shandy* (1760–67), which parodies the form of the novel by doing away with a conventional plot.

▶19TH CENTURY

The novel continued to develop in England during the 1800's and achieved great popular success. Novelists in other countries, notably France, Russia, and the United States, also made important contributions. The century produced some of the world's greatest and best-loved novels.

England

Sir Walter Scott and Jane Austen are the two most important English novelists of the early 1800's. Scott wrote historical novels about the Middle Ages and about the Lowlanders and Highlanders of Scotland. *Waverley* (1814), *The Heart of Midlothian* (1818), and *Ivanhoe* (1819) are among the best known of his many novels. His books have action and adventure and give fascinating pictures of the past. Jane Austen's novels are very different from Scott's. Her *Pride and Prejudice* (1813) and *Emma* (1816) are about well-to-do people living quietly in English villages. She is most admired for her witty dialogue, well-drawn characters, and cleverly worked-out plots.

Two sisters, Charlotte and Emily Brontë, were remarkable English novelists. Charlotte's *Jane Eyre* (1847) is the story of a poor but self-reliant governess. Emily's *Wuthering Heights* (1847) is about two people who have a passionate love affair that finally destroys them both.

The most famous writers under the reign of Queen Victoria (1837–1901) were William Makepeace Thackeray, Charles Dickens, George Eliot, and Thomas Hardy. Thackeray's best-known book is *Vanity Fair* (1847–48). It criticizes the crude ambitions and manners of English society.

Dickens was a very popular novelist with a fiery and intense imagination. His novels often criticize social conditions in England. They are full of humor, adventure, and sentiment and contain dozens of memorable characters. Most of his novels were first published in weekly installments, which were eagerly awaited by readers. Three of Dickens' best-known works are *David Copperfield* (1849–50), *A Tale of Two Cities* (1859), and *Great Expectations* (1861).

George Eliot is the pen name of Mary Ann Evans, whose best book is *Middlemarch* (1871–72). It is a long novel about life in a small city and shows how various people, after a long struggle, find a place for themselves in the world.

Thomas Hardy's finest novels are *The Return of the Native* (1878) and *Tess of the D'Urbervilles* (1891). He shows his characters against the great background of the natural world. These are dark and somber books, in which an evil fate pursues the main characters to their doom.

France

The greatest French novelists of the 1800's are Stendhal, Honoré de Balzac, Victor Hugo, and Gustave Flaubert. Stendhal in *The Red and the Black* (1830) tells about the dull life in France after the Napoleonic Wars and shows how remarkable people revolted against that dullness. Balzac wrote *The Human Comedy* (1827–47), a series of interconnected novels and stories that present the whole range of French life. Hugo was the most passionate and poetic of these novelists. His most famous novel is *Les Misérables* (1862), a dark tale of suffering. The heroine of Flaubert's *Madame Bovary* (1856) tries without success to escape the boredom of small-town life.

Russia

The novel in Russia gained its first importance with Aleksander Pushkin's *Captain's Daughter* (1836), a short historical novel. Nikolai Gogol's *Dead Souls* (1842) is the first great Russian comic novel. The hero, a most ordinary man, meets a series of mad, extravagant characters. Ivan Turgenev's *Fathers and Sons* (1862) is written in a clear and graceful style. It is about the conflict between older and younger people.

Captain Ahab's relentless search for the white whale that took off his leg leads to disaster in *Moby Dick*, an exciting novel of the sea by Herman Melville.

Leo Tolstoi and Fëdor Dostoevski are two of the world's greatest novelists. Tolstoi's *War and Peace* (1865–69) describes Napoleon's invasion of Russia and the way one generation grows up while another is growing old. His *Anna Karenina* (1875–77) joins a story about an unhappy love affair to a story about a happy marriage. Dostoevski's novels are powerful studies in crime, guilt, religious torment, and faith. His most famous novels are *Crime and Punishment* (1866) and *The Brothers Karamazov* (1879–80).

The United States

The first significant American novels were written by James Fenimore Cooper. He wrote a series of novels about the adventures of the American frontiersman Natty Bumppo; *The Last of the Mohicans* (1826) is the best known.

Nathaniel Hawthorne is most famous for *The Scarlet Letter* (1850) and *The House of the Seven Gables* (1851). His chief themes are sin, mystery, and repentance. He writes in a clear, firm style, but his ideas are complicated. His basic concern is the welfare of the human soul. He is the first American novelist to rank with writers such as Dickens and Thackeray in England.

Herman Melville wrote *Moby Dick* (1851), which is considered one of the great American novels. The book can be enjoyed as a tale of the sea, but it also raises deep questions about the nature of human existence. It explores the problem of whether the world is ultimately good or evil.

Mark Twain is best known for his humor and for his easy, conversational style in such novels as *The Adventures of Tom Sawyer* (1876) and *A Connecticut Yankee in King Arthur's Court* (1889). In *The Adventures of Huckleberry Finn* (1884), Huck and the runaway slave Jim have humorous adventures. But the hardships and cruelty they experience show the dark side of American life.

Henry James lived in England and often wrote about Americans in Europe. His theme was the reaction of the innocent American to the ancient culture of Europe. *The American* (1877), *The Portrait of a Lady* (1881), and *The Ambassadors* (1903) are among his most widely read books. James developed theories about the nature of the novel that influenced many later writers.

▶MODERN NOVELS

By the 20th century, the novel had become a nearly universal literary form. Writers from many countries wrote outstanding novels, creating a new variety of styles and subjects. Often, modern novelists broke with earlier traditions and experimented with new techniques, adding to the diversity.

Early 1900's

Two of the most important English novelists of the early 1900's were Joseph Conrad and D. H. Lawrence. Both were less interested in describing what their characters did than in showing what they felt and thought. Conrad's books, such as *Lord Jim* (1900), often have a surface plot of adventure in exotic lands. But underneath they are about the moral choices that shape people's lives. In *Sons and Lovers* (1913) and *Women in Love* (1920), Lawrence examines the ways men and women develop emotionally in their relationships with one another.

The Irish writer James Joyce went even further in portraying the inner lives of his characters. He used a technique called **stream of consciousness**, which attempts to represent the flow of thoughts and feelings that pass through a person's mind. Joyce's use of this technique can be seen in his novel *Ulysses* (1922), which describes one day in the lives of two fictional Dubliners. The stream-of-consciousness technique was used by other modern novelists, notably the English writer Virginia Woolf. Her novels include *Mrs. Dalloway* (1925) and *To the Lighthouse* (1927).

Other European novelists also experimented with new techniques and subjects. The French novelist Marcel Proust wrote *Remembrance of Things Past* (1913–27), which explores in depth the workings of human memory and emotion. Two important authors writing in German were Franz Kafka and Thomas Mann. In his novels *The Trial* (1925) and *The Castle* (1926), Kafka portrays a frightening world of isolation and despair. Mann frequently wrote about the conflicts between artists and society. One of his best-known works is *The Magic Mountain* (1924).

In the United States, many novelists were interested in realistically describing problems of American society. Edith Wharton criticizes the materialism of New York high society in *The House of Mirth* (1905) and describes a tragedy on a New England farm in *Ethan Frome* (1911). Theodore Dreiser wrote *Sister Carrie* (1900) and *An American Tragedy* (1925), powerful novels about American urban life. Sinclair Lewis attacked the narrow-mindedness and spite of small-town life in

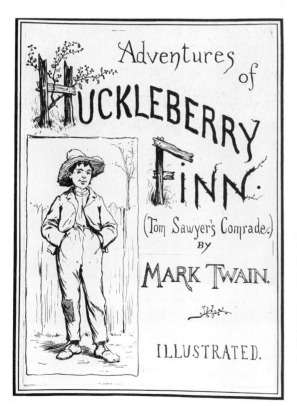

Left: In Mark Twain's *Adventures of Huckleberry Finn*, an orphan boy encounters both the good and the bad in American society. *Below:* An American farming family travels west in search of work in *The Grapes of Wrath*, John Steinbeck's novel of the Great Depression.

his novels *Main Street* (1920), *Babbitt* (1922), and *Arrowsmith* (1925).

In *This Side of Paradise* (1920) and *The Great Gatsby* (1925), F. Scott Fitzgerald describes the extravagance and self-delusion of wealthy Americans of the 1920's. John Steinbeck is best known for *The Grapes of Wrath* (1939), which recounts the struggles of an American farming family during the Depression of the 1930's.

Ernest Hemingway's novels of disappointed love and heroic human endurance include *The Sun Also Rises* (1926), *A Farewell to Arms* (1929), and *For Whom the Bell Tolls* (1940). His style is brief, objective, and dramatic.

William Faulkner wrote a series of novels set in Yoknapatawpha County, a fictional area of Mississippi. These works, which include *The Sound and the Fury* (1929), *Light in August* (1932), and *Absalom, Absalom* (1936),

continue to influence modern novelists, particularly southern writers.

Later 1900's

The years following World War II (1939–45) saw a burst of activity from writers around the world. The horror and destruction of the war profoundly affected the way people viewed the world. As a result, much postwar literature is characterized by a dark and gloomy outlook.

In France, existentialism, a philosophical movement that gained prominence in the 1930's, continued to influence novelists. Existentialists believed that people must create their own moral values and take full responsibility for their lives. Albert Camus dramatized existentialist views in brief, sharply etched novels, including *The Stranger* (1942), *The Plague* (1947), and *The Fall* (1956). Another

Clockwise from left: Outstanding modern novelists include Aleksandr Solzhenitsyn (Soviet Union), Alice Walker (United States), Gabriel García Márquez (Colombia), and John Updike (United States).

writer influenced by existentialism was the Irish-born Samuel Beckett, who lived in France and wrote many of his works in French. His novels, such as *Molloy* (1950) and *Malone Dies* (1952), focus on the lack of meaning in human life.

Germany's major postwar novelist is Günter Grass, whose books satirize German culture. The Czech writer Milan Kundera also comments on postwar European life in such novels as *The Book of Laughter and Forgetting* (1979). Important postwar Italian novelists include Italo Calvino and Pier Paolo Pasolini.

The tradition of Russian fiction was seriously disrupted by the Revolution of 1917 and later events. The official Soviet school of writing, socialist realism, limited original expression in favor of spreading Soviet doctrine. Still, some outstanding novelists emerged. Mikhail Sholokhov became internationally known for his lengthy novel *The Quiet Don* (1928–40). Two other writers produced great works at the cost of government disapproval. Boris Pasternak won worldwide acclaim for *Dr. Zhivago* (1957), but the novel was banned in the Soviet Union until 1988. Aleksandr Solzhenitsyn wrote about life in Soviet prison camps in *The First Circle* (1964) and other novels. He was expelled from the Soviet Union in 1974.

England's leading postwar novelists include Graham Greene, who explored moral problems in *The Heart of the Matter* (1948) and many other books. William Golding's *Lord of the Flies* (1954) and Anthony Burgess' *A Clockwork Orange* (1962) investigate the dark side of human nature. Other outstanding English novelists of the later 1900's were Kingsley Amis, Margaret Drabble, Iris Murdoch, and Muriel Spark.

England's historical position as a powerful and far-reaching empire has led to a tradition of English-language literature in former colonies throughout the world. Two highly regarded African novelists writing in English are the Nigerians Chinua Achebe and Wole Soyinka. V. S. Naipaul, a Trinidadian of Indian descent who settled in England, has written impressive novels on the heritage of colonialism, including *A Bend in the River* (1979).

Canada has produced English-language novelists of international stature, including Margaret Atwood and Mordecai Richler. Canada also has a tradition of French-language literature. Notable Canadian novelists writing in French include Roger Lemelin and Gabrielle Roy.

In the United States, the first major novelist to emerge after World War II was Norman Mailer. His acclaimed first novel, *The Naked and the Dead* (1948), was based on his wartime experiences.

Two popular American novelists of the 1950's and 1960's were J. D. Salinger and Kurt Vonnegut, Jr. Salinger's *The Catcher in the Rye* (1951) dramatizes the frustration and loneliness of an adolescent boy. Vonnegut's novels, which mingle science fiction and social satire, include *Cat's Cradle* (1963) and *Slaughterhouse-Five* (1969).

Jewish life in America was the focus of novels by Saul Bellow, Bernard Malamud, and Philip Roth. Bellow won the Nobel prize for literature in 1976. His novels include *The Adventures of Augie March* (1953) and *Humboldt's Gift* (1975).

Black American writers have made important contributions to the novel. Ralph Ellison, in *Invisible Man* (1952), and James Baldwin, in *Go Tell It on the Mountain* (1953) and other works, eloquently express the black American experience. Later black writers, notably Toni Morrison (*Tar Baby*; 1981) and Alice Walker (*The Color Purple*; 1982), continued to explore aspects of black life.

John Updike produced carefully crafted novels chronicling middle-class suburban life. Among his many works are *Rabbit, Run* (1960), *Couples* (1968), and *Roger's Version* (1986). Equally prolific was Joyce Carol Oates. Her novels portray characters who live intensely and act on their feelings, often with violent results.

Some of the most innovative novels of the later 1900's were produced by Latin American writers. They often used a technique called "magical realism," in which dream-like elements combine with the everyday. The Colombian Gabriel García Márquez was one of the finest modern novelists writing in Spanish. His novels include *One Hundred Years of Solitude* (1967) and *Love in the Time of Cholera* (1987). Other Latin American novelists include Brazil's Jorge Amado, Mexico's Carlos Fuentes, and Peru's Mario Vargas Llosa.

MASON COOLEY
College of Staten Island
City University of New York

November

November was the ninth month of the ancient Romans' ten-month year, so its name came from *novem,* the Latin word for "nine." In the Northern Hemisphere, November is a month of cold winds and gray skies. Winter is on the way.

Place in the year: 11th month.
Number of days: 30.
Flower: Chrysanthemum.
Birthstone: Topaz.
Zodiac signs: Scorpio, the Scorpion (October 23– November 21), and Sagittarius, the Archer (November 22– December 21).

1
- Anniversary of the Revolution in Algeria

2
- **Daniel Boone** born 1734
- **Marie Antoinette** born 1755
- **James K. Polk** born 1795
- **Warren G. Harding** born 1865
- North Dakota became the 39th state, 1889
- South Dakota became the 40th state, 1889
- Balfour Declaration stated Britain's intention of establishing a Jewish state in Palestine, 1917
- Radio station KDKA in Pittsburgh began first regular radio broadcasts, 1920
- *All Souls' Day*

3
- **William Cullen Bryant** born 1794
- U.S.S.R. launched Sputnik II with dog on board, 1957
- Independence Day in Dominica; Panama

4
- Erie Canal formally opened in New York state, 1825
- Iranian militants seized 90 hostages at U.S. Embassy in Tehran, 1979
- *Will Rogers Day* in Oklahoma
- Constitution Day in Tonga

5
- Gunpowder Plot to blow up British Parliament failed, 1605. Now celebrated as Guy Fawkes Day in England

6
- Abraham Lincoln elected president of the U.S., 1860
- First intercollegiate modern football game, Rutgers defeating Princeton at Rutgers, 1869

7
- **Marie Curie** born 1867
- **Konrad Lorenz** born 1903
- Lewis and Clark sighted Pacific Ocean, 1805
- General William Henry Harrison defeated Indians in Battle of Tippecanoe, 1811
- Last spike driven in Canadian Pacific Railway, 1885

8
- **Christiaan Barnard** born 1922
- Montana became the 41st state, 1889

9
- Congress of Industrial Organizations (CIO) established, 1935
- Largest power failure in history blacked out New York City, parts of eight states, and parts of Canada for several hours, 1965

10
- **Martin Luther** born 1483

11
- Washington became the 42nd state, 1889
- Armistice signed ending World War I, 1918
- Tomb of the Unknown Soldier dedicated at Arlington, Virginia, 1921
- *Veterans Day*
- Independence Day in Angola
- Remembrance Day in Canada

12
- **Auguste Rodin** born 1840
- **Sun Yat-sen** born 1866
- Second launching of U.S. space shuttle Columbia became first re-use of a space vehicle, 1981

13
- **Robert Louis Stevenson** born 1850
- Mariner 9, U.S. unmanned spacecraft, orbited Mars and became first man-made object to orbit another planet, 1971

14
- **Robert Fulton** born 1765
- **Claude Monet** born 1840
- **Jawaharlal Nehru** born 1889
- **Sir Frederick Grant Banting** born 1891
- **Aaron Copland** born 1900

15
- **William Pitt, Earl of Chatham,** born 1708
- **Georgia O'Keeffe** born 1887
- Draft of Articles of Confederation adopted by Continental Congress, 1777

16
- Oklahoma became the 46th state, 1907
- U.S. officially recognized the Soviet Union, 1933

17
- Congress first met in Washington, D.C., 1800
- Suez Canal opened, 1869

18
- Standard time began in U.S., 1883

- Murder of five Americans in Jonestown, Guyana, followed by mass suicides and murders of more than 900 members of Jim Jones's People's Temple, 1978
- Independence Day in Morocco

19
- **Ferdinand de Lesseps** born 1805
- **James A. Garfield** born 1831
- Abraham Lincoln delivered Gettysburg Address, 1863
- Prince of Monaco Holiday in Monaco

20
- **Sir Wilfrid Laurier** born 1841
- **Robert F. Kennedy** born 1925
- Nuremberg Trials, trying Nazi offenders for crimes against humanity, began, 1945

21
- **Voltaire** born 1694
- **William Beaumont** born 1785
- Mayflower Compact signed, 1620
- North Carolina ratified the Constitution, 1789

22
- **George Eliot** born 1819
- **Charles de Gaulle** born 1890
- President John F. Kennedy assassinated in Dallas, Texas, 1963
- Independence Day in Lebanon

23
- **Franklin Pierce** born 1804
- Labor-Thanksgiving Day in Japan

24
- **Baruch Spinoza** born 1632
- **Zachary Taylor** born 1784
- **Henri de Toulouse-Lautrec** born 1864
- Lee Harvey Oswald, accused assassin of President Kennedy, killed by Jack Ruby while in

custody of Dallas Police, 1963
- Anniversary of the New Regime in Zaire

25
- **Andrew Carnegie** born 1835
- **Pope John XXIII** born 1881
- Independence Day in Suriname

26
- First national Thanksgiving Day in the U.S. proclaimed, 1789

28
- **William Blake** born 1757
- Independence Proclamation Day in Albania
- Independence Day in Mauritania

29
- **George Brown** born 1818
- **Louisa May Alcott** born 1832
- Commander Richard E. Byrd made first flight over South Pole, 1929
- Major changes in the Roman Catholic liturgy, including the use of English in many parts of the mass, became effective in the U.S., 1964
- *Nellie Tayloe Ross's Birthday* in Wyoming

30
- **Jonathan Swift** born 1667
- **Cyrus Field** born 1819
- **Mark Twain** born 1835
- **Sir Winston Churchill** born 1874
- Independence Day in Barbados
- National Day in Benin

First Tuesday following the first Monday in November: *Election Day.* **First Saturday after November 11:** *Sadie Hawkins Day.* **Fourth Thursday:** *Thanksgiving Day.* **Third week of November:** *National Children's Book Week.*

The calendar listing identifies people who were born on the indicated day in boldface type, **like this.** You will find a biography of each of these birthday people in *The New Book of Knowledge.* In addition to citing some historical events and historical firsts, the calendar also lists the holidays and some of the festivals celebrated in the United States. These holidays are printed in italic type, *like this.* See the article HOLIDAYS for more information.

Many holidays and festivals of nations around the world are included in the calendar as well. When the term "national holiday" is used, it means that the nation celebrates an important patriotic event on that day—in most cases the winning of independence. Consult *The New Book of Knowledge* article on the individual nation for further information on its national holiday.

A nuclear power plant (*above*) uses the energy contained in the nucleus of the atom—the most powerful source of energy known—to produce electricity. Technicians in a computerized control room (*right*) keep close watch on the plant's operation. Because it does not pollute the air or use up scarce supplies of oil and coal, nuclear energy has great promise. But problems of safety and cost remain to be solved.

NUCLEAR ENERGY

Nuclear energy is the energy contained in the center, or nucleus, of an atom. The nucleus is the most powerful source of energy that exists. Until the 1930's, scientists did not know how to release this energy. Since then, people have put nuclear energy to many constructive uses. Nuclear energy is used in scientific research and in medical treatments. It powers satellites and submarines, and it is used to produce electricity. People have also put nuclear energy to destructive uses, through the creation of nuclear weapons.

Nuclear energy has great promise. It also poses great risks. Understanding the risks and benefits requires some knowledge of the source of nuclear energy: atoms and the particles that make them up.

▶ATOMIC STRUCTURE

All substances are made up of atoms. The atom is the basic unit of a chemical element, and the atoms that make up one element are different from the atoms that make up another element.

Atoms themselves are made up of smaller **subatomic particles**. The nucleus (plural: nuclei) consists of two kinds of particles, **protons** and **neutrons**, bound closely together. Clouds of smaller particles called **electrons** surround the nucleus. Each electron carries a negative electrical charge. Each proton carries a positive charge. (Neutrons have no charge.) Opposite electrical charges attract each other, and this attraction holds the electrons and the nucleus together as an atom.

Atoms of different elements may join in clusters to form **molecules** of various substances. The atoms join together by exchanging or sharing electrons. Their nuclei remain unchanged. Thus it is the electrons that determine how an atom behaves chemically—that is, in what ways it may combine.

The forms of energy we are most familiar with result from reactions that involve electrons. For example, when wood burns, molecules in the wood are pulled apart. Their atoms are combined in new ways with oxygen from the air. In the process, **chemical energy** is released.

In contrast, nuclear energy involves changes in the nucleus of the atom. To understand how this energy is released, we need to take a closer look at the nucleus.

Inside the Nucleus

The nucleus contains most of the atom's **mass**. (Mass is the total amount of matter in a substance.) Atoms of the same element all have the same number of protons—for example, all oxygen atoms have eight protons, and all hydrogen atoms have one proton. But atoms of the same element may contain different numbers of neutrons. A hydrogen nucleus may have one proton and no neutrons, one proton and one neutron (a form called deuterium, or heavy hydrogen), or one proton and two neutrons (a form called tritium).

These various forms of hydrogen are called **isotopes** of hydrogen. In the same way, there may be different isotopes of other elements. (To indicate an isotope, scientists use a notation that shows the **mass number**—the total number of protons and neutrons—along with the symbol for the element. Ordinary hydrogen is H-1, deuterium H-2, and tritium H-3.)

THE THREE ISOTOPES OF HYDROGEN

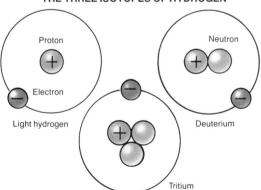

Proton

Neutron

Electron

Light hydrogen

Deuterium

Tritium

With its single proton, hydrogen is the lightest element. The heaviest natural element is uranium. Its isotopes include uranium 235 and uranium 238. Scientists have made heavier elements in the laboratory. But these elements are not found in nature because they are unstable—they begin to change almost as soon as they are formed.

These changes are related to conflicting forces in the nucleus. The positively charged protons and uncharged neutrons are held together by a powerful attraction called the **strong force**. At the same time, however, the protons repel each other—just as particles with opposite charges attract each other, those with the same charge tend to push each other away.

In the very heavy elements that scientists have created, the nuclei are very large and have many protons. In such nuclei, the tendency of the protons to repel each other overpowers the strong force. Thus the nuclei begin to break down into smaller nuclei and individual particles. This process is called **radioactivity**. A few natural elements, including uranium, are also radioactive.

▶NUCLEAR REACTIONS

Radioactivity is an example of a nuclear reaction—a change in the nucleus. It is considered a **spontaneous** nuclear reaction because it takes place without the action of any outside force. The unstable nuclei continue to give off particles until they reach a stable state. In this way, uranium gradually changes into lead, a lighter and more stable element.

Radioactivity was discovered by the French scientist Antoine Henri Becquerel in 1896. As scientists learned more about this process, they discovered that similar reactions can be **induced**, or made to happen. If a uranium 235 nucleus is struck by a free neutron, for example, it may split. The result will be two nuclei of lighter elements. Some stray neutrons are also released.

In early studies, scientists observed that the total mass of the particles left after a nuclear reaction was often less than the mass of the original nucleus. What had happened to the missing mass? It had been converted to energy. (The idea that mass and energy are two forms of the same thing had been proposed by Albert Einstein in 1905. To read more about this idea, see the article RELATIVITY in Volume QR.)

In the same way that heavy nuclei can break apart, light nuclei can combine. In both cases, the nuclei are seeking to reach a more stable state—elements with medium mass tend to be the most stable. And in both cases, small amounts of mass can be converted to large amounts of energy. Thus nuclear energy can be released in two types of reactions: fusion (the joining of nuclei) and fission (the splitting of a nucleus.)

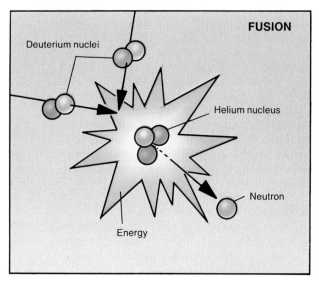

FUSION

Deuterium nuclei

Helium nucleus

Neutron

Energy

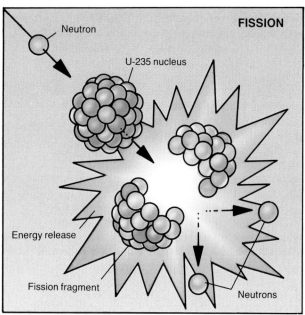

FISSION

Neutron

U-235 nucleus

Energy release

Fission fragment

Neutrons

Nuclear Fusion

In nuclear fusion, two light nuclei combine, or fuse, to form a heavier nucleus. When two deuterium nuclei fuse, for example, helium is formed, and energy is given off.

Fusion reactions power the sun and other stars. But these reactions have proved difficult to duplicate in a controlled, continuous way on earth. To fuse, two nuclei must be pushed together. But because each nucleus carries a positive charge, the nuclei tend to repel each other instead.

This tendency of the nuclei to repel each other can be overcome by enormous pressures and temperatures of millions of degrees. At these extremes, matter is in a state called **plasma**, in which atoms break up into free electrons and free nuclei. The particles move so fast in the intense heat that they overcome the tendency to repel each other.

Fusion achieved at high temperatures is called **thermonuclear fusion**. Humans use it in nuclear weapons (see the article NUCLEAR WEAPONS in this volume). Attempts to use it for peaceful purposes, such as the production of power, have failed.

The plasmas required for thermonuclear fusion are difficult to produce and contain. A device called a **tokamak**, invented in the Soviet Union in 1969, uses a magnetic field to confine the plasma in a doughnut shape. But **magnetic confinement**, as this method is called, requires extremely strong magnetic fields. These fields generally use more energy than the fusion produces.

Another technique, called **inertial confinement**, uses laser beams or beams of charged particles. The beams are directed at tiny pellets that hold deuterium or another light element. They cause the pellet to heat rapidly, forcing the nuclei together. So far, this technique too has failed.

In 2005, the United States and five other nations announced that France had been chosen as the site of the International Thermonuclear Experimental Reactor (ITER). ITER uses a tokamak design. If ITER maintains a fusion reaction, it will become a test power plant.

Nuclear Fission

In nuclear fission, a single nucleus is split into two nuclei of lighter elements. In the process, a small amount of mass is converted into

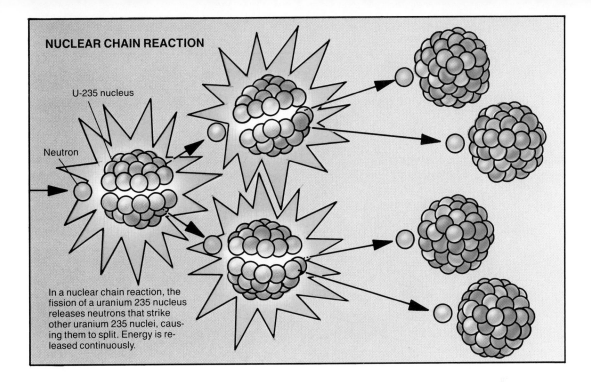

NUCLEAR CHAIN REACTION

U-235 nucleus

Neutron

In a nuclear chain reaction, the fission of a uranium 235 nucleus releases neutrons that strike other uranium 235 nuclei, causing them to split. Energy is released continuously.

a great amount of energy. The fission of a given amount of uranium 235 produces about 160,000 times as much energy as the burning of the same amount of coal. Thus the discovery that energy could be produced through nuclear fission was truly monumental.

The fission of a single nucleus would not be of much use. But in the right conditions, fission can develop into a **chain reaction**. For example, the fission of a uranium 235 nucleus releases two or three neutrons. These neutrons can hit other nuclei of uranium 235 and cause them to break up, releasing energy and neutrons. In this way the reaction builds.

For the chain reaction to continue, the uranium 235 must be arranged so that most of the neutrons that are released encounter other nuclei and cause further fission. When material is arranged so that a chain reaction can take place, the arrangement is called a **critical assembly**. The amount of uranium 235 or other fuel required to keep the reaction going is called the **critical mass**.

In nuclear weapons that make use of fission, the critical assembly is designed to release a sudden, enormous burst of energy. But a critical assembly can also be designed to produce continuous, controllable energy. This is the idea behind a nuclear reactor. The development of nuclear reactors has made fission an important source of energy, chiefly for the production of electrical power.

▶**NUCLEAR POWER**

At an electric power plant, fanlike machines called turbines drive generators that produce electricity. In most plants, these turbines are powered by steam. Some form of energy is needed to boil water and produce the steam. In a traditional power plant, this energy is produced by burning fossil fuels, such as coal or oil. In a nuclear power plant, the source of the energy is a nuclear reactor.

Nuclear Reactors

Various types of nuclear reactors are used in power production. In all types, however, the central part of the reactor is the **core**, which contains the fuel, the moderator, and the coolant. Other important parts of the reactor include the control rods and the containment structure.

Fuel. The fuel used in a reactor is generally a form of uranium. Uranium ores are mined, and the uranium is separated from the ores at mills near the mines. Natural uranium is a mixture of isotopes. It is less than 1 percent uranium 235, which is the isotope used for fission.

Before uranium is used in U.S. reactors, it is **enriched**, or processed to increase the level of uranium 235. (Canadian reactors, which have a slightly different design, use natural uranium as fuel.) The fuel is then formed into small pellets and put into long, thin metal

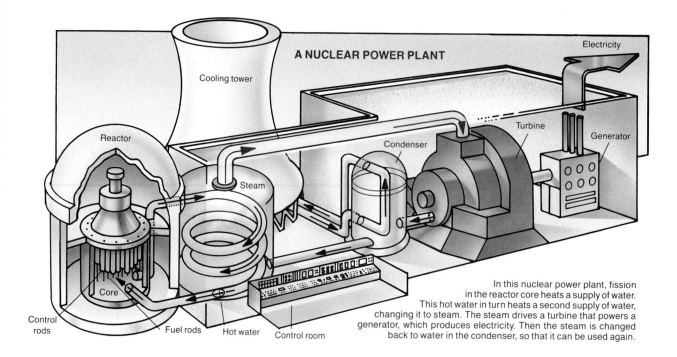

A NUCLEAR POWER PLANT

Electricity

Cooling tower

Reactor

Steam

Turbine

Generator

Condenser

Core

Control rods

Fuel rods

Hot water

Control room

In this nuclear power plant, fission in the reactor core heats a supply of water. This hot water in turn heats a second supply of water, changing it to steam. The steam drives a turbine that powers a generator, which produces electricity. Then the steam is changed back to water in the condenser, so that it can be used again.

rods. As many as 50,000 of these fuel rods, bundled into groups called **fuel assemblies**, stand upright in the reactor core.

One type of reactor, the **breeder reactor**, produces as well as consumes fuel. In a breeder reactor, free neutrons produced by fission are absorbed by uranium 238, which is transformed into plutonium. Plutonium is highly fissionable and can be used in weapons as well as in reactors. For security and safety reasons, breeder reactors are not used for civilian power production in the United States. France is the only country that uses breeder reactors in this way.

Moderator. The moderator is a substance that surrounds the fuel rods. Its purpose is to slow the speed of the free neutrons that are released in fission. By slowing the neutrons, the moderator increases the chance that they will be absorbed by the fuel and cause fission.

Most U.S. reactors use ordinary water as a moderator. Canadian reactors use **heavy water**. (Water is a mixture of hydrogen and oxygen. In heavy water, deuterium takes the place of the ordinary hydrogen.) Besides slowing the free neutrons, ordinary water absorbs some of these particles. Heavy water absorbs fewer free neutrons, so that more

Above: Inside a nuclear power plant, fission in the reactor core is used to heat water, changing it to steam. The steam powers a turbine that drives a generator to produce electricity. After the steam leaves the turbine, it is cooled and condensed back into water, so that it can be used again. *Right:* Fuel rods from a nuclear reactor remain dangerously radioactive even after most of their fuel is used up. Spent rods are stored in pools of water that has been treated to absorb radiation.

neutrons are available to cause fission. This is why Canadian reactors are able to use natural uranium as fuel.

A type of reactor that was common in the former Soviet Union and some other countries uses blocks of graphite (a form of carbon) as a moderator. Breeder reactors use fast neutrons and generally have no moderator.

Coolant. The coolant carries away heat produced by fission in the core. In reactors that use ordinary or heavy water as a moderator, the same fluid acts as the coolant.

In a **boiling water reactor**, the heat from the core turns the coolant into steam, which drives the turbines for electric power production. The steam then passes through a condenser, which cools it and turns it back into water. In a **pressurized water reactor**, the water that acts as the moderator and coolant is kept under pressure so that it cannot boil, even at very high temperatures. This water is used to heat a second supply of water and turn it into steam for driving the turbines.

Reactors that rely on graphite as a moderator must use another substance as a coolant. This may be water or a gas, such as carbon dioxide, that is blown through the core. A common type of breeder reactor uses liquid sodium as a coolant.

Control Rods. To produce a steady supply of energy, the chain reaction in a nuclear reactor must be carefully controlled. If too little fission takes place, the reaction will die out. If there is too much fission, the reaction may begin to run out of control.

To regulate the chain reaction, nuclear reactors are equipped with control rods that can be lowered into the core. The control rods are made of a material such as the metal cadmium that absorbs free neutrons. The more control rods are lowered, the slower the reaction becomes. In most designs, the control rods will drop into the core automatically in an emergency, to shut the reactor down.

Containment. The reactor is housed in a **reactor vessel** with heavy steel walls. This vessel is generally placed in a **containment building** with walls, floor, and roof of thick concrete. These structures are designed to prevent the escape of radioactive materials.

▶ **SAFETY AND WASTE DISPOSAL**

The makeup of the fuel assembly in a reactor makes it virtually impossible that the core could explode like a nuclear bomb. However, should a reactor fail in some way and release radioactive material, exposure to radiation could harm people, animals, and crops over a wide area. Radiation could poison food and water supplies and make its effects felt for years.

Thus the enormous energy and the radioactive materials contained in a reactor are sources of concern. The safe handling of nuclear fuel and the wastes produced by nuclear reactors are also important issues.

Reactor Safety. Nuclear reactors are designed with many safety features. For example, most reactors have emergency cooling systems that automatically flood the core with cold water if it begins to overheat. Reactor operators are highly trained, and constant watchfulness is part of the operation of all plants. Reactor construction and operation are closely regulated by governments. (In the

Nuclear wastes raise important safety concerns. Low-level wastes, including clothing and equipment exposed to radiation, are buried at special disposal sites.

United States, the agency that oversees reactors is the Nuclear Regulatory Commission.)

Despite these measures, serious accidents have occurred at nuclear reactors. The most feared type of accident involves loss of a reactor's coolant. When this happens, the core can heat to enormous temperatures, and the fuel rods can melt. In a full **core meltdown**, the molten fuel could burn through the floor of the containment structure and enter the ground, where it could pollute water supplies.

So far, this has not happened. In a serious accident in 1979 at the Three Mile Island nuclear plant, near Harrisburg, Pennsylvania, about half the fuel melted. But the accident was brought under control before the fuel broke through the reactor vessel, and little radioactivity was released. The reactor was permanently shut down.

A Soviet worker hoses radioactive dust off buildings near Chernobyl. In 1986, a power plant there had one of the worst nuclear accidents on record.

An even more serious accident took place in the Soviet Union in 1986, at the Chernobyl power plant near Kiev. The reactor's graphite moderator overheated, causing a series of explosions and fires. The roof was blown off the building, and radioactive material was released into the air. Over 30 people were killed immediately, and hundreds of nearby residents developed severe radiation-related illnesses.

In 1999, Japan experienced its worst nuclear accident at a fuel processing plant in the town of Tokaimura. Workers mixed too much uranium at once, setting off an uncontrolled chain reaction. Although it was brought under control, dozens of people were exposed to radiation.

Accidents such as these have produced worldwide concern. Designers have proposed several ways to improve safety. One proposal is to build smaller reactors and to submerge them in pools of borated water (water containing boron, which can absorb radiation). If the reactor vessel were to crack, this water would enter the reactor and stop the chain reaction.

Human error has been the main cause of nuclear accidents. Much of the daily operation of nuclear plants is handled by computers. The accidents at Three Mile Island, Chernobyl and Tokaimura showed that it is important to have well-educated operators and well-designed computer systems to help operators make the right decisions in an emergency.

Fuel and Waste Handling. Nuclear fuel travels through many steps from the mine to the reactor and to its eventual disposal. Together, these steps make up the **nuclear fuel cycle**. Because the fuel is radioactive, each step raises risks of radiation exposure.

In recent years, regulations have improved safety. For example, large quantities of mill tailings (material left over from milling operations, in which uranium is separated from its ore) were once allowed to lie in heaps. Dust from the heaps blew away, exposing people for miles around to radiation. Regulations now require these heaps to be covered.

The disposal of spent fuel from nuclear reactors poses a more difficult problem. After fuel rods have been in place about three years, most of the uranium 235 is used up. But the rods contain highly radioactive materials, including some unused uranium 235 and plutonium. The fuel rods can be processed to recover this material, and this is done in France. In the United States, commercial reactors were barred from reprocessing fuel in the 1970's, for security and safety reasons. Instead, spent fuel is stored in water pools at the reactors. By the end of 1987, almost 16,000 tons of spent fuel had been stored in this way.

The materials in spent fuel are **high-level nuclear wastes**. These wastes will remain radioactive for thousands of years. Thus people need to find safe ways of storing them. In a plan developed by the U.S. Department of Energy, spent fuel and other high-level nuclear wastes would be stored in deep underground rock formations. Some of the wastes would first be melted together with other materials to form a glasslike substance (a process called **vitrification**).

Besides high-level wastes, reactors produce **low-level wastes**—building materials, equipment, and clothing that may have absorbed radiation. This material is not as harmful as high-level waste, but there is a lot of it. It is stored at special disposal sites.

▶HISTORY

Scientists began searching for a way to set off a nuclear chain reaction in the 1930's. Several researchers succeeded in splitting atomic nuclei at this time. But it was two Austrian scientists, Lise Meitner and Otto Frisch, who in 1939 first explained the release of energy obtained in nuclear fission.

During World War II, the United States government supported work in nuclear fission by a number of scientists. The goal of this program, called the Manhattan Project, was to produce an atomic bomb before Nazi Germany could do so. As part of this work, the Italian-born scientist Enrico Fermi headed a team of researchers at the University of Chicago. They created the first artificially produced nuclear chain reaction in 1942.

The first use of nuclear energy was in weapons. Scientists were quick to realize nuclear energy's potential for other uses, however. The first nuclear-powered submarine, the USS *Nautilus*, was launched in 1954. The world's first nuclear power plant began operation in England two years later. A commercial nuclear power plant was built in the United States near Pittsburgh, Pennsylvania, in 1957. That same year, the International Atomic Energy Agency was set up by the United Nations to promote the peaceful use of nuclear energy. This agency, with headquarters in Vienna, Austria, also attempts to prevent the use of nuclear materials for war.

During the 1960's and 1970's, utility companies turned increasingly to nuclear power. By the end of the 1980's, more than 100 nuclear plants were providing just under 20 percent of the electricity used in the United States. The percentage of electricity provided by nuclear energy was much higher in some countries—more than 70 percent in France, 66 percent in Belgium, and almost 50 percent in Sweden, for example.

In the United States, only a few nuclear plants were built after 1975, however. Interest in nuclear power declined for three reasons. First, demand for electricity did not grow as much as had been expected. Second, the cost of building and running a safe nuclear power plant proved to be very high. Third, public support for nuclear power fell off as concern over the safety and cost of nuclear power plants grew.

Concern over these issues has grown in other countries, too. For example, Sweden halted construction of new nuclear power plants after the Three Mile Island accident in 1979. Because it does not pollute the air or use up the world's limited supplies of fossil fuels, nuclear energy continues to have great promise. But its future will depend on how the problems of safety, waste disposal, and cost are solved.

Meanwhile, scientists continue to experiment with nuclear fusion. Fusion fuels are more plentiful than fission fuels—deuterium, for example, can be extracted from seawater. Thus fusion might one day provide an almost limitless source of energy. And scientists think that the waste problems associated with fusion would be less severe than those that result from fission.

BALA R. NAIR
Westinghouse Electric Corporation
INDIRA NAIR
Carnegie Mellon University

See also ATOMS; ELEMENTS, CHEMICAL; ENERGY; FISSION; MATTER; NUCLEAR WEAPONS; POWER PLANTS; RADIOACTIVE ELEMENTS; URANIUM.

NUCLEAR FISSION. See FISSION.

A mushroom cloud rises in the air in a test of a nuclear bomb. With their vast potential for destruction, nuclear weapons have deeply affected the modern world.

NUCLEAR WEAPONS

Nuclear weapons are the most powerful weapons in the world. The explosion of a nuclear bomb produces destruction on a scale far vaster than the explosion of a conventional bomb. And nuclear weapons can produce harmful effects that last far longer, and cover a far larger area, than the immediate effects of the explosion itself.

Nuclear weapons have been used in combat only twice, by the United States against Japan at the end of World War II. Along with the United States, Russia, Ukraine, China, France, Britain, India, and Pakistan acknowledge having nuclear weapons. Together these countries have enough weaponry to threaten all of civilization.

The world has never experienced a nuclear war, in which countries attack each other with nuclear weapons. Based on what they know about these weapons, however, scientists think that the results of such a war would be devastating. Thus nuclear weapons have had a deep and troubling effect on the world.

▶ **HOW NUCLEAR WEAPONS WORK**

The power of nuclear weapons comes from nuclear energy—energy released from the nucleus, or center, of an atom. The energy may be released in two ways: through the splitting of the nucleus, or **nuclear fission**, and through the joining of two nuclei, or **nuclear fusion**. (You will find descriptions of these processes in the articles NUCLEAR ENERGY and FISSION.)

Fission Weapons. Fission weapons (also called atomic weapons) make use of nuclear fission to produce an explosion. In these weapons, many nuclei undergo fission so rapidly that, in effect, they split at the same time and release an enormous amount of energy. This is accomplished through a **chain reaction**.

A chain reaction begins with the fission of a few nuclei. Each nucleus is made up of particles called protons and neutrons. When the nucleus splits, most of these particles go to form lighter nuclei. Several neutrons are also released, along with a great deal of energy. The free neutrons strike other nuclei nearby, causing them to split and release neutrons. These neutrons in turn produce still more fission, and the chain reaction quickly builds.

Only a few materials will support a chain reaction. Fission weapons contain materials such as uranium 235 and plutonium 239. These are **fissionable** forms of uranium and plutonium—that is, forms that readily undergo fission. The materials used in weapons are produced in special factories.

A chain reaction also requires a certain amount of fissionable material. (Scientists use the term **critical mass** to describe the amount that is needed.) A fission bomb contains separate pieces of fissionable material, each too small to support a chain reaction. The bomb also contains a conventional explosive. When this explosive is set off, it pushes the pieces of fissionable material together with great force, starting the chain reaction.

Some of the materials used in weapons, especially uranium 235, are also used to produce fission in nuclear reactors. But the material in

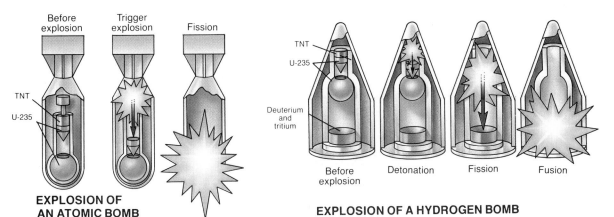

**EXPLOSION OF
AN ATOMIC BOMB**

An atomic bomb is triggered by an explosive such as TNT. This pushes pieces of fissionable material such as uranium 235 together, starting a chain reaction.

EXPLOSION OF A HYDROGEN BOMB

A hydrogen bomb is triggered by the explosion of a fission device. This causes nuclei of deuterium and tritium (forms of hydrogen) to fuse, releasing energy.

a reactor is far less concentrated than the material in a bomb. It is also arranged so that the reaction takes place in a slow, controlled way. In a bomb, the entire chain reaction takes place in less than a millionth of a second. Huge amounts of energy are released in an enormous explosion.

Fusion Weapons. Fusion bombs are often called hydrogen bombs because they depend on the fusion of many hydrogen nuclei. Fusion releases even more energy than fission (for the same weight of nuclear material). It is also more difficult to achieve. For fusion to take place, the hydrogen nuclei must be confined and heated to temperatures of millions of degrees. Because of the heat, fusion weapons are also known as **thermonuclear** weapons.

The conventional explosives that are used to trigger atomic bombs are not powerful enough to set off thermonuclear explosions. Instead, thermonuclear weapons use fission explosions to trigger the fusion.

A thermonuclear weapon depends on materials such as deuterium and tritium, which are forms of hydrogen that will undergo fusion more readily than ordinary hydrogen. The weapon also contains a fission bomb. The fission bomb is set off first, and its explosion produces extremely high temperatures and pressures. These forces make the deuterium and tritium nuclei fuse almost all at once, producing a massive explosion.

▶**KINDS OF NUCLEAR WEAPONS**

People often speak of nuclear weapons in terms of **kilotons** (thousands of tons) and **megatons** (millions of tons). These terms refer not to the weight of the weapons but to their

strength (or **yield**) as compared to the strength of a well-known conventional explosive, TNT (trinitrotoluene). A one-kiloton weapon produces an explosion equal to the explosion of 1,000 tons of TNT. The explosion of a one-megaton bomb releases the same amount of energy as a million tons of TNT.

The first nuclear weapons were atomic bombs with forces of about 20 kilotons or less. Today a single missile can carry a thermonuclear warhead with a yield of 25 megatons. And weapons with more than twice that yield have been built. Powerful weapons such as these are **strategic** nuclear weapons. They are designed to destroy cities, industrial centers, and large military installations. Strategic weapons are made to be dropped from planes or delivered by missiles, some of which can travel halfway around the world.

Tactical nuclear weapons have much shorter ranges and much lower yields. They are mostly battlefield weapons, such as anti-aircraft missiles and artillery shells that are designed for use against enemy troops and tanks. The yield of a battlefield nuclear weapon may be as little as a tenth of a kiloton or as much as several kilotons.

Most nuclear weapons are designed to explode in the air just over a target. (The explosion point is sometimes called **point zero**, and the target area beneath it is called **ground zero**.) Space-based nuclear weapons have been proposed, although such weapons have not been built. In one type, a nuclear explosion would be used to trigger an X-ray laser— a powerful, focused beam of X rays. This beam could be used to destroy enemy satellites and missiles over a wide area.

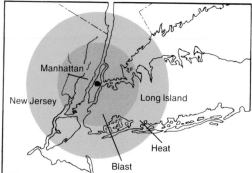

Nuclear weapons have devastating effects. *Left:* A single atomic bomb, dropped by the United States in 1945, destroyed most of the Japanese city of Hiroshima.

Below: If a 20-megaton nuclear bomb exploded over mid-town New York City, the blast could severely damage buildings as much as 10 miles (16 kilometers) away. Heat could cause serious burns and ignite fires up to 20 miles (32 kilometers) away.

Manhattan

New Jersey

Long Island

Heat

Blast

▶ EFFECTS OF NUCLEAR WEAPONS

The effects of a nuclear explosion are so awesome that they are difficult to imagine. In 1945, a single atomic bomb destroyed most of the city of Hiroshima, Japan, and killed or injured more than half the people. A second bomb caused similar destruction in the Japanese city of Nagasaki. Most of what people know about the effects of nuclear weapons was learned in these explosions and in tests conducted in isolated areas where no people live.

The effects of a nuclear explosion vary with the yield of the weapon. Scientists are still unsure of all the effects, but they know that a powerful nuclear explosion causes destruction in several main ways.

Blast. The enormous release of energy in a nuclear explosion heats the air very quickly. The hot air expands rapidly, creating a shock wave (or blast) that travels out from the site of the explosion. This blast accounts for half the energy released by the explosion. It can flatten buildings near the explosion site and cause damage for miles around. The force of the explosion can also produce a large crater in the ground.

Heat. A nuclear explosion creates a fireball with temperatures of millions of degrees. The temperatures are high enough to instantly destroy almost anything near the site of the explosion. Heat accounts for about a third of the energy released in the explosion. The heat from the fireball can set off raging fires over a wide area. Meanwhile, dust and dirt are sucked into the fireball. Because hot air rises, the dust and dirt rise with the fireball, creating a huge, mushroom-shaped cloud.

Radiation. Along with the blast and heat, large amounts of harmful radiation are released in a nuclear explosion. About half of this radiation is called **prompt radiation** and is mostly in the form of neutrons and gamma rays (high-energy rays that, like X rays, are very penetrating). The radiation can kill people and animals near the site of the explosion. Even several miles away, people can become sick from exposure to radiation. And radiation can produce diseases such as cancer that take years to develop.

The **delayed radiation** effects of a nuclear explosion can be widespread and long-lasting. The explosion produces vast quantities of tiny particles that are **radioactive**—that is, they continue to give off radiation. These particles coat everything within range of the explosion. They also coat the dust and dirt that are drawn into the mushroom-shaped cloud. In this way the particles enter the atmosphere, where they may be carried for many miles.

Eventually the particles fall back to earth as radioactive **fallout**. The fallout from a nuclear explosion could harm people hundreds of miles away from the explosion site. It could contaminate soil, water, and food supplies over large areas. And the particles would remain radioactive for a very long time, even centuries.

The radiation produced by a nuclear weapon can vary with the design of the weapon. For example, some thermonuclear weapons are considered "cleaner" than others because they produce less radioactive fallout. A type of weapon called a **neutron bomb** (or enhanced radiation weapon) releases less of its energy as blast and more in the form of neutron radiation. Thus a neutron bomb does less damage to buildings and to tanks and other military equipment. But its effects on people and other living things are deadly.

Effects in Space.   The height at which a nuclear explosion takes place is a factor in its effects. For example, a bomb that exploded high above the ground would draw up less dirt and dust and thus would produce less fallout. If a nuclear weapon were exploded in space, there would be no air or other material to produce shock waves, fires, or radioactive dust. The main effect of the explosion would be an enormous burst of radiation (mostly X rays and gamma rays). The radiation could destroy satellites many miles away.

The explosion would also produce an **electromagnetic pulse**—a powerful burst of electric current that is one of the most curious nuclear effects. The pulse is produced as gamma rays enter the atmosphere and interact with it. If a nuclear weapon were exploded just above the atmosphere (or very high in the atmosphere), an electromagnetic pulse would travel to the ground.

The pulse could destroy or damage electric and electronic equipment—computers, television and radio equipment, communications networks, electrical circuits in homes and offices—for hundreds of miles around. Thus it would be possible for one country to use a nuclear weapon to disrupt communications and many other important aspects of life in another country.

Effects of Nuclear War.   So far we have described the effects of a single nuclear explosion. The combined effect of many such explosions—as might be seen in a nuclear war —is unknown. But people can estimate how terrible a nuclear war would be.

For example, scientists have estimated what the results would be if several key U.S. military targets were attacked with nuclear weapons at about the same time. If the combined

yield of the explosions were 400 megatons, the scientists think that half the country's population might be killed, mostly from the long-term effects of radiation.

A full-scale nuclear war would generate fires on an enormous scale and would reduce large areas to ashes. Huge quantities of smoke and dust would be sent up into the atmosphere. Some scientists think that this would lead to a severe change in the world's climate. The clouds of dust and smoke would circulate in the atmosphere for years, blocking sunlight. Without the warmth of the sun, much of the world would grow cooler. A **nuclear winter** lasting several years might affect as much as half the world.

Scientists agree that the massive use of nuclear weapons would produce vast amounts of radioactive material, which would also circulate in the atmosphere. Fallout might spread throughout the world and continue to rain down to earth for years.

▶**HISTORY**

The first nuclear weapons were built by scientists working in the United States during World War II. The U.S. Government supported their work under a secret program called the Manhattan Project. President Franklin D. Roosevelt gave the order to begin work on the first atomic bomb, and physicist J. Robert Oppenheimer directed the project. At the time the project was launched, the United States feared that scientists in Nazi Germany were developing a similar weapon. Their goal was to produce the weapon first, and they succeeded in doing so.

The first explosion of an atomic bomb was a test conducted on July 16, 1945, in the desert of New Mexico. Germany had surrendered two months before, but the United States was still at war with Japan. Less than a month after the test explosion, on August 6 and August 9, United States planes dropped atomic bombs on the Japanese cities of Hiroshima and Nagasaki. On August 10, Japan announced that it was ready to surrender. (The formal surrender took place on September 2.)

Because the Hiroshima and Nagasaki bombs hastened Japan's surrender, nuclear weapons have been credited with shortening the war. The decision to use the bombs has been questioned, and it is still debated. But in any case, the explosion of the first atomic bombs marked the start of what has become known as the nuclear age.

For a few years after World War II, the United States was the only country to have nuclear weapons. Then, in 1949, the Soviet Union exploded its first atomic bomb. The two countries were soon involved in an arms race, with each trying to build more (and more powerful) nuclear weapons than the other. The United States exploded the first hydrogen bomb in 1952. The Soviet Union tested its own hydrogen bomb about nine months later.

Soon other countries obtained nuclear weapons. But the number of these countries has remained small, chiefly because the knowledge and materials needed to produce nuclear weapons are difficult to obtain. Britain has had U.S.-made nuclear weapons since the early 1950's. France and China developed their own nuclear weapons in the 1960's. In the 1970's, India exploded what it called a "peaceful nuclear device." After India conducted more nuclear tests in the late 1990's, neighboring Pakistan exploded its own nuclear devices in several tests. South Africa had also developed nuclear weapons, but it dismantled them by the early 1990's. Belarus and Kazakhstan had nuclear weapons but gave them to Russia in the early 1990's after the breakup of the Soviet Union. Other countries suspected of developing the ability to produce nuclear weapons include Israel, Iran, Iraq, and North Korea.

The nuclear weapons that these countries have are only a fraction of those held by the United States, Russia, and Ukraine. As of the late 1990's, they had over 15,000 strategic warheads—fewer than the 50,000 U.S. and Soviet warheads in the late 1980's, but still enough to destroy each country several times.

▶ NUCLEAR ARMS AND POLICY

With each confrontation between countries that have nuclear weapons has come concern over the possibility of a nuclear war. If such a war should break out, the effects would reach around the world. Thus the question of how to reduce or eliminate the nuclear threat remains one of today's most important questions.

Nuclear Strategy. Some people believe that because of the terrible force of nuclear weapons, there will never be a full-scale nuclear war. This view is based on a theory called *m*utual *a*ssured *d*estruction (MAD). According to the MAD theory, no country will use nuclear weapons if there is a strong chance that the other side will counter with a similar attack —because the only outcome would be complete destruction for both sides.

In this view, nuclear weapons serve as a **deterrent**, or method of preventing attack. Simply by having nuclear weapons, a country can prevent another country from staging a nuclear attack against it. Both the United States and the former Soviet Union relied on this theory. Each country continually sought to improve its nuclear force, so that the other side would not be able to overpower it.

The large-scale use of nuclear weapons would have disadvantages besides the threat of counterattack. For example, if a country were to succeed in conquering another country with a large nuclear attack, fallout and other long-lasting effects could make the conquered land of little use to the winners.

However, a **limited nuclear war**—one in which few nuclear strikes were made or only battlefield weapons were used—would not produce such widespread destruction. Some experts believe that if nuclear weapons are used in combat, it will be in a limited war. But there is debate over whether a limited nuclear war could be controlled. A small nuclear attack might be followed by a larger counterattack. Responses would follow one after another, and the war might soon escalate, or build, into a full-scale nuclear conflict.

Arms Control. To many people, the surest way to eliminate or reduce the threat of nuclear war is to eliminate the weapons, or at least to reduce their numbers. Almost from the time the first atomic bomb was exploded, there has been strong public pressure for the control of nuclear arms. Various groups at various times have called on governments to freeze (or halt) the growth of their nuclear arsenals, to reduce the numbers of nuclear weapons they have, or to ban nuclear weapons outright. Many government leaders have also pressed for limits on nuclear weapons. But progress toward these goals has been slow.

In the 1960's, the United States and the Soviet Union began a long series of negotiations on cutting back the nuclear arms each held. These *Strategic Arms Limitation Talks* (SALT) led to a treaty, signed in 1972, that set limits on the numbers of certain kinds of nuclear weapons. A second SALT treaty was signed in 1979. But the SALT II treaty was contro-

Opponents of nuclear arms march in New York City. Many people would like to see all such weapons eliminated, but there are obstacles to full nuclear disarmament.

versial. The U.S. Senate never approved it, and the U.S. Government terminated it.

In late 1987, the two countries signed the *I*ntermediate-range *N*uclear *F*orces (INF) Treaty, which banned nuclear missiles with ranges of about 300 to 3,400 miles (500 to 5,500 kilometers). Missiles in this range could travel from the Soviet Union to Western Europe but not to the United States.

The INF Treaty was a milestone. It was the first time that the two powers had agreed to reduce the size of their nuclear arsenals and destroy missiles. It also set up strict procedures for **verification** (making sure that both sides carried out the agreement).

In 1991, the United States and the Soviet Union signed the *St*rategic *A*rms *R*eduction *T*reaty (START), cutting long-range nuclear missiles. A second START treaty was signed by Russia and the United States in 1993. In 1996, the United Nations, including all the major powers, approved the Comprehensive Test Ban Treaty, banning all nuclear testing.

In 1972, the United States and the Soviet Union signed a treaty, agreeing not to build *a*nti*b*allistic *m*issile (ABM) systems. An ABM system is designed to intercept and destroy enemy missiles that have been fired but have not yet reached their targets. The reasoning behind the treaty was that a country with an ABM system might believe that it could survive a nuclear attack and thus might be more likely to start a nuclear war. (In 1983 the United States proposed a space-based antimissile system called the Strategic Defense Initiative, but so far only short-range battlefield antimissile systems have been developed.) In 2002 the United States withdrew from the ABM treaty, citing the need for a missile defense system in the wake of the war on terrorism.

Fallout from test explosions became a worldwide concern in the 1950's. In 1963, an international treaty banned the testing of nuclear weapons in the atmosphere, in space, and under water. Since then most tests have been conducted underground. In addition, the United States and the Soviet Union agreed to limit the size of their underground tests to less than 150 kilotons. They were also among some 120 countries that signed a nuclear nonproliferation agreement. These countries pledged to work to prevent the spread, or proliferation, of nuclear weapons.

Despite the progress that has been made toward arms control, the agreements signed so far provide only limited protection against the threat of nuclear war. Such agreements are fragile and can easily be broken. The risk that more countries will obtain nuclear weapons remains. It is even possible that nuclear weapons might fall into the hands of terrorists outside government control.

Many people would like to see all nuclear weapons eliminated. But nuclear weapons cannot be "disinvented"—the materials and knowledge needed to make them are available. And as long as countries feel threatened, they will not easily give up their right to protect themselves by any available means. For example, in 2003 North Korea threatened to test and make use of its nuclear weapons unless the United States offered to sign a nonaggression treaty.

BENOIT F. MOREL
Carnegie Mellon University

See also DISARMAMENT; MISSILES.

Visual patterns such as the one shown on this tumbling block quilt are often based on mathematical formulas that produce precise sequences of colors and shapes.

NUMBER PATTERNS

Numbers and number patterns have fascinated people since ancient times, when it was thought that numbers had magic powers. Since then, the study of number patterns and relationships has been an important part of mathematics.

The ability to recognize and use patterns of all types plays a key role in the learning process in almost every field, and looking for a pattern is a strategy used by all good problem solvers. In music, for example, recognizing chord patterns makes it easier to learn and memorize musical compositions. In team sports, identifying patterns of play helps athletes and coaches plan strategies for competition. In mathematics, patterns are used to study topics ranging from arithmetic to geometry, algebra, and statistics.

The study of patterns is especially important today because we encounter incredible amounts of information every day. As the amount of data increases, so does the difficulty of examining and making sense of it. Often computers are needed to display data as a graph or mathematical "picture" so that patterns can be more easily recognized.

▶ LOOKING FOR PATTERNS

Interesting number patterns can be discovered by carefully examining the **multiples** of certain numbers. (A multiple is the product of a given number and another number.) For example, can you find any patterns formed by the first nine multiples of 9? Examine the multiplications shown below.

$$9 \times 1 = 09$$
$$9 \times 2 = 18$$
$$9 \times 3 = 27$$
$$9 \times 4 = 36$$
$$9 \times 5 = 45$$
$$9 \times 6 = 54$$
$$9 \times 7 = 63$$
$$9 \times 8 = 72$$
$$9 \times 9 = 81$$

Look at the units digits in the list. From top to bottom, they read 9, 8, 7, 6, 5, 4, 3, 2, 1. Reading the tens digits from top to bottom they are the opposite: 0, 1, 2, 3, 4, 5, 6, 7, 8. Will these patterns continue for more multiples of 9? Try the next nine multiples. Except for the repeating 9's in the digits in the tens place in the next two multiples, 90 and 99, you should see consistent patterns. Being familiar with patterns such as these can be of help when you memorize the multiples of 9 or multiply by 9 to solve a problem.

Are there other numbers whose multiples have interesting patterns? You may want to try making similar lists and looking for patterns.

1	2	3	4	5	6	7	8	9	10
11	12	13	14	15	16	17	18	19	20
21	22	23	24	25	26	27	28	29	30
31	32	33	34	35	36	37	38	39	40
41	42	43	44	45	46	47	48	49	50
51	52	53	54	55	56	57	58	59	60
61	62	63	64	65	66	67	68	69	70
71	72	73	74	75	76	77	78	79	80
81	82	83	84	85	86	87	88	89	90
91	92	93	94	95	96	97	98	99	100

Figure 1. Lattice

▶ LATTICES

Many patterns can be explored by placing numbers on a grid, or **lattice**, a regular geometric arrangement of points or objects. One of the simplest lattices shows an arrangement of numbers from 1 to 100 in rows of ten.

Using the lattice in Figure 1, touch each number that is a multiple of 5. Can you visualize the pattern this makes? The multiples of 5 are all located in two columns on the grid, the column beginning with 5 and the column beginning with 10.

Now do the same for the multiples of 11. This time a completely different pattern is made. The multiples of 11 go across the columns on a **diagonal**, or slant. You may wish to find patterns for other multiples in the same way.

Here is a different way to find patterns on a lattice. Make a copy of the chart in Figure 1. Color all the multiples of 2 blue. Then color all the multiples of 3 yellow. When you are finished, note that some of the numbers appear green. Can you explain why? It is because you colored the multiples of 2 blue and the multiples of 3 yellow, and blue and yellow make the color green. The numbers that appear green are multiples of both 2 and 3, and 2 and 3 are **factors**, or divisors, of 6. So, the green numbers are multiples of 6.

▶ PASCAL'S TRIANGLE

One of the most famous lattices in mathematics is a triangle named after the French mathematician and physicist Blaise Pascal, who lived during the 1600's.

There are dozens of patterns to be found in this triangle. Before reading about some of these patterns, see if you can discover the way the triangle is constructed. Start at the top of the triangle in Figure 2, and travel down the rows, searching for a pattern.

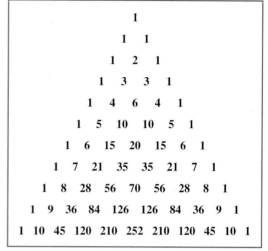

Figure 2. Pascal's Triangle

Constructing Pascal's Triangle

In order to study the patterns, we will number the rows and examine a smaller part of the triangle. In Figure 3, we have numbered the rows of Pascal's triangle starting with 0 so that the second number in each row after Row 0 is the same as the row number.

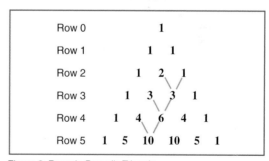

Figure 3. Rows in Pascal's Triangle

Notice that each row begins and ends with the number 1. Other numbers are found by adding the two closest numbers in the row above. For example, in Row 3 the third number is found by adding the numbers above it, 2 + 1. The third number in Row 4 is found by adding 3 + 3, and the third number in Row 5 is found by adding 4 + 6.

The diagonals of Pascal's triangle contain many patterns. The outside diagonals are all

1's. The second diagonal is made up of the counting numbers: 1, 2, 3, ... (The three dots . . . are called an ellipsis and indicate that the numbers continue in the same pattern without end.) The third diagonal contains numbers known as the triangular numbers: 1, 2, 6, 10, ... Triangular numbers are discussed below in the section Numbers as Shapes.

Row Sums in Pascal's Triangle

Now examine the sums of the numbers in each row of Pascal's triangle in Figure 4. No-

Row Number							Row Sum
Row 0				1			Sum = 1
Row 1			1		1		Sum = 2
Row 2			1	2	1		Sum = 4
Row 3		1	3	3	1		Sum = 8
Row 4	1	4	6	4	1		Sum = 16
Row 5	1	5	10	10	5	1	Sum = 32

Figure 4. Sums of Rows in Pascal's Triangle

tice that each sum is a **power** of 2. (A power of a number indicates how many times the number is to be multiplied by itself. For example, 2^3 is read 2 to the third power. It means $2 \times 2 \times 2$, or 8.)

Look at Row 3. The sum of the numbers in Row 3 is 8, or 2^3. As you can see, the row number and the power of 2 that represents the sum of the numbers in that row are the same.

Tossing Coins

The numbers and patterns we have been examining in Pascal's triangle are useful in many areas of mathematics. Mathematicians use this triangle to solve problems about **probability**, that is, how likely it is that a given event may occur or not occur.

Here is how Pascal's triangle can be used to predict how many ways one or more tossed coins may fall. First of all, the sum of the numbers in each row of the triangle tells us the total number of ways that one, two, three, or more coins can fall. For example, as you can see in Figure 5, the sum of the numbers in Row 1 (1 + 1 = 2) tells us that one coin can fall in two ways—either heads or tails. The sum of the numbers in Row 2 (1 + 2 + 1 = 4)

indicates that two coins can fall four ways, and so forth.

In addition, the individual numbers in the rows of the triangle show the different combinations of heads and tails that are possible for different numbers of coins. In Figure 5, the numbers in the outcome column correspond to the numbers in Rows 1, 2, 3, and 4 of Pascal's triangle. Look at the numbers in the outcome column for Row 2. The first number, 1, indicates that when two coins are tossed, there is only one way for the coins to fall with two heads up:

The second number, 2, indicates that there are two ways for the coins to fall with one head up and one tail up:

Number of the Row in Pascal's Triangle	Number of Coins Tossed	Number of Ways for Each Outcome (H = heads, T = tails)	Total Number of Ways for Each Outcome
1	1	1 1 1 H 0 H 0 T 1 T	2
2	2	1 2 1 2 H 1 H 0 H 0 T 1 T 2 T	4
3	3	1 3 3 1 3 H 2 H 1 H 0 H 0 T 1 T 2 T 3 T	8
4	4	1 4 6 4 1 4 H 3 H 2 H 1 H 0 H 0 T 1 T 2 T 3 T 4 T	16

Figure 5. Using Pascal's Triangle to Predict Coin Toss Patterns

The third number, 1, indicates that there is one way for the coins to fall with two tails up:

The numbers in the rows of Pascal's triangle can also be used to find the mathematical probability that you will get two, one, or no heads when you toss two coins. This is how it is done. The total of the numbers in Row 2 in Figure 5 is 4 (1 + 2 + 1 = 4). So the probability that the coins will fall with two heads and no tails is one chance in four, which can also be expressed as $\frac{1}{4}$. The probability that the coins will fall with one head and one tail is two chances in four, which can also be expressed as $\frac{2}{4}$ or $\frac{1}{2}$. The probability that the coins will fall with no heads and two tails is one chance in four, or $\frac{1}{4}$.

Using Figure 5, can you figure out what the probability is that three coins will fall with two heads and one tail? The answer is three chances in eight, or $\frac{3}{8}$.

▶ **NUMBER SEQUENCES**

Number sequences, or ordered lists of numbers, provide another source for studying patterns. Many number sequences exist in the world of the mathematician and the scientist —and in your everyday world, too. A mathematician in New Jersey who collects number sequences has compiled a list of about 5,000 different sequences.

Arithmetic Sequences

There are different types of number sequences. The sequence 2, 6, 10, 14, 18, . . . is an example of one type of number sequence. What is the difference between the first two numbers in the sequence? What is the difference between the next two numbers? In both cases, the difference is 4. This sequence forms an **arithmetic sequence** because there is a common difference, 4, between any term, or member, in the sequence and the next term. Different arithmetic sequences will have different numbers as the common difference, or different starting numbers.

Arithmetic sequences pop up frequently in everyday activities. For example, if you save $4 from a part-time job every week, how much money will you have in your savings at the end of the second week? The third week? The fourth week? Your savings will accumulate in an arithmetic sequence or progression: $4, $8, $12, $16 . . . .

Geometric Sequences

Here is an example of another type of number sequence: 1, 3, 9, 27, 81 . . . . What is the relationship between 1 and 3? Between 3 and 9? Between 9 and 27? You can say that 3 is three times greater than 1, 9 is three times greater than 3, and 27 is three times greater than 9. The sequence in this case is a **geometric sequence** because there is a common ratio, 3, between each successive pair of numbers.

If you save $4 one week and then double the amount each week, how much money will you have in your savings at the end of the second week? The third week? The fourth week? Your savings will accumulate in a geometric sequence or progression: $4, $8, $16, $32 . . . . As you can see, numbers grow faster in a geometric sequence than they do in an arithmetic sequence.

Fibonacci Sequence

Fibonacci was the nickname of Leonardo of Pisa, an Italian mathematician who lived in the early 1200's. Fibonacci is best known for the sequence of numbers that bears his name. He discovered the sequence as he was working out a problem about the breeding of rabbits. It is a special sequence that is neither arithmetic nor geometric.

The Fibonacci sequence of numbers begins 1, 1, 2, 3, 5, 8, 13, ... Can you figure out what the next three numbers will be? Each new number is found by adding the two preceding numbers. So the next three numbers will be 21, 34, and 55.

Surprisingly, the Fibonacci numbers are found in art and nature. Artists use ratios of Fibonacci numbers to create pleasing rectangles in painting and architecture and to represent proportions of the human body. In nature, consecutive spirals of a pinecone, a pineapple, and the seeds of a sunflower head occur in the same sequence as Fibonacci numbers. The numbers of leaves or branches on many plants also occur in consecutive Fibonacci numbers.

FINDING PATTERNS IN FIBONACCI NUMBERS

Many interesting relationships among the Fibonacci numbers can be discovered by exploring their patterns. Here are a few for you to try.

1. Write the first ten Fibonacci numbers in a row:

    1, 1, 2, 3, 5, 8, 13, 21, 34, 55

    Add the first three numbers. Write the sum. Compare the sum to the fifth number in the row.

    Next, add the first four numbers and write the sum. Compare the sum to the sixth number in the row. What is the pattern?

    Can you find the sum of the first five numbers without adding them?

2. Consider this group of three consecutive Fibonacci numbers: 1, 2, 3. **Square** the middle number (multiply the number by itself). Then multiply the two outer numbers. What do you notice?

    Try this with a different set of three consecutive Fibonacci numbers: 2, 3, 5. What do you notice?

    Is the pattern always the same?

    Try a few more examples on your own. How would you state the pattern?

3. This time, consider a group of four consecutive Fibonacci numbers: 1, 2, 3, 5. Multiply the two middle numbers. Then multiply the two outer numbers. Compare the two products. What do you notice?

Do the same with the numbers: 5, 8, 13, 21. What do you notice?

Try a few more examples. What is the pattern?

4. You may want to experiment in a similar way with five or six or more consecutive Fibonacci numbers to discover other patterns.

(The answers are on the last page of the article.)

▶NUMBERS AND THEIR FACTORS

There are many relationships to be found among the counting numbers. Some relate to the factors of the numbers. The factors, or divisors, of a counting number divide the number evenly. For example, the factors of 6 are 1, 2, 3, and 6, because these numbers divide 6 evenly. The factors of 4 are 1, 2, and 4.

Numbers with exactly two factors are called **prime numbers**. For example, 2 is a prime number because its only factors are 1 and 2. Numbers with more than two factors are known as **composite numbers**. A 4 is a composite number because it has three factors, 1, 2, and 4. The number 1 does not fit into either category, because it has only one factor, 1.

Prime Numbers

The prime numbers are important to many branches of mathematics, and they have been studied by many prominent mathematicians. Going back to the time of the ancient Greeks, mathematicians have been asking: "How many primes are there?" This is a hard question. It has been proven that there are an **infinite**, or endless, number of primes, so there is no method that we can use to find them all.

A much easier question to answer is: "How many even primes are there?" The only even prime is 2. The number 2 is a prime because it has exactly two factors, 1 and 2. Every even number greater than 2 has more than two factors, because such a number is a multiple of 2 (which is one factor) and some other counting number greater than 1 (and that number must have at least two factors).

The Sieve of Eratosthenes

More than 2,000 years ago, a Greek mathematician named Eratosthenes discovered an interesting way to find all the prime numbers between 1 and 100.

Using a chart like the lattice in Figure 1, Eratosthenes circled the smallest prime number, 2, and then crossed out all the numbers on the chart that were multiples of 2. Then he circled the second prime, 3, and crossed out all the multiples of 3. He continued in this manner, next circling 5 and crossing out its multiples, until he came to the end of the chart. The circled numbers on the chart were prime numbers. Numbers that are not primes were sifted out. This method of finding primes is called the **sieve of Eratosthenes**.

Modern mathematicians used a slightly different version of Eratosthenes' chart to find prime numbers, and in the process they proved

1	2	3	4	5	6
2	3	4	5	6	7
8	9	10	11	12	13
14	15	16	17	18	19
20	21	22	23	24	25
26	27	28	29	30	31
32	33	34	35	36	37
38	39	40	41	42	43
44	45	46	47	48	49
50	51	52	53	54	55
56	57	58	59	60	61
62	63	64	65	66	67
68	69	70	71	72	73
74	75	76	77	78	79
80	81	82	83	84	85
86	87	88	89	90	91
92	93	94	95	96	97
98	99	100			

Figure 6. A Version of the Sieve of Eratosthenes

something interesting. You may want to try what they did. Copy the chart in Figure 6. Use the method described in this article to find the primes. When you have finished, there should be 25 primes circled. Did you find them all? Do you notice any patterns?

All of the numbers in Columns 1, 3, and 5 are multiples of 2. And all of the numbers in Columns 2 and 5 are multiples of 3. Since the numbers in Column 5 are divisible by both 2 and 3, and 2 and 3 are factors of 6, the numbers in Column 5 are also divisible by 6.

The results of this exploration helped mathematicians understand that all prime numbers between 1 and 100 that are greater than 3 are located immediately before or after a number in Column 5. So, they must be either one more or one less than some multiple of 6. This discovery helped mathematicians locate new prime numbers above 100.

Goldbach's Conjecture

Many **conjectures**, or statements that have not been proven yet, have been made concerning prime numbers. In the 1700's, the German mathematician Christian Goldbach made the conjecture that every even number greater than

2 could be expressed as the sum of two prime numbers. For example, $4 = 2 + 2$, $6 = 3 + 3$, and $8 = 3 + 5$. Goldbach's conjecture has been tested on numbers in the millions, but no one has been able to prove that the conjecture is always true. On the other hand, no one has been able to find an even number that could not be written as the sum of two primes.

Looking for Large Primes

The sieve of Eratosthenes can be extended beyond 100 to find larger primes, but the task gets harder and harder. The development of computers has helped mathematicians discover large prime numbers. Computers have been especially useful in the discovery of **Mersenne primes**, which are named for Father Marin Mersenne, who studied them during the 1600's. Mersenne primes are of the form $2^p - 1$, where p is a prime number. For example, if $p = 3$, then $2^3 - 1$, or 7, is a prime number.

The Greek mathematician Euclid knew of four primes of the Mersenne type: $2^2 - 1$, or 3; $2^3 - 1$, or 7; $2^5 - 1$, or 31; and $2^7 - 1$, or 127. Between 1461 and 1876, six more such primes were found, the greatest of which was $2^{127} - 1$, which has 39 digits. In 1994 the 33rd Mersenne prime was discovered. This prime, $2^{859,433} - 1$, has 258,716 digits and would require eight newspaper pages of print for a listing of its digits.

Perfect Numbers

The ancient Greeks, especially Pythagoras and his followers, spent many hours studying the patterns formed by the sum of the **proper factors** of prime and composite numbers. A factor is considered a proper factor if it is less than the number itself. For example, the proper factors of 4 are 1 and 2; their sum is 3.

If the sum of the proper factors of a number is equal to the number itself, the number is called a **perfect number**. The number 6 is the smallest perfect number, because the sum of its proper factors is 6 ($1 + 2 + 3 = 6$). Before reading the next paragraph, try to find the next perfect number. It might help you to know that it is less than 30.

Pythagoras knew of four perfect numbers: 6, 28 (there is your answer), 496, and 8,128. The fifth perfect number is 33,550,336 and was not found until 1,400 years later.

By 1965 only 20 perfect numbers had been found. Then in the years 1969 and 1970, with the help of a computer, a 17-year-old, Roy N. Ferguson, found the next three perfect numbers. In 1979 the 27th perfect number was discovered. It has 13,395 digits.

▶ NUMBERS AS SHAPES

Many numbers have fascinating dot patterns. The Pythagoreans studied patterns made by numbers by arranging dots or pebbles in the sand. For example, four dots can be arranged in the shape of a square, and three dots can be arranged to make a triangle. Numbers that can be represented in this way, that is, in the shape of **polygons** (closed figures with straight sides), are called **polygonal numbers** or **figurate numbers**.

Square Numbers

Numbers, such as 4, that can be represented by dots arranged in a square are called **square numbers**. The dot figures made by the first four square numbers—1, 4, 9, and 16—are shown in Figure 7.

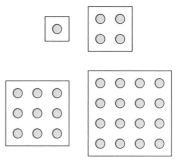

Figure 7. Four Square Number Figures

Note that there is one dot for the first square number, 1, and four dots for the second square number, 4, and so forth.

Now consider the relationship between the number of rows and the number of columns for each square number. Can you see a pattern for drawing the square numbers? To be square, the dot figure must have the same number of rows as it has columns.

Figure 8. Figure for Fifth Square Number

How would you draw the fifth square number? You would arrange the dots in five rows and five columns, as in Figure 8. What is the fifth square number? Instead of counting all the dots, you can simply multiply the number of rows, 5, by the number of columns, 5, to get 5 × 5 = 25. You have squared 5.

We can also look at the square numbers in a geometric way. Look at Figure 9. The first

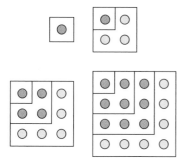

Figure 9. Square Numbers from Odd Number Sums

square number is a square with one dot. The second square number is found by adding an L-shaped figure called a **gnomon** to the first square number. This gnomon contains three dots, so the second square number, 4, is the sum of 1 and 3, which are the first two odd numbers. Adding a gnomon with five dots makes the third square number. The third square number, 9, is the sum of 1 + 3 + 5, which are the first three odd numbers. Look at

the figure for the fourth square number. What numbers produce the sum that is the fourth square number? The first four odd numbers, 1 + 3 + 5 + 7, produce the sum of 16, which is the fourth square number. Can you see the pattern? The sums of consecutive odd numbers produce the square numbers.

Triangular Numbers

Numbers, such as 3, that can be represented by dots arranged in a triangle are called **triangular numbers**. Figure 10 shows the figures made by the first four triangular numbers: 1, 3, 6, and 10. Notice that 1, the first number in the sequence, is considered both a triangular number and a square number. What kind of pattern is found in the figures below? Notice how each figure is formed. The figure for the second triangular number, 3, has one dot in the first row and two dots in the second row.

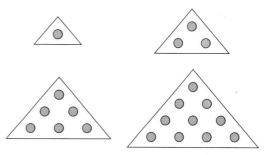

Figure 10. Figures for Triangular Numbers

Did you know that . . .

it is possible to add all the counting numbers from 1 through 100 in a minute or two—without using a calculator?

When Carl Friedrich Gauss, one of the greatest mathematicians of all time, was in grade school in Germany in the late 1700's, he and his classmates were asked to find the sum of the first 100 counting numbers. While his classmates began the tedious process of adding the numbers in order, Gauss found a shortcut and

computed the answer in minutes. It is thought that he wrote the sum backward and forward, leaving out the middles, as in the illustration, and then added vertically.

Gauss reasoned that there would be 100 sums of 101, for a total of 10,100. Since he had written the sum of the numbers twice, the true sum was 10,100 ÷ 2, or 5,050.

Because 5,050 is the sum of all the counting numbers from 1 through 100, it is a triangular number.

$$1 + 2 + 3 + \ldots + 98 + 99 + 100$$
$$100 + 99 + 98 + \ldots + 3 + 2 + 1$$
$$101 + 101 + 101 + \ldots + 101 + 101 + 101$$

The sum of 1 + 2 is 3. The third triangular number is the sum of 1 + 2 + 3, and the fourth is the sum of 1 + 2 + 3 + 4. Can you predict what the fifth triangular number is? Following the pattern, it would be the sum of 1 + 2 + 3 + 4 + 5, or 15.

Whenever you add consecutive counting numbers starting from 1, the sum will be a triangular number.

Other Polygonal Numbers

Pentagonal, or five-sided, numbers and other larger polygonal numbers can be thought of as combinations of square numbers and triangular numbers. In the dot patterns in Figure 11 below, notice that the third pentagonal number is made up of the third square number. The second triangular number is on top.

Figure 11. Pentagonal Numbers

  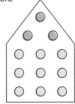

Cannonball Numbers

Geometrical patterns in three dimensions are possible using **cannonball numbers**. Cannonball numbers are formed by stacking the terms, or members, of polygonal numbers. For example, the square numbers can be stacked on top of each other to form a pile, like stacking real cannonballs in a square pyramid, as in Figure 12. Each layer of the stack

Figure 12. Square Cannonball Numbers

is a square number. So the first square cannonball number, as you can see, is 1, and the second is 1 + 4, or 5. The third square cannonball number has three layers, with one cannonball on top, four in the middle layer, and nine in the bottom layer (the middle cannonball in the bottom layer cannot be seen), for a total of 1 + 4 + 9, or 14. The third square cannonball number is 14.

Triangular cannonball numbers can be made by stacking the triangular numbers into triangular pyramids.

The study of patterns such as those in this article can increase our understanding of mathematical concepts and relationships. It can also be a fascinating and entertaining activity to pursue in our leisure hours.

Dr. Carol R. Findell
Associate Professor and Program Coordinator
Mathematics Education, Boston University

Answers to Finding Patterns in Fibonacci Numbers

1. The sum is 4. The number 4 is one less than the fifth number, 5.

   The sum is 7. The number 7 is one less than the sixth number, 8.

   The sum of any group of Fibonacci numbers, taken consecutively from the first number to the last number, is one less than the Fibonacci number located two places after the last number in the group.

   The sum is 12.

2. 2 squared is 4, and 1 × 3 = 3. The product of the outer numbers is one less than the middle number squared.

   3 squared is 9, and 2 × 5 = 10. The product of the outer numbers is one more than the middle number squared.

   The pattern varies.

   If you take any three consecutive Fibonacci numbers, square the middle number, and then multiply the outer numbers, the product of the outer numbers is alternately one more or one less than the square of the middle number.

3. 2 × 3 = 6, and 1 × 5 = 5. The product of the middle numbers is one more than the product of the outer numbers.

   8 × 13 = 104, and 5 × 21 = 105. The product of the middle numbers is one less than the product of the outer numbers.

   If you take any four consecutive Fibonacci numbers, multiply the two middle numbers, and then multiply the two outer numbers, the first product is alternately one less or one more than the second product.

NUMBER PUZZLES AND GAMES

A world without numbers is impossible to imagine. Numbers are everywhere and you use them every day, most often for practical reasons. But for people who like to solve puzzles and play games, mathematics has another purpose. It can be used to create number puzzles and games that provide very entertaining ways to pass the time.

For thousands of years, puzzle solvers have matched their brain powers against the baffling schemes of the puzzle makers. If you want to test your brain power, you have come to the right place. Here you will find puzzles to unravel and games to play. Try one and then another. If you need solutions, you will find them at the end of this article.

 **THE CLASSICS**

What is a classic puzzle? It is a puzzle that has bewildered generations of solvers. Here are three classic puzzles. Years ago, your parents or grandparents may have tried to solve them. Did they succeed? Not everyone does. Will you solve them? There is only one way to find out. Try them.

1. Cats and Mice

Do you know one of the things Egyptians were writing down 3,000 years ago? Number puzzles. In 1858 a man named A. Henry Rhind discovered an ancient Egyptian scroll. This scroll contains the oldest known puzzle in the world. Here it is, only revised a bit for present-day puzzle solvers.

There was once a small village with just seven houses. In each house there lived seven cats. Each cat killed seven mice. If they had lived, each mouse would have eaten seven stalks of wheat. Each wheat stalk had seven kernels of grain. If houses, cats, mice, stalks, and kernels were added together, what number would you get?

2. Sisters, Sisters, Sisters

Puzzle makers were hard at work in ancient China, too. Here is a family puzzle that dates back more than 1,500 years.

Three sisters live in three different cities. The sisters visit their mother whenever they can. The oldest sister visits every five days, the middle sister visits every four days, and the youngest sister visits every three days. If all three sisters left their mother's house this morning, how many days will pass before all four women come together again?

3. Tower of Hanoi

The Tower of Hanoi is a famous puzzle. This is how it works. Draw three circles on a sheet of paper. Label the circles like this:

Put a quarter in Circle A. On top of the quarter, put a nickel. On top of the nickel, put a dime.

Your job is to move the tower from Circle A to either Circle B or Circle C. Move one coin at a time. Never place a larger coin on top of a smaller one. It is possible to transfer the tower in just seven moves. Can you do it? If you manage this task, try something harder. Make a four-story tower by sliding a penny between the dime and nickel. You can transfer this tower in 15 moves.

Try creating a five-story tower by adding a half-dollar. It is possible to transfer this building in 31 moves.

Here is a story concerning this puzzle. In ancient days, a Hindu god built a tower composed of 64 golden disks. He placed the tower in a temple and told the priests to move it from one location to another. They had to obey the same rules you followed. The god instructed the priests to work nonstop day and night and declared that the world would vanish the moment the priests finished their task. How long did the priests work? Can you guess? The answer is surprising.

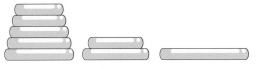

The next puzzles are mathematical, but you do not add, subtract, multiply, or divide to solve them. Instead, you arrange numbers, cards, or pennies in special ways. These puzzles may take time to solve, but do not give up on them. You can do them all, if you try.

4. Numbers in Boxes

This puzzle seems easy. All you do is place numbers in boxes. Sometimes, though, arranging numbers can present quite a challenge. Are you ready for this one? If so, copy this grid on a sheet of paper.

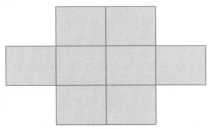

Now, arrange the numbers 1, 2, 3, 4, 5, 6, 7, and 8 in the boxes. You will put a single number in each box. There is only one rule. You may not put consecutive numbers next to each other either vertically, horizontally, or diagonally. You must not put 3 next to 2 or 4, or 5 next to 4 or 6, for instance.

Perhaps you will find the answer quickly. That does not usually happen with this puzzle, though. You may be tempted, therefore, to peek at the solution. Avoid the temptation. Instead, give the puzzle another try. This time, perhaps, the numbers will fall into place.

5. Cards in Order

Here is a mind-bending puzzle. Take an ace and one each of the 2, 3, 4, 5, 6, 7, 8, 9, and 10 cards from a deck of cards. You must arrange this mini-deck in a special way. With the deck properly organized, you will turn over the first card and place it face up on a table. This card must be an ace. Then slide the second card to the bottom of the deck without turning it over.

You flip over the third card. It must be a 2. Then slide the fourth card to the bottom of the deck. Keep up this pattern until you have turned over all ten cards. You have arranged the deck perfectly, if you turn over all ten cards in numerical order. They will appear in order from ace to 10.

6. Pennies at Home

To play Pennies at Home, you need eight pennies and a playing board. The board consists of five squares drawn in a row. Label the right-hand square HOME. Place two pennies apiece in the other four squares.

Your job is to get the pennies safely HOME. To do this, take all the coins from any square and drop them one by one into the squares to the right. Here is how the board might look after your first move.

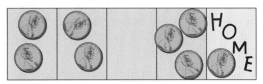

If you still have pennies in your hand after you drop one in the HOME square, circle around the board and begin dropping pennies again. Never take pennies away from HOME. But you can move pennies from any other square. On any move, if the last penny you drop lands in a square already occupied by pennies, you can continue the game. If that last penny lands in an empty square, though, the game ends and you fail the challenge. Can you arrange to bring all the pennies HOME before that happens? It is not easy, but it can be done.

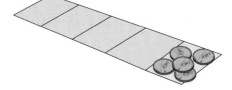

With the right numbers, you can discover amazing facts. You can estimate what your adult height may be or find out how much you would weigh on the planet Mars. The next activities show you how this is done—in case you want to know.

7. How Tall Will You Grow?

Would you like to know how tall you will be when you are fully grown? There is no way to predict your exact adult height, but there is a simple method for getting a good estimate. First, change your height from feet and inches to just inches. (There are 12 inches in a foot.) Then find your age on the chart below. Multiply the height you are now by the growth factor for your age and sex. This gives you an estimate of your grown-up height in inches. Then change the inches back to feet and inches.

Age	Girls	Boys
8	1.28	1.39
9	1.23	1.33
10	1.19	1.28
11	1.14	1.23
12	1.07	1.19
13	1.03	1.15

8. Another Weigh

How much do you weigh? If you travel to other planets in our solar system, you will discover something strange. Although you will stay the same size as you move from planet to planet, your weight will change. Visit Jupiter and you will weigh much more than you weigh on Earth. Visit Pluto and you will weigh a lot less. You can figure out your interplanetary weight without booking passage on the space shuttle. Look at this chart. It shows a special weight factor for each planet.

Planet	Wt. Factor	Planet	Wt. Factor
Jupiter	2.50	Mars	.38
Pluto	.06	Saturn	1.08
Mercury	.38	Uranus	.91
Venus	.91	Neptune	1.19

To find your weight on another world, simply multiply your Earth weight by the weight factor for your favorite planet. Whatever the product, that's your other-worldly weight.

Imagine you weigh 100 pounds on Earth, you will weigh 100 × 2.5, or 250 pounds, on Jupiter. On the other hand, you will weigh 100 × .06, or a mere 6 pounds, on Pluto.

Here are some number jokes and humorous puzzles. After you discover the answers, share the silliness with a friend.

9. Letter Play

Can you take two letters from FIVE and still have four left?

10. Number Play

If two is company and three makes a crowd, what are four and five?

11. A Corn-y Story

There is a basket in a barn filled with nine ears of corn. Every day a rabbit sneaks into the barn and hops out with three ears. Why does it take this rabbit nine days to empty the basket?

12. Clockworks

Have you heard of Lewis Carroll? He wrote the book *Alice In Wonderland*. In addition to writing books, Lewis Carroll liked inventing puzzles. Here is one of his sillier ones.

Imagine you have two clocks. One is broken. The hands do not move at all. The other clock loses one minute every day. You can keep one. Which one should you select?

Keep the broken clock, Lewis Carroll said, and throw the other away. Carroll had a logical reason for saying this. Can you figure out his reason? That is your puzzle.

Would you like to amaze your friends and family? It is easy to astound one and all, if you know the right number tricks.

13. I Know Your Number

This is a simple but impressive trick.

Tell a friend to select any five-digit number, as long as none of the digits repeat. Next tell your friend to rearrange the digits in any order to make another five-digit number. Then your friend should subtract the smaller five-digit number from the larger one and then add all the digits in the resulting number. If this sum is a one-digit number, your friend can stop. If not, your friend should add the digits again and keep adding until only a one-digit number is the result. Your friend must not tell you the result. Instead, say that you have been reading your friend's mind and that you already know the number. What is the number? It is 9.

This is a good trick, because no matter what five-digit number your friend selects, the final number will be 9. Try it yourself and you will see. You know the answer is always 9, but your friend, who does not, will be amazed by your mind reading. Your friend will beg to know how you managed the trick. Do not tell. Instead, smile and say, "It is all in the math!"

14. A Dice Trick

Tell a friend to roll a pair of dice, and make sure the two numbers are hidden from you.

After the dice are rolled, instruct your friend to multiply the number on top of one of the dice by 2. Then add 3 to the result, and multiply the sum by 5. To this amount your friend should add the number on top of the second of the dice. Finally, tell your friend to multiply the entire amount by 10 and tell you the total. Now you can tell your friend which two numbers were rolled on the dice!

How do you know these numbers? Here is how. No matter what numbers were on the dice, your friend's total will be a three-digit number that ends with a zero. Drop the zero and think of the remaining two digits as a new number. Subtract 15 from that number. You have a two-digit answer. Each digit is one of the numbers your friend rolled with the dice.

Imagine your friend rolls a 2 and a 6. When you multiply 2 times 2, you get 4. Then you add 3 to the 4 and get 7. Then you multiply 7 by 5 and get 35. When you add in the 6, you get 41. Finally, you multiply the 41 by 10 and get 410. When you drop the zero, you get 41. Then subtract 15 from 41 and you get 26. Remember, your friend rolled a 2 and a 6. There they are in the 26. Astounding!

Sometimes only logical thinking can get you out of a difficult situation. That is certainly the case with Sally, who must solve two logic puzzles to escape from the castle of an evil wizard.

15. Which Door?

A wizard leads Sally to an underground room. Sally finds herself facing two doors. She must walk through one of them. If she picks the wrong one, she will land in a dreary dungeon. If she picks the right door, she will take a big step toward freedom. There are two trolls in the room with her. One troll always tells the truth. The other troll always lies. Sally has no idea which troll lies and which one tells the truth. The wizard instructs her to ask one troll one question. If she asks the right question, she will discover freedom's door. What question should Sally ask?

16. Which Pill?

With your help, Sally selects the correct door. But her troubles are not over. The wizard shows her seven pills. They are all the same size and color, but they are not identical. Six of the pills are poisonous. The seventh pill is an escape-the-wizard pill. This pill weighs a bit more than the others. The wizard gives Sally a balance scale and orders her to swallow one pill. Sally can use the scale twice before she selects her pill. Can you help Sally find the escape pill?

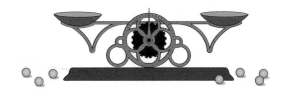

Some number problems are easy. They are so easy, it is silly to call them problems. You will not find any problemless problems here. These problems should give you a bit of a brain strain. If you manage to solve them, you have accomplished something big.

17. Where Are Those Signs?

Look at this strange number sentence:

$$2 \;\square\; 4 \;\square\; 6 \;\square\; 8 \;\square\; 13 \;\square\; 57 = 110$$

You can turn this sentence into a true equation if you insert the right addition, subtraction, and multiplication signs in the boxes.

$$2 \times 4 \times 6 - 8 + 13 + 57 = 110$$

Here are two more unsigned problems ready for you to complete.

$$5 \;\square\; 5 \;\square\; 5 \;\square\; 5 \;\square\; 5 = 30$$

$$1 \;\square\; 234 \;\square\; 5 \;\square\; 678 \;\square\; 9 = 899$$

These last two problems are the hardest yet. Why? There are no boxes showing where the signs belong. You must find the right spots yourself. Put an addition sign here and a subtraction sign there, or group the 8's to make larger numbers, until you make the equation work.

$$8 \; 8 \; 8 \; 8 \; 8 \; 8 \; 8 \; 8 = 1,688$$

$$1\;0\;2\;0\;3\;0\;4\;0\;5\;0\;6\;0 = 30$$

18. Digits Everywhere

Take a look at this equation:

$$\square\square\square + \square\square\square + \square\square\square + \square = 1,368$$

What is missing? Numbers. Use each of the digits 0 through 9 to fill the boxes and make a true equation.

$$123 + 456 + 789 + 0 = 1,368$$

Try the next four problems on your own. For each equation, fill the boxes with the digits 0 through 9. It will be hard to get every digit placed correctly, but you can do it.

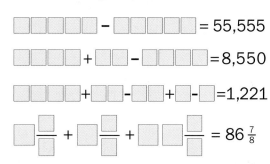

$$\square\square\square\square\square - \square\square\square\square\square = 55,555$$

$$\square\square\square\square + \square\square - \square\square\square\square = 8,550$$

$$\square\square\square\square + \square\square - \square\square + \square - \square = 1,221$$

$$\square\tfrac{\square}{\square} + \square\tfrac{\square}{\square} + \square\square\tfrac{\square}{\square} = 86\tfrac{7}{8}$$

19. Number Pyramids

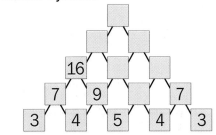

This is a number pyramid. It is not finished. It needs more numbers. To complete the pyramid, add the numbers on the bottom level to discover what numbers should be on the next level. For example, start on the left of the bottom row: 3 + 4 = 7. This number, 7, is the first number on the left of the next level of the pyramid. Pyramids can get very complicated, especially when numbers are missing in the bottom row. Then you must subtract your way down the pyramid.

Copy the pyramid above and the three pyramids below. Try to reach the top of each one. Watch out for the fraction and decimal pyramids. They are especially tricky.

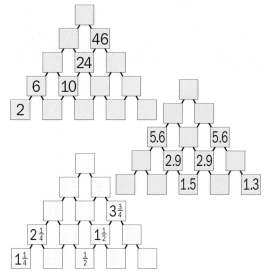

Here are two games meant for two players. Round up a friend and start the action.

20. Pig

For this game, you need one playing dice, or die, that you and your opponent will take turns rolling. Let us say you go first. You can roll the die as often as you want during your turn unless you happen to roll the number 1. Each time you roll, you add the number on the die to the sum of all the numbers you rolled during that round. If you roll a 1, however, you lose all of your points, and you must pass the die to your opponent.

Naturally you do not want to roll a 1. So, if you think you might toss this dangerous number, hand the die to your opponent. That way, your turn ends, but you get to keep your points. Your opponent rolls the die as often as he or she wants, or until a 1 is rolled. Then the die returns to you. Again, you roll and add new points to your old score. But if you roll a 1, it is a wipeout. You lose all the points you had collected so far, and you must pass the die back to your opponent. How do you win Pig? You must top 60 points before your opponent does. For a harder game, you can go for 100 points.

Why is the game called Pig? Well, if you make a pig of yourself and roll the die too often, you know what will happen. You will probably toss that horrible 1. Generosity, a willingness to share the die, therefore, is the key to victory in a game of Pig.

21. A Number Board
Copy this game board on a sheet of paper:

6	5	9
4	1	3
8	2	7

You and your opponent each need three tokens for this game. For tokens you can use two objects of different shapes, or two different coins such as pennies and dimes, or two of anything else you would enjoy using. Take turns putting your tokens on the board. Whenever you place a token in a square, you score points. If you place a token in the 3 square, you get 3 points. If you place one in the 2 square, you get 2 points.

After you and your opponent have placed all six tokens, take turns sliding tokens to adjoining squares. You can slide vertically, horizontally, or diagonally. You score more points with each move. The game ends when one person arranges his or her three tokens in a vertical, horizontal, or diagonal row—just like in tic-tac-toe. When the game ends, the player with the highest score wins. In this game, then, if you have a lower score than your opponent, do your best to avoid putting your three tokens in a row. But if you have the higher score, go for it.

1. Cats and Mice
There are 7 houses in the village. There are $7 \times 7 = 49$ cats. There are $49 \times 7 = 343$ mice. There are $7 \times 343 = 2,401$ stalks. There are $7 \times 2401 = 16,807$ kernels. Add it all up, and you get 19,607.

2. Sisters, Sisters, Sisters
In 60 days the sisters and their mother will come together again. Why? 60 is the smallest multiple of 5, 4, and 3.

3. Tower of Hanoi
To transfer a three-coin tower, begin by moving the dime to Circle C and the nickel to Circle B. Move the dime to Circle B and the quarter to Circle C. Move the dime to Circle A and the nickel to Circle C. Move the dime to Circle C. You are finished in seven moves.

There is a pattern that works no matter how tall the tower. Number the coins or disks. In a three-level tower, the dime is 1, the nickel is 2, and the quarter is 3. Odd numbered disks must move from Circle A to Circle C on their first moves. Even numbered disks must go from Circle A to Circle B. Disk 1 must change places every second move. Disk 2 must change places every fourth move. Disk 3 changes places every eighth move, and disk 4 every sixteenth move. Keep up the pattern for each new disk and the tower will shift.

As for the Hindu priests, it will take them 18,446,744,073,709,551,615 moves to transfer the tower. If they move one disk every second, this job will take more than 500,000,000,000 (500 billion) years.

4. Numbers in Boxes

	3	5	
7	1	8	2
	4	6	

5. Cards in Order
Place the deck from top down in this order: Ace, 6, 2, 10, 3, 7, 4, 9, 5, 8.

6. Pennies at Home
Here is one way to get the pennies HOME. Each digit stands for the number of pennies in a square. At first, you have 2 2 2 2 0. Change 2 2 2 2 0 **to** 2 2 0 3 1 **to** 3 3 0 0 2 **to** 3 0 1 1 3 **to** 3 0 0 2 3 **to** 4 0 0 0 4 **to** 0 1 1 1 5 **to** 0 0 2 1 5 **to** 0 0 2 0 6 **to** 0 0 0 1 7 **to** 0 0 0 0 8.

9. Letter Play
Erase **F** and **E** from **FIVE**. What do you get? IV. That is 4 written in Roman numerals.

10. Number Play
Four and five make nine, of course.

11. A Corn-y Story
Every day the rabbit leaves the barn with one ear of corn and its own two ears.

12. Clockworks
If a clock loses one minute a day, it almost never shows the exact time. A broken clock shows the right time twice a day, making it the better choice.

15. Which Door?
Sally's question should be, "Which door will the other troll say leads to the dungeon?" She can ask either troll. The lying troll will point to freedom's door, because he will lie about the truthful troll's answer. The truthful troll will also point to freedom's door, because he will report the lying troll's response truthfully. Either way, Sally has her answer.

16. Which Pill?
Sally should begin by weighing three pills on the right side of the scale and three pills on the left side. If the scale balances, then the heavier pill (the escape-the-wizard pill) is not on the scale and Sally should swallow it. If the scale tips, then the heavier pill is on the side that is tipping. That means Sally must focus on these three pills. She should put one pill on the left side, one pill on the right side, and leave the third pill off the scale. If the scale tips, Sally will know which pill is heavier. If the scale balances, Sally should swallow the third pill.

17. Where Are Those Signs?
Some problems have more than one solution. Did you find different ways to solve the problems? If so, good for you.

$$5 \times 5 - 5 + 5 + 5 = 30$$
$$1 + 234 - 5 + 678 - 9 = 899$$
$$888 - 88 + 888 = 1,688$$
$$10 + 20 - 30 + 40 + 50 - 60 = 30$$

You can make up your own Where Are Those Signs puzzles. Write a problem and its answer. Then rewrite it removing every sign except the equals signs. Trade problems with a friend.

18. Digits Everywhere
$$98,765 - 43,210 = 55,555$$
$$9,876 + 24 - 1,350 = 8,550$$
$$1234 + 56 - 78 + 9 - 0 = 1221$$
$$9\tfrac{1}{2} + 6\tfrac{3}{4} + 70\tfrac{5}{8} = 86\tfrac{7}{8}$$

19. Number Pyramids
These are the completed pyramids.

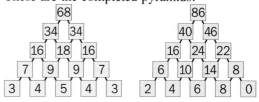

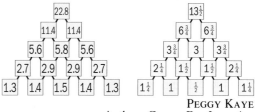

PEGGY KAYE
Author, *Games For Learning*
and *Games For Math*

Different types of activities require the use of different kinds of numbers. The counting, or natural, numbers may be used to count how many objects there are in a group or collection.

a number, too. Other kinds of numbers have names like -40 (negative 40) or $\sqrt{2}$ (the square root of 2). Some numbers do not even look like numbers. To mathematicians, scientists, and engineers, for example, the symbol e can be a number.

What Is a Counting Number?

The numbers people discovered first are called the **counting numbers**, or **natural numbers**. The word "counting" tells one of the main ways these numbers are used. To count the number of something, perhaps the number of apples in a basket, you begin by saying the names of the counting numbers in order: "one, two, three, four, five, six. . . ." and so on. When you reach the last apple, the number name you have said is the same as the number of apples in the basket. For example, if there were only nine apples in the basket you would say the number name "nine."

Numbers are ideas, and the names of the counting numbers are really names for number ideas. There are many ways to make pictures of them. One way occurred about 30,000 years ago, when people used stone tools to scratch notches or lines on bones to represent number ideas. In this method, the first thing to be counted is shown as a short scratch. Then another scratch is made for the second thing. As each thing is counted, another scratch is made on the bone. Using that method,

means the same as the number name "ten," and like the word "ten," the bone scratches could mean ten of anything—ten apples, or ten animals, or ten days.

Another way people used to show counting numbers is still used in mathematics today.

NUMBERS AND NUMBER SYSTEMS

Numbers are one of the oldest ideas developed by human beings, older even than writing. We know that numbers were being used 30,000 years ago by people who were still using stone axes as tools. Today we no longer have much use for stone axes, but we do need numbers every day of our lives. Of course, our knowledge of numbers and how to use them has grown tremendously since those early times. For us, numbers have become very powerful tools.

▶ WHAT ARE NUMBERS?

A stage magician may ask a person to "pick a number, any number," and then try to guess that number. If you were asked, what number would you pick? Nearly everyone picks a number such as 7 or 13 or 100. Those are all good choices. But there are other possible choices that seem very different from numbers such as 7 or 13. For example, a person could pick $\frac{3}{4}$ (three-fourths), a fraction. A fraction is

Here is how it worked in one of the earliest civilizations, which existed in the region that is now made up of the countries Turkey, Syria, and Iraq.

To count the number of sheep in a flock before shepherds took it to pasture, a small piece of clay was shaped for each sheep. The clay was then baked to harden it. The pieces of clay, called **tokens**, were put into a clay envelope, and that was baked, too. Weeks later, when the shepherds returned with the flock, the envelope was cracked open so that they could check how many sheep there were in the flock when they left. If they could still match one token for each sheep and one sheep for each token, the shepherds knew that none of the sheep had been lost.

So you can think of a counting number as part of a process of starting with one thing and then adding one more of the same thing over and over. This is the "scratches on bone" way to think about it. Another way is to think of a counting number as part of a process in which you match the objects in one group with the objects in another so that every object has one match and there are no objects left over. This is the "tokens and sheep" way to think about it. Mathematicians call this way one-to-one correspondence.

Number or Numeral?

Numbers are ideas, but scratches on bones, tokens, and number words such as "one" or "ten" are real things, not ideas. They are ways we use to represent number ideas. Numerals are also real things. They are signs or symbols often used to represent number ideas. There are many kinds of numerals.

Some numerals used today are like the scratches on bones that people used long ago. They are called "tallies," and they are usually made like this:

These numerals also have the names "one, two, three, four, five, six, seven, eight, nine." A more common way to write numerals is to use what are called the Hindu-Arabic numerals. They are 1, 2, 3, 4, 5, 6, 7, 8, 9. Another way to write numerals is to use what are called Roman numerals, which you sometimes see on clocks or in dates. They are I, II, III, IV,

V, VI, VII, VIII, IX. All three sets of numerals represent the same number ideas. (To read more about them, see the article NUMERALS AND NUMERATION SYSTEMS in Volume N.)

To calculate distances on a map, numbers may be added, subtracted, multiplied, or divided. These four operations are used to find solutions to a wide variety of mathematical problems.

Zero

One number familiar to you is not used in counting. It was given the name "zero," and it is often written by using the numeral 0. You use zero to answer questions such as, "If you had ten pens and you gave all of them away to your friends, how many pens would you have left?" The number zero can also be used to mark a starting point on a scale. Or it can set a particular point on a scale. For example, when a weather report says that the temperature is zero degrees, it does not mean that the temperature is nothing or that there is no temperature. It means that the temperature is at a level that is neither above nor below zero.

Although zero is an important number idea, it was not recognized for a long time. Mathematicians in India were the first to use zero as a number, and they also introduced the

Can you recognize where you would see numbers the way they are shown above? They can be found on objects people see every day. You can find them listed at the end of this article.

numeral 0. The earliest use of the numeral 0 that has been found is on an Indian monument dated A.D. 876.

▶ WHAT IS A NUMBER SYSTEM?

Numbers are most useful when they can be combined in various ways. The counting numbers can always be combined by addition and multiplication, and the result is always another counting number. For example, 3 and 6 are counting numbers and so is 9, which is the sum of 3 + 6. The product of 3 × 6 is 18, and 18 is a counting number. However, counting numbers can be combined by subtraction or division only some of the time. The result of 6 − 3, for example, is 3, and 3 is a counting number. The result of 3 − 6, however, is −3, or negative 3, which is not a number we use in counting. In the same way, if you divide 6 by 3, the answer, called the quotient, is a counting number. But the quotient of 3 divided by 6, which is .5, is not.

A set of numbers, the operations that can be used with those numbers, such as addition, subtraction, multiplication, and division, and the rules for using the operations form a **number system**. The counting numbers with addition and multiplication form a very simple number system, but there are many other systems. For example, if you include zero with the counting numbers, you have a more complete system called **whole numbers**.

Number System Rules

Each number system obeys certain rules. Mathematicians agree, however, that every number system that includes the counting numbers must follow the same rules as the counting numbers do.

Closure Properties. In the system of counting numbers, if you add two numbers, the sum of the numbers must also be a counting number. For example, 5 and 7 are counting numbers, so the sum of 5 + 7, which is 12, is a counting number. If you multiply two numbers in this system, the product of the two numbers must also be in the system. For example, because 8 and 4 are counting numbers, the product of 8 × 4, or 32, must be a counting number. These two rules are called **closure properties**. In the counting numbers system, the result of an addition or multiplication with counting numbers always turns out to be another counting number, so the system is said to be **closed**. Like the counting numbers, the system of whole numbers is also closed for addition and multiplication.

Commutative Properties. In both the counting numbers and the whole numbers systems, the order in which numbers are added makes no difference. When you add 2 + 3, you get the same sum as when you add 3 + 2.

If we let the letter a stand for any number at all and let b stand for any number also, then we can say that $a + b = b + a$. The sum is the same no matter in what order a and b are added. This is called the **commutative property of addition**.

There is also a **commutative property of multiplication**. Thus 3 × 5 = 5 × 3, and 4 × 9 = 9 × 4. To state this in general terms you would write, $a \times b = b \times a$, where a and b stand for any two numbers.

It is helpful to remember the commutative property when you are using the basic addition or multiplication facts to solve problems. For every fact, such as 4 + 7 = 11, there is a companion fact, such as 7 + 4 = 11, with the numbers being added in reverse order. This means you have to know and remember only 50 basic addition facts instead of 100. The same is true for multiplication facts.

Associative Properties. How do you add 3 + 6 + 5? You can add only two numbers at a time. Do you first add 6 to 3 and then add 5? Or do you begin by adding 5 to 6 and then add this sum to 3? Either method gives you the same result. It makes no difference how you group neighboring numbers when you add them. This is known as the **associative property of addition**.

Parentheses may be used for grouping numbers. You may write:

$$(3 + 6) + 5, \text{ or } 3 + (6 + 5).$$

Using either method, the sum is 14. The general way to state this rule is to say that for any of the whole numbers, including those called the counting numbers,

$$(a + b) + c = a + (b + c).$$

The associative property can be helpful when you add numbers such as $7 + 8$. Think of 8 as $7 + 1$. Since you probably always remember $7 + 7 = 14$, it may be easier to add $(7 + 7) + 1 = 15$, than it is to remember $7 + 8 = 15$.

There is also an **associative property of multiplication**. It may be stated as:

$$(a \times b) \times c = a \times (b \times c).$$

The Distributive Property. Another property of the whole numbers system connects multiplication to addition. Look at the statement $3 \times (4 + 7) = (3 \times 4) + (3 \times 7)$. When you add 4 to 7 and multiply the sum by 3, you obtain the same answer, 33, as when you multiply 4 and 7 each separately by 3 and then add the two products.

This property is used in arithmetic when you use multiplication to find the product of two numbers. For example, the steps followed in multiplying 5×23 use the fact that 23 can be expressed as $20 + 3$. The multiplication has this pattern: $5 \times (20 + 3) = (5 \times 20) + (5 \times 3) = 100 + 15 = 115$. This property of the system of whole numbers or of counting numbers is called the **distributive property** and may be written as:

$$a \times (b + c) = (a \times b) + (a \times c).$$

Identity Elements. Thus far, all the properties described have been true in both the counting numbers system and the whole numbers system. Another property true for both systems concerns the number 1 when it is used in multiplication. The product or result of any number multiplied by 1 is the number being multiplied. What is 5×1? The answer is 5. What is 15×1? The answer is 15. To state this in general, when a stands for any counting number or whole number, $a \times 1 = a$, and $1 \times a = a$. This is called the **identity property for multiplication**, and the number 1 is called the **identity element for multiplication**.

The counting numbers do not have an identity property for addition, but the whole numbers do. What is $3 + 0$? The answer is 3. The sum of any number and zero is the number itself. In general, when a stands for any whole number, $a + 0 = a$, and $0 + a = a$. The number 0 is the **identity element for addition**.

▶ **INTEGERS**

The whole numbers are a useful system, but adding one more property to the system of whole numbers produces a more complete system. The new property or rule is known as the **additive inverse property**. It states that for every number there must be another number that when added to it results in a sum of 0. For any number represented by a, the number shown as $-a$ is the **additive inverse**, or opposite, of a, and $a + (-a) = 0$. This new number system is called the **integers**. The integers include the whole numbers, just as the whole numbers include the counting numbers.

A good way to picture the integers is with a thermometer. The 0 on a thermometer marks the starting point on a scale. Numbers above

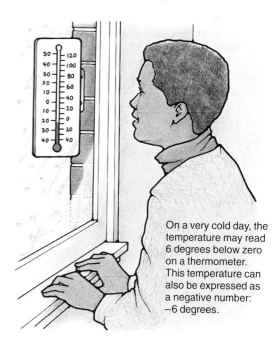

On a very cold day, the temperature may read 6 degrees below zero on a thermometer. This temperature can also be expressed as a negative number: -6 degrees.

What is infinity?

What is the largest number you can think of? One million—1,000,000? One billion—1,000,000,000? You may have heard that infinity is the biggest possible number, but that is not true. There is no biggest real number, or counting number, or any other kind of number.

Think of the largest number of things that you might think of counting, such as the number of stars in the sky, or the grains of sand on a beach, or all of the atoms in the universe. Although these would be big numbers, they are not infinity. We might estimate the number of atoms in the universe to be 1 followed by 80 zeros. That is an enormous number, but you can add 1 to it to get a larger number, and add 1 to that number to get an even larger number. There is no limit to how many times you can keep adding 1. That is why there is no greatest counting number.

What is infinity, if it is not a big number? One kind of infinity may be thought of as the endless process of finding an ever bigger number. It means that a set of numbers keeps getting larger without ever reaching a final largest number. Mathematicians show this type of infinity by the "lazy 8" symbol.

It is sometimes called potential infinity because it may be approached but never reached.

0 are the same as the counting numbers. Numbers below 0 are the additive inverses of the counting numbers. A figure often used in mathematics to show the integers is similar to a thermometer lying on its side. It is called a **number line**.

Numbers to the right of 0 are represented by points with equal spaces between them, which are labeled with the counting numbers. The additive inverses are placed to the left of 0. They are called **negative numbers**. They are written as -1, -2, and so on. What looks like a subtraction sign is a negative sign.

When the counting numbers are considered as part of the integers, they are called **positive numbers**. A positive number is sometimes shown with a $+$ in front of it, which looks like the addition sign but it is called a positive sign. Notice, however, that 0 is neither positive nor negative.

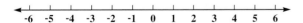

We frequently have occasion to do operations with integers. Suppose you are playing a game in which you can win or lose points. At first you gain 4 points, then you lose 9 points. To find your total score, you must add a positive and a negative number. To do this, the numbers can be written in parentheses as $(+4)$ and (-9). The sum of the numbers is indicated with the use of an addition sign:

$$(+4) + (-9) = ?$$

This addition can easily be done with the help of the number line. As you use the number line, it will help if you think of positive and negative numbers as moves in certain directions. Starting at 0, you move four units in the positive direction, to the right, arriving at $+4$. From $+4$ you move nine units in the negative direction, to the left. You find that you are at -5. Thus $(+4) + (-9) = (-5)$. The direction and length of each move along the number line may be shown with arrows.

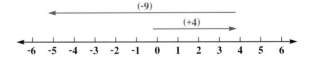

You can also subtract and multiply positive and negative numbers using a number line.

▶RATIONAL NUMBER SYSTEM

When you are using the operation of division, it is not always possible to get an exact answer when you are using the counting numbers, the whole numbers, or the integers. For example, the quotient, or result, of $13 \div 3$ (13 divided by 3) is between 4 and 5. This is because $12 \div 3$ is 4, and $15 \div 3$ is 5, and 13 is between 12 and 15. But there are no integers between 4 and 5.

To do the division, you need to use a new set of numbers that includes all the integers. To explain this new set of numbers in general terms, we let a stand for any number. Then we say that for every number a (except 0) there is a number $\frac{1}{a}$. The rule that shows the relationship between these two numbers can be shown by the equation $a \times \frac{1}{a} = 1$. This rule is called the **multiplicative inverse property**, and the number $\frac{1}{a}$ is called the **multiplicative inverse** of a. For example, $\frac{1}{4}$ is the multiplicative inverse of 4. If we use 4 in the equation, we have $4 \times \frac{1}{4} = 1$. The number $\frac{1}{4}$ is also called a **fraction**.

People have been using a number system that includes the multiplicative inverse property for a very long time. This practice goes back to when trading was used to buy and sell goods. For example, the hide of a cow might be traded for five bushels of grain plus half of another bushel of grain. Since there are 2 half bushels or units in a whole bushel or unit of grain, we write $\frac{1}{2}$ (one-half) to show the part left over. The 2 shows how many equal parts there are in a whole unit. The 1 shows how many parts are left over. In another situation, a person may have picked 8 apples and traded away 5 of them. It takes 8 equal parts to make a whole unit this time, so the person would have traded away $\frac{5}{8}$ (five-eighths) of the apples and would have $\frac{3}{8}$ (three-eighths) of them left.

We call $\frac{1}{4}$, $\frac{1}{2}$, $\frac{3}{8}$, and $\frac{5}{8}$ fractions, and the numbers represented by fractions are called **rational numbers**. A rational number can be expressed as the quotient, or ratio, of two integers. Since the rational numbers are quotients of the integers, rational numbers can be positive or negative. For example, 6 can be expressed as $\frac{6}{1}$ or by other fractions, such as $\frac{12}{2}$ or by $\frac{-18}{-3}$.

Every rational number can be represented on a number line, although they crowd each other so closely that not all of them can be labeled. For example, suppose you squeeze in the rational numbers $\frac{2}{3}$ and $\frac{3}{4}$, which are very close to one another. In between them, however, is the average of $\frac{2}{3}$ and $\frac{3}{4}$, which is $\frac{17}{24}$. Furthermore, in between $\frac{2}{3}$ and $\frac{17}{24}$ is their aver-

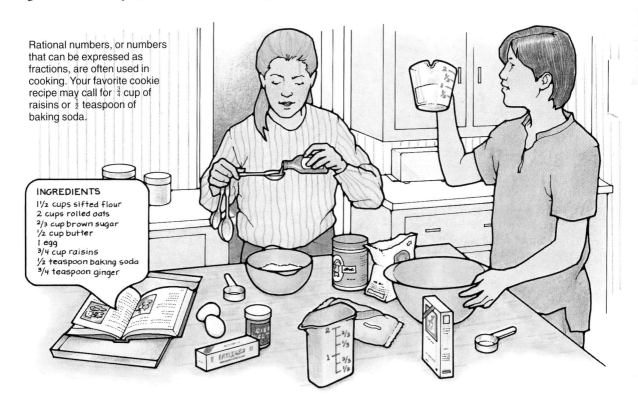

Rational numbers, or numbers that can be expressed as fractions, are often used in cooking. Your favorite cookie recipe may call for $\frac{3}{4}$ cup of raisins or $\frac{1}{2}$ teaspoon of baking soda.

INGREDIENTS
1½ cups sifted flour
2 cups rolled oats
⅔ cup brown sugar
½ cup butter
1 egg
¾ cup raisins
½ teaspoon baking soda
¾ teaspoon ginger

age, and so on. Mathematicians use the word "dense," or crowded, to describe this property of the rational number system.

Here is a number line with some of the points for rational numbers labeled on it.

▶REAL NUMBERS

Even though the rational numbers are dense on the number line, there are still points on the line that cannot be identified with rational numbers. This astonishing discovery was made by the ancient Greeks, who proved that numbers such as the square root of 2, shown as $\sqrt{2}$, are not rational numbers. The square root of a number is a number that if multiplied by itself produces the original number. No rational number multiplied by itself produces 2. The number must exist, however, since it can be shown to be the length of the diagonal of a certain type of square. Therefore, in addition to the rational numbers there are **irrational numbers**.

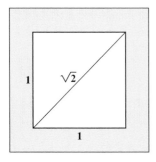

The length of the diagonal of a 1 inch (1") square is $\sqrt{2}$, the square root of 2. Such numbers are called irrational numbers.

Irrational numbers can be represented by numerals called **infinite decimals**. For example, $\sqrt{2}$ can also be written as the infinite decimal 1.41421356 . . . . The three dots before the period mean that there are always more decimal places that can be calculated. With infinite decimals, it is possible to locate irrational numbers on the number line.

The irrational numbers and the rational numbers together form what is called the **real number system**. The real numbers can account for all of the points on a number line, and they include all the numbers that people use for most purposes.

In addition to being defined as any number that can be represented by a point on a number line, real numbers can also be defined as any positive or negative number that can be shown by an infinite decimal. An integer such as -2 can be shown by the repeating infinite decimal -2.0000 . . . . Each decimal place after the point is filled with a 0. A rational number such as $\frac{5}{7}$ can be written as a repeating infinite decimal also, but in this case there is a pattern of six digits that repeats:

$$\frac{5}{7} = 0.714285\ 714285\ 714285\ \ldots\ .$$

▶COMPLEX NUMBERS

Although the real numbers include all the numbers people use in daily life, there are still other kinds of numbers. For example, there is no real number that is equal to $\sqrt{-1}$, or the square root of negative 1. Indeed, no square root of a negative number is a real number. Any real number multiplied by itself always gives a positive result. Thus there is no real number that when multiplied by itself will give -1 as a result. Mathematicians, therefore, invented new numbers that are the square roots of negative numbers. Since such square roots are not real numbers, they are called **imaginary**. Imaginary numbers can be defined in terms of $\sqrt{-1}$, which is also shown as the letter i. For example, $\sqrt{-4}$ is the same as $2\sqrt{-1}$ but is written as $2i$.

There is no imaginary number system, but the imaginary numbers and the real numbers together form part of a larger system called the **complex number system**. All the complex numbers can be written in the form $a + bi$. Here a and b can be any of the real numbers and $i = \sqrt{-1}$.

The complex numbers and the real numbers obey all the properties of the rational numbers —associative, closure, commutative, distributive, identity, and inverse for both addition and multiplication. Since there is no larger set of numbers that also has all of these properties, the complex number system is the end of the number systems.

BRYAN BUNCH
Instructor of Mathematics, Pace University
Coauthor, *The Timetables of Science*

See also ARITHMETIC; DECIMAL SYSTEM; FRACTIONS AND DECIMALS; MATHEMATICS; NUMBER PATTERNS; NUMBER PUZZLES AND GAMES; NUMERALS AND NUMERATION SYSTEMS.

(Answers to question about numbers on common objects: A highway sign; the recycling code on the bottom of a plastic bottle; numbers on a digital clock; the identification and price code on a product.)

This ancient stone carving tells about a journey taken by an Egyptian pharaoh, Amenhotep III, in 1450 B.C. It contains many number symbols. You can see the Egyptian symbols representing the number 743 in the third row from the bottom, on the left side.

NUMERALS AND NUMERATION SYSTEMS

Whenever we write a number, we are writing a symbol for that number. This symbol is called a **numeral**.

A numeral is not the same thing as a number. When we say "two," for example, we are expressing the idea of "a thing and another thing," an amount or a quantity that can also be expressed by a number, the number two. That number can be shown as a word, spelled "t-w-o," or as a numeral, the numeral 2.

Numerals and the rules we use to combine them make up a system called a **numeration system**. One numeration system includes the numerals 1, 2, 3, 4, 5, 6, 7, 8, 9, and 0. These ten symbols are also called **digits**, a term that comes from the Latin word for "finger" or "toe." This word recalls the use of fingers and toes in early counting systems. Digits can be combined to write larger numbers. For instance, you can combine the digits 1 and 4 to write the numeral 14, which represents the number fourteen.

This numeration system is not the only system of numerals, however. Numbers may not change, but the numerals used for writing them have changed many times over the years. Some of these other numeration systems are still used today.

▶ EARLY NUMERATION SYSTEMS

Human beings used numbers long before they invented writing. People who lived 40,000 years ago probably used a simple sign language to show numbers to one another. For example, they might have raised two fingers to show that there were two deer, five fingers on one hand to show five deer, and all the fingers on both hands to show ten.

The earliest written numerals that we know of were merely scratches on bones, rocks, or pieces of wood. Eventually these scratches became part of a **tally mark numeration system**. In a tally system, the number 3, for instance, is written with three strokes, or tally marks, like this: ///. To make it easier to count the marks, they were later arranged in groups of five. The symbol for 5 was written with the fifth line drawn through the other four: ////. The number 16 would thus be shown as //// //// //// /.

▶ ADDITIVE SYSTEMS

As civilizations progressed, so did their numeration systems. Tally marks or strokes were not an efficient way to record large quantities or numbers, so new numeration systems were developed.

The Egyptian Numeration System

One of the oldest numeration systems was developed in ancient Egypt more than 5,000 years ago. The Egyptians used vertical strokes to represent the numbers from 1 through 9, but they also invented special **hieroglyphics**, or picture-writing symbols, to represent certain numbers larger than 9.

Figure 1 shows the special symbols used by the Egyptians. Notice that there was no symbol for zero but that each of the special symbols stood for a power of ten. That means that each successive symbol in the system depicts a number that is ten times greater than the one before it.

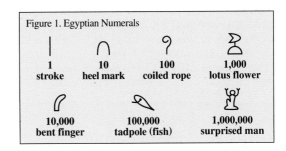

Figure 1. Egyptian Numerals

1 stroke	**10** heel mark	**100** coiled rope	**1,000** lotus flower
10,000 bent finger	**100,000** tadpole (fish)	**1,000,000** surprised man	

403

The Egyptians wrote larger numbers by writing several symbols next to each other in a row. Because the total value of the number represented was determined by adding the values of all the symbols in the row, the Egyptian numeration system is called an **additive system**. For example, here is a number written with Egyptian numerals:

| | | ∩ ∩ ∩ ∩ ∩

To work out the value of the number, add 1 + 1 + 10 + 10 + 10 + 10 + 10 = 52. The total value of the written symbols is the number 52.

In this system, the order in which the symbols were written was not important. It seems, however, that most Egyptian numerals were written with the symbols going from smallest to largest in left-to-right order.

Roman Numerals

The people of ancient Rome developed their numeration system almost 3,000 years ago. Their system began as a series of tally-like marks that looked like this: I, II, III, and so on. Because these strokes were hard to count when large numbers were involved, the Romans devised other symbols to represent groups of strokes. The Roman numerals are shown in Figure 2.

Figure 2. Roman Numerals			
I =	1	C =	100
V =	5	D =	500
X =	10	M =	1,000
L =	50		

In the Roman system, the number 8 is written VIII and the number 107 is written CVII. In the beginning the positions of the symbols did not matter. The general practice was to group like symbols and to write them in left-to-right order from largest to smallest.

Like the Egyptian system, the Roman numeration system is an additive system. To find the value of a number in the Roman system, the values of all the symbols shown are added. So, to find the value of MCCLXVI, add 1,000 + 100 + 100 + 50 + 10 + 5 + 1 = 1,266. The numeral MCCLXVI represents the number 1,266.

In order to make numbers easier to read, the Romans later made certain changes in their system. If a numeral with a lesser value was written to the left of a numeral with a greater value, the lesser value was subtracted from the greater. For example, the symbol I written to the left of a V meant "subtract one from the five." So the number 4 was represented as IV instead of as IIII. Nine was represented as IX instead of as VIIII. Following the same rule, XL meant 50 minus 10, or 40. However, if a numeral with a lesser value was written to the right of a numeral with a greater value, the two of them were added, so LX meant 50 plus 10, or 60.

Computation with Roman numerals was not easy. Imagine trying to add XXVII (27) to CXLVI (146). You might try lining the numerals up like this:

$$\begin{aligned} &\text{XXVII} \\ + \; &\text{CXLVI} \end{aligned}$$

This does not work because symbols with like values are not in line with each other. For this reason, the Romans, like many people in ancient civilizations, did their computing with the aid of an **abacus**. An abacus is a simple calculating machine made of beads strung on wires in a frame. With the help of an abacus, Roman numerals could be added and subtracted. However, multiplying or dividing with these numerals required enormous mathematical skill. (For more information about the abacus, see ABACUS in Volume A.)

Roman numerals were commonly used until the late 1600's, and they are still used to write dates and show time on some clocks.

▶MULTIPLICATIVE SYSTEMS

Both the Egyptian and the Roman numeration systems were additive systems. In other ancient civilizations, a different kind of numeration system was developed.

Many people who lived in Greece about 2,500 years ago used a system of numeration called the **Herodianic** or **Attic** system. Greeks using this system wrote large numbers by combining certain symbols. For example, the symbol for 5 and the symbol for 100 were combined to show 5 times 100, forming the symbol that represented the number 500:

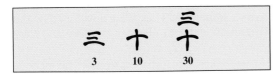

Γ	H	⊓⊦
5	10	500

Since symbols such as these indicated a multiplication, the Herodianic numeration system is called a **multiplicative system**. Multiplicative systems are usually additive as well.

The traditional Chinese numeration system, which dates back to the 200's B.C., also used multiplicative grouping. In this system, symbols represent each of the numbers 1 through 9, as well as the numbers 10, 100, 1,000, and other powers of ten. In the Chinese system, the symbol for 3 might be combined with the symbol for 10. This combination meant 3 times 10, or 30.

三	十	𠧧
3	10	30

Computing with multiplicative systems, however, was no easier than computing with additive systems.

▶POSITIONAL NUMERATION SYSTEMS

As civilizations advanced, a more efficient numeration system was developed. This system made it easier to represent large numbers, and it simplified the process of computation. One system that evolved is called a **positional**

numeration system, or a **place-value system**, because the value of a particular symbol depends not only on the symbol but also on its position or place in the number.

The Babylonian Numeration System

In about 3000 B.C., the Babylonians developed one of the first positional numeration systems. It was based on the number 60 and numbers were grouped by sixties. The Babylonian system is therefore called a **base-sixty system**, and 60 is called the **base number**.

The Babylonians wrote on soft clay tablets with an instrument shaped like a wedge, so their numerals were wedge-shaped. In the Babylonian numeration system, there were two basic numerals. A vertical wedge mark represented 1, and a horizontal wedge mark pointing to the left represented 10.

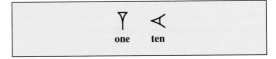

Y	◁
one	ten

Numbers less than 60 were written by combining the symbols for 1 and 10. The numeral for 12, for example, would be written:

◁ Y Y
twelve

To write numbers greater than 60, the Babylonians used a place-value system. The number 85, for instance, would be written as a two-place numeral:

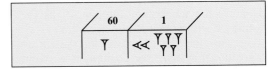

The first place on the right was the ones place. The next place to the left had a value of 60. So, to the Babylonian, the above numeral meant 1 sixty plus 2 tens and 5 ones, or 85.

The greatest two-place numeral in the Babylonian system was represented as 59 sixties and 59 ones, or the number 3,599. When a number greater than 3,599 was needed, the Babylonians had to use three-place numerals. Since the system was based on the number 60, the third place value was 60 times the second place value, or 3,600.

At first there was no symbol for zero in the Babylonian system. Without a zero **place-holder**, or symbol used to indicate a missing value, it was difficult to determine the value of the number represented by a numeral. The early Babylonians tried to show a difference by leaving a space for a missing value. If the space was not large enough, however, the reader could easily make a mistake. Imagine how hard it would be if we did not have a zero symbol in our numeration system. It would not always be possible to tell whether "3 6" meant 36 or 306.

Even after a symbol for zero was introduced into the Babylonian system, it was used only to indicate a missing value within a numeral, not at the end of one. Figuring out what number was meant could still be confusing.

Although the Babylonian system is no longer used, we still use a base-sixty system when we measure time as 60 seconds in a minute and 60 minutes in an hour.

The Mayan Numeration System

The Mayan civilization existed in parts of Mexico and Central America for about 3,000 years, from about 1500 B.C. to A.D. 1500. It is thought that the mathematics of the Maya was fairly advanced and complex, but existing records show only how they used mathematics in their calendar and in astronomy.

The Mayan numeration system probably dates back to the A.D. 300's, and it was primarily a base-twenty system. It used only three symbols: a dot representing 1, a horizontal bar representing 5, and a symbol that looked like a clamshell representing 0. Figure 3 shows the numbers 1 through 19 as they would be written by the Maya.

Because the Mayan numeration system was a positional system, the position of a symbol indicated its value. In the Mayan system, place value increased vertically from the bottom to the top. The bottom row in a Mayan numeral was the ones row. The next row up was the twenties row. That meant that any numeral in the second row was to be multiplied by 20.

When the Maya wanted to write the number 20, they first wrote their clamshell symbol for zero. Above that they put a single dot, the symbol for 1. The dot occupied the second row or place in the numeral and meant "1 twenty." To write the number 21, one dot was placed in the first row and one dot was placed in the second row.

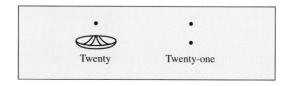

Twenty   Twenty-one

Although the Mayan numeration system was based on the number 20, it was not entirely a base-twenty system. In a base-twenty system, each place value would be 20 times the value of the previous place. The Maya made one exception to this rule. Usually the third place or position had a value of 18 times 20, instead of 20 times 20. It is believed that this exception was made because the system was used most often to count the days in the calendar, and the Mayan year had 18 months with 20 days in each month.

Hindu-Arabic Numerals and the Decimal System

The numerals we ordinarily use—1, 2, 3, 4, 5, 6, 7, 8, 9, 0—are known as **Hindu-Arabic numerals**. They were developed by the Hindus in India in about A.D. 600, and they

Figure 3. Mayan Numerals

1	2	3	4	5	6	7	8	9	10

11	12	13	14	15	16	17	18	19

were introduced to the Western world by the Arabs about 1,300 years ago. Originally there were only nine symbols in the Hindu system, but then a symbol for zero was added. The Hindus also devised a positional numeration system called the **decimal system**.

The decimal system is a positional, or place-value, system based on the number 10. The word "decimal" comes from a Latin word meaning "ten." In the Hindu-Arabic decimal system, the ten symbols, or digits, from 0 through 9 can be combined to write numbers of any size. The value of each digit depends not only on the digit itself but also on its place or position in the number.

In **whole numbers** (zero and all of the numbers we use for counting), the last digit in the number is in what is called the ones place. The place to its left is called the tens place, the next position is called the hundreds place, and the next is called the thousands place. Then going from left to right, each place has a value ten times the value of the one directly to its right.

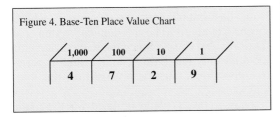

Figure 4. Base-Ten Place Value Chart

1,000	100	10	1
4	7	2	9

In our base-ten system, in the number 4,729, which digit has the greatest value? Which digit has the least value? Look at Figure 4. You can see that the 9 in 4,729 means 9 times 1, or 9 ones. The 2 means 2 times 10, or 20. The 7 means 7 times 100, or 700. The 4 means 4 times 1,000, or 4,000. In this number, the digit 4 has the greatest value because it is in the thousands place. The digit 9 has the least value because it is in the ones place.

The symbol for zero is important in the decimal system. We can see immediately, for example, that the numerals 110 and 101 represent two different numbers. In the numeral 110, the zero indicates that the ones place is empty. In the numeral 101, the zero tells us that the tens place is empty.

The invention of the zero and the invention of the decimal system made it possible to add, subtract, multiply, and divide whole numbers easily without the aid of an abacus. (More information about these computing operations is in the article ARITHMETIC in Volume A.)

▶ **OTHER POSITIONAL SYSTEMS**

The numeration systems discussed here are not the only numeration systems possible. People have developed and used other systems with different number bases. The base number for a system can be 2 or 12 or 16 as well as 10 or 20 or 60. Examining systems with other base numbers can help us understand the base-ten decimal system better.

The Base-Five System

It is thought that the Hindu-Arabic decimal system probably grew out of a counting system based on the ten fingers of both hands. Suppose this system had been based on the number of fingers on one hand. In this base-five system, numbers or objects would be grouped by fives rather than by tens.

WONDER QUESTION

Who invented zero?

The discovery of the need for zero and the invention of a symbol for zero are among the most important mathematical advances of all time. No one knows exactly when or where the idea of zero originated, but about 300 B.C. the Babylonians, who lived in that part of the world now called Iraq, used a zero symbol. The symbol

showed that there was an empty place, or a missing value, within a number. A zero used in this way is called a placeholder.

The people of the ancient Mayan civilization in what is now Central America also had a symbol for a zero used as a placeholder. Their symbol looked like a clamshell or a closed eye:

It was the Hindus of India, however, who were the first to use zero as a number. To the Hindus, zero was a number representing "nothing," and they used zero as the answer to a problem such as 2 minus 2 equals 0. The symbol

is still used today, and it was also invented by the Hindus. It first appears on a tablet dated A.D. 876.

The Hindu zero, along with the Hindu decimal numeration system, made methods of computing efficient and precise.

If there were 13 objects, for example, there would be two groups of five objects and three objects left over:

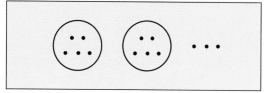

The numeral to express this idea would be written 23_{five}, and we would say its name as "two-three base-five." The 2 in the numeral means 2 times 5, or 2 fives. We can say that 2 is in the fives place. The 3 means 3 times 1, or 3 ones, and we can say that 3 is in the ones place. The small "five" to the right of and just below the 23 is called a **subscript**. It tells us that we are in the base-five system.

The first ten numerals in the base-five numeration system are shown in Figure 5, along with their decimal or base-ten equivalents.

Figure 5. First Ten Base-Five Numerals

Base-Five Numerals	Decimal Numerals
1_{five}	1
2_{five}	2
3_{five}	3
4_{five}	4
10_{five}	5
11_{five}	6
12_{five}	7
13_{five}	8
14_{five}	9
20_{five}	10

How many digits are there in base-five? Just as there are ten digits in our base-ten decimal system, there are five digits in base-five: 0, 1, 2, 3, and 4. Can you tell why? Think about our decimal place-value system. When we reach ten in any place or position, we trade it for one of the next place. For example, when we reach the number ten, we write it as 10, showing 1 ten and no ones. When we reach the fifth number in base-five, we have to write a two-place numeral, 10_{five}, to show 1 five and zero ones.

If you had 24 objects, what base-five numeral would you write? You would write 44_{five}

because in 24, there are 4 groups of five and 4 left over. What would happen if you had 25 objects? The base-five numeral would be written 100_{five}. Why do you need a three-place numeral? Because 25 is 5 times 5, or five groups of five, and five of any place value must be traded for one of the next place. In Figure 6, you can see that 100_{five} means 1 twenty-five, with zero fives and zero ones left over.

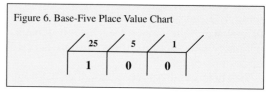

Figure 6. Base-Five Place Value Chart

Although counting systems based on the number 5 have been used by people in the past, the base-five numeration system is not in common use today.

The Duodecimal System

A base-twelve system is called a **duodecimal system**. The word "duodecimal" comes from the Latin word "duodecim," which means "twelve." The duodemical system requires twelve digits. Since the decimal system includes only ten digits, one of which is zero, two new digits must be invented for this system.

The symbol **T** could be used for the tenth digit and the symbol **E** for the eleventh digit. In Figure 7 you will find the first twelve duodecimal numerals as well as their decimal equivalents.

Figure 7. Duodecimal Numerals

Duodecimal Numerals	Decimal Numerals
1_{twelve}	1
2_{twelve}	2
3_{twelve}	3
4_{twelve}	4
5_{twelve}	5
6_{twelve}	6
7_{twelve}	7
8_{twelve}	8
9_{twelve}	9
T_{twelve}	10
E_{twelve}	11
10_{twelve}	12

In the base-twelve system, the value of each position or place is twelve times the value of the place to its right. The first place is the ones place, and the second place is the twelves place. The twelfth numeral, therefore, is a two-place numeral: 10_{twelve}. Can you figure out the value of the third place? It is 12 times 12, or 144. The first three-place numeral would be written: 100_{twelve}.

Some people believe that everyone should learn and use the duodecimal numeration system. They think that division would be easier with a duodecimal system because 12 can be divided by 1, 2, 3, 4, and 6, and 10 can only be divided by 1, 2, and 5. A base-twelve system is used today to count objects by the dozen (12) or by the gross (144).

The Binary System

The base-two numeration system is called the **binary system**. "Binary" is a word based on the Latin word for "two." The binary system has only two digits: 0 and 1. In the binary system, the value of each position or place is two times the value of the place to its right. So the far-right place is the ones place, the position to its left is the twos place, the next position to the left is the fours place, and so on. Can you tell what decimal number is represented by the binary numeral in Figure 8?

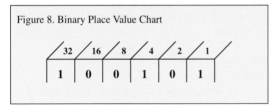

Figure 8. Binary Place Value Chart

To find the number, you compute:

$$(1 \times 32) + (0 \times 16) + (0 \times 8) + (1 \times 4) + (0 \times 2) + (1 \times 1) = 37$$

The six-place binary number 100101 has the same value as the two-place decimal number 37. As you can see, binary numbers quickly become very long. The binary system is not a handy one to use in solving everyday mathematics problems. Just writing the numbers would take a lot of time.

The binary system is, however, a good system for computers to use to transmit information. Computers operate by means of a number of "on-off" switches that control the flow of electricity. The base-two numeral 1 indicates

that a switch is "on" and electricity can pass through. The numeral 0 indicates that a switch is "off." Because computers work very quickly, they have no trouble managing the long binary numbers.

The Hexadecimal System

In the **hexadecimal system**, numbers are grouped by sixteens. The word "hexadecimal" comes from the Greek word for six and the Latin word for ten. Just as the duodecimal system requires two new one-place numerals, the hexadecimal system needs six additional one-place numerals, or digits. These six digits are **A, B, C, D, E,** and **F**. They have the same values as the base-ten numbers 10, 11, 12, 13, 14, and 15.

In the hexadecimal system, the value of each position or place is 16 times the value of the position to its right. The first place on the far right is the ones place, the next position to the left is the sixteens place, and the next position is the two hundred fifty-sixes place. Figure 9 shows that in this system, $24B_{sixteen}$ has the same value as the decimal number 587.

Figure 9. Hexadecimal Numeral

$$2 \quad 4 \quad B_{sixteen}$$

(1×11)	$=$	11
(4×16)	$=$	64
(2×256)	$=$	512
		$\overline{587_{ten}}$

Computers often store information using hexadecimal numbers.

Dr. Carol R. Findell
Associate Professor and Program Coordinator
Mathematics Education, Boston University

See also ABACUS; ARITHMETIC; COMPUTERS; MATHEMATICS, HISTORY OF; NUMBERS AND NUMBER SYSTEMS; ROMAN NUMERALS.

Answers to "Can You Read and Write Egyptian Numerals?"

a) 21,365

b) 2,030

c) 1,000,728

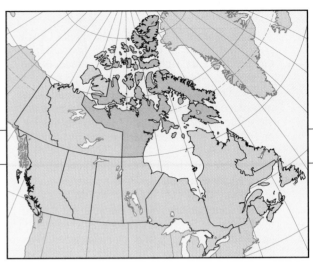

NUNAVUT

Nunavut's flag (above) features an inuksuk, *which symbolizes the stone monuments that guide people on land and mark sacred and other special places. The* Niqirtsuituq, *or North Star, appears in the upper right corner. Both of these elements also appear on the territorial coat of arms (opposite page), where they are joined by other symbolic figures, including the caribou (land), narwhal (sea), igloo (traditional life), and crown (government).*

Nunavut is Canada's largest and newest territory, making up nearly one-fifth of the country's area. Nunavut was created on April 1, 1999, when the Northwest Territories was divided into a western part, still known as the Northwest Territories, and an eastern part, known as the territory of Nunavut. The word *Nunavut* means "our land" in Inuktitut, the language of the Inuit (formerly known as Eskimos).

Nunavut is located in northeastern Canada near the Arctic Ocean. The territory extends over a vast area consisting of more than 770,000 square miles (2 million square kilometers) and includes all the islands in Hudson and James bays. Greenland lies to the east. Manitoba forms the territory's southern border, while the Hudson Strait separates Nunavut from Quebec. Nunavut's neighbor across the North Pole is Russia.

Nearly 60 percent of Nunavut lies north of the Arctic Circle. Because of this, the region has long nights during the winter and long days during the summer. On or about June 21 (summer solstice, the longest day of the year and the beginning of summer), the sun remains above the horizon for 24 hours at the Arctic Circle. It never rises above the horizon on or about December 21 (winter solstice, the shortest day of the year and the beginning of winter).

▶ THE LAND

Nunavut can be divided into two geographic areas: the Arctic mainland and the Arctic Archipelago. The Arctic mainland is part of the Canadian Shield, which is a rocky, hilly area. The Arctic Archipelago is made up of a number of islands in the Arctic Ocean, including Baffin Island, the largest island in Canada and the fifth largest island in the world. Nunavut's northernmost island is Ellesmere Island. Its northern tip is less than 500 miles (800 kilometers) from the North Pole. The Belcher Islands are the southernmost islands in Hudson Bay. Permafrost, or permanently frozen ground, is found throughout the territory.

A dogsledder harnesses a member of his team as he prepares to take his *qamutik*, or wooden sled, out for a run in Iqaluit, Nunavut's capital.

FACTS AND FIGURES

Location: Northern Canada. **Latitude**—83° 07' N to 51° 39' N. **Longitude**—61° 16' W to 120° 40' W.

Organized as Territory: April 1, 1999.

Population: 26,745 (2001 estimate).

Capital and Largest City: Iqaluit, pop. 5,236 (2001 estimate).

Physical Features: Area—808,185 sq mi (2,093,190 km²). **Rivers**—Back, Coppermine, Thelon, Kazan, Dubawnt. **Lakes**—Baker, Hazen, Nettiling, Amadjuak, Nueltin, Yathkyed. **Islands**—Baffin, Ellesmere, Devon, Southampton. **Highest point**—8,584 ft (2,616 m), Barbeau Peak.

Industries and Products: Mining; fishing; tourism; arts and crafts.

Government: Partially self-governing territory. **Head of government**—shared between the leader elected by the territorial council and the commissioner appointed by the federal government. **Territorial representation in federal parliament**—1 elected member of the House of Commons. **Voting age for territorial elections**—18.

Climate

Nunavut has an arctic climate. Winter lasts for at least 10 months. In mid-winter, temperatures often drop to –8°F (–22°C). The coldest temperature ever recorded at Alert, Canada's northernmost center in the Arctic, was –58°F (–50°C). Winter weather is characterized by clear skies, although storms do occur. Arctic blizzards, which can arise suddenly, are fierce snowstorms with intensely cold and strong winds.

During the short summer, few days have temperatures above 70°F (20°C), and freezing temperatures can occur any time. In July and August, the temperature is usually below 50°F (10°C).

Nunavut lies above the tree line, a region known as the tundra. Tundra vegetation consists of dwarf shrubs, sedges, heath, and lichens. The vegetation is a food source for such animals as caribou, musk ox, lemming, arctic ground squirrel, and arctic hare.

▶ THE PEOPLE AND THEIR WORK

Nunavut is the native homeland of the Inuit, who make up nearly 85 percent of the total population. In 2001, its population was almost 27,000, making Nunavut the least populated

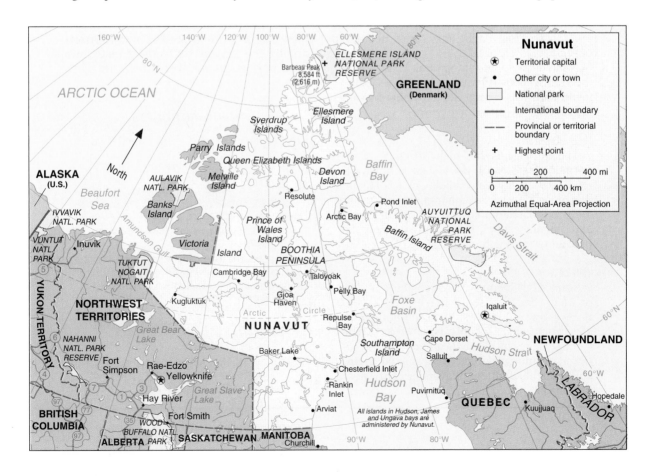

territory in Canada. The remaining 15 percent includes descendants of other native groups, Europeans, and métis (people of mixed Indian and European ancestry).

Industries and Products

Although about 85 percent of the people are employed by the federal, territorial, and local governments, unemployment is a serious problem. Nunavut has few resources. Without fertile land and forests, the territory's natural wealth lies in its minerals, petroleum deposits, and wildlife. Minerals are found in the Canadian Shield, and oil and gas deposits exist in the Arctic Islands. However, since the cost of developing and marketing these resources is so high, most of these have not been developed. Two lead and zinc mines have been opened, one at Nansivik on the northern tip of Baffin Island and the other at Polaris on Little Cornwallis Island.

Hunting for caribou and seal is a traditional aspect of the Inuit culture that provides fresh meat for Inuit families and a modest income from seal pelts. The fur industry is based on seal, white fox, and polar bears. Fishing is also important to Nunavut's economy. Most commercial fishing takes place at the mouths of the main rivers flowing into the Arctic Ocean and Hudson Bay. Arctic char is the most important commercial fish.

Nunavut abounds in natural beauty, and the tourist industry, while still small, is growing. Inuit artists receive some income by selling carvings and other native art.

Transportation

The airplane is the main form of transportation, since no highways or railways extend from southern Canada into Nunavut. Air service reaches all communities as well as the two isolated mining sites. Ships bring food and building supplies to approximately 80 percent of the communities.

▶ EDUCATION

Some 42 elementary and secondary schools provide education for Nunavut's 8,000 students. However, many students do not graduate from high school. Nunavut's Arctic College offers further educational opportunities. Government grants are available to enable students to attend universities elsewhere in Canada.

▶ PLACES OF INTEREST

Nunavut's main museum, the Nunatta Sunaqutangit, is in Iqaluit. It features Inuit prints and sculptures. Other museums are located in Arctic Bay and Pangnirtung. The Kekerten Historic Park, south of Pangnirtung, features a reconstructed whaling station from the 1800's. Other towns have local museums and visitor centers with historic and artistic displays. The territory also has two national parks and reserves—Auyuittuq (meaning "the land that never melts") and Ellesmere Island.

▶ CITIES

Most of Nunavut's inhabitants live in settlements (very small villages). Iqaluit, the capital, is the largest city, with a population of about 5,300. Iqaluit is located on the southern part of Baffin Island. Rankin Inlet, the second largest settlement, has a population of about 2,200.

▶ GOVERNMENT

Nunavut elected 19 members to the Legislative Assembly in February 1999. The following month, the new assembly chose Paul Okalik as the first premier of Nunavut. The territory has no political parties. As a territorial government, Nunavut has powers assigned to it by the federal government in Ottawa. These powers extend over health care, hous-

---

IMPORTANT DATES

1576	English navigator Martin Frobisher explored Baffin Island.
1880	Britain transferred the Arctic islands to Canada.
1926	The Arctic Islands Game Preserve was established.
1939	During World War II (1939–45), the United States built a military base at Frobisher Bay.
1976	The idea of Nunavut was proposed to the Canadian government.
1982	Over half of the Northwest Territories' residents voted in favor of dividing the Northwest Territories.
1992	Residents of the Northwest Territories approved a plan to create an Inuit-controlled territory.
1993	The Nunavut Act and the Nunavut Land Claims Agreement Act were passed by Parliament.
1995	In a plebiscite, Iqaluit was chosen to be Nunavut's capital.
1999	The territory of Nunavut was established.

ing, renewable resources, and social services. Nunavut residents elect one member to the Canadian House of Commons to represent their interests in Ottawa.

Nunavut is divided into three administrative regions: Qikiqtaaluk (formerly known as Baffin), Kivalliq (formerly Keewatin), and Kitikmeot.

Each year, the government of Nunavut receives a large grant from the federal government. With this financial support, Nunavut is able to operate its government and provide basic services to its residents.

▶ HISTORY

Native peoples first came to Nunavut from Alaska's Arctic coast some 5,000 years ago. These early hunters were searching for seal and other marine life. The Thule peoples arrived about 1,000 years ago. The present-day Inuit are descendants of the Thule. About A.D. 1000 the Vikings explored the coast of North America and probably made contact with the Thule.

In 1576, Sir Martin Frobisher, an English navigator who searched for the Northwest Passage, was the first European to set foot in the area that is now Nunavut. Many explorers arrived after Frobisher, including John Davis and Henry Hudson. Samuel Hearne, who worked for the Hudson's Bay Company, made a long overland trek to the Arctic Ocean from the Prince of Wales Fort, a fur-trading post at the mouth of the Churchill River on Hudson Bay. He was searching for the source of copper reported by Indians trading at the fort. In 1770, Hearne began a journey with a group of natives, the Chipewyan, whose chief, Matonabbee, knew the route to the copper deposits. When they had reached the shores of the Arctic Ocean, they found no great deposits. Hearne and the Chipewyan returned to the mouth of Churchill River in 1772.

In 1845, Sir John Franklin, who had explored the Arctic coast twice before, began a search for the Northwest Passage. After entering the Arctic Ocean, Franklin's ships were locked into heavy ice, and he and his men perished. During the search for Franklin, the British admiralty mapped most of the islands in the Arctic Archipelago. In a voyage that took three years (1903–06), Roald Amundsen became the first person to sail through the Northwest Passage.

On April 1, 1999, Inuit children joined in a celebration to welcome Nunavut into the Canadian confederation of provinces and territories.

For more information, see the article NORTHWEST PASSAGE in this volume.

Recent Events

The quest for a separate homeland for the Inuit began in the 1970's. The Tungavik Federation of Nunavut, representing the interests of the Inuit, successfully negotiated with the Canadian government for the right to govern themselves. This included the right to determine their own school systems, economic policies, and land rights. In 1993, the Canadian Parliament passed the Nunavut Land Claims Agreement Act and the Nunavut Act. The Nunavut Act established a separate territory for the Inuit. A transition period from 1992 to 1999 was designed to help the Inuit prepare for Nunavut's new government and to train Nunavut's residents for job opportunities created by the new government.

The Nunavut Land Claims Agreement Act of 1993 represents the largest land claims settlement in Canada. Under this agreement, the Inuit surrendered their claim to lands and waters in Nunavut in exchange for a number of benefits, including a cash settlement, a trust fund to prepare the Inuit for new government jobs, title to selected lands, and mineral rights.

In February 1999, more than 10,000 people, representing 88 percent of those eligible to vote, elected the 19 members of Nunavut's first legislative assembly. The assembly met the following month to select a premier, a cabinet, and a deputy of the assembly. On April 1, 1999, the new government officially began its first session.

R. M. BONE
University of Saskatchewan

NURSERY RHYMES

All over the world children delight in hearing and reciting nursery rhymes (often called Mother Goose rhymes). Each year new editions of nursery rhymes are published. Several reasons can be given for their great popularity. First, the subjects of the rhymes are extremely varied. Bad boys, crooked men, old women, birds, dogs, cats, frogs, kings, and queens all appear in nursery rhymes. Many rhymes tell a good story, full of action and

JACK AND JILL

Jack and Jill
Went up the hill,
To fetch a pail of water;
Jack fell down,
And broke his crown,
And Jill came tumbling after.

fun. The wildly exaggerated humor appeals to children. The rhymes also have a definite rhythm that children love. Sometimes a refrain is repeated, and sometimes combinations of sounds make lovely poetry. Rhymes may be funny, sad, serious, or silly. In short, there is a jingle for every taste and mood.

Nursery rhymes have been passed from one generation to another. Hardly a child grows up without learning by heart "Hey Diddle, Diddle," "Pat-a-cake, Pat-a-cake," or "Jack and Jill." Even before they really understand what the words mean, children are amused by "This Little Pig Went to Market" or lulled to sleep by "Rock-a-bye, Baby."

The name "Mother Goose" first appeared on the frontispiece of Charles Perrault's collection of fairy tales *Contes de ma Mère l'Oye* ("Tales of My Mother Goose") in 1697, but it is possible that the name had been known for

THE OLD WOMAN IN A SHOE

There was an old woman who lived in a shoe,
She had so many children she didn't know what to do;
She gave them some broth without any bread;
She whipped them all soundly and put them to bed.

a long time. In French villages, older women were probably given the task of keeping the geese. Since these women were also the village storytellers, they might have been called *ma mère l'oye*. Some believe the original Mother Goose was the mother of the French emperor Charlemagne (742–814). This woman, who was called Goose-Footed Bertha, was famous for the tales she told her children.

In Boston's Old Granary Burying Ground, a tombstone marks a grave that is said to be Mother Goose's. A woman named Mistress Goose (Vergoose or Vertigoose) lived in Boston, Massachusetts, toward the end of the 1600's. She was the mother-in-law of Thomas Fleet, a Boston printer. Fleet is reported to have published in 1719 a book called *Songs for the Nursery; or Mother Goose's Melodies for Children*. It was a collection of the

HEY DIDDLE, DIDDLE

Hey diddle, diddle,
The cat and the fiddle,
The cow jumped over the moon;
The little dog laughed
To see such sport,
And the dish ran away with the spoon.

MISS MUFFET

Little Miss Muffet
Sat on a tuffet,
Eating her curds and whey;
There came a big spider,
Who sat down beside her
And frightened Miss Muffet away.

rhymes his mother-in-law sang to her grandchildren. No copy of the Fleet volume has ever been discovered, however, so scholars do not accept the story as true.

John Newbery of London prepared a collection of nursery rhymes before he died in 1767. It was published in 1781 under the title of *Mother Goose's Melody: or, Sonnets for the Cradle*. In 1785 Isaiah Thomas of Massachusetts published a reprint of the Newbery edition for American children. These two books contain the first written versions, but we know that many of the rhymes are really much older.

Most nursery rhymes were never intended for the nursery. During the 1500's in England, adults sang ballads, rounds (songs in which people sing the identical words but begin at different times), and other types of folk songs. Mothers sang the songs to their infants, and so the songs were brought into the nursery. The people of Elizabethan England also liked to tell riddles. Many of these riddles became part of the literature of the nursery. Other rhymes referred to political events and were recited or sung in taverns and marketplaces. Children hearing them would seize upon a catchy refrain or appealing phrase and make the musical rhymes their own.

Probably the only nursery rhymes meant especially for children are the rhymes that mothers sang to their children at bedtime,

HUMPTY DUMPTY

Humpty Dumpty sat on a wall,
Humpty Dumpty had a great fall;
All the King's horses and all the King's men
Couldn't put Humpty together again.

the rhymes that taught the children how to count or say the alphabet, and the rhymes that accompanied the games mothers and children played together.

Children in every country have nursery rhymes. The jingles often reflect the history or customs of the people. English rhymes refer repeatedly to London, Wales, Queen Anne, King George, and many other places and people familiar to English children. American nursery-rhyme collections include the well-known "Yankee Doodle," which appeared during the American Revolution (1775–83), and "Mary's Lamb," supposedly based on a true incident.

Reviewed by EFFIE LEE MORRIS
San Francisco Public Library

See also CHILDREN'S LITERATURE; NONSENSE RHYMES.

MARY'S LAMB

Mary had a little lamb,
Its fleece was white as snow;
And everywhere that Mary went
The lamb was sure to go.
It followed her to school one day,
That was against the rule;
It made the children laugh and play
To see a lamb at school.

NURSES AND NURSING

Nurses are health-care professionals dedicated to caring for those who are sick or injured. They also work to prevent illness and educate people on good health practices. Nurses make up the largest number of health-care professionals in the United States, working as members of health-care teams that provide services in many different settings. Although most nurses are women, the number of male nurses is growing. The word "nurse" comes from the Latin word meaning "to nourish," and concern for the well-being of others is at the core of the profession.

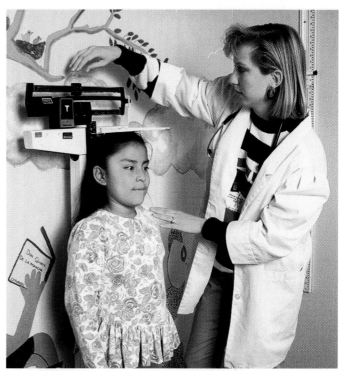

A nurse weighs and measures a girl during an annual physical. Nurses care for the sick or injured and also help healthy people stay well.

▶ **TYPES OF NURSES**

The three main categories of nurses are registered nurses, advanced practice nurses, and licensed practical (vocational) nurses. Within each of these categories are nurses who specialize in specific types of care.

Most **registered nurses** (RN's) work directly with patients. They typically evaluate and record a patient's symptoms, reactions, and progress; work with other caregivers during patient examinations, treatments, and surgery; and administer medication. They also assist in patient recovery and rehabilitation and educate patients on their health needs and self care.

Advanced practice registered nurses (APRN's) are registered nurses who have completed specialized education and received a master's degree in nursing. The scope of their practice is governed by state laws; some states allow them to work more independently than others. APRN's include nurse practitioners, clinical nurse specialists, certified nurse midwives, and certified registered nurse anesthetists.

Most advanced practice nurses are **nurse practitioners** (NP's). NP's diagnose and treat common and chronic illnesses, providing a level of care previously provided only by physicians. They perform physical examinations, order laboratory tests, and prescribe medications and treatments for illnesses and injuries. They specialize in areas of practice such as pediatrics (care of children) or geriatrics (care of the elderly). In most states, NP's must work closely with physicians and follow protocols (sets of rules) that guide their practice.

Clinical nurse specialists (CNS's) have in-depth knowledge and skills in a specific area of expertise and care for patients who require a more specialized approach. Because of their clinical expertise, many CNS's are employed by hospitals as nurse educators and nurse experts. They can also practice independently, such as in psychotherapy. They assist other nurses, keep their skills current, solve complex patient care problems, and provide patient education.

Certified nurse midwives (CNM's) care for women throughout their pregnancies (unless there are special circumstances), deliver babies, and provide care to mothers and newborns after birth. Demand for the services of CNM's has increased in recent years. CNM's work in hospitals, clinics, their own offices, doctors' offices, and birthing centers and may even deliver babies in patients' homes.

Certified registered nurse anesthetists (CRNA's) administer anesthesia and monitor patients during surgery. They may practice independently or with anesthesiologists (physicians who specialize in anesthesia).

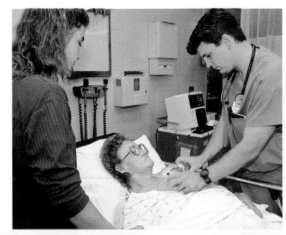

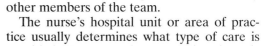

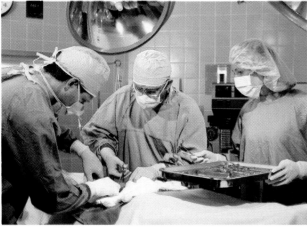

may determine that the patient needs care by other members of the team.

The nurse's hospital unit or area of practice usually determines what type of care is provided. For example, nurses in obstetric units help deliver babies. Operating-room nurses prepare patients for surgery and assist the surgical team during the operation. After surgery, they monitor patients' vital signs and administer post-operative treatments.

Many RN's, LPN's, and nursing assistants work in long-term-care facilities such as nursing homes. They care for people with long-term disabilities, chronic illness, or memory loss. Long-term-care patients are often elderly; geriatric nursing has become more important as the number of older people in the population has increased.

Home-health-care nurses, assistants, and aides provide care in patients' homes. They may be employed by visiting nurse associations, county health departments, or private agencies. These nurses may also care for people with long-term disabilities, chronic illness, or memory loss, as well as those who need shorter-term care after hospitalization. This type of nursing has become more important because people no longer stay in hospitals as long as they once did.

Nurses also work in schools. They provide first aid, conduct vision and hearing tests, administer medications, and teach classes in hy-

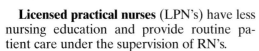

Licensed practical nurses (LPN's) have less nursing education and provide routine patient care under the supervision of RN's.

Nursing assistants (NA's) are not nurses, but nurses' aides. They are trained to provide basic care such as feeding and bathing under the supervision of RN's and LPN's.

▶ **WHERE NURSES WORK**

Nurses work in many different settings, from hospitals and nursing homes to schools and factories.

Most nurses work in hospitals as part of a health-care team that includes physicians, administrators, dietitians, social workers, physical therapists, pharmacists, and many others. Nurses in this setting help patients who need emergency care and those who are acutely (severely or suddenly) ill. They are usually responsible for providing nursing care and carrying out medical directives prescribed by doctors. They identify the patient's symptoms and may take independent action, or they

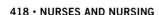

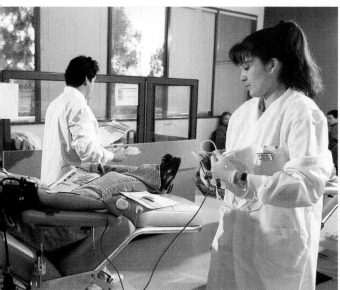

prevent the spread of disease. Many public health nurses also provide direct patient care, particularly for patients with special needs. They may teach diabetics to give themselves insulin injections, for example, or advise the elderly about diet and nutrition.

Some nurses work in the military, caring for active and retired service people and their families. In the U.S. Army, Navy, and Air Force, registered nurses may enter as commissioned officers. A number of military nurses have achieved high rank, even becoming admirals and generals. Nurses also serve in foreign countries with organizations such as the Peace Corps, the World Health Organization, and the International Red Cross. Many nurses are engaged in international missionary work.

Nurses work in many different settings and often specialize in specific types of care. *Clockwise from bottom left:* An operating room nurse assists surgeons. A geriatric nurse examines an elderly woman in a nursing home. A visiting nurse checks a patient's blood pressure during a home visit. Public health nurses monitor blood donors. Nurses working overseas immunize children and adults.

Nurses who are not involved in direct patient care may use their knowledge and skills in other ways. For example, nurse attorneys—registered nurses who have earned a law degree and passed the bar examination—often practice as staff attorneys in hospitals and other health-related agencies, join medical malpractice law practices, or practice law independently. Nurse attorneys may also help develop public health policy at the state and national level.

Some nurses teach in colleges and universities at the undergraduate and graduate level, in hospital schools, and in programs that train licensed practical nurses. Nurse educators must meet the same requirements as other faculty in the college or university, and a doctorate in nursing is often required.

giene and health. They also help evaluate children who may have physical or emotional problems that require extra medical care. The school nurse may be a public health nurse on the staff of a local agency or a nurse employed by the school system.

Occupational health nurses work in factories, large companies, department stores, and other work sites. They treat workers who are injured on the job and provide follow-up care. Occupational health nurses also teach workers about health-care practices and how to prevent accidents, injuries, and illness. They conduct safety and environmental surveys and routine physical examinations.

Public health nurses are concerned with the health of populations as well as of individuals. They may develop and carry out programs for entire cities or regions, including areas that are underserved. The goal of these programs is to promote good health and help

Other nurses become managers and administrators, directing nursing services in hospitals, clinics, nursing homes, home health agencies, public health departments, and health centers. They also serve as deans, directors, and department heads in nurse-education programs.

▶ **HISTORY OF NURSING**

People have nursed the sick and injured since ancient times. Often, this was consid-

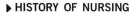

ered part of a woman's domestic duties, although men have served as nurses too.

In Europe, and later in North America, Christianity influenced the growth of nursing. From the early days of the Christian religion, there was a close connection between nursing and the church. The first church workers concerned with nursing were called deaconesses. They were unmarried women or widows who visited and cared for the sick and comforted families in mourning.

Many hospitals were started by the church, and nursing was done by men and women in religious orders. During the Crusades of the Middle Ages, nursing orders of monks and knights tended the sick and wounded. But in the 1500's, many monasteries in Europe, especially in England, were closed. A dark period in nursing began. Hospitals were often staffed by uneducated women who were ill-fed and overworked.

The upturn in nursing began in 1633, when St. Vincent de Paul founded the secular (nonreligious) nursing order of the Daughters of Charity in Paris. The members spread to many parts of the world.

In the mid-1800's, Florence Nightingale, an English nurse, began her pioneering work in health care, which emphasized training for nurses and better patient care based on her research. Hailed as a heroine for her care of English soldiers during the Crimean War (1853–56), she inspired women around the world to become nurses. This was particularly true in the United States during the Civil War (1861–65), when nurses were urgently needed to care for sick and wounded soldiers. In 1860, Nightingale established the first school of nursing at St. Thomas's Hospital in London. Graduates of this school helped in the development of nursing and health care in many other countries. Schools based on the Nightingale model were started in the United States and Canada in the early 1870's. (For more information, see the biography of Florence Nightingale in this volume.)

In the late 1800's and early 1900's, the demand for nurses was fueled by the growth of industry. During this time, many people moved from farms to cities to work at factories and mills. Workplace injuries and illness from unsafe working conditions increased significantly, as did health problems caused by living in unclean, overcrowded cities. Many workers had also moved away from their families, which had traditionally provided care. As a result, unpaid nursing was replaced by women who were paid to care for the sick, usually in hospitals. Despite Nightingale's influence, many of these nurses re-

Top: Florence Nightingale, an Englishwoman, was the founder of modern nursing.

Left: From the early days of Christianity, a close connection existed between nursing and the church. The church started many hospitals, and nursing was often done by men and women in religious orders.

ceived only minimal training and worked under extremely difficult conditions.

Over the next several decades, the number of hospitals and nursing schools grew, and standards of nursing care became stricter. Hospitals, which had often hired nursing students, began hiring only nursing school graduates. During World War II (1939–45), an increased need for educated nurses led to the creation of the Cadet Nurse Corps, which granted free tuition, books, and uniforms, plus an allowance, to students in participating schools. As a result, thousands of young women were recruited into nursing.

After World War II, medical care became more specialized, as did nursing. By the end of the 1900's, the field had changed considerably. Due to rising health-care costs, nurses were providing more of the care previously provided by doctors, but at less expense. They also cared for people in a wider range of settings (rather than just in hospitals) to further reduce health-care costs. These included patients' homes, outpatient facilities (which treat and discharge patients the same day), nursing homes and assisted living facilities, and community health centers and clinics. In addition, it became increasingly necessary to update knowledge and skills, in response to the rapid expansion of information and medical technology in the health-care field.

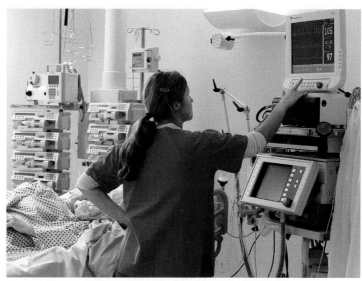

An intensive care nurse checks a patient's monitors. Due to the rapid advances in medical technology, nurses must continually update their knowledge and skills.

▶ CAREERS IN NURSING

The growing demand for nurses makes nursing one of the most sought-after health-care careers. According to the U.S. Bureau of Labor Statistics, more new jobs are expected to be created for registered nurses over the next several years than for any other occupation. The greatest need is for nurses with bachelor of science nursing degrees who can provide care in a variety of settings, such as hospitals, schools, clinics, and nursing homes. There is also a need for nurses who specialize in specific areas such as neonatal (newborn) care, obstetrics, emergency medicine, geriatrics, mental health, and surgery.

Students interested in nursing should discuss nursing education programs with their parents, school guidance counselors, and nurses they may know. They should read about nursing careers as much as possible. High school students can learn about nursing by volunteering in hospitals or joining organizations that expose them to careers in the health-care field, such as the American Red Cross.

In the United States, students must graduate from an approved nursing program and pass a licensing examination to get a nursing license. The purpose of this is to protect the public by making sure the nurse has met minimum standards of knowledge and of safe practice.

Three types of programs prepare students to become RN's in the United States. They are bachelor of science degree programs, associate degree programs, and diploma programs. Graduation from high school is required for all three. The program should be accredited by the National League for Nursing (NLN) or the American Association of Colleges of Nursing (AACN).

Students who receive bachelor of science degrees usually major in nursing. This degree is called a BSN. BSN's are offered in senior colleges and universities and take four academic years. The curriculum combines nursing education with general education in the liberal arts and sciences. Graduates may enter master's degree programs to prepare for more advanced positions.

Associate degree programs are two-year programs offered by junior or community colleges. Students take both liberal arts and technical courses and receive faculty-supervised experience in hospitals.

Diploma programs, which are becoming less common, are usually offered by hospitals or other health institutions. The course of study takes two or three years and includes study of the sciences and the theory and practice of nursing.

Graduates of diploma and associate degree programs who decide they want advanced study are eligible to apply to programs that offer bachelor's or master's degrees in nursing.

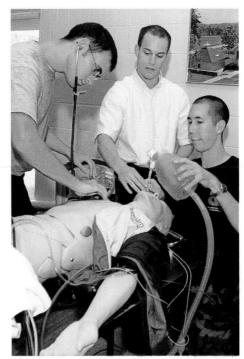

Nursing students practice medical procedures on a dummy. The demand for nurses makes nursing one of the most sought-after health-care careers.

Most advanced practice nursing specialties require a master's degree in the specialty area. Some programs prepare nurses to be clinical specialists in certain areas, such as mental health, geriatrics, pediatrics, or obstetrics. Other programs prepare nurses for careers in teaching or administration. Nurse scientists and researchers, deans of college and university programs, and faculty members in graduate schools usually must have doctoral degrees.

All nurses must keep their skills up to date. Continuing education programs are usually available through nurses' associations, hospitals, and colleges.

The licensed practical nurse program is usually offered by vocational schools in the public education system, in junior or community colleges, or in hospitals. The program usually takes a year to complete, but may vary from 9 to 18 months.

Nursing assistants were originally trained on the job to relieve nurses of some of the simpler but necessary tasks of patient care. However, nursing assistant programs are now offered by various agencies and community colleges.

▶ **NURSING ORGANIZATIONS**

In many countries, professional nurses join together to form nursing associations. The national nurses' associations of many countries make up the International Council of Nurses (ICN), which is headquartered in Geneva, Switzerland. The ICN works with nurses and their countries to improve nursing education and service.

In the United States, the American Nurses' Association (ANA) is the professional association of registered nurses. The National League for Nursing (NLN) is an organization of several groups concerned with nursing. It includes nurses, health-care professionals, health agencies, schools, and citizens interested in nursing. The NLN works to improve the quality of nursing education and service. It is also one of two accrediting associations for all schools of nursing in the United States. (Accreditation ensures that specific standards have been met by the program.) The second accrediting organization is the American Association of Colleges of Nursing (AACN) Commission on Collegiate Nursing Education (CCNE). It accredits baccalaureate and graduate nursing programs.

In addition to these, there are many national organizations for nurses in specialized fields, such as surgery, emergency medicine, and occupational health.

Practical nursing has several organizations. The NLN has a Council of Practical Nursing Programs. There are also the National Federation of Licensed Practical Nurses and the National Association for Practical Nurse Education and Service.

PATRICIA ROWELL, PH.D., R.N.
PAMELA C. HAGAN, M.S., R.N.
American Nurses' Association

See also HOSPITALS.

NUTRITION

Eating is one of life's pleasures, but it is also a necessity. Human beings, like all living things, depend on food for the energy that powers all of the body's functions. Nutrition is the science that deals with how the body uses food to function normally and to nourish life.

▶ THE ESSENTIAL NUTRIENTS

Though food contains many different chemicals, there are certain essential elements called **nutrients** that we must obtain from food to function normally. Our bodies use these nutrients for energy and growth and to repair damaged tissues.

There are six main groups of nutrients that are vital to the health of the human body: **proteins**, **carbohydrates**, **fats**, **vitamins**, **minerals**, and **water**. While all the essential nutrients help cells function normally, proteins, carbohydrates, and fats are the nutrients that supply the body with energy, which is measured in **kilocalories** (a unit of 1,000 **calories**). One calorie equals the amount of heat energy required to raise the temperature of 1 gram of water by 1 degree Celsius (1.8 degrees Fahrenheit). Although food energy is technically described in kilocalories, it is most often expressed simply as "calories."

Proteins

Proteins are made from long chains of chemical substances known as **amino acids**. There are 22 different amino acids, all of which contain carbon, oxygen, hydrogen, and nitrogen. From these amino acids, the body can make countless different proteins. The body can make 13 of the amino acids on its own; the other 9 amino acids must be obtained from the food we eat. These are called **essential amino acids**.

Just as carbohydrates and fats can be used as a source of energy, so can protein. Each gram of protein provides 4 units of energy, or calories. However, the body needs protein for several more important reasons. Proteins are very important for the growth and repair of all body tissue. The need for protein is greater at certain stages of life, such as during adolescence when a person is growing, or when a person is recovering from an illness or accident. Proteins are

By making good eating choices, we are more likely to achieve proper growth and development and to maintain good health throughout our lives.

needed to make numerous body tissues and substances, including bones, skin, organs, enzymes, antibodies, and hormones.

Human beings are able to get the protein they need from animal or plant sources. Foods from animal sources, such as meat, fish, poultry, cheese, milk, and eggs, contain all the essential amino acids and so are considered **complete proteins**. Because these foods contain such large amounts of protein, people who eat animal products daily are more likely to eat too much protein rather than not enough.

Plant foods do not contain all the essential amino acids, so they are considered **incomplete proteins**. **Vegetarians**, people who eat plant foods rather than foods from animal sources, can still obtain adequate protein from the foods they eat. In a vegetarian diet, foods with incomplete proteins are combined in such a way that all the amino acids are obtained. For example, both black beans and rice are missing different essential amino acids. Alone, each one would be an incomplete protein source, but they form a complete protein when they are combined.

MYTHS AND FACTS

Myth: Bodybuilders should take amino acid supplements in order to obtain adequate protein.

Fact: Though weight training increases the body's need for protein due to the building of lean muscle, an athlete can easily obtain adequate protein from food sources.

SEEKING NUTRITIONAL NEWS AND ADVICE

More and more people are aware of the part that diet plays in promoting well-being and preventing disease. They search for nutritional information using a variety of sources. Many times the information is confusing or contradictory, but there are several reliable sources that can help you make healthful choices.

One of the best sources of nutritional advice is a registered dietitian or a nutritionist. A registered dietitian (who may also be called a certified or licensed dietitian) has completed a bachelor's degree in nutrition from an accredited college, gained practical experience as an intern, and passed a national exam prepared by the American Dietetic Association (ADA). While anyone can call themselves a nutritionist, a qualified nutritionist should have at least a bachelor's degree in nutrition. Though many dietitians and nutritionists work for hospitals, convalescent homes, and other institutions and agencies, a growing number of these practitioners are in private practice, where they see clients individually or in groups.

The expert advice of a dietitian or nutritionist can also be found in other settings, even your own home. Qualified experts write articles for newspapers and popular magazines on a variety of topics. Some television stations have weekly programs on nutrition that are hosted by registered dietitians.

In addition to dietitians and nutritionists, other reliable sources of nutritional information include hot-lines and newsletters published by universities or institutions, such as clinics. The ADA has a consumer hot-line that you can call regarding questions on nutrition. Nutritional newletters, such as the *Tufts University Diet & Nutrition Letter* and the *University of California at Berkeley Wellness Letter*, are also authoritative sources of information.

Carbohydrates

Carbohydrates are chemical compounds made up of carbon, oxygen, and hydrogen. There are two basic forms of carbohydrates: simple and complex. Sugars, such as glucose and fructose, are simple carbohydrates. Starches (in plants) and glycogens (in humans and other animals), which are formed from long chains of sugar particles, are complex carbohydrates. Because there is a great deal of starch in plants and very little glycogen in animals, plant starch is the complex carbohydrate that is referred to as a nutrient.

Most of the energy we need for our daily activites is obtained from this nutrient group, which provides 4 calories per gram of carbohydrate. Simple carbohydrates are broken down, or digested, quickly and are used by the body for immediate energy. Sugars are found in a variety of foods, including milk and milk products, fruits, table sugar, honey, syrups, jams, and jellies.

While sugars are a ready supply of energy, starches must be broken down into sugars before the body can use them for energy. Starches are found in bread, cereals, potatoes, pasta, rice, and other grains such as bulgur and cous cous. These complex carbohydrate foods provide a steady supply of energy.

MYTHS AND FACTS

Myth: A vegetarian diet is always healthier than a meat-based diet.

Fact: If not well planned, a vegetarian diet can contain protein sources that are high in saturated fat and cholesterol, such as cheese and eggs. Care must be taken to include legumes, tofu and other soy products, low-fat cheese, as well as eggs in moderation. With inadequate knowledge of vegetarian nutrition, an individual's diet may fall short in protein, calcium, iron, and vitamin B_{12}.

Fats

There are three kinds of fat: **saturated fats**, **monounsaturated fats**, and **polyunsaturated fats**. Like carbohydrates, fats are made up of carbon, oxygen, and hydrogen. They are also like carbohydrates in that they are an energy source. In fact, fats are the body's most concentrated sources of energy. They deliver approximately 9 calories—more than twice as many calories as proteins or carbohydrates.

In addition to being an energy source, fats circulate or store the vitamins A, D, E, and K. Fats are also a source of fatty acids that the body cannot produce. These essential fatty acids are necessary for the building of cell membranes. Fats also enhance the aroma of food, and since they take longer to digest than proteins and carbohydrates, foods with fats satisfy the feeling of hunger longer. Oils, butter, margarine, cheeses, whole milk, cream, meats, fish, poultry, nuts, and seeds all contain fats.

Vitamins

Vitamins are nutrients that do not provide energy but are essential in helping cells function normally. They are found naturally in most foods and may also be added to processed foods. There are two general types of vitamins: fat-soluble vitamins and water-soluble vitamins. The **fat-soluble vitamins**, which are dissolved and stored in fats, are A, D, E, and K. The **water-soluble vitamins**, which are dissolved and stored in water, are vitamin C and a group of eight others called the B-complex vitamins.

Each of the 13 vitamins has several important functions. For example, vitamin C fights infections, maintains collagen (the protein in connective tissue), aids in absorption of the mineral iron, and prevents cell damage. Other vitamins help the body release energy from food; maintain the health of the eyes, skin, bones, and nervous system; and help produce substances such as hormones and enzymes.

The human body uses very small amounts of vitamins every day. Yet there are differences in the requirements of individuals. Some individuals, such as pregnant women or strict vegetarians, need to take supplemental vitamins and minerals. Before taking supplements on your own, seek guidance from a registered dietitian or your physician to determine if your diet is lacking in certain nutrients. (For more information about these nutrients and minerals, you can read the article VITAMINS AND MINERALS in Volume U-V.)

Consumers need to carefully examine claims promoting a supplement as having "magical" properties that will cure a variety of conditions and ills.

Minerals

Minerals are naturally occurring substances that are found in water and soil and are taken in by plants as they grow. We obtain minerals when we eat plants or plant-eating animals.

There are 21 minerals that our bodies need daily for optimum health. Minerals are divided into two groups: major minerals and trace minerals. The 7 **major minerals** are present in the body in amounts of approximately a teaspoon, while the 14 **trace minerals** are present in smaller amounts. Both groups are equally important, since each mineral has a vital role in maintaining health.

Minerals perform a variety of functions. They are important in regulating chemical reactions and building and maintaining bones, teeth, hemoglobin in red blood cells, and cell fluids. They perform their tasks independently or as part of a team. Some, such as calcium, perform tasks in both ways. Calcium acts independently to aid blood clotting. With phosphorus, magnesium, and fluoride, calcium is vital for maintaining the health of bones and teeth.

The death of singer Karen Carpenter, from the effects of anorexia nervosa, attests to the dangerous, and sometimes fatal, results that can occur when an individual suffers from an eating disorder.

Water

Unlike some of the other nutrients, water does not supply the body with energy. Nevertheless, it has several important functions that make it, perhaps, the most important nutrient of all. Water provides the environment for all of the body's chemical processes to take place. As a component of blood, it transports nutrients to all the cells of the body and carries waste away from them. This tasteless liquid is crucial for cooling the body. It also carries waste out of the body as urine.

The human body needs about 2 1/2 quarts (2.5 liters) of water a day to function. An individual can live without other nutrients for up to several weeks but would not survive for much longer than a week without water. Luckily, water is readily available. Along with the water we drink, we also get water from beverages and fruits and vegetables. Other solid foods also contain water, but in much smaller quantities than in fruits and vegetables.

▶ CHOOSING A HEALTHY DIET

A healthy way of eating is important for well-being. Food nourishes our bodies as well as our senses and emotions. It is an important part of life's celebrations. Most families have holiday traditions, religious or cultural, that include food. Our families and societies supply us with our knowledge about food. It is also what determines our relationship with

Americans have a great variety of foods from which to choose to obtain the best balance of nutrients for the body's needs.

food and, subsequently, our eating choices.

In food-centered societies, food is used to entertain, celebrate, and show appreciation. It is also used as a reward and for comfort. Yet many societies also value thinness, especially in females. These mixed messages not only can make it difficult to make healthy choices about food but can play a part in eating disorders, such as anorexia nervosa (a disorder in which an individual, fueled by the fear of becoming obese, refuses to eat).

Another consideration in making food choices is the understanding of our nutritional needs. Adolescents have special nutritional needs. A growing adolescent requires a tremendous amount of calories and a large amount of all nutrients to support growth. Calcium and iron are especially important during this time. The only people that have greater nutritional needs than adolescents are

Nutritional needs change throughout a person's life span. The rapid growth that infants (*left*), pregnant women (*below*), and adolescents (*bottom*) experience requires additional nutrients as well as additional calories.

pregnant women. During pregnancy, protein, calories, folic acid, vitamin B$_{12}$, calcium, phosphorus, magnesium, and iron are in great demand. While the elderly do not require the large nutritional intake of adolescents or pregnant women, they do have special needs. Limited incomes, physical obstacles (such as poorly fitting dentures), and disorders that affect how nutrients are absorbed within the digestive system are some of the problems that affect the diet of the elderly.

Nutritionists, the scientists who study nutrition, have also learned that there are elements in addition to nutrients that help maintain health and prevent illness. One such element is fiber, the indigestible part of fruits, vegetables, and cereal grains that does not supply energy. Though not a true nutrient, fiber is very important since it helps other foods pass through the digestive system. Studies show that fiber-rich diets are crucial for maintaining the condition of the colon, preventing constipation, reducing the risk for colon cancer, and preventing diverticulosis (an inflammation in the intestinal wall).

Several tools exist that provide individuals with helpful information for choosing a balanced, healthful diet. These include the Dietary Reference Intakes (DRI's), the Dietary Guidelines for Americans, the Food Guide Pyramid, and food labels.

The Dietary Reference Intakes (DRI's)

The Dietary Reference Intakes are the standards for the calorie and nutrient intakes of healthy individuals. Developed by the Food and Nutrition Board of the National Academy of Sciences, the DRI's expand upon the Recommended Daily Allowances (RDA's), which have been published since 1941. The DRI's describe the average daily consumption levels for proteins, calories, vitamins, and minerals. The levels are set high enough so that there are stored amounts of nutrients, which can be used during short periods of time when nutrient intakes are not sufficient.

The DRI's provide a generous margin of safety for healthy people, with separate recommendations for infants, children, females, males, and women who are pregnant or nursing. Nutrient requirements can change along with a change in an individual's physical condition. When an individual is ill, recovering from surgery, or living with a chronic disor-

der, the DRI for a certain nutrient may increase or decrease.

Dietary Guidelines for Americans

The Dietary Guidelines provide advice for healthy Americans two years of age and older about making healthy diet and lifestyle choices. The U.S. Department of Agriculture (USDA) and the U.S. Department of Health and Human Services first published them in 1980, and they are reviewed and revised every five years. There are ten guidelines.

- Aim for a healthy weight.
- Be physically active every day—do at least 30 minutes of moderate exercise daily.
- Use the food pyramid to guide your food choices.
- Choose a diet with plenty of grain products, especially whole grains.
- Eat a variety of fruits and vegetables daily.
- Keep food safe to eat by separating raw meats and eggs from ready to eat foods, cooking foods to a safe temperature, and refrigerating perishable foods promptly.
- Follow a diet low in saturated fat and cholesterol and moderate in total fat.
- Eat and drink sugars in moderation. High-sugar foods and drinks supply an abundance of calories but few nutrients.
- Limit salt and salty flavorings.
- If you drink alcoholic beverages, do so in moderation. That means one drink daily for women and two for men.

The Food Guide Pyramid

The USDA introduced the Food Guide Pyramid in 1992. It grouped foods together based on the kinds of nutrients they provide and was intended to help consumers follow

the USDA's nutritional guidelines. A revised pyramid was released in 2005 (see illustration). The new pyramid, called MyPyramid, is a symbol that includes six bands of color, covering all the food types: the five food groups (grains; vegetables; fruits; milk products; and meats and beans) and oils. The widths of the bands suggest how much each food type should contribute to your diet.

The new pyramid does not include recommended daily portions. Instead, consumers are encouraged to choose a personalized plan based on their age, sex, and activity level. A planning tool is available at the MyPyramid Web site.

Food Labels

The Nutrition Labeling and Education Act, passed by Congress in 1990, resulted in standardized nutritional labels on all packaged and processed foods. A label must cite serving size and quantity per serving of the following: total calories, total fat, total carbohydrates, protein, saturated fat, cholesterol, complex carbohydrates, sugars, dietary fiber, and the number of calories from fat. It also provides information on vitamins A and C and the minerals calcium, iron, and sodium.

Labels also provide Daily Values (DV's). They are the recommended amounts of certain nutrients that a person consuming 2,000 or 2,500 calories a day should eat as part of a healthy diet. You can compare the amount of a nutrient that a particular product contains to what you should be eating each day according to the DV closer to your caloric needs. All labels provide DV's for total fat, saturated fat, cholesterol, sodium, carbohydrate, and fiber.

The Food and Drug Administration has an additional responsibility: It helps

MyPyramid
STEPS TO A HEALTHIER YOU
MyPyramid.gov

GRAINS   VEGETABLES   FRUITS   MILK   MEAT & BEANS

Nutrition Facts

Serving Size 1oz (28g/About 39 pieces)
Serving Per Container 16

Amount Per Serving

Calories 160   Calories from Fat 120

	% Daily Value*
Total Fat 14g	21%
Saturated Fat 2g	9%
Polyunsaturated Fat 4g	
Monounsaturated Fat 8g	
Cholesterol 0mg	0%
Sodium 0mg	0%
Potassium 200mg	6%
Total Carbohydrate 6g	2%
Dietary Fiber 3g	11%
Sugars 1g	
Protein 8g	

Vitamin A 0% • Vitamin C 0%
Calcium 0% • Iron 2% • Niacin 20%
Folate 20% • Phosphorus 10%
Magnesium 15% • Copper 15%

* Percent Daily Values are based on a 2,000 calorie diet. Your daily values may be higher or lower depending on your calorie needs:

		Calories	2,000	2,500
Total Fat	Less than		65g	80g
Sat Fat	Less than		20g	25g
Cholesterol	Less than		300mg	300mg
Sodium	Less than		2,400mg	2,400mg
Potassium			3,500mg	3,500mg
Total Carbohydrate			300g	375g
Dietary Fiber			25g	30g

Calories per gram:
Fat 9 • Carbohydrate 4 • Protein 4

INGREDIENTS: PEANUTS.

SATISFACTION GUARANTEED
PLEASE INCLUDE CODE NUMBER FROM
SIDE OF LABEL IN ALL CORRESPONDENCE   **Glass Recycles**

By regulating the information on food labels, the U.S. government makes sure that consumers can compare products and find the ones that best fit their nutritional needs.

consumers by regulating health claims and descriptive terms, such as low fat, that appear on food labels. There are nine groups of terms that manufacturers can use on their products, each with a strict definition. Whether you are trying to eat a more balanced diet, manage your weight, or follow a special regime for health reasons, reading labels will help supply the information you need to make the choices that are best for you.

▶ **NUTRITION AND DISEASE**

Our nutritional concerns are much different from those of our ancestors. Before the 1900's, many people around the world, in developed and developing countries, died from deficiency diseases (illnesses caused from a lack of certain nutrients). While deficiency diseases still account for much of the poor health of people in developing countries, diseases of excess are the most serious threats to nutritional health for people in developed countries.

Deficiency Diseases

When the diet has low amounts of proteins and calories, protein-calorie malnutrition occurs. If the diet is severely lacking in proteins, the condition is called **kwashiorkor**. If the diet is severely lacking in calories, then the condition is called **marasmus**. Both conditions have serious effects on the body, including weight loss, failure to grow, and the wasting of tissues. Left untreated, these conditions can be fatal. It is difficult to determine the extent of these deficiencies accurately. They are most common in developing countries. In the United States, instances of kwashiorkor and marasmus are occasionally found in neglected infants or in individuals in low-income households.

Protein-calorie malnutrition can also accompany certain diseases and conditions. Tuberculosis, stomach and intestinal diseases that interfere with the intake or absorption of food, and trauma, such as surgery, can lead to an inadequate intake of proteins and calories.

Vitamin and mineral deficiencies can be the result of poor diets. The most common vitamin deficiencies are **beriberi** (a vitamin B_1 deficiency), **pellegra** (a niacin deficiency), **rickets** (a vitamin D deficiency), and **xerophthalmia** (a vitamin A deficiency). The most common mineral deficiencies include **iron-deficiency anemia** and **goiter**, an enlargement of the thyroid gland that results from a lack of iodine.

Diseases of Excess

Today many people develop illnesses, such as heart disease, obesity, and cancer, that have been linked to dietary excesses. For example, it is well accepted that a diet high in saturated fat and cholesterol (a waxy, fatlike substance found in many animal foods) raises blood cholesterol.

MYTHS AND FACTS

Myth: A high-protein, low-carbohydrate diet is the most successful regime for promoting weight loss.

Fact: A high-protein, low-carbohydrate diet is not safe. The quick weight loss that occurs with this regime is caused by the loss of water and lean muscle. The body breaks down muscle to amino acids and converts it to the sugar it needs. This type of diet can elevate blood cholesterol, lower blood sugar, cause mineral imbalances, stress the kidneys, and cause other metabolic abnormalities.

UNDERSTANDING NUTRITIONAL CLAIMS

Claims promoting the nutritional value of a product are a familiar sight on a food label. Because many of the same terms, such as low fat, have been used on a variety of products that differ greatly from one another, it has not been easy to understand exactly what they mean. Labeling regulations established by the Food and Drug Administration now spell out the meaning of specific terms and how they can be used. Below are some basic terms with their definitions.

Fortified, enriched, added, or more are claims that mean a food must have at least 10 percent more of the Daily Value for a particular nutrient, such as protein, dietary fiber, or an essential vitamin or mineral, that either was not originally in the food or was present in smaller amounts.

Free as part of a description, such as fat free, means that a product does not contain that nutrient or contains an insignificant amount. The term can be used for a product that contains less than 0.5 grams per serving of fat, saturated fat, or sugar; less than 2 milligrams (mg) of cholesterol; or 5 mg of sodium.

Without label regulations, advertisers could easily mislead consumers by noting certain nutritional facts about a product while hiding others.

Fresh can only be used with food that is raw, contains no preservatives, and has never been frozen, heated, or processed.

Healthy is a term that can be used on a label if a food is both low in fat and saturated fat and a serving does not contain more than 480 mg of sodium and more than 60 mg of cholesterol.

High and good source emphasizes the presence in a product of certain nutrients for which higher levels are desirable. For example, high fiber means that a product must equal 20 percent or more of the Daily Value for fiber in a single serving. A good source of fiber means a serving contains 10 to 19 percent of the Daily Value for fiber.

Lean and extra lean describes the fat content of meat, poultry, seafood, and game. For foods to be considered lean, they must have less than 10 grams of fat, 4 grams of saturated fat, and 95 mg of cholesterol per serving; to be considered extra lean, less than 5 grams of fat and 2 grams of saturated fat.

Light or lite applies to a nutritionally altered food product and means that it contains one-third fewer calories or half the fat or sodium of the regular food product. Light can also be used to describe other qualities, including taste, color, or smell, but it must clearly specify to which it refers, for example, "light in taste."

Low means that a food, such as a low-fat food, can be eaten frequently without exceeding the Daily Value guidelines for calories or a specific nutrient, such as total fat, cholesterol, and sodium.

Reduced (or less) is a comparison term. It means that a food has 25 percent less of a nutrient or calories than the regular food. For instance, reduced-fat salad dressing must have 25 percent less fat than the regular salad dressing.

Cholesterol is necessary for cell metabolism. But high levels of unused cholesterol circulating in the blood accumulates in the walls of the arteries. Eventually it forms a **plaque**, or hard node. As the plaque builds up, the arteries narrow and harden, producing a condition called **atherosclerosis**. The results of atherosclerosis can be high blood pressure, heart attack, or stroke.

Everyone suffering from a deficiency disease unfortunately does not have the same opportunity to improve their nutritional status as someone with a disease of excess. We can make the choice to change our eating behaviors. With good nutritional habits, we can prevent disease and increase our chances for an active and healthful life.

MARIA GUGLIELMINO
Registered Dietitian
Author, *Diet and Nutrition Report*

See also BODY CHEMISTRY; FOOD REGULATIONS AND LAWS; FOOD SHOPPING; VITAMINS AND MINERALS.

NUTS

A nut is the fruit of a tree. Like all kinds of fruit, a nut contains the seed of its tree. Some fruits, like the apple, have a number of small seeds. Other fruits, such as the peach or the walnut, have one large seed. Some fruits are soft and fleshy; others are dry and hard. When we eat certain fleshy fruits, such as apples and peaches, we eat the soft outer part and throw the seeds away. When we eat certain other fruits, like walnuts and hickory nuts, we eat the kernel of the seed and throw away the hard, dry outer shell and its covering.

According to botanists, a nut is a tree fruit that has a single seed with its kernel enclosed in a dry, hard shell. Its shell does not split open when the fruit is ripe. Walnuts, butternuts, hickory nuts, hazelnuts, chestnuts, acorns, and pecans are true nuts.

Popularly we call any seed that has a kernel inside a hard or brittle shell a nut. This includes almonds, coconuts, Brazil nuts, water chestnuts, cashew nuts, and pistachio nuts. Peanuts, also called groundnuts, are not really nuts at all. The peanut produces underground pods from aboveground flowers and actually belongs to the bean family.

Tree nuts have been used for food for thousands of years. The trees themselves, and their branches and flowers, have been used on religious occasions since biblical times. The Bible tells us that walnuts were grown in King Solomon's garden and that Joseph's brothers carried pistachio nuts to Egypt.

It is believed that early peoples ate nuts as a regular part of their diet. Since nuts are high in protein, some nutritionists believe that nuts will be widely used in the future to help feed people during food shortages.

The oldest method of cooking nuts is to roast them in their shells in hot sand or ashes. Many campers use this method even today.

▶THE PARTS OF A NUT

A nut kernel is protected by its woody shell. The shell keeps the kernel from drying, from injury, and from attacks by bacteria, fungi, and insects. Most nuts have a hull, or a fleshy fruit part, that grows over them. The hulls of some nuts dry and split as the nut matures.

The kernel is usually made up of an embryo, an endosperm, and a thin, skinlike seed

Walnuts and the smaller filberts, or hazelnuts, are two of the many kinds of nuts grown in tropical, subtropical, and temperate climate zones of the world.

coat called a pellicle. The embryo is the part of the kernel that would grow into a new plant if the nut were planted under suitable conditions. The endosperm, when present, is a food-storage organ and may take up most of the kernel. But when mature, most nuts have no endosperm, and the food is stored in the seed leaves (cotyledons) of the embryo.

▶USES FOR HULLS AND SHELLS

The hulls and shells of some nuts serve very useful purposes. Almond hulls are sometimes used as food for livestock. From coconut husks comes a fiber known as coir, which is used for cordage, mattress stuffing, brushes, and mats. Most shells burn well and may be used for fuel. Finely ground almond, pecan, and walnut shells may be used as metal cleaners. They remove oil and metal cuttings from machined parts and residues from jet engines.

▶USES FOR KERNELS

The kernels of nuts contain all the food materials, except water, that are needed to start the growth of seedling trees. Most oily nuts have a large percentage of fat and protein and a small amount of carbohydrates. Oily kernels usually have 50 percent fat. Some have as much as 70 percent. The amount of protein in nut kernels usually ranges from 10 percent to 25 percent, which is similar to the protein content of beef. Thus nuts may in part substitute for meat in the diet. Nuts are generally high in phosphorus, potassium, and iron. Some nuts also provide a high level of certain vitamins.

▶ COMMERCIAL NUT GROWING

Nuts have always served as food for people. Traces of nuts have been found in the excavations of cave dwellings. Nuts were well known to the people of Old Testament times. Jacob sent almonds and pistachio nuts as gifts to his son Joseph. Early Romans and Greeks ate hazelnuts, acorns, chestnuts, and almonds. At the same time, walnuts were growing in the gardens of China.

Nuts have been used as food in North America since very early days. American Indians used many nuts, including acorns. They crushed the kernels and soaked out the bitter, astringent materials that were not good to eat.

In the early days, nuts were harvested from wild native trees and from seedlings grown from these trees. It was not until late in the 19th century that trees were grafted or budded in North America. Budding and grafting are techniques that enable people to increase the number of trees that produce superior nuts. Buds or short sticks (scions) containing buds are taken from the best trees and then set into the stem of a seedling, where they grow.

As the trade for nuts developed, growers learned better ways to grow, pack, and store nuts to keep them from spoiling. As knowledge of raising nuts grew, commercial orchards of grafted trees became more common.

Of all countries, the United States has most fully developed the commercial production of certain nuts, specifically almonds, Persian walnuts, filberts, and pecans. The trees are planted in orchards and are cultivated. Cultivation increases yields and reduces production costs. In the United States and other countries, nuts such as Brazil nuts, hickory nuts, pine nuts, and black walnuts are harvested chiefly from wild seedling trees. Commercial plant-

ings for these nuts either are not economical or are in the early stages of development.

Two kinds of nuts, coconuts and peanuts, are the basis of such large industries that there are separate articles about them. The other commercially important nuts are described on the following pages. Some nuts, not so important commercially, have specialized uses. These nuts are included in the chart.

▶ ALMOND

The almond is one of the oldest and best-known edible nuts. There are two kinds, the sweet and the bitter. The sweet almond is used for food, and the oil of bitter almonds is used for food flavoring. Almond shells are called hard, soft, or paper shells. The paper-shelled almonds are especially popular.

Almonds grow best where there are long, hot summers and mild, but not warm, winters. The nut harvest is largest when the rainfall during the season is low and the trees are properly cultivated and watered. Budded trees of selected varieties are planted in orchards to produce sweet almonds. Bitter almonds are produced by certain seedling trees.

Almonds are closely related to peaches. The kernel of the almond nut looks much like the kernel inside the shell of a peach seed. But the flesh of the mature almond fruit becomes dry and leathery and splits open, while that of the peach is soft and juicy and does not split.

Almonds ripen in early fall. When most of the hulls have split, the fruits, or nuts, are harvested. Large canvas sheets are spread under the trees, and the trees are jarred with rubber mallets or a power shaker to shake the nuts down.

The almonds are hulled and dried before they are delivered to a processing plant. If the almonds are to be sold with their shells on, they are usually bleached. Most almonds are sold as kernels after their shells are removed.

Italy produces the most almonds. Many are produced in Spain and the state of California in the United States. They are also grown in Iran, Portugal, and Morocco.

▶ BRAZIL NUT

The Brazil nut comes from a gigantic tree of the Amazon River basin. The tree grows as high as 23 to 45 meters (75 to 150 feet) and has a trunk 1 to 2 meters (3 to 6 feet) in diameter. The tree blossoms from October to March. About 14 months after blossoming, the fruit ripens. The harvest begins in November and may last until June.

The fruit of the Brazil nut tree is a roundish pod about 10 to 15 centimeters (4 to 6 inches) in diameter. The pod is very hard and woody. It contains from 8 to 24 nuts. Each nut is brown and triangular, with a thin, brittle shell. It is about 3 to 5 centimeters (1 to 2 inches) long.

The vast numbers of wild trees in Brazil could produce a plentiful supply of nuts. But there are problems in obtaining the nuts. The nuts must be transported through the jungle to the river waterways. And harvesting the nuts is dangerous because the pods containing them are large and fall from a great height. The people who gather the nuts must wait for calm days before they go under the trees to pick up the fruits.

The fruit is split open with a machete, and the nuts are taken out. When they are washed in water, the imperfect nuts float and may be easily removed. The good nuts are dried, placed in baskets, and sent by boat to a collector. The collector sells the nuts to an exporter, who ships them to other countries.

▶ CASHEW

The cashew tree is a native of tropical America. Early European explorers of the Americas carried cashews to the tropical areas of the Old World. Today, the principal commercial producing areas are in southwest India, Mozambique, East Africa, and tropical America. Most of the nuts are shelled in India, which is the principal source of the nut kernels.

The cashew nut grows at the end of a fleshy "apple." The nut is bean-shaped and has an outer and an inner shell. Between the shells is a poisonous and irritating oil. (The plant is a relative of poison ivy.) The oil is removed when the nuts are roasted in the shelling process.

The fruit is pulled from the tree by a long bamboo pole with a hook on the end. The nuts are broken off the "apples" and transported to processing plants, where they are shelled and their kernels are packed.

Because the cashew tree can grow well under poor conditions, it has been planted in waste areas not suited to other crops. Increas-ing demand for the nuts has caused growers to try to find better ways to raise the trees. But few trees are grown under modern orchard conditions. Most of the nuts are harvested from seedling trees.

▶ CHESTNUT

There are four important species of chestnuts, each named for the area to which it is native. They are the American, Chinese, European, and Japanese chestnuts. The four types are much alike. The chestnut is a brown nut. One to three or more grow inside a prickly bur, maturing about three or four months after blossom time.

Chestnuts are high in starch and relatively low in oil and protein. Unlike most other nuts, they are very perishable and are best stored under refrigeration. If they are kept too moist, they mold. If kept too dry, they dry out. Chestnuts are especially valuable as a food in mountainous parts of southern Europe, where grain cannot be grown.

The American chestnut, an important forest tree, was almost completely destroyed by a fungus introduced about the year 1900 from Asia. This fungus causes a bark disease called chestnut blight. Only the Chinese and Japanese species are resistant to the blight. The disease has also occurred in Europe, especially in Italy and France. But in recent years the blight seems to have been controlled by natural forces in Europe. Scientists are experimenting to see whether the same control can be used in the United States so that the American chestnut tree can again be grown.

▶ FILBERT, OR HAZELNUT

Filberts, or hazelnuts, are native to Europe. They require a temperate climate. The most important producing areas are Turkey, Italy, Spain, and the western parts of Oregon and Washington in the United States.

The trees are cultivated in orchards. In the wild the filbert is generally a bush. Many suckers grow up from the roots. When allowed to produce suckers, the bush will grow only about 4.5 meters (15 feet) high. If the suckers are removed and grown as trees, they may grow twice that tall. The trees flower in February or March. The nuts are ready to harvest in August or September. The nuts either drop naturally or are shaken from the trees.

PECAN

The pecan is a species of hickory tree. It is native to an area of North America, ranging from southeastern Iowa down the Mississippi River and its tributaries to the rivers of Texas and rivers nearby in Mexico. Some trees grow to a great age and are often 45 meters (150 feet) high, with branches that spread 30 meters (100 feet) or more. They grow best in a climate where long, hot summers are followed by cool winters.

Beginning in the late 1800's, grafted trees were planted in orchards. Today, the United States produces most of the pecans of the world. Mexico and South Africa are also important producers.

Pecan trees flower in April or May, and the nuts mature from September to November. A single nut is in a hull that splits into four sections when it is mature. The nuts usually are olive-shaped. The nuts of the best varieties have thin shells that are easily cracked so that the kernel may be removed.

Before harvesting the nuts, the ground under the trees is cultivated—or the grass or weeds are mowed—so the nuts may be more easily gathered. The mature nuts drop from their hulls or are knocked from the trees with bamboo poles or are shaken down by mechanical shakers. The nuts are then gathered by hand or machine.

PISTACHIO

The pistachio nut is also called the green almond. The nut is oval, with a smooth, thin, brittle shell and light green or creamy yellow kernel. The pistachio tree is a native of Turkey, Syria, and other countries nearby. It needs long, hot summers, cool winters, and moderate soil moisture. The chief growing areas are Tur-

SOME IMPORTANT NUTS

NUT	SCIENTIFIC NAME	ORIGIN	NATURE OF PLANT	REGION OF PRODUCTION	WILD OR CULTIVATED	PRINCIPAL USE
African oil palm nut	*Elaeis guineesis*	Tropical West Africa	Medium palm tree	Tropical Africa, Southeast Asia, Brazil	Wild and cultivated	Edible and industrial oils
Almond	*Prunus amygdalus*	Mediterranean Basin	Small tree	Italy, Spain, United States, Portugal	Cultivated	Food; hulls for stock food
Babassu	*Orbignya oleifera*	Brazil	Palm tree	Brazil	Wild	Nuts for cooking oil and soap; shells for fuel
Betel nut (areca nut)	*Areca catechu*	Malay Peninsula	Palm tree	Tropics of Asia; eastern Pacific islands	Cultivated and wild	Chewing nut
Brazil nut (cream-nut; para nut)	*Bertholletia excelsa*	Brazil	Large tree	Northern South America	Wild	Food
Butternut	*Juglans cinerea*	United States, Canada	Medium tree	United States, Canada	Wild and cultivated	Food
Candlenut (lumbang)	*Aleurites moluccana*	Tropical Pacific islands	Small tree	Tropical Pacific islands	Wild, some cultivated	Industrial oil
Cashew	*Anacardium occidentale*	West Indies, tropical America	Small tree	India, East Africa, tropical America	Wild and cultivated	Food
Castanopsis	*Castanopsis* (various species)	Southeast Asia, western North America	Bush to large tree	Southeast Asia, western North America	Wild	Food
Chestnut	*Castanea* (various species)	Europe, China, United States, Japan	Medium to large tree	China, Europe, Japan	Wild and cultivated	Food
Chufa (tiger; earth almond; rush nut; ground almond)	*Cyperus esculentus*	Southern Europe	Grass or rushlike herbs	Spain, Africa, southeastern United States	Wild and cultivated	Food
Coconut	*Cocos nucifera*	Islands of Indian Ocean	Large palm tree	Most tropical countries	Wild and cultivated	Food; beverage; oils; fiber
Cola (kola)	*Cola acuminata*	Tropical Africa	Large tree	Tropical West Africa, South America	Wild and cultivated	Chewing nut; stimulant; beverages; flavoring
Filbert; hazelnut; cobnut	*Corylus* (various species)	Europe, United States	Bush and small tree	Turkey, Italy, Spain, United States	Wild and cultivated	Food

key, Iran, Afghanistan, Italy, Syria, and California in the United States.

Sometimes, grafted trees of selected varieties are grown. These grafted trees are cultivated. But most pistachio trees are seedlings and receive little attention.

The clusters of mature fruits hang on the trees, making it easy to harvest them all at one time. The fruit clusters are knocked off with a pole or pulled from the tree by hand. The fruits are squeezed between the fingers to remove the hulls from the nuts. When the nuts are placed in water, the bad nuts float. The good nuts are dried and either roasted and salted or shelled and sold as kernels.

▶ WALNUTS

There are many different kinds of walnuts. Two are of commercial importance—the Persian (often called the English) and the eastern black. The Persian walnut is a native of Iran but grows in many countries of the world. This is the walnut generally found in the shell, although it is also sold as kernels.

The eastern black walnut has a hard shell and is difficult to crack. Only its kernels are offered for sale in retail markets. The eastern black is a native of the eastern United States. Both kinds of trees produce good nuts. Their wood is used for furniture and gunstocks. Indeed, black walnut is the most valuable hardwood grown in the United States.

The trees grow best in deep, fertile, and well-drained soil. They need fairly long, hot summers, followed by moderately cold winters. Good rainfall is needed. Most commercial Persian walnuts are produced in California in the United States and in France, Italy, and Turkey. The black walnut is produced only in the United States.

NUT	SCIENTIFIC NAME	ORIGIN	NATURE OF PLANT	REGION OF PRODUCTION	WILD OR CULTIVATED	PRINCIPAL USE
Ginkgo	*Ginkgo biloba*	China, Japan	Medium tree	China, Japan	Wild and cultivated	Food
Hickory (many common names)	*Carya* (various species)	United States	Medium to large trees	United States; Ontario, Canada	Wild and cultivated	Food
Litchi (Chinese)	*Litchi chinensis*	Southern China	Medium tree	Southern China, India	Cultivated	Food
Macadamia (Queensland nut; Australian nut; bush nut)	*Macadamia* two species: *ternifolia* and *tetraphylla*	Southern Australia	Medium tree	Southern Australia, Hawaii, Southern California	Wild and cultivated	Food
Oyster	*Telfairia occidentalis*	Tropical Africa	Woody-stemmed climbing vine	Tropical East Africa	Wild and cultivated	Food
Peanut (groundnut)	*Arachis hypogaea*	South America	Herbaceous annual	India, China, United States, Brazil, Nigeria	Cultivated	Edible oil, food
Pecan	*Carya illinoensis*	Southern United States	Large tree	United States, northern Mexico, South Africa	Wild and cultivated	Food
Pili (Java almond)	*Canarium* (various species)	Southeast Asia	Medium to large trees	Southeast Asia	Wild	Food
Pine nut (Indian; piñon; pignolia)	*Pinus* (about 15 species)	Europe, Asia, western United States	Medium to large trees	Europe, Asia, western United States	Wild	Food
Pistachio (pistache; green almond)	*Pistacia vera*	Mediterranean Basin	Small tree	Turkey, Iran, Italy, Syria, Afghanistan	Wild and cultivated	Food
Tung	*Aleurites fordii*	China	Medium tree	China, Brazil, United States, Argentina, Japan	Cultivated	Paint oil (poisonous to eat)
Walnut, eastern black; Persian (English)	*Juglans* (various species)	United States, Japan, Iran	Medium and large trees	United States, France, Italy, Turkey	Wild and cultivated	Food
Water chestnut	*Trapa natans*	Southern China	Water plant	China	Cultivated	Food

Persian walnuts are commercially grown in orchards of grafted trees. The amount of cultivation and care they are given depends on the area in which they are grown. Black walnuts usually are not produced in orchards. But they are being more widely planted for the two purposes of nut and wood production.

The fleshy hull of the Persian walnut splits and releases the nut at maturity. Harvesting in commercial orchards in California is done largely with mechanical shakers and sweepers. The husk of the black walnut must be removed at harvest. Most nuts are picked up by hand and then mechanically hulled.

RICHARD A. JAYNES
Connecticut Agricultural Experiment Station
See also COCONUT; PEANUTS AND PEANUT PRODUCTS.

NYASALAND. See MALAWI.

NYLON AND OTHER SYNTHETIC FIBERS

In 1938, a giant chemical-manufacturing company announced an exciting discovery. After ten years of patient research and experiments, its scientists had been able to make a new, silklike fiber out of coal, air, and water. At first the new material, which was given the name nylon, was looked on as a luxury. It was used in place of silk in such things as women's stockings and dresses. Today nylon and other synthetic fibers are used in countless products.

Synthetic fibers can do many things that natural fibers cannot do. They may be stronger, may wash better, or may hold their shape better. Synthetic fibers are used for warm sweaters that can be washed in a washing machine instead of having to be washed carefully by hand. They are used to make blankets, suits, and carpets that will not be damaged by moths. They are used for ropes that lift great weights.

Most synthetic fibers have an interesting property—when they become hot, they soften. When they are heated more, they melt. This property is useful because creases that are ironed into pants or skirts made of these fibers last for a long time. On the other hand, care must be taken not to wash or iron synthetic fibers at too high a temperature.

▶ **TYPES OF SYNTHETIC FIBERS**

Synthetic fibers are often called man-made fibers because they are made by people. There are three main types of synthetic fibers—regenerated, true synthetic, and mineral.

Regenerated Fibers

These fibers are made by taking molecules from natural materials, such as wood or cotton, and rearranging the molecules in a different form. (A molecule is a combination of two or more atoms that make up a particular substance.)

Most regenerated fibers are made from cellulose, the natural substance that forms the chief part of the walls of plant cells. Some natural fibers are also made of cellulose—cotton and linen are two important examples. The cellulose for regenerated fibers comes mostly from wood pulp and from cotton fibers that are too short to be spun into thread.

Rayon, the most important regenerated cellulose fiber, was one of the first synthetic fibers to be developed. It was invented as a low-priced substitute for silk. Most rayon produced today is of a type called **viscose** rayon. It is used in women's dresses and underwear and in some industrial uses where strength and low price are important. Most disposable bedsheets, towels, and diapers contain a great deal of rayon.

Acetate is another type of rayon. Its fibers are not as strong as those of viscose, but they have the advantage of not wrinkling as easily. Acetate is used in underwear, dresses, and shirts; in home furnishings; and in cigarette filters.

True Synthetic Fibers

These fibers are completely synthetic—even their molecules are not found in nature. The true synthetics are made from such raw materials as coal, petroleum, water, air, and alcohol. They are actually plastics in the form of long, thin strands.

The true synthetic fibers are much alike in many ways. All of them are strong, and they can take a great deal of bending. They are elastic, so they spring back into shape after they have been stretched. Most of them soften and then melt when heated. They absorb very little water, so they dry quickly. But this quality also makes them feel clammy and uncomfortable to some people. Like other synthetic fibers, they resist insects, rot, mildew, and many chemicals.

Nylon is one of the most widely used synthetic fibers. It is strong and smooth and durable. Nylon fibers are also elastic. Pure nylon is used in women's stockings and underwear. It is also used in ropes, fishing lines and nets, carpets, and tire cords. Natural fibers like wool are sometimes blended with nylon to make fabrics last longer. Wool socks, for instance, may have nylon added to the toes and heels, which get most of the wear. One type of nylon, called aramid, is noted for its resistance to heat and fire. It is also exceptionally tough and strong. Aramid is used in fire fighters' clothing, airplane carpets and upholstery, and many other products. In its solid form, nylon is a tough, smooth, slippery plastic. It is used in machine parts such as gears and bearings because it needs no lubrication.

Polyester fibers have become the most widely used synthetic fibers. They are almost as strong as nylon and somewhat stiffer. Polyester fibers are often mixed with cotton and wool. They are used in clothing to make it resistant to wrinkling. Such clothing is often smooth when it comes out of a dryer after laundering, and it can be worn all day with little wrinkling. Polyester is also used in carpeting, tire cords, knitted fabrics, and filling for padded garments and sleeping bags.

Acrylic fibers can be made very light and fluffy. They are used in soft, woolly products such as sweaters, blankets, carpets, socks, and imitation fur coats.

Olefin fibers are made from the soft, waxy plastics called polypropylene and polyethylene. Olefins are very resistant to deterioration from chemicals, perspiration, and weather. As plastics, they are widely used in food containers, toys, squeeze bottles, and many other familiar items. As fibers, they are used in indoor-outdoor carpets, webbing for outdoor furniture, ropes, and sandbags.

Spandex is made from polyurethane, the material used for foamed plastic ice buckets, picnic containers, and cushions. Spandex fibers are very elastic. They can be stretched over and over again and still return to their original length. They are used in stretch clothing such as bathing suits and girdles.

Mineral Fibers

These fibers are made from substances such as glass and metals. They are being used more and more because they resist fire and many chemicals.

Glass fibers can be made very fine. They do not burn. They can also stand a very heavy pull. Unfortunately, they break easily when they are bent. Glass fibers are used in fireproof draperies. Embedded in plastic, they are used in airplanes, boat hulls, and furniture. Much glass fiber is used as insulation for houses, stoves, and refrigerators.

Metallic fibers are often coated with a transparent plastic film so that they do not tarnish. They are used for decorative purposes in table linens, laces, and other items.

▶ **MANUFACTURE**

Synthetic fibers contain atoms of only a few chemical elements. Carbon and hydrogen

---

How are synthetic fibers named?

Have you ever been confused by the many names of synthetic fibers? There is good reason to be. But in the United States there is a plan to the way synthetic fibers are named. The fibers are divided into different types, according to the basic chemicals from which they are made. Each type has been given a name, defined by law, called a **generic** name. (The word "generic" means "belonging to a class.") "Polyester" and "acrylic" are two examples of generic names.

The generic name of the fiber must appear on the label that every garment carries. If you know the qualities of the generic types of fibers, the generic name on the label of a garment will tell you what you are getting.

Besides the generic name, every label usually carries the trade name of the fiber. If you look at the label of a shirt, you may see the words "Dacron polyester." The word "Dacron" is a trade name belonging to one company. For that reason it should be spelled with a capital D. Fortrel and Kodel are trade names of polyester fibers made by other companies.

Before labels carried generic names, shoppers had to memorize a whole list of trade names. This was difficult. Nylon alone, for example, has more than 25 different trade names. Some of them are listed in the table at the end of this article.

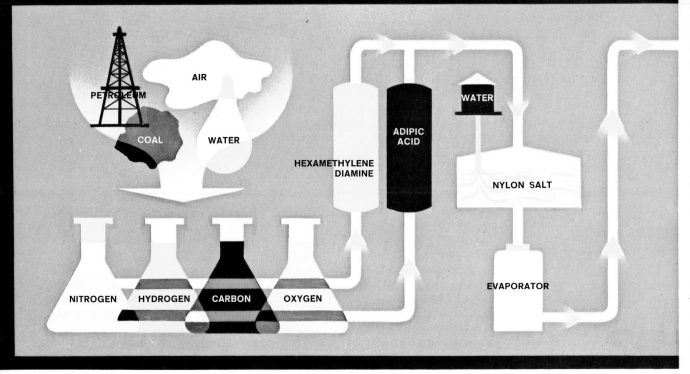

Steps in the manufacture of nylon, from raw material to finished product.

are always present. There can also be oxygen, nitrogen, or chlorine. The kinds of atoms that are present and the way they are arranged in the molecules determine how the fiber will behave.

Despite their differences in chemical makeup, all synthetic fibers are manufactured in much the same way. First, chemicals are mixed to produce a viscous (gluey) liquid. This liquid is then forced through tiny holes in a metal nozzle called a **spinneret**. The liquid comes through the holes as long, thin strands, or **filaments**. The filaments harden in the air or in a chemical bath. Then the fibers are stretched. Stretching makes the molecules in the fiber line up in the same direction. This makes the fiber much stronger. Next, the filaments are washed to rid them of excess chemicals. Then they are bleached and dried. Finally they are wound on spools.

The filaments can be made very long—they grow as long as there is material to force through the spinneret holes. They can be made so fine as to be almost invisible or as thick as a straw.

Filaments may be used singly. A single filament is called a **monofil**. Thick monofils are used in webbing for outdoor furniture and as bristles for brushes. Thin ones are used in sheer stockings. But usually filaments are

twisted together into yarn. The yarn in an automobile tire may contain several hundred filaments.

Filament yarns are used where great strength is required, as in parachutes, ropes, and tire cords. They are also used in fancy dress fabrics and in upholstery fabrics, where their shine and smoothness are desirable. But fabrics made from filaments are usually quite thin and transparent. In clothing, these fabrics lie close to the skin, and they may feel uncomfortable.

To solve these problems, filaments often are cut into shorter pieces, 3 to 15 centimeters (1 to 6 inches) in length. Yarns are spun by twisting these shorter fibers together. Such yarns are called **staple yarns**. Staple yarns have more air between their fibers than filament yarns. They are also thicker and less transparent. Fabrics made of staple yarns do not lie as close to the skin as those made of filament yarns, so they are more comfortable. Fiber ends stick out of the fabric and trap air. The trapped air acts as an insulator and makes the fabric feel less hot, cold, or clammy.

Staple yarns can be spun of mixtures of natural and synthetic fibers. Such mixed yarns combine the advantages of several fibers. For instance, polyester-cotton blends wear

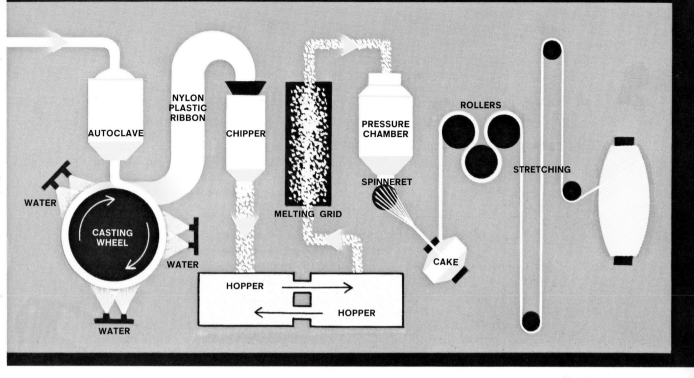

well and resist wrinkling because of the polyester fibers in them. They are comfortable and not too transparent because of the cotton. They are used in shirts, slacks, blouses, dresses, sheets, and other items where previously only cotton was used.

Another way to produce synthetic fiber yarns that are thicker and less transparent is to form little loops or arcs in the filaments by a process called **texturizing**. Such yarns are used in sweaters, sport clothing, and carpets.

▶ HISTORY

For many hundreds of years people have been fascinated by the way that silkworms and spiders spin long, smooth filaments. The animals do this by forcing a liquid through tiny body openings. The process looks simple, but people could not copy it until fairly recently.

According to legend, about 2,000 years ago a curious Chinese stuck a needle into a silk gum. (Silk as it comes from the silkworm is covered with a sticky gum.) When the person pulled the needle away, a fine thread of gum came with it. The gum hardened in the air to become a silk fiber. You can make fibers at home this way with rubber cement. But obviously this is not a practical way to manufacture fibers on a large scale.

An Englishman named Louis Schwalbe is credited with having been the first person to succeed in spinning artificial fibers. Schwalbe was not able to produce a practical fiber because the necessary materials had not yet been invented. But in 1842 he introduced the spinneret, with which filaments could be spun.

The First Regenerated Fibers

About the same time, chemists learned how to dissolve wood pulp and cotton fibers to obtain the cellulose in them. Fibers of cellulose were first made in 1855 by Georges Audemars of Switzerland. But the chemical processes turned the cellulose into nitrocellulose, a powerful explosive. Fabrics made from it easily burst into flame.

Two researchers, working separately, succeeded in making fibers from a less flammable form of nitrocellulose. One was Sir Joseph Swan (1828–1914), an English chemist, physicist, and inventor. Swan was looking for a material to make filaments for electric light bulbs. He thought that an artificial fiber might be the answer. The other person was a French count, Hilaire de Chardonnet (1839–1924). Chardonnet was interested in creating new fibers for use in textiles. He was a good businessman as well as a good scientist. His first

SOME IMPORTANT SYNTHETIC FIBERS

GENERIC NAME	SOURCE	TRADE NAMES	MAIN USES
Acetate	Cellulose	Celanese, Estron, Loftura, and others	Clothing; pillows; upholstery; cigarette filters
Acrylic	Acrylonitrile	Acrilan, Creslan, Orlon, and others	Clothing, including furlike coats and knitted items; blankets; carpets; upholstery
Aramid	Polyamide	Kevlar, Nomex	Flame-resistant clothing; filters; tires
Fluorocarbon	Tetrafluoro-ethylene	Teflon	Sewing thread; protective clothing; surgical applications; filters
Mineral Fiber	Glass; metals	Fiberglass, Lurex, X-Static	Curtains; draperies; filters; materials resistant to fire and insects
Modacrylic	Acrylonitrile	Elura, SEF, Verel	Draperies; flame-resistant children's sleepwear; furlike coats; work clothes
Nylon	Polyamide	Antron, Cantrece, Crepeset, Enkalure, Qiana, and others	Clothing; carpets; draperies; hosiery; upholstery; tents; tires; ropes
Olefin	Olefins	Herculon, Marvess, Vectra, and others	Carpets; webbing for outdoor furniture; filters; ropes
Polyester	Ethylene glycol and terephthalic acid	Dacron, Fortrel, Kodel, and others	Clothing; sheets; ropes; sails; carpets; tires
Rayon	Cellulose	Avril, Enkrome, Fibro, and others	Clothing; upholstery; disposable Items; bedding
Saran	Vinylidene chloride	Bolta, Saran, Velon	Screening; luggage; protective clothing; draperies; doll hair
Spandex	Polyurethane	Lycra, Monvelle	Girdles; bathing suits; support hose
Vinyon	Vinyl chloride	Vinyon HH	Embossed carpets; pressed felts

plant opened in 1890 in Besançon, France. Later he opened plants in several other countries. Better, safer fibers have since taken the place of Chardonnet's nitrocellulose, but Chardonnet is known as the person who started the industry.

One safer fiber was developed in England in 1892. The fiber was named viscose because the manufacturing process used a viscous cellulose solution. Today viscose is better known as rayon. Acetate was first made in 1899, but it was not developed fully enough for use in fabrics until about 1920.

Completely Synthetic Fibers

Many years after the invention of regenerated fibers, chemists learned how to make their own polymers. (A polymer is a long chain of molecules. Cellulose is a natural polymer. All synthetic fibers consist of polymers of one kind or another.) The next step was to create polymers that had the right properties for use in fibers.

The person who invented the first synthetic fiber was an American scientist, Wallace H. Carothers (1896–1937). The work started in the laboratories of E.I. du Pont de Nemours and Company in 1928. Ten years later—a short time as scientific developments go—Du Pont announced nylon. This was the first fiber made by combining atoms into molecules, molecules into polymers, and polymers into fibers, rather than using polymers made by nature.

Some ten additional types of synthetic fibers have been developed since nylon appeared. And chemists continue to work to develop other synthetic fibers. They are looking for fibers that will be lower in price, stronger, and more resistant to chemicals and heat. Resistance to heat and light are especially important for the fibers used in space capsules. Chemists are also trying to develop new fibers that will combine the good qualities of the older materials—for instance, a fiber that is as strong as nylon and that can absorb water as well as viscose rayon can. In the years since Chardonnet's plant opened, much has been done. But the future will probably bring even better and cheaper fibers.

JOHN F. KRASNY
National Bureau of Standards

See also FIBERS; PLASTICS; TEXTILES.

Index

HOW TO USE THE DICTIONARY INDEX

See the beginning of the blue pages in Volume 1.

Napoleon I (cont.)
  stabled horses in what is now the Prado   P:424
  tomb in Paris   P:73
  wars with Austria   H:3
  map(s)
    empire in 1812   N:12
  picture(s)   E:366; F:417; W:270
    coronation   N:11
    Coup d'État of 18 Brumaire   F:473
    diamond necklace   J:99
    political cartoon about Embargo of 1807   J:70
    political cartoon about failed Russian campaign   N:12
    portrait by Jacques Louis David   N:10
    troops retreating from Moscow   R:370
    Waterloo, Battle of   N:14
Napoleon II (son of Napoleon I and Marie-Louise)   N:11
Napoleon III (emperor of France)   F:417; N:14
  completed the buildings of the Louvre   L:333
  Franco-Prussian War   F:452
  Mexican empire set up under Maximilian   J:142;
    M:249–50, 427
  town-planning for Paris   P:75
Napoleonic Code (of laws)   F:416, 473; L:85; N:11
  Louisiana's legal system is partly based on   L:314
  Quebec's legal system   S:506
Napoleonic Wars   N:11–13; S:484
Napster (file-sharing program)   R:124
Nara (Japan)   J:41
Narayan, R. K. (Indian author)   I:142
Narayanan, K. R. (president of India)   I:119
Narcissus (in Greek mythology)   G:367
  picture(s)   R:319
Narcissus (plant)   G:42
  picture(s)   G:36
Narcissus and Goldmund (book by Hermann Hesse)   H:125
Narcosis (illness from breathing compressed air in deep-sea
    diving)   U:23
Narcotics (drugs)   D:333–34; N:15
Narcotics, Bureau of (of the United States)   N:15
Narcotics squads (of police departments)   P:363
Narmada River (India)   I:124–25
Narmer (king of ancient Egypt) *see* Menes
Narodnaya, Mount (Russia)   R:362
Narragansett Bay (Rhode Island)   R:214, 215, 219
  picture(s)   R:215
Narragansetts (Indians of North America)   I:177; R:224, 225;
    T:173–74
Narrative poems (poems that tell a story)   L:259; P:353 *see
    also* Ballads
Narrow-gauge railroads   R:78
Narrow-spectrum antibiotics   A:308
Narváez, Pánfilo de (Spanish soldier and explorer)   F:271
Narwhals (whales)   I:416; W:150–51
Naryn River (Kyrgyzstan–Uzbekistan)   K:314
NASA *see* National Aeronautics and Space Administration
NASA Hubble Space Telescope *see* Hubble Space Telescope
Nash, Ogden (American humorist)   H:291
Nashua (New Hampshire)   N:159
Nashville (capital of Tennessee)   N:16; T:79, 81, 83
  country music   C:572, 573; R:262a; T:74, 80
  picture(s)   N:16; T:83
    country music   T:80
Naskapi (Indians of eastern Canada)   I:177, 190
Nasrids (Moorish dynasty in Spain)   S:381
Nassau (capital of the Bahamas)   B:16, 17
Nasser, Gamal Abdel (president of Egypt)   E:105; N:17
  picture(s)   E:105
Nasser, Lake (High Dam Lake) (Egypt)   E:102; L:32; N:261
Nast, Thomas (American political cartoonist)   C:127; N:17
  picture(s)
    Tammany Hall cartoon   C:127
    Tilden-Hayes election cartoon   H:70
Nasturtiums (flowers)   F:281
Natchez (Indians of North America)   I:178; M:359

Natchez (Mississippi)   M:357, 360
  picture(s)   M:358
Natchez Trace (overland trail)   M:358; O:271; P:260; T:81
  map(s)   O:273
  picture(s)   M:358
Natchez Trace Parkway   M:358; T:82
Natchitoches (Louisiana)   L:327
Nathan (Hebrew prophet)   B:161
Nathan, Sellapan Rama (president of Singapore)   S:181
Natick (Massachusetts)   M:148
Nation, Carry (American temperance leader)   P:484 *profile*
National Aeronautics and Space Administration (NASA)
    S:338–39, 340d
  astronauts   A:466
  "Earth Science Enterprise"   S:363
  Great Observatories   S:367–68
  "New Millennium" missions   S:351
National Agricultural Library (Washington, D.C.)   L:178
National AIDS Policy, Office of (United States)   P:451
National Air and Space Museum (Washington, D.C.)
    P:273–74; S:340a
National American Woman Suffrage Association   A:299;
    W:212a
National and Capodistrian University of Athens (Greece)
    A:476d
National anthems and patriotic songs   N:18–23 *see also* the
    facts and figures section of country articles
  Olympic Games awards ceremony   O:110
National Archery Association   A:362
National Archives (United States)   G:76d; N:24
  picture(s)   N:24; W:33
    display of the Declaration of Independence   D:57
National Assembly (France)   P:372
National Association for the Advancement of Colored People
    (NAACP)   A:79i, 79j, 79m; C:326; N:25–26
  Du Bois, W. E. B.   D:344
  Hooks, Benjamin L.   H:221
  Jackson, Lilly May Carroll   M:132
  Johnson, James Weldon   J:118
  Spingarn Medal   S:409–10
National Association of Amateur Oarsmen   R:341
National Association of Colored Women   W:212b
National Association of Intercollegiate Athletics   B:96
National Association of Mexican War Veterans   U:121
National Association of Realtors   R:113
National Association of Secondary School Principals (NASSP)
    N:42
National Audubon Society *see* Audubon Society, National
National Autonomous University of Mexico   U:226
National Ballet of Canada   B:32; C:69
National Bank Act (United States, 1863)   B:53
National banks   B:53
National Baseball Hall of Fame and Museum (Cooperstown, New
    York)   B:88
National Basketball Association (NBA)   B:99
National battlefields, battlefield parks, and battlefield site (of the
    United States)   N:54
National Black Caucus of State Legislators   C:326
National Broadcasting Corporation (NBC)   R:60
National budget (U.S. federal government)   C:367, 368;
    E:62–63; U:205
National Button Society   B:484
National Cancer Institute (NCI)   C:95
National Cathedral (Washington, D.C.)   W:32
  picture(s)
    stained-glass window   S:418
National cemeteries (of the United States)   N:27–29, 54;
    V:322
  Tomb of the Unknown Soldier   U:227
  Who can be buried in a U.S. national cemetery?   N:29
National Center for Complementary and Alternative Medicine
    A:194e; M:210
National Civil Rights Museum (Memphis, Tennessee)   M:217

National Collegiate Athletic Association
  basketball   **B:**96, 98
  football   **F:**360
  gymnastics events   **G:**433
  soccer   **S:**221
National Congress of Parents and Teachers *see* Parents and
    Teachers, National Congress of
National Conventions *see* Conventions, political
National Council of the Boy Scouts of America   **B:**359
National Crime Information Center   **F:**76; **H:**226
National Dance Company of Guinea
  picture(s)   **G:**406b
National Day (China)   **C:**261
National Defense Act (United States, 1916)   **N:**42
National Drug Control Policy, Office of (United States)   **P:**451
National Economic Council (of the United States)   **P:**451
National Education Association (NEA)   **H:**196; **L:**17
National Endowment for the Arts (NEA)   **T:**159
National Environmental Prediction Center (U.S.)   **W:**93
National Federation of Business and Professional Women's Clubs
    W:212b
National Federation of State High School Associations   **B:**96
National FFA Foundation   **F:**104
National FFA Organization *see* FFA (Future Farmers of America)
National Film Board of Canada   **C:**66–67, 69
National Fire Protection Association   **F:**149, 153
National Football Conference   **F:**360
National Football League   **F:**360, 364
National Forest System (of the United States)   **N:**30–34 *see
    also* Forests and forestry; National Park System; the
    places of interest section of state articles
  forests part of national public lands reserves   **P:**517
  Nebraska National Forest was planted by people   **N:**85
  Roosevelt, Theodore   **R:**331
  wonders of the national forests   **N:**31
  Wyoming's forests   **W:**338
  map(s)   **N:**33
National Freshwater Fishing Hall of Fame (Hayward, Wisconsin)
    W:200
National Gallery (London)   **N:**35
  picture(s)   **N:**35
National Gallery of Art (Washington, D.C.)   **N:**36–38; **W:**33
  East Building   **U:**136
  grants from the A. W. Mellon Trust   **F:**391
  Pei, I. M.   **P:**118
  picture(s)   **N:**36
National Gallery of Canada (Ottawa)   **N:**39–40
  picture(s)   **O:**250
National Genealogical Society (NGS)   **G:**76d
National Geographic (magazine)   **N:**41
National Geographic Society   **N:**41
National Grandparents Day   **H:**170
National grasslands (in the United States)   **N:**30, 32
  Dust Bowl restoration   **D:**356
  Thunder Basin National Grassland   **W:**338
  vegetation in South Dakota   **S:**316
  map(s)   **N:**33
National Guard (of the United States)   **N:**41–42; **T:**117; **U:**101,
    105, 108
  picture(s)   **N:**41
  flood assistance   **U:**105
National Health Service (United Kingdom)   **U:**54
National High School Rodeo Association   **R:**280
National Highway Traffic Safety Administration   **C:**534; **T:**293
National historical parks (of the United States)   **N:**54
National Historical Publications and Records Commission (United
    States)   **N:**24
National historic sites (of the United States)   **N:**47, 53
National Hockey League (NHL)   **I:**28–29, 30, 31–32
National holidays   **H:**167–69
  table(s)   **H:**166
National Honor Society   **N:**42
National Ignition Facility (California)   **L:**46d
National Independent Union Council   **L:**17
National Indoor Football League (NIFL)   **F:**364

National Industrial Recovery Act (United States, 1933)
    H:275; **R:**324
National Institute for Occupational Safety and Health (NIOSH)
    O:13
National Institutes of Health (NIH)   **H:**79; **N:**43; **P:**514
  Human Genome Project   **G:**86, 91
National Intercollegiate Rodeo Association   **R:**280
Nationalism
  Africa, history of   **A:**68–69
  American literature   **A:**207–8
  Asia, history of   **A:**455–56
  Europe, history of   **E:**366–67
  genocide, justification of   **G:**96
  India, history of   **I:**133
  Ireland, history of   **I:**324
  Latin America, literature of   **L:**67–68
  medieval papacy and   **R:**290
  Middle East   **M:**304–5
  Nazism   **N:**78–81
  Palestine   **J:**107; **P:**40d–41, 42–43
  Quebec separatist movement   **Q:**17
  Reformation as a nationalist movement   **C:**291; **P:**492;
    R:291
  Scotland   **S:**88
Nationalist China *see* Taiwan
Nationalists (in Northern Ireland)   **N:**336, 337; **U:**61
Nationalists (in Spain)   **S:**393
Nationalization *see* Government ownership
National Junior Honor Society   **N:**42
National Labor Relations Act (Wagner Act) (United States, 1935)
    L:7; **N:**138h; **R:**324; **U:**195
National Labor Relations Board (NLRB)   **L:**7
National Labor Unions (NLU)   **L:**12–13
National lakeshores (of the United States)   **N:**55
  Wisconsin's Apostle Islands National Lakeshore   **W:**200
National land reserve   **P:**517
National League (baseball)   **B:**84, 87, 93
  World Series records   **B:**86
National League for Nursing   **N:**421, 422
National Liberation Front (FLN) (Algeria)   **A:**188
National Liberation Front (NLF) (Vietnam)   **V:**338
National libraries   **L:**178–79
National Library of Canada (Ottawa)   **C:**53; **L:**178–79
National Library of Medicine (Washington, D.C.)   **L:**178
National Little Britches Rodeo Association   **R:**280
National Marine Fisheries Service (United States)   **F:**221
National Memorial Cemetery of the Pacific (Hawaii)   **H:**215;
    N:29
National memorials (of the United States)   **N:**52 *see also* the
    places of interest section of state articles
National military parks (of the United States)   **N:**52
National monuments (of the United States)   **N:**45, 47, 50–51
    see also the places of interest section of state articles
National Museum of the Middle Ages (Paris, France)   **P:**70
National Nuclear Security Administration (United States)
    E:218
National Oceanic and Atmospheric Administration (NOAA)
    C:455; **T:**242; **W:**94
National Open *see* U.S. Open
National Organization for Women (NOW)   **C:**326; **F:**475; **N:**43;
    W:213
National Origins Act (United States, 1929)   **I:**91
National Palace (Mexico City)   **M:**253
National parks (Canada)   **C:**54 *see also* the names of parks;
    the places of interest section of province articles
  Banff National Park (Alberta)   **B:**46
  Jasper National Park (Alberta)   **J:**54
National Park Service (of the United States)   **N:**45, 47, 50
National Park System (of the United States)   **N:**44–57;
    P:77–78 *see also* National Forest System; the names
    of parks; the places of interest section of state articles
  Glacier National Park (Montana)   **G:**220
  Grand Canyon National Park   **G:**290–92
  How do areas qualify to become part of the National Park
    System?   **N:**52

National Park System (cont.)
   Interior, United States Department of the **I:**256
   national cemeteries **N:**28
   national parks, list of **N:**46
   What is the largest U.S. national park? **N:**49
   Yellowstone National Park **Y:**355
   Yosemite National Park **Y:**362–63
   map(s) **N:**46
National parkways (of the United States) **N:**55
National Pest Control Association **H:**264
National Police Services (Canada) **R:**343
National preserves (of the United States) **N:**48
National Public Radio **R:**56
National Radio Astronomy Observatory (Green Bank, West
   Virginia) **W:**134
National Railroad Passenger Corporation *see* Amtrak
National Recovery Administration (NRA) **N:**138h; **R:**324
National recreation areas (of the United States) **N:**32, 34, 55
National reserves (of the United States) **N:**54
National resources *see* Natural resources; individual country
   articles
National rivers (of the United States) **N:**55
National Road *see* Cumberland Road
Nationals (persons loyal to or protected by a nation without
   regard to citizenship) **C:**322
National Safety Council **S:**3
National scenic trails (of the United States) **N:**55
National seashores (of the United States) **N:**55
   Padre Island National Seashore (Texas) **T:**132
   picture(s)
      Cumberland Island National Seashore **G:**135
National Security Act (United States, 1947) **D:**84; **U:**110
National Security Council (of the United States) **P:**451
   vice president a member of **V:**330
National Security Medal (American award)
   picture(s) **D:**70
National Senior Citizens Law Center **C:**326
National Socialism *see* Nazism
National Socialist German Workers' Party *see* Nazism
National Space Institute **V:**391
National Technical Institute for the Deaf (Rochester, New York)
   D:51
National Telecommunications and Information Administration
   (NTIA) **C:**455
National Television Systems Committee (NTSC) **T:**65
National Theatre (London, England) **T:**160; **U:**49
National Theatre School (Montreal) **C:**69
National Transportation Safety Board **T:**290
National Underground Railroad Freedom Center (Cincinnati,
   Ohio) **O:**70
National Urban League **A:**79j; **C:**326
National Vocational Agricultural Teachers' Association **F:**104
National Weather Service (of the United States) **T:**242; **W:**92,
   93, 94
National wild and scenic rivers (of the United States) **N:**55
National Woman's Loyal League **W:**212
National Woman's Party **P:**101; **W:**212b
National Woman Suffrage Association **W:**212a
National Women's Football Association (NWFA) **F:**364
National Zoological Park (Washington, D.C.) **W:**34; **Z:**393
Nation at Risk, A (United States government study) **T:**38
Nation of Islam *see* Black Muslims
Nations (of the world) **W:**254
   child development, influences on **C:**224
   international law **I:**267–68
   international relations **I:**269–70
   natural resources, distribution of **N:**65–66
   map(s)
      political entities shown **W:**256–57
Native American Rights Fund **C:**326
Native Americans *see* Indians, American
Native cat (marsupial) **M:**115
Native land claims *see* Land claims
Native ore (metal found in an almost pure state) **O:**217

Native Son (novel by Richard Wright) **A:**217; **W:**327
Nativity (birth of Christ) **C:**299, 300
Nativity (painting by the Master of Flémalle)
   picture(s) **D:**361
Nativity, The (painting by Gentile da Fabriano)
   picture(s) **J:**85
NATO *see* North Atlantic Treaty Organization
Natron (saltlike substance used in mummification) **M:**512
Natural (in music) **M:**537
Natural bridge (rock bridge or arch)
   Natural Bridge (Kentucky) **K:**220
   Natural Bridge (Virginia) **V:**354
   Utah **U:**250
Natural Bridges National Monument (Utah) **U:**250
Natural clay (modeling material) **C:**354
Natural fibers **F:**108–9, 112
Natural foods **H:**79
Natural gas **N:**58–60
   Alaska **A:**152
   Algeria **A:**187
   Canada's Interior Plains **C:**61
   energy supply **E:**221
   Europe's natural resources **E:**360
   fuels **F:**487–88, 490
   helium, source of **H:**106
   Kansas **K:**178, 180, 183
   lighting **L:**233–34
   Netherlands **N:**120a, 121
   North American mineral resources **N:**292
   Oklahoma **O:**85, 88
   petroleum and petroleum refining **P:**171
   public utility **P:**522
   United Kingdom **U:**53, 57
   United States production **U:**91, 94
   White, Israel Charles **W:**139
   picture(s)
      processing in Algeria **A:**187
Natural gas vehicles (NGV's) **N:**59
Natural habitat exhibits (in zoos) **Z:**389–90
Natural history, museums of **M:**523; **P:**110
Natural immunity **I:**95
Naturalism (in art)
   Africa, art of **A:**71, 72
   Italy, art of **I:**393
Naturalism (in literature) **R:**114
   American literature **A:**213
   drama **D:**303–4
   Dreiser, Theodore **D:**324
   fiction **F:**114
   France, literature of **F:**441
   Ghosts (play by Ibsen) **I:**2
   Spanish literature **S:**390
   Strindberg, August **S:**467
   Zola, Émile **Z:**387
Naturalism (in music) **O:**147–48
Naturalistic observation (in psychology) **P:**502
Naturalists (people who study nature) **N:**67–68, 70
   Burroughs, John **B:**457
Naturalization (admission of an alien to citizenship) **N:**61
   Alien Act of 1798 **A:**14
   citizenship **C:**322, 323–24
Natural killer cells (in the immune system) **I:**96
Natural language books (in reading programs) **R:**109–10
Natural law, theory of **C:**325
Natural levees (river deposits) **R:**238
Natural monopolies **P:**520
Natural numbers *see* Counting numbers
Natural resources **N:62–66** *see also* Conservation; Fishing
   industry; Forests and forestry; Mines and mining; Soils;
   Water supply; individual continent, country, province,
   and state articles
   Arctic region **A:**380
   conservation of **C:**523–27
   economic factor of production **E:**57

endangered species   **E:**208–11
environment, quality of   **E:**299–306
forests and forestry   **F:**374–77
geologists at work   **G:**119
mountains, importance of   **M:**507
National Forest System, conflicts over multiple use and
wilderness use in   **N:**32–34
oceans, uses of the   **O:**28
trade and commerce   **T:**264–65
trees   **T:**300–311
water pollution   **W:**62–67
Natural selection (Darwinian theory of evolution)   **E:**372, 375,
376, 377–78, 378
Darwin's ideas   **D:**38–39; **S:**67
genetics and evolution   **G:**81–82
implications for biology   **B:**203
life, adaptations in   **L:**197–98
science, milestones in   **S:**72
Natural sign (in musical notation)   **M:**535
Natural State (nickname for Arkansas)   **A:**406, 407
Natural Tunnel (Virginia)   **V:**354
Nature (book by Emerson)   **A:**209
Nature (journal)   **S:**68
Nature, balance of *see* Balance of nature
Nature, study of   **N:**67–70
Burroughs, John   **B:**457
holidays celebrating nature   **H:**161–63
witchcraft and nature spirituality   **W:**209
Nature centers (natural history museums with outdoor exhibits)
M:523
Nature Conservancy (organization)   **P:**317
Naughty Marietta (operetta by Herbert)   **M:**553; **O:**168
Nauplius (crustacean larva)   **C:**602
Nauru   **N:**71
map(s)   **N:**71
picture(s)
flag   **F:**236
Nautical measure   **W:**117
Nautical mile (measure of distance)   **W:**115
Nautiloids (early invertebrates)   **F:**386
Nautilus (fictional submarine in Jules Verne's *Twenty Thousand
Leagues Under the Sea*)
picture(s)   **S:**79
Nautilus, **USS** (nuclear submarine)   **N:**373; **S:**476; **U:**118
base in Connecticut   **C:**514
first ship to reach North Pole   **A:**381
picture(s)   **S:**474; **U:**117
Nautilus equipment (for weight training)   **W:**107
Nautiluses (mollusks) *see* Chambered nautiluses
Nauvoo (Illinois)   **M:**457; **S:**205
Navajo (Indians of North America)   **I:**184–85
Arizona   **A:**397, 400, 405
language used as code in World War II   **N:**194
New Mexico   **N:**184, 190, 193
originally came from Canada   **R:**33
turquoise used in jewelry   **G:**75
witches, beliefs about   **W:**208
picture(s)   **U:**243, 246
blanket   **W:**98b
handmade rug   **R:**355
jewelry   **J:**96
Navajo National Monument (Arizona)   **A:**400
picture(s)   **A:**400
Naval Academy, United States *see* United States Naval Academy
Naval Forces Central Command (of the United States Navy)
U:111
Naval Forces Europe (of the United States Navy)   **U:**111
Naval Reactors, Office of (United States)   **E:**218
Naval War College, United States (Newport, Rhode Island)
R:217
Navaratri (Hindu holiday)   **R:**154, 155
Navarre, Marguerite de (French writer)   **F:**437
Navassa (outlying area of the United States in the Caribbean)
U:84
Nave (part of a church)   **A:**369; **C:**134; **I:**392

Navel (belly button)   **J:**95; **R:**179
Navel orange   **O:**187
Navigation   **N:**72–77
airplane navigation systems   **A:**117–20
bats use echolocation   **B:**103
boating and sailing rules   **B:**267; **S:**11
Coast Guard aids to navigation   **U:**124–25
fish may use sense of smell to navigate   **F:**194
Greenwich Observatory   **G:**374b
gyroscope   **G:**437
Henry the Navigator directed improvements in   **E:**403
latitude and longitude   **L:**77–78
lighthouses and lightships   **L:**227–29
maps and globes   **M:**92–99
migration of animals   **H:**197, 200–202
ocean currents are relied on   **O:**18
radar   **R:**39
satellites, artificial   **S:**54
sextants   **O:**183
space navigation   **S:**340k–340L
submarine navigation   **S:**475
transportation needs   **T:**283
trigonometry, uses of   **T:**313
What is a ship's log?   **N:**73
Navigation Acts (Britain, 1650 to 1750)   **D:**58; **U:**176
Navigation dams   **D:**16
Navratilova, Martina (American tennis player)   **T:**97 *profile*
picture(s)   **T:**97
Navratri (Hindu festival)   **H:**141
Navy, Canadian *see* Royal Canadian Navy
Navy, United States *see* United States Navy
Navy Cross (American award)   **D:**69
picture(s)   **D:**70
Navy Department (of the United States Navy)   **U:**111
Nawang Gombu (Sherpa guide and mountaineer)   **E:**371
Nayanars (a people of India)   **H:**142
Nazarbayev, Nursultan (president of Kazakhstan)   **K:**201
Nazarene, Church of the   **P:**494
Nazarenes (group of German painters)   **R:**303
Nazareth (Israel)   **J:**85, 86; **M:**119
Nazca (ancient Indian civilization of Peru)   **I:**109, 170
Nazism   **N:**78–81 *see also* Fascism; Hitler, Adolf
genocide   **G:**96
Germany's Third Reich   **G:**162–63
Goering, Hermann Wilhelm   **W:**302
Hitler, Adolf   **H:**153–54
Holocaust   **H:**173–74; **W:**298
Jewish population in Europe   **G:**149–50
persecution of Jews   **J:**106
racism   **R:**34c
rise of dictators before World War II   **W:**294
Un-American Activities Committee, House   **U:**13
picture(s)
war crimes trials at Nuremberg   **I:**268
Nazi-Soviet Nonaggression Pact (1939)   **U:**42
picture(s)
cartoon ridiculing pact   **U:**42
NBA *see* National Basketball Association
NBC *see* National Broadcasting Corporation
NCCAM *see* National Center for Complementary and Alternative
Medicine
NCI *see* National Cancer Institute
Ndadaye, Melchior (Burundi president)   **B:**459
Ndayizeye, Domitien (Burundi president)   **B:**459
Ndebele (Matabele) (a people of Africa)   **S:**272; **Z:**381, 383
picture(s)
house   **A:**76
N'Djamena (capital of Chad)   **C:**181
NEA *see* National Endowment for the Arts
Neagh, Lough (lake, Northern Ireland)   **U:**53
Neanderthal human   **P:**440, 441, 442
Ice Age   **I:**12–13
religious rituals may have been practiced   **R:**145

Neanderthal human (cont.)
   map(s)
      where remains have been found   **P:**439
   picture(s)   **P:**439
      grave   **P:**440
Neapolitan mastiffs (dogs)   **D:**247
   picture(s)   **D:**247
Neap tides   **O:**19; **T:**195
Near Earth Asteroid Rendezvous (NEAR) Shoemaker (space probe)
    C:451; **S:**359, 360
Near-Earth Asteroid Tracking (NEAT)   **C:**450
Near East *see* Middle East
Nearsightedness (eye defect)   **E:**431; **L:**46c, 150, 151
NEAT *see* Near-Earth Asteroid Tracking
Nebraska   **N:**82–95; **S:**438
   map(s)   **N:**93
   picture(s)
      cattle   **N:**83
      Chimney Rock   **N:**94
      football fans   **N:**87
      fossil beds   **N:**87
      grain elevator   **N:**83
      irrigated farmland   **N:**86
      Lincoln   **N:**91
      Omaha   **N:**89
      schoolchildren raising flag   **N:**83
Nebraska, University of   **N:**86, 87
   picture(s)
      football fans   **N:**87
Nebraska National Forest   **N:**85, 90
Nebrija, Antonio de (Spanish author)   **S:**387
Nebuchadnezzar II (king of Babylon)   **A:**233; **B:**5; **M:**232;
    W:217
Nebulas (large clouds of gases)   **A:**474; **N:**96; **U:**211, 213
   formation of stars   **S:**430
   picture(s)   **S:**428
Neck bones   **M:**66
Necker, Jacques (Swiss-born French statesman)   **F:**468
Neck injuries   **F:**160
Necklaces (jewelry)   **J:**94, 98
   picture(s)   **J:**95, 96, 99, 100
      diamonds and emeralds   **G:**69
      Indian art   **D:**72
Nectar (of flowers)   **F:**284, 285, 286
   bees make nectar into honey   **B:**116, 117; **H:**210, 211
   food of butterflies and moths   **B:**478
Nectaries (glands of a plant)   **F:**284
Nectarines (fruits)   **P:**107
Needfire (to cure diseases of cattle)   **F:**142
Needham, James (American trader)   **T:**84
Needlecraft (art or craft of creating designs on fabric)   **F:**14;
    N:97–101 *see also* Crocheting; Embroidery; Knitting;
    Sewing
Needle guns   **G:**420
Needle lace   **L:**19
Needle-nose pliers (tools)   **T:**230
Needlepoint (form of embroidery)   **N:**100
Needles   **N:**102
   embroidery needles   **N:**97
   knitting needles   **K:**278
   needlepoint needles   **N:**100
   sewing needles   **S:**129
Needles, phonograph   **H:**132; **S:**267
Needle telegraph   **T:**51
Needlework *see* Needlecraft
Nefertiti (Nefretiri) (queen of ancient Egypt)   **E:**116
Negative charges (of electricity)   **E:**135–36
Negative cutters (for motion pictures)   **M:**485
Negative ion *see* Anion
Negative numbers (those less than zero)   **A:**183; **M:**164;
    N:400, 402
Negatives (in photography)   **P:**211, 215, 216
   color separation in printing   **P:**472–73
   lithographic plates   **P:**475

Negev (area of Israel)   **I:**371, 372
   picture(s)   **I:**370
Negoi Peak (Romania)   **R:**297
Negotiation (bargaining to settle a dispute)   **A:**349
Negrillos (a people of Africa) *see* Pygmies
Negritos (a people of New Guinea and the Philippines)   **A:**445
Negritude (African cultural movement)   **A:**76c–76d
Negro, Río (Uruguay)   **S:**280; **U:**238
Negroes *see* African Americans; Blacks
Negros Island (Philippines)   **P:**185
Negro spirituals *see* Spirituals
Nehemiah (book of the Old Testament)   **B:**163
Nehru, Jawaharlal (India's first prime minister)   **N:**103
   memorial in Delhi   **D:**104
   picture(s)   **I:**133; **P:**40a, 459
Neighborhoods (in cities)   **C:**312, 314
Neisse River (Europe)   **P:**359
Nekhen (ancient Egyptian kingdom)   **A:**234
Nekrasov, Viktor (Russian author)   **R:**384
Nekton (actively swimming marine animals)   **O:**25
Nelson (New Zealand)   **N:**241
Nelson, Byron (American golfer)   **G:**258 *profile*
   picture(s)   **G:**258
Nelson, Horatio, Lord (English admiral)   **N:**104
   column in Trafalgar Square   **L:**294
   Napoleon I   **N:**10, 11
   saved England from invasion by sea   **E:**249
Nelson, Willie (American singer and composer)   **C:**573
   picture(s)   **C:**573
Nelson A. Rockefeller Empire State Plaza (Albany, New York)
   picture(s)   **N:**221
Nelson River (Canada)   **C:**57; **M:**81
Nematocysts (stinging cells)   **J:**72
   picture(s)   **J:**73
Nematodes (worms) *see* Roundworms
Nemean lion (in Greek mythology)   **G:**366
Nemesias (flowers)
   picture(s)   **G:**50
Nemesis (in astronomy) *see* Death star
Nemesis (in Greek mythology)   **G:**367
Nemours (mansion, Delaware)   **D:**96
   picture(s)   **D:**89
Nemunas River (Lithuania)   **L:**262
Nene *see* Hawaiian goose
Nennius (Welsh priest and historian)   **A:**438b
Neo-Babylonian empire   **A:**233; **M:**232
Neoclassicism (in art and architecture)
   architecture   **A:**372–73
   France   **F:**428
   furniture   **F:**511, 512–13
   Germany   **G:**171
   Italian art   **I:**403
   Latin America   **L:**63
   romanticism a reaction against   **R:**302
   sculpture   **S:**101–2
   picture(s)
      bedroom at Fontainebleau   **F:**509
      Prado museum   **P:**423
Neoclassicism (in literature)   **E:**276
   drama, history of   **D:**301
   Spanish literature stifled by   **S:**389
Neoclassicism (in music)   **M:**398
Neodymium (element)   **E:**175; **M:**32
Neoimperialism (in international relations)   **I:**102
Neolithic Age *see* New Stone Age
Neon (gaseous element)   **N:**105, 106
   elements   **E:**175
   gases in industry   **G:**61
   lighting   **L:**224
   liquid gases   **L:**253
   neon lamps   **E:**150–51; **L:**236
   spark chambers   **C:**563
   picture(s)
      neon sign   **G:**61
Neoplasms *see* Tumors

Neoplasticism (school of modern painting)   **M:**393, 410
Neoprene (synthetic rubber)   **R:**346
Neoprimitivism (in art)   **R:**378–79
Neorealism (in films)   **M:**493
Nepal   **N:**107–10
   Everest, Mount   **E:**370–71
   Himalayas   **H:**137, 138
   Hinduism   **H:**142
   map(s)   **N:**107
   picture(s)
      dyers' market   **D:**375
      Fish Tail Mountain   **W:**217
      flag   **F:**236
      handicrafts and textiles   **N:**109
      Kathmandu   **N:**110
      terraced fields   **N:**107
      yak   **N:**108
Nepalese (a people of south central Asia)   **N:**107
Nepali (language)   **N:**107
Nephrite (gem mineral)   **G:**73; **J:**11
Nephritis (kidney disease)   **D:**197–98; **K:**244
Nephron (part of the kidney)   **D:**198; **K:**243
   diagram(s)   **K:**242
Nepisiguit River (New Brunswick)   **N:**138–38a
Nepotism (giving favors to relatives)   **R:**290
Neptune (planet)   **N:**111–14; **P:**281–82
   discovery   **A:**471
   observing Neptune   **P:**281
   radiation belts   **R:**49
   radio astronomy   **R:**69
   relationship with Pluto   **P:**343–44
   sometimes is outermost planet   **P:**341–42; **S:**241
   space probes   **O:**10; **S:**360
   picture(s)   **N:**111
Neptune (Roman god) *see* Poseidon
Neptunium (element)   **E:**175
Neritic zone (of the ocean)   **O:**23
Nernst, Walther (German chemist and teacher)   **L:**35
Nero (Roman emperor)   **N:**114; **R:**316
   Olympic Games   **O:**104
   persecution of Christians   **C:**288; **R:**286
   used emerald as lens   **M:**286
   picture(s)   **C:**288
Neruda, Pablo (Chilean poet)   **C:**254; **L:**69; **P:**352
   "Alturas de Machu Picchu," excerpt from   **L:**69
   picture(s)   **L:**57; **P:**352
Nerva (Roman emperor)   **R:**316
Nerve cells *see* Neurons
Nerve net (nervous system of simple animals)   **B:**363
Nerves *see* Nervous system
Nervous system   **B:**287, 288–89; **N:**115–18
   anesthesia   **A:**255–56
   autism is a neurological disorder   **A:**526–27
   birds   **B:**224
   brain   **B:**362–69
   coelenterates   **J:**72
   crocodilians' sensory organs   **C:**592
   drugs act on   **D:**334; **N:**15
   fish   **F:**191–92
   insects   **I:**238–39
   multiple sclerosis   **D:**197
   phenylketonuria   **D:**199
   rabies   **D:**201
   sleep   **S:**198
   syphilis may damage   **D:**206
   tissues of the body   **B:**275
   tooth nerves   **T:**43
   picture(s)
      multiple sclerosis damage   **D:**197
Ness, Loch (lake, Scotland)   **L:**32, 281; **S:**86; **U:**53
   picture(s)   **C:**131
Nesting dolls (Russian folk art)
   picture(s)   **R:**363
Nestor (Russian monk and chronicler)   **R:**380

Nests
   ants   **A:**321–22
   birds   **B:**228–30
   eagles   **E:**2
   fish   **F:**196
   flightless birds   **O:**243
   herons, bitterns, and egrets   **H:**124
   insects   **I:**246–47
   penguins   **P:**121
   rabbits and hares   **R:**25
   picture(s)
      bees   **B:**121
Netanyahu, Benjamin (Israeli political leader)   **I:**376
Net force (in physics)   **C:**365
Netherland dwarf rabbits   **R:**25
Netherlands   **N:**119–21
   Amsterdam   **A:**225
   art *see* Dutch art; Flemish art
   Christianity, history of   **C:**293
   Christmas customs   **C:**301
   delta made by three rivers   **R:**236
   dredging operations   **D:**321–22
   East India Company   **E:**47
   education, history of   **E:**81
   flood control   **F:**255
   food   **F:**331
   homosexuals can legally marry   **H:**204
   houseboats   **H:**189
   ice skating   **I:**44
   Indonesia, history of   **I:**211–12
   Jews, history of the   **J:**105
   music *see* Dutch and Flemish music
   national anthem   **N:**18
   Pilgrims (Separatists) sheltered in Leyden   **P:**344; **T:**170
   Spain, history of   **S:**377
   Suriname   **S:**517
   Where and what are the Low Countries?   **E:**349
   William (kings and princes)   **W:**173–74
   World War II   **W:**296–97, 312, 316
   map(s)   **N:**120a
   picture(s)
      Amsterdam   **A:**225; **N:**120c
      bicycle transportation   **N:**120
      cheese market   **N:**120
      costumes, traditional Dutch   **C:**373
      dairy farm   **N:**120b
      Europoort   **E:**361; **N:**120b
      fishing industry   **N:**120b
      flag   **F:**236
      gardens   **G:**43
      tulips   **E:**350
      windmills   **E:**349
Netherlands Antilles (Dutch West Indies) (island group in the Caribbean Sea)   **C:**113; **N:**120d
Netherlands East Indies *see* Indonesia
Net income *see* Profit
Neto, Agostinho (Angolan president)   **A:**260
Nets (for fishing)   **F:**218–19; **O:**40
   picture(s)   **N:**287, 293
Netscape Navigator (Web browser)   **C:**493
Networking protocol (of computers)   **C:**487
Networks (for radio and television broadcasting)   **J:**136; **R:**56, 59; **T:**68
Networks (in topology)   **T:**237
Networks (of computers)   **C:**486, 487, 491
   electricity in communications   **E:**147
   telecommunications   **T:**46, 49–50
   video games   **V:**332c
Netzahualcóyotl (Texcoco ruler)   **I:**172
Neuchâtel, Lake (Switzerland)   **L:**32
Neuharth, Allen (American journalist)   **J:**139 *profile*
Neuilly, Treaty of (1919)   **W:**291
Neumann, Balthazar (German architect)   **G:**171
Neural networks (computer programs)   **C:**492
Neurilemma (of peripheral nerve cells)   **N:**117

Neurobiology   **B:**203
Neurology see Nervous system
Neurons (nerve cells)   **B:**288; **N:**115, 117–18
  brain   **B:**362, 363, 367, 368
  some are over 3 feet long   **C:**159
  picture(s)   **B:**363
Neurophysiology (physiology of nervous system)   **B:**199
Neurotransmitters (chemicals in the nervous system)   **B:**363, 368
Neuschwanstein (castle in Germany)
  picture(s)   **G:**149
Neutering (of dogs)   **D:**260
Neutral (chemical term)   **C:**202, 204
Neutral (Indians of North America)   **I:**175
Neutral (transmission position)   **A:**549
Neutrality (nonalignment of nations)   **I:**269
  policy of Asian nations   **A:**456
  Sweden   **S:**529
  Switzerland   **S:**546
  War of 1812   **W:**8
  Wilson's policies before World War I   **W:**182
Neutrality Act (United States, 1939)   **W:**295
Neutrino (subatomic particle)   **A:**489
Neutron bomb   **N:**377
Neutrons (atomic particles)   **A:**485, 488; **C:**201, 202, 203, 204
  cosmic rays   **C:**562
  elements   **E:**166
  fission   **F:**222
  nuclear energy   **N:**366, 367, 370–71
  physics, history of   **P:**239
  radiation   **R:**43
  radiation of a nuclear explosion   **N:**376
  radioactive elements   **R:**64
Neutron stars   **A:**473, 474; **M:**178; **P:**539; **S:**432–33
Neutrophils (white blood cells)   **B:**259, 260–61
Nevada   **G:**251; **N:122–36**
  Mead, Lake   **L:**32
  map(s)   **N:**133
  picture(s)
    cacti   **N:**123
    Carson City   **N:**132
    desert   **N:**124
    Hoover Dam   **N:**126
    Lake Mead National Recreation Area   **N:**123
    Lake Tahoe   **N:**125
    Las Vegas   **N:**123
    Native American powwow   **N:**129
    Nevada, University of   **N:**129
    Pyramid Lake   **N:**127
    railroad museum   **N:**126
    Reno   **N:**131
    sheep   **N:**130
    Virginia City   **N:**126
Nevada, University of   **N:**129
Nevada City (Montana)   **M:**436
  picture(s)   **M:**436
Nevada Fall (California)   **W:**59
Nevado Mismi (stream in Peru that is the source of the Amazon River)   **A:**198
Nevado Sajama (highest mountain in Bolivia)   **B:**307
Neve, Don Felipe de (Spanish colonial governor)   **L:**307
Nevelson, Louise (Russian-American sculptor)   **M:**396b; **N:**137; **S:**105; **U:**135
  picture(s)   **I:**93
    Mirror-Shadow VII (sculpture)   **S:**105
    Mrs. N's Place (sculpture)   **U:**135
Neves, Tancredo de Almeida (Brazilian political figure)   **B:**384
Neville, Richard (English statesman) see Warwick, Earl of
Nevis (Caribbean island) see Saint Kitts and Nevis
Nevsky, Alexander (Russian hero) see Alexander Nevsky
Nevsky Prospekt (avenue in Saint Petersburg, Russia)   **S:**18a
  picture(s)   **R:**365; **S:**18b
New Age (belief system)   **R:**152

New Amsterdam (Dutch settlement in America, now New York City)   **N:**121, 210, 222; **T:**175; **U:**174
  fairs, history of   **F:**18
  Peter Minuit's purchase from the Indians   **N:**234
  Stuyvesant, Peter   **S:**472
Newark (New Jersey)   **N:**173, 174
  picture(s)   **N:**174
Newars (a people of Nepal)   **N:**107, 110
New Bedford (Massachusetts)   **F:**221; **M:**145
Newberry Library (Chicago, Illinois)   **I:**67; **L:**178
Newbery, Chantelle (Australian diver)   **O:**119
Newbery, John (English publisher)   **C:**229, 232; **N:137**, 415
Newbery Medal (book award)   **C:11–12**, 232
New Book of Knowledge, The (encyclopedia)   **E:**206, 207
New Britain (volcanic island in Pacific)   **P:**9
New Brunswick (Canada)   **C:**82; **N:138–38g**
  map(s)   **N:**138d
  picture(s)
    farm   **N:**138b
    Fredericton   **N:**138e
    Hartland Covered Bridge   **N:**138e
    Hopewell Rocks Provincial Park   **N:**138a
    paper and pulp mill   **N:**138c
    Saint John   **N:**138f
New Brunswick, University of (Canada)   **C:**52; **N:**138d
  picture(s)   **N:**138e
New Caledonia (Pacific island)   **C:**539; **P:**9
New Castle (Delaware)   **D:**99, 101
  picture(s)   **D:**98
Newcastle (New South Wales, Australia)   **A:**511
Newcastle (Newcastle-upon-Tyne) (England)   **U:**60
Newcastle (Wyoming)   **W:**340
New Castle County (Delaware)   **D:**88, 90, 92, 93, 95, 102
"New Colossus, The" (poem by Emma Lazarus)
  excerpt from   **L:**169
New Comedy (period in Greek literature)   **G:**357
Newcomen, Thomas (English inventor)   **I:**220–21
  piston engine   **E:**229
  steam engine   **I:**280; **S:**444; **W:**77
New Criticism (literature study method)   **W:**12
New Deal (program of Franklin D. Roosevelt)   **N:**138h; **R:**323–24; **U:**194–95
  agricultural price supports   **F:**61
  Depression, Great   **D:**120
  modifies capitalism   **C:**103
  Montana   **M:**441
  policies of political parties   **P:**371
  recovery from 1929 depression aided by   **D:**122
  Un-American Activities Committee, House   **U:**13
New Delhi (capital of India)   **D:**103–5; **I:**123, 129, 139
  picture(s)   **D:**104
New Democratic Party (in Canada)   **C:**75
New Denmark (New Brunswick)
  picture(s)
    farm   **N:**138b
New Echota (Georgia)   **G:**140
New Economic Policy (NEP) (in Soviet history)   **R:**372; **U:**41–42
New England (northeastern United States)   **N:**139 see also Connecticut; Maine; Massachusetts; New Hampshire; Rhode Island; Vermont
  American literature   **A:**207–8, 209, 213
  Boston   **B:**339–42
  colonial life   **C:**409–19
  early schools   **E:**81–82
  farm life in colonial America   **C:**413–14
  homes and housing, history of   **H:**194
  Indian wars   **I:**202
  Puritans   **P:**550–51
  Smith, John, explored   **S:**205
  thirteen American colonies   **T:**170–74
  United States, history of the   **U:**174, 175
  witch hunts   **W:**209
New England Anti-Slavery Society   **A:**6
New England Historic Genealogical Society   **G:**76d

New England Primer, The (colonial textbook)   C:229, 233;
      E:82; P:551
New England Wild Flower Society   E:306
Newfoundland, Memorial University of *see* Memorial University
      of Newfoundland
Newfoundland and Labrador (Canada)   N:140–47
   advection fogs   F:290
   Canada, history of   C:79
   Ericson, Leif   E:311–12
   landforms of Canada   C:54–55
   Nunatsiavut (Inuit self-governing region)   I:276
   provincial government   C:78
   Viking settlements in   E:311–12; V:343
   map(s)   N:144
   picture(s)
      fishing   N:143
      L'Anse aux Meadows   N:147
      logging   N:143
      outport   N:142
      puffins on Gull Island   N:145
      St. John's   N:146
      Torngat Mountains   N:142
New France (early Canada)   C:79–81; Q:17
   art and architecture   C:71–72
   Cartier, Jacques   C:126
   French and Indian War   F:462
   fur trade in the New World   F:519–20
   Saint Lawrence River   S:14
New Freedom (program of Woodrow Wilson)   W:180, 181
New Georgia (one of the Solomon Islands)   S:252, 253
New Granada (Spanish viceroyalty)   C:408; S:293
Newgrange (Ireland)   I:322
New Guinea   N:148–49; P:5
   cassowaries are a form of money   O:245
   Indonesia   I:207
   Papua (Irian Jaya)   I:209, 212
   Papua New Guinea   P:58d–59
   World War II   W:308, 309
   map(s)   N:149
   picture(s)   N:148
New Hampshire   C:422; N:150–63; T:174
   map(s)   N:161
   picture(s)
      Adams, Mount   N:152
      canoe on lake   N:154
      cargo ship in Portsmouth harbor   N:157
      Concord   N:158, 159
      covered bridge   N:152
      Dartmouth College   N:155
      fall foliage   N:151
      Franconia Notch   N:158
      hikers on mountain   N:154
      Manchester   N:157
      Mount Washington Cog Railway   L:288; N:158
      Old Man of the Mountain   N:151
      Portsmouth   N:158
      snow-covered inn   N:156
      snowshoers at Squam Lake   N:151
      White Mountain National Forest   N:31
New Hampshire, University of   N:155
New Hampshire Grants (land purchases in Vermont history)
      V:318
New Harmony (Indiana)   I:152, 157; O:283
New Haven (Connecticut)   C:512, 513, 515, 516, 517, 520,
      521
   picture(s)   C:513
New Hebrides *see* Vanuatu
Ne Win, U (Burmese military and political leader)   M:561
New Ireland (volcanic island in the Pacific)   P:10
New Jersey   N:164–79
   colonial life in America   C:419
   fairs, history of   F:18
   Livingston family   L:273, 274
   thirteen American colonies   T:176

Wilson's accomplishments as governor   W:180
   map(s)   N:177
   picture(s)
      agriculture   N:166
      Atlantic City   N:165, 172
      chemical plant   N:170
      Delaware Water Gap   N:166
      George Washington Bridge   N:165
      Giants Stadium   N:172
      Jersey City   N:174
      Newark   N:174
      Port Elizabeth   N:173
      Princeton University   N:169
      Sandy Hook Light   N:172
      shore   N:165, 168
      Six Flags Great Adventure   N:172
      Trenton   N:175
New Jersey Plan (for United States Constitution)   U:146
New Kingdom (1570–1070 B.C., ancient Egypt)   E:109
New London (Connecticut)   U:125
New Look (in fashion)   C:379
New Madrid (Missouri)   M:379
Newman, Arnold (American photographer)   P:215 *profile*
   picture(s)
      self-portrait   P:215
Newman, Barnett (American sculptor)   S:105
Newman, James (American astronaut)   S:348 *profile*
   picture(s)   S:349
Newman, John Henry, Cardinal (English theologian)   E:284
Newman, Larry (American balloonist)   B:36
Newman, Paul (American film actor)   M:490 *profile*
New Mexico   N:180–94
   Anasazi   A:227
   Carlsbad Caverns   C:155–56
   Compromise of 1850   C:479
   Dust Bowl   D:355
   Hispanic Americans   H:148
   map(s)   N:191
   picture(s)
      Albuquerque   N:189
      Carlsbad Caverns   N:188
      cattle ranching   N:186
      Chaco Culture National Historical Park   N:188
      Llano Estacado   N:182
      people   N:184
      rock formations   N:181
      Sangre de Cristo Mountains   N:182
      Santa Fe   H:145; N:181, 189
      Santa Fe Opera House   N:185
      Taos Pueblo   I:183; N:188
      Very Large Array   N:187; O:10; R:66
      White Sands National Monument   N:188
New Mexico, Museum of (Santa Fe)   N:185, 188
New moon   M:447
   picture(s)   M:448
New Negro, The (anthology of black writers' works)   A:215
New Negro Movement *see* Harlem Renaissance
New Netherland (Dutch colony in America)   N:210, 221–22,
      234; S:472; T:174–76
New novel (in French literature)   F:443
New Orleans (Louisiana)   N:195–96
   aquarium   A:337
   Audubon Park Zoo   Z:390
   Civil War   C:338
   hurricane Katrina   B:469
   jazz   J:58, 59; L:320
   Laffite's smuggling operations   L:23
   Louisiana, cities of   L:319, 321, 323
   Louisiana, history of   L:318, 327, 328
   Louisiana World Exposition (1984)   F:17
   Mardi Gras   C:116; H:163
   places of interest   L:322
   picture(s)
      American flag raising (1803)   T:105

New Zealand (cont.)
  gold discoveries **G:**252
  immigration **I:**94
  Niue **P:**10
  Olympic Games (1976) **O:**111
  Sutherland waterfall **W:**59
  Tokelau **P:**10
  map(s) **N:**236
  picture(s)
    Christchurch **N:**240
    flag **F:**236
    geothermal power plant **N:**238
    hot spring **N:**237
    Milford Sound **N:**235
    Mount Cook **N:**237
    people **N:**235
    rugby players **N:**237
    sheep ranch **A:**92; **N:**239
    volcano **V:**384
    Wellington **N:**240
NEXRAD (Next-Generation Radar) **R:**39; **W:**90
Next Generation Space Telescope *see* James Webb Space
  Telescope
Next of kin (a person's nearest relatives) **L:**89
Nezahualcóyotl (Mexico) **M:**247
Nez Percé (Indians of North America) **I:**188
  Appaloosa horses developed by **H:**240
  Chief Joseph **I:**59
  Idaho **I:**46
  Indian wars **I:**205
  Montana defeat **M:**428, 436, 440
Nez Perce National Historic Park (Idaho–Montana) **I:**54;
  M:436
Ngalops (a people of Bhutan) **B:**155
Ngo Dinh Diem (president of Vietnam) **V:**334d, 336
Ngo Dinh Nhu (Vietnamese leader) **V:**336
Ngola (ruler of ancient Kimbundu kingdom) **A:**260
Ngo Quyen (Vietnamese rebel) **V:**334c
NGO's (Nongovernmental organizations) **D:**184
Ngouabi, Marien (president of the Congo) **C:**506
Nguyen Cao Ky (Vietnamese military and political leader) *see*
  Ky, Nguyen Cao
Nguyen Khanh, General (Vietnamese leader) **V:**336
Nguyen That Thanh (Vietnamese political leader) *see* Ho Chi
  Minh
Nguyen Van Thieu (Vietnamese army officer and political leader)
  see Thieu, Nguyen Van
NGV's *see* Natural gas vehicles
NHL *see* National Hockey League
Nhu *see* Ngo Dinh Nhu
Niacin (a B-complex vitamin) **V:**370c
  table(s) **V:**372
Niagara (warship) **P:**134
Niagara Escarpment (Ontario) **O:**124
Niagara Falls **N:**242–43; **W:**59
  picture(s) **N:**211, 243; **O:**132; **W:**218
Niagara Movement (of African American intellectuals) **D:**344
Niagara Peninsula (Canada) **O:**127
Niagara River (Canada–United States) **C:**56; **N:**213
Niamey (capital of Niger) **N:**252
  picture(s) **N:**251
Niantics (Indians of North America) **R:**224
Niari River (Congo) **C:**505
Niaux Cave (France) **P:**436
Nibelungenlied (German romance) **A:**490; **G:**176; **N:**281
Nibelungs, Song of the *see* Nibelungenlied
Nicaea, Council of (325) **C:**289, 528; **E:**43; **R:**286
Nicaea (Iznik) (ancient city in Turkey) **P:**411
Nicaragua **N:**244–48
  Central America **C:**172, 173, 174, 175
  guerrilla warfare **G:**400
  Iran-Contra Affair **I:**310
  lakes **L:**32–33
  Latin America **L:**49

  Ortega, Daniel **O:**231
  map(s) **N:**244
  picture(s)
    flag **F:**237
    Mombacho and Lake Nicaragua **N:**245
    slum **P:**419
Nicaragua, Lake (Nicaragua) **L:**32–33; **N:**245, 287
  picture(s) **N:**245
Nice (France) **C:**182; **F:**410
Nicene Creed **L:**151; **R:**286
Niche (an animal's role in its community) **A:**268; **P:**434
Nicholas, Saint (patron saint of Russia) **S:**18d *profile*
  Austria's favorite holiday **A:**519
  Christmas customs **C:**297, 301
Nicholas V (antipope) **R:**293
Nicholas I, Saint (pope) **R:**292
Nicholas II (pope) **R:**292
Nicholas III (pope) **R:**293
Nicholas IV (pope) **R:**293
Nicholas V (pope) **R:**293
Nicholas I (emperor of Russia) **C:**587; **N:**248; **R:**370
  Hermitage Museum **H:**122
  Jews conscripted for military service **J:**106
  picture(s) **N:**248
Nicholas II (emperor of Russia) **N:**249; **R:**365, 370–71; **U:**33,
  39, 40, 41
  World War I **W:**288
  picture(s) **R:**371; **W:**278
Nicholas Nickleby (book by Charles Dickens) **D:**151
Nicholson, Ben (English painter) **E:**263
Nicholson, Jack (American actor) **M:**491 *profile*
  picture(s) **M:**491
Nicias, Peace of (421 B.C.) **P:**120a
Nickel **N:**249–50
  alloys **A:**192, 193
  batteries **B:**103b–103c
  Canada is world's leading source **C:**61
  elements **E:**175
  Manitoba **M:**82
  nickel-producing regions of North America **N:**293
  table(s) **M:**235
Nickel cadmium batteries **E:**143
Nickelodeons (early motion picture theaters) **M:**488
Nickels (coins) **C:**400
Nickel silver **K:**285
Nicklaus, Jack (American golfer) **G:**258 *profile,* 260
  picture(s) **G:**258
Nicknames **N:**7 *see also* Names
  folklore **F:**306–7
  state **U:**80 *see also* individual state articles
Nicobar Islands (India) **I:**366
Nicodemus (in New Testament) **B:**161
Nicolet, Jean (French explorer) **N:**250; **W:**204
Nicosia (capital of Cyprus) **C:**617
Nicotine (chemical) **D:**329; **T:**215
Niello (engraving technique) **D:**75; **G:**303
Nielsen, Carl (Danish composer) **D:**112
Niemeyer, Oscar (Brazilian architect) **B:**382; **L:**65
Niepce, Joseph Nicéphore (French photography pioneer) **D:**2;
  P:211
  picture(s)
    world's first successful photograph **P:**211
Niepce de Saint-Victor, Abel (French inventor) **P:**211
Nietzsche, Friedrich (German philosopher) **G:**180
Niflheim (wintry realm in Norse mythology) **N:**278, 280
Niger **N:**251–52
  map(s) **N:**251
  picture(s)
    boys on camelback **A:**56
    flag **F:**237
    Niamey **N:**251
    skyscraper and traditional homes **A:**58
Nigeria **N:**253–58
  folk dance **F:**300, 302

gems **G:**71
harvest festival Iriji **H:**161
literature **A:**76b, 76d
Organization of Petroleum Exporting Countries **O:**222
population growth **P:**387
poverty caused by corrupt rule **P:**419
sculpture of Ifé and Benin cultures **A:**71
sculpture of Nok culture **A:**70–71; **P:**411
sculpture of Yoruba peoples **A:**72
talking drum **A:**78
map(s) **N:**254
picture(s)
    flag **F:**237
    Igbo people **N:**258
    Jebba **N:**255
    Lagos **N:**256
    market in Lagos **N:**254
    Muslims praying before mosque **A:**57
    Nok sculpture **P:**411
    oil tanker **N:**256
    people **N:**253
    traditional wedding costumes **A:**55
    village **N:**253
    Yoruba sculpture **A:**72
Niger-Kordofanian languages **A:**56
Niger River (Africa) **A:**48; **G:**406a; **M:**61; **N:**255; **R:**244
picture(s) **N:**255, 256; **R:**244
Night
early time measurement **T:**200
Earth's period of rotation **E:**9
length of during the seasons **S:**109, 110–11
Night blindness (eye disorder) **E:**431; **V:**370b
Night-blooming cereus *see* Cereus
Nightclubs **D:**27
picture(s)
    Memphis (Tennessee) **T:**78
Night crawlers (worms) *see* Earthworms
Nighthawks (birds) **H:**128
picture(s) **B:**235
Nighthawks (painting by Edward Hopper)
picture(s) **U:**133
Nightingale, Florence (English nurse) **C:**587; **N:259,** 420; **S:**443
picture(s) **N:**259, 420
Nightjars (birds) **H:**128
Nightmares (frightening dreams) **D:**320; **M:**222
Night monkeys *see* Douroucoulis
Nightshade family (of plants) **P:**316; **V:**290
potatoes **P:**403
tobacco **T:**214–15
tomatoes **T:**223
Night-vision devices **E:**160, 162
photography **P:**209
picture(s) **E:**161
photography **P:**208
"Night Will Never Stay, The" (poem by Eleanor Farjeon) **F:**124
Nihavend, Battle of (642) **P:**157
Nihon (Japanese name for Japan) **J:**40
Nihon-gi (sacred book of Shinto) **R:**151–52
Niihau (one of the Hawaiian Islands) **H:**50, 60
Nijinsky, Vaslav (Russian ballet dancer and choreographer) **B:**29, 30
Nike (in Greek mythology)
Winged Victory of Samothrace **G:**352
picture(s)
    Winged Victory of Samothrace **L:**333; **S:**95
Nikolais, Alwin (American choreographer) **D:**32
Nile, Battle of the (1798) **N:**10, 104
Nile crocodiles
picture(s) **C:**593
Nile River (Africa) **N:260–61**
Africa, great rivers of **A:**48, 54
Aswan High Dam **L:**32
early agriculture **A:**97–98

Egypt **E:**102
Egyptian civilization **A:**234–35; **E:**107; **R:**241
flood waters used to good advantage **F:**255
Middle East **M:**300
source in Lake Victoria **L:**27, 34
Sudan **S:**478
Uganda **U:**5
What and where are the Mountains of the Moon? **A:**61
map(s) **N:**261
picture(s) **A:**48; **R:**236–37
    agriculture **A:**63; **M:**301
    delta **E:**18
    Egypt **E:**99
    feluccas **N:**260
    irrigation ditches **F:**257
    women carrying water **W:**73
Nilo-Saharan languages **A:**56
Nilotic people (of Africa) **A:**55; **E:**330; **S:**478; **U:**4
Nimba, Mount (highest peak in Ivory Coast) **I:**419
Nimble Free Hand to the Rescue (painting by Dubuffet)
picture(s) **F:**432
Nimbostratus clouds **C:**385; **W:**87
picture(s) **C:**384
Nimeiry, Gaafar al- (Sudanese president) **S:**480
Nimitz, Chester William (American naval officer) **W:**301
profile, 308
picture(s) **W:**301
Nimrod (Biblical character) **B:**161
Nimrud (city in ancient Assyria)
picture(s) **A:**228; **M:**304
Nin, Anaïs (American author) **D:**150
Niña (ship of Christopher Columbus) **C:**446, 448; **E:**404
Nine ball (pocket billiards game) **B:**179–80
Nine Figures Climbing Trees (painting)
picture(s) **F:**298
Nine Men's Morris (game) **G:**13
911 (emergency telephone number) **A:**199; **F:**157
Ninepins (bowling game) **B:**350
Nineteen Eighty-Four (novel by George Orwell) **E:**289; **O:**234; **S:**82
Nineteenth Amendment (to the United States Constitution) **U:**158; **V:**393
Anthony, Susan B. **A:**299
civil rights **C:**326
Tennessee **T:**87
women's rights movement **W:**212a–212b
Ninety-five theses (of Luther) **L:**346; **R:**130
Ninety Six National Historic Site (South Carolina) **S:**304
Nineveh (capital of ancient Assyria) **A:**233, 462
Mosul (Iraq) **I:**314
public library of clay tablets **L:**171
Nine-volt batteries **B:**103b
Niño, El (Pacific Ocean current) *see* El Niño
Nintendo (Japanese video-game company) **V:**332b
Ninth Amendment (to the United States Constitution) **B:**182, 183
Ninth Symphony (of Beethoven) **C:**284; **G:**186
Nintoku (Japanese emperor) **O:**236
Niobid Painter (Greek artist) **G:**350–51
Niobium (element) **E:**175
Niobrara River (Nebraska) **N:**82, 84
Niord (Norse god) **N:**278–79
Nipisiguit River (New Brunswick) *see* Nepisiguit River
Nipmucks (Indians of North America) **R:**224
Nipper (Victor Talking Machine Company's trademark dog) **P:**195
picture(s) **P:**195
Nippon (Japanese name for Japan) **J:**40
NIRA *see* National Industrial Recovery Act
Nirvana (state of perfect happiness)
Buddha **B:**423
Buddhism **B:**423, 424; **R:**149, 150
Nisei Week (Japanese American festival) **A:**458
Nishkin Bottles (for collecting seawater samples) **O:**39
Niter *see* Saltpeter

Nitrates (salts of nitric acid)   **C:**158, 252, 255; **O:**17
Nitric acid   **A:**9; **O:**289
Nitrile (synthetic rubber)   **R:**346
Nitro (West Virginia)   **W:**132
Nitrocellulose (Gun cotton) (explosive)   **N:**439–40; **P:**327–28
Nitrogen (chemical element)   **N:**262
  acid rain   **A:**10
  air is a mixture of oxygen and nitrogen   **G:**56
  air pollution   **A:**123
  atmosphere contains   **A:**480
  bends, the   **U:**22–23
  carbon-14 decays back to   **R:**76
  cirrhosis of the liver   **L:**270
  elements   **E:**175
  fertilizers   **F:**96, 97; **G:**85
  formula   **C:**201
  industrial uses   **G:**59
  liquid gases   **L:**253
  liver removes from amino acids   **L:**268–69
  ocean water, dissolved in   **O:**17
  refrigeration   **R:**134, 135
  soils, elements in   **S:**236
Nitrogen fixation (part of the nitrogen cycle)   **G:**85; **N:**262; **P:**314
Nitrogen oxides (air pollutants)   **A:**9, 123
Nitroglycerin (explosive)   **E:**420–21, 422
Nitrous oxide (laughing gas)
  anesthesia   **A:**254, 255, 256
  atmosphere   **A:**480
  Davy, Sir Humphrey   **D:**44
  medicine, history of   **M:**208a, 208c
Nits (lice eggs)   **H:**263
Nitschke, Ray (American football player)   **F:**363 *profile*
  picture(s)   **F:**363
Niue (Pacific island)   **P:**10
Nivelle, Robert (French army officer)   **W:**287, 288
Nixon, Francis (English inventor)   **T:**143
Nixon, Lewis (American naval architect)   **R:**41
Nixon, Patricia Ryan (wife of Richard M. Nixon)   **F:**180; **N:**262b, 262f
  picture(s)   **F:**180; **N:**262c, 262f
Nixon, Richard Milhous (37th president of the United States)   **N:**262a–262f; **U:**201–2
  China, visit to   **C:**272
  impeachment question   **I:**99
  role in Alger Hiss case   **S:**408; **U:**13
  television debates with Kennedy   **K:**208
  vice presidency   **V:**330 *profile*
  Vietnam War   **V:**338
  Watergate   **W:**60–61
  picture(s)   **E:**124, 129; **F:**368; **N:**262a; **P:**452; **U:**201
    with Bill Clinton   **N:**262f
    on college football team   **N:**262b
    with family   **N:**262c
    with John Kennedy   **K:**207; **N:**262c
    with Mao Zedong   **N:**262e
    with Nikita Khrushchev   **N:**262c
    resignation   **N:**262f
    with Spiro Agnew   **N:**262d
Nixon, Tricia (daughter of Richard Nixon) *see* Cox, Tricia Nixon
Niza, Marcos de (Italian missionary)   **A:**402
Nizhniy Novgorod (Russia)   **F:**18; **R:**359, 365
Nkrumah, Kwame (first president of Ghana)   **G:**198
Nkurunziza, Pierre (Burundi president)   **B:**459
NKVD (Soviet People's Commissariat for Internal Affairs)   **U:**42
NMR *see* Magnetic resonance imaging
No (Japanese drama) *see* Noh
NOAA Weather Radio   **W:**94
Noah's Ark (Bible story)   **B:**168–69
  picture(s)   **B:**162
    cameo representation   **J:**99
Nobel, Alfred Bernhard (Swedish chemist and manufacturer)   **E:**420–21; **N:**263
  picture(s)   **N:**263
Nobelium (element)   **E:**175

Nobel prizes   **H:**287; **N:**263–71; **S:**453
Nobile, Umberto (Italian aviator)   **A:**226
Nobility (social class)   **C:**131–32
Noble gases   **G:**61; **N:**105–6
  atoms   **A:**487
  filament lamps   **L:**235
  periodic table   **E:**167
"Noble savage" (Rousseau's ideal)   **E:**296
Noboa Bejarano, Gustavo (president of Ecuador)   **E:**69
Nobunaga (Oda Nobunaga) (Japanese general and statesman)   **J:**43; **O:**236
Nocake (colonial American corn food)   **C:**411
No Child Left Behind Act (United States, 2002)   **E:**86–87
Nocks (notches on the tail of an arrow)   **A:**361
Noctilio bats   **B:**101–2
Nocturnal animals
  bats   **B:**101
  lizards   **L:**275–76
  lobsters   **L:**280
  moths   **B:**475
  red light exhibits in zoos   **Z:**390
Nocturne (in music)   **M:**542
Nodes (of plants)   **L:**113; **P:**304
Nodosaurus (dinosaur)   **D:**176
Nodules (of plants)   **P:**314
Noëls (French Christmas carols)   **C:**118
Noether, Emmy (German mathematician)   **A:**184
No fault coverage (in automobile insurance)   **I:**251
No fault divorce   **D:**230
Noguchi, Isamu (American sculptor)
  picture(s)
    New York City statue   **S:**91
Noh (Nō) (Japanese drama)   **D:**298; **J:**32, 53
  Japanese theater   **T:**162
  picture(s)   **D:**297
Noise   **N:**271; **S:**263
  airports seek to control noise   **A:**129
  deafness caused by   **D:**48
  disease caused by   **D:**198–99
  white noise (electronic sound)   **E:**156
Nok (early African culture, Nigeria)   **N:**257
  sculpture   **A:**70–71; **P:**411
  picture(s)
    sculpture   **P:**411
Nokia Corporation   **F:**137
  picture(s)   **F:**137
Nolde, Emil (German painter)   **M:**391
Nomadism (of desert-dwelling animals)   **H:**197
Nomads   **N:**272
  Afghanistan   **A:**43
  Arabs   **A:**343, 344
  Australian Aborigines   **A:**7, 498
  Bedouin   **S:**550
  desert people and cultures   **D:**129, 130
  Djibouti   **D:**232
  Genghis Khan unites Mongol tribes   **G:**94
  gypsies   **G:**434–35
  helped spread languages   **L:**39
  homes of   **H:**189
  Iraq   **I:**311–12
  Kazakhstan   **K:**200
  Lapland's mountain people   **L:**44
  Masai   **K:**229
  Mauritania   **M:**179
  Mongolia   **M:**416
  Morocco   **M:**458
  Niger   **N:**251
  ranch life, origins of   **R:**102
  Sahara inhabitants   **S:**7
  Saudi Arabia   **S:**58a, 58b
  semi-nomadic people of Africa   **A:**63
  Somalia   **S:**254
  Southwest Asia   **A:**451
  Suriname Indians   **S:**516

North American Current I:35
North American F-100 (supersonic fighter plane) A:567
North American Free Trade Agreement (NAFTA) (1992) I:271;
    N:305; U:205
    Bush, George B:465
    Canada C:65, 85
    Clinton, William C:367
    Mexico M:245
    picture(s)
        signing N:304
North American Soccer League S:218b
North American X-15 (research plane) A:567
North Asia A:441
North Atlantic Drift (section of the Gulf Stream) A:479; E:348;
    G:413
North Atlantic Treaty Organization (NATO) N:305
    Canadian forces in C:70
    Clinton administration C:368
    Cold War C:401
    de Gaulle withdraws French forces D:87; F:420
    Eisenhower was first commander of E:124
    headquarters (Brussels, Belgium) B:134
    Truman's help in shaping T:326
    picture(s)
        meeting on Yugoslavian civil war I:269
North Battleford (Saskatchewan) S:49
North Borneo see Sabah
North Carolina C:421; N:306–21; T:177–78
    map(s) N:316
    picture(s)
        Biltmore Estate N:314
        Blue Ridge Mountains N:307
        Bogue Sound N:308
        Cape Hatteras lighthouse N:307
        Charlotte N:315
        farm N:309
        fisheries N:313
        fox hunting N:307
        people N:310
        Raleigh N:315, 317
        swamplands N:308
        swinging bridge N:314
        tobacco farming N:313
        USS North Carolina Battleship Memorial N:314
        Wright Brothers National Memorial N:314
North Carolina, University of N:310, 311
North Carolina State University N:310–11
North Church (Boston, Massachusetts) see Old North Church
North Dakota N:322–35
    map(s) N:332
    picture(s)
        Badlands N:323
        Bismarck N:330
        bison N:323
        Fargo N:329
        Fort Union Trading Post N:331
        Frontier Village N:331
        Knife River Indian Villages N:331
        Lake Sakakawea N:325
        Medora Musical N:327
        prairie farm N:323; P:427
        Red River of the North N:325
        university N:327
        wheat farming N:328
North Dakota, University of N:326–27
North Dakota State University N:327
Northeast Passage (Arctic sea route) A:380; E:414; H:273
North Equatorial Current A:479; G:413
Northern Alliance (Afghan fighting force) T:116–17
Northern Anatolian (Pontic) Mountains (Turkey) T:345
Northern bobwhites (birds) Q:4a
Northern Colorado, University of (Greeley, Colorado) C:434
Northern flicker (bird)
    picture(s)
        nest B:229

Northern fur seals F:518; H:199
Northern goshawks (birds) H:64
Northern Hemisphere L:77
    air motion W:81
    constellations C:529–30
    equator divides the hemispheres E:308
    Gulf Stream G:413
    has two-thirds of the world's land surface C:538
    hurricanes H:302, 303
    month by month see individual month articles
    ocean currents E:19
    seasons E:9; S:109, 110, 111
    trade winds T:268
    winds W:187, 188, 189
    map(s)
        glaciation during Ice Ages I:11
Northern Ireland N:336–37
    historical, cultural, and scenic places U:54
    Ireland, history of I:324
    land features U:52, 53
    United Kingdom, government of the U:61
    map(s) N:336
    picture(s)
        Belfast N:336
        Bloody Sunday anniversary N:337
        farmers U:46
        Giant's Causeway R:265; U:53
Northern lights see Aurora borealis
Northern Marianas see Marianas, Northern
Northern Mountains (North Korea) K:295
    picture(s) K:294
Northern Quebec Inuit Association I:276
Northern Rhodesia (now Zambia) Z:377, 378
Northern Spy (variety of apple) A:331
Northern Territory (Australia) A:513
Northern Virginia, Confederate Army of C:339, 340–41
    Stuart, Jeb S:470
North Korea see Korea, North
North Little Rock (Arkansas) A:413, 415
Northmen (Norsemen) (Scandinavian peoples who plundered
        Europe in the Middle Ages) S:58g see also Vikings
    first recorded explorers of the Arctic A:380
    Norse gods and goddesses N:277–81
    people of France F:404
    sagas in Scandinavian literature S:58h
North Platte River (United States) W:336–37
North Pole A:378, 379
    Amundsen, Roald A:226
    Earth's axis E:9; G:436
    exploration and discovery A:380–81; E:414
    Henson, Matthew H:115
    Peary, Robert E., was first to reach North Pole P:117
    seasonal positions S:109
North Saskatchewan River (Canada) S:43
North Sea O:46
    picture(s)
        petroleum rig E:360
North Star (Polaris) C:530; G:436, 437
    navigation N:75
    position seen from equator E:308
North Star, The (newspaper published by Frederick Douglass)
    A:79g
North Star State (nickname for Minnesota) M:326, 327
Northumberland Strait (Canada) C:54, 57; N:138, 138c, 350
North Vietnam see Vietnam, Democratic Republic of
Northwest Angle (section of Minnesota) M:326; T:104, 107
Northwest Coast Indians (of Canada) C:71; M:577
North West Company (fur traders) F:520–21, 523
    Alberta, history of A:171
    Canada's Nor'Westers C:82–83
    Mackenzie's explorations for the company M:5
Northwestern Ice Yachting Association I:20
North-West Mounted Police see Royal Canadian Mounted Police
Northwest Ordinance (Ordinance of 1787) (United States history)
    O:75; P:259; U:177; W:140–41

Novosibirsk (Russia)   R:359, 365
NOW *see* National Organization for Women
Nowshāk, Mount (Afghanistan)   A:43
Noyce, Robert (American inventor)   I:285
Ntaryamira, Cyprien (Burundi president)   B:459
Ntibantunganya, Sylvestre (Burundi president)   B:459
N-type (Negative type) semiconductor   E:159; T:275
    diagram(s)   T:274
Nu, U (Burmese statesman)   M:561
Nubia (ancient region in present-day Sudan)   A:235
Nubian Desert (Africa)   S:478
Nuclear accidents   F:36; N:372
Nuclear batteries (devices that produce electricity)   B:103c
Nuclear chemistry   C:205
Nuclear disarmament   C:401; D:181, 182
Nuclear energy   E:221; N:366–73
    changes in atomic nuclei   M:178
    chemistry, history of   C:211
    cosmic rays   C:562–63
    Einstein's theory of relativity   R:139, 143
    energy, forms of   E:213, 216
    Energy, United States Department of   E:218
    fallout from nuclear explosions   F:35–36
    Fermi's reactor   F:92
    first chain reaction was at University of Chicago   C:221
    fission   F:222–23
    hazardous radioactive wastes   H:73
    International Atomic Energy Agency   U:69
    nuclear fusion   I:289
    nuclear submarines   S:475–76
    nuclear weapons   N:374–79
    radioactive elements   R:65
    rocket power   R:262
    Rutherford's theory of the atom   R:387
    ships, nuclear-powered   S:154, 159
    star energy   S:430, 431
    uranium   U:231
    uranium deposits in North America   N:294
Nuclear Energy, Science, and Technology, Office of (United
    States)   E:218
Nuclear engineers   E:226
Nuclear family   F:37–38, 40
Nuclear fission *see* Fission (of atomic nuclei)
Nuclear fuels   F:490
Nuclear fusion   E:216, 222; N:368
    changes in atomic nuclei   M:178
    hydrogen as an energy source   H:316
    lasers, uses of   L:46d
    nuclear weapons   N:375
    plasma and fusion   I:289
    radioactive radiation   R:46
    stars   S:431
    sun's interior   S:491
Nuclear magnetic resonance imaging *see* Magnetic resonance
    imaging
Nuclear Nonproliferation Act (United States, 1978)   G:237;
    K:298
Nuclear Nonproliferation Treaty (1968)   D:182; N:379
Nuclear physics (branch of physics that studies nuclear energy)
    N:366–73
    Alvarez, Luis Walter   A:195
    engineering   E:226
Nuclear power plants   E:221; F:490; N:369–73
    environment, problems of   E:300, 305
    Europe, importance in   E:360
    fallout   F:36
    first American plant built in Pennsylvania   P:133
    France   F:409
    Geiger counters   G:68
    Maine   M:45
    public utilities   P:521
    Seabrook (New Hampshire)   N:163
    steam turbines   T:342
    Sweden   S:527
    water pollution   W:67

picture(s)
    Three Mile Island   P:133
Nuclear reactions (of atomic nuclei)   N:367–69
    cosmic rays   C:562
    fission   F:222–23
    sun   S:491
Nuclear reactors   N:369–73 *see also* Meltdown
    fallout   F:36
    fission   F:222–23
    rockets   R:262
    picture(s)
        Korea, North   K:296
Nuclear submarines   S:475–76; U:114
    picture(s)   S:473
Nuclear test ban *see* Nuclear disarmament
Nuclear weapons   N:374–79 *see also* Atomic weapons;
    Neutron bomb
    Cold War   C:400, 401
    control through disarmament   D:181, 182
    Cuban missile crisis   C:611
    fallout   F:35–36
    Indian nuclear tests   I:134
    Iran suspected of producing illegal weapons   I:310
    Korea, North   K:298, 303
    missiles carry nuclear warheads   M:345, 348, 349
    Oppenheimer, J. Robert   N:232–33
    Pakistan   P:40a
    Pauling's opposition to   P:102
    peace movements   P:106
    Russia–United States reduction treaty   B:468
Nuclear winter   N:377
Nucleic acids (in body chemistry)   B:295, 297–98; L:200
    body, human   B:273
    in cell nucleus   C:160
    how antibiotics work   A:308–9
    viruses   V:362, 364, 366
Nucleoli (of cells)   C:160; L:200
Nucleons (atomic particles)   A:485; R:43
Nucleotides (nucleic acid chains)   B:297–98, 299
Nucleus (of a comet)   C:452
Nucleus (of a galaxy)   M:309
Nucleus (of the cell)   C:160, 161, 162; L:200
    bacteria lack nuclei   B:11
    body, human   B:273, 274
    genes, location of   G:78
    microbes   M:274
    nuclear membrane   L:200
    plant cells   P:294
    protozoans   P:495, 497
Nucleus (plural: nuclei) (of the atom)   A:485, 487
    chemical terms   C:204
    chemistry, history of   C:211
    chemistry of the atom   C:201, 202
    electricity and the makeup of atoms   E:135
    elements, atomic numbers of   E:166
    fission   F:222–23
    nuclear energy   N:366–73
    radiation   R:43
    radioactive elements   R:64
    Where does fission take place?   F:223
Nude (in art)   D:316
Nude Descending a Staircase, No. 2 (painting by Duchamp)
    D:344
Nudibranchs (mollusks)   M:406, 407
Nuer (language)   A:56
Nuer (people of Sudan)   F:303
Nueva San Salvador (El Salvador)   E:197
Nuggets (chunks of solid gold)   G:248, 251
Nujoma, Sam (president of Namibia)   N:9
Nuku'alofa (capital of Tonga)   T:224
Nullarbor Plain (Australia)   A:505
Nullification (in United States history)   U:182
    Calhoun's theory   C:17
    Jackson opposes   J:6–7

PHOTO CREDITS

The following list credits the sources of photos used in THE NEW BOOK OF KNOWLEDGE. Credits are listed, by page, photo by photo—left to right, top to bottom. Wherever appropriate, the name of the photographer has been listed with the source, the two being separated by a dash. When two or more photos by different photographers appear on one page, their credits are separated by semicolons.

143 Wilson—First Light.
143 © Lorraine C. Parow—First Light; © John Eastcott/Yva Momatiuk—Valan Photos.
145 © Francis Lepine—Valan Photos
146 © Ken Straiton—First Light
147 © Wayne Wegner—First Light
148 © Kal Muller—Woodfin Camp & Associates
149 © SuperStock
151 © William Johnson; © Craig Blouin; © William Johnson.
152 © Craig Blouin—f/Stop Pictures; © William Johnson.
154 © David Brownell (all photos on page).
155 © Michael Quan—f/Stop Pictures
156 © William Johnson
157 © Candace Cochrane—Positive Images; © John Gauvin—Studio One.
158 © David Brownell; © Don & Pat Valenti—f/Stop Pictures; © Patricia J. Bruno—Positive Images; © Paul Rezendes—Positive Images.
159 © William Johnson
162 The Bettmann Archive; The Granger Collection; Courtesy of the Manchester Historic Association.
163 NASA
165 © Bob Krist; © R. Macia—H. Armstrong Roberts; © Gene Ahrens—Bruce Coleman Inc.
166 © Michael Baytoff; © Bob Krist.
168 © Jim Mejuto—FPG International; © Kelly-Mooney—Courtesy of the New Jersey State Aquarium at Camden.
169 © Mary Ann Brockman
170 © C. C. Lockwood—Bruce Coleman Inc.
171 © Bob Krist
172 © Fridmar Damm—Leo de Wys; © Steve Hurwitz—Bruce Coleman Inc.; © Tom Hevezi—Allsport; © Photri.
173 © Donald Brewster—Bruce Coleman Inc.
174 © Phil Degginger—Bruce Coleman Inc.; © R. Krubner—H. Armstrong Roberts.
175 © D. Campione—H. Armstrong Roberts
178 Brown Brothers
179 The Granger Collection; © Courtesy of the Clara Maass Foundation.
181 © Buddy Mays—Travel Stock; © Marcia Keegan—The Stock Market; © Byron Crader—Root Resources.
182 © Tom Bean; © Buddy Mays—Travel Stock.
184 © Buddy Mays—Travel Stock (all photos on page).
185 © Murrae Haynes—The Santa Fe Opera Theater
186 © Buddy Mays—Travel Stock; © Sandia National Laboratories.
187 © Buddy Mays—Travel Stock
188 © Buddy Mays—Travel Stock; © Jacques Jangoux—Peter Arnold, Inc.; © Buddy Mays—Travel Stock; © Byron Crader—Root Resources.
189 © James Blank—The Stock Market; © Reinhard Brucker.
192 North Wind Picture Archives; The Bettmann Archive.
193 UPI/Bettmann Newsphotos; © Joe Munroe—Photo Researchers.
194 AP/Wide World Photos
195 © Bob Daemmrich—The Image Works
197 © David Woods—The Stock Market
198 © David R. Frazier
199 © Joseph Sohm—The Stock Market; © Steve Elmore—Tom Stack & Associates.
200 © Cynthia Johnson—Liaison Agency; © David R. Frazier.
201 © David R. Frazier
202 © Phillip Jones Griffiths—Magnum Photos; © David R. Frazier.
203 © Jan Halaska—Photo Researchers
204 The Granger Collection (all photos on page).
205 © Courtesy of the *Chicago Tribune*, Chicago Online (all photos on page).
208 © Tomas Muscionico—The Stock Market
210 © Tom Tracy—Photo Network
211 © David Barnes—The Stock Market; © Steve Winter—Black Star; © Michal Heron—The Stock Market.
212 Finger Lakes Association; © Abram G. Schoenfeld—Photo Researchers.
213 © Piotr Kapa—The Stock Market
214 © David Alan Harvey—Woodfin Camp & Associates; © Farrell Grehan—Photo Researchers; © Rafael Macia—Photo Researchers.
216 © Martha Cooper—The Viesti Collection, Inc.; © Jim Anderson—Woodfin Camp & Associates.
217 © Robert B. Shaver—NFL Photos
218 © Rafael Macia—Photo Researchers; © Nubar Alexanian—Woodfin Camp & Associates.

219 © Mark Weidman
220 © T. J. Florian—Photo Network; Courtesy of the City of Rochester.
221 © David L. Brown—The Stock Market
224 Courtesy of the John Jay Homestead
225 UPI/Bettmann Newsphotos
226 © Richard Drew—AP/Wide World Photos
228 © Hiroji Kubota—Magnum Photos
229 © Paul Fusco—Magnum Photos; © Katrina Thomas—Photo Researchers; © Catherine Karnow—Woodfin Camp & Associates.
230 © Michael Tamborrino—The Stock Market; © Eleni Mylonas—The Viesti Collection, Inc.
231 © Cynthia Matthew—The Stock Market; © Alan Schein—The Stock Market.
232 AP/Wide World Photos; © Stan Honda—AP/Wide World Photos.
233 AP/Wide World Photos
234 © Matt Moyer—AP/Wide World Photos
235 © Bryan Peterson—Taxi/Getty Images; © Gisela Damm—eStock Photo; © Picture Finders Ltd./eStock Photo.
237 © Steve Vidler—eStock Photo; © Ross Setford—Fotopress/AP/Wide World Photos; © David Noton—Masterfile.
238 © Studio Carlo Dani—Animals Animals/Earth Scenes; © Steve Vidler—eStock Photo; © Jon Arnold—Danita Delimont, Agent.
239 © Andris Apse—Bruce Coleman Inc.
240 © Jon Arnold—Danita Delimont, Agent; © Yoshio Tomii—SuperStock.
241 © Bachmann—Photo Researchers
243 © Michele Burgess—SuperStock
245 © Douglas Faulkner
246 © John Hoagland—Liaison Agency
247 AP/Wide World Photos
248 The Granger Collection
251 © John Elk III—Bruce Coleman Inc.
253 © SuperStock; © Marc and Evelyne Bernheim—Woodfin Camp & Associates.
254 © Betty Press—Woodfin Camp & Associates
255 © Marc and Evelyne Bernheim—Woodfin Camp & Associates
256 © Chris Hondros—Getty Images; © Georg Gerster—Photo Researchers.
257 © British Museum, London/Werner Forman Archive/Art Resource, NY
258 © Terence Spencer—TimePix
259 London Stereoscopic Company/Hulton/Archive by Getty Images
260 © SuperStock
261 © Michael A. Vaccaro
262a © Bachrach; The Bettmann Archive; NASA; UPI/Bettmann Newsphotos.
262b UPI/Bettmann Newsphotos
262c AP/Wide World Photos; UPI/Bettmann Newsphotos; UPI/Bettmann Newsphotos.
262d © W. Miller—Magnum Photos
262e © C. W. Owen—Black Star
262f © Wally McNamee—Woodfin Camp & Associates; © The White House.
263 © Phil Degginger—Stone/Getty Images
268 © CERN/P. Loiez—Science Photo Library/Photo Researchers.
271 © Douglas Fisher—The Image Bank
272 © Harrison Forman
274 From *Cautionary Verses* by Hilaire Belloc, copyright 1931 by Hilaire Belloc, renewal copyright 1959 by Eleanor Jebb Belloc, Elizabeth Belloc, and Hilaire Belloc, illustrations by B.T.B. and Nicholas Bentley, reprinted by permission of Alfred A. Knopf, Inc.
275 Illustration by L. Lesle Brooke from *Nonsense Songs* by Edward Lear, reproduced with permission of the publisher, Frederick Warne & Company
276 Illustration from *Nonsense Omnibus*, written and illustrated by Edward Lear, reproduced with permission of Frederick Warne & Company
277–278 William Geise
282 © Wendell Metzen—Bruce Coleman Inc.; © Alison Forbes—New England Stock Photo; © M. Timothy O'Keefe—Tom Stack & Associates.
283 © Norman Owen Tomalin—Bruce Coleman Inc.; © T. Davis/W. Bilenduke—Stone; © David Hiser—Stone; © Will & Deni McIntyre—Photo Researchers; © Grace Davies—Photo Network; © Alison Forbes—New England Stock Photo.
284 © Gary Irving—Stone; © David Muench—Stone; © Gary Braasch—Stone.
285 © D. Holden Baily—Tom Stack & Associates; © Gary Irving—Stone.
286 © Pete Souza—Liaison Agency; © Terry Donnelly—Tom Stack & Associates; © Jim

287 Schwabel—Photo Network.
287 © Robert Frerck—Stone; © John Hyde—Bruce Coleman Inc.
288 © Cotton Coulson—Woodfin Camp & Associates
290 © John Hyde—Bruce Coleman Inc.; © Brian Stablyk—Stone; © Erwin & Peggy Bauer—Bruce Coleman Inc.
291 © Art Wolfe—Stone
292 © François Gohier—Photo Researchers
293 © François Gohier—Photo Researchers; © Arthur Tress—Photo Researchers.
294 © Bob Thomas—Stone; © Bruce Hands—Stone; © Robert Frerck—Woodfin Camp & Associates; © John Cancalosi—Tom Stack & Associates; © M. Timothy O'Keefe—Bruce Coleman Inc.; © Frank Wing—Liaison Agency.
295 © W. Perry Conway—Tom Stack & Associates; © Thierry Cazabon—Stone; © Jeff Greenberg—Stock, Boston; © Kaluzny/Thatcher—Stone.
296 © Pascal Quittemelle—Stock, Boston
298 © Nigel Atherton—Stone
299 © Joseph Nettis—Stock, Boston
300 © Jean-Claude Carton—Bruce Coleman Inc.; © Vince Streano—Stone.
301 © David R. Frazier—Photo Researchers; © Michael Rosenfeld—Stone.
303 © David J. Sams—Stock, Boston; © Peter Skinner—Photo Researchers.
304 © Poulides/Thatcher—Stone; © Dirk Halstead—Liaison Agency.
307 © William Strode—Woodfin Camp & Associates; © Murray & Associates, Inc.—Picturesque; © SuperStock.
308 © SuperStock; © Bob Glander—SuperStock.
309 © Buddy Mays—Travel Stock
310 © Jane Howard—Photo Researchers
311 © Chip Henderson—Picturesque; © Murray & Associates, Inc.—Picturesque.
313 © Bill Weems—Woodfin Camp & Associates; © Steve Murray—Picturesque; © Murray & Associates, Inc.—Picturesque.
314 © SuperStock; © Cameramann International Ltd.; North Carolina Travel & Tourism Division; © Joseph A. DiChello, Jr.
315 © APS Services—H. Armstrong Roberts; © Chip Henderson—Picturesque.
317 © Murray & Associates, Inc.—Picturesque
319 © Ernest H. Robl
320 © Eric Preau—Corbis-Sygma
321 © Tom McHugh—Photo Researchers; The Granger Collection; UPI/Bettmann Newsphotos.
323 © Grant Heilman—Grant Heilman Photography; © Stephen Trimble—Root Resources; © Stan Osolinski—Dembinsky Photo Associates.
325 © Sheldon Green (all photos on page).
327 © Jeff Greenberg; © Sheldon Green; © Sheldon Green; © Sheldon Green.
328 © Sheldon Green (all photos on page).
329 © Sheldon Green
330 © Sheldon Green
331 © Sheldon Green; © Sheldon Green; © Mary Borkhuis.
333 Courtesy of the State Historical Society of North Dakota
334 Courtesy of the State Historical Society of North Dakota; Courtesy of the State Historical Society of North Dakota.
335 © Focus on Sports; © Sheldon Green.
336 © Courau/Explorer—Photo Researchers
337 © Karim Daher—Liaison Agency
339 UPI/Bettmann Newsphotos; The Bettmann Archive; © Owen Beattie—University of Alberta.
341 © Wayne Lankinen—Bruce Coleman Inc.
342 © Tessa MacIntosh—Spectrum
344 © Terje Rakke—The Image Bank/Getty Images; © Masakatsu Yamazaki—HAGA/The Image Works; © Brian Lawrence—SuperStock.
346 © Georg Gerster—Photo Researchers; © Trygve Bolstad—Panos Pictures.
347 © Jan Butchofsky-Houser/Housertock
348 © Erland Aas—SCANPIX/AP/Wide World Photos
349 © Dagli Orti—Viking Ship Museum, Oslo/The Art Archive
351 © Leonard Lee Rue III—Photo Researchers
352 Canapress Photo; © Miller Comstock, Inc.
353 © Pam Hickman—Valan Photos; © Warren Gordon—Miller Comstock, Inc.
354 © Eric Hayes—Miller Comstock, Inc.
356 © Arthur Burchell—Valan Photos
358 The Bettmann Archive
360 The Granger Collection